Successful Technological Integration for Competitive Advantage in Retail Settings

Eleonora Pantano
Middlesex University London, UK

A volume in the Advances in E-Business Research (AEBR) Book Series

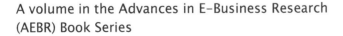

An Imprint of IGI Global

Managing Director:	Lindsay Johnston
Managing Editor:	Austin DeMarco
Director of Intellectual Property & Contracts:	Jan Travers
Acquisitions Editor:	Kayla Wolfe
Production Editor:	Christina Henning
Development Editor:	Brandon Carbaugh
Typesetter:	Amanda Smith
Cover Design:	Jason Mull

Published in the United States of America by
Business Science Reference (an imprint of IGI Global)
701 E. Chocolate Avenue
Hershey PA, USA 17033
Tel: 717-533-8845
Fax: 717-533-8661
E-mail: cust@igi-global.com
Web site: http://www.igi-global.com

Library of Congress Cataloging-in-Publication Data

CIP Data Pending
ISBN 978-1-4666-8297-9 (hardcover)
ISBN 978-1-4666-8298-6 (ebook)

This book is published in the IGI Global book series Advances in E-Business Research (AEBR) (ISSN: 1935-2700; eISSN: 1935-2719)

British Cataloguing in Publication Data
A Cataloguing in Publication record for this book is available from the British Library.

All work contributed to this book is new, previously-unpublished material. The views expressed in this book are those of the authors, but not necessarily of the publisher.

For electronic access to this publication, please contact: eresources@igi-global.com.

Advances in E-Business Research (AEBR) Book Series

In Lee
Western Illinois University, USA

ISSN: 1935-2700
EISSN: 1935-2719

MISSION

Technology has played a vital role in the emergence of e-business and its applications incorporate strategies. These processes have aided in the use of electronic transactions via telecommunications networks for collaborating with business partners, buying and selling of goods and services, and customer service. Research in this field continues to develop into a wide range of topics, including marketing, psychology, information systems, accounting, economics, and computer science.

The **Advances in E-Business Research (AEBR) Book Series** provides multidisciplinary references for researchers and practitioners in this area. Instructors, researchers, and professionals interested in the most up-to-date research on the concepts, issues, applications, and trends in the e-business field will find this collection, or individual books, extremely useful. This collection contains the highest quality academic books that advance understanding of e-business and addresses the challenges faced by researchers and practitioners.

COVERAGE

- Semantic Web
- Trends in E-business Models and Technologies
- Virtual Organization
- Web Advertising
- Global E-business
- Web Service-Based Business Systems
- Electronic Supply Chain Management
- Online Consumer Behavior
- E-business Standardizations
- Interorganizational Information Systems

IGI Global is currently accepting manuscripts for publication within this series. To submit a proposal for a volume in this series, please contact our Acquisition Editors at Acquisitions@igi-global.com or visit: http://www.igi-global.com/publish/.

Titles in this Series

For a list of additional titles in this series, please visit: www.igi-global.com

Strategic E-Commerce Systems and Tools for Competing in the Digital Marketplace
Mehdi Khosrow-Pour (Information Resources Management Association, USA)
Business Science Reference • copyright 2015 • 263pp • H/C (ISBN: 9781466681330) • US $185.00 (our price)

The Evolution of the Internet in the Business Sector Web 1.0 to Web 3.0
Pedro Isaías (Universidade Aberta (Portuguese Open University), Portugal) Piet Kommers (University of Twente, The Netherlands) and Tomayess Issa (Curtin University, Australia)
Business Science Reference • copyright 2015 • 407pp • H/C (ISBN: 9781466672628) • US $235.00 (our price)

RFID Technology Integration for Business Performance Improvement
In Lee (Western Illinois University, USA)
Business Science Reference • copyright 2015 • 337pp • H/C (ISBN: 9781466663084) • US $225.00 (our price)

Integrating Social Media into Business Practice, Applications, Management, and Models
In Lee (Western Illinois University, USA)
Business Science Reference • copyright 2014 • 325pp • H/C (ISBN: 9781466661820) • US $225.00 (our price)

Electronic Payment Systems for Competitive Advantage in E-Commerce
Francisco Liébana-Cabanillas (University of Granada, Spain) Francisco Muñoz-Leiva (University of Granada, Spain) Juan Sánchez-Fernández (University of Granada, Spain) and Myriam Martínez-Fiestas (ESAN University, Perú)
Business Science Reference • copyright 2014 • 393pp • H/C (ISBN: 9781466651906) • US $215.00 (our price)

Trends in E-Business, E-Services, and E-Commerce Impact of Technology on Goods, Services, and Business Transactions
In Lee (Western Illinois University, USA)
Business Science Reference • copyright 2014 • 347pp • H/C (ISBN: 9781466645103) • US $185.00 (our price)

Interdisciplinary Perspectives on Business Convergence, Computing, and Legality
Reema Khurana (Institute of Management Technology-Ghaziabad, India) and Rashmi Aggarwal (Institute of Management Technology-Ghaziabad, India)
Business Science Reference • copyright 2013 • 354pp • H/C (ISBN: 9781466642096) • US $165.00 (our price)

Research and Development in E-Business through Service-Oriented Solutions
Katalin Tarnay (University of Pannonia, Hungary & Budapest University of Technology and Economics, Hungary) Sandor Imre (Budapest University of Technology and Economics, Hungary) and Lai Xu (Bournemouth University, UK)

www.igi-global.com

701 E. Chocolate Ave., Hershey, PA 17033
Order online at www.igi-global.com or call 717-533-8845 x100
To place a standing order for titles released in this series, contact: cust@igi-global.com
Mon-Fri 8:00 am - 5:00 pm (est) or fax 24 hours a day 717-533-8661

Editorial Advisory Board

Table of Contents

Section 1
Store Design and Atmosphere

Detailed Table of Contents

Section 1
Store Design and Atmosphere

Chapters included in this section show how the adoption of advanced technologies changes the store atmosphere, by enriching the traditional (physical) points of sale with new digital and exciting environments and innovative interactive tools. Meaningful examples are further presented. In addition, this section proposes the usage of these technologies also for the design of new efficient stores.

Chapter 1
    Anthony Kent, University of Lincoln, UK
    Charles Dennis, University of Lincoln, UK
    Marta Blasquez Cano, University of Manchester, UK
    Eva Helberger, University of the Arts London, UK
    Josko Brakus, University of Leeds, UK

The aim of this chapter is to develop knowledge of retail environments through an overview of the most used technologies in retailing and the contribution of in-store technologies to the experience of the fashion store environment. The chapter commences with an overview of the influence of multichannel development, consumer-facing technologies, and their adoption by fashion retailers. The second part examines the use of digital signage and its contribution to atmospherics in a department store. The researchers have used a mixed method approach, with observational techniques drawn first from ethnographic methodology, and second, a quantitative approach to consumers' environmental response behavior. The results indicate a limited use of innovative in-store technologies and reliance on conventional technological media in fashion stores. Secondly, digital signage demonstrates both communication and experiential effects. The chapter concludes with a discussion of convergence between the virtual and physical store environments and the implications for theory and management.

Chapter 2

Gianpiero Di Blasi, Università degli Studi di Torino, Italy
Eleonora Pantano, Middlesex University London, UK

The emerging need to make more attractive physical stores for catching new clients and maintaining the existing ones pushes retailers to develop efficient practices for acquiring knowledge from consumers and involving them in the points of sales' design. The final users' needs and preferences are considered a core in design process. This chapter proposes a system for involving consumers in the store design process through an innovative cloud participatory platform. It is a low cost hardware/software architecture offering a user-friendly interface able to be adopted by audiences with different background. Results show the consumers' interest to contribute in the design by using such technologies and providing a large amount of detailed information useful for future appealing stores' development. Finally, this chapter shows how the inclusion of modern low-cost game technologies in retail industry might provide ripper effects in several disciplines such as human-computer interaction, marketing, and management.

Chapter 3

Ingrid Poncin, Catholic University of Louvain (UCL), Belgium
Marion Garnier, SKEMA Business School - Université de Lille, France
Virginie Maille, SKEMA Business School - Université de Lille, France

The Merchant Virtual Universe (MVU), which hyperrealistically reproduces the environment of a real shopping mall, is proving to be an innovative retail setting. It offers a competitive advantage by providing a satisfying and compelling online experience. This chapter examines immersion processes in an MVU and studies their evolution over time. The researchers collected qualitative and quantitative data from users throughout successive visits to a 3D virtual shopping mall. The data highlight the special role of perceived realism and sense of presence in allowing users to become immersed. The results confirm the links among realism, presence, and immersion, as well as their influence on satisfaction. They further illustrate the process as time passes: Realism is the strongest factor of immersion at the beginning of the experience but over time is replaced by presence. This work confirms that MVU designers must consider the importance of realism of the virtual environment.

Chapter 4

Patrizia Cherubino, IULM University, Italy & BrainSigns srl, Italy
Anton Giulio Maglione, Sapienza University, Italy
Ilenia Graziani, BrainSigns srl, Italy & Sapienza University, Italy
Arianna Trettel, BrainSigns srl, Italy
Giovanni Vecchiato, BrainSigns srl, Italy & Sapienza University, Italy
Fabio Babiloni, BrainSigns srl, Italy & Sapienza University, Italy

The purpose of this chapter is to share scientific methods for the quantitative measurement of emotion through the recording of physiologic and cerebral variables of consumers in relation to advertising stimuli and during the purchase in the store. For this reason, the authors describe the way to estimate the emotion along the visit of a shop by using the approach-withdrawal index. It demonstrates how it is possible to describe the variation of the appreciation of a shop visit by two groups of persons. The specific contribution to the scientific literature is the use of such approach-withdrawal index and the estimation of the emotion linked with the visit of a large point of sale (e.g. a supermarket). The proper use of these methodologies can provide information related to cognitive and emotional aspects of persons involved in the appreciation of products in retail points of sale.

Section 2
Consumers' and Employees' Behaviour, Adoption, and Acceptance

The chapters included in this section provide an overview of the response towards the introduction of technology-based innovations from both consumers' and employees' perspectives. In particular, this section describes their behaviour in terms of adoption and acceptance, decision-making process, and store/channel choice.

Chapter 5
Hyunjoo Im, University of Minnesota – Twin Cities, USA
Young Ha, California State University – Long Beach, USA

Mobile technology is becoming a critical part of marketing practices and many retailers aim to engage consumers through mobile coupons. In this context, it is critical to understand what drives consumers to use mobile coupons. Technology adoption research offers insights for both researchers and practitioners into this matter. This chapter critically reviews guiding theories, Technology Acceptance Theory and Innovation Diffusion Theory, as well as important literature on technology adoption to discuss evolution and application of technology adoption research. Five perception variables (perceived usefulness, perceived ease of use, perceived enjoyment, subjective norm, compatibility) and three individual characteristics (personal innovativeness, perceived risk, gender) are selected as most relevant determinants of consumers' intention to adopt and use mobile coupons. Limitation of technology adoption research and possible future research avenues are discussed.

Chapter 6
Tasha L. Lewis, Cornell University, USA
Suzanne Loker, Cornell University, USA

Technology use in apparel retail stores is on the rise and changing the way that employees work and customers shop. In spite of increased use, advanced technology deployed within apparel retail stores has yet to match the rapid pace of growth for technologies adopted by apparel consumers enabled by mobile devices and sophisticated digital applications. Apparel retail employees are the first line of contact for customers and are often engaged with them at several points in the service interaction, including assisting with the initial selection of apparel based on customers' desired product features, the try-on of clothing, and unique in-store services like personal shopping. In this chapter, the authors examine employee usage intent for technologies supportive of these various points of service interaction. The likelihood of employee usage of technology as well as employee characteristics that influenced the extent of technology adoption were also measured.

Chapter 7

This chapter gives insight into consumers' online and offline fashion shopping behavior, consumers' omni-channel usage during the shopping process, and consumer fashion shopper segments. Based on a literature review, omni-channel shopping behavior during the shopping process was operationalized. Subsequently, an online survey was developed to collect information of 2124 consumers living in the catchment areas of five regional Dutch shopping centers in 2013. Results of the analyses confirm previous findings and contribute additional evidence that suggests relations between consumers' omni-channel shopping behavior during the shopping process and socio-demographics and psychographics. Furthermore, results show that channel usage in the previous phase of the shopping process has a major influence on the channel usage in the following phases of the shopping process. By using the TwoStep clustering technique, six fashion shopper segments are found and described, with one of them a clear omni-channel shopper segment. The results provide information for retailers to know the type of consumers they reach through various channels to offer the right information, on the right channel, during the various phases of the shopping process.

Increasingly, brick and mortar retailers compete with their counterparts by enriching the point of sale through technological innovations that make use of customer-owned mobile devices. So, for example, IKEA, the world's largest furniture retailer, has introduced an interactive mobile app that provides the customer with additional insights in a personalized and convenient way: by scanning quick response codes in the printed catalogue, 3D objects, pictures, text, or videos are provided on the customer's smartphone or tablet. They inform about a furniture's interior or its potential usage, give planning aids, or visualize the furniture in alternative surroundings. In this chapter, the perceived usefulness, ease of use, and attitude towards such new technology-based innovations are discussed. Customers' perceptions are measured by applying a modified technology acceptance model. Traditional customer surveys as well as online customer reviews are analyzed. The results are encouraging: the mobile app is seen as an enrichment of the shopping experience but can be improved. Both data collection formats lead to similar results.

Section 3
Innovation Management and Innovative Strategies

This section offers a collection of recent studies proposing some promising strategies for the successful adoption of innovations in retail settings. Findings contribute to the body of literature on innovation and technology management for retailing and broaden the understanding of adoption dynamics in general. In particular, they offer a management perspective of the innovative force characterizing retail sector, and the possible strategies for creating new services within the financial sustainability standpoint.

Chapter 9

Philipp Spreer, University of Gottingen, Germany
Katrin Kallweit, University of Gottingen, Germany

Service excellence is one of the key differentiators for retailers in the digital environment. To ensure a high level of service quality at the point of sale, retailers contemplate the implementation of Self-Service Information Technologies (SSITs). This chapter 1) examines the mediation effect of service quality within the technology acceptance model and 2) identifies relevant segments based on the level of acceptance and the perception of the service quality provided by an SSIT. Building on data from a laboratory experiment using a fully functional application for Tablet PCs, the partial least squares approach and a combined hierarchical and non-hierarchical cluster analysis were used. The findings reveal that the perceived service quality partially mediates the effect of the attitude towards using on the intention to reuse. Moreover, two distinct segments are identified: the "occasional handymen" and the "enthusiastic experts," who differ significantly in terms of SSIT acceptance.

Chapter 10

Milena Viassone, University of Turin, Italy

In recent years, the issue of innovation in marketing channels has assumed an increasing importance, but this topic has been considered in reference to specific areas of innovation or to single categories of subjects within channels. Despite this, there is a lack of contributions that provide guidelines to excel in innovative retail channels. This chapter aims at describing the set of features of benchmark firms awarded for the innovation in retail channels and proposing an illustrative framework to be followed by retailers who choose the path of innovation. This objective is carried out throughout a systematic analysis of related literature both on innovation and benchmark in retail channels and throughout the analysis of 127 benchmark retailers awarded with two important prizes for innovation in the period 2011-2014. Results allow the creation of a set of best practices for innovative retailers, thus providing an important contribution to this topic.

Chapter 11

Michael Lewrick, University Ulm, Germany
Maktoba Omar, Edinburgh Napier University, UK
Robert Williams Jr., Susquehanna University, USA
Nathalia C. Tjandra, Edinburgh Napier University, UK
Zui-Chih Lee, Susquehanna University, USA

The retail industry market environment is very competitive; thus, in order to maintain their competitive advantage retailers are required to continuously come up with innovative offerings and systems. This chapter aims to provide useful insights for the retailers regarding the correlation between market orientation and innovation. The chapter illustrates the differences in start-up and mature companies, and reveals new insights with regard to market orientation and its constituent elements, and its relationship with both incremental and radical innovations. Readers learn that strong competitor orientation, a key ingredient of market orientation, has a positive relationship to incremental innovation for start-up companies, but it is counterproductive for mature companies, where a strong customer orientation is associated with radical innovation. The focus is to understand the dynamics of the entrepreneur versus manager during the transition process as a company grows.

Fashion retail is recognised for its strong capabilities in product innovation, while also having the potential to improve the governance of technology-based process innovation. This chapter proposes a model perspective in management of technology and innovation, including special requirements of fashion retailing. In particular, this chapter discusses the context of fashion retailing understood as product and brand-based characteristics. A case study-based methodology is then used to guide an analysis of antecedents and (expected) outcome of fashion retail innovation. IT-based innovation dominates, but innovation is suggested to include a broader scope of technologies. Contrary to innovation maturity models, this chapter proposes to consider innovation as a continuous refinement between dynamic capabilities and absorptive capacity where technologies must be adapted to the special characteristics of the fashion retail industry.

Chapter 13

The main purpose of this chapter is to address two important areas for successfully managing retail businesses—financial sustainability and innovative technology—in order to find out in which ways they affect each other. In order to clarify the financial sustainability of innovative technologies and the ways innovative technologies contribute in achieving financial sustainability in a retail company as a whole, it has been explored in grocery retailing in the Republic of Croatia. The results of a study among the top retail companies operating in the Croatian market suggest that innovative technology has the highest priority in their strategic and financial planning as one of the four fundamental pillars of financial sustainability. However, the results also indicated a long payback period after the implementation of new technological solutions.

Chapter 14

Kijpokin Kasemsap, Suan Sunandha Rajabhat University, Thailand

This chapter explores the roles of corporate marketing strategies and brand management in the global
retail industry, thus describing the concepts of marketing strategy, international retail marketing strategy,
retail marketing mix, and internationalization; the relationship between corporate marketing strategies
and internationalization; the challenges of retail marketing mix in the fashion retail industry; the overview
of brand management; and the significance of brand management in the global retail industry. The
implementation of corporate marketing strategies and brand management is critical for modern organizations
that seek to serve suppliers and customers, increase business performance, strengthen competitiveness,
and achieve continuous success in global business. Therefore, it is necessary for modern organizations
to examine their corporate marketing strategies and brand management applications, create a strategic
plan to regularly check their practical advancements, and rapidly respond to the corporate marketing
strategies and brand management needs of customers in the global retail industry.

Foreword

Successful Technological Integration for Competitive Advantage in Retail Settings comprises research, insights, and practices on a topic that researchers do not explore very often: the link between technology and marketing in the retail sector.

We are all aware of the numerous technologies that have affected the retail sector, even if these technologies very often did not originate in the retail domain, but were adapted to suit retail companies. Nevertheless, these technologies have already modified the way business is done in retailing. Further, it is very difficult to accurately forecast the changes that will occur within just the next five to ten years, let alone in the long term, which is totally unpredictable.

This up to date collection of papers from different countries and various fields of specialization focuses on five main topics:

- The continuous innovation process in retailing and the issues of funding and maintaining the pace of innovation;
- The effect of technologies on the consumer experience, especially on the social interaction, which is one of the main elements of the consumer experience;
- The evolution of the interaction between customers and retailers, specifically the mediating role of shop assistants;
- How technology and innovations can provide retailers with a competitive advantage;
- The retailer's dilemma: Investing in innovation, or adapting to the sector specificities, innovations and other domains' technologies.

My personal observations are first of all related to one of the most ancient retail strategy concepts – scale economies. From the beginning of modern retail in the mid-19th century, the economies of scale concept was strictly linked to the retailers' size and their ability to negotiate lower prices than their competitors could provide with their suppliers. Very soon a second element became relevant: The ability to increase the inventory and the capital turn-over to sustain the virtuous circle of sales volume, cost reduction, price reduction and sales growth. This managerial innovation required companies to introduce "technologies" to manage their inventory turn-over and to very efficiently control the capital they invested in their retail company.

More than 150 years after the birth of the department store, the real competitive advantage is no longer size, but companies' capacity to be innovative, flexible and capable as well as to exploit technologies better than their competitors. A few current retail champions have within a short time acquired a place in the rankings of the world's top retailers, while other—well reputed and long-established—retailers have disappeared, or are facing difficult challenges to maintain their place in the market. Size does, of course, still matter, but more in the sense of generating resources to invest in order to improve the company's efficiency and competitive advantage than in the previous sense of the balance of power between retailers and manufacturers.

The second point I want to emphasise is linked to one of the main sections of the book: Funding innovations and technology adoption. This issue is a true dilemma for many retail companies whose financial performances are shrinking due to the world economic crisis and the on-going price war in many developed markets, but which are also forced to invest in innovations that could help them maintain their position in the market.

This observation leads to another point: The pervasiveness of technology and innovation in retail companies. We have seen the integration of technologies into stores, but also into the entire supply chain in order to manage branches dispersed throughout the world and as a tool to demonstrate retail brands' omni-channel presence to consumers.

Certain in-store technologies are partially replacing tasks that store personnel previously performed, for example, automatic cash systems and self-scanning systems. In other cases, these technologies are aimed at improving the interaction between the sales assistants and the customers in order to offer the latter the personalized service available in online channels. Technologies therefore not only help retailers reduce their operating costs, but simultaneously help improve the customer experience.

The customer experience is perhaps the key issue for every technology integration in retailing. Many researchers have studied the evolution of consumer behaviour through the diffusion of technologies that allow everybody to make purchases everywhere, at any time and to share their impressions, intentions and opinions in real time before, during and after their purchase. Researchers have also analysed new ways to create a relationship between brands and consumers, while some of their publications have illustrated innovative forms of attachment to brands.

Technologies and their integration into retailers' day-to-day operations should improve the relationship between a brand and its consumers, both current and potential; simultaneously, technologies should help retailers suggest experiences to their customers that can differentiate a brand from all others in the market. A positive experience is a key factor in order to create attention and build a strong and lasting relation with customers.

Customer experience is perhaps easier to create in a physical store, while technologies can help reinforce the set of store experiences already studied in the "sensory retail" stream of research. In future it will be essential for retailers to propose a unique store experience, well differentiated from the experiences available through other channels; conversely, the risk of stores becoming irrelevant or mere show rooms before customers make their purchases online, could become a reality.

Finally, I highlight the differences between developed and developing markets.

All the main retailers in the world are international, even if their level of internationalization and the weight of the foreign markets regarding turnover and profitability differ greatly. With the advent and diffusion of technologies in all the main retail company sectors, the question arises whether these technologies should be adopted around the world, or whether the technological level should be adapted to different countries' requirements. Some adaptations may be compulsory, due to the host market's limitations, but the cultural acceptance of some technologies, or the social and cultural habits that are still very important in certain "non-western" markets may justify other modifications.

This is another challenge for researchers and managers trying to integrate retailing and technology.

I believe Successful Technological Integration for Competitive Advantage in Retail Settings provides scholars and managers with many contributions regarding the fast changing retail sector where the customer not only has to remain centre stage, but marketing and management theories and practices also have to integrate the evolutions and the disruptions that technologies and their application introduce to businesses.

Daniele Pederzoli
NEOMA Business School, France

Daniele Pederzoli *has a degree from the University of Bologna (Italy) and a PhD from the University of Rennes I (France). He is currently Professor of Marketing and Director of the Bachelor in Retail Management programme at NEOMA Business School, France. He started working in the retail sector as Head of the Retail Unit of a training and consulting company in Italy at the end of the 1970s. After the completion of his PhD, he became an Associate Professor at the Rouen Business School in France. He has authored or co-authored four books in the field of retail marketing and shopping centre management. He has also published 14 articles in academic journals and more than 30 communications at academic congresses in France and internationally. He has also written more than 100 articles for managerial marketing and retail reviews. His current research interests are international retailing and relations between brands, stores, and consumers in the luxury sector.*

Preface

In recent years, progresses in technology have made available a large amount of technical innovations for improving retail process, while the demand of innovative services is increasing more than in the past. As a consequence, this innovative force pushes retailers to innovate to successfully compete.

As a result, many interactive systems have been introduced in traditional points of sale, such as self-service technologies, touch screen displays, mobile applications for mobile devices (i.e. virtual catalogues for smart phones), intelligent shopping trolleys fixed and portable RFID (Radio Frequency IDentification), etc. (Demirkan & Spohrer, 2014; Rese, Schreiber, & Baier, 2014). For instance, groceries and department stores have introduced self-service technologies equipped with RFID systems for self-checkouts; stores for electronics have introduced interactive touch-screen displays for providing information on products and related prices, promotions, and location within the store; others have introduced applications for mobile phones for supporting consumers to find stores, items, creating a wish list, etc.; a few retailers also created completely new virtual stores based on ubiquitous computing, such as the Spanish Pickbe, which allows consumers to access its products directly from mobile while they are located in a certain area (such as a certain metro stop). Another consistent part of retailers had not introduced yet technological innovations in their stores (Pantano & Viassone, 2014). The main advantages for consumers related to such innovation lie in the possibility to achieve constantly updated information on available products and service, which consumers can access through entertaining, high interactive, and user-friendly interfaces (Bodhani, 2012; Chattaramental, 2012; Oh, Teo, & Sambamurthy, 2013; Wang, 2012; Papagiannidis, Pantano, See-to, & Bourlakis, 2013). As a consequence, stores look more appealing and attractive providing consumers with a new and exciting shopping experience (Demirkan & Spohrer, 2014).

Similarly, these technologies may provide retailers with information on consumers' behaviour and preferences, useful for managing data, predicting market trends, developing customized services and advertising campaign, reducing cost of personnel (for example moving some services traditionally executed by salesforce to the automatic system) (Evans, 2011; Pantano, 2014).

However, critical issues may arise while innovating, due to the difficulties of retailers to define efficient management strategies for successfully absorbing the innovative technologies. In fact, retailers tend to outsource the Research and Development function. As a consequence, they are usually the adopters of innovations produced by other manufacturing companies through expensive and dynamic strategies (Pantano, 2014). Introducing innovation within the points of sale also involves some risks, concerning the high level of uncertainty emerging from consumers' effective usage of the technology, monetary investment (costs), time consuming, complexity of the process, risk of obsolescence of technology, and the changes in the store layout and atmosphere (Alkemade & Suurs, 2012; Pantano et al., 2013).

For these reasons, current retailers show a consistent heterogeneity in innovating strategies.

Despite these restraining conditions (i.e. risks related to consumers' acceptance, monetary investment, risks of fast obsolescence of the technology, etc.), the wave of innovative technologies available for improving selling goods is making available many interactive and innovative systems. In particular, these systems are able to support both consumers while shopping and retailers for achieving fast and update information on market trends, selling process, and creating new adaptable and direct marketing strategies.

This book intends to provide useful insight into technology and innovation management for retailing, by taking advantage from the most recent researches in this sector, in order to provide a framework for understanding the phenomenon and guidelines for identifying the best technologies for enhancing the retail process, and the best strategies to manage such technologies (in terms of introduction, adoption, acceptance, etc.).

Hence, it provides an integrative view able to support both practitioners (retailers and developers) and scholars with different backgrounds but all interested in understanding (1) how consumers accept and interact with new technologies, (2) developers design new usable, interactive, and efficient interfaces and systems, (3) how marketers and managers define more successful strategies based on a better usage of the technology, and (4) how the technology changes the interactions and the perception of all the actors involved in the process (e.g. consumers, frontend employees, and retailers), etc.

THE CHALLENGES

Hence, the retail scenario enriched with novel technologies poses new questions to both scholars and practitioners:

- To what extent will a continuous innovation in retailing be feasible and financially sustainable?
- Will the role of physical seller be totally replaced by more realistic interfaces?
- How can the capacity of absorbing technological innovations by retailers be measured and increased?
- Will the advanced technologies modify the meaning of shopping as social experience?
- When should a retailer be pioneer or simply an adopter?
- How can the impact of these technologies on retailing be measured?

Therefore, innovation and technology management, traditionally related to industrial engineering topics, can be successfully integrated for the definition of new successful retail strategies, while the challenges they solicit a way for adequate understanding of the new competitive scenario.

The studies collected in this book aim at answering to some of these questions, by proposing on one hand the retailers' management strategies and on the other one the consumers' standpoint, with emphasis on the effect of the technology-enriched retail scenario on their experience.

TARGET AUDIENCE

The book should provide an integrative view of the emerging innovative scenario in retailing. Due to its focus on current hot topics for scholars and practitioners, the book would be an important tool for both retailers and developers, and for scholars of several fields such as Economics, Management, Psychology, Industrial Engineering, Sociology, and Computer Science.

ORGANIZATION OF THE BOOK

The book is organized into 3 sections and 14 chapters

The first section focuses on the influence of new technologies on store design and atmosphere. In particular, four chapters are included in this section showing to what extent the advanced technologies can change the store atmosphere by enriching the traditional (physical) points of sale with new digital and exciting environments and innovative interactive tools. The description and analysis proposed are then supported by meaningful examples. In addition, this section proposes the usage of these technologies also in the design of new efficient stores.

The first chapter describes the new retail environments after the introduction of advanced technologies, with emphasis on the digital signage and multichannel development effects on the store atmosphere for fashion retailers, by presenting some evidences from UK market.

The following chapter investigates the use of cloud computing for new store design by outlining to what extent new technologies might successfully involve consumers in the design process and in the final service co-creation by starting from an experiment taking place in a university laboratory.

The third chapter focuses on a particular technology, the merchant virtual universe, which reproduces virtually a real shopping mall. The research analyses the realistic online experience, with emphasis on the feeling of immersion in the new retail environment by outlining the fundamental role of immersion, realism, and sense of presence on consumers' satisfaction.

The fourth chapter aims at illustrating the usage of neuroimaging for deeply understanding the effect of certain marketing stimuli within a point of sale, with emphasis on the cognitive and emotional aspects of consumers involved in the evaluation of products available within the store.

The second section focuses on consumers and employees' acceptance of advanced technologies within the point of sale. The chapters included in this section provide an overview of consumers and employees' response in terms of adoption and acceptance, decision-making process, and store/channel choice.

The first chapter included in this section focuses on consumers' acceptance of mobile coupon. Starting from the Technology Acceptance Theory and Innovation Diffusion Theory, it outlines the determinants in terms of perception variables and individual characteristics.

Chapter 6 focuses on apparel stores, with emphasis on employee's behavior after the introduction of advanced technologies able to support their work, by measuring the determinants of technology adoption.

Chapter 7 investigates the emerging phenomenon of omnichannel shopping, based on the usage of online and offline channels (i.e. magazines, friends, physical store, etc.) by consumer for achieving information able to support the shopping experience. In particular, this chapter analyses the usage of multiple channels during shopping process.

The following chapter focuses on consumers' acceptance of a new technology consisting of an interactive application for mobile phone that allows to scan the codes available in the printed catalogue to access to 3D virtual reconstruction of products and interact with them from their own mobile. This app enhances the shopping experience and represents a promising research area for further improvements.

The last section of the current book is based on innovation management and innovative strategies, by offering a collection of chapters investigating the possible strategy for successfully adopting innovations in retail settings. The presented findings contribute to the body of innovation and technology management for retailing and broaden the understanding of adoption dynamics in general. In particular, they offer a management perspective of the introduction of technological innovations in retail settings by emphasizing the innovative force characterizing the sector and the possible strategies for creating new services within the financial sustainability standpoint.

The first chapter included in this section outlines to what extent the service excellence is one of the key elements for retailers for differentiating in the digital environment, starting from a laboratory experiment based on mobile application and related tablet computers.

The following chapter proposes an investigation of current strategies of retailers who adopted innovative retail channel strategies, by analysing 127 retailers between 2011 and 2014.

Similarly, the subsequent chapter focuses on the topics of market orientation, innovation and their reciprocal relationships with business success in retail industry with emphasis on the difference between radical and incremental innovation for profitably strategies.

Chapter 12 investigates the expected outcomes from innovating in fashion retail by considering innovation maturity models, absorptive capacity, and dynamic capabilities.

The following chapter analyses the financial sustainability of innovating in retail settings by taking into account the case of Croatian groceries. One of the outcomes shows to what extent there is a long payback period after the adoption of new technological innovations.

The last chapter included in the book explores the role of corporate marketing strategies and brand management in retail industry with emphasis on the fashion sector.

The book aims at integrating previous findings that mainly focused on consumers and technology by adding also an innovation management and corporate perspective. This publication is intended to provide a comprehensive vision of the current competitive scenario in retailing and to propose management strategies for successfully competing.

Eleonora Pantano
Middlesex University London, UK

REFERENCES

Alkemade, F., & Suurs, R. A. A. (2012). Patterns of expectations for emerging sustainable technologies. *Technological Forecasting and Social Change*, *79*, 448–456.

Bodhani, A. (2012). Shops offer thee-tail experience. *Eng. Technol.*, *7*(5), 46–49.

Chattaraman, V., Known, W.-S., & Gilbert, J. E. (2012). Virtual agents in retail websites: Benefits of simulated social interaction forolder users. *Computers in Human Behavior*, *28*(6), 2055–2066.

Demirkan, H., & Spohrer, J. (2014). Developing a framework to improve virtual shopping in digital malls with intelligent self-services sytems. *Journal of Retailing and Consumer Services*, *21*(5), 860–868.

Evans, J. R. (2011). Retailing in perspective: The past is a prologue to the future. *International Review of Retail, Distribution and Consumer Research*, *2*(1), 1–31.

Oh, L.-B., Teo, H. H., & Sambamurthy, V. (2012). The effect of retail channel integration through the use of information technologies on firm performance. *Journal of Operations Management*, *30*(5), 368–381.

Pantano, E. (2014). Innovation drivers in retail industry. *International Journal of Information Management*, *34*, 344–350.

Pantano, E., Iazzolino, G., & Migliano, G. (2013). Obsolescence risk in advanced technologies for retailing: A management perspective. *Journal of Retailing and Consumer Services*, *20*(1), 225–233.

Pantano, E., & Viassone, M. (2014). Demand pull and technology push perspective in technology-based innovations for the points of sale: The retailers evaluation. *Journal of Retailing and Consumer Services*, *21*(1), 43–47.

Papagiannidis, S., Pantano, E., See-to, E., & Bourlakis, M. (2013). Modelling the determinants of a simulated experience in a virtual retail store and users' product purchasing intentions. *Journal of Marketing Management*, *29*(13/14), 1462–1492.

Rese, A., Schreiber, S., & Baier, D. (2014). Technology acceptance modeling of augmented reality at the point of sale: Can surveys be replaced by an analysis of online reviews? *Journal of Retailing and Consumer Services*, *21*(5), 869–876.

Wang, M. C.-H. (2012). Determinants and consequences of consumer satisfaction with self-service technology in a retail setting. *Managing Service Quality*, *22*(2), 128–144.

Section 1
Store Design and Atmosphere

Chapters included in this section show how the adoption of advanced technologies changes the store atmosphere, by enriching the traditional (physical) points of sale with new digital and exciting environments and innovative interactive tools. Meaningful examples are further presented. In addition, this section proposes the usage of these technologies also for the design of new efficient stores.

Chapter 1

Branding, Marketing, and Design:
Experiential In-Store Digital Environments

Anthony Kent
University of Lincoln, UK

Marta Blasquez Cano
University of Manchester, UK

Charles Dennis
University of Lincoln, UK

Eva Helberger
University of the Arts London, UK

Josko Brakus
University of Leeds, UK

ABSTRACT

The aim of this chapter is to develop knowledge of retail environments through an overview of the most used technologies in retailing and the contribution of in-store technologies to the experience of the fashion store environment. The chapter commences with an overview of the influence of multichannel development, consumer-facing technologies, and their adoption by fashion retailers. The second part examines the use of digital signage and its contribution to atmospherics in a department store. The researchers have used a mixed method approach, with observational techniques drawn first from ethnographic methodology, and second, a quantitative approach to consumers' environmental response behavior. The results indicate a limited use of innovative in-store technologies and reliance on conventional technological media in fashion stores. Secondly, digital signage demonstrates both communication and experiential effects. The chapter concludes with a discussion of convergence between the virtual and physical store environments and the implications for theory and management.

INTRODUCTION

Mobile connectivity provides new opportunities for browsing and shopping; mirroring computer-based online sales growth, fashion clothing has become the most popular category in m-commerce (Mercer, 2013). According to industry reports (Bain, 2011; Deloitte, 2011; Marketing Week 2013; Retail Week 2013, 2014) retailers can stimulate store-based consumption by integrating the physical and the virtual store experience through the installation of new and interactive technology into their physical stores. This integration offers consumers services that they have become accustomed to online, including personalized recommendation, reviews, price transparency,

DOI: 10.4018/978-1-4666-8297-9.ch001

videos and products in addition to a sensory and immersive experience that the online store cannot provide. In the general context of marketing communications, targeted communications have grown while mass media advertising has declined (Vranca, 2009).

To the authors' knowledge, to date no retailers with substantial investment in store technology publish information on their return on investment. Therefore no conclusion can yet be drawn from prior research concerning whether in-store technology profitably drives sales (Bearne, 2014). Nevertheless, the rapid development of online and mobile technologies and their pervasiveness, merit further examination. Consequently, the chapter commences with an assessment of the application of interactive technologies in store environments, and their contribution to in-store consumer experience. In doing so this study expands on Verhoef et. al.'s (2009) model for customer experience management, by examining in more detail which elements of the customer retail experience are permeated by the use of technology.

One technological element of the in-store environment that has become well-established is digital signage. This type of signage consists of screens in public places showing video (Dennis, Newman, Michon, Brakus, & Wright, 2010). Content may include advertisements, community information, entertainment and news. Digital signage aims to talk to shoppers while they are captive and in the mood to buy (Dennis et al., 2010). Interest in bringing advertisements into stores is growing (Burke, 2009) and many retailers have launched digital signage networks, which can also generate substantial advertising revenues (Signs of the Times, 2006).

Newman, Dennis and Zaman (2006) investigated the acceptability of digital signage to shoppers, reporting that it creates a more modern image, increases enjoyment and provides useful information, although for a minority it can be considered boring and incapable of commanding their attention. Dennis et al. (2010) subsequently explained that such signage has a significant, positive, total effect on mall consumer spending and to some extent has a positive effect on shoppers' approach behaviors, such as spending (Dennis, Michon, Brakus, Newman & Alamanos, 2012).

In this context of personal and mobile but also retailer-led technologies and new opportunities that arise to re-define consumer experiences of the fashion store, the objectives of this chapter fall in two parts. The first is to assess the extent to which interactive technologies are used by retailers in the fashion sector, and their influence on customer experience; and further to evaluate the convergence of online and physical retailing. The second part of this chapter has the objectives of assessing the role of a specific technology in-store, digital signage, its influence on consumers' brand experience of the store environment, its influence on their behavior and their spending.

Background

Technologies in Retailing: The Influence of Multichannel

The digital revolution has empowered consumers, raising expectations for different experiences and changing behaviors (Deloitte, 2011; Pine & Gilmore, 2011; Rosenblum & Rowen, 2012). As the internet offers more choice, the consumer now holds more power throughout different stages of the shopping process: in decision-making, at the point of purchase and in product ownership (PwC, 2011), they are more demanding and expect more from their shopping experiences (Mathwick et al. 2002; OXIRM, 2006).

The rapid growth of the internet has led to the concept and realization of multichannel retailing, which includes all the activities involved in the sale of products or services through more than one channel (Zhang et al., 2010). A multichannel retailer requires a consistent brand experience across all points of interaction with the consumer (Bagge, 2007). The implication that an evaluation of brand touchpoints and the integration between experiences across channels is a crucial success factor, has given rise to a further conceptualization, omnichannel (Bain, 2011). For retail brands, integration strategies require attention to online sites and physical stores, but also other points of contact including catalogues, telephone sales, mobile apps and social media.

Consumers too have come to consider their shopping experience as a whole (Interbrand, 2012) and look for an integrated and consistent experience between channels (Roy et al., 2005; Zhang et al., 2010). In this way consumers communicate with retailers through multiple media, especially in their use of highly interpersonal channels (Kumar & Venkatesan, 2005).Consequently, exploratory shopping behavior characterizes multichannel retailing (Kumar & Venkatesan, 2005, Rohm & Swaminathan, 2004). However, lack of experiential information and physical interaction with the product is one of the main barriers to buying fashion online (Merle, Senecal, & St-Onge, 2012; Retail Week, 2012) because fashion clothing is a category that requires multisensory engagement (Citrin, Stem, Spangenberg, & Clark, 2003).

Digital mediating technologies have significantly changed the online shopping experience, with Image Interactive Technologies such as augmented reality, virtual fitting rooms or 3D virtual models helping consumers to evaluate clothes online and as a consequence, reduce the risk associated with the process. Secondly, these technologies have contributed to an interactive online experience accompanied by atmospheric cues that increase the level of pleasure felt by the shopper (Eroglu, Machleit, & Davis, 2003) and generate a positive attitude towards fashion shopping (Yang & Young, 2009).

While retailers have been slow to adopt innovative technologies and many stores today are not even mobile or digitally enabled (Deloitte, 2011), increasingly, technology demonstrates the capacity to blur the boundaries between the in-store and online shopping experiences (Merle et al., 2012). This presents a number of challenges for physical store retailing. The most fundamental is the decline of bricks-and-mortar stores as the dominant distribution channel (Clifford, 2012). The ability to shop online results in fewer visits by the consumer to stores (Ernst & Young, 2001), a reduction in the average length of time consumers spend in a store (Chu & Lam, 2007) and a decline in their sales (Mintel, 2012). Consequently, there are increasing concerns about the store's viability in its capacity as a 'showroom' for online purchasing. Nevertheless from the retailers' perspective it remains the primary point of contact with the consumer (Chu & Paglucia, 2002) and for consumers, shopping in stores prevails as the most popular place to buy clothes. It is estimated that the physical store will continue to be the main point of sale for the next five years, but it is important to acknowledge that stores are becoming just one part of a larger and more connected customer experience (Deloitte, 2011).

Technology has the power to transform the appearance of a store, causing the store to appear more futuristic and providing the opportunity of introducing new services and providing customized messages to consumers as much as introducing new entertainment tools (Pantano & Naccarato, 2010). In-store technology redefines the store experiences and store layouts through innovations such as click-and-collect services, radio frequency identification, shopping assistant services or more advanced technologies such as consumers' mirrors or interactive fitting rooms that connect with social networks (Drapers, 2012, and Pantano & Naccarato, 2010). However, retailers should not lose sight of the service dimension of their operations in additional to their customer experience, and must focus on technology that is relevant for consumers and that provides real value for them (Euromonitor International, 2009).

There are then, both functional and hedonic considerations to the use of in-store technologies. The introduction of new elements stimulating consumers' interest and attention are important to inspire consumers, and to create more pleasurable in-store experiences (Bäckström & Johansson, 2006). Technology can create an attractive environment making the shopping experience engaging and memorable (Deloitte, 2011, Drapers, 2012, and Kozinets et al., 2002). Ballantine et al. (2010) refer to the use of attractive stimuli in the store, such as the use of interactive product displays to attract attention and engage customers. Interactive devices, including store-ordering hubs, iPads, and display screens in general, provide opportunities to browse online from the store (Bäckström & Johansson, 2006, and WGSN, 2012), create a new merchandise layout, make products more accessible and convenient to buy (Euromonitor International, 2009) and influence consumers' expectations on search efficiency (Pantano & Naccarato, 2010).

In the fashion industry, sensory elements are especially important as consumers look not only to touch and trial clothes (Underhill, 2008) but also for entertainment when they buy clothing. Therefore a convenient, relaxing and enjoyable in-store environment makes shopping a pleasurable experience (Chu & Lam, 2007) and in this, technology can make a clear contribution (Pantano & Naccarato, 2010).

However, despite the emphasis on channel integration and the role of technologies in mediating experiences, there is a lack of specific research about how this integration takes place in the physical store space. Pantano and Naccarato (2010) reviewed interactive technologies that are present in the store and affect the shopping experience. They include the 'most-used' technologies in point of sale and relate these technologies with other studies to make some inferences about possible influences on consumer behavior. However Pantano and Naccarato (2010) did not explain the criteria to determine the use of technologies in the physical space, nor did they explicitly situate their work in a theoretical framework. For their part, Brynjolfsson, Hu, and Rahman (2013) conducted an empirical study through data obtained from a medium-sized retail

company but without specifying the theoretical frameworks or methodologies applied. They refer to different technologies used in a multichannel environment and suggest strategies for different types of retailers, although those authors do not fully explain how the integration should take place. Finally, aside from academic papers, a number of industry reports have described the presence and role of technology in the store (Deloitte, 2011; Omnico, 2013; Retail Week, 2012). The reports provide a broad overview and valuable insights into the strategic development of technologies in multi and omnichannel retailing. These deserve closer examination and conceptualization, and so the next section turns to a detailed assessment of brand experience and the place of a specific technology, digital signage, in this field.

Brand Experience in Retailing

Shopping is not just obtaining tangible products but also experience and enjoyment (Martineau, 1958). Dennis, Murphy, Marsland, Cockett & Patel (2002) find that service and experiential attributes, for example store layout, cleanliness, and atmosphere, are more associated with shoppers' choices than is merchandise. Enjoyment and entertainment are important benefits (Babin, Darden, & Griffin, 1994; Yoo, Park, & MacInnis, 1998), valued by consumers, and reflected in spending (Donovan, Rossiter, & Marcoolyn, 1994).

Marketers can use experience providers, for example visual identity, communication, product presence, websites, atmospherics, and service to create customer experiences (Schmitt, 1999). In the marketing literature, the concept of experience is explored from a number of perspectives: shopping, consumption, customer/consumer, service, product, and brand experience (Puccinelli et al., 2009; Skard, Nysveen, & Pedersen, 2011; Verhoef et al., 2009). Notwithstanding, we agree with Zarantonello and Schmitt (2010) that brand experience spans all contexts in which the concept of experience has been applied in marketing.

Service or product experiences refer to specific offerings and shopping experience refers to a specific phase in the consumer cycle. Therefore, we consider brand experience to be the conceptually-broadest experience construct, especially considering that brand could be either product-based or service-based and that both customers and non-customers may have experiences with a brand (Brakus et al., 2009; Skard et al., 2011). An ad and the stimuli that the ad focuses on (e.g. logo, brand characters, verbal slogan, jingle), for example, can evoke a 'brand experience' (Schmitt, 2012).

Brakus et al. (2009) focus on multiple sources of brand experiences acknowledging that a series of touchpoints between the product or service brand and the consumer creates an experience (Duncan & Moriarty, 2006). Brand experiences are 'subjective, internal consumer responses (sensations, feelings, and cognitions) and behavioral responses evoked by brand-related stimuli that are part of a brand's design and identity, packaging, communications, and [retail] environments' (Brakus et al., 2009 p. 53). The role of context can be found in the theory of mind modularity (Pinker, 1997) that the mind is not a universal processor of context-free information, but consists of context-dependant special-purpose computational modules responding to specific environmental cues, inspired the brand experience construct. Sensory experience refers to sensory stimulation; affective experience to moods, feelings, and emotions; intellectual experience to intellectual stimulation (analytical reasoning and/or divergent thinking); and behavioral experience to bodily interactions with the environment.

Brand experiences are inherently valuable and have a positive impact on consumer satisfaction, stated loyalty, and brand-consumer relationship (Brakus et al., 2009; Chang & Chieng, 2006). Eisingerich and Rubera (2010) argue that in western societies brand self-relevance and innovativeness have a greater effect on brand commitment compared to other elements such as customer orientation and social responsibility. Brand self-relevance is a key

element in Schmitt's psychological brand model (2012), which has five layers that represent the psychological engagement of consumers with brands. Inner layers represent utilitarian engagement; middle layer self-relevance to consumers; and outer layer social engagement with a brand. Brand choice can also be influenced by experienced emotions (Esch et al., 2012). When consumers feel emotionally attached to a brand they are likely to be more loyal (Thomson, MacInnis, & Park, 2005) and willing to spend more social and financial resources on it (Park, MacInnis, Priester, Eisingerich, & Iacobucci, 2010). Digital Signage messages high in affective content could facilitate affective engagement with a brand and therefore positive approach.

When consumers perceive a brand as a source of compelling experiences, they derive additional perceived value over functional and economic value (Pine & Gilmore, 1999; Zhang & Schmitt, 2001). When experiences lead to stimulating, pleasurable outcomes, evoked brand experiences should affect not only past-directed satisfaction judgments, but also subsequent behavior (Brakus et al., 2009). Therefore, evoked experiences should positively affect consumers' attitudes towards an ad and approach towards the advertiser.

Brand experiences are neither belief-based nor evaluative judgments about the brand. Rather, they include internal responses such as sensations, feelings, divergent (imaginative) thoughts and 'approach' as well as convergent (analytical) thoughts triggered by brand-related stimuli (Brakus et al., 2009). Therefore most brand experiences are not cognitive, except for high-order intellectual, analytical thoughts and reasons.

Brand attitudes are general evaluations based on beliefs (Fishbein & Ajzen, 1975), while brand experiences result from consumer interactions or communications with (e.g.) advertisements or shopping environments (Brakus et al., 2009; Chang & Chieng, 2006). Overall brand attitudes are general and do not elucidate the nature of brand experience. However, brand experiences can result in brand evaluations and may develop into attitudes.

Atmospherics

Experience cannot be understood without an appreciation of the role of atmospherics, defined as the conscious designing of space to create certain effects in buyers (Kotler, 1972). With 'designing of space' it embraces every aspect of the environment that can influence consumers' experience: a positive store atmosphere is essential to the creation of experience (Hoffman and Turley, 2002). Adopting a holistic approach, atmospherics have a direct effect on the customer experience (Ballantine et al., 2010; Biehl-Missal and vom Lehn, 2014; Michon, Yu, Smith, & Chebat, 2007; Puccinelli et al., 2009; Underhill, 2008) influencing psychological and behavioral shopping outcomes (Bitner, 1992; Donovan & Rossiter, 1982; Turley and Milliman, 2000).

Atmospherics have been widely acknowledged to influence consumer perceptions of value of stores and specific products (Babin et al., 1994). From a behavioral perspective, atmospherics influence shoppers' approach or avoidance behaviors (Donovan & Rossiter, 1982). Atmosphere has an impact on shoppers' affect, their emotional affinity to the store (Parsons, 2010) and increases consumers' satisfaction and mood (Babin & Darden, 1996; Chebat & Michon, 2003), and customer patronage (Babin & Attaway, 2000). Further, in specialty fashion stores, the environment can influence shopper orientation resulting in different behaviors (Scarpi, 2006).

In this context, atmosphere is perceived in a bodily way and has an objective status but is always part of a subjective reality (Böhme, 1993, 2001). Atmospheric cues emanate from a physical source, and such sources can be external or internal to the store, where layout, store design, and point of purchase materials contribute to material elements of the atmosphere (Turley & Milliman, 2000). In the case of retail stores, their atmosphere may be consciously designed by the retailer to cause certain moods and behaviors in the consumer, although its effects are intangible and always formed by subjective perception (Böhme, 2001).

Puccinelli et al. (2009) following Baker, Grewal, and Parasuraman (2009) simplify the classification of atmospherics and refer to three primary sets of cues: design, ambient and social cues. Design cues include both external and internal variables while social cues refer to employees and the presence of other customers. Ambient cues include aspects such as lighting, store layout, music or the use of technology in the store. This physical dimension has particular managerial relevance as it is manufactured and controlled by the retailer to deliver experience for both employees and customers (Zeithaml, Bitner, & Gremler, 2009). Further, the physical dimension uses measurable stimuli, which facilitates the micro planning of the store atmosphere.

The second part of this chapter examines these issues in more detail to show how atmospheric cues affect consumers' cognitive and emotional reactions and their approach behavior in the store (Morrison, Gan, Dubelaar & Oppewal, 2011; Walsh, Shiu, Hassan, Michaelidou & Beatty, 2011). To examine the problem in more detail, the current research focuses on a ubiquitous in-store technology, digital signage, as a provider of in-store customer experiences (Schmitt, 1999).

Digital signage networks are relatively new as a retail atmospheric stimulus. Limited prior research on digital signage has demonstrated that such screens may be considered as experiential cues themselves because they enhance the environment since shoppers perceive them as being high-tech, modern and attractive (Newman, Dennis, Wright and King, 2010). Shoppers also welcome information provided by digital signage (Newman et al., 2006). In line with Schmitt's (1999) notion of experience providers, digital signage may also be used to build the product- and/or service-brand experience via specific cues and imagery used in the broadcast messages. This section focuses on the ability of in-store digital signage messages to build service-brand experiences (in this case for a travel agent), in contrast to previous research focusing on tangible products (Burke, 2009). The role of digital signage is more specific, as it has a direct communication function, and its contribution to the experience of the store may not be explicitly defined.

Digital signage should constitute an effective marketer-manipulable atmospheric stimulus, acting as an experience provider for shoppers (Schmitt, 1999). If the broadcast message is hedonic, the evoked experience will be affective. If it is functional, utilitarian information to help shoppers with decision making, the evoked experience will be intellectual, likely consisting of analytic, convergent reasoning about the service or product.

An important question concerns the extent to which the process between consumers' exposure to an environmental stimulus and their approach behavior is mediated by cognition and affect and whether initial reactions are cognitive or affective (c.f. Chebat & Michon, 2003). The sequence of cognition and affect is not clearly defined by research in this field (Dennis et al., 2010; Kaltcheva & Weitz, 2006) and can be explained through the psychology of experience, the complex relationship between *erlebnis*, the immediacy of sensing and feeling, and *erfahrung*, the presence of fact finding, and the interplay between these two as experiencing and experienced in a state of mind (Jantzen, 2013). Sometimes affect comes first (e.g., Bosmans, 2006; Demoulin, 2011; Morrison et al., 2011), sometimes cognitions (e.g., Babin, Chebat & Michon, 2004; Chebat & Michon, 2003; Jang & Namkung, 2009; Walsh et al., 2011). The order may depend on type of stimulus (Morrin & Chebat, 2005).

So, the researchers predict that digital signage advertisements with cognitive content (providing utilitarian information), evoking intellectual brand experience among consumers, will be directly associated with increased approach towards the advertiser. Moreover, evoked intellectual experience will be indirectly associated with increased approach towards the advertiser by positively af-

fecting attitude towards the ad. Similarly, digital signage advertisements with affective content (providing hedonic information) will evoke affective brand experience, which will be directly associated with increased approach behavior towards the advertiser. Moreover, the evoked affective experience will be indirectly associated with increased approach behavior towards the advertiser by positively affecting attitude towards the advertisement.

Consistent with research on pleasant atmospheric stimuli (e.g., music, scent and lighting) on consumers' attitudes during shopping, we predict that a message with pleasant, affective, hedonic cues, unlike the cognitive content, will result in positive attitude towards the ad. Consumers tend to choose to process pleasant, affect-laden incidental cues, as they are unlikely to devote sufficient cognitive resources (Shiv & Fedorikhin, 1999). Note that in a previous study on digital signage, most respondents were unable to recall specific content (Dennis et al., 2010). Therefore, consumers intuitively 'infer' attitude from (positive) affect, using the 'affect-as-information' heuristic (Pham, 2004).

ISSUES

The research for this chapter was undertaken in London's West End shopping area. This is the traditional centre for retailing in London and one of the top shopping destinations with the highest sales density in the UK (OXIRM, 2013). In recent years, fashion retail has become more significant as one of the major thoroughfares, Regent St. has seen the conscious development of flagship fashion stores (Kent and Brown, 2009). The concentration of retail showcases and their function as brand beacons demonstrates a high level of investment in the brand experience. Therefore these stores might well be expected to demonstrate engagement with the latest technologies.

Media reports provided a broad overview and an initial categorization of different ways that the 'physical' and 'digital' stores integrate, and the technologies that might be evident in support of such integration. For the first stage of the research, a sample of fashion stores in the main shopping streets, Oxford St., Bond St. and Regent St. formed the basis of an ethnographic study. Observations were made of the types of technologies, their spatial connectivity and use in department stores, high-street retailers and luxury retailers, and the research was further informed by purposive sampling of fashion stores in nearby Covent Garden.

Although academic and industry researchers increasingly emphasize engagement with customers through mobile devices there is limited evidence of this in practice in the fashion retail sector. The rapid adoption of touchscreen smartphones and tablets by consumers suggests that retailers might develop ways to interact with consumers and that 'screens' in general have an increasing level of acceptance as an interface. However, the most evident in-store technologies are digital signage video screens and illuminated light boxes. These installations extend from small to large single screens and on a larger scale still, to multiple screens, such as the digital theatre in the Burberry flagship store in Regent St.

Retailers use display technologies with a variety of objectives. Firstly, a limited number of retailers show video images of their collections on fashion catwalks and larger number use single images to promote specific pieces from their current collections. Often screens have the obvious communication function to convey a myriad of brand clues, by showing the advertising campaigns for the brand, how the products are handmade to convey the luxury element of the brand, or hedonistic content customizing the product to communicate young and creative brand values. Secondly, retailers use the screens to contribute to the atmosphere in the store, as in the case of the Calvin Klein store in Regent Street that shows images of a glacier on large screens around the store. Finally, screens are used for purely informative purposes, for example as signage to indicate where the stock is located, to demonstrate product features and one or more styling options.

The screens are often prominently positioned behind the till or on the back wall facing the store entrance, alternatively they are attached to pillars in the store. Sometimes the screens form part of the window display as well. But a relationship between the type of retailer and the location and size of the screens is not evident; nor is the size of retailer related to the content of the screen. Where big screens are used, they present mood visuals or catwalks but there are some exceptions, such as Desigual that uses a big screen to communicate sales reductions. Many department stores follow a different strategy due to the fact that their display space is more compromised: they convey very different brands so generally each brand displays its own screens with its collections, advertising or promotional campaigns. One exception is the massive Harrods store, where display space at the escalators is used for digital signage screens, as reported in the second part of this chapter. Screens have been present in store environments for some considerable time. However the omnipresence of digital signage video screens across all type of stores (multiple, luxury, independent, department small, medium and large) is notable. The proliferation of screens signals a more technical store environment aimed at meeting the visual expectations of the consumer accustomed to online media.

One of the most important aspects that facilitate cross-channel capabilities in the store is the offer of free wi-fi as consumers nowadays consider their own smartphones to constitute an important form of technology to facilitate their shopping (Deloitte, 2011). In fact, smartphones offer significant opportunities to drive consumers to the store through the offer of free wi-fi and location-based services technology (Drapers, 2012). There are two dimensions in the way stores offer this facility: one is wi-fi as a facility enabling customers to connect to the internet for free, while the other, an integrative service, purposefully takes the consumer to the company website and offers an alternative range and information function that could be cross-referenced in the store.

Where wi-fi is available it is predominantly offered only as a connective service, thereby missing the opportunity to provide a more integrated branded experience. The integrative service was available at only two of the London West End (UK) fashion stores. A considerable number of stores do not offer wi-fi, which confirms the observation that London's West End retailers tend not to use new technologies, even though consumers are more likely to shop in stores that offer them. Some of those retailers, however, offer digital points-of-sale to buy online from the store, typically in department stores and some younger fashion retailers such as Urban Outfitters, although not consistently through its stores in this area, New Look and Diesel in Covent Garden. Burberry was found to be the only luxury West End fashion retailer offering this option.

The influence of multichannel retailing is most evident in the click-and-collect function. However, there are major differences between stores in how this point of delivery forms part of the store design. Smaller retailers do not have a specific delivery point and consumers need to collect their items at the till. In other cases, even if the click-and-collect point at the till is adequately indicated, the collection can take place elsewhere. The best example is the delivery point in department stores that leverage their space to offer specific collection points, and demonstrate a more integrated approach to multichannel experience. Most of the stores that do not offer click and collect do not have an integrated stock system, consequently the stock cannot overlap or interchange between the physical retail stores and the online stores. Several store managers mentioned that this is something that they are looking into providing; however no further information was given on the barriers for integrating stock systems.

Some retailers offer innovative technologies that link physical and virtual channels in the store with the expectation of an effect on consumer engagement. These technologies often include some form of touchscreen drawing on consumers' growing familiarity with these devices. Such is the case of the "Selfridge Denim Bar", a huge tactile screen that gives the opportunity to choose the jean that best suits each consumer based on different criteria. Once the perfect jeans have been chosen, consumers can see them on the in-store screen and share with friends through social networks. And of course, consumers can try the garment on in the store and then buy it through their preferred channel.

The most advanced examples of a multichannel-inspired experience were found in the New Look store in Oxford Street. This store's displays include garments that can only be purchased online and the transaction can be done from the store through the use of QR codes and smartphones. Throughout the store digital and printed advertising promote the online site and multiple interactive points allow consumers to access the online store there-and-then. Niketown is a point of reference in the use of technology with hedonic and utilitarian purposes, providing a fully integrated omnichannel experience in their store at Oxford Circus. Examples include touch screens with information about the product, mobile apps, interaction with social networks and a lab for runners that measure the way customers run to offer the more suitable trainer.

In the luxury sector, which generally does not demonstrate a high level of adoption of technologies, Burberry provides a good case study of channel integration. Its digital theatre, magic mirrors and the iPads carried by every shop assistant differentiate it from other luxury retailers.

The second stage of research for this chapter concerned the predominant technology that was identified earlier: digital signage video screens. This part of the study was conducted in the Harrods flagship department store in Knightsbridge.

The Harrods store is the biggest user of digital signage in this prestigious shopping area, having over 150 screens that, in addition to enhancing the store atmosphere and promoting Harrods merchandise, provide a substantial media income to Harrods from advertisers. The study explored shoppers' reactions to cognitive as opposed to affective digital signage advertisements and their approach behavior in the store.

Digital signage was researched using pleasant imagery including a tropical landscape to provide sensory affective experience, eschewing narrative material such as the use of humour in order to reduce individual inconsistencies across the sample that might be caused by the different ways in which participants may perceive a message (e.g. different senses of humour between participants). A commercial specialist created three advertisements:

1. **High-Cognitive/Low Affect (C):** Details and price of a tropical island holiday in mainly text form with the logo of an upscale private travel company;
2. **High Affect/Low Cognitive (A):** Video of a seaplane landing in a beautiful tropical lagoon next to a golden sand beach, with the same logo; and
3. **High Cognitive/High Affect (CwA):** Combining video and text from the first two.

Shoppers were intercepted near permanently-installed digital signage. Respondents were asked to participate in a study about their shopping experience. The advertisement concerned a real service of the upscale in-house private travel company, targeting customers of the store.

The (C) and (CwA) advertisements were perceived as more utilitarian than (A); and similarly (A) and (CwA) were perceived as more hedonic than (C). Exposing shoppers to either (A) or (CwA) significantly increased hedonic evaluations of the ad compared to (C) but there was no significant difference between effects of (A) and (CwA). Similarly,

exposing shoppers to either (C) or (CwA) significantly increased shoppers' utilitarian evaluations of the ad compared to (A), but there was no significant difference between the effects of (C) and (CwA). Utilitarian evaluations were significantly greater than hedonic evaluations of (C). Hedonic evaluations were significantly greater than utilitarian evaluations of (A). There was a small, conceptually irrelevant difference between shoppers' utilitarian and hedonic evaluations of (CwA) advertisement.

In determining the attitude towards the advertisement and approach towards the advertiser, exposing shoppers to either (A) or (CwA) significantly increased attitude to the advertisement compared to (C), but there was no significant difference between effects of (A) and (CwA). Exposing shoppers to either (A) or (CwA) significantly increased approach to the advertiser compared to (C). In both cases there was no significant difference between effects of (A) and (CwA)

Digital signage had a significant effect on shoppers' expected spending on their trip to the store. Exposing shoppers to either (A) or (CwA) significantly increased expected spending. The effect remained after controlling for classification variables for which spend varied, that is age and first visit or not. There was also a significant effect of the content on the expected number of items bought by shoppers on this trip. Exposing shoppers to either (A) or (CwA) significantly increased the expected number of items bought.

SOLUTIONS AND RECOMMENDATIONS

At an overarching level, a significant issue concerns the extent to which technologies mediate the experience of the retail store. Two different dimensions can be conceptualized, in which the 'real' and 'virtual' merge in the store. Firstly, an experiential dimension, in which the role of the atmospherics and the creation of a superior shopping experience are the most important elements that define the stores' space. Secondly, real and virtual dimensions mainly defined by cross-channel services, to provide a more utilitarian service, notably through click and collect points.

From the findings of the research, it can be concluded that four different levels of technology are present in the physical store:

Level 1: No technology.

There is no presence of consumer-facing technology in the store. Some of the stores without any technology might be cautious or cost restrained. In other cases the aim is to maintain their focus on a well understood human service-oriented in-store experience strategy.

Level 2: Technology as an element of in-store design.

For some stores technology is a tool at the service of design in order to communicate a distinct brand experience. It is the case of stores that use big screens to create a mood, for example, Hollister, or even fashion brands that show catwalks that communicate fashion credibility. This group includes retailers that use technology to provide a more pleasurable shopping experience or with informative purpose.

In these first two levels there is no a real integration with online operations and the objective is to communicate brand experience through the store environment with a focus on hedonic experience. The next two levels provide a degree of integration between the virtual and physical worlds.

Level 3: Technology as a facilitator.

Retailers that offer functional technologies and cross-channel capabilities for example Wi-Fi and click and collect services.

Level 4: Technology as a means to merge physical and virtual channels.

These retailers are working toward a multichannel integration. The merging of channels provides both hedonic and utilitarian value in the shopping experience. Technology is at the service of the consumer but it offers an enjoyable and different experience as well. The best examples observed are New Look, Selfridges, Nike Town and Burberry.

However, the presence of technology appears to be related to brand positioning. Luxury fashion brands used significantly less interactive technology than other high street brands possibly being influenced by perceptions of exclusivity, issues with global online distribution, and also the age of the target audience. On the other hand most luxury brands used their digital signage screens to convey information on how the products were made, catwalk videos or lifestyle images often from their advertising campaigns.

Based on these findings, it can be argued that there are two main trends in the way retailers manage the in-store experience with brand image objectives. On the one hand retailers offer a physical experience that cannot be replicated online; this means offering a shopping environment that enables consumers to feel they are engaged with the brand, which presents the brand as "premium" experience. On the other hand, there are retailers that strive towards an integration of the physical and digital channels with the objective of offering a totally integrated experience of the brand; these retailers make an extensive use of technology in the store, which promotes a cross-channel experience. These trends represent two extremes whilst a substantial number of retailers observed are placed towards the middle.

Video screens and light boxes displaying still photographic images have a relatively long history in fashion stores, comprising the most common technology element in those stores. They have a limited functional effect as a lighting medium, which achieves its greatest impact in otherwise low-lit stores. They are consistently used to communicate the retail brand by highlighting new clothing lines, ranges, and runway shows: in this sense they are an extension of point of sale material, as illuminated posters.

However the definition of the images, the intensity of screens and possibilities to create a dynamic environment of changing images, distinguishes them from physical promotional materials. They do however, (in common with other technological installations) have a physical form. Applying Verhoef's et al.'s (2009) categorization, digital signage video screens and light boxes have to be located as an element of the store's design, contributing to the store atmosphere. On the other hand, touchscreens make a different contribution to the store through the possibilities for interaction, and in this respect form a dimension of Verhoef's et al.'s (2009) service interface. Their primary function is an in-store look-up point for information about products and their availability. However, with the integration of online services, the category of Service Interface turns out to be more problematic than Verhoef and colleagues anticipate.

The availability and promotion of click-and-collect service points indicate their emergence as a significant interface with customers. They are conceptualized by their functionality and currently have a minimal contribution to the designed element of the store. The provision of wi-fi as a technological mediator of in-store experience, extends the service interface beyond the store's physical boundaries. The opportunities to create virtual interfaces are neglected by Verhoef et al. as they focus on passive and active self-service technologies, their examples being drawn from shopping carts and self-service checkouts, and their impact on experience.

A third dimension of experience relevant to this research is a social one. Wi-fi enables co-created services but it too has an under-developed role in co-creating social environments and accessing social communities. The possibilities through accessing the virtual environment in-store, are realized in the use of interactive mirrors and touchscreens.

Touchscreens therefore have multiple experiential functions, as a service interface and as an underexploited opportunity for the store to create and contribute to their customers' social networks.

McQ merges these categories as it uses interactive mirrors to achieve both hedonic and functional objectives, they allow the consumer to access new opportunities to construct their identity and communicate it through mobile and social media. A similar effect is achieved by Selfridges Denim bar. Moreover interactive touchscreens have an atmospheric aspect through their attractive appearance, and offer interactive services through look-up functions, product information and browsing. They engage the consumer on a cognitive and interactive level eliciting active participation and in some cases also adding educational, emotional and entertaining dimensions.

Although there is limited evidence for the physical and virtual environments merging in international flagship stores, this research contributes to a reinterpretation of Verhoef et al.'s categorization of experience. Although there was limited evidence from the stores investigated for this chapter, the social environment, the retail atmosphere and service interface demonstrate signs of merging through the use of store-based technologies. To an even more limited extent, the use of personal mobile technologies – smartphones – points to a different form of merger between online and offline, the physical and virtual store. However these developments are at an early stage of adoption, the extent to which technology permeates the service interface and environment appears to be less for the retailers studied in this chapter than other case studies and industry reports have suggested.

Digital signage video screens are an effective, marketer-manipulable retail atmospheric stimulus. Well-designed advertisements that play to the strength of digital signage with moving, pleasant images can increase shoppers' approach behaviors towards an advertiser and the total service experience. Findings in this regard are more conclusive than previous studies, which have been based either on a small qualitative sample (Newman et al., 2006) or a questionnaire survey in a single condition (Dennis et al., 2010).

The findings are important because they demonstrate the effectiveness of a digital signage advertisement that stimulates pleasure (little functional information), and evokes affective experience. Previous studies have concerned more functional, 'features-and-benefits' content and have mainly focused on tangible products (Burke, 2009). Evoked affective experience seems to be a stronger predictor of approach behavior than evoked intellectual experience. Moreover, customers' affective experiences are more strongly associated with positive attitudes and approach behaviors than are cognitive based experiences. This is consistent with 'primacy of affect' – when consumers allocate few processing resources, as towards digital signage incidental informational cues, they are more likely to be led by their 'hearts' than 'heads'. Consumers often make decisions by misattributing 'evaluation of' as 'liking' (Pham, 2004) affect-laden options; and allocating insufficient deliberative processing resources to assess and reason about 'functional' features of the same options (Shiv & Fedorikhin, 1999).

In retail digital signage, deliberation may be relatively low (in the Dennis et al. (2010) study, most respondents were unaware of having viewed specific advertisements, yet still considered that digital signage contributed to positive image). This lends emphasis to our finding of the strength of the evoked affective experiences. Digital signage, evoking affective, sensory brand-experience, provides a different theoretical explanation of how marketing communications influence consumers than the one that existing mass-media models provide.

The study of digital signage has strong theoretical implications, suggesting that brand-related stimuli in store digital signage trigger not only deliberative processes and brand attitudes; but they also evoke experiences that stimulate senses, evoke feelings and elicit approach behavior (Brakus et al., 2009). In contrast, the theoretical focus of the traditional communication models (DAGMAR (Colley, 1961); Elaboration Likelihood Model (Petty & Cacioppo, 1986); Rossiter & Percy's (1997) Grid) has concerned attitudes, rather than experiences. Such models assume that processing of communication messages is mostly deliberative, resulting in high-order responses including elaborations, categorizations, inferences, recall, arguments and counter-arguments. Based on those responses, consumers construct attitude towards the message and then towards the advertised brand.

FUTURE RESEARCH DIRECTIONS

The research literature together with the findings presented in this chapter demonstrate that retailers are in an exploratory phase of converging their communication and distribution channels. Online communication and technology should be permeating the service interface and environment. In the context of Verhoef et al.'s (2009) experiential model and research agenda in a limited number of stores the social environment, retail atmosphere and service interface are increasingly merged through the use of technologies.

Due to the lack of detailed research in this field this paper focuses on the presence of different types of technology in the physical store; there is a need to understand the impact of these technologies on consumers (Pantano, 2010). A further step will be to extend observations to shoppers in order to know how they interact with technology and how that interaction affects their experience of the retail store. The methodology of in store observation also has limitations and could be expanded with in depth interviews with shoppers to explore customer perception.

It would also be interesting for practitioners to further explore the extent to which in-store technology drives sales and which technology does so more than others. Similarly the impact that technology has on brand perception and word of mouth needs to be considered. Another line of inquiry is to investigate other forms of technology as part of the store, and in particular the mediating role of smartphone apps in the service interface and social environment and how consumers use mobile devices during their purchasing journey.

Digital signage video screens can have two beneficial effects for a retailer. The first effect is the communication effect; that is, the cues contained in the broadcast messages evoke specific experiences in customers that, in turn, positively affect the attitude towards the advertiser and consumers' approach behaviour. This is especially true if the messages contain affective or a mix of affective and intellectual cues.

Secondly, digital signage has an additional 'umbrella effect'. That is, it enhances the shopping experience which, in turn, results in an increase in intended spending (the umbrella effect). This result is consistent with Brakus et al. (2009) who claim that evoked experiences are inherently valuable for consumers. If consumers desire to make an experience last longer, that desire could affect the length of stay in the shop and the purchase intentions or other outcome variables (see Brakus et al. (2009) for effect of experience on satisfaction and loyalty; Iglesias, Singh, & Batista-Foguet (2011) for effect on propensity to recommend; and Stuart-Menteth, Wilson, & Baker (2006) for effect on affective commitment). Moreover, the particular attractiveness that digital signage adds to shoppers on their first visit to the store may have important implications for store loyalty by generating repeat business. This addresses Puccinelli, Deshpande and Isen's (2007) question of whether the effect of store atmospherics is greater on newcomers.

In the second part of this study, shoppers were asked to view the digital signage, rather than passing it by in the natural course of their shopping trip. They may not have perceived it if it had only been 'wallpaper' as digital signage has to compete with other stimuli in the store. However, the affective ad carried no cognitive information which thus effectively forced superficial 'wallpaper' processing. We recommend further research into the effects of natural (rather than forced) wallpaper or peripheral processing.

This research is focused on a specific context; flagship stores and centrally located shopping streets in London. It can be extended to other less significant shopping locations and to observe other cities around the world to determine the role that cultural expectations play in the integrated offer of retailers.

CONCLUSION

This chapter advances knowledge of in-store experiences, specifically brand experience and proposes new directions for research. From the results recorded here, it appears that there is a gap between media and industry reports concerning multichannel integration and use of interactive technologies compared with the actual levels of implementation. Nearly all retailers have an online site, and this is mostly acknowledged in-store. For UK-based retailers products are replicated in both sites, achieving a level of integration between the ranges. This is not always the case with international fashion brands where the online range is managed from another country, and reflects clothing sold in Europe with some products available in the UK.

Further, the research demonstrates that in-store technologies have an experiential and utilitarian or functional use. The most commonly used are based upon more conventional photo and digital signage video screens, which has been demonstrated to be effective both as advertising communications and in contributing to the image of a store.

Digital signage video screens and light boxes are conventional in-store communication media and as such pose a low risk to the retailer. Prior to the publication of this book, little information has been available on the effectiveness of more advanced in-store technology. The dimensions of technological integration in this chapter point to continuing opportunities to achieve competitive advantage from the exploitation of relatively convention technologies, and that technological integration into fashion stores is in an early stage of development. The authors hope that this chapter and, indeed, the book as a whole, will stimulate further uptake of and research into in-store technologies.

REFERENCES

Babin, B. J., & Attaway, J. S. (2000). Atmospheric affect as a tool for creating value and gaining share of customer. *Journal of Business Research*, *49*(2), 91–100. doi:10.1016/S0148-2963(99)00011-9

Babin, B. J., Chebat, J. C., & Michon, R. (2004). Perceived appropriateness and its effect on quality, affect, and behavior. *Journal of Retailing and Consumer Services*, *11*(5), 287–298. doi:10.1016/j.jretconser.2003.09.002

Babin, B. J., & Darden, W. R. (1996). Good and bad shopping vibes: Spending and patronage satisfaction. *Journal of Business Research*, *35*(3), 201–106. doi:10.1016/0148-2963(95)00125-5

Babin, B. J., Darden, W. R., & Griffin, M. D. (1994). Work and/or fun: Measuring hedonic and shopping value. *The Journal of Consumer Research*, *20*(4), 644–656. doi:10.1086/209376

Bäckström, K., & Johansson, U. (2006). Creating and consuming experiences in retail store environments: Comparing retailer and consumer perspectives. *Journal of Retailing and Consumer Services*, *13*(6), 417–430. doi:10.1016/j.jretconser.2006.02.005

Bagge, D. (2007). *Multichannel retailing: The route to customer focus*. London: IBM Global Business Services.

Bain. (2011). *Omnichannel retailing*. Retrieved November 20, 2013, from http://www.bain.com/Images/Bain%202011%20Holiday%20Series_Issue%233.pdf

Baker, J., Grewal, D., & Parasuraman, A. (2009). The influence of store environment on quality inferences and store image. *Journal of the Academy of Marketing Science*, *22*(4), 328–339. doi:10.1177/0092070394224002

Ballantine, P. W., Jack, R., & Parsons, A. G. (2010). Atmospheric cues and their effect on the hedonic retail experience. *International Journal of Retail & Distribution Management*, *38*(8), 641–653. doi:10.1108/09590551011057453

Bearne, S. (2014). In-store tech, sales driver or hype. *Business of Fashion*. Retrieved November 20, 2013, from http://www.businessoffashion.com/2014/06/store-tech-sales-driver-hype.html?utm_source=Subscribers&utm_campaign=6da089d3b1-&utm_medium=email&utm_term=0_d2191372b3-6da089d3b1-417168977)

Biehl-Missal, B., & vom Lehn, D. (2014). Aesthetic atmospheres in museums: A critical marketing perspective. In M. Henning (Ed.), *Museum media/international handbook of museum studies*. Chichester, UK: Wiley-Blackwell.

Bitner, M. J. (1992). Servicescapes: The impact of physical surroundings on customers and employees. *Journal of Marketing*, *56*(April), 57–71. doi:10.2307/1252042

Böhme, G. (1995). *Atmosphäre, Essays zur neuen Ästhetik*. Frankfurt: Suhrkamp.

Böhme, G. (2001). *Aisthetik, Vorlesung über Ästhetik als allgemeine Wahrnehmungslehre*. München: Wilhelm Fink Verlag.

Bosmans, A. (2006). Scents and sensibility: When do (in)congruent ambient scents influence product evaluations? *Journal of Marketing*, *70*(3), 32–43. doi:10.1509/jmkg.70.3.32

Brakus, J. J., Schmitt, B. H., & Zarantonello, L. (2009). Brand experience: What is it? How do we measure it? And does it affect loyal*ty*? *Journal of Marketing*, *73*(3), 52–68. doi:10.1509/jmkg.73.3.52

Brynjolfsson, E., Hu, Y. J., & Rahman, M. S. (2013). Competing in the age of omnichannel retailing. *MIT Sloan Management Review*, *54*(4), 1–7.

Burke, R. R. (2002). Technology and the customer interface: What consumers want in the physical and virtual store. *Journal of the Academy of Marketing Science*, *30*(4), 411–432. doi:10.1177/009207002236914

Burke, R. R. (2009). Behavioral effects of digital signage. *Journal of Advertising Research*, *49*(2), 180–185. doi:10.2501/S0021849909090254

Chang, P. L., & Chieng, M. H. (2006). Building consumer-brand relationship: A cross-cultural experiential view. *Psychology and Marketing*, *23*(11), 927–959. doi:10.1002/mar.20140

Chebat, J. C., & Michon, R. (2003). Impact of ambient odors on mall shoppers' emotions, cognition and spending: A test of competitive causal theories. *Journal of Business Research*, *56*(7), 529–539. doi:10.1016/S0148-2963(01)00247-8

Chu, A., & Lam, M. C. (2007). Store environment of fashion retailers: a Hong Kong perspective. In T. Hines & M. Bruce (Eds.), Fashion marketing (2nd ed.; pp. 151-167). Oxford, UK: Elsevier.

Chu, J., & Paglucia, G. (2002). *Enhancing the customer shopping experience*. London: IBM Institute for Business Value.

Citrin, A. V., Stem, D. E. Jr, Spangenberg, E. R., & Clark, M. J. (2003). Consumer need for tactile input: An internet retailing challenge. *Journal of Business Research*, *56*(11), 915–922. doi:10.1016/S0148-2963(01)00278-8

Clifford, E. (2012). *Fashion online*. Mintel.

Colley, R. H. (1961). *Defining advertising goals for measured advertising results*. New York, NY: Association of National Advertisers.

Deloitte. (2011). *Store 3.0*. Retrieved November 20, 2013, from http://www.deloitte.com/assets/Dcom-MiddleEast/Local%20Assets/Documents/Industries/Consumer%20Business/me_consumer_business_store_3.0_11.pdf

Demoulin, N. T. M. (2011). Music congruency in a service setting: The mediating role of emotional and cognitive responses. *Journal of Retailing and Consumer Services*, *18*(1), 10–18. doi:10.1016/j.jretconser.2010.08.007

Dennis, C. (2005). *Objects of desire: Consumer behavior in shopping centre choices*. Basingstoke, UK: Palgrave Macmillan.

Dennis, C., Michon, R., Brakus, J., Newman, A., & Alamanos, E. (2012). New insights into the impact of digital signage as a retail atmospheric tool. *Journal of Consumer Behaviour*, *11*(6), 454–466. doi:10.1002/cb.1394

Dennis, C., Murphy, J., Marsland, D., Cockett, W., & Patel, T. (2002). Measuring image: Mall case studies. *International Review of Retail, Distribution and Consumer Research*, *12*(4), 353–373. doi:10.1080/09593960210151153

Dennis, C., Newman, A., Michon, R., Brakus, J., & Wright, L. T. (2010). The mediating effects of perception and emotion: Digital signage in mall atmospherics. *Journal of Retailing and Consumer Services*, *17*(3), 205–215. doi:10.1016/j.jretconser.2010.03.009

Donovan, R. J., & Rossiter, J. (1982). Store atmosphere: An environmental psychology approach. *Journal of Retailing*, *58*(1), 34–57.

Donovan, R. J., Rossiter, J., Marcoolyn, G., & Nesdale, A. (1994). Store atmosphere and purchasing behavior. *Journal of Retailing*, *70*(3), 283–294. doi:10.1016/0022-4359(94)90037-X

Drapers. (2012). *Technology in fashion.* Retrieved November 20, 2013, from http://www.drapersonline.com/news/news-headlines/technology-in-fashion/

Duncan, T., & Moriarty, S. (2006). How integrated marketing communication's "touchpoints" can operationalize the service dominant logic. In R.F. Lusch & S.L. Vargo (Eds.), The service-dominant logic of marketing (pp. 236-244). New York: M.E. Sharpe.

Eisingerich, A. B., & Rubera, G. (2010). Drivers of brand commitment: A cross-national investigation. *Journal of International Marketing, 18*(2), 64–79. doi:10.1509/jimk.18.2.64

Ernst and Young. (2001). *Global online retailing.* Retrieved November 20, 2013, from https://www2.eycom.ch/publications/items/globalonlineretailing/de.pdf

Eroglu, S., Machleit, K., & Davis, L. (2003). Empirical testing of a model of online store atmospherics and shoppers responses. *Psychology and Marketing, 20*(2), 139–150. doi:10.1002/mar.10064

Esch, F. R., Moll, T., Schmitt, B., Elger, C. E., Neuhaus, C., & Weber, B. (2012). Brands on the brain. Do consumers use declarative information or experienced emotions to evaluate brands? *Journal of Consumer Psychology, 22*(1), 75–85. doi:10.1016/j.jcps.2010.08.004

Euromonitor International. (2009). *Global retailing: New concepts in retailing: The thin line between success and failure.* London: Euromonitor International.

Fishbein, M., & Ajzen, I. (1975). *Belief, attitude, intention, and behavior: An introduction to theory and research.* Reading, MA: Addison-Wesley.

Iglesias, O., Singh, J. J., & Batista-Foguet, J. M. (2011). The role of brand experience and affective commitment in determining brand loyalty. *Journal of Brand Management, 18*(8), 570–582. doi:10.1057/bm.2010.58

Interbrand. (2012). *What's in store for 2012?* London: Interbrand.

Jang, S. S., & Namkung, Y. (2009). Perceived quality, emotions, and behavioral intentions: Application of an extended Mehrabian-Russell model to restaurants. *Journal of Business Research, 62*(4), 451–460. doi:10.1016/j.jbusres.2008.01.038

Jantzen, C. (2013). Experiencing and experiences: A psychological framework. In J. Sundbo & F. Sørensen (Eds.), *Handbook on the experience economy* (pp. 146–170). Cheltenham, UK: Edward Elgar. doi:10.4337/9781781004227.00013

Kaltcheva, V., & Weitz, B. (2006). When should a retailer create an exciting store environment? *Journal of Marketing, 70*(1), 107–118. doi:10.1509/jmkg.2006.70.1.107

Keller, K. L. (2003). Brand synthesis: The multidimensionality of brand knowledge. *The Journal of Consumer Research, 29*(4), 595–600. doi:10.1086/346254

Kent, A. M., & Brown, R. (2009). *Flagship marketing, concepts and places.* Abingdon, UK: Routledge.

Kotler, P. (1973). Atmospherics as a marketing "tool". *Journal of Retailing, 49*(4), 48–64.

Kozinets, R. V., Sherry, J. F., DeBerry-Spence, B., Duhachek, A., Nuttavuthisit, K., & Storm, D. (2002). Themed flagship brand stores in the new millennium: Theory, practice, prospects. *Journal of Retailing, 78*(1), 17–29. doi:10.1016/S0022-4359(01)00063-X

Kumar, V., & Venkatesan, R. (2005). Who are the multichannel shoppers and how do they perform? Correlates of multichannel shopping behavior. *Journal of Interactive Marketing, 19*(2), 44–62. doi:10.1002/dir.20034

Martineau, P. (1958). The personality of the retail store. *Harvard Business Review, 36*(1), 47–55.

Mathwick, C., Malhotra, N. K., & Rigdon, E. (2002). The effect of dynamic retail experiences on experiential perceptions of value: An Internet and catalog comparison. *Journal of Retailing, 78*(1), 51–60. doi:10.1016/S0022-4359(01)00066-5

Mercer, J. (2013). *E-commerce-UK.* London: Mintel.

Mercier, P., Jacobsen, R., & Veitch, A. (2012). *Retail 2020, competing in a changing industry.* Boston, MA: Boston Consulting.

Merle, A., Senecal, S., & St-Onge, A. (2012). Whether and how virtual try-on influences consumer responses to an apparel web site. *International Journal of Electronic Commerce, 16*(3), 41–64. doi:10.2753/JEC1086-4415160302

Michon, R., Yu, H., Smith, D., & Chebat, J. (2007). The shopping experience of female fashion leaders. *International Journal of Retail & Distribution Management, 35*(6), 488–501. doi:10.1108/09590550710750359

Mintel. (2012). *Clothing retailing Europe.* London: Mintel.

Morrin, S., & Chebat, J. C. (2005). Person-place congruency: The interactive effects of shopper style and atmospherics on consumer expenditures. *Journal of Service Research, 8*(2), 181–191. doi:10.1177/1094670505279420

Morrison, M., Gan, S., Dubelaar, C., & Oppewal, H. (2011). In-store music and aroma influences on shopper behavior and satisfaction. *Journal of Business Research, 64*(6), 558–564. doi:10.1016/j.jbusres.2010.06.006

Neslin, S. A., Grewal, D., Leghorn, R., Shankar, V., Teerling, M. L., Thomas, J. S., & Verhoef, P. C. (2006). Challenges and opportunities in multichannel customer management. *Journal of Service Research, 9*(2), 95–112. doi:10.1177/1094670506293559

Newman, A., Dennis, C., Wright, L. T., & King, T. (2010). 'Shoppers' experiences of digital signage – A cross-national qualitative study. *Journal of Digital Contents Technology and its Applications, 4*(7), 50-57.

Newman, A., Dennis, C., & Zaman, S. (2006, Fall). Marketing images and consumers' experiences in selling environments. *Marketing Management Journal,* 515-599.

Newman, A. J., & Patel, D. (2004). The marketing directions of fashion retailers. *European Journal of Marketing, 38*(7), 770–789. doi:10.1108/03090560410539249

Omnico. (2013). *Omni-channel retailing.* London: Omnico Retail.

OXIRM. (2006). *The future of retail business models.* Oxford, UK: Oxford Institute of Retail Management.

OXIRM. (2013). *The state of UK retail places.* Oxford Institute of Retail Management. Retrieved November 20, 2013, from http://oxford-institute.sbsblogs.co.uk/2013/07/19/diversity-and-the-uks-high-streets

Pantano, E. (2010). New technologies and retailing: Trends and directions. *Journal of Retailing and Consumer Services, 17*(3), 171–172. doi:10.1016/j.jretconser.2010.03.004

Pantano, E., & Naccarato, G. (2010). Entertainment in retailing: The influences of advanced technologies. *Journal of Retailing and Consumer Services, 17*(3), 200–204. doi:10.1016/j.jretconser.2010.03.010

Park, C. W., MacInnis, D. J., Priester, J., Eising-erich, A. B., & Iacobucci, D. (2010). Brand attachment and brand attitude strength: Conceptual and empirical differentiation of two critical brand equity drivers. *Journal of Marketing*, *74*(6), 1–17. doi:10.1509/jmkg.74.6.1

Petty, R. E., & Cacioppo, J. T. (1986). *The elaboration likelihood model of persuasion*. In L. Berkowitz (Ed.), Advances in experimental social psychology (pp. 123–205). New York, NY: Academic Press.

Pham, M. T. (2004). The logic of feeling. *Journal of Consumer Psychology*, *14*(4), 360–369. doi:10.1207/s15327663jcp1404_5

Pine, B. J., & Gilmore, J. H. (1998, July-August). Welcome to the experience economy. *Harvard Business Review*.

Pine, B. J., & Gilmore, J. H. (1999). *The experience economy: Work is theatre and every business a stage*. Cambridge, MA: Harvard Business School Press.

Pine, B. J., & Gilmore, J. H. (2011). *The experience economy*. Cambridge, MA: Harvard Business Press.

Pinker, S. (1997). *How the mind works*. New York, NY: Norton.

Puccinelli, N. M., Deshpande, R., & Isen, A. M. (2007). Should I stay or should I go? Mood congruity, self-monitoring and retail context preference. *Journal of Business Research*, *60*(6), 640–648. doi:10.1016/j.jbusres.2006.06.014

Puccinelli, N. M., Goodstein, R. C., Grewal, D., Price, R., Raghubir, P., & Stewart, D. (2009). Customer experience management in retailing: Understanding the buying process. *Journal of Retailing*, *85*(1), 15–30. doi:10.1016/j.jretai.2008.11.003

PwC (2011). *"Pick'n'Mix": Meeting the demands of the new multichannel shopper*. London: PwC.

PwC and Kantar. (2012). *Retailing 2020: Winning in a polarized world*. Retrieved November 20, 2013, from www.pwc.com/us/retailandconsumer

Retail Week. (2012). *Ecommerce in fashion: How retailers are driving online sales*. Retrieved November 20, 2013, from http://www.retail-week.com/retail-week-ecommerce-in-fashion/5042018.article

Retail Week. (2013). *Multichannel now, 2013*. London: Retail Week.

Retail Week. (2014). *Multichannel, unraveling touchpoints*. Retrieved November 20, 2013, from http://www.retail-week.com/multichannel/analysis-tracking-shopper-journeys-across-the-multichannel-landscape/5060398.article

Rohm, A., & Swaminatham, V. (2004). A typology of online shoppers based on shopping motivations. *Journal of Business Research*, *57*(7), 748–757. doi:10.1016/S0148-2963(02)00351-X

Rosenblum, P., & Rowen, S. (2012). The 2012 retail store: In transition. *Retail Systems Research*. Retrieved November 20, 2013, from http://www.rsrresearch.com/2012/05/09/the-2012-retail-store-in-transition-2/

Rossiter, J., & Percy, L. (1997). *Advertising communications and promotion management* (2nd ed.). New York, NY: McGraw-Hill.

Roy, R., Zhao, M., & Dholakia, N. (2005). Multichannel retailing: A case study of early experiences. *Journal of Interactive Marketing*, *19*(2), 63–74. doi:10.1002/dir.20035

Scarpi, D. (2006). Fashion stores between fun and usefulness. *Journal of Fashion Marketing and Management*, *10*(1), 7–24. doi:10.1108/13612020610651097

Schmitt, B. (1999). Experiential marketing. *Journal of Marketing Management*, *15*(1-3), 53–67. doi:10.1362/026725799784870496

Schmitt, B. (2012). The consumer psychology of brands. *Journal of Consumer Psychology*, *22*(1), 7–17. doi:10.1016/j.jcps.2011.09.005

Shiv, B., & Fedorikhin, A. (1999). Heart and mind in conflict: The interplay of affect and cognition in consumer decision making. *The Journal of Consumer Research*, *26*(3), 278–292. doi:10.1086/209563

Signs of the Times. (2006, November 3). *The Economist*, p. 378.

Skard, S., Nysveen, H., & Pedersen, P. E. (2011). *Brand and customer experience in service organizations: Literature review and brand experience construct validation* (Working Paper No. 09/11). Institute for Research in Economics and Business Administration, Bergen: SNF.

Stuart-Menteth, H., Wilson, H., & Baker, S. (2006). Escaping the channel silo: Researching the new consumer. *International Journal of Market Research*, *48*(4), 415–437.

Thomson, M., MacInnis, D. J., & Park, C. W. (2005). The ties that bind: Measuring the strength of consumers' emotional attachments to brands. *Journal of Consumer Psychology*, *15*(1), 77–91. doi:10.1207/s15327663jcp1501_10

Turley, L. W., & Milliman, R. E. (2000). Atmospheric effects on shopping behavior: A review of the experimental evidence. *Journal of Business Research*, *49*(2), 193–211. doi:10.1016/S0148-2963(99)00010-7

Underhill, P. (2008). *Why we buy: The science of shopping - Updated and revised for the internet, the global consumer, and beyond*. New York, NY: Simon and Schuster.

Verhoef, P., Lemon, K., Parasuraman, A., Roggeveen, A., Tsiros, M., & Schlesinger, L. (2009). Customer experience creation: Determinants, dynamics and management strategies. *Journal of Retailing*, *85*(1), 31–41. doi:10.1016/j.jretai.2008.11.001

Vranca, S. (2009, September 21). WPP chief tempers hopes for ad upturn. *Wall Street Journal*, p. B1.

Walsh, G., Shiu, E., Hassan, L. M., Michaelidou, N., & Beatty, S. E. (2011). Emotions, store-environmental cues, store-choice criteria, and marketing outcomes. *Journal of Business Research*, *64*(7), 737–744. doi:10.1016/j.jbusres.2010.07.008

Yang, K., & Young, A. (2009). The effects of customised site features on Internet apparel shopping. *Journal of Fashion Marketing and Management*, *13*(1), 28–139. doi:10.1108/13612020910939923

Yoo, C., Park, J., & MacInnis, D. J. (1998). Effects of store characteristics and in-store affective experiences on store attitude. *Journal of Business Research*, *42*(3), 253–263. doi:10.1016/S0148-2963(97)00122-7

Zarantonello, L., & Schmitt, B. H. (2010). Using the brand experience scale to profile consumers and predict consumer behavior. *Journal of Brand Management*, *17*(7), 532–540. doi:10.1057/bm.2010.4

Zeithaml, V., Bitner, M., & Gremler, D. (2009). *Services marketing* (5th ed.). New York, NY: McGraw-Hill.

Zhang, J., Farris, P., Irvin, J., Kushwaha, T., Steenburgh, T., & Weitz, B. (2010). Crafting integrated multichannel retail strategies. *Journal of Interactive Marketing*, *24*(2), 168–180. doi:10.1016/j.intmar.2010.02.002

Zhang, S., & Schmitt, B. H. (2001). Creating local brands in multilingual international markets. *JMR, Journal of Marketing Research*, *38*(3), 313–325. doi:10.1509/jmkr.38.3.313.18869

ADDITIONAL READING

Burke, R. R. (2002). Technology and the customer interface: What consumers want in the physical and virtual store. *Journal of the Academy of Marketing Science*, *30*(4), 411–432. doi:10.1177/009207002236914

Dahlström, P., & Edelman, D. (2013). *The coming era of on-demand marketing*. New York, NY: McKinsey & Company.

Deloitte. (2011). *Store 3.0*. Retrieved November 20, 2013, from http://www.deloitte.com/assets/Dcom-MiddleEast/Local%20Assets/Documents/Industries/Consumer%20Business/me_consumer_business_store_3.0_11.pdf

Dennis, C., Michon, R., Brakus, J. J., Newman, A., & Alamanos, E. (2012). New insights into the impact of digital signage as a retail atmospheric tool. *Journal of Consumer Behaviour*, *11*(6), 454–466. doi:10.1002/cb.1394

Dennis, C., Newman, A., Michon, R., Brakus, J. J., & Wright, L. T. (2011). Modelling shopper responses to retail digital signage. In E. Pantano & H. Timmermans (Eds.), *Advanced technologies management for retailing: Frameworks and issues* (pp. 22–43). Hershey, PA: IGI Global. doi:10.4018/978-1-60960-738-8.ch003

Fernández-Sabiote, E., & Román, S. (2012). Electronic commerce research and applications adding clicks to bricks: A study of the consequences on customer loyalty in a service context. *Electronic Commerce Research and Applications*, *11*(1), 36–48. doi:10.1016/j.elerap.2011.07.007

Kaltcheva, V., & Weitz, B. (2006). When should a retailer create an exciting store environment? *Journal of Marketing*, *70*(1), 107–118. doi:10.1509/jmkg.2006.70.1.107

Kent, A. M., & Brown, R. (2009). *Flagship marketing, concepts and places*. Abingdon: Routledge.

Lee, I. (Ed.). (2014). *Trends in e-business, e-services and e-commerce*. Hershey, PA: IGI Global. doi:10.4018/978-1-4666-4510-3

Lusch, R. F., & Vargo, S. L. (2006). Service-dominant logic: Reactions, reflections and refinements. *Marketing Theory*, *6*(3), 281–288. doi:10.1177/1470593106066781

Newman, A., Dennis, C., Wright, L. T., & King, T. (2010). Shoppers' experiences of digital signage – a cross-national qualitative study. *Journal of Digital Contents Technology and its Applications*. *4*(7): 50-57.

Newman, A., Dennis, C., & Zaman, S. (2006). Marketing images and consumers' experiences in selling environments. *Marketing Management Journal, (Fall)*: 515-599.

Omnico (2013). *Omni-channel retailing*. London: Omnico Retail.

Pine, B. J., & Gilmore, J. H. (2011). *The experience economy*. Cambridge, MA: Harvard Business Press.

Retail Week. (2013). *Multichannel Now 2013*. London: Retail Week.

Reynolds, J., Cuthbertson, C., & Bell, R. (Eds.). (2004). *Retail strategy*. Abingdon: Routledge.

Sundbo, J., & Sørensen, F. F. (Eds.). (2013). Handbook on the experience economy. Cheltenham: Edward Elgar.

Turley, L. W., & Chabat, J.-C. (2002). Linking retail strategy atmospheric design and shopping behavior. *Journal of Marketing Management*, *18*(1-2), 125–144. doi:10.1362/0267257022775891

Van Bommel, E. Edelman, D., & Ungerman, K., (2014). Digitizing the consumer decision journey. New York NY: McKinsey & Company.

Verhoef, P., Lemon, K., Parasuraman, A., Roggeveen, A., Tsiros, M., & Schlesinger, L. (2009). Customer experience creation: Determinants, dynamics and management strategies. *Journal of Retailing*, *85*(1), 31–41. doi:10.1016/j.jretai.2008.11.001

Yoo, W.-S., Lee, Y., & Park, J. (2010). The role of interactivity in e-tailing: Creating value and increasing satisfaction. *Journal of Retailing and Consumer Services*, *17*(2), 89–96. doi:10.1016/j.jretconser.2009.10.003

Zhang, J., Farris, P. W., Irvin, J. W., Kushwaha, T., Steenburgh, T. J., & Weitz, B. A. (2010). Crafting integrated multichannel retailing strategies. *Journal of Interactive Marketing*, *24*(2), 168–180. doi:10.1016/j.intmar.2010.02.002

KEY TERMS AND DEFINITIONS

Affect: An emotional state in contrast to cognition. It is a dimension of behavior, disposing a consumer favorably, or otherwise, towards a product or service.

Atmospherics: The conscious designing of space and intangible environmental elements to create certain effects in buyers.

Brand Attitude: General evaluations by consumers towards brands based on their beliefs.

Brand Experience: Subjective, internal consumer responses (sensations, feelings, and cognitions) and behavioral responses evoked by brand-related stimuli that are part of a brand's design and identity, packaging, communications, and retail environments.

Cognition: Mental processes concerned with thinking and knowing, but also interpretation and empathy.

Digital Signage: Consists of screens in public places showing video. Content may include advertisements, community information, entertainment and news. It aims to talk to shoppers while they are captive and in the mood to buy.

Multichannel: All the activities that involve the sale of products or services via more than one channel. A multichannel retailer requires a consistent brand experience across all points of interaction with the consumer.

Technology: In-store electronic devices kiosks, iPads, display screens and in general, opportunities to make the store more attractive, enable consumers to browse online, and make products more accessible and convenient to buy.

Chapter 2
Consumers' Involvement on (Re)Engineering Store Design:
A Cloud Approach

Gianpiero Di Blasi
Università degli Studi di Torino, Italy

Eleonora Pantano
Middlesex University London, UK

ABSTRACT

The emerging need to make more attractive physical stores for catching new clients and maintaining the existing ones pushes retailers to develop efficient practices for acquiring knowledge from consumers and involving them in the points of sales' design. The final users' needs and preferences are considered a core in design process. This chapter proposes a system for involving consumers in the store design process through an innovative cloud participatory platform. It is a low cost hardware/software architecture offering a user-friendly interface able to be adopted by audiences with different background. Results show the consumers' interest to contribute in the design by using such technologies and providing a large amount of detailed information useful for future appealing stores' development. Finally, this chapter shows how the inclusion of modern low-cost game technologies in retail industry might provide ripper effects in several disciplines such as human-computer interaction, marketing, and management.

INTRODUCTION

In recent years, marketing orientation has dramatically shifted from a product orientation to a consumer orientation (Tajeddini, 2010), by considering consumers as the core of the process. According to past studies (Wright et al., 2006), putting end-users perspective, with emphasis on their experience, as the starting point for the design represents the basic element for successful strategies. This approach is able to define new strategies that posit consumers' needs and preferences as the fundamental for developing new successfully products and services (Tajeddini, 2010; Reychav and Weisberg, 2009), by actively involving final users into the design (Iversen et al., 2012; Bullinger et al., 2010; Nuttavuthisit, 2010; Bonner, 2010). To achieve this goal, the business

DOI: 10.4018/978-1-4666-8297-9.ch002

activities are mainly directed to meet consumers' expectations, by identifying, analysing, understanding and answering their needs in through understanding their preferences and expectations. In this direction, a successful strategy is devoted to identify the best practice for involving them in the service/product co-creation process. In fact, their active participation increases the acceptance of the final product (Wang et al., 2011; Lian and Lin, 2008). Hence, understanding consumers' involvement allows marketers and developers to create new customized products and services with benefits for consumers' acceptance (Wang et al., 2006; Edvardsson et al., 2012).

Modern technologies enhance this process by both offering novel and exciting platforms able to catch users' attention and motivate them to be active participants in the design process, and providing more visual information and interactive tools (Kim et al., 2007). For instance, immersive technologies support designers in deeply understanding the expectations and perceptions of end-users through a realistic experience able to solicit the knowledge sharing (both from consumer to consumer and from consumer to designer), with benefits for the quality of the final outcome (Loke and Robertson, 2009).

Since previous studies outlined significant differences between retailers' opinions and consumers' needs regarding the elements able to improve the shopping experience (Backstrom and Johansson, 2006), identifying the best practice for integrating the two perspectives is emerging as a critical factor for the design of new efficient stores. For instance, consumers pay more attention towards layout, price, products selection, whereas retailers mainly focus on technological solutions for enhancing design elements (Backstrom and Johansson, 2006; Kourouthanassis et al., 2007). For this reason, a successful approach to design requires a strong dialog between the different perspectives coming from different backgrounds (Wright et al., 2006; Dahan and Hauser, 2002). Previous researches on improving the physical store tested the effectiveness of the new solutions by inviting consumers

to physically visit it and express judgments on the aesthetic and shopping experience, thus after the effective realization (Wang et al., 2011; Vieira, 2010). This procedure is expensive in terms of cost and time. Other studies tried to test the consumers' preferences before the effective realization, for instance in the designing of shopping centres, by exploiting the use of virtual reality tools (Borgers et al., 2010; Parker and Lehmann, 2011), and applying the subsequent results to the actual design. In this case, the developer has not a direct interaction with consumers and only take into account their final suggestions.

The aim of this chapter is to deeply understand to what extent consumers can be successfully involved also in the design of a new point of sale for increasing the quality of the final output, by proposing a new participatory platform able to support the (re)design of shopping experiences and of more attractive stores. In particular, the purpose is to reconsider the retailing process and consumer experience by focusing on a consumer-driven store design perspective.

The first part of the chapter concerns the current advanced technologies for involving consumers in the co-creation of products and services, with emphasis on virtual and augmented reality; whereas the second one focuses on the new platform based on the cloud participation as supporting tools for enhancing retail processes in each phase of the store design process. Suggestions for academics and practitioners are further proposed.

THEORETICAL BACKGROUND

Virtual Reality and Immersive Technologies

Many recent studies identified the vital role of online platforms and virtual reality tools for successfully involving users to participate into design process. The majority of these researches focused on virtual communities for enhancing the interaction between developer and final user (Light and Akama, 2012, Fueller et al., 2011), due to the fact that a virtual reality-based scenario is less expensive and more flexible if compared to the development of a real world simulation scenario (e.g. flight simulators) (Kozak et al., 1993). For this reason, the virtual reality environments have been successfully exploited for training in several sectors, such as medicine (it is largely used for surgical trainees), education and learning; manufacturing and prototyping, etc. (Kozak et al., 1993; Piccoli et al., 2001; Seymour et al., 2002; Valerio Netto and De Oliveira, 2002; Grantcharov et al., 2004; Rubio et al., 2005; Reznick and MacRae, 2006; van der Meijden and Schijven, 2009).

Recent advances in virtual reality developed also new 3D imaginary visual worlds with a high level of realism, generated by a computer, which users can explore through special input devices (e.g. data gloves, motion capture systems, etc.) for interacting with the environment and having the feeling of immersion in the digital scenario (Dede, 2009; Pantano and Servidio, 2012). Hence, there is a sort of shift from the real setting to a virtual one. Understanding the main differences (and analogies) between real and virtual scenario is an ancient and critical problem. Date back to the ancient Greek era, Plato (428 B.D.- 348 B.D.) reflects on the concepts of real and virtual, on what is real and what is the fruit of our imagination ("The Republic", VII book). Although the similarity between the Plato's cave and the current world seems bizarre, it is particularly evident that: "today we are not encircled by shadows but by images. It is true that images are there in order to show the truth, but when they show it, they also hide it. The virtual reality is a contradiction in terms: if the reality is *reality* it cannot be virtual. We live in a kind of virtual cave in which we are entered for our will" (Saramago, 2003). Hence, attempts of *realistic* simulations of reality already emerged in the ancient age, despite without the technological tools current available for the effective simulation of imaginary worlds.

More recently, in the last century many improvements have been done in the field of virtual reality. For instance, in the '30s, the first algorithms in military context have been developed to simulate the fight environment for bomber aviators; whereas in the 1965 Ivan Sutherland (Sutherland, 1965) proposed a system in which synthetic images are presented to the viewer by two screens directly connected to human's eyes.

As anticipated, to date, the current advances in Information and Communication Technologies provide innovative tools for enriching user's experience, such as control movement sensors, haptic systems, etc., with benefits for successfully introducing virtual reality into many applicative contexts:

1. **Entertainment:** For the creation of fantastic worlds or physically impossible scenes concerning the cinematographic industry and videogames (Zyda, 2005; Weibel et al., 2008; Zhou et al., 2013);

2. **Education and Learning:** For the creation of attractive training environments for defence, sport, medicine, psychotherapy, etc., as well as for the simulation of dangerous, expensive or impossible experiences such as in biology, astronomy, and chemistry (Gurusamy et al., 2009; Virvou et al., 2005; Moreno, 2006; Dede, 2009; Dalgarno and Lee, 2010; Pantano, 2011);

3. **Arts and Cultural Heritage:** For the reproduction of lost monuments and scenes, the fruition of art handwork into new contests and novel ways, the tourist promotion, etc. (Pantano and Servidio, 2011; Sylaiou, 2010; Karoulis et al., 2006);

4. **Built Environment:** For the simulation of traffic and new urban design (Bullinger et al., 2010), etc.

In these scenarios, hybrid forms of virtual reality such as 'augmented' or 'mixed' reality have been created to improve the benefits of virtual reality and the realism of the digital context (e.g. the sense of realism and immersion in the virtual space). This is an enriched vision of virtual reality, consisting of a user interface based on a 3D space embedded within the real (physical) world (Seo and Lee, 2013; Lee et al., 2010). Despite the great advantages in adopting VR-based systems, there are still some problems to overcome for:

- **Obtaining Realistic Data and Models:** The reproduction of particular scenarios such as archaeological parks requires specific information, that only a professional and expert team could provide, concerning both the scientific/cultural part and the 3D modelling techniques;
- **Having Efficient Computing Equipment:** The virtual simulations require huge resources for computing and advanced technologies;
- **Having Exciting Output Devices:** 3D monitors, auditory speakers, etc. able to catch users' attention (i.e. the technology should be able to recognize user's behaviour, in terms of control gestures, camera tracking, etc. through tracker systems in order to reply with the most effective output).

One of the most important aspects of any virtual, immersive environment is the interaction between the human and the computer, usually called HCI (Human-Computer Interaction). Humans need to communicate actions, intents, goals and choices to the machine, conversely computers have to inform the users about the environment, their internal state, the answers to the users' queries and so on. This communication may involve explicit dialog, even if in the most current computer systems the communication is more implicit, freeform and imperceptible. Modern user interfaces are based on 3D interaction that is an HCI in which the user's tasks are performed directly in a 3D spatial context.

Although the use of virtual and immersive technologies generates such contextual richness that could improve the design process, the outlined findings and knowledge could be hard to be included into the design process, by suggesting a new challenge for the current researches (Kieldskov and Stage, 2012).

Collaborative Platforms for Gaming

Despite the original purpose of being only an entertaining tool, the game platforms have acquired the role of core of multimedia entertainment for a huge segment of population. In fact, the most advanced platforms for gaming are based on superior graphics interfaces, realistic tools for interacting with computer and cloud computing technology with benefits for the final quality of the game in terms of interface, functionalities and ease of use (Das et al., 2010). The most recent ones propose advanced and high realistic interfaces that support also the sharing of several typologies of contents, such as movies, music, and game online with other users, as well as the possibility to collaborate for improving the game experience.

Among the current available platforms, Xbox is a meaningful example. Its technical features, in terms of computing power and innovative control system, allow a huge number of users to develop and share novel and more exciting and attractive videogames. Xbox was Microsoft's first foray into the gaming console market. It was released between November 2001 and March 2002 worldwide (The Xbox official site, 2013). The second edition of the Xbox, called Xbox 360, was launched in November 2005; the name Xbox 360 is supposed to reflect that it was designed to be the "centre of your entertainment experience" (The Xbox official site, 2013); therefore, the number is referred to 360 degrees of a circle. Presumably, it was also a way to integrate a 3 into the title to suggest its ability to compete with the Xbox's main competitor PlayStation 3. The Xbox runs a custom operating system that exposes APIs similar to APIs found in Windows. The system is based on the Windows NT architecture that powered Windows 2000.

Kinect is an innovative motion sensing input device developed by Microsoft for the Xbox 360. Based on a webcam-style add-on peripheral, it enables users to control and interact with the console without the need to touch a game controller, through a natural user interface using gestures and spoken commands. The project, firstly announced on June 2009 under the code name "Project Natal", is aimed at broadening the Xbox 360's audience beyond its typical gamer base. Kinect is based on a system able to interpret specific gestures, making completely hands-free control of electronic devices by using an infrared projector and camera and a special microchip to track the movement of objects and individuals in three dimensions. This 3D scanner system (Light Coding) employs a variant of image-based 3D reconstruction. The Kinect sensor is a horizontal bar connected to a small base with a motorized pivot. The device provides a full-body 3D motion capture, facial recognition and voice recognition capabilities. The depth sensor consists of an infrared laser projector combined with a monochrome CMOS sensor, which captures video data in 3D under any ambient light conditions. The sensing range of the depth sensor is adjustable, and the Kinect software is capable of automatically calibrating the sensor based on gameplay and the player's physical environment. Finally, Xbox Live is the online multiplayer gaming and digital media delivery service created and operated by Microsoft for the Xbox (The Xbox Live official site, 2013). It was first made available in November 2002. Since Xbox is an advanced console for developing realistic videogames, Kinect supports interactivity, and Xbox Live is an online and collaborative platform for gaming (where vendor and client can develop together the final product), it is possible to integrate the benefits of these technologies and synthetize them efficiently in a new environment with several purposes.

Cloud Computing and Cloud Collaboration

Cloud computing can be viewed as the result of evolution and adoption of several technologies and paradigms (Armbrust, 2010). It is an emerging computational approach consisting of the use of computing resources (hardware and software) delivered as a service through Internet. Cloud computing entrusts remote services with user's data, software and computation, with the aim to allow users to achieve benefit from these technologies without any specific knowledge of each one. In particular, end users interact with cloud-based applications through a web browser or a lightweight application while the business software and user's data are stored on servers at a remote location. In this scenario, Gmail and GoogleDrive are two meaningful examples: through Gmail the user access to email management (i.e. consulting, archiving, writing, etc.) by using the web browser or the ad-hoc applications available in any smartphone, while the data (the mails) are safety stored on the Google servers (this functionality overcomes the problems of storage on the physical mobile devices that may have a limited capacity of memorizing and computing); through GoogleDrive the user may write, modify and share the documents (especially googledocs) with other users avoiding the further problems concerning the size of document attachment (i.e. some providers limits the size of the attached file to a limited number of MByte).

The concept of cloud computing is not totally new. It dates back to the late 1950s, when large-scale mainframe have become available in academia and enterprises, accessible via terminal computers, which required hardware with no internal computational capacities used only for communications. To make more efficient use of costly mainframes and overcome this problem, the practice of sharing CPU time on a mainframe has become a standard approach known in the industry as time-sharing (Strachey, 1959). In fact, this methodology allowed multiple users to share both the physical access to the computer from multiple terminals, and to share the CPU time. As a main benefit, there was a dramatically reduction of periods of inactivity on the mainframe, which guaranteed a large return on the investment.

Subsequently, as computers became more prevalent, academics and practitioners explored modalities for

1. Making large-scale computing power available to more users through time sharing,
2. Experimenting with algorithms to provide the optimal use of the infrastructure, and
3. Developing platform and applications with prioritized access to the CPU and efficiency for the end users (Corbató, 2012).

Although the term is rather vague and seems to be used in different contexts with different meanings, three types of cloud computing services can be figured out (Magoulès, 2009):

- **SaaS (Software as a Service):** It consists in the use of programs installed on a remote server, often through a web server, this term is conceptually similar to the term ASP (Application service provider);
- **DaaS (Data as a Service):** With this service a large amount of data are made available via the web (this is also currently known as Open Data);
- **PaaS (Platform as a Service):** Instead of one or more individual programs a complete software platform is performed remotely; this platform can be a collection of different services, programs, libraries, etc. (for example Google App Engine);
- **IaaS (Infrastructure as a Service):** This type of cloud is almost a synonym for Grid Computing, but with one essential feature: the resources are used on request then the platform needs it.

Despite cloud computing was born to solve business problems, it is recently used for several research areas such as the bioinformatics, due to the huge benefits not limited to the cost/time saving, which can be summarized as follows (Wall et al., 2010; Afgan et al, 2011):

- Companies can avoid upfront infrastructure costs, and focus on projects that differentiate their businesses instead of their infrastructure;
- Companies can get their applications up and running faster, with improved manageability and less maintenance, and enables IT to more rapidly adjust resources to meet fluctuating and unpredictable business demand;
- Users can achieve a better quality of the final storage service;
- Users are able to access their data from everywhere, by reducing the risk of data loss.

Due to these huge benefits, the idea of cloud computing can be further exploited in a cooperative and collaborative scenario: not only for sharing information, but also for putting together information for creating a new product. In fact, cloud collaboration is a new, innovative way of sharing and co-authoring documents through the use of cloud computing (Graham, 2011; Diffina et al, 2010). In this context, collaboration refers to the ability of employees to work together/simultaneously on a particular task.

Despite the benefits of cloud collaboration, noteworthy threat lays on the users' data storage on the cloud provider's server, which could allow an unauthorized access to the data with negative consequence for privacy concerns. In fact, this is a critical issue in the current literature that would require further investigations, and a risk that may discourage users' acceptance of this technology.

An interesting example of cloud collaboration can be found in (Han, 2013), by focusing on the new content-centric collaboration platform able to support automated content-centric collaboration on cloud system, which the author named as "active content collaboration platform". This platform supports event-driven automatic collaboration and a modularized and extensible architecture, and provides a scalable high-performance architecture. Hence, cloud collaboration technologies allow users to upload, comment and collaborate on documents and even improve or edit the document itself, evolving the document within the cloud. Though these technologies, documents are uploaded into a central "cloud" for storage and others can then access and modify/improve them.

THE IMMERSIVE (CLOUD) STORE

System Architecture

Starting from the above-mentioned characteristics of cloud computing and cloud collaboration concepts, the system proposed in this chapter is based on the characteristics of an immersive store (i.e. the large use of 3D visualization techniques), for involving consumers actively in the design process of a new store. The first prototype of immersive store, based on immersive technologies, was ideated and created by developers and subsequently tested on final consumers (Pantano and Servidio 2012). Hence consumers were involved only to judge the final product. In opposite, in the current work, we involved consumers from the first phase of the development of the new store, by considering them as active participants, in order to evaluate the quality of both the design process and the final output during each phase of the process (Figure 1).

After the user has logged into the system, he/she had to perform one of the following steps:

- To select a store project (created by the same user or by another user);
- To create a new store project.

Store project creation further involves the following tasks:

1. **Selection of a Floor Plan:** Selected among different alternatives already developed through an ad hoc software for PC desktop computers. Currently the user can select a floor plan among a set of five standard floor plans;
2. **Selection of the Store Type the User Wants to Design:** This is mandatory due to the peculiarities characterizing each typology of store. Currently the user can create only clothing stores.

The system requires only a limited number of (low-cost) hardware: each workspace is equipped with Xbox 360 and Kinect (as described in the previous sections), while the Xbox Live manages the interaction among the different users (the cloud collaboration). We assumed these technologies as low cost if compared to the other systems usually employed in the design process. Given the gradual lowering pricing of the game consoles, this system is much cheaper if compared with proprietary solutions based on significantly more complex hardware architectures. For our experiments, we created some fulfilled workspaces for users attending the experiment in a laboratory at University of Calabria (Italy).

User Interaction

As anticipated, the system allows the interaction among users (like in an online videogame), as well as between user and environment, which reproduces the possible future store. Each user has the possibility to add, remove, replace, and "model" several objects/furniture for creating a new environment/store simultaneously (such as: benches, shelves, fitting rooms, etc.). Furthermore, for each kind of furniture, user can select among different alternatives concerning the materials (i.e. glasses or wood for shelves, etc.), as well as the dimension (Figure 2, top-left).

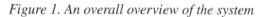

Figure 1. An overall overview of the system

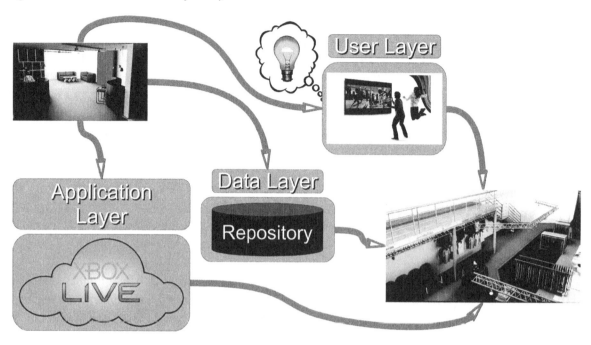

Figure 2. Top-left: screenshot of the software during the store creation (a detail of the software running a version for computer desktop visualization); middle-right: preliminary version of the possible future store, before consumers' involvement in design process; bottom-left: the final version of the store realized through the users' active involvement in the design process

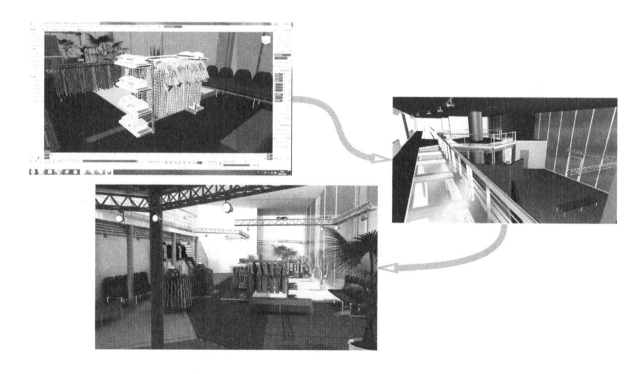

The interaction system is driven by arms and legs gestures, while new objects can be selected through an icons-accessible menu. After this preliminary phase concerning the definition of basic elements of the store, user can "browse" the environment (by simulating the gesture of walking), stand in front of an object, edit the related position and dimension (by spreading, tightening and rotating the arms) and delete the item if preferred (by portray a cross symbol on the chest). Similarly, user may select and add objects to sell (currently only clothes) from a database of possible items (created from standard primitives and subsequently improved through 3D graphics tools). In particular, the available goods are strictly linked to the selected furniture, (i.e. if users sat furniture with coat hangers, the system requires the positioning of clothes too)

Hence, the system allows the multi-user mode for interacting with other users. In fact, several users may interact with the same environment at the same time. In this case, the system represents the other users as an avatar (users see each other like an avatar) for supporting the interaction among actors (i.e. consumers, developers, managers, etc.) and promoting the cooperation. Furthermore, the system synchronizes the changes added by each user and keeps the coherence of the virtual store.

Design Process Implementation through Users' Interaction

The preliminary version of the future point of sale shows an empty surface based on two floors that could be defined according to users' preferences. The space contains some walls, shelves, and sofas to recall a retail environment without focusing on a specific product (Figure 2, middle-right).

We recruited 35 undergraduate volunteer students during the standard activities at University of Calabria (Italy). Sample could access and participate to the experiment between January and March 2014. We asked participants to explore a potential new store and make the preferred changes through the available tools, and to provide their evaluation of the experience through a subsequent questionnaire. Hence, they were free to take part in the experiment as active actors of the design process.

We scheduled 6 sessions of 1 hour for 5 different groups, consisting of 7 participants each one provided our system (the first group attended also to the last session). Before starting each section, a developer explained the main functionalities of the system and the aim of the research. A developer and a retailer were always present during each section. The members of the same group worked simultaneously from different stations (equipped with the system and the required tools and located in different corner of the lab, in order to allow the interaction among participants only via the system).

The experiment ended when participants didn't add significant changes to the previous version of the store. Since the participants of the first group started the effective design process by adding the first items and choosing the typology of store, this group has been also involved in the last section to evaluate the quality of the final product. The version emerging from the 6th section is the definitive one (Figure 2, bottom-left).

After completing the project, we asked all 35 participants to explain through semi-structured questions:

1. The motivations to take part to the experiment,
2. The level of satisfaction of the experience, and
3. Their evaluation of the final outcome. Users' responses have been investigated through software for content analysis.

Majority of respondents (92%) appreciated the idea to participate to the design of new store because usually they consider that retailers do not take their opinion into account, because they consider the idea of cloud collaboration for a new store very innovative and entertaining. Furthermore, the 94% of respondents felt satisfied with both the process, which perceived as very interactive and ease, and the final store, which perceived as high focused on their preferences. The model of store emerging from this interactive process has been further compared with the one that has been developed previously in Pantano and Servidio (2012) without involving consumers in the whole process. In particular, 100 undergraduate students who didn't attend the past experiments were asked to rank the two different models according to 5 parameters (attractive, interesting, influencing the entry decision, stimulating curiosity), after the virtual exploration of 15 minutes for each model. The 93% of respondents preferred the version realized through the participatory design.

DISCUSSION

The described experiment shows to what extent it is possible to employ a cloud approach also for developing new stores through a participatory platform involving consumers. The new store arising from the collaboration among users, developers and retailers is a new and highly customized environment based on consumers' preferences, which is expected to be more appreciated by consumers if compared to a store developed in a traditional and not participatory design process.

Three aspects of our research emerge from a theoretical standpoint: the

1. Efficient consumers' involvement in the new store design process,
2. The efficient management of consumer knowledge, and
3. The increased quality of consumers-developer interaction.

1. Efficient Consumers' Involvement in the New Store Design Process

Participants showed enthusiasm in attending the experiment, due to both the new novel and interactive visual tools used for creating the new environment, and the possibility to provide creative contributions that retailers/developer could take into account for developing a new store based on their preferences. Hence, they were immersed in the design experience, and their perspective was the starting point for the design, as anticipated by previous researches identifying this element as the basic one for a successful design (Wright et al., 2006; Tajeddini, 2010; Reychav and Weisberg, 2009; Wang et al., 2011; Lian and Lin, 2008). In fact, users' suggestions in defining products, furniture and layout become part of the creative process, whose outcome would be a new point of sale able to attract a wider number of consumers. The platform has been perceived as a sort of entertaining environment, a game, which users felt free to enjoy. Due to the ease of use of the system tools, the enjoyable tools (i.e. we used tools usually part of game console), the quality of interface, and enhanced interaction modalities motivated users in participating to our experiment, the respondents got an active role into the design process and appreciated their new role of *co-creator*, in accordance with previous studies (Dahan and Hauser, 2002; Bonner et al., 2010; Bullinger et al.; 2010).

In particular, users added several improvements to the first version of the system, such as the changes of lights and color, locating the single items on the shelves, etc.. Since they introduced these changes in real-time, it is hard to determine the exact number of contributions they added, whereas it is easy to define the quality of the final outcome. As a consequence, the store emerged from their interactions is expected to meet a huger acceptance by the market.

Although past works highlighted that the findings and knowledge generated through virtual and immersive technologies could be hard to be included into the design process (Kieldskov and Stage, 2012), our findings showed to what extent users' knowledge might be efficiently integrated in the process in-real time and it may be included in the creation of a new store. For these reasons, our platform is a powerful tool for easily and efficiently integrating consumers' point of view in the (whole) design process, with benefits for the quality of the final store.

2. Efficient Management of Consumer Knowledge

Since the experience is enriched with several stimuli, consumers' perceptual and emotional aspects are involved, with benefits for the entertainment perception. As a consequence, they are willing to provide more judgments and personal opinions, which represent that part of knowledge modeled through the improvements of the virtual store. While consumers interact with the system and modify the environment, they provide knowledge on their preferences and needs that retailers can easily exploit for developing a more efficient store. Therefore, also the tacit (not codified) knowledge seems to emerge, with benefits for retailers who have access to a wider amount of information on potential clients. These findings are consistent with past studies (Edvardsson et al., 2012) that stated how the new situational contexts represented by a participatory platform solicit consumers' contributions. In fact, our participatory platform based on cloud computing supports users in expressing their knowledge through visual and interactive tools, by transferring their opinions and preferences in a final product (the fully furnished store). For instance, starting from users' changes to the store layout (in terms of walls and physical constraints removing), we realized their preference of open spaces that could make easier and funnier the exploration. Moreover, the idea of open space provides a feeling of free exploration, which enhances consumers' satisfaction. Similarly, from the changes added to the relaxing area (a small

area furnished with sofas, etc.), we understood the role of this space during the shopping experience for both male and female target. Thus, we may assume the importance consumers give to the possibility to relax while shopping offered by the presence of sofas, coffee corners, etc..

The tool we propose allows also testing and investigating consumers in-store behavior, in order to evaluate in advance the behavior in the future stores before its effective realization. In fact, the quantity and quality of users' changes to the initial model shows how it could be perceived and implemented by consumers for better meeting their needs. In our experiment, we proposed a generic empty store as starting point, but a further advanced version of the store reproducing the real one can advance the knowledge on how it can be efficiently improved for fitting consumers' expectations in the real context, thus the evaluation phase is simultaneous with the development one. This practice allows saving time and money, by reducing the cost and the time involved the traditional store evaluation phase that takes place after the physically realization (Wang et al., 2011; Vieira, 2010).

3. Increased Quality of Consumer-Developer Interaction

As anticipated by Edvardsson et al. (2012), the knowledge achieved from the collaborative experience represents the result of the successful cooperation among different actors. In our experiment, customers, developers and retailers cooperated for achieving the mutual goal (the creation of a new efficient store). Their effort has been integrated in a common development process in order to accomplish the value-creation through a new service.

In addition to the role of established online platforms such virtual communities for enhancing the interaction between developer and final users (Light and Akama, 2012; Fueller et al., 2011), we propose a new system able to overcome the boundaries between the role of retailer, developer and consumer, by providing an innovative platform where all participants have the same possibilities, tools and functions for improving the scenario. In this way, users (consumers) feel free to interact with the system and with the others participants, by considering their work important like the work of the others without taking into account their original role (i.e. if they are retailers or developers, etc.). In fact, from the final product it is not possible to distinguish the changes made by retailers, consumers, or developers. Since also a retailer and a developer attended the last session and they didn't make change, the final outcome can be considered as similarly appreciated by the all categories of actors. Although the different actors involved in the process may have different points of views and show different behaviours triggered by different background and roles (Backstrom and Johansson, 2006; Kourouthanassis et al., 2007; Wright et al., 2006), our system efficiently integrates the various perspectives by giving them the possibility to equally contribute to the final store, thus it synthetizes these perspectives in a unique product accepted by the different categories of actors. Hence, this system based on cloud collaboration fosters and stimulates the sharing knowledge between retailers and consumers. The final outcome is both a possible future store largely appreciated by consumers and retailers, and an efficient channel able to support the dialog between the different perspectives involved in the design process. Retailers may take into account these emergent elements for the definition of new in-store retail strategies.

CONCLUSION AND FUTURE WORKS

This chapter shows a new approach for developing/designing more efficient stores through the cloud computing and cloud collaboration approach. One of the main advantages of our platform lays on the high level of collaboration and cooperation among involved actors, who work together for designing a new store, within a low cost technological scenario.

The benefits of our system can be summarized as follows:

- The use of gesture makes simple selecting, positioning and editing the objects with respect to the old classic 'point & click' model of the traditional desktop systems;
- The proposed hardware/software architecture is really cheap and accessible;
- The system is based on game console ease of use and largely diffused among youth;
- The cloud collaboration system reduces the cost while increasing the opportunity to interact directly with managers, retailers, final consumers, and developers in an efficient and direct way, in order to achieve a better output. In fact, all participants are informed in real-time about the advancements of the process.

Therefore, our system shows how a cloud computing approach, already successfully exploited in several sectors (Wall et al., 2010; Afgan et al, 2011), might become a powerful tool also for retail industry, by offering a new collaborative system in retail patronage. In fact, results highlight to what extent the outcome emerging from the collaboration seems to be more appreciated by consumers if compared with the store fully designed by the developer. In the one hand, it confirms that involving users increases the acceptance of the final product (Wang et al., 2011; Lian and Lin, 2008); in the other one it underlines the larger consumers' acceptance of high customized products (Wang et al., 2006; Edvardsson et al., 2012), while considering the new store as the final product.

Despite the important issues emerging from our study, there are some limitations that should be taken into account. Since our system is still a prototype, its access is still limited to the laboratory at university, thus people cannot access by private home for attending the experiment (design process). A further development might consist of making the access available from personal computer equipped with the technology for the 3D visualization and interaction, in order to involve a wider number of potential consumers and to increase the quality and quantity of contributions with benefits for the quality of the final store.

In addition, some open questions still remain concerning the legal aspect of the design outcome. Who will be the legal owner of the participatory project? How do preserve the process from the access of possible competitors, by also preserving the access of not-authorized people to the whole process and to the final outcome before the physical realization of the store? In this sense, it would be useful to state some particular agreements in order to limit the spread of news before the completion of the project.

REFERENCES

Afgan, E., Baker, D., Coraor, N., Goto, H., Paul, I. M., Makova, K. D., & Taylor, J. et al. (2011). Harnessing cloud computing with Galaxy Cloud. *Nature Biotechnology*, *29*(11), 972–974. doi:10.1038/nbt.2028 PMID:22068528

Armbrust, M., Fox, A., Griffith, R., Joseph, A. D., Katz, R., Konwinski, A., & Zaharia, M. et al. (2010). A view of cloud computing. *Communications of the ACM*, *53*(4), 50–58. doi:10.1145/1721654.1721672

Backstrom, K., & Johansson, U. (2006). Creating and consuming experiences in retail store environments: Comparing retailer and consumer perspectives. *Journal of Retailing and Consumer Services*, *13*(6), 417–430. doi:10.1016/j.jretconser.2006.02.005

Bonner, J. M. (2010). Customer interactivity and new product performance: Moderating effects of product newness and product embeddedness. *Industrial Marketing Management*, *39*(3), 485–492. doi:10.1016/j.indmarman.2008.11.006

Borgers, A., Brouwer, M., Kunen, T., Jessurun, J., & Janssen, I. (2010). A virtual reality tool to measure shoppers' tenant mix preferences. *Computers, Environment and Urban Systems*, *34*(5), 377–388. doi:10.1016/j.compenvurbsys.2010.04.002

Bowman, D. A., Kruijff, E., LaViola, J. J. Jr, & Poupyrev, I. (2004). *3D user interfaces: Theory and practice*. Redwood City, CA: Addison Wesley.

Bullinger, H.-J., Bauer, W., Wenzel, G., & Blach, R. (2010). Towards user centred design (UCD) in architecture based on immersive virtual environments. *Computers in Industry*, *61*(4), 372–379. doi:10.1016/j.compind.2009.12.003

Corbató, F. J., Merwin-Daggett, M., & Daley, R. C. (1962). An experimental time-sharing system. In *Proceedings of Spring Joint Computer Conference* (pp. 335-344). New York, NY: ACM.

Dahan, E., & Hauser, J. R. (2002). The virtual customer. *Journal of Product Innovation Management*, *19*(5), 332–353. doi:10.1016/S0737-6782(02)00151-0

Dalgarno, B., & Lee, M. J. W. (2010). What are the learning affordances of 3-D virtual environments? *British Journal of Educational Technology*, *41*(1), 10–30. doi:10.1111/j.1467-8535.2009.01038.x

Das, S., Agrawal, D., & Abbadi, A. E. (2010). G-Store: A scalable data store for transactional multi key access in the cloud. In *Proceedings of the 1st ACM Symposium on Cloud Computing* (pp. 163-174). New York, NY: ACM. doi:10.1145/1807128.1807157

Dede, C. (2009). Immersive interfaces for engagement and learning. *Science*, *323*(5910), 66–69. doi:10.1126/science.1167311 PMID:19119219

Diffina, J. (2010). Cloud collaboration - Using Microsoft SharePoint as a tool to enhance access services. *Journal of Library Administration*, *50*(5-6), 570–580. doi:10.1080/01930826.2010.488619

Dudley, J. T., Pouliot, Y., Chen, R., Morgan, A. A., & Butte, A. J. (2010). Translational bioinformatics in the cloud - An affordable alternative. *Genome Medicine*, *2*(8), 51–57. doi:10.1186/gm172 PMID:20691073

Edvardsson, B., Kristensson, P., Magnusson, P., & Sundstrom, R. (2012). Customer integration within service development - A review of methods and an analysis of insitu and exsitu contributions. *Technovation*, *32*(7-8), 419–429. doi:10.1016/j.technovation.2011.04.006

Fuller, J., Hutter, K., & Faullant, R. (2011). Why co-creation experience matters? Creative experience and its impact on the quantity and quality of creative contributions. *R & D Management*, *41*(3), 259–273. doi:10.1111/j.1467-9310.2011.00640.x

Graham, M. (2011). Cloud collaboration - Peer-production and the engineering of the internet. In S. Brunn (Ed.), *Engineering earth* (pp. 67–83). Berlin: Springer. doi:10.1007/978-90-481-9920-4_5

Grantcharov, T. P., Kristiansen, V. B., Bendix, J., Bardram, L., Rosenberg, J., & Funch-Jensen, P. (2004). Randomized clinical trial of virtual reality simulation for laparoscopic skills training. *British Journal of Surgery*, *91*(2), 146–150. doi:10.1002/bjs.4407 PMID:14760660

Gurusamy, K. S., Aggarwal, R., Palanivelu, L., & Davidson, B. R. (2009). Virtual reality training for surgical trainees in laparoscopic surgery. *Cochrane Database of Systematic Reviews*, *1*, 1–74. PMID:19160288

Han, B. J., Jung, I. Y., Kim, K. H., Lee, D. K., Rho, S., & Jeong, C. S. (2013). Cloud-based active content collaboration platform using multimedia processing. *EURASIP Journal on Wireless Communications and Networking*, *2013*(63), 63–76. doi:10.1186/1687-1499-2013-63

Iversen, O. S., Leong, T. W., Wright, P., Gregory, J., & Bowker, G. (2012). Working with human values in design. In *Proceedings of the 12th Participatory Design Conference* (pp. 143-144). New York, NY: ACM. doi:10.1145/2348144.2348191

Karoulis, A., Sylaiou, S., & White, M. (2006). Usability evaluation of a virtual museum interface. *Informatica*, *17*(3), 363–380.

Kim, J., Fiore, A. M., & Lee, H.-H. (2007). Influences of online store perception, shopping enjoyment, and shopping involvement on consumer patronage behaviour towards an online retailer. *Journal of Retailing and Consumer Services*, *14*(2), 95–107. doi:10.1016/j.jretconser.2006.05.001

Kjeldskov, J., & Stage, J. (2012). Combining ethnography and object-orientation for mobile interaction design: Contextual richness and abstract models. *International Journal of Human-Computer Studies*, *70*(3), 197–217. doi:10.1016/j.ijhcs.2011.10.004

Kourouthanassis, P. E., Giaglis, G. M., & Vrechopoulos, A. P. (2007). Enhancing user experience through pervasive information systems: The case of pervasive retailing. *International Journal of Information Management*, *27*(5), 319–335. doi:10.1016/j.ijinfomgt.2007.04.005

Kozak, J. J., Hancock, P. A., Arthur, E. J., & Chrysler, S. T. (1993). Transfer of training from virtual reality. *Ergonomics*, *36*(7), 777–784. doi:10.1080/00140139308967941

Lee, J. Y., Rhee, G. W., & Seo, D. W. (2010). Hand gesture-based tangible interactions for manipulating virtual objects in a mixed reality environment. *International Journal of Advanced Manufacturing Technology*, *51*(9-12), 1069–1082. doi:10.1007/s00170-010-2671-x

Lian, J.-W., & Lin, T.-M. (2008). Effects of consumer characteristics on their acceptance of online shopping: Comparisons among different product types. *Computers in Human Behavior*, *24*(1), 48–65. doi:10.1016/j.chb.2007.01.002

Light, A., & Akama, Y. (2012). The human touch: participatory practice and the role of facilitation in designing with communities. In *Proceedings Series of the 12th Participatory Design Conference* (pp. 61-70). New York, NY: ACM. doi:10.1145/2347635.2347645

Loke, L., & Robertson, T. (2009). Design representations of moving bodies for interactive, motion-sensing spaces. *International Journal of Human-Computer Studies*, *67*(4), 394–410. doi:10.1016/j.ijhcs.2008.11.003

Magoulès, F. (2009). *Fundamentals of grid computing: Theory, algorithms and technologies*. Chapman & Hall/CRC. doi:10.1201/9781439803684

Microsoft. (2014). *Xbox official site*. Retrieved March 18, 2014 from http://www.xbox.com

Microsoft. (2014). *Xbox Live official site*. Retrieved March 18, 2014 from http://www.xbox.com/live

Mollet, N., & Arnaldi, B. (2006). Storytelling in virtual reality for training. *Lecture Notes in Computer Science*, *3942*, 334–347. doi:10.1007/11736639_45

Moreno, R. (2006). Learning in high-tech and multimedia environments. *Current Directions in Psychological Science*, *15*(2), 63–67. doi:10.1111/j.0963-7214.2006.00408.x

Nuttavuthisit, K. (2010). If you can't beat them, let them join: The development of strategies to foster consumers' co-creative practices. *Business Horizons*, *53*(3), 315–324. doi:10.1016/j.bushor.2010.01.005

Pantano, E. (2011). Virtual cultural heritage consumption: A 3D learning experience. *International Journal of Technology Enhanced Learning*, *3*(5), 482–495. doi:10.1504/IJTEL.2011.042100

Pantano, E., & Servidio, R. (2011). The role of pervasive environments for promotion of tourist destinations: The users' response. *Journal of Hospitality and Tourism Technology*, *2*(1), 50–65. doi:10.1108/17579881111112412

Pantano, E., & Servidio, R. (2012). Modeling innovative points of sales through virtual and immersive technologies. *Journal of Retailing and Consumer Services*, *19*(3), 279–286. doi:10.1016/j.jretconser.2012.02.002

Parker, J. R., & Lehmann, D. R. (2011). When shelf-based scarcity impacts consumer preferences. *Journal of Retailing*, *87*(2), 142–155. doi:10.1016/j.jretai.2011.02.001

Piccoli, G., Ahmad, R., & Ives, B. (2001). Web-based virtual learning environments: A research framework and preliminary assessment of effectiveness in basic it skills training. *MIS Quarterly: Management Information Systems*, *25*(4), 401–426. doi:10.2307/3250989

Reychav, I., & Weisberg, J. (2009). Going beyond technology: Knowledge sharing as tool for enhancing customer-oriented attitudes. *International Journal of Information Management*, *29*(5), 353–361. doi:10.1016/j.ijinfomgt.2008.11.005

Reznick, R. K., & MacRae, H. (2006). Teaching surgical skills- Changes in the wind. *The New England Journal of Medicine*, *355*(25), 2664–2669. doi:10.1056/NEJMra054785 PMID:17182991

Rubio, E. M., Sanz, A., & Sebastian, M. A. (2005). Virtual reality applications for the next-generation manufacturing. *International Journal of Computer Integrated Manufacturing*, *18*(7), 601–609. doi:10.1080/09511920500069259

Saramago, J. (2003). *The cave*. Harvest Books.

Seo, D. W., & Lee, J. Y. (2013). Direct hand touchable interactions in augmented reality environments for natural and intuitive user experience. *Expert Systems with Applications*, *40*(9), 3784–3793. doi:10.1016/j.eswa.2012.12.091

Seymour, N. E., Gallagher, A. G., Roman, S. A., O'Brien, M. K., Bansal, V. K., Andersen, D. K., & Blumgart, L. H. et al. (2002). Virtual reality training improves operating room performance results of a randomized, double-blinded study. *Annals of Surgery*, *236*(4), 458–464. doi:10.1097/00000658-200210000-00008 PMID:12368674

Silaiou, S., Mania, K., Karoulis, A., & White, M. (2010). Exploring the relationship between presence and enjoyment in a virtual museum. *International Journal of Human-Computer Studies*, *68*(5), 243–253. doi:10.1016/j.ijhcs.2009.11.002

Strachey, C. (1959). Time sharing in large fast computers. In *Proceedings of the International Conference on Information Processing* (pp. 336-341). Academic Press.

Sutherland, I. E. (1965). The ultimate display. In *Proceedings of the Congress of the International Federation of Information Processing* (pp. 506-508). Academic Press.

Tajeddini, K. (2010). Effect of customer orientation and entrepreneurial orientation on innovativeness: Evidence from the hotel industry in Switzerland. *Tourism Management*, *31*(2), 221–231. doi:10.1016/j.tourman.2009.02.013

Valerio Netto, A., & De Oliveira, M. C. F. (2002). Virtual reality for machine tool prototyping. *Proceedings of the ASME International Mechanical Engineering Congress and Exposition*, *13*, 15-22.

Van der Meijden, O. A. J., & Schijven, M. P. (2009). The value of haptic feedback in conventional robot-assisted minimal invasive surgery and virtual reality training: A current review. *Surgical Endoscopy and Other Interventional Techniques*, *23*(6), 1180–1190. doi:10.1007/s00464-008-0298-x PMID:19118414

Vieira, V. A. (2010). Visual aesthetic in store environment and its moderating role on consumer intention. *Journal of Consumer Behaviour*, *9*(5), 364–380. doi:10.1002/cb.324

Virvou, M., Katsionis, G., & Manos, K. (2005). Combining software games with education: Evaluation of its educational effectiveness. *Journal of Educational Technology & Society*, *8*(2), 54–65.

Wall, D. P., Kudtarkar, P., Fusaro, V. A., Pivovarov, R., Patil, P., & Tonellato, P. J. (2010). Cloud computing for comparative genomics. *BMC Bioinformatics*, *11*(1), 259–271. doi:10.1186/1471-2105-11-259 PMID:20482786

Wang, H.-C., Pallister, J. P., & Foxall, G. R. (2006). Determinants of consumer loyalty in B2C e-commerce. *Technovation*, *26*(12), 1366–1376. doi:10.1016/j.technovation.2005.11.003

Wang, Y. J., Minor, M. S., & Wei, J. (2011). Aesthetics and the online shopping environment: Understanding consumer responses. *Journal of Retailing*, *87*(1), 46–58. doi:10.1016/j.jretai.2010.09.002

Weibel, D., Wissmath, B., Habegger, S., Steiner, Y., & Groner, R. (2008). Playing online games against computer-vs. human-controlled opponents: Effects on presence, flow, and enjoyment. *Computers in Human Behavior*, *24*(5), 2274–2291. doi:10.1016/j.chb.2007.11.002

Wright, P., Blythe, M., & McCarthy, J. (2006). User experience and the idea of design in HCI. *Lecture Notes in Computer Science*, *3941*, 1–14. doi:10.1007/11752707_1

Zhou, J.-Y., Song, A.-B., & Luo, J.-Z. (2013). Evolutionary game theoretical resource deployment model for P2P networks. *Journal of Software*, *24*(3), 526–539. doi:10.3724/SP.J.1001.2013.04229

Zyda, M. (2005). From visual simulation to virtual reality to games. *Computer*, *38*(9), 25–32. doi:10.1109/MC.2005.297

ADDITIONAL READING

Abernathy, W. J., & Clark, K. B. (1985). Innovation: Mapping the winds of creative destruction. *Research Policy, 14*(1), 3–22. doi:10.1016/0048-7333(85)90021-6

Backstrom, K. (2011). Shopping as leisure: An exploration of manifoldness and dynamics in consumers shopping experiences. *Journal of Retailing and Consumer Services, 18*(3), 200–209. doi:10.1016/j.jretconser.2010.09.009

Baxter, R. J., & Berente, N. (2010). The process of embedding new information technology artifacts into innovative design practices. *Information and Organization, 20*(3-4), 133–155. doi:10.1016/j.infoandorg.2010.04.001

Bezes, C. (2013). Effect of channel congruence on a retailer's image. *International Journal of Retail & Distribution Management, 41*(4), 254–273. doi:10.1108/09590551311330537

Boeck, H., & Fosso Wamba, S. (2008). RFID and buyer-seller relationships in the retail supply chain. *International Journal of Retail & Distribution Management, 36*(6), 433–460. doi:10.1108/09590550810873929

Campbell, C.S., Maglio, P.P., & Davis, M.M. (2011). From self-service to super-service: a resource mapping framework for co-creating value by shifting the boundary between provider and customer. *Information Systems and E-Business Management, 9,*173.191.

Chebat, J.-C., Gelinas-Chebat, C., & Therrien, K. (2008). Gender-related wayfinding time of mall shoppers. *Journal of Business Research, 61*(10), 1076–1082. doi:10.1016/j.jbusres.2007.09.021

Dabholkar, P. A. (1996). Consumer evaluations of new technology-based self-service options: An investigation of alternative models of service quality. *International Journal of Research in Marketing, 13*(1), 29–51. doi:10.1016/0167-8116(95)00027-5

Davis, M. M., Spohrer, J. C., & Maglio, P. P. (2011). How technology is changing the design and delivery of services. *Operation Management Research, 4*(1-2), 1–5. doi:10.1007/s12063-011-0046-6

Eastlick, M. A., Ratto, C., Lotz, S. L., & Mishra, A. (2012). Exploring antecedents of attitude toward co-producing a retail checkout service utilizing a self-service technology. *International Review of Retail, Distribution and Consumer Research, 22*(4), 337–364. doi:10.1080/09593969.2012.690775

Floh, A., & Madlberger, M. (2013). The role of atmospheric cues in online impulse-buying behaviour. *Electronic Commerce Research and Applications, 12*(6), 425–439. doi:10.1016/j.elerap.2013.06.001

Gefen, D., Karahanna, E., & Straub, D. W. (2003). Inexperience and experience with online stores: The importance of tam and trust. *IEEE Transactions on Engineering Management, 50*(3), 307–321. doi:10.1109/TEM.2003.817277

Gilboa, S., & Vilani-Yaetz, I. (2013). Shop until you drop? An exploratory analysis of mall experiences. *European Journal of Marketing, 47*(1/2), 239–259. doi:10.1108/03090561311285538

Grewal, D., Baker, J., Levy, M., & Voss, G. B. (2003). The effects of wait expectations and store atmosphere evaluations on patronage intentions in service-intensive retail stores. *Journal of Retailing, 79*(4), 259–268. doi:10.1016/j.jretai.2003.09.006

Hauser, J., Tellis, G. J., & Griffin, A. (2006). Research on Innovation: A review and agenda for Marketing Science. *Marketing Science, 25*(6), 687–717. doi:10.1287/mksc.1050.0144

Heitz-Spahn, S. (2013). Cross-channel free riding consumer behaviour in a multichannel environment: An investigation of shopping motives, sociodemographics and product categories. *Journal of Retailing and Consumer Services, 20*(6), 570–578. doi:10.1016/j.jretconser.2013.07.006

Herhausen, D., Schogel, M., & Schulten, M. (2012). Steering customers to the online channel: The influence of personal relationships, learning investments, and attitude toward the firm. *Journal of Retailing and Consumer Services, 19*(3), 368–379. doi:10.1016/j.jretconser.2012.03.012

Hilton, T., & Hughes, T. (2013). Co-production and self-service: The application of Service-Dominant Logic. *Journal of Marketing Management, 29*(7-8), 861–881. doi:10.1080/0267257X.2012.729071

Kelly, P., Lawlor, J., & Muvey, M. (2013). Customer decision-making processes and motives for self-service technology usage in multi-channel hospitality environments. *International Journal of Electronic Customer Relationship Management, 7*(2), 98–116. doi:10.1504/IJECRM.2013.056491

Kim, J.-E., & Kim, J. (2012). Human factors in retail environments: A review. *International Journal of Retail & Distribution Management, 40*(11), 818–841. doi:10.1108/09590551211267593

Ko, E., & Kincade, D. H. (2007). Do quick response technology-based attributes make a difference in consumer satisfaction with apparel retail stores? *Journal of the Textile Institute, 98*(6), 491–499. doi:10.1080/00405000701476302

Kotler, P. (1974). Atmospheric as a marketing tool. *Journal of Retailing, 49*(4), 48–64.

Lee, H., Fairhurst, A., & Cho, H. J. (2013). Gender differences in consumer evaluations of service quality: Self-service kiosks in retail. *Service Industries Journal, 33*(2), 248–265. doi:10.1080/02642069.2011.614346

Ngo, L. V., & O'Cass, A. (2013). Innovation and business success: The mediating role of customer participation. *Journal of Business Research, 66*(8), 1134–1142. doi:10.1016/j.jbusres.2012.03.009

Noon, B. M., & Mattila, A. S. (2009). Consumer reaction to crowding for extended service encounters. *Managing Service Quality, 19*(1), 31–41. doi:10.1108/09604520910926791

Nuttavutshit, K. (2014). How consumers as aesthetic subjects co-create the aesthetic experience of the retail environment. *Journal of Retailing and Consumer Services, 21*(4), 432–437. doi:10.1016/j.jretconser.2014.03.003

Oh, L.-B., Teo, H.-H., & Sambamurthy, V. (2012). The effects of retail channel integration through the use of information technologies on firm performance. *Journal of Operations Management, 30*(5), 368–381. doi:10.1016/j.jom.2012.03.001

Pan, Y., & Zinkhan, G. M. (2006). Determinants of retail patronage: A meta-analytical perspective. *Journal of Retailing, 82*(3), 229–243. doi:10.1016/j.jretai.2005.11.008

Pantano, E. (2014). Innovation drivers in retail industry. *International Journal of Information Management, 34*(3), 344–350. doi:10.1016/j.ijinfomgt.2014.03.002

Pantano, E., & Migliarese, P. (2014). Consumer' collaborative innovation for supporting retailers' decision making: a new immersive approach for store design. In G. Philips-Wren, S. Carlsson, A. Respicio, & P. Brezillon (Eds.), *DSS2.0-Supporting decision making with new technologies* (pp. 381–391). IOS Press.

Pantano, E., & Migliarese, P. (2014). Exploiting consumer-employee interactions in technology-enriched retail environments through a relational lens. *Journal of Retailing and Consumer Services*, *21*(6), 958–965. doi:10.1016/j.jretconser.2014.08.015

Pantano, E., & Timmermans, H. (2014). (in press). What is smart for retailing? *Procedia*. *Environmental Sciences*.

Pantano, E., & Viassone, M. (2014). Demand pull and technology push perspective in technology-based innovations for the points of sale: The retailers evaluation. *Journal of Retailing and Consumer Services*, *21*(1), 43–47. doi:10.1016/j.jretconser.2013.06.007

Papagiannidis, S., Pantano, E., See-To, E. W. K., & Bourlakis, M. (2013). Modelling the determinants of a simulated experience in a virtual retail store and users' product purchasing intentions. *Journal of Marketing Management*, *29*(13-14), 1462–1492. doi:10.1080/0267257X.2013.821150

Petiot, J.-F., & Dagher, A. (2011). Preference-oriented form design: Application to cars' headlights. *International Journal of Interactive Design and Manufacturing*, *5*(1), 17–27. doi:10.1007/s12008-010-0105-5

Pramatari, K., & Theotokis, A. (2009). Consumer acceptance of RFID-enabled services: A model of multiple attitudes, perceived system characteristics and individual traits. *European Journal of Information Systems*, *18*(6), 541–552. doi:10.1057/ejis.2009.40

Reinstaller, A., & Sanditov, B. (2005). Social structure and consumption: On the diffusion of consumer good innovation. *Journal of Evolutionary Economics*, *15*(5), 505–531. doi:10.1007/s00191-005-0265-9

Sha, D. Y., Perng, D. B., & Lai, G. L. (2013). Study of using smart digital content technology in retail store. *Applied Mechanics and Materials*, *411-414*, 2161–2166. doi:10.4028/www.scientific.net/AMM.411-414.2161

Sharma, A. (2001). Consumer decision-making, salespeople's adaptive selling and retail performance. *Journal of Business Research*, *54*(2), 125–129. doi:10.1016/S0148-2963(99)00090-9

Shen, Y.-C., Chang, S.-H., Lin, G. T. R., & Yu, H.-C. (2010). A hybrid selection model for emerging technology. *Technological Forecasting & Social Science*, *77*(1), 151–166. doi:10.1016/j.techfore.2009.05.001

Spies, K., Hesse, F., & Loesch, K. (1997). Store atmosphere, mood and purchasing behaviour. *International Journal of Research in Marketing*, *14*(1), 1–17. doi:10.1016/S0167-8116(96)00015-8

Verganti, R. (2008). Design, meanings, and radical innovation: A metamodel and a research agenda. *Journal of Product Innovation Management*, *25*(5), 436–456. doi:10.1111/j.1540-5885.2008.00313.x

Verhoef, P., Neslin, S. A., & Vroomen, B. (2007). Multichannel customer management: Understanding the research-shopper phenomenon. *International Journal of Research in Marketing*, *24*(2), 129–148. doi:10.1016/j.ijresmar.2006.11.002

Verhoef, P. C., Lemon, K. N., Parasuraman, A., Roggeveen, A., Tsiros, M., & Schlesinger, L. A. (2009). Customer experience creation: Determinants, dynamics and management strategies. *Journal of Retailing*, *85*(1), 31–41. doi:10.1016/j.jretai.2008.11.001

Veryzer, R. W. Jr. (1998). Discontinuous innovation and the new product development. *Journal of Product Innovation Management*, *15*(4), 304–321. doi:10.1016/S0737-6782(97)00105-7

Vrechopoulos, A. P. (2010). Who controls store atmosphere customization in electronic retailing? *International Journal of Retail & Distribution Management, 38*(7), 518–537. doi:10.1108/09590551011052115

Walter, F. E., Battiston, S., Yildirim, M., & Schweitzer, F. (2012). Moving recommender systems from on-line commerce to retail stores. *Information System E-Business Management, 10*(3), 367–393. doi:10.1007/s10257-011-0170-8

Weber, M. E. A., Weggeman, M. C. D. P., & van Aken, J. E. (2012). Developing what customers really need: Involving customers in innovations. *International Journal of Innovation and Technology Management, 9*(3), 1250018. doi:10.1142/S0219877012500186

Xie, J., & Shugan, S. M. (2001). Electronic Tickets, Smart Cards, and Online Prepayments: When and How to Advance Sell. *Marketing Science, 20*(3), 219–243. doi:10.1287/mksc.20.3.219.9765

KEY TERMS AND DEFINITIONS

Cloud Collaboration: A way of sharing and co-authoring computer files through the use of cloud computing. Cloud collaboration allows uploading, commenting and collaborating on documents and even amending the document itself.

Cloud Computing: An approach consisting in the use of computing resources (hardware and software) delivered as a service through Internet.

Consumer's Co-Creation: Consumers' active participation to the service/product creation process. Consumers are not only the final users of the product/service, but actively participate in its delivering. A meaningful example is related to the self-service technologies, when consumers use automatic cash-desks for self-checkout.

Human-Computer Interaction: Involves the study, planning, design and uses of the interaction between people and computers. It is the intersection of computer science, behavioral sciences, design and several other fields of study.

Immersive Cloud Store: A new tool for supporting retailers and developed based on the integration of immersive technologies (with emphasis on established immersive stores) and could platforms. This new scenario involves consumers in the store design from the first phase of the development.

Immersive Technologies: Technologies able to blur the line between the physical and digital (or simulated) world, thereby creating a sense of immersion.

Innovation Management: Discipline allowing organization to manage processes while innovating. It involves a set of tools and practices that allow managers and engineers to manage the innovation, including search, select, developing, implementation, evaluation. Its focus is to allow organization to respond to external (e.g. market) or internal opportunity, and employ creative efforts to transfer in new ideas, processes or products/services.

Participatory Design: An approach to design aimed at actively involving all stakeholders (e.g. developer, users, etc.) in the process, in order to achieve a satisfactory outcome for all actors.

Retailing: The sale of goods and services from individual or organizations to end-users (consumers). It can take places in fixed locations like points of sale, door-to-door, online, through mobile, etc. while the emerging technologies are proposing new retail channels, which may be further integrated in new shopping environments.

Store Design: A discipline aimed at designing store environments/retail spaces, by focusing on store atmosphere, layout, products displaying and location, etc.

Technology Management: It is a discipline that allows organization to manage technological fundamentals for creating competitive advantages. Hence, it focuses on the deep understanding of the future benefits for organization emerging from technology adoption.

Chapter 3
A Merchant Virtual Universe as an Innovative Retail Setting:
A Dynamic Perspective on the Immersion Process

Ingrid Poncin
Catholic University of Louvain (UCL), Belgium

Marion Garnier
SKEMA Business School - Université de Lille, France

Virginie Maille
SKEMA Business School - Université de Lille, France

ABSTRACT

The Merchant Virtual Universe (MVU), which hyperrealistically reproduces the environment of a real shopping mall, is proving to be an innovative retail setting. It offers a competitive advantage by providing a satisfying and compelling online experience. This chapter examines immersion processes in an MVU and studies their evolution over time. The researchers collected qualitative and quantitative data from users throughout successive visits to a 3D virtual shopping mall. The data highlight the special role of perceived realism and sense of presence in allowing users to become immersed. The results confirm the links among realism, presence, and immersion, as well as their influence on satisfaction. They further illustrate the process as time passes: Realism is the strongest factor of immersion at the beginning of the experience but over time is replaced by presence. This work confirms that MVU designers must consider the importance of realism of the virtual environment.

INTRODUCTION

Ever since the publication of Holbrook and Hirschman's (1982) work, growing research interest has focused on the shopping experience; recent studies in the area of e-commerce reflect this trend. Consumer researchers have identified online experience as a potential source of differentiation and growth (Hoffman & Novak, 1996; Childers, Carr, & Peck, 2001; Mathwick, Malhotra

DOI: 10.4018/978-1-4666-8297-9.ch003

& Rigdon, 2001; Rose, Clark, Samouel & Hair, 2012). The evolution of multimedia and Internet technologies has created new perspectives and rich user experiences, such as virtual universes. These three-dimensional (3D) interactive digital environments allow users to view, move around in, and experience an imaginary world (Van Schaik, Turnbull, Van Wersch & Drummond, 2004) that may or may not look like the real world (Barnes & Mattsson, 2008). In the virtual universe, an avatar acts as the graphic representation of the user, interacting freely and directly with the environment, and possibly with other avatars (Bretonès, Quinio & Réveillon, 2010). Virtual universes have changed many of the ways that people play, work, and live. They also are changing the ways they shop and consume (Ward & Saren, 2008).

Building on the success and effectiveness of virtual universes that support social interaction (Second Life) or action-oriented gaming (World of Warcraft), online retailers have gradually adopted various Massively Multiplayer Online Role-Playing Game (MMORPG) techniques. Designing and using 3D flashes may enrich consumers' experiences (Li, Daugherty & Biocca, 2001) and steadily increase sales (Demery, 2006). Similarly, exposure to flagship brand stores within social virtual worlds positively influences brand attitude and real-life purchase intent (Haenlein & Kaplan, 2009). Other studies (Poncin & Garnier, 2012) show that merchant virtual universes (MVUs) or websites that integrate virtual reality devices (Charfi & Volle, 2011; Merle, Senecal & St-Onge, 2012) are a source of satisfaction and positive intentions (new visit, purchase). Such innovative devices and tools in Internet retail settings create realistic retail experiences that can provide retailers with a competitive advantage.

Research is now focusing on what participates to "virtual experience," or experience within a virtual context. Moving beyond the study of objective environmental factors, such as atmospheric elements or avatars (Poncin & Garnier, 2010; Garnier & Poncin, 2013), researchers are beginning to discuss the role

of human responses to the system. A qualitative study (Charfi & Volle, 2011) has suggested that psychological immersion (Schultze, 2010) is the "heart" of the experience in e-commerce websites using virtual reality devices. Internet users might be fully accessing the experiences offered by websites because they are immersed, that is, experiencing intense moments. This immersion may be having a positive effect on various responses such as attitudes, satisfaction, and buying intentions. Can this hypothesis be confirmed quantitatively, in an MVU? Little is known about the factors that induce user immersion in the virtual experience. Most research focuses on immersion in non-merchant, non-mediated activities, such as attending a classical music concert (Carù & Cova, 2006), or mediated activities that are not interactive, such as watching a movie (Fornerino, Helme-Guizon & Gotteland, 2008). Immersion in a computer-mediated merchant activity, using a technical device to interact with the virtual environment, may be quite different. Furthermore, there do not appear to be any studies of the factors that may change over time during the immersion process. A better understanding of what MVU immersion is, and of the factors that facilitate or impair consumer immersion in an experience, could contribute to the improvement of MVUs.

With these objectives in mind, this study examines the role of perceived realism and sense of presence suggested by Van Schaik et al. (2004) as immersion (involvement) factors in a gaming virtual universe. Three studies explore these ideas and reveal a link between perceived realism and presence immersion, then explore the influence of these factors on satisfaction with the MVU. The studies also indicate that perceived realism is the strongest factor of immersion at the beginning of the immersion experience, but over time, it gets replaced by presence. As the results show, the influence of immersion (as well as its antecedents, realism, and presence) on satisfaction weakens over time. This chapter offers an in-depth understanding of how an innovative technology such as an MVU can offer retailers a competitive advantage.

BACKGROUND

Immersion and Its Effects in an MVU

Scholars with an interest in experience come from many academic fields, including communication, psychology, cognitive science, computer science, engineering, philosophy, arts, and marketing. These scholars have provided various conceptualizations to express the idea of experience. Guided by Schultze (2010), who points to the key role of "psychological immersion, i.e., involvement and emotional engagement" to understand online experiences, the focus of this chapter is "psychological immersion," and "perceived immersion." The latter is a human response to the system, unlike Slater's (1999, 2002) interpretation of immersion, which refers to the objective property of the system's technology, "the extent to which it is capable of delivering an illusion of reality to the senses" (Slater & Wilbur, 1997), which is measured independently from the human experience that it engenders (Sanchez-Vives & Slater, 2005).

This state of psychological immersion may occur in a wide variety of activities; it has been studied in non-mediated contexts, such as listening to a concert (Carù & Cova, 2006) or shopping in a store (Arnould, Price & Zinkhan 2002). Immersion has also been studied in mediated contexts, such as watching a movie (Fornerino, et al., 2008), or in computer-mediated contexts, such as gaming or online navigation (Charfi & Volle, 2011). No matter the context, immersion appears as an intense moment experienced by the consumer. Individuals immersed in mediated activities such as watching a movie disconnect from the real world and lose awareness of who they are in real life, in favor of another self within the experiential context (Fornerino et al., 2008). A similar conceptualization appears in the literature dedicated to computer-mediated activities, which defines the psychological state of immersion as "the degree to which a virtual environment submerges the perceptual system of the user" (Biocca & Delaney, 1995). The individuals

are "involved" (Palmer, 1995), "absorbed" (Quarrick, 1989), or "engaged, engrossed" (Lombard & Ditton, 1997). Immersion can range from partial to total, possibly until a state of "flow" is reached (Fornerino et al., 2008; Hoffman & Novak, 1996). The online context defines this point as, "the state occurring during network navigation which is:

1. Characterized by a seamless sequence of responses facilitated by machine interactivity,
2. Intrinsically enjoyable,
3. Accompanied by a loss of self-consciousness,
4. Self-reinforcing" (Hoffman & Novak, 1996).

Researchers have stated the importance of immersion (or similar concepts such as the flow studied most often in a computer-mediated context). In non-mediated activities, it has been observed that immersion in a structured immersion program or an immersion camp positively influences oral language development pace and language proficiency, as well as the desire to learn more (Chen & Wu, 2007). Similarly, the visit experience at a museopark may depend on immersion (Mencarelli & Pulh, 2012). In a context of mediated activities such as movie consumption, immersion appears to lead to full access to the offered experience (Fornerino et al., 2008). Likewise, attitude toward the brand in an advertisement is more positive when the viewer feels immersed (Bhatnagar & Fang, 2011). Various studies of online environments have demonstrated the positive influence of immersion, or flow (Hoffman & Novak, 2009; Mollen & Wilson, 2010; Rose et al., 2012). Notably, in their qualitative study, Charfi and Volle (2011) concluded that immersion is the "heart" of the experience of MVUs that integrate virtual reality features and devices. They found that it increases satisfaction, elicits positive emotions or intentions (such as ordering a product or service on the website or filling in a contact form), results in direct contact with the brand, and generates positive talk about the brand. The same pattern of results is predicted for an MVU.

Further investigation focuses on factors that may intervene in the course of the immersion process. Van Schaik et al. (2004) suggested the role of realism and presence in allowing users to become immersed in a gaming virtual universe. Are these factors involved in the consumption experience of an MVU?

Perceived Realism in the Experience of an MVU

All virtual universes share common features:

- Multi-user shared spaces,
- A graphic interface that represents a world,
- Real-time interaction,
- Possibility for the user to act on,
- Environmental persistence, and
- Socialization resulting from conversation support, groups, and neighborhoods.

They can nevertheless differ in their orientation (with or without a specific goal) and, if there is a goal, in nature (play, socialization, or utilitarian purposes). They can also differ according to the realism of the environment and activities within the world (realistic or imaginary).

Common language mistakenly treats "real" and "virtual" as opposites. Tisseau (2001) defines the virtual as "what is potential within the real, what has all essential conditions to its realization" (Cadoz, 1994). The virtual, then, should be opposed to the *actual* (what is specifically here and now), not to the real. According to Papagiannidis, Pantano, See-To and Bourlakis (2013), "current advances in computer graphics provide new tools for enhancing the realism of the virtual experience and make it more similar to the real one" (p. 1463). Various studies in psychology, philosophy and consumer behavior (Poncin & Garnier, 2010; El Kamel & Rigaux-Bricmont, 2011) show that in leisure life-simulation, or MVUs, real and virtual are intimately linked and even complementary. To what extent should a virtual universe, and specifically an MVU, be realistic?

MVUs belong to the category of virtual universes that have a utilitarian aim and are fully realistic, with regard to the environment and the activities within the universe. Using a personalized avatar, the consumer enters a 3D shop or shopping mall that mimics a "real" location (paths, shelves, product display). The consumer can wander, view and manipulate products (using images or 3D models), and even try on clothing. The consumer can also chat online with other customers of the shopping mall or shop, interact with virtual agents in shops, and purchase products for home delivery, just as in any distance ordering or traditional online purchase. In addition to hedonic activities (such as window shopping or exhibition visits), MVUs focus on purchase and consequently on utilitarian features and activities such as data collection, purchase decisions, and payment. They combine a realistic purchase experience with a direct and concrete effect onw reality, because purchased products are not virtual and will be received by home delivery.

This strong link with reality should require the MVU to be sufficiently realistic, that is, to faithfully reproduce the perceptible reality. Yee, Ellis, and Ducheneaut (2009) state that some virtual universes (e.g., collaborative work) need a more realistic representation of familiar artifacts than others, such as gaming virtual universes that can be totally imaginary or fanciful. Such universes tend to deliver an accurate representation of reality. For example, a collaborative work virtual universe will include a round table and chairs for a meeting, even if avatars representing the participants do not need to sit down. This realistic representation of a work environment creates an anchor point for participants and enhances credibility of the professional virtual universe (Yee, Ellis, & Ducheneaut, 2009). At this stage, the notion of hyperreality (Baudrillard, 1994) offers an interesting and converging point of view as well as further arguments to understand the experience in an MVU as a realistic virtual universe.

Hyperreality is defined as "a reality that is different from the perceptible objective reality that leads to inability to make the difference between what is real and what is false…. This copy of the real can be authentic or an improved reproduction of an existing reality, or can be an original reality without any equivalent" (Graillot, 2005). This reality, created by simulation, is used mostly in art (realist reproductions), tourism (simulated environments, such as Disneyland parks, that reproduce physical or sensory elements of the real; Graillot, 2005), or even retailing (furniture showrooms and displays in shops; Edvardsson, Enquist, & Johnston, 2003). Virtual universes, and by extension MVUs, can therefore be considered as simulacra, places to simulate the real and create an experience in a hyperreal way. Throughout literature, hyperreality appears as an important facet of the consumption experience and its connection to nostalgia (e.g., Badot & Cova, 2003; Firat & Venkatesh, 1995; Haenlein & Kaplan, 2009; Ritzer, 2005). Research has shown that it is fundamental for those hyperreal environments to be realistic—and even overly realistic—to enhance the experience (Graillot, 2005).

These findings regarding visual fidelity of the visual environment, along with the findings of Yee et al. (2009) regarding the necessity of realistic representation for some contexts (including the merchant context), suggest that the realism attributed to an MVU as a hyperreal setting is highly involved in the consumption experience, through the feeling of immersion. Van Schaik et al. (2004) found a positive but moderate correlation between realism (realness) and immersion (involvement) in a gaming virtual universe; might the same link (or an even more positive one) be observed in an MVU context?

Sense of Presence in the Experience of an MVU

The term "telepresence," now commonly known as "presence," as developed by NASA and robotic engineers, refers to the illusion of being, by means of a telecommunication system, in another physical place, in which a person can act in the synchronized way that she or he would in the physical space in which she or he actually resides (e.g., Biocca & Delaney, 1995; Minsky, 1980). Many researchers, including Steuer (1992), Held and Durlach (1992), Sheridan (1992), Ellis (1996), and Slater and Wilbur (1997), have adopted this definition. Therefore, presence commonly refers to the "illusion of being in a distant place," that is, in the mental state in which "a user feels physically present within the computer-mediated environment" (Slater & Seed, 2000) or has the psychological sense of "being there" (Schultze, 2010). The International Society of Presence Research specifies that "even though part or all of the individual's current experience is generated by and/or filtered through human-made technology, part or all of the individual's perception fails to accurately acknowledge the role of the technology in the experience" (Riva, 2009), and "the virtuality of the experience is unnoticed" (Lee, 2004). However, there is some confusion regarding presence, due to various ways of conceptualizing the term. Lombard and Ditton (1997) note that presence is a multi-faceted phenomenon (see Lombard & Ditton, 1997; Schultze, 2010). Although some researchers (Rieunier, 1998; Van Schaik et al., 2004) add an attentional or involvement component, this work associates this component with immersion, in accordance with Schultze (2010). Moreover, the social component (sense of social presence) suggested by other researchers (Wang, Baker, Wagner, & Wakefield, 2007; Yoo & Alavi, 2001), is not applied to this work, due to the characteristics of the MUV (beta version) used in the study. For purposes of this study, presence refers only to the sense of "being there."

Research demonstrates that presence is involved in experience of gaming virtual universes (Schultze, 2010). Might it also be involved in an MVU context?

The next part of this chapter presents three studies that address that question. It examines the retail experience during successive visits to an MVU (a 3D shopping mall), in which the consumer is represented by an avatar, and offers and products of various stores and brands are presented. Quantitative data collected during the first visit confirm the influence of immersion on satisfaction in the context of an MVU. Researchers also collected qualitative data during this visit to understand fully the involvement of perceived realism and sense of presence in the MVU experience. Subsequent visits to the same website over a two-month period led to more detailed study of the immersion processes and their evolution.

STUDY 1: THE EFFECTS OF IMMERSION IN THE MVU

In 2012, Pantano and Servidio observed customer interactions in a new immersive-environment point of sale system and found that customer experience played a key role in consumer satisfaction with the technology. Papagiannidis et al. (2013) also found a positive association between consumer experience and satisfaction when modeling the determinant of a simulated experience in a virtual retail store. Therefore, the first hypothesis is that immersion in an MVU has the same positive effects as those observed in non-virtual online environments, (Hoffman & Novak, 2009; Mollen & Wilson, 2010; Rose et al., 2012) or in environments that integrate virtual reality features and devices (qualitative study by Charfi & Volle, 2011). Specifically,

H1: The more consumers are immersed in the MVU, the stronger their satisfaction with the MVU.

The Study 1 objective was to test this hypothesis quantitatively, using data collected in partnership with a 3D shopping mall (see illustrations in Appendix 1), before its launch at the end of 2011.

Method

A group of 286 undergraduate students (ages 18 to 25 years, 63% female) received extra credit for participating in this study. They were required to visit the online shopping mall as intensively as possible (minimum 40 minutes; average 80 minutes; maximum 120 minutes). All participants were first-time visitors to the MVU, as the website was in a beta test version. Interactions with other visitors were not possible in this version.

The post-visit questionnaire used in the study included a measure of immersion on a scale adapted from Fornerino et al. (2008); the scale measures engagement (ignoring all solicitations for attention that are external to the activity of visiting the website). The scale, developed in the context of movie consumption, is non-virtual but mediated. Satisfaction with the MVU also was measured (adapted from Oliver, 1980). Answers were based on five-point Likert scales. The Cronbach's alpha values for the scales were satisfactory (0.84 and 0.82, respectively). SmartPLS2 was used to analyze the data. This structural equation modeling (SEM) tool allowed us to test the psychometric properties of the measurement model (reliability and validity of every scale), estimate the parameters of the structural model (strength of the relation between the various variables of the model), and test theoretical assumptions. It involved no assumptions about the population (Fornell & Bookstein, 1982). Although the sample size in the first study was substantial, the sample size in the third set of dynamic data was small. Thus, in the interests of homogeneity, all analyses were carried out using PLS.

Results

Scores for variables are around average ($M_{Immersion}$ = 2.41; $M_{Satisfaction}$ = 3.04). Taking into account the lack of studies on the topic and other measures of the variables in a similar context, there have

Figure 1. Structure of the three studies

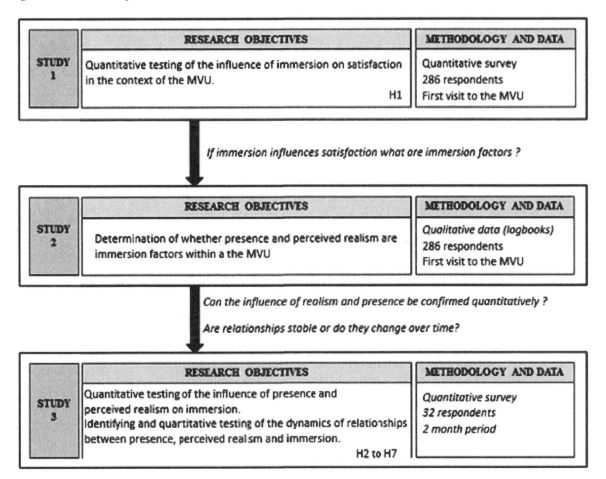

not been any comparison standards for assessing whether the scores should be regarded as weak or strong.

First, the psychometric qualities of the measurement model are satisfactory. Note that, to respect all the criteria of the model validity, it was necessary to remove one item from the immersion scale (see Appendix 3). Subsequently, the results indicate that the scales are strong and reliable (see Table 1). The composite reliability for all the scales (between 0.88 and 0.89) exceeds the minimum threshold (Burton-Jones & Hubona, 2006; Fornell & Larcker, 1981). Second, the average variances extracted (AVE) are superior to 0.5, as recommended (Fornell & Larcker, 1981). Third, the discriminant validity of the different

constructs is also satisfactory, because the square roots of the AVE (see Table 2, in bold) are greater than any other values. Finally, convergent validity is also verified (Yoo & Alavi, 2001). Each item is more strongly correlated with its own latent variable than with other variables in the model, and each coefficient of level weighting is greater than or equal to 0.7 (see Table 3).

Table 1. Estimation of the reliability of measurement model

	AVE	Composite Reliability	Cronbach's Alpha
Immersion	0.608	0.885	0.839
Satisfaction	0.736	0.891	0.820

Table 2. Discriminant validity of the scales of measure

	Immersion	Satisfaction
Immersion	**0.779**	
Satisfaction	0.536	**0.858**

Table 3. Convergent validity of the scales of measure

	Immersion	Satisfaction
Immersion2	**0.65**	0.31
Immersion3	**0.85**	0.56
Immersion4	**0.81**	0.32
Immersion5	**0.75**	0.37
Immersion6	0.83	0.45
Satisfaction1	0.49	**0.89**
Satisfaction2	0.46	**0.87**
Satisfaction3	0.43	**0.81**

The next step is the examination of the general characteristics of the variables of the model to test the hypothesis. As shown in Figure 2, and as predicted, immersion has a significant and positive influence on satisfaction ($\beta = 0.536$; Adjusted $R^2 = 0.288$; t = 7.794; $p < 0.001$; these results come from the bootstrap process). H1 is therefore validated.

The data show the same pattern of results found by Fornerino and colleagues (2008) in a movie consumption context, and by Charfi and Volle (2011) in their qualitative study in e-commerce websites using virtual reality devices, but the results are produced in a quantitative fashion and in the specific context of an MVU.

STUDY 2: PERCEIVED REALISM AND SENSE OF PRESENCE IN THE EXPERIENCE OF AN MVU

Method

This study relies on the analysis of qualitative data collected during Study 1 visits. It aims to determine the role of realism and presence in the MVU ex-

perience. Immediately following their completion of the questionnaire used in Study 1, participants were required to complete a logbook to describe their visits. Eleven open-ended questions (see Appendix 2) invited them to describe their a priori expectations regarding a 3D merchant website, their first impressions and emotions arising from the website and the visit, changes in feelings and impressions toward the website during the visit, what they had appreciated (or not appreciated) about the website, and their intentions to return to the site. Respondents were also invited to illustrate their answers with screenshots. A total of 260 logbooks were completed and analyzed (1052 pages). The first step was a content analysis conducted by two independent coders, using NVIVO9 software. The analysis was based on the logbook's themes, using both identical coding units and free emerging coding. The content was structured around the two themes of perceived

Figure 2. Visit 1

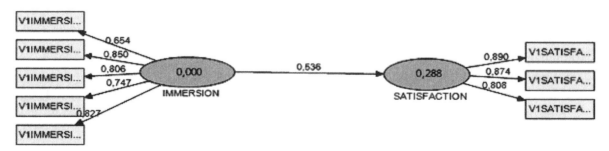

realism and presence as part of the experience. The second step was to compare and discuss the analysis of each coder to reach consensus.

Results

Narrative analysis identifies various perceptions, depending on the previous experiences of shopping or of virtual universes.

The realism of the MVU appears to be a strong anchor point for the experience.

The analysis confirms the search for and identification of anchor points; the narratives clearly highlight references from the "real" that serve as such. While 10% of the respondents stated they had no specific expectations before the visit, the remainder (90%) declared three main types of expectations that can be related to three "realities" experienced in the past.

Of the group with specific expectations, 25% of the respondents made a direct link with video games and virtual worlds such as *Second Life*:

Visually, I immediately thought about the game 'The Sims' or to the virtual world 'Second Life' — *Nathan*

I was pleasantly surprised of the reality of the shopping mall as well as feeling like in a videogame in which I'm the heroine of the game. — *Margaux.*

About 30% of the specific-expectation group had expectations related to their previous experiences with two-dimensional (2D) merchant websites:

I was expecting to be able to click on products to have the product sheet and the price. — *Binda*

Retailers are real ones and when you want details about a product, there is the 'add to cart' that appears. — *Malorie.*

The remaining 30% of the specific-expectation group referred to real shopping malls:

This shopping mall looks like those already existing, shops, some green outdoor spaces, benches. — *Camille*

Being able to wander from shop to shop would make you feel like being in a shopping mall in which shops are next to one other. — *Elodie*

Respondents compared the MVU to a real mall (authentic or reproducing an existing reality):

I was expecting to enter a 'cyber' shopping mall that would be a representation of reality, with the possibility to move freely, to make encounters, to have fun and obviously to make various purchases. — *Charles-Henri*

Nevertheless, although references to existing realities appear in the majority of responses, the narratives also compared the MVU to an original reality without any equivalent, in line with the notion of hyperreality previously evoked:

I've found the environment very pleasant ... it's a new experience I was longing to try. — *Camille*

The significant volume of narrative produced by this study shows the importance of realism in the MVU context, through the process of forming expectations and comparison with a search for anchor in a well-known reality (Poncin & Garnier, 2010).

In their logbooks, many respondents commented on the realism of the MVU and their satisfaction with it. More than 70% of respondents reported a positive first impression regarding realism:

I've found the place very friendly, we had the impression of being in a realistic world. — *Sabrina*

I was pleasantly surprised to see that visually the environment and the quality of drawings were far better than what I had imagined. – Pauline

This positive impression is associated with the process of making the MVU one's "home" or "reality":

This world seemed welcoming, especially because of bright colors and above all very near to reality. —Laetitia

In particular, the MVU seems to meet expectations regarding graphic realism:

I found drawings were well done, rather realistic"—Charlotte; "I was surprised by the precision with which the mall was realized. —Hugo

I appreciated the beautiful visuals... I've seen products, displaying was not necessarily attractive but the shopping mall atmosphere was pretty harmonious. —Luc

The virtual visit displays fairy-like colors (luminosity, sun, bright colors) that are relaxing and comforting in those rainy days at the moment. — Claire

In addition to commenting on visual stimuli, participants compared their sensations and perceptions to their anchor points (Carù & Cova, 2006). This comparison results in a positive or negative evaluation of the experience, and, through this, the perception of a more or less important distance with the environment. This response reflects the literature (Dinh, Walker, & Hodges, 1999; Slater & Wilbur, 1997) that states that sensory elements from the real should be copied and identical within the virtual world, so that the virtual world resembles the real world and the user can feel like the actor of the experience. This clearly refers to a sense of presence. Moreover, the analysis highlights the importance of sensory and social stimuli, as well as action, to feeling present and fully living the experience.

Participants referred to the quality of the sensory experiences, drawing particular attention to gaps between the virtual experience and a real experience. In 3D displays, vision is highly stimulated, but the senses of touch and hearing are under-solicited, compared with reality. In a store, touch is important (Underhill, 2007). Computer-mediated activities do not allow the experience of touching. Tisseron (2008) explains: "In a virtual universe ... everything is deliciously or desperately visual, according to your capacity to be satisfied with that" (p. 170). The fact that nothing can be touched, even with an avatar, bothers visitors:

I had the feeling of not being able to manipulate anything ... impossible to take products. —Margaux

I like the concept a lot, I could buy products I know but I wouldn't buy an object that necessitates a selection by touch, like clothing. — François

Respondents also mentioned the lack of sound. On one hand, visitors were happy not to face the noise pollution of real shopping malls:

This place is calm and peaceful, you don't have the usual noise of the shopping mall, I find it positive. — Madeline

On the other hand, some respondents commented that the absence of sound altered the realism of the environment (Madeline added, "Even if it diminishes realism"), and many of them found the silence burdensome. Some specifically noted the absence of music (which literature has shown to be an important factor in sales spaces; Rieunier, 1998):

Without music, it's boring. — Laura

Others even associated silence with emptiness and death ("A shopping mall is somewhere noisy, but here it's cold like a dead place," — Emeric), as referenced by Rouzé (2004). A greater number of respondents also highlighted the impression of loneliness that springs from silence:

Where are the noises, where are the people, I really do not have the feeling of being in a shopping mall on a Saturday morning, I'm alone. — Marion

These responses confirm the findings of Schifferstein and Desmet (2007), who show that perceived silence can induce a feeling of disconnection; in the context of this study, this may be the feeling of being less present.

Respondents also mentioned this feeling of loneliness as a more global perception ("The website on a whole does not give the impression of life and society" —Pierre) or as the absence of other people moving about or interacting:

The absence of people has tarnished the image of a welcoming and convivial place. — Laetitia

Although this is a predictable result, as no interactions or encounters were possible due to the beta testing situation, it is notable that interactivity—representing the notion of social presence—was mentioned frequently; 87% of respondents would have liked to be able to interact with fellow clients or sales agents.

Respondents also referred to presence by identifying action as a main element of their experience:

I like being able to totally control the visit: to be able to move, to go where we want. — Fanny

I really had the feeling of doing my shopping in a real garden which was very pleasant. — Sophie

I wandered around in other places to see the shops. — Pauline

I tried to put products in the basket for the first time; it was ok. — Damien

Such verbs of action (e.g., moving, doing) can be related to the feeling of presence.

The analysis of these narratives reveals the importance of sensory stimulation and action to the creation of an experience of presence that is rich and immersive. It shows how realism and presence are involved in the experience of an MVU. However, there is a further question: can the roles of realism and presence be specified within the process of immersion?

STUDY 3: THE ROLE OF REALISM AND PRESENCE DURING THE IMMERSION PROCESS IN AN MVU

The next step is to examine the specific roles of sense of perceived realism and presence in the immersion process and their evolution over time.

Sense of Presence as an Antecedent of Immersion in an MVU

As previously noted, presence commonly refers to the "illusion of being in a distant place," that is, the psychological sense of "being there" (Schultze, 2010). When individuals feel present, they have the perceptual illusion of a non-mediated technology (Lombard & Ditton, 1997) and experience.

The analysis of the qualitative discourse collected in Study 2 identified the roles of various facets of presence. (Because the beta version of the website used in the study did not allow any interaction with others, the role of the social component of presence was not included in the study; the analysis focused on the sensory component that appeared in the participants' responses.) The analysis of qualitative Study 2 responses identified the roles of action and control (Moon et al., 2013) in feeling present and fully living the experience. In prior literature, some researchers are interested in presence as a feeling of being in a world created by computer displays. Others, in line with the framework of embodied cognition (which states that understanding the world means conceptualizing it in terms of actions; Lakoff, 1987, 1999), refer to the phenomenon of acting within this world (Flach & Holden, 1988; Zahorik & Jenison, 1998). Some researchers (e.g., Sanchez-Vives & Slater, 2005; Slater & Seed, 2000) have adopted this conceptualization. Thus, *being there* should be the ability to *do* there (Slater & Seed, 2000). It is through action—the thought, conscious or not, of doing—that the user feels present.

In this research, the focus is on presence as the perception of being in the *physical* MVU place: sensing it and being able to act in it.

Presence induces the consumer to learn how to manage actions within the new environment and consecutive sensory stimulations (Auvray & Fuchs, 2007). The user is no longer passive; the facts of being actor and active favor a more successful experience (Carù & Cova, 2003, 2006a, 2006b). Users feel deeply immersed in the experience. A sense of presence may therefore be regarded as a condition for immersion to develop.

The influence of presence on immersion has already been considered in several works (e.g., Schultze, 2010; Slater, 1999; Slater & Wilbur, 1997; Van Schaik et al., 2004). However, no research has directly focused on the sensory and action facets of presence. For instance, Van Schaik et al. (2004) observed a correlation between immersion (involvement) and presence, but without consideration of the sensory and action components of presence. These components have not been studied in the context of an MVU.

Thus, the proposal is that presence is an antecedent of immersion in an MVU:

H2: The stronger consumers' feeling of presence in the MVU, the deeper their immersion in the MVU.

Perceived Realism as an Antecedent of Presence and Immersion in an MVU

According to several researchers, perceived realism could be an antecedent of presence. Most research has focused on sensory realism. As suggested by Joy and Sherry (2003), any experience is closely linked to the ability to feel with precision: "If you use only one of the senses, you perceive only one fifth of the aesthetic experience. On the other hand, in synesthesia, several senses are included and a more holistic appreciation is consequently possible." The more convincing the sensory data from the virtual environment, the greater the user's immersion. Virtual universes can create an illusion of reality, especially if they offer users the stimuli that fit what they expect from the universe (Rosenblom, 2003). The greater the number of human senses stimulated by a medium, the greater the capability of the medium to produce a sense of presence (Lombard & Ditton, 1997). Research has shown that the greater the level of visual realism, the greater the sense of presence (Dinh, Walker, & Hodges, 1999). Schultze (2010) explains that, in causal terms, the basic model of presence's antecedents looks something like this: technological features - realism/sensory fidelity - presence.

However, this influence may not be specific to sensory realism. As suggested by Joy and Sherry (2003), synesthesia—the mobilization of several senses to perceive an experience—is necessary. Furthermore, in models of perception, reconstruction and adaptation, individuals using a virtual environment will be able to perceive and attribute to the environment a certain degree of reality and consequently determine extent to which the virtual environment faithfully reproduces the "real world". The user will then perceive a certain degree of "global" realism of the virtual environment, that is, the extent to which it resembles the real world. Consequently, the evidence for sensory realism may be extended to perceived realism in general.

By regarding perceived realism as an antecedent of presence, and regarding presence as an antecedent of immersion (H2), the prediction is that perceived realism should also influence immersion through presence. This hypothesis converges with suggestions by Li et al. (2003), Suh and Lee (2005), and Charfi and Volle (2011) that new technologies such as Rich Media tools, 2D or Web 2.0 can—thanks to their realism—help the consumer live an immersive experience by proxy, accessed through hyperreal simulacra.

The influence of realism on presence has never been studied, though its influence regarding immersion has been demonstrated by Van Schaik et al. (2004). When measured in a gaming virtual universe, the researchers found the correlation between "realness" (realism) and immersion (involvement) to be positive but moderate. As realism appears to be more important in an MVU context, a stronger link with immersion may be observed. Thus,

H3: The stronger consumers' feeling of presence in the MVU, the deeper their presence/immersion in the MVU.

Given the evidence for the influence of presence and realism, the evolving nature of the influence over time can be further investigated. The next step is to examine the evolution of these immersion mechanisms.

The Evolution of Immersion Mechanisms Over Time

As noted previously, technologies associated with the virtual universe introduce a physical distance between organic action points (physical action of the user) and distant action points (action within the virtual universe). Through these technologies, the user perceives information from the virtual environment (distant perception). This information is converted into physical stimulation (Auvray & Fuchs, 2007) that is interpreted by the individual. This sequence implies a progressive learning process. As in the real world, experience springs from automatic actions that users acquire as time goes by (Auvray & Fuchs, 2007) and that accumulate (Ling, Chai, & Piew, 2010).

It can be imagined, therefore, that the role of realism and sense of presence in immersion mechanisms evolves, as the process of the individual's appropriation of the environment takes place. It is probable that the influence of presence on immersion is stronger over time. As the user becomes familiar with the environment, and learns how to use it and act in it, the cumulative nature of the experience leads to a stronger influence of the sense of presence on the ability of the user to feel immersed. Thus:

H4: The relationship between presence and immersion strengthens over time.

As time passes, and as a result of the learning process, the environment becomes a well-known place—a well-known reality. Users perceive the virtual environment as a new reality, a new world in which they feel an increasing sense of belonging and presence. The suggestion, therefore, is that the influence of perceived realism on presence becomes stronger with time. Thus:

H5: The role of realism as an antecedent of presence strengthens over time.

Conversely, there may be a decrease in the influence of perceived realism on immersion, as time passes. Once individuals have begun to appropriate a website, they tend to give less and less attention to original "real-world" anchor points that, according to Carù and Cova (2006), are essential during nesting operations. These anchor points evolve according to new investigations of the website by the users. Consequently, perceived realism is no longer related to the external world but to anchor points previously created within the virtual environment and the sense of presence. Realism should therefore be less and less necessary for immersion. As realism's influence on presence increases, the influence of realism on immersion may decrease. Thus:

H6: The role of realism as an antecedent of immersion decreases over time.

The further prediction is that, over time, shoppers who are deeply immersed will take their satisfaction from other elements. During initial visits, the newness of the immersion experience and the challenge of discovering and appropriating the MVU can be intrinsically satisfying. But in subsequent visits, something more may be needed to maintain a satisfying relationship: variety, new challenges, new things to do, new products, and other novel features. Consequently, the importance of immersion to satisfaction may decline as other commercial features become more important.

H7: Over time, immersion is less and less a factor of satisfaction.

The authors believe that this is the first study of the evolution of immersion mechanisms over time. The next study tests this series of hypotheses (H2–H7).

Method

A second study of visits to the MVU during a two-month period was conducted following the first study. It studies quantitatively the dynamic process of immersion

Of the 286 participants in the first study, 50 volunteered to continue their experience in the virtual mall. During a two-month period following the first study, 32 participants finally visited the MVU at least four times. To prevent selection bias, the researchers verified that this sample matched the Study 1 sample on measures of immersion and satisfaction. The current hypotheses were tested using the same (Study 1) questionnaire, with responses submitted following Visit 2 and Visit 4. First, the questionnaire was used to measure immersion (Cronbach's αs of 0.933 and 0.946, respectively, for Visits 2 and 4) and satisfaction (Cronbach's αs of 0.882 and 0.942, respectively), using the same scales as Study 1. Second, perceived realism was measured, by adapting a scale from Potter (1988). (Although this scale does not include items related to social realism, the measure appeared unnecessary, as the beta version of the website did not allow interaction with other users.) After deleting one item, αs were 0.786 and 0.790, respectively, for Visits 2 and 4. Finally, the researchers measured presence. Although several scales were available in the literature (e.g., Carlin, Hoffman, & Weghorst, 1997; Ellis et al., 1997; Regenbrecht, Schubert, & Friedmann, 1998; Schubert, Friedmann, & Regenbrecht, 2001; Slater, Usoh, & Steed, 1994; Towell & Towell, 1997; Witmer & Singer, 1994), not all components of these scales were relevant. For instance, the scale used by Schubert et al. (2001) includes a "realness" component that the study had already included as a measurement of the antecedent of full immersion. The component of involvement, a consequence of presence (Schulze, 2010), measured by Schubert et al. (2001), and Witmer and Singer (1998), was already taken into account in the study's immersion scale. The study focused on sensory and action items adapted from Witmer and Singer (1998)'s scale. As the website did not produce any sound, and no technological tool enabled touch as in Witmer and Singer's study, items involving the senses of hearing and touch were excluded. To respect the rules of model quality in PLS (i.e. AVE > 0.5 and α > 0.7), some items were deleted (see Appendix 3). Cronbach's αs were 0.717 and 0.752, respectively, for Visits 2 and 4.

Results

The researchers analyzed data from the second and the fourth visits to the MVU. As in Study 1, the sample size of Study 2 did not fit requirements for classical regression models; therefore, the analysis was carried out using PLS.

Table 4. Estimation of the reliability of the measurement model

	AVE		Composite Reliability		Cronbach's Alpha	
	V2	V4	V2	V4	V2	V4
Immersion (5 items)	0.79	0.83	0.95	0.96	0.93	0.95
Presence (4 items)	0.54	0.57	0.82	0.84	0.72	0.75
Perceived Realism (4 items)	0.60	0.59	0.86	0.85	0.79	0.79
Satisfaction (3 items)	0.81	0.90	0.93	0.96	0.88	0.94

Table 5. Discriminant validity of the scales of measure

	Immersion	Presence	Perceived Realism	Satisfaction
Immersion	**0.88** **0.91**			
Presence	0.45 0.72	**0.73** **0.75**		
Perceived realism	0.50 0.65	0.35 0.55	**0.77** **0.77**	
Satisfaction	0.62 0.51	0.48 0.50	0.49 0.41	**0.90** **0.95**

The first examination is of the psychometric qualities of the measurement model. In accordance with Visit 1, the analyses have been computed using only five items for immersion. Moreover, to respect the standard of the reliability, one item from the perceived realism scale was also removed. All psychometric indicators are satisfactory for both Visit 2 and Visit 4. More precisely, the scales are strong and reliable (see Table 4). The composite reliability for all the scales and the AVE exceed the recommended minimum thresholds. The discriminant validity of the different constructs is also satisfactory for Visit 2 and Visit 4, because the square roots of the AVE (in bold) are greater than the other values (see Table 5). The convergent validity is verified; items are more strongly correlated with their own latent variable than with other variables, and their coefficient of level weighting is greater than or equal to 0.7 (see Table 6).

The hypotheses were then tested.

Figure 2 and Figure 3 illustrate the results for Visit 2 and Visit 4, respectively (see Appendix 5 for detailed results). All results are products of the bootstrap process.

As predicted, sense of presence has a significant and positive influence on immersion for both Visit 2 ($\beta = 0.31$; Adjusted $R^2 = 0.34$; t = 5.88; $p < 0.001$) and Visit 4 ($\beta = 0.52$; Adjusted $R^2 = 0.61$; t = 7.43; $p < 0.001$). H2 is therefore validated. Van Schaik et al. (2004) previously observed the influence of "presence" on immersion (involvement) but did not identify the sensory and action components of presence that this qualitative study found to be important to the MVU context. This influence has been demonstrated in a gaming virtual universe but not in the context of an MVU. Similarly, as predicted, R^2 and β increase between Visit 2 and Visit 4, indicating that the influence of presence on immersion increases over time. H4 is therefore validated. This finding represents a substantial contribution to the field; it is the first evidence of this evolving relationship.

Perceived realism also appears as a presence factor for both Visit 2 ($\beta = 0.35$; Adjusted $R^2 = 0.126$; t = 5.53, $p < 0.001$) and Visit 4 ($\beta = 0.54$; Adjusted $R^2 = 0.34$; t = 10.19, $p < 0.001$). Realism is an antecedent of immersion for both Visit

Figure 3. Visit 2

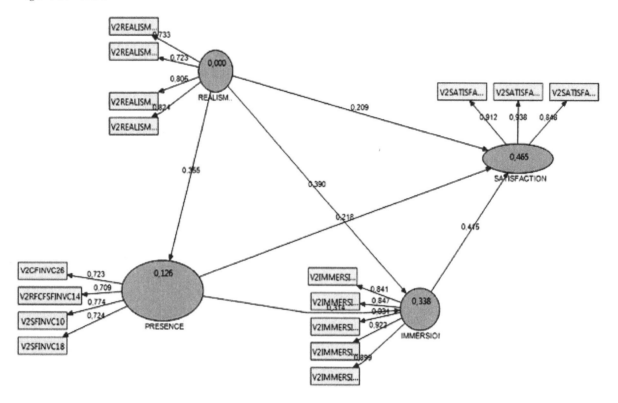

2 (β = 0.39; Adjusted R² = 0.34; t = 4.47; *p* < 0.001) and Visit 4 (β = 0.37; Adjusted R² = 0.61; t = 5.16; *p* < 0.001). H3 is therefore validated. The link between realism and immersion is as suggested by theories, according to which presence result from sensory matching between reality and the virtual environment, and more globally as suggested by Van Schaik et al. (2004), in a gaming virtual universe. This link has not been studied with regard to MVUs, though Schubert et al. (2001) and Van Schaik et al. (2004) examined realism as a presence component (but not an independent antecedent). With regard to the evolving role of realism over time, as predicted, the link (R² and β) between realism and presence increases between Visit 2 and Visit 4; the influence of realism on presence strengthens as time passes. H5 is therefore validated. Conversely, the link (R² and β) between realism and immersion decreases between Visit 2 and Visit 4; the influence of realism on immersion diminishes as time

goes by. H6 is therefore validated. Until now, this evolving relationship has never been studied.

After observing the influence of realism and presence on immersion, the respective roles of those factors can be compared. As shown by the R² and β results, the influence of realism is greatest at Visit 2, while the influence of presence becomes the greatest by Visit 4. This could be due, as previously suggested, to various appropriation and learning processes and the cumulative nature of experience that make realism more important during discovery of the MVU, but also leads to presence being more important once the MVU is familiar.

Observations also reveal that immersion is decreasingly a determinant of satisfaction over time. Although this influence remains significant and positive during the two visits, R² and β decrease between Visit 2 (β = 0.42; Adjusted R² = 0.465; t = 5.265; *p* < 0.001) and Visit 4 (β = 0.25; Adjusted R² = 0.302; t = 2.13; *p* < 0.001). Notably,

Table 6. Convergent validity of the scales of measure

Cross Loading	Immersion	Presence	Perceived Realism	Satisfaction
V2presence1(V2CFINVC26)	0.253424	0.722590	0.232017	0.356945
V2immersion2	0.841169	0.410293	0.411509	0.583317
V2immersion3	0.846704	0.501927	0.399494	0.445008
V2immersion4	0.931393	0.393762	0.412852	0.598200
V2immersion5	0.922435	0.380476	0.537265	0.586018
V2immersion6	0.899426	0.333239	0.461122	0.526039
V2Realism1	0.268374	0.235273	0.732547	0.519573
V2realism2	0.239199	0.029913	0.722686	0.084165
V2realism4	0.406588	0.387758	0.824129	0.322951
V2Realism5	0.524076	0.708732	0.204532	0.419681
V2presence2(V2RFSFINVC14)	0.380699	0.485484	0.509082	0.511307
V2satisfaction1	0.573069	0.485484	0.509082	0.911853
V2satisfaction2	0.568000	0.396830	0.423206	0.938346
V2satisfaction3	0.528265	0.48236	0.396190	0.847674
V2presence3(V2SFINVC10)	0.393402	0.774372	0.332323	0.285928
V2presence4(V2SFINVC18)	0.259257	0.723872	0.279185	0.181213
V4presence1 (V4CFINVC26)	0.433358	0.660253	0.238407	0.408449
V4immersion2	0.949822	0.705751	0.573321	0.537302
V4immersion3	0.924540	0.601431	0.598166	0.486484
V4immersion4	0.852896	0.579239	0.498209	0.413058
V4immersion5	0.874970	0.721819	0.649442	0.452153
V4immersion6	0.937436	0.647614	0.634293	0.412002
V4Realism1	0.371131	0.307400	0.738703	0.293091
V4realism2	0.304634	0.337595	0.708290	0.013594
V4realism4	0.238343	0.250460	0.766618	0.359554
V4Realism5	0.781948	0.601824	0.845547	0.446183
V4presence2(V4RFSFINVC14)	0.501566	0.693699	0.244250	0.188666
V4satisfaction1	0.463739	0.446135	0.410993	0.957828
V4satisfaction2	0.481951	0.491030	0.420903	0.949862
V4satisfaction3	0.498585	0.477954	0.346564	0.933590
V4presence3(V4SFINVC10)	0.577759	0.814566	0.411772	0.459722
V4presence4 (V4SFINVC18)	0.639608	0.842173	0.642258	0.414723

R^2 and β do not really decrease between Visit 1 and 2 (Visit 1: $\beta = 0.536$; Adjusted $R^2 = 0.288$; t $= 7.794$; $p < 0.001$). However, strict comparisons between Visits 1 and Visit 2 are difficult, taking into account the difference in sample size (286 and 32, respectively). Furthermore, because immersion is a learning process, participants may not have been fully immersed at the end of Visit 1. Analysis of the results shows that the direct influence of immersion factors on satisfaction also disappears as time passes. There is an influence of realism ($\beta = 0.209$; Adjusted $R^2 = 0.465$; t =

2.17; $p < 0.001$) and presence ($\beta = 0.22$; Adjusted $R^2 = 0.465$; t = 2.54; $p < 0.000$) on satisfaction during Visit 2, but this influence disappears by Visit 4 (realism: $\beta = 0.110$; Adjusted $R^2 = 0.302$; t = 0.992; n.s.; presence: $\beta = 0.26$; Adjusted $R^2 = 0.302$; t=1.937; n.s.). It may be that once shoppers are well immersed, they take their satisfaction from elements other than immersion. During first visits, novelty, discovery, and immersion can be intrinsically enjoyable and satisfying. In subsequent visits, variety, new challenges, and new things to do (e.g., in games such as MMOR-PGs that regularly offer updates, new places, and new quests to users) are essential to a satisfying relationship. Consequently, the importance of immersion for satisfaction may decline as other commercial features become more important. In the test website, for example, there should have been products to buy or novelties to sample in shops or new activities. Until now, research has not quantitatively studied the dynamic character of the immersion process.

SOLUTIONS AND RECOMMENDATIONS

From a managerial point of view, the findings confirm that MVU designers must be aware of the importance of realism to the virtual environment. Especially during first visits, realism appears to be a basic condition of "entering" the environment, feeling present in it, being immersed in it, and being satisfied with it. Developers of such websites should therefore try to maximize imitation of the "real" world, or at least maximize the credibility of the MVU design as a faithful representation of reality. This realism can make up for the virtuality of the MVU and the absence of any human contact, giving such innovative retail settings a potential advantage.

For many consumers, shopping in an MVU is a new experience; they can be surprised or disoriented. For developers, encouraging appropriation by reproducing and simulating well-known realities is key. Namely, developers should try

Figure 4. Visit 4

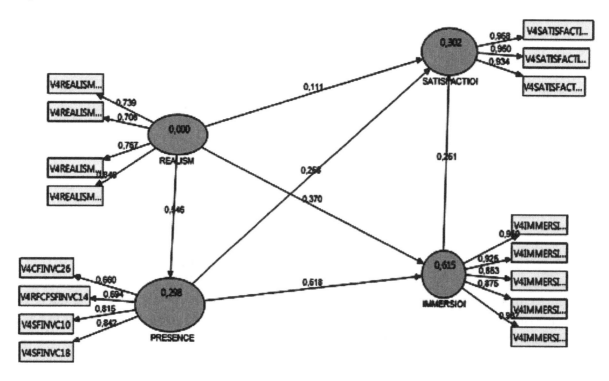

to reproduce real store designs, classic presentations of products and classic arrangements and features of physical retail environments (e.g., a mall). Although some designers may think that futurist or fantasy designs are suitable to the innovative image of the MVU, firms wishing to adopt MVUs as a new retail setting should be aware that causing additional user disorientation could be damaging. They should avoid futurist or fantasy designs, as they may decrease perceived realism and all of its positive correlates related to immersion and satisfaction—thereby reducing their competitive advantage.

Furthermore, the research results suggest that the graphic quality of an MVU, beyond being realistic, should also be of good quality. Given the increasing familiarity of consumers with 3D graphics (as in high quality animation), perceived realism results from sharp, highly refined graphics, free-flowing movements and animations or high quality colors. Although this may increase the development cost of the MVU, it may ensure consumer adoption and profitability over time. Realism is also derived from sensory elements. Consequently, it is important for developing sensory realism. Uses of background noises, footstep sounds, or music in the design may contribute to the faithful reproduction of reality. The feeling of social presence may also contribute to the representation of reality.

Realism can also spring from the ability of the user to interact with the environment. As suggested by Ardelet and Brial (2011) and Rose et al. (2012), it can come from devices that allow consumers to interact with other shoppers (Aljukhadar, Senecal, & Daoust, 2012). Similar to the exchange and discussion possibilities of traditional commerce, interactivity features increase the feeling of social presence among visitors. This feeling reinforces the relationship with the retailer, through identification with others, and fosters the feeling of trust (Aljukhadar,

Senecal, & Ouellette, 2010) and control that is so important online. MVU developers should therefore try to favor interactions between consumers by providing tools such as chat, meetings, and other exchanges, as well as virtual sales agents (preferably animated) to reproduce the presence of human sales agents. Moreover, as suggested by Pantano and Servidio (2012), a highly customized, interactive, and enjoyable virtual interface is a better alternative than a standard (real) service that is deficient (e.g., insufficient sales staff).

In the case of virtual environments, the rapid evolution of technology allows true progresses in a relatively short term, provided that the development is not to the detriment of transactional functions (Charfi & Volle, 2011). As shown by the results, the process leading to satisfaction takes time, and also evolves over time. Although realism, immersion, and presence are important when consumers are discovering the innovative retail setting, the range of graphic, sensory, and social imitations cannot be sufficient to maintain a competitive advantage over time. Instead, over time realism, presence, and immersion become less important; to satisfy their shoppers, MVUs must renew the experience over time.

Two main recommendation arise from these results. First, because consumers may need time to become familiar with and convinced by the MVU, a long-term, sustainable strategy is needed. Second, the innovative effect of such a retail setting will be insufficient over time (satisfaction may eventually spring from factors such as functionalities, product or service offerings, or commercial features such as price policy, selling processes, and trust and loyalty-building features), so a solid strategic and operational marketing plan is needed to ensure competitive advantage in the long term. Given the cumulative nature of experience, a long-term strategy based on a coherent differentiation for competitive advantage is therefore necessary.

FURTHER RESEARCH DIRECTIONS

This work has some limits that researchers should try to overcome. The first limitation results from the test MVU itself. The beta test version of the website used as the test did not offer a complete experience. For instance, participants did not have the opportunity to hear sounds or to interact with other shoppers or sales agents. Although (as mentioned in the discussion of the results of Study 2), the presence or absence of others (feeling of social presence) seems important in such a context, this component was not integrated into the study. The results may be more comprehensive with a more sophisticated MVU, and the factor of social presence could be interesting to study. A second limitation results from the precariousness of the sense of presence and immersion. Although the role of realism and sense of presence may globally evolve as observed, "glitches" can cause frequent breaks in presence (Garau, Friedman, Ritter, Widenfeld, Antley, Brogni, & Slater, 2008) or immersion (Carù & Cova, 2006). Users may feel present, and perhaps immersed, at a given time, but suddenly lose this sense (e.g., because they notice how uncomfortable their chairs are, or because they are thinking of their work; Carù & Cova, 2006). Research shows that "brief sequences of appropriation facilitated mini-immersion episodes instead of a single, large-scale, immediate and all-encompassing dive into the deep end." (Carù & Cova, 2006, p.13). Similarly, Ijsselsteijn and de Ridder (1998) found that the extent of presence experienced in a virtual environment changes continuously. Slater, Usoh, and Steed (1994) measured breaks in presence, that is, shifts away from feeling located in a virtual experience to being aware of the physical world. Measurements taken at a given time at the end of each visit do not take into account these mini-interruptions. To succeed, research will have to try to measure immersion "live," as it is perceived (i.e., as the experience goes along). A third limitation is the sample size in Study 3. This problem stems from the difficulty of embedding the same participants in successive studies over time. In addition to raising questions about the representativeness and significance of the results, this sample size does not permit the analysis of the moderating nature of individual characteristics. The study by Charfi and Volle (2011), for example, cites involvement of the visitor as a potential source of immersion. Similarly, by showing that novices give more importance to spatial and aesthetic characteristics of the selling environment, Hoffmann and Novak (2009) question the role of the visitor's expertise. Numerous variables, individual as well as relative to the "real" environment, could therefore influence and moderate the appropriation pace of the environment, as well as the evolution of the individual's experience as time goes by. The study of those variables is a research perspective to be considered.

CONCLUSION

The evolution of multimedia and Internet technologies has transformed the e-commerce landscape. The transfer of interactive techniques from MMORPGs to online shopping malls, showrooms and online shopping websites has accelerated, along with the enrichment of the online consumer experience that is central for online shopping growth (Rose et al., 2012). Adding to the growing body of work over last decade regarding virtual universes, the aim of this work is to better understand the immersion mechanisms in an MVU and their evolution over time.

Qualitative and quantitative data collected during successive visits over a two-month period in a hyperreal commercial virtual universe confirm that, in an MVU context, immersion can be a relevant factor due to its strong link to satisfaction with the MVU. Furthermore, with regard to the immersion process, this research confirms the global links among realism, presence, and immersion, as well as the influence of these factors on satisfaction. In so doing, it highlights the role of perceived realism and sense of presence that has only been suggested in literature, but never actually demonstrated, specifically in an MVU context. Prior to these studies, researchers had not examined this entire pattern. Another major contribution of this research is the observation of the processes over time. At the beginning of the immersion experience (Visit 2), realism is a stronger factor of immersion than presence. However, over time, the influence of realism becomes non-significant, while the influence of presence increases and becomes the strongest antecedent of immersion. In addition, the influence of immersion, as well as its antecedents—realism and presence—on satisfaction lessens over time. To the best of the authors' knowledge, this is the first study to examine the evolution of immersion processes; previous studies have not highlighted this evolution over time. The results lead to the conclusion that the claim by Charfi and Volle (2011)—that immersion is the "heart of the experience"—is true, especially during first visits. Over time, shoppers are likely to derive satisfaction from other factors, such as offers and services, or a highly differentiating marketing strategy, just as any other retail setting. This strategy is necessary to sustain an MVU over time, as technological innovation alone is insufficient to maintain a long-term perspective.

This chapter provides concrete recommendations regarding MVU design and related development strategies. It offers specific advice on how to build a comprehensively realistic 3D online retail setting, incorporating graphic, sensory, and social features. The recommendations reinforce the importance of a strong differentiating marketing and commercial strategy over time, to ensure that the competitive advantage created by the innovative retail setting persists.

ACKNOWLEDGMENT

The authors dedicate special thanks to Idées-3Com, creators of the 3D shopping mall for their help in this research.

REFERENCES

Aljukhadar, M., Senecal, S., & Daoust, C.-E. (2012). Using recommendation agents to cope with information overload. *International Journal of Electronic Commerce, 17*(2), 41–70. doi:10.2753/JEC1086-4415170202

Aljukhadar, M., Senecal, S., & Ouellette, D. (2010). Can the media richness of a privacy disclosure enhance outcome? A multifaceted view of trust in rich media environments. *International Journal of Electronic Commerce, 14*(4), 103–126. doi:10.2753/JEC1086-4415140404

Ardelet, C., & Brial, B. (2011). Influence of the recommendations of Internet users: The role of social presence and expertise. *Recherche et Applications en Marketing, 26*(3), 45–69. doi:10.1177/076737011102600303

Arnould, E. J., Price, L., & Zinkhan, G. (2002). *Consumers*. New York: McGraw-Hill.

Auvray, M., & Fuchs, P. (2007). Perception, immersion et interactions sensorimotrices en environnement virtuel. Intellectica, 45(1), 23-35.

Badot, O., & Cova, B. (2003). Néo-marketing, 10 ans après: Pour une théorie critique de la consommation et du marketing réenchantés. *Revue Française du Marketing, 195*(5), 79–94.

Barnes, S., & Mattsson, J. (2008). Brand value in virtual worlds: An axiological approach. *Journal of Electronic Commerce Research, 9*(3), 195–206.

Baudrillard, J. (1994). *Simulacra and simulation*. University of Michigan.

Bhatnagar, N., & Fang, W. (2011). Is self-character similarity always beneficial? *Journal of Advertising, 40*(2), 39–50. doi:10.2753/JOA0091-3367400203

Biocca, F., & Delaney, B. (1995). Immersive virtual reality technology. In F. Biocca & M. R. Levy (Eds.), *Communication in the age of virtual reality* (pp. 57–124). Hillsdale, NJ: Lawrence Erlbaum Associates.

Bretonès, D. D., Quinio, B., & Réveillon, G. (2010). Bridging virtual and real worlds: Enhancing outlying clustered value creations. *Journal of Strategic Marketing, 18*(7), 613–625. doi:10.1080/0965254X.2010.529157

Burton-Jones, A., & Hubona, G. (2006). The mediation of external variables in the technology acceptance model. *Information & Management, 43*(6), 706–717. doi:10.1016/j.im.2006.03.007

Cadoz, C. (1994). *Les réalites virtuelles*. Paris: Dominos Flammarion.

Carlin, A. S., Hoffman, H. G., & Weghorst, S. (1997). Virtual reality and tactile augmentation in the treatment of spider phobia: A case report. *Behaviour Research and Therapy, 35*(2), 153–158. doi:10.1016/S0005-7967(96)00085-X PMID:9046678

Carù, A., & Cova, B. (2003). Approche empirique de l'immersion dans l'expérience de consommation: Les opérations d'appropriation. *Recherche et Applications en Marketing, 18*(2), 47–65. doi:10.1177/076737010301800203

Carù, A., & Cova, B. (2006a). Expériences de marque: Comment favoriser l'immersion du consommateur? *Décisions Marketing, 41*(1), 43–52.

Carù, A., & Cova, B. (2006b). How to facilitate immersion in a consumption experience: Appropriation operations and service elements. *Journal of Consumer Behaviour, 5*(1), 4–14. doi:10.1002/cb.30

Chen, B., & Wu, W. V. (2007). Extolling the virtues of language immersion in whole-family camps. *The Business Review, Cambridge, 7*(2), 77–83.

Childers, T., Carr, C., Peck, J. C., & Carson, S. (2001). Hedonic and utilitarian motivations for online retail shopping behavior. *Journal of Retailing, 77*(4), 511–535. doi:10.1016/S0022-4359(01)00056-2

Choi, J., Lee, H. J., & Kim, Y. C. (2011). The influence of social presence on customer intention to reuse online recommender systems: The roles of personalization and product type. *International Journal of Electronic Commerce, 16*(1), 129–153. doi:10.2753/JEC1086-4415160105

Demery, P. (2006). As consumers flock to high bandwidth, e-retailers shake, rattle and roll. *Internet Retailer*. Retrieved July 2013 from http://www.internetretailer.com/article.asp?id=17145

Dinh, H. Q., Walker, N., & Hodges, L. (1999). Evaluating the importance of multi-sensory input on memory and the sense of presence in virtual environments. In *Proceedings of the IEEE Virtual Reality Conference 1999* (pp. 222–228). IEEE. doi:10.1109/VR.1999.756955

Edvardsson, B., Enquist, B., & Johnston, R. (2003). Cocreating customer value through hyperreality in the prepurchase service experience. *Journal of Service Research, 10*(10), 1–13.

El Kamel, L., & Rigaux-Bricmont, B. (2011). Les apports du postmodernisme à l'analyse des univers virtuels comme expérience de consommation: Cas de Second Life. *Recherche et Applications en Marketing, 26*(3), 71–92. doi:10.1177/076737011102600304

Ellis, S. R. (1996). Presence of mind: A reaction to Thomas Sheridan's "Further musings on the psychophysics of presence". *Presence (Cambridge, Mass.), 5*(2), 247–25. PMID:11539412

Ellis, S. R., Dorighi, N. S., Menges, B. M., Adelstein, B. D., & Jacoby, R. H. (1997). In search of equivalence classes in subjective scales of reality. In M. J. Smith, G. Salvendy, & R. J. Koubek (Eds.), *Design of computing systems: Advances in human factors ergonomics* (pp. 873–876). Elsevier.

Firat, A. F., & Venkatesh, A. (1995). Liberatory postmodernism and the reenchantment of consumption. *The Journal of Consumer Research, 22*(3), 239–267. doi:10.1086/209448

Flach, J. M., & Holden, J. G. (1998). The reality of experience. *Presence (Cambridge, Mass.), 7*(1), 90–95. doi:10.1162/105474698565550

Fornell, C., & Bookstein, F. L. (1982). Two structural equation models: LISREL and PLS applied to consumer exit-voice theory. *JMR, Journal of Marketing Research, 19*(4), 440–452. doi:10.2307/3151718

Fornell, C., & Larcker, D. (1981). Evaluating structural equation models with unobservable variables and measurement error. *JMR, Journal of Marketing Research, 18*(1), 39–50. doi:10.2307/3151312

Fornerino, M., Helme-Guizon, A., & Gotteland, D. (2008). Movie consumption experience and immersion: Impact on satisfaction. *Recherche et Applications en Marketing, 23*(3), 93–111. doi:10.1177/205157070802300306

Garau, M., Friedman, D., Ritter Weidenfeld, H., Antley, A., Brogni, A., & Slater, M. (2008). Temporal and spatial variations in presence: Qualitative analysis in interviews from an experiment on breaks in presence. *Presence (Cambridge, Mass.), 17*(3), 293–309. doi:10.1162/pres.17.3.293

Garnier, M., & Poncin, I. (2013). *Identification to the avatar in a commercial 3D virtual world: A dynamic perspective*. Lille, France: European Advances in Consumer Research, July, Barcelona.

Graillot, L. (2005). Réalités (ou apparences?) de l'hyper-réalité: Une application au cas du tourisme de loisirs. *Recherche et Applications en Marketing, 20*(1), 43–63. doi:10.1177/076737010502000103

Haenlein, M., & Kaplan, A. M. (2009). Flagship brand stores within virtual worlds: The impact of virtual store exposure on real-life attitude toward the brand and purchase intent. *Recherche et Applications en Marketing, 24*(3), 57–79. doi:10.1177/076737010902400304

Held, R. M., & Durlach, N. I. (1992). Telepresence. *Presence (Cambridge, Mass.), 1*(1), 109–112.

Hoffman, D., & Novak, T. (1996). Marketing in hypermedia computer-mediated environments: Conceptual foundations. *Journal of Marketing, 60*(3), 50–68. doi:10.2307/1251841

Hoffman, D. L., & Novak, T. P. (2009). Flow online: Lessons learned and future prospects. *Journal of Interactive Marketing, 23*(1), 23–34. doi:10.1016/j.intmar.2008.10.003

Holbrook, M. B., & Hirschman, E. C. (1982). The experiential aspects of consumption: Consumer fantasies, feelings and fun. *The Journal of Consumer Research, 9*(2), 132–140. doi:10.1086/208906

IJsselsteijn, W. A., & de Ridder, H. (1998). *Measuring temporal variations in presence*. Ipswich, UK: British Telecom Laboratories.

Joy, A., & Sherry, J. Jr. (2003). Speaking of art as embodied imaginations: A multisensory approach to understanding aesthetic experience. *The Journal of Consumer Research, 30*(2), 259–282. doi:10.1086/376802

Lakoff, G. (1987). *Women, fire, and dangerous things*. Chicago: University of Chicago Press. doi:10.7208/chicago/9780226471013.001.0001

Lakoff, G., & Johnson, M. (1999). *Philosophy in the flesh: The embodied mind and its challenge to Western thought*. New York: Basic Books.

Lee, K. M. (2004). Presence explicated. *Communication Theory*, *14*(1), 27–50. doi:10.1111/j.1468-2885.2004.tb00302.x

Li, H., Daugherty, T., & Biocca, F. (2001). Characteristics of virtual experience in electronic commerce: A protocol analysis. *Journal of Interactive Marketing*, *15*(3), 13–30. doi:10.1002/dir.1013

Li, H., Daugherty, T., & Biocca, F. (2003). The role of virtual experience in consumer learning. *Journal of Consumer Psychology*, *13*(4), 395–407. doi:10.1207/S15327663JCP1304_07

Ling, K. C. H., Chai, L. T., & Piew, T. H. (2010). The effects of shopping orientations, online trust and prior online purchase experience towards customers' online purchase intention. *International Business Research*, *3*(3), 63–76. doi:10.5539/ibr.v3n3p63

Lombard, M., & Ditton, T. (1997). At the heart of it all: The concept of presence. *Journal of Computer-Mediated Communication*, *3*(2). Retrieved from http://jcmc.indiana.edu/vol3/issue2/lombard.html

Mathwick, C., Malhotra, N., & Rigdon, E. (2001). Experiential value: Conceptualization, measurement and application in the catalog and internet shopping environment. *Journal of Retailing*, *77*(1), 39–56. doi:10.1016/S0022-4359(00)00045-2

Mencarelli, R., & Pulh, M. (2012). Web 2.0 et musées. *Decisions Marketing*, *65*(65), 77–82. doi:10.7193/DM.065.77.82

Merle, A., Senecal, S., & St-Onge, A. (2012). Whether and how virtual try-on influences consumer responses to an apparel web site. *International Journal of Electronic Commerce*, *16*(3), 41–64. doi:10.2753/JEC1086-4415160302

Minsky, M. (1980). Telepresence. *Omni (New York, N.Y.)*, *2*(9), 45–52.

Mollen, A., & Wilson, H. (2010). Engagement, telepresence and interactivity in online consumer experience: Reconciling scholastic and managerial perspectives. *Journal of Business Research*, *63*(9/10), 919–925. doi:10.1016/j.jbusres.2009.05.014

Moon, J. M. D., Hossain, D., Sanders, G. L., Garrity, E. J., & Jo, S. (2013). Player commitment to massively multiplayer online role-playing games (MMORPGs): An integrated model. *International Journal of Electronic Commerce*, *17*(4), 7–38. doi:10.2753/JEC1086-4415170401

Oliver, R. L. (1980). A cognitive model of the antecedents and consequences of satisfaction decisions. *JMR, Journal of Marketing Research*, *17*(4), 460–469. doi:10.2307/3150499

Palmer, M. T. (1995). Interpersonal communication and virtual reality: Mediating interpersonal relationships. In F. Biocca & M. R. Levy (Eds.), *Communication in the age of virtual reality* (pp. 277–302). Hillsdale, NJ: Lawrence Erlbaum.

Pantano, E., & Servidio, R. (2012). Modeling innovative points of sales through virtual and immersive technologies. *Journal of Retailing and Consumer Services*, *19*(3), 279–286. doi:10.1016/j.jretconser.2012.02.002

Papagiannidis, S., Pantano, E., See-To, E., & Bourlakis, M. (2013). Modelling the determinants of a simulated experience in a virtual retail store and users' product purchasing intentions. *Journal of Marketing Management*, *29*(13-14), 1462–1492. doi:10.1080/0267257X.2013.821150

Poncin, I., & Garnier, M. (2010). L'expérience sur un site de vente 3D. Le vrai, le faux et le virtuel: À la croisée des chemins. *Management et Avenir*, *2*(32), 173–191. doi:10.3917/mav.032.0173

Poncin, I., & Garnier, M. (2012). Immersion in a new commercial virtual environment: The role of the avatar in the appropriation process. In Z. Gürhan-Canli, C. Otnes, & R. Zhu (Eds.), *Advances in consumer research*. Association for Consumer Research.

Potter, W. J. (1988). Developing an instrument to measure perception of reality in television content. *Journal of Broadcasting & Electronic Media, 32*, 23–41. doi:10.1080/08838158809386682

Quarrick, G. (1989). *Our sweetest hours: Recreation and the mental state of absorption.* Jefferson, NC: McFarland.

Regenbrecht, H. T., Schubert, T. W., & Friedmann, F. (1998). Measuring the sense of presence and its relations to fear of heights in virtual environments. *International Journal of Human-Computer Interaction, 10*(3), 233–249. doi:10.1207/s15327590ijhc1003_2

Rieunier, S. (1998). L'influence de la musique d'ambiance sur le comportement du client: Revue de la littérature, défis méthodologiques et voies de recherches. *Recherche et Applications en Marketing, 13*(3), 57–77. doi:10.1177/076737019801300305

Ritzer, G. (2005). *Enchanting a disenchanted world: Revolutionizing the means of consumption.* Thousand Oaks, CA: Pine Forge Press.

Riva, G. (2009). Is presence a technology issue? Some insights from cognitive science. *Virtual Reality (Waltham Cross), 13*(3), 159–167. doi:10.1007/s10055-009-0121-6

Rose, S., Clark, M., Samouel, P., & Hair, N. (2012). Online customer experience in e-retailing: An empirical model of antecedents and outcomes. *Journal of Retailing, 88*(2), 308–322. doi:10.1016/j.jretai.2012.03.001

Rouzé, V. (2004). *Les musiques diffusées dans les lieux publics: Analyse et enjeux de pratiques communicationnelles quotidiennes.* (Doctoral Dissertation). Université Paris 8, St-Denis, France. Retrieved July, 2013 from http://tel.archives-ouvertes.fr/docs/00/63/52/96/PDF/thA_se_sans_annexe.pdf

Sanchez-Vives, M. V., & Slater, M. (2005). From presence to consciousness through virtual reality. *Nature Reviews. Neuroscience, 6*(4), 332–339. doi:10.1038/nrn1651 PMID:15803164

Schifferstein, H.N.J., & Desmet, P.M.A. (2007). The effects of sensory impairments on product experience and personal well-being. *Ergonomics, 50*(12), 2026–2048. doi:10.1080/00140130701524056 PMID:17852370

Schubert, T. W., Friedmann, F., & Regenbrecht, H. (2001). The experience of presence: Factor analytic insights. *Presence (Cambridge, Mass.), 10*(3), 266–281. doi:10.1162/105474601300343603

Schultze, U. (2010). Embodiment and presence in virtual worlds: A review. *Journal of Information Technology, 25*(4), 434–449. doi:10.1057/jit.2010.25

Sheridan, T. B. (1992). Musings on telepresence and virtual presence. *Presence (Cambridge, Mass.), 1*(1), 120–125.

Slater, M. (1999). Measuring presence: A response to the Witmer and Singer presence questionnaire. *Presence (Cambridge, Mass.), 8*(5), 560–565. doi:10.1162/105474699566477

Slater, M. (2002). Presence and the sixth sense. *Presence (Cambridge, Mass.), 11*(4), 435–439. doi:10.1162/105474602760204327

Slater, M., & Steed, A. (2000). A virtual presence counter. *Presence (Cambridge, Mass.), 9*(5), 413–434.

Slater, M., Usoh, M., & Steed, A. (1994). Depth of presence in virtual environments. *Presence (Cambridge, Mass.)*, *3*(2), 130–144.

Slater, M., & Wilbur, S. (1997). A framework for immersive virtual environments (five): Speculations on the role of presence in virtual environments. *Presence (Cambridge, Mass.)*, *6*, 603–617.

Steuer, J. (1992). Defining virtual reality: Dimensions determining telepresence. *Journal of Communication*, *42*(4), 73–93. doi:10.1111/j.1460-2466.1992.tb00812.x

Suh, K.-S., & Lee, Y. E. (2005). The effects of virtual reality on consumer learning: An empirical investigation. *Management Information Systems Quarterly*, *29*(4), 673–697.

Tisseau, J. (2001). *Réalité virtuelle: autonomie in virtuo*. Habilitation à Diriger des Recherches, Informatique, Université de Rennes 1.

Tisseron, S. (2008). *Virtuel, mon amour: Penser, aimer, souffrir, à l'ère des nouvelles technologies*. Paris: Albin Michel.

Towell, J., & Towell, E. (1997). Presence in text-based networked virtual environments or "MUDS". *Presence (Cambridge, Mass.)*, *6*(5), 590–595.

Underhill, P. (2007). *La science du shopping: comment le merchandising influence l'achat*. Paris: Village mondial.

Van Schaik, P., Turnbull, T., Van Wersch, A., & Drummond, S. (2004). Presence within a mixed reality environment. *Cyberpsychology & Behavior*, *7*(5), 540–552. doi:10.1089/1094931042403145 PMID:15667049

Wang, L. C., Baker, J., Wagner, J. A., & Wakefield, K. (2007). Can a retail web site be social? *Journal of Marketing*, *71*(3), 143–157. doi:10.1509/jmkg.71.3.143

Ward, J. L., & Saren, M. (2008). Second Life: Contours of a virtual marketing landscape. In *Proceedings of European Marketing Academy Conference*. University of Brighton.

Witmer, B. G., & Singer, M. J. (1994). *Measuring immersion in virtual environments*. ARI Technical Report 1014. Alexandria, VA: U.S. Army Research Institute for the Behavioral and Social Sciences.

Witmer, B. G., & Singer, M. J. (1998). Measuring presence in virtual environments: A presence questionnaire. *Presence (Cambridge, Mass.)*, *7*(3), 228–240. doi:10.1162/105474698565686

Yee, N., Ellis, J., & Ducheneaut, N. (2009). The tyranny of embodiment. *Artifact*, *2*, 1–6.

Yoo, Y., & Alavi, M. (2001). Media and group cohesion: Relative influences on social presence, task participation, and group consensus. *Management Information Systems Quarterly*, *25*(3), 371–390. doi:10.2307/3250922

Zahorik, P., & Jenison, R. L. (1998). Presence as being-in-the-world. *Presence (Cambridge, Mass.)*, *7*(1), 78–89. doi:10.1162/105474698565541

ADDITIONAL READING

Ahn, T., Ryu, S., & Han, I. (2007). The impact of web quality and playfulness on user acceptance of online retailing. *Information & Management*, *44*(3), 263–275. doi:10.1016/j.im.2006.12.008

Alba, J., Lynch, J. W. B., Janiszewski, C., Lutz, R., Sawyer, A., & Wood, S. (1997). Interactive home shopping: Consumer, retailer, and manufacturer incentives to participate in electronic marketplace. *Journal of Marketing*, *61*(3), 38–53. doi:10.2307/1251788

Babin, B. J., Darden, W. R., & Griffin, M. (1994). Work and /or fun measuring hedonic and utilitarian, shopping value. *The Journal of Consumer Research*, *20*(4), 644–655. doi:10.1086/209376

Bailenson, J., Yee, N., Merget, D., & Schroeder, R. (2006). The effect of behavioral realism and form realism of real-time avatar faces on verbal disclosure, non-verbal disclosure, emotion recognition and copresence in dyadic interaction. *Presence (Cambridge, Mass.)*, *15*(5), 259–372.

Barlow, A. K. J., Siddiqui, N. Q., & Mannion, M. (2004). Development in information and communication technologies for retail marketing channels. *International Journal of Retail & Distribution Management*, *32*(3), 157–163. doi:10.1108/09590550410524948

Garnier, M., & Poncin, I. (2013). The avatar in marketing: Synthesis, integrative framework and perspectives. *Recherche et Applications en Marketing*, *28*(1), 85–115. doi:10.1177/2051570713478335

Kaplan, A. M., & Haenlein, M. (2009). The fairyland of Second Life: Virtual social worlds and how to use them. *Business Horizons*, *52*(6), 563–572. doi:10.1016/j.bushor.2009.07.002

Novak, T. P., Hoffman, D., & Yung, Y.-F. (2000). Measuring the customer experience in online environments: A structural modeling approach. *Marketing Science*, *19*(1), 22–44. doi:10.1287/mksc.19.1.22.15184

Parmentier, G., & Rolland, S. (2009). Les consommateurs des mondes virtuels: Construction identitaire et expérience de consommation dans Second Life. *Recherche et Applications en Marketing*, *24*(3), 43–56. doi:10.1177/076737010902400303

Poncin, I., & Ben Mimoun, M. S. (2014). The impact of "e-atmospherics" on physical stores. *Journal of Retailing and Consumer Services*, *21*(5), 851–859. doi:10.1016/j.jretconser.2014.02.013

Scarpi, D. (2012). Work and fun on the Internet: The effects of utilitarianism and hedonism online. *Journal of Interactive Marketing*, *26*(1), 53–67. doi:10.1016/j.intmar.2011.08.001

Senecal, S., Gharbi, J. E., & Nantel, J. (2002). The Influence of flow on hedonic and utilitarian shopping values. In S. Broniarczyk & K. Nakamoto (Eds.), *Advances in Consumer Research 29* (pp. 483–484). Provo, UT: Association for Consumer Research.

KEY TERMS AND DEFINITIONS

Avatar: A virtual character that represents the consumer in the virtual universe.

Hyperreality: "A reality that is different from the perceptible objective reality that leads to inability to make the difference between what is real and what is false ….This copy of the real can be authentic or an improved reproduction of an existing reality, or can be an original reality without any equivalent" (Graillot, 2005).

Merchant Virtual Universe (MVU): An online 3D retail setting that reproduces a store or shopping mall, in which consumers can window-shop, purchase products and services, participate in activities and interact with other consumers. In MVUs, consumers are usually represented by avatars.

Perceived Realism: The extent to which the MVU is perceived as realistic, that is, that it faithfully reproduces the perceptible real.

Presence: Commonly refers to the "illusion of being in a distant place," that is, the mental state in which "a user feels physically present within the computer-mediated environment'' (Slater & Steed, 2000), the psychological sense of "being there" (Schultze, 2010).

Psychological Immersion: "The degree to which a virtual environment submerges the perceptual system of the user" (Biocca & Delaney, 1995). Immersion can be from partial to total, possibly until reaching a state of "flow" (Fornerino, Helme-Guizon & Gotteland, 2008; Hoffman & Novak, 1996), defined in an online context as "the state occurring during network navigation which is: 1) characterized by a seamless sequence of responses facilitated by machine interactivity, 2) intrinsically enjoyable, 3) accompanied by a loss of self-consciousness, 4) and self-reinforcing" (Hoffman & Novak, 1996).

Synesthesia: The mobilization of several senses to perceive an experience.

APPENDIX 1: ILLUSTRATIONS OF A 3D COMMERCIAL WEBSITE (MVU)

Figure 5. A 3D shop

Figure 6. Outdoor spaces of the 3D shopping mall

APPENDIX 2: VISIT 1 LOGBOOK

Instructions

1. Visit the Shopping Mall website as extensively as possible. Create your avatar, have a walk, observe, try!
2. During the visit, make a screen copy of your avatar and keep it as an image file (.bmp or .jpeg).
3. Then you must fill in this visit logbook as soon as you finish the visit.
4. Fill it in spontaneously. Answer the questions in as free and as detailed a manner as possible. There are no good or wrong answers. All your comments are important.
5. To answer the questions, fill in the dedicated frames.

Part 2: Website Visit

1. What were you expecting before visiting the website?
2. Describe your avatar:
3. How have you created your avatar? Did you personalize it? *If yes, how and why? What do you think of it? What do you feel toward this avatar? If no, why did you choose not to do it?*
4. What was your first impression when arriving on the website?
5. Tell us about your visit of the website. What did you do? What did you see?
6. Was your first impression confirmed during this visit? Has it evolved? Why? What did you feel during this visit?
7. Did you meet other visitors? What happened?
8. Did you visit a shop? If yes, which one? What is your opinion about this new kind of shop? What are your feelings?
9. What did you like in this visit and this website? Why? What did you not like? Why?
10. What would be your expectations regarding this kind of website? What would you like to find? What are the opportunities for improvement regarding the current version of the website?
11. Did you have any technical problems or difficulties during the visit? If yes, which ones? Describe each difficulty in a detailed manner. How have you resolved the problem or how did it resolve? Have those difficulties had an impact on your experience of visiting the website?

APPENDIX 3: FINAL SCALES

Perceived Realism

- The virtual shopping mall presents things as they are in life.
- What happens in the virtual shopping mall does not look like everyday life.
- The virtual shopping mall does not depict life as it is for real.
- The virtual shopping mall makes me live experiences as if I was really there.

Presence

- How compelling was your sense of objects moving through space?
- How completely were you able to actively survey or search the environment using vision?
- How compelling was your sense of moving around inside the virtual environment?
- How quickly did you adjust to the virtual environment experience?

Immersion

- For some moments, I lost consciousness of what was around me.
- During the visit of the website, my body was in front of the computer but my mind was in the world created by the site.
- The virtual shopping mall made me forget realities of the outside world.
- During the visit, what happened before the visit or what would happen after, did not matter.
- The virtual shopping mall made me forget my immediate environment.

APPENDIX 4: OVERVIEW AND PATH COEFFICIENTS FOR VISIT 2

Table 7. Overview for Visit 2

	AVE	Composite Reliability	R-Square	Cronbachs Alpha
Immersion	0.790364	0.949538	0.338131	0.933218
Presence	0.537020	0.822515	0.125726	0.717144
Perceived Realism	0.596644	0.855018		0.786615
Satisfaction	0.810173	0.927436	0.465235	0.882054
	Communality	**Redundancy**		
Immersion	0.790364	0.146656		
Presence	0.537020	0.069358		
Perceived Realism	0.596644			
Satisfaction	0.810173	0.276534		

Table 8. Path coefficients (mean, STEDEV, t-values) for Visit 2

	Original Sample (O)	Sample Mean (M)	Standard Deviation (STDEV)	Standard Error (STERR)	T-Statistics
Immersion -> Satisfaction	0.415438	0.419964	0,078900	0.078900	5.265392
Presence -> Immersion	0.314305	0.313954	0.053439	0.053439	5.881587
Presence -> Satisfaction	0.217779	0.221672	0.085831	0.085831	2.537307
Perceived Realism ->Immersion	0.390314	0.388899	0.087264	0.087264	4.472814
Perceived Realism ->Presence	0.3545479	0.381081	0.064058	0.064058	5.535292
Perceived Realism -> Satisfaction	0.209215	0.208885	0.096269	0.096269	2.173225

APPENDIX 5: OVERVIEW AND PATH COEFFICIENTS FOR VISIT 4

Table 9. Overview for Visit 4

	AVE	Composite Reliability	R-Square	Cronbachs Alpha	Communality	Redundancy
Immersion	0.825746	0.959438	0.614550	0.946830	0.825746	0.391717
Presence	0.572481	0.841283	0.297651	0.752799	0.572481	0.157805
Perceived Realism	0.587502	0.850116		0.790254	0.587502	
Satisfaction	0.897088	0.963165	0.301921	0.942592	0.897088	0.172295

Table 10. Path coefficients (mean, STEDEV, t-values) for Visit 4

	Original Sample (O)	Sample Mean (M)	Standard Deviation (STDEV)	Standard Error (STERR)	T-Statistics
Immersion -> Satisfaction	0.250987	0.242273	0.117866	0.117866	2.129429
Presence -> Immersion	0.518496	0.515170	0.069799	0.069799	7.428455
Presence -> Satisfaction	0.2575150	0.273819	0.132926	0.132926	1.937285
Perceived Realism ->Immersion	0.369604	0.368977	0.071607	0.071607	5.161547
Perceived Realism ->Presence	0.545574	0.553663	0.053542	0.053542	10.189677
Perceived Realism -> Satisfaction	0.110586	0.106233	0.111396	0.11396	0.992732

Chapter 4
Measuring Cognitive and Emotional Processes in Retail:
A Neuroscience Perspective

Patrizia Cherubino
IULM University, Italy & BrainSigns srl, Italy

Arianna Trettel
BrainSigns srl, Italy

Anton Giulio Maglione
Sapienza University, Italy

Giovanni Vecchiato
BrainSigns srl, Italy & Sapienza University, Italy

Ilenia Graziani
BrainSigns srl, Italy & Sapienza University, Italy

Fabio Babiloni
BrainSigns srl, Italy & Sapienza University, Italy

ABSTRACT

The purpose of this chapter is to share scientific methods for the quantitative measurement of emotion through the recording of physiologic and cerebral variables of consumers in relation to advertising stimuli and during the purchase in the store. For this reason, the authors describe the way to estimate the emotion along the visit of a shop by using the approach-withdrawal index. It demonstrates how it is possible to describe the variation of the appreciation of a shop visit by two groups of persons. The specific contribution to the scientific literature is the use of such approach-withdrawal index and the estimation of the emotion linked with the visit of a large point of sale (e.g. a supermarket). The proper use of these methodologies can provide information related to cognitive and emotional aspects of persons involved in the appreciation of products in retail points of sale.

INTRODUCTION

It is well known from neuroscience that the cerebral systems related to emotion in humans play a vital role and often unconscious (that is subtracted from the conscious cognitive control) during the decisions that we generate every day. Very often the emotions perceived during sensory stimulation to which we are subjected in everyday life do not manifest themselves in our conscious control, while driving our behavior instead perceived as "spontaneous" or natural.

DOI: 10.4018/978-1-4666-8297-9.ch004

Often we are not able to rationally justify our purchasing behavior, which often differ greatly from our original intent in favor of a purchase "decided on the spot" on the basis of purely instinctive motivations. The reason for this behavior of "decision-making" seemingly out of control during the conscious rational choice of goods or services is based on the fact that the different emotional systems in the brain of humans can easily access to the centers of decision behavior without be subjected to the filter of the cognitive part of the brain. The emotion is therefore a very important factor in the decision to purchase a good or a service, as well as plays a vital role in the perception of a product. It therefore seems clear that the possibility to understand and to measure the emotion induced by an advertising, as well as to measure the emotion induced by the vision of a logo can be extremely important for a company that invests on advertising.

To measure the emotion induced by a product or an image in a consumer, however, can be a difficult exercise. In fact, there may be a problem of "self-perception" of the emotion itself: as we have already said a perceived emotion cannot simply become apparent to our conscious attention while instead is inducing a precise behavior. When this happens it is typical to collect verbal reports from the consumers such as "I cannot explain why I made this choice," or similar. Another problem related to the perception of the emotion in the consumers is related to the ability by the consumer to describe properly the emotion perceived during the observation of a product or a service. Another possible issue is related to the will of the interviewed to share with the others the own emotion related to the product or service consumption. It appears clear from these previous possible issues, that an objective measure of the emotion could be of some help in the evaluation of the correct proposition of goods and services in the retail to the consumers.

The technological and methodological innovations of this paper is that the emotions (and the related processes in the brain that occurs during such emotions) can be measured during the exposition of the subjects to the advertisements or during the purchase decision in the store. In addition, this can be performed in ecologic conditions close to what happens in the normal life. This is possible thanks to advanced technological devices able to measure brain and emotional activities outside of the scientific laboratories of the universities or the research centers.

The real advantage of the quantitative measure of emotional during the use of advertising in selected groups of users is the possibility to better modulate the advertising message on the point of sale recognizing its strengths and weaknesses. The relevance of this contribution for companies lies in the information that the quantitative measure of emotion:

1. It is possible out of scientific laboratories and universities;
2. It is able to operate effectively for the improvement of the advertising messages and the corporate communications;
3. Is able to provide information not directly obtainable by the processes of explicit verbalization of the respondents.

The measurement of emotions and the relative brain processes associated with the instinctive perception of advertising can thus provide additional evidence to the measurement of the efficacy of the advertising obtained via other typical methods of marketing research.

The purpose of this chapter is then to share scientific methods for the quantitative measurement of emotion through the recording of physiologic and cerebral variables of consumers in relation to advertising stimuli and during the purchase in the store. For this reason we describe the way to estimate the emotion along the visit of a shop by using the approach-withdrawal index, described in the following pages. It will be demonstrated how using such index it can be possible to describe the variation of the appreciation of a shop visit by two groups of persons. The specific contribution to the scientific literature is the use of such approach-withdrawal index and the estimation of the emotion linked with the visit of a large point of sale (e.g. a supermarket).

Background

In the last two decades, different techniques and devices have been developed to measure thoughts and feelings, by measuring the brain activity through the collection of the hemodynamic or electromagnetic signature of activated neural networks. Since last 10 years, unsolved problems and questions related to the evaluation of economic transactions, reached the neuroscience labs. Therefore, neuroscience researchers began to cooperate with economists in order to evaluate the brain activity during the generation of economic value judgments. What can cognitive neuroscience teach economics on the base of these last decades of common research? Cognitive neuroscience deconstructs the picture of perfectly rational humans, which are deliberating their choices by weighting costs and benefits until a deliberative equilibrium is reached. Although humans are definitely capable of conscious deliberation, many, if not most, economically relevant decision processes are characterized by certain other features such as automatic, fast and effective cognitive processes, which are not under direct volitional control (Bargh and Chartrand, 1999). Second, they are under the influence of unrecognized and finely tuned affective mechanisms, which often play a decisive role in action (Damasio et al., 1996; Davidson et al., 1990; Panksepp, 2004). Third, many of these processes have been shaped by evolution in order to serve social purposes (BCacioppo, 2002). Thus, decision-making and evaluation in economic contexts

will be influenced by mechanisms dedicated to social interaction (Braeutigam et al., 2004). Hence, the incorporation of neuroimaging into the decision-making sciences has generated the interest not only of economists but also of marketing scientists. The line of reasoning was that if the neuroscientist could "image" the brain at work during the perception of particular concepts of value for the economists, such as the "perceived value" of choices to be made, then the same could be attempted for concepts useful in marketing. In fact, images of activated brain areas during the appreciation of concepts, such as the "brand" or simply during the observation of advertisements, was attempted and successively largely explored by different brain imaging devices. Todays, there are high hopes that neuroimaging technology could solve some of the problems that marketers faced. In particular, a prominent hope is that neuroimaging will both streamline marketing processes and save money. Another hope is that neuroimaging will reveal information about consumer preferences that is unobtainable through conventional methods. In this context, the most popular brain imaging method adopted in the neuromarketing field is the functional Magnetic Resonance Image (fMRI), a technique that returns a sequence of images of the cerebral activity by means of the measure of the cerebral blood flow. It is very well known that the hemodynamic measurements of the brain activity allow a level of localization of the activated brain structures on the order of few cubic millimeters, being capable to detect activations also in deep brain structures. However, the lack of time resolution, due to the intrinsic nature of the measured signal, makes the fMRI unsuitable to follow the brain dynamics on the base of its sub seconds activity. However, there are other brain imaging techniques that allow to follow on a millisecond base the brain activity during the exposition to relevant marketing stimuli, such as electroencephalography (EEG), although characterized by a spatial resolution of square centimeters. To overcome this problem, high-resolution EEG technology (hrEEG) has been developed to enhance the poor spatial information content of the EEG activity in order to detect the brain activity with a spatial resolution of a square centimeter and the unsurpassed time resolution of milliseconds (Babiloni et al., 2004). In addition, EEG devices are also relatively inexpensive, robust and even wearable by the subject, making such technology of interest for the evaluation of marketing stimuli. Nowadays, researchers are attempting to investigate the signs of the brain activity correlated with an increase of attention, memory and emotional engagement during the observation of commercial advertisements (Vecchiato et al., 2010; Langleben et al., 2009). In fact, indirect variables of emotional processing could be gathered by tracking variations of the activity of specific anatomical structures linked to the emotional processing activity in humans, such as the pre- and frontal cortex (PFC and FC respectively; Davidson, 2004). The PFC region is structurally and functionally heterogeneous but its role in the generation of the emotions is well recognized. Specifically, findings suggest that the left PFC is an important brain area in a widespread circuit that mediates appetitive approach, while the right PFC appears to form a major component of a neural circuit that instantiates defensive withdrawal (Davidson, 2004; Balconi et al., 2009). In addition, it is very well know the role of the frontal areas in cognitive processes such as memory and attention in complex tasks (Werkle-Bergner et al., 2006; Klimesch, 1999). Moreover, by monitoring autonomic activity such as the heart rate (HR) it is possible to assess the emotional state of the subject (Montano et al., 2009).

The way in which such amount of information from neuroscience could be useful to the marketing studies in retail point of sale is suggested by the well-known fact that at least the 70% of the new products launched worldwide (including cars, shoes, clothes etc.) failed within the first six months. This happens simply because people are not saying (or are not able to say) the truth when they are interviewed with respect to the product they have tasted or watched previously. There are a lot of reasons for that behavior, but this disability to proper report the own feelings related to the product is usually a huge obstacle to the correct collection of information from consumers, at the base of solid marketing actions. Thus, the application of neuroscience-based methodologies allows to the researchers to gain information not available otherwise related to the unconscious and spontaneous reaction of the consumers in front of the product stimuli. Of course such kind of information is just a part of the whole story related to the acquisition of consumer's habit in front of the product.

In the present context, the object of our research was to describe methodologies available to analyze the brain activity and the emotional engagement occurring during the "naturalistic" observation of products in the point of sale. Hence, the final goal was to link significant variations of the EEG and autonomic variables with cognitive and emotional reactions to the presented and observed products. In order to do that, different indexes could be employed to summarize the performed measurements, later used in the statistical analysis.

CEREBRAL PROCESSES RELEVANT IN THE RETAIL

Main Cerebral Events that Occur in a Visit of a Shop

The aim of the application of neuroimaging techniques in cognitive neuroscience is to understand how brain functioning mediates cognition and human behavior such as decision-making, reward processing, memory, attention, approach and withdrawal motivation and emotional processing.

The use of advanced neuroimaging techniques allows an increasingly precise identification of neural responses across specific brain regions. The importance of such anatomical localization is due to the potential relevance of certain brain regions for consumer research given the role they play in different cognitive and emotional functions.

The idea is to use the amount of knowledge already developed so far in neuroscience to interpret the cerebral events related to purchase occurring during the visit of a store or a shop. In the following, it will be described some main cerebral processing that have place during a purchase in a store with a description of the possible cerebral regions involved in such processing.

In the successive section it will be described how such processes could be measured in a store.

Decision-Making

A central question within consumer research is about consumer decision-making and the way consumers assess different product alternatives based on perceived benefits and costs. Several regions of the prefrontal cortex (PFC), situated in the frontal lobe of the brain, might be related to this question due to the critical role they play in the underlying processes of human decision-making. Specifically, there is evidence of both the orbitofrontal cortex (OFC) and the ventromedial prefrontal cortex (VMPFC) being involved in the processing of different alternatives and potential outcomes through the assessment of their (perceived) value (Tremblay & Schultz, 1999). In particular, the OFC is associated with the evaluation of trade-offs and the expected capacity of outcomes to satisfy one's needs (Wallis, 2007). It also plays a central role in making choices about appropriate behaviors, especially when one is faced with unpredictable situations (Elliott, Dolan, & Frith, 2000). Finally, the dorsolateral prefrontal cortex (DLPFC) also plays a critical role in decision-making as it is known for being involved in cognitive control over emotions (Rilling, King-Casas, & Sanfey,

2008). In particular, it is involved in the control of impulses for complying with social norms while the ventrolateral prefrontal cortex (VLPFC) could play a role in motivating this social norm compliance by representing the threat of punishment from others (Rilling & Sanfey, 2011). Interestingly, the cognitive effort in the PFC appears to be lower when a sure gain is expected com- pared with risky decisions. Measuring the activity of these regions may therefore provide useful insights about the neural foundations of consumer choices and marketing constructs such as perceived value.

Reward Processing

Another set of brain regions of particular interest for consumer research consists of those part of the reward system of the brain. They indeed respond to subjectively attractive rewards such as food (Berridge, 1996), money (Knutson, Adams, Fong, & Hommer, 2001) and drugs (Wise & Rompré, 1989). In other words, an attractive product design or a favourite brand that is able to act as a rewarding stimulus within consumers' brains may trigger the psychological motivations that influence purchase behaviour. A way of monitoring the processing of rewarding stimuli is to measure the activation of the striatum, a striped mass of white and grey matter located in the basal ganglia inside the forebrain. Although a major function of the striatum is movement planning and control, it also plays a role in the reward system of the brain. Thus, there is evidence of the role of the striatum and its components (putamen, caudate nucleus and nucleus accumbens) in the evaluation of actual rewards with respect to one's expectations (Knutson & Wimmer, 2007) and the influence of social factors on the reward-related activity in this region (Fliessbach et al., 2007). Also part of the reward system is the ventral tegmental area (VTA). It is responsible for transmitting dopamine, a neurotransmitter, to other brain regions, thus enabling the modulation of decision-making and playing a role in goal-seeking behaviors (Fields, Hjelmstad, Margolis, & Nicola, 2007).

Attention and Memory

The amount of information consumers are exposed to is enormous, yet our processing capacity is limited. Each second we are exposed to an estimated 11 million bits of information that reach us through all our senses, yet humans are capable of processing only around 50 bits of that information, letting most of the input go by unnoticed (Wilson, 2002). How consumers represent, attend to, and perceive incoming information may have a profound influence on their behavior. One of the key questions at this stage, discussed next, is what consumers pay attention to (i.e., focus on) once there are exposed to a number of rapidly identified choice alternatives (i.e., brand, communications). Attention is the mechanism responsible for selecting the information that gains preferential status above other available information. Recent review of attention in neuroscience indicates that four conceptual components are fundamental to attention: bottom-up or saliency filters, top-down control, competitive visual selection, and working memory (Plassmann et al., 2012). The brain mechanisms involved in attention and visual processing could also be of interest to consumer research since advertising, logos and product designs all possess an important aesthetic component (e.g. shapes, colours) that is processed by the brain in the form of a visual stimulus. The aforementioned prefrontal cortex is responsible for directing and focusing attention and has been shown to connect with the neurons in charge of processing visual stimuli in the vision centre of the brain, called the occipital lobe (Armstrong, Fitzgerald, &Moore, 2006). Similarly, the study of memory-related mental processes might provide useful findings in relation to variables influencing consumer behaviour such as product experience, brand awareness and advertising recall. Most importantly, the hippocampus, located in the temporal lobe, plays a major role in the formation of different forms of memory and

is a central region for memory processing and consolidation (McGaugh, 2000), thus involved in long-term memory. In particular, it is key to the acquisition and recall of declarative memory (Eichenbaum, 2000). Additionally, the amygdala, situated next to the hippocampus to which it is closely related, plays an important role as a modulator of the memory system, particularly in the consolidation of memory (McGaugh, 2000).

Approach and Withdrawal Motivation

Human fMRI studies have shown that activity in the orbitofrontal cortex (OFC), in particular its medial parts, at the time a reward is being enjoyed correlates with subjective reports about the pleasantness or valence of the experience. An interesting open question is which neural systems encode negative experiences. Several studies have found that unpleasantness of taste might the correlated with brain activity in the lateral OFC and left dorsal anterior insula/operculum. O'Doherty and colleagues found that the size of abstract punishments (i.e., losing money) activated lateral parts of the ODC (O'Doherty, Kringelbach, Rolls, Hornak, & Andrews, 20101). One problem in investigating negative experience is to dissociate it from intensity. This problem arises due to the negativity bias of intensity: negative experiences is to dissociate it from intensity. This problem arises due to the negativity bias of intensity: negative experiences are usually also perceived to be more intense and thus are often confounded, in particular for visual stimuli such as facial or object attractiveness. Using a different methodological approach to investigate positive vs. negative emotional experiences, neuromarketing studies are based on the idea that there is a left-right asymmetry of the frontal electroencephalography (EEG) signals (Davidson, Rkman, Saron, Senulis, & Friesen, 1990). These and related studies suggest that relatively greater activity in the left frontal region is associated with either positive emotional experience or the motivational drive to approach an object (Harmon-Jones, 2003). Although there are strong correlations between frontal EEG asymmetry and personality traits, the degree to which the asymmetry changes from one moment to another is questionable. Some studies have applied this approach to measure moment-to-moment fluctuations in emotional responses to advertisements without accounting for autocorrelations in time or multiple statistical comparisons. However, the validity of such approaches is unclear, as hemispheric asymmetry is also an index of working memory load (Habib, Nyberg, & Tulving, 2003). Further research to investigate the neural representation of positive vs. negative experienced values is needed (Plassmann et al., 2012).

According to the neuroscience literature, human behaviour relies on two motivational systems, whether behaviour is motivated by an anticipated desirable outcome or a possible aversive outcome. Specifically, EEG studies have provided important empirical support about the left frontal cortex being involved in a system that motivates approach behaviour (Davidson, 2004). Reversely, the right frontal cortex has been shown to be involved in a system that motivates withdrawal behaviour (Davidson, 2004). Thus, studies suggest that a greater activity in the left frontal region with respect to the right frontal region is associated with approach motivation, which is in turn generally associated with positive emotions, although the latter should be applied with caution as not always the case (Harmon-Jones, 2003). On the contrary, a relatively greater activity in the right frontal region is associated with withdrawal motivation, which is in turn generally associate d with negative emotions (Harmon-Jones, 2003). Consequently, the interest for consumer research is the possibility to monitor the left–right asymmetry of consumers' brains so as to interpret their motivational responses to marketing stimuli and thus potentially infer the attractiveness of products and brands.

Emotional Processing

A central brain region for emotional responses is the amygdala. In particular, it is involved in the processing of negative emotions and unknown stimuli, as well as in aversive responses to inequity (Rilling & Sanfey, 2011). It is also known as a locus of aversive and fear memory (Maren & Quirk, 2004). To a minor extent, it has equally been shown to process positive emotions, usually in relation to rewarding stimuli. Another key emotion-related region is the insula (or insular cortex). It plays a role in the processing of negative experiences such as the perception and expectation of risks, especially when making decisions for which a social or financial risk is expected (Preuschoff, Quartz, & Bossaerts, 2008; Knutson & Bossaerts, 2007). Likewise, the activation of the insula has been associated with anger and disgust in response to unfair economic situations. Additionally, as well as being involved in the evaluation process of stimuli, the aforementioned OFC plays a role in experiencing and anticipating the emotion of regret when outcomes differ from expectations (Coricelli et al., 2005). Finally, it is worth mentioning another area involved in emotional processing, the cingulate cortex, which includes the cingulate gyrus. Studies indeed suggest that the anterior cingulate evaluates emotional and motivational information and integrates it in the decision-making process (Bush, Luu, & Posner, 2000). Moreover, the anterior cingulate has been associated with the experience of an internal conflict between alternative options, its activation possibly being due to a conflict between cognitive and emotional motivations. The role of emotions in decision-ma king has been further explained through neurological and cognitive frameworks such as the somatic marker theory. Overall, the study of these brain mechanisms is likely to be central in consumer neuroscience due to the importance of the emotional component of purchase decisions in traditional consumer research. However, this will need to account for the complexity of the interconnected cerebral networks involved in emotions as there is not a single brain region responsible for emotional processes and no single brain region is activated in relation to one particular type of emotions (Phan, Wager, Taylor, & Liberzon, 2002).

It is worth of noticing as the emotional processing will impact on the variation of some physiological variables, such as the heart rate and the activity of the eccrine glands of the palm of the hands. This last variable is called Galvanic Skin Response (GSR). Variation of the heart rate and of the GSR return information about the "emotion" perceived by the user according to the theory of the affective emotional plane proposed by Barrett and Russel (1999). In such theory the attributes of a perceived "emotion" are related to its arousal level and its valence. These arousal and valence qualities are the independent components of all the emotions perceived by humans. These different qualities of the emotion could be gathered in humans by measuring the variation of the heart rate for the valence of the emotion, and by measuring the activity of the eccrine glands of the hand for the arousal level.

MEASURING THE DECISION-MAKING AND THE EMOTION IN THE RETAIL STORES

So far several cerebral processes relevant in the retail have been described: decision-making, approach and withdrawal motivation, emotion are neural activities that play a role during the retail visit. The aim of this particular section of the chapter is to describe how such cerebral processes could be measured at the state of the art actually. Once such processes could be measured in the store, with the needed time resolution, the intensity of such processes could be put in relation with the specific events occurring within the store. For instance, the measurement of the emotional level before the decision to purchase a product, or before

the removal of a product from the basket could return valuable insight about the mechanisms of acceptance or rejection of the goods offered on the shelf within the retail.

Among the different neuroimaging methods available, the measure of the neuroelectrical activity of the brain by using a net of electrodes disposed on the head (electroencephalogram, EEG) presents several advantages when compared to the other available neuroimaging methodologies. In particular, the measurement of the cerebral activity with the use of EEG allows to follows with an appropriate time-resolution the development of the brain processes during the shop visit. The consumer could wear a cap with the electrodes and the cerebral activity will be gathered by a lightweight device (the EEG acquisition device). In such a way the collection of the brain activity could be related in time to the events occurring in the shop to the consumer. In fact, the EEG is able to track the cerebral activity on the base of the second time resolution or less. Such kind of time-relation cannot be possible by using other neuroimaging methodology such for instance the functional Magnetic Resonance Imaging (fMRI), that was unable to obtain an image of the cerebral activity with a time resolution lower than tens of seconds. In addition to the EEG, that return information about the possible occurrence of cerebral events related to the decision-making as well as to the approach/withdrawal activity in the store, there is also the possibility to follow the emotional processes occurring there. Such emotional processes are followed by measuring the alteration of body markers including the heart rate (with the electrocardiogram, ECG) and the activity of the hand sweat glands. These body markers are strictly related to the variation of the emotions perceived by the consumers during the visit of the shop and the relative purchases. Of course, the measuring of the cerebral activity and the related emotions could be performed also by using other neuroimaging devices, such as for instance the functional Magnetic Resonance Imaging (fMRI). However, in this case since the fMRI device cannot be moved (it is an installation of the weight of thousands kilograms) the retail visit could be performed just virtually by the consumer. In such condition the consumer lies supine within the fMRI device while a retail scenario would be projected on his/her pair of glass. Although possible, the measurement of the retail visit with fMRI device is then quite cumbersome to realize and without the needed time resolution to solve the fine temporal details of the decision making related to the product purchase.

The EEG and the physiological signals (heart rate, GSR) could be then measured in normal consumer during a visit of a retail. Information returned by these measurements are related to the time-varying appreciation of the goods reviewed by the consumer within the shop during the visit, as indexed by the approach-withdrawal EEG activity (Davidson, 2000). In fact, with this particular cerebral index it is possible to evaluate the profile of appreciation of the different goods during the visit of a shelf.

In particular, the methodology to perform such data collection are explained technically in the following paragraph.

EEG Recordings and Signal Processing

The cerebral activity was recorded by means of a portable EEG system (BEmicro and Galileo software, EBneuro, Italy). Informed consent was obtained from each subject after explanation of the study, which was approved by the local institutional ethics committee. Electrodes were arranged according to an extension of the 10-10 international system. Recordings were initially extra-cerebrally referred and then converted to an average reference off-line. We collected the EEG activity at a sampling rate = 256 Hz while the impedances kept below 5 kΩ. Each EEG trace was then converted into the Brain Vision format (BrainAmp, Brainproducts GmbH, Germany) in

order to perform signal pre-processing such as artefacts detection, filtering and segmentation. The EEG signals have been band pass filtered at 1-45 Hz and depurated of ocular artefacts by employing the Independent Component Analysis (ICA). The EEG data have been re-referenced by computing the Common Average Reference (CAR). Individual Alpha Frequency (IAF) has been calculated for each subject in order to define the alpha as alpha = [IAF-2, IAF+2].

Approach-Withdrawal Index

In order to define an approach-withdrawal index (AW) according to the theory related to the earlier introduced EEG frontal asymmetry theory, we computed such imbalance as difference between the average EEG power of right and left channels. The formula we used is the following:

$$AW = \frac{1}{N_P} \sum_{i \in P} \chi_{\alpha i}^2(t)$$
$$-\frac{1}{N_Q} \sum_{i \in Q} y_{\alpha i}^2(t) == AveragePower_{\alpha right, frontal}$$
$$-AveragePower_{\alpha left, frontal}$$

$$(1)$$

where $x_{\alpha i}$ and $y_{\alpha i}$ represent the ith EEG channel in the alpha band that have been recorded from the right and left frontal lobes, respectively. In addition, P = {Fp2,AF6,AF4,F4} and Q = {Fp1,AF7,AF3,F5}, N_P and N_Q represent the cardinality of the two sets of channels. In such a way, an increase of AW will be related to an increase of interest and vice versa. The AW signal of each subject has been z-score transformed and then averaged to obtain an average waveform.

Emotional Index

The emotional index is defined by taking into account the GSR and HR signals. As far as the construction of such variable concerns, we refer to affects circumplex (Russel and Bartlett, 1999) where the coordinates of a point in this space are defined by the HR (horizontal axis) and the GSR (vertical axis). As presented in the Introduction section, several studies have highlighted that these two autonomic parameters correlate with valence and arousal, respectively.

In order to have a mono-dimensional variable, we describe the emotional state of a subject by defining the following Emotional Index (EI):

$$EI = 1 - \frac{\beta}{\pi} \qquad (2)$$

where

$$\beta = \begin{cases} \dfrac{3}{2}\pi + \pi - \vartheta, GSR_z \geq 0, HR_z \leq 0 \\ \dfrac{\pi}{2} - \vartheta, otherwise \end{cases} \qquad (3)$$

GSR_z, HR_z represent the z-score variables of GSR and HR respectively; ϑ, in radians, is measured as arctang (HRz, $GSRz$). Therefore, the angle β is defined in order to transform the domain of ϑ from $[-\pi, \pi]$ to $[0, 2\pi]$ and obtain the EI varying between $[-1, 1]$. This is why we have two ways to calculate β. According to Equations 2 and 3 and the affect circumplex, negative *($HR_z < 0$)* and positive *($HR_z > 0$)* values of the EI are related to negative and positive emotions, respectively, spanning the whole affect circumplex.

However, it remains mandatory to understand which particular good on the shelf is responsible for the variation of the approach-withdrawal activity recorded in the user. To this purpose the use of a particular device able to return the information about the eye-gaze of the consumer within the shop is highly recommendable. Such device is called eye-tracking and it is able to collect the movement of the eye-gaze with a frequency of 30 up to 60 times per second. In this way it is possible to collect "where" the consumer looks within

the shop and at the same time which particular cerebral activity is experienced. In addition to the EEG measurements and the eyetracker device, a couple of electrodes on the hand could return in real time also the profile of the variation of the heart rate of the consumer during the retail visit (for the valence of the perceived emotion) as well as the variation of the perceived arousal level. Such variation of the heart rate and arousal are then correlated to the quality of the emotion perceived by the consumer during the observation of the good in the store, with a time resolution of a couple of seconds. It is of interest to underline that the emotional information provided by the heart rate collection are different from those obtained by the approach-withdrawal evaluation, being the same different in perception that exists between the words "emotional" and the word "feeling" in the English vocabulary. In particular, the "emotional" attitude of the consumer in front of a good is indexed by the variation of his/her heart rate and eccrine glands activity (according to a well-established theory in psychology for valence and arousal of an emotion) while the "cerebral" interest of the consumer for the good is instead indexed by the approach-withdrawal EEG value.

The experimental setup needed to perform such multimodal recording of the cerebral and eye activity of a consumer within the visited shop is presented in Figure 1, in a case for a consumer within the retail food store. Different information are available by the acquisition of the cerebral and emotional feedback of the consumer during the decision-making moments related to the choice of a bottle of wine: his appreciation of the particular bottle, as indexed by the approach-withdrawal EEG activity and the appreciation of particular of the bottle's shape, that attracts more the eye-gaze. In addition, the emotion perceived related to the wine is then also measured by the electrodes measuring heart rate and cutaneous hand impedance (for arousal). As a consequence, an entire complete set of information about the perceived emotion and interest of the consumer within the store is available with a time-resolution of one second.

Figure 1. Experimental setup

It is possible then to follow the cerebral and emotional processes of a consumer within a store during his/her visit. Such processes are indexed by specific variables that could be quantitatively characterized and analyzed. In addition, through a standard normalization procedures (Zar, 1994) the values of such emotional and cerebral indexes could be averaged across different consumers, without be subjected to the large inter-subject variability usually exhibited by the biological indexes. This is obtained by shifting from the original variables collected to their z-score values, obtained by estimating the average and the standard deviation values of such variables in the analyzed sample. By using these normalization procedure and the related z-scores, it is then possible to obtain average cerebral and emotional profile of appreciation of goods during a predetermined visit of the shop for one population. In addition to that, it is possible to describe the perceived cerebral and emotional appreciation of the shop visit for two distinct population groups, such as a group of normal consumers (group A) and another group of consumers that have a fidelity card of the shop (group B). In this case, the possibility to characterize the perceived emotion and cerebral processes of these two groups of consumers within the shop will open new perspectives about the understanding of their behavior beyond the mere description of their purchases.

For instance, Figure 2 represents the possible outcome of an experiment performed by using the recording of cerebral and emotional processes during the visit of a food store in two groups of consumers as described above (A and B). The x-axes of the Figure 2 present the predetermined path that all the participants of the groups A and B performed across the shop, while the y-axes represent the levels of the average cerebral appreciation for the persons belonging to the group A and B across different areas of the store

It could be appreciated that the different population have a similar appreciation profile but in the section in which a group could have different benefit from the other (e.g. section wines and liquor). It could be concluded that population A (normal customers) generated levels of appreciation lower than usual customers (group B) during a visit in the shop. Such information could be used by the management of the retail to promote specific actions to increase the level of satisfaction of the customers belongs to the A group.

Figure 2. Possible outcome

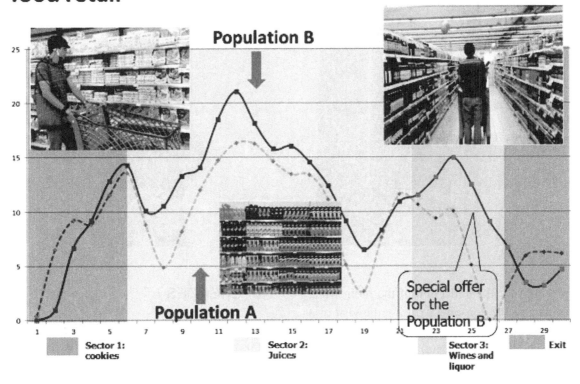

CONCLUSION AND FUTURE RESEARCH DIRECTIONS

In this chapter we have demonstrated the possibility to collect cerebral and emotional activity during the visit of a point of sale. The technology employed relies on the use of advanced indexes pointing at two particular psychological brain states, the appreciation/withdrawal from a stimulus and the emotion measured with the body markers, through EEG, EKG and GSR. Another important point is that in the present chapter a contribution to the literature of the estimation of the emotion from the collection of EKG and GSR has been described, through the use of the Equations 2-3. Such approach could return valuable information as derived from normal subjects visiting the point of sale.

It became evident that the possibility of measuring emotional and cerebral activity in consumer during their visit of the shop will open new areas of research in order to better understand the cerebral processes underlying the decision of purchase in the point of sale.

While up to some years ago such mobile measurements were cumbersome for the consumer, forced to bring with him/her a very heavy computer on the back of shoulder, today the situation appear much better. Lightweight devices are available for the measurements of the cerebral activity during the visit of shops or even museums and other educational or entertainment sites (such as cinemas, theatre, etc.) as demonstrated in the following Figure 3. In such Figure the equipment employed for the collection of cerebral and emotional activity during the visit of an art gallery is displayed.

Figure 3. Lightweight devices

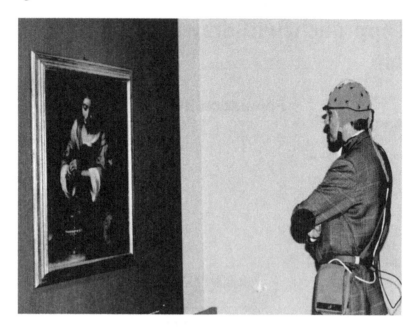

The future for the collection of the biometrical reactions of the consumers during the visit of a retail will be of very light (ideally of the size of a modern mobile smartphone) and will return even in real time the engage of the users during the shopping experience. Such amount of data will be of paramount importance to characterize from the "consumers" point of view the most interesting areas of the point of sale from the cerebral and from an emotional perspective.

ACKNOWLEDGMENT

This work was in part supported by a grant of the Italian Minister of Foreign Affairs with a bilateral project between Italy and China "Neuropredictor" and by a project supported by PRIN2012 to Fabio Babiloni and Giovanni Vecchiato.

REFERENCES

Armstrong, K. M., Fitzgerald, J. K., & Moore, T. (2006). Changes in visual receptive fields with microstimulation of frontal cortex. *Neuron, 50*(5), 791–798. doi:10.1016/j.neuron.2006.05.010 PMID:16731516

Babiloni, F., Mattia, D., Babiloni, C., Astolfi, L., Salinari, S., Basilisco, A., & Cincotti, F. et al. (2004). Multimodal integration of EEG, MEG and fMRI data for the solution of the neuroimage puzzle. *Magnetic Resonance Imaging, 22*(10), 1471–1476. doi:10.1016/j.mri.2004.10.007 PMID:15707796

Balconi, M., Brambilla, E., & Falbo, L. (2009). BIS/BAS, cortical oscillations and coherence in response to emotional cues. *Brain Research Bulletin, 80*(3), 151–157. doi:10.1016/j.brainres-bull.2009.07.001 PMID:19591907

Berridge, K. C. (1996). Food reward: Brain substrates of wanting and liking. *Neuroscience and Biobehavioral Reviews*, *20*(1), 1–25. doi:10.1016/0149-7634(95)00033-B PMID:8622814

Braeutigam, S., Rose, S. P., Swithenby, S. J., & Ambler, T. (2004). The distributed neuronal systems supporting choice-making in real-life situations: Differences between men and women when choosing groceries detected using magnetoencephalography. *The European Journal of Neuroscience*, *20*(1), 293–302. doi:10.1111/j.1460-9568.2004.03467.x PMID:15245501

Bush, G., Luu, P., & Posner, M. I. (2000). Cognitive and emotional influences in anterior cingulate cortex. *Trends in Cognitive Sciences*, *4*(6), 215–222. doi:10.1016/S1364-6613(00)01483-2 PMID:10827444

Cacioppo, J. T. (2002). Social neuroscience: Understanding the pieces fosters understanding the whole and vice versa. *The American Psychologist*, *57*(11), 819–831. doi:10.1037/0003-066X.57.11.819 PMID:12564179

Chartrand, T. L., & Bargh, J. A. (1999). The chameleon effect: The perception-behavior link and social interaction. *Journal of Personality and Social Psychology*, *76*(6), 893–910. doi:10.1037/0022-3514.76.6.893 PMID:10402679

Coricelli, G., Critchley, H. D., Joffily, M., O'Doherty, J. P., Sirigu, A., & Dolan, R. J. (2005). Regret and its avoidance: A neuroimaging study of choice behavior. *Nature Neuroscience*, *8*(9), 1255–1262. doi:10.1038/nn1514 PMID:16116457

Damasio, A. R., Everitt, B. J., & Bishop, D. (1996). The somatic marker hypothesis and the possible functions of the prefrontal cortex. *Philosophical Transactions of the Royal Society of London. Series B, Biological Sciences*, *351*(1346), 1413–1420. doi:10.1098/rstb.1996.0125 PMID:8941953

Davidson, R. J., Ekman, P., Saron, C. D., Senulis, J. A., & Friesen, W. V. (1990). Approach-withdrawal and cerebral asymmetry: Emotional expression and brain physiology. I. *Journal of Personality and Social Psychology*, *58*(2), 330–341. doi:10.1037/0022-3514.58.2.330 PMID:2319445

Davidson, R. J., Shackman, A. J., & Maxwell, J. S. (2004). Asymmetries in face and brain related to emotion. *Trends in Cognitive Sciences*, *8*(9), 389–391. doi:10.1016/j.tics.2004.07.006 PMID:15350238

Eichenbaum, H. (2000). A cortical-hippocampal system for declarative memory. *Nature Reviews. Neuroscience*, *1*(1), 41–50. doi:10.1038/35036213 PMID:11252767

Elliott, R., Dolan, R. J., & Frith, C. D. (2000). Dissociable functions in the medial and lateral orbitofrontal cortex: Evidence from human neuroimaging studies. *Cereb Cortex*, *10*(3), 308–317. doi:10.1093/cercor/10.3.308 PMID:10731225

Fields, H. L., Hjelmstad, G. O., Margolis, E. B., & Nicola, S. M. (2007). Ventral tegmental area neurons in learned appetitive behavior and positive reinforcement. *Annual Review of Neuroscience*, *30*(1), 289–316. doi:10.1146/annurev.neuro.30.051606.094341 PMID:17376009

Habib, R., Nyberg, L., & Tulving, E. (2003). Hemispheric asymmetries of memory: The HERA model revisited. *Trends in Cognitive Sciences*, *7*(6), 241–245. doi:10.1016/S1364-6613(03)00110-4 PMID:12804689

Harmon-Jones, E. (2003). Early career award. Clarifying the emotive functions of asymmetrical frontal cortical activity. *Psychophysiology*, *40*(6), 838–848. doi:10.1111/1469-8986.00121 PMID:14986837

Klimesch, W. (1999). EEG alpha and theta oscillations reflect cognitive and memory performance: A review and analysis. *Brain Research. Brain Research Reviews*, *29*(2-3), 169–195. doi:10.1016/S0165-0173(98)00056-3 PMID:10209231

Klimesch, W., Doppelmayr, M., & Hanslmayr, S. (2006). Upper alpha ERD and absolute power: Their meaning for memory performance. *Progress in Brain Research*, *159*(1), 151–165. doi:10.1016/S0079-6123(06)59010-7 PMID:17071229

Knutson, B., & Bossaerts, P. (2007). Neural antecedents of financial decisions. *The Journal of Neuroscience*, *27*(31), 8174–8177. doi:10.1523/JNEUROSCI.1564-07.2007 PMID:17670962

Knutson, B., Fong, G. W., Adams, C. M., Varner, J. L., & Hommer, D. (2001). Dissociation of reward anticipation and outcome with event-related fMRI. *Neuroreport*, *12*(17), 3683–3687. doi:10.1097/00001756-200112040-00016 PMID:11726774

Knutson, B., Rick, S., Wimmer, G. E., Prelec, D., & Loewenstein, G. (2007). Neural predictors of purchases. *Neuron*, *53*(1), 147–156. doi:10.1016/j.neuron.2006.11.010 PMID:17196537

Knutson, B., & Wimmer, G. E. (2007). Splitting the difference: How does the brain code reward episodes? *Annals of the New York Academy of Sciences*, *1*(1104), 54–69. doi:10.1196/annals.1390.020 PMID:17416922

Langleben, D.D., Loughead, J.W., Ruparel, K., Hakun, J.G., Busch-Winokur, S., Holloway, M.B., … Lerman, C. (2009). Reduced prefrontal and temporal processing and recall of high "sensation value" ads. *Neuroimage*, *46*(1), 219-25.

Maren, S., & Quirk, G. J. (2004). Neuronal signalling of fear memory. *Nature Reviews. Neuroscience*, *5*(11), 844–852. doi:10.1038/nrn1535 PMID:15496862

McGaugh, J. L. (2000). Memory-A century of consolidation. *Science*, *287*(5451), 248–251. doi:10.1126/science.287.5451.248 PMID:10634773

Montano, N., Porta, A., Cogliati, C., Costantino, G., Tobaldini, E., Casali, K. R., & Iellamo, F. (2009). Heart rate variability explored in the frequency domain: A tool to investigate the link between heart and behavior. *Neuroscience and Biobehavioral Reviews*, *33*(2), 71–80. doi:10.1016/j.neubiorev.2008.07.006 PMID:18706440

O'Doherty, J., Kringelbach, M. L., Rolls, E. T., Hornak, J., & Andrews, C. (2001). Abstract reward and punishment representations in the human orbitofrontal cortex. *Nature Neuroscience*, *4*(1), 95–102. doi:10.1038/82959 PMID:11135651

Panksepp, J., Nocjar, C., Burgdorf, J., Panksepp, J. B., & Huber, R. (2004). The role of emotional systems in addiction: A neuroethological perspective. *Nebraska Symposium on Motivation*, *50*(1), 85–126. PMID:15160639

Phan, K. L., Wager, T., Taylor, S. F., & Liberzon, I. (2002). Functional neuroanatomy of emotion: A meta-analysis of emotion activation studies in PET and fMRI. *NeuroImage*, *16*(2), 331–348. doi:10.1006/nimg.2002.1087 PMID:12030820

Plassmann, H., Zoëga Ramsøy, T., & Milosavljevic, M. (2012). Branding the brain: A critical review and outlook. *Journal of Consumer Psychology*, *5*(1), 85–115.

Preuschoff, K., Quartz, S. R., & Bossaerts, P. (2008). Human insula activation reflects risk prediction errors as well as risk. *The Journal of Neuroscience*, *28*(11), 2745–2752. doi:10.1523/JNEUROSCI.4286-07.2008 PMID:18337404

Rilling, J. K., King-Casas, B., & Sanfey, A. G. (2008). The neurobiology of social decision-making. *Current Opinion in Neurobiology*, *18*(2), 159–165. doi:10.1016/j.conb.2008.06.003 PMID:18639633

Rilling, J. K., & Sanfey, A. G. (2011). The neuroscience of social decision-making. *Annual Review of Psychology*, *62*(1), 23–48. doi:10.1146/annurev.psych.121208.131647 PMID:20822437

Russell, J. A., & Barrett, L. F. (1999). Core affect, prototypical emotional episodes, and other things called emotion: Dissecting the elephant. *Journal of Personality and Social Psychology*, *76*(5), 805–819. doi:10.1037/0022-3514.76.5.805 PMID:10353204

Tremblay, L., & Schultz, W. (1999). Relative reward preference in primate orbitofrontal cortex. *Nature*, *398*(6729), 704–708. doi:10.1038/19525 PMID:10227292

Vecchiato, G., De Vico Fallani, F., Astolfi, L., Toppi, J., Cincotti, F., Mattia, D., & Babiloni, F. et al. (2010). The issue of multiple univariate comparisons in the context of neuroelectric brain mapping: An application in a neuromarketing experiment. *Journal of Neuroscience Methods*, *191*(2), 283–289. doi:10.1016/j.jneumeth.2010.07.009 PMID:20637802

Wallis, J. D. (2007). Orbitofrontal cortex and its contribution to decision-making. *Annual Review of Neuroscience*, *30*(1), 31–56. doi:10.1146/annurev.neuro.30.051606.094334 PMID:17417936

Werkle-Bergner, M., Müller, V., Li, S. C., & Lindenberger, U. (2006). Cortical EEG correlates of successful memory encoding: Implications for lifespan comparisons. *Neuroscience and Biobehavioral Reviews*, *30*(6), 839–854. doi:10.1016/j.neubiorev.2006.06.009 PMID:16904180

Wilson, M. A. (2002). Hippocampal memory formation, plasticity, and the role of sleep. *Neurobiology of Learning and Memory*, *78*(3), 565–569. doi:10.1006/nlme.2002.4098 PMID:12559835

Wise, R. A., & Rompre, P. P. (1989). Brain dopamine and reward. *Annual Review of Psychology*, *40*(1), 191–225. doi:10.1146/annurev.ps.40.020189.001203 PMID:2648975

Zar, J. H. (2000). *Biostatistical analysis*. New York: Prentice Hall.

ADDITIONAL READING

Giovanni Vecchiato. (2013). *Arianna Trettel, Patrizia Cherubino and Fabio Babiloni, Neuroelectrical Brain Imaging Tools for the Study of the Efficacy of TV Advertising Stimuli and their Application to Neuromarketing*. Springer International.

Stephen Genco. (2013). *Andrew Pohlmann, Peter Steidl, Neuromarketing For Dummies*. Wiley.

Thomas Ramsoy. (2014). *Introduction to Neuromarketing & Consumer Neuroscience*. Kindle Edition.

KEY TERMS AND DEFINITIONS

Electroencephalography: (**EEG**): The recording of electrical activity along the scalp. EEG measures voltage fluctuations resulting from ionic current flows within the neurons of the brain.

Emotion: In psychology and philosophy, emotion is a subjective, conscious experience characterized primarily by psychophysiological expressions, biological reactions, and mental states. Emotion is often associated and considered reciprocally influential with mood, temperament, personality, disposition, and motivation.

Eyetracker: A non-invasive device able to follow the human eye-gaze during the exploration of a picture, a shelf or other goods. Mobile eye-tracker are wear on the head as glass while non-portable eyetracker devices are solidal with the computer screen.

Eyetracking: The process of measuring either the point of gaze (where one is looking) or the motion of an eye relative to the head.

Functional Magnetic Resonance Imaging or Functional MRI (fMRI): A functional neuroimaging procedure using Magnetic Resonance Imaging technology that measures brain activity by detecting associated changes in blood flow. This technique relies on the fact that cerebral blood flow and neuronal activation are coupled.

Neuromarketing: A new field of marketing research that studies consumers' sensorimotor, cognitive, and affective response to marketing stimuli.

Neuroscience: The scientific study of the nervous system. Traditionally, neuroscience has been seen as a branch of biology. However, it is currently an interdisciplinary science that collaborates with other fields such as chemistry, computer science, engineering, linguistics, mathematics, medicine and allied disciplines, philosophy, physics, and psychology.

Section 2
Consumers' and Employees' Behaviour, Adoption, and Acceptance

The chapters included in this section provide an overview of the response towards the introduction of technology-based innovations from both consumers' and employees' perspectives. In particular, this section describes their behaviour in terms of adoption and acceptance, decision-making process, and store/channel choice.

Chapter 5
Determinants of Consumers' Mobile Coupon Adoption:
A Critical Review of Theories and Literature

Hyunjoo Im
University of Minnesota – Twin Cities, USA

Young Ha
California State University – Long Beach, USA

ABSTRACT

Mobile technology is becoming a critical part of marketing practices and many retailers aim to engage consumers through mobile coupons. In this context, it is critical to understand what drives consumers to use mobile coupons. Technology adoption research offers insights for both researchers and practitioners into this matter. This chapter critically reviews guiding theories, Technology Acceptance Theory and Innovation Diffusion Theory, as well as important literature on technology adoption to discuss evolution and application of technology adoption research. Five perception variables (perceived usefulness, perceived ease of use, perceived enjoyment, subjective norm, compatibility) and three individual characteristics (personal innovativeness, perceived risk, gender) are selected as most relevant determinants of consumers' intention to adopt and use mobile coupons. Limitation of technology adoption research and possible future research avenues are discussed.

INTRODUCTION

With nearly 56% of US adults being smartphone users (Smith, 2013), retailers now acknowledge the importance of integrating mobile technology into marketing. Emergence of mobile technology enables retailers to communicate with consum-

ers in an innovative way, and retailers develops various mobile marketing practices including SMS (Short Message Service) messages, mobile applications, mobile coupons, and other location-based services. As consumers become increasingly resistant to marketing messages, the effectiveness of traditional mass marketing techniques has

DOI: 10.4018/978-1-4666-8297-9.ch005

been questioned. To overcome this challenge, retailers are turning to mobile marketing. Mobile marketing messages can be highly personalized with the content of information and the timing (Scharl, Dickinger, & Murphy, 2005). The fact that consumers are rarely parted from their phones makes mobile marketing ubiquitous and personal (Karjaluoto, Jayawardhena, Kuckertz, & Kautonen, 2008). Moreover, with GPS capability, mobile phones allow retailers to send information to potential consumers based on the actual location of the devices, which retailers can use to increase relevance of information. Because of these advantages, mobile marketing is viewed as a more effective tool than other marketing methods (Dickinger & Kleijnen, 2008; Shankar, Venkatesh, Hofacker, & Naik, 2010). Recent statistics on mobile marketing practices seem to provide support for the superiority of mobile marketing over others. Ninety-eight percent of consumers who receive SMS marketing messages open the messages while only 22 percent read email marketing messages (Wachs, 2013). As consumers have access to the Internet almost all the time, 90% of shoppers with smartphones use their mobile phones while shopping at a brick-and-mortar store to compare prices, find deals and coupons, read product reviews, or communicate with friends (eMarketer, 2013).

Among mobile marketing practices, mobile couponing is particularly promising. Mobile coupons are digital coupons delivered to mobile devices of consumers for monetary benefits to encourage consumers to purchase a product or service (MMA, 2007). Mobile coupons, just like traditional paper-based coupons, promote sales. However, mobile coupons possess different characteristics from the traditional coupons. Unlike the traditional coupons that require considerable time and effort for searching and clipping, mobile coupons are delivered to the devices and easily stored in the devices. Consumers can actively visit a retailer's website or search the web to download coupons that they are interested in. Some consum-

ers install mobile applications that push coupons to them based on their interests and locations. As these examples illustrate, downloading, saving, and redeeming the mobile coupons is much easier and more convenient than clipping and remembering to carry traditional coupons (Sharl et al., 2005), and researchers have expected mobile coupons would be far more successful than traditional paper-based coupons (Shankar et al., 2010; Sharl et al., 2005). Indeed, mobile coupons enjoy a higher redemption rate (10%) than traditional coupons (1% or less) (Juniper Research, 2012). About one third of consumers who received mobile coupons are likely to visit brick-and-mortar stores for apparel, electronics, and consumer packaged goods (ROI Research Inc., & Microsoft, 2011), which presents retailers with opportunities to engage and increase contacts with target consumers. Mobile coupons also can lure consumers to the retail stores because GPS-enabled mobile devices allow retailers to offer mobile coupons when consumers are near their retail stores (Okazaki & Taylor, 2008). Another important benefit of mobile coupons is the consumer data mobile coupons supply retailers with. With mobile coupons, retailers not only can drive sales by attracting the consumers to their stores but also can obtain an accurate data of the customers who visited and redeemed the coupons (Olenski, 2013). Therefore, it is apparent that retailers need to incorporate mobile coupons into their marketing communication strategy. However, some consumers do not still respond to the mobile coupons, and it is necessary to understand what determines consumers' decision to adopt mobile coupons so that retailers can design and distribute mobile coupons to maximize benefits from these opportunities.

The current chapter is to discuss theoretical models and complex factors that guide us to understand consumers' decisions to use mobile technology, particularly mobile coupons. In this chapter, mobile couponing is viewed as a part of new technology and the focus is on the key issues related to mobile technology and technology adoption. Understanding consumer intention to use mobile technology in a retail context provides a valuable insight for retailers who face rapid changes in the omni-channel environment.

Two theories, Technology Acceptance Model and Innovation Diffusion Theory, have been used to explain why individuals adopt a technology or innovation. Because mobile couponing is a new technology/innovation, it is reasonable to rely on these two popular theories to investigate reasons why individuals do or do not adopt mobile coupons. In this chapter, these theories are reviewed to discuss the core concepts and assumptions as well as how the theories have been modified and extended over time. Then, the determinants of consumers' technology adoption were identified in the context of mobile coupons based on two theories and previous literature. The chapter particularly highlights the beliefs, perceptions and personal trait variables that affect individuals' decisions to adopt mobile coupons, and summarizes their relationships and examines some inconsistent findings from previous literature. The chapter concludes with a summary of discussions, limitations of technology adoption research and future research avenues.

THEORETICAL BASIS

In order to predict consumers' adoption of mobile coupons, researchers often resorted to two theories, Technology Acceptance Model and Innovation Diffusion Theory. Mobile technology is still relatively new, and not all consumers have adopted the technology. Mobile coupon users need to be comfortable in using smartphone functions to some degree. There are two major ways for consumers to obtain mobile coupons. First, consumers can initiate the search for coupons, and browse and download the coupons via the internet browser on their mobile devices. Second, consumers can purchase mobile applications that provide mobile coupons based on consumers' needs. For this

method, consumers should be able to know how to find the applications from the mobile application store and to install the application. Therefore, the ability to use smartphones is a necessary condition for mobile coupon usage. Although the number of smart phone users grew steadily worldwide for the past few years (eMarketer, 2014), some consumers may not use mobile coupons because of their inability to use smartphones. Thus, mobile marketing and mobile couponing can be considered as a technology or an innovation from the consumer's perspective.

Technology Acceptance Model (TAM)

Technology Acceptance Model (TAM) is an individual's motivational model that explains a user's adoption of a technology. Conceptually, an individual's decision to use an information system is triggered by the user's motivation to use the system. Davis (1985) proposed that subjective evaluation of characteristics of a system determines the level of motivation to use the system, which, in turn, predicts actual use of the system. Grounded on Theory of Reasoned Action, Davis (1989) developed TAM, a simple motivational model that explains one's acceptance of a system with his/her beliefs about the characteristics of the system, attitudes towards the system, and behavioral intention. TAM posits actual adoption of a technology is dependent on two beliefs, namely, perceived ease of use and perceived usefulness. That is, a user decides to adopt a new system when he/she perceives the system is easy to use and useful. These perceptions/beliefs regarding the system are proposed to form either favorable or unfavorable attitude towards using the system, which subsequently predicts behavioral intention and actual usage. The author also proposed that perceived ease of use positively influences perceived usefulness. This initial model was later simplified by dropping attitude because the empirical data suggested beliefs (i.e., perceived usefulness and perceived ease of use) directly

Figure 1. Variations of TAM

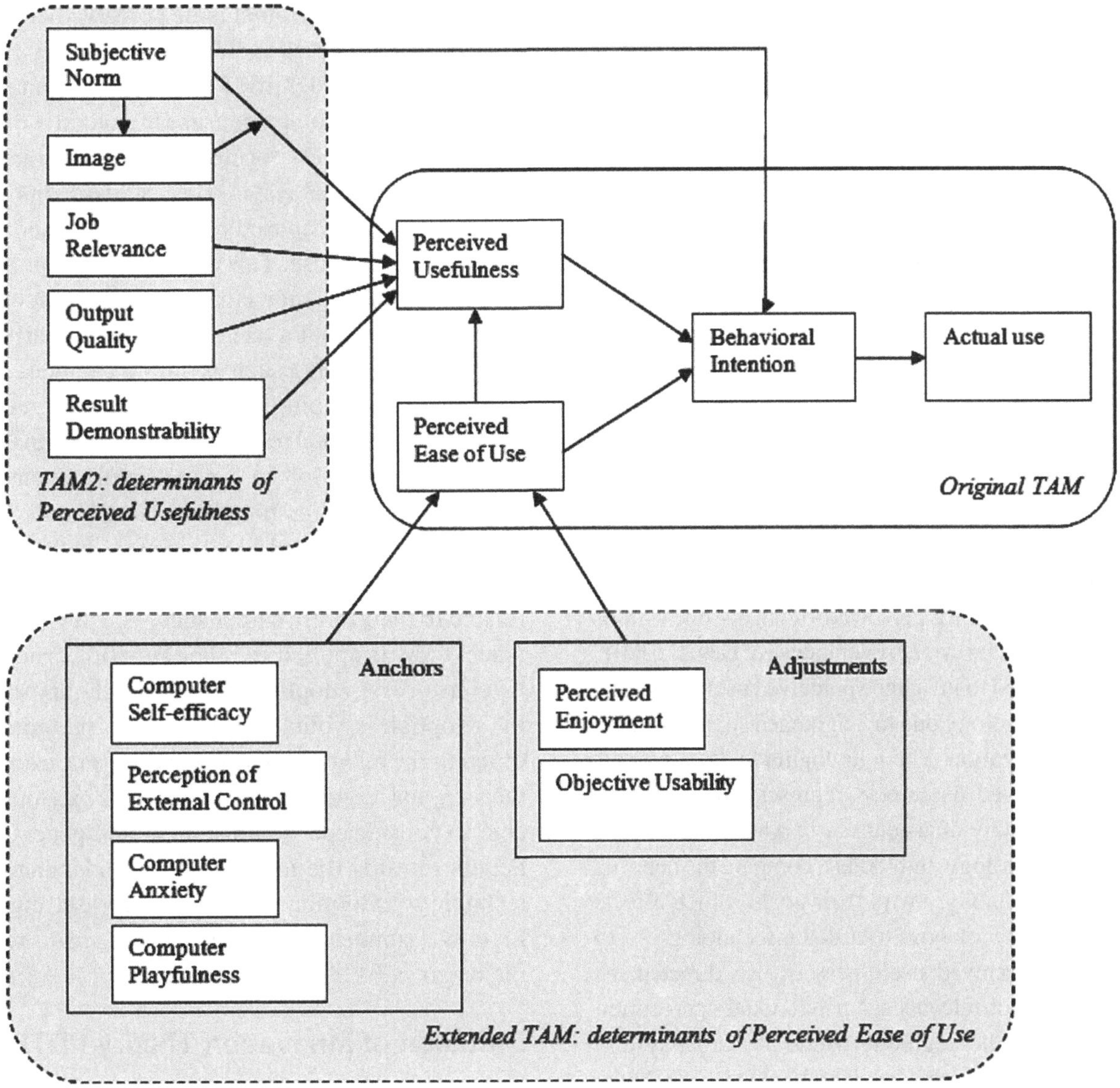

predicted behavioral intention without mediation of attitude (Venkatesh & Davis, 1996). Numerous researchers used this refined TAM as a theoretical basis when investigating system adoption (see the original TAM in Figure 1).

TAM is a widely accepted framework for technology adoption research, with the article presented the model being cited over 20,000 times (Davis, 1989). The model has proven itself to be effective and robust by being adopted in a myriad of technology adoption contexts. Despite of the broad applicability of TAM, researchers have also acknowledged that TAM is limited in its predictive power because of its parsimony. The simple nature of the model prevented researchers from identifying the reasons why beliefs are formed. Also, the model fails to capture hedonic motivation of consumers. Therefore, efforts were made to extend TAM to increase the specificity of the model to be able to provide ways to facilitate individuals' technology adoption.

One such effort is TAM2, an extended TAM developed by Venkatesh and Davis (2000). Recognizing the importance of identifying determinants of perceived usefulness, they attended to social influence and cognitive assessment. They proposed three social factors (i.e., subjective norm, voluntariness, and image) and four cognitive determinants (job relevance, output quality, result demonstrability, and perceived ease of use) that influence perceived usefulness (see Figure 1). TAM2 suggests that perceived usefulness of a technology is affected by social pressure. Subjective norm, a belief that important others think what he/she should do, has been an important predictor of behavioral intention (Fishbein & Azjen, 1975). Voluntariness refers to the context of technology adoption – whether the users were forced to adopt a technology or not. Image, "the degree to which use of an innovation is perceived to enhance one's status in one's social system (Venkatesh & Davis, 2000)" is proposed to influence perceived usefulness of a new technology due to heightened social status in an organization. The four cognitive determinants of perceived usefulness represent the cognitive process individuals engage in when evaluating a new technology. Individuals compare the benefits of the technology with their goals, which affects their belief of how useful the technology is to them. Perceived usefulness is also directed affected by job relevance, "an individual's perception regarding the degree to which the target system is applicable to his/her job (Venkatesh & Davis, 2000)", and output quality, "how well the technology performs (Venkatesh & Davis, 2000)". Result demonstrability "the tangibility of the results of using the innovation (Moore & Benbasat, 1991)" affects perceived usefulness because individuals can clearly see what adoption of the new technology can do. The authors tested TAM2 for three different time periods and in diverse contexts to test the model in both voluntary and mandatory information system adoption situations. They confirmed the importance of subjective norm, particularly in a mandatory setting.

In addition, Venkatesh (2000) extended TAM by identifying determinants of perceived ease of use. In the extended TAM, two groups of determinants are identified to address personal beliefs regarding computer usage in general (i.e., anchors) and beliefs formed through interaction with the target system (i.e., adjustments). Both beliefs are proposed to influence a user's perceived ease of use. This extended TAM provides more insights for intrinsic motivation of individuals to adopt a technology, particularly in a voluntary setting such as online commerce and mobile shopping. Because the original TAM was developed to explain users' information system adoption in a work environment, the adoption was assumed mandatory. Also, individuals' successful adoption of the technology and increasing job performance is directly related to their future career success. However, when TAM is applied to other situations such as consumers' adoption of mobile shopping, the adoption is voluntary. Moreover, the goal of using the technology is quite different from the original context. Thus, it seems reasonable to consider personality traits and general beliefs towards the technology to understand technology adoption in a voluntary setting. Figure 1 summarizes modifications made to the original TAM.

Diffusion of Innovation Theory (IDT)

Even though TAM has been used broadly to illustrate the adoption of a new information technology, its parsimony is found to be a major limitation. Since Rogers' (2003) diffusion of innovation theory (IDT) suggests a more comprehensive set of perceived characteristics of a new technology, it is eligible to provide valuable insights into the factors influencing mobile coupon service adoption.

Rogers' (2003) diffusion of innovation theory proposes the innovation decision-making process (DMP) describing five stages of technology adoption:

1. Knowledge,
2. Persuasion,
3. Decision,
4. Implementation, and
5. Confirmation.

Five stages illustrate how a consumer recognizes a new technology, develops an attitude toward it, adopts it, implements the decision, and confirms the decision.

According to the DMP (Rogers, 2003), in the knowledge stage, an individual recognizes the existence of a new technology (e.g., mobile coupon service) and obtains knowledge of the technology. Here, personal variables such as personal innovativeness, gender, subjective norm, and previous experience, play an important role. Consumers may be seeking information regarding a new technology in accordance with their existing situations and personal needs and interests. For example, consumers with high level of innovativeness may obtain the knowledge of mobile coupon services earlier than those with low level of innovativeness. More specific information related to each personal variable will be discussed in the later sections (see the section 'determinants of technology adoption').

In the persuasion stage, consumers become more emotionally involved with the technology as they form positive or negative attitudes toward it based on the information obtained in the knowledge stage. How consumers interpret the information received during the knowledge stage affects attitude formation. Therefore, evaluating perceived characteristics of the new technology becomes especially important in developing positive or negative attitudes toward the technology in the persuasion stage. Consumers may mentally relate the new technology to their current or future situation and evaluate its perceived characteristics before deciding to adopt or reject it. The key outcome of the persuasion stage in the DMP is an attitude (either positive or negative) toward the new technology.

The DMP emphasizes the importance of five perceived characteristics evaluated by consumers during the persuasion stage:

1. Relative advantage (i.e., usefulness in TAM),
2. Compatibility,
3. Complexity (i.e., ease of use in TAM),
4. Trialability, and
5. Observability (Rogers, 2003).

'Relative advantage' measures the degree of advantages or disadvantages gained from the use of a new technology. It is often expressed as the usefulness of the new technology in TAM (Davis, 1989; Moore & Benbasat, 1991). If consumers perceive the new option (e.g., mobile coupon service) to be more useful than currently available options (e.g., paper coupons, online coupon code), a positive attitude will be formed toward the new option. 'Compatibility' designates the fit between the new option and the existing situations and beliefs. If consumers find that the new technology is compatible with their current lifestyles and their needs and interests, there will be a great possibility to adopt such option rapidly. 'Complexity' deals with the easiness of using the new technology. If the new technology is difficult to use, its adoption level will be low. 'Trialability' is the degree to which the new technology can be available for trial. If consumers have a chance to experiment with the new option and find out how it works, they may feel more comfortable using such option and easier to adopt it in the future. 'Observability' is related to the visibility of the new technology to others. If the results of adopting the new technology are easily observed and communicated to others, its adoption rate will be fast (Rogers, 2003). Previous research (Moore & Benbasat, 1991; Tornatzky & Klein, 1982) confirmed that relative advantage (usefulness), compatibility, and complexity (ease of use) are more reliable contributors than trialability and observability to consumer adoption across a broad range of technology types. When the new

Figure 2. Five stages of the Decision Making Process (DMP)

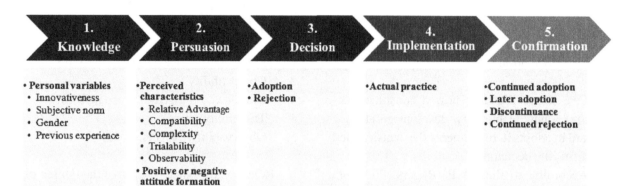

technology is perceived to be easy to use, useful, and compatible with an individual's current needs and lifestyle, more favorable attitudes will be developed.

In the decision stage, consumers may decide to adopt or reject the target technology in accordance with their attitude formed in the persuasion stage. Consumers who formed positive attitude toward the technology may decide to make full use of it, whereas those with negative attitude may decide not to adopt the technology. Recent research confirms that attitudes toward mobile coupon services positively influence consumers' intention to use mobile coupon services in the future (Ha & Im, 2014).

Once the decision is being made, in the implementation stage, consumers put their decision into actual practice (e.g., actual use of mobile coupon service for shopping). At this stage, consumers may still have a certain level of uncertainty about the consequences of the new technology, which will lead to active information seeking to answer further questions about the new option (e.g., what problems am I going to encounter when I use mobile coupon services? and how can I solve them?).

In the confirmation stage, consumers seek reinforcement for the decision previously made and may alter their decision if exposed to contradictory messages about the new technology. Therefore, discontinuance or later adoption of

the technology may occur during this stage of the decision process. In general, consumers are looking for information that will support the decision already made (an example of selective exposure) to prevent dissonance. Figure 2 illustrates the decision making process (DMP) adopted for the mobile coupon service adoption.

DETERMINANTS OF TECHNOLOGY ADOPTION

Both TAM and IDT have served researchers over years in identifying major determinants of users' technology adoption. The main determinants were often directly drawn from these theories in the previous research, but researchers also recognized a need to expand the set of antecedents. Researchers have incorporated additional determinants to these theoretical models to explain technology adoption in a wide range of situations such as healthcare professionals' adoption of PDA (Yi, Fiedler, & Park, 2006), information system adoption in an organization (Karahanna, Straub, & Chervany, 1999; Venkatesh & Davis, 2000), word processing software adoption (Davis, Bagozzi, & Warshaw, 1989), online shopping adoption (Yi et al., 2006), adoption of wireless technology for job performance (Yen, Wu, Cheng, & Huang, 2010) and computer-based assessment adoption

Table 1. Beliefs/perception scales: PU and PEOU

Construct	Item
Perceive Usefulness (Agarwal & Prasad, 1998)	Using XXX would make it easier to do my work.
	Using XXX would help me to accomplish tasks more quickly.
	Using XXX would improve the quality of the work I do.
	Using XXX would give me greater control over my work.
	Using XXX would enhance my effectiveness in the MBA program and/or my job.
Relative Advantage (Karahanna et al., 1999)	If I were to adopt XXX, it would enable me to accomplish my tasks more quickly.
	If I were to adopt XXX, the quality of my work would improve.
	If I were to adopt XXX, it would enhance my effectiveness on the job.
	If I were to adopt XXX, it would make my job easier.
Ease of Use (Agarwal & Prasad, 1998)	My interaction with XXX is clear and understandable.
	I believe it would be easy to get XXX to do what I want it to do.
	Overall, I believe XXX would be easy to use.
	Learning to use XXX would be easy for me.
Perceived Ease of Use (Venkatesh & Davis, 2000)	My intention with XXX is clear and understandable.
	Interacting with XXX does not require a lot of my mental effort.
	I find XXX to be easy to use. I find it easy to get XXX to do what I want it to do.

Note. Specific technologies in the scales are replaced by XXX. Some items were designed to address a system adoption within an organization. In consumer research, it is advised to modify the items to be applicable to shopping situations.

in e-learning (Park, 2009; Terzis & Economides, 2011). As a result, technology adoption literature has introduced numerous determinants of technology adoption in addition to the variables identified by TAM and IDT. The following section highlights the findings from the previous technology adoption research by discussing selected determinants that are most important and relevant to the context of mobile coupon adoption.

Perceptions/Beliefs about Mobile Coupons and the Technology

Perceived Usefulness/ Relative Advantage

Perceived usefulness is one of two key determinants of technology acceptance in TAM. Perceived usefulness (PU) is defined as "the prospective user's subjective probability that using a specific application system will increase his or her job performance within an organizational context (Davis et al., 1989)". This construct is very goal-oriented and similar to relative advantage from IDT (see Table 1 to compare measurement items). Both PU and relative advantage refer to the degree of an individual's belief that adopting the target technology would be beneficial when compared with the current situation (Yi et al., 2006). Research consistently found that perceived usefulness or relative advantage predicts technology adoption (e.g., Moore & Benbasat, 1991).

Although perceived usefulness in the early TAM research was understood in the context of job performance, it can be applied to the consumer context. When consumers believe a new technology helps them to achieve their goals, they are likely to develop positive attitudes toward the target technology. Because consumers' goals (e.g., finding the product of interest, purchasing the right product) are not as critical as job performance, perceived usefulness may become less significant in making a technology adoption decision. However, all consumers are driven to accomplish their shopping goals. Thus, it is reasonable to believe that perceived usefulness is an important determinant of technology adoption in a retail context.

Previous research confirmed the significance of PU in technology adoption in various situations. It has been noted that PU is the most important determinant of technology adoption in diverse research settings such as when the new technology is for jobs (Yi, Jackson, Park, & Probst, 2006), businesses (Yen et al., 2010), online auction shopping (Stern, Royne, Stafford, & Bienstock, 2008), and mobile marketing (Rohm, Gao, Sultan, & Pagani, 2012). Particularly, in the context of mobile service adoption, PU is found to be a critical predictor of consumers' attitude toward mobile service adoption (Shankar et al., 2010).

Perceived Ease of Use/Complexity

Perceived ease of use (PEOU) is the other belief variable from TAM which predicts one's adoption of a new technology. PEOU is defined as "the degree to which the prospective user expects the target system to be free of effort (Davis et al., 1989)". PEOU addresses the issue of complexity of a technology in IDT. A complex technology will be perceived as more difficult to use, reducing PEOU. Thus, PEOU and complexity will be inversely related. It was conceived that PEOU directly predicts PU because an easy-to-use technology would be less difficult to use and adopt, which would help a user enhance job performance (and thus, the technology becomes useful) (Venkatesh & Davis, 2000).

PEOU was found to have less impact as users get used to the technology (Karahanna et al., 1999). Although the majority of research finding suggests a stronger influence of PU than PEOU on behavioral intention, a recent study investigating

mobile coupon adoption intention reported an opposite result (Im & Ha, 2013). The importance of PU is drawn from the goal, whether it is to perform a job or to complete a shopping task. The context of mobile coupon adoption is different from this traditional notion of tasks because the decision to receive mobile coupons does not necessarily lead to actual purchases. Consumers can decide to receive coupons for potential future shopping trips or for informational purposes without committing to purchases. The decision is relatively casual and care-free because there is not as much financial and social risk involved. Similarly, in a study that investigated consumers' intention to adopt handheld internet devices for personal uses, Bruner and Kumar (2005) reported a significant importance of PEOU in predicting PU and a positive affect, fun, which was the strongest predictor of attitude towards adoption. Thus, the inconsistent result in the mobile coupon context may suggest the importance of PEOU in the unique situation.

Compatibility/Job Relevance

Compatibility, the degree to which an individual believes a technology to be compatible with his/her needs and values, is a perceived characteristic of an innovation. Compatibility, along with relative advantage and complexity, is one of three innovation characteristics drawn from IDT that are consistently found to predict innovation adoption (Yi et al., 2006). Compatibility is analogous to job relevance, one of four cognitive instrumental determinants of PU in TAM2 proposed by Venkatesh and Davis (2000). People assess usefulness of a technology by evaluating a match between the goals and projected results of using the technology. Thus, job relevance, "an individual's perception regarding the degree to which the target system is applicable to his or her job" (Venkatesh & Davis, 2000) closely resembles compatibility of a technology with one's work or life. Others (Yen et al., 2010) have employed task-technology fit (TTF) to address the fit between a technology and

Table 2. Beliefs/perceptions scales: compatibility and PE

Construct	Item
Compatibility (Agarwal & Prasad, 1998)	Using XXX would be compatible with all aspects of my work.
	I think that using XXX would fit well with the way I like to work.
	Using XXX would fit into my workstyle.
Compatibility (Ha & Im, 2014)	Mobile coupon services fit into my shopping style.
	Mobile coupon services fit well with the way I like to shop.
Job Relevance (Venkatesh & Davis, 2000)	In my job, usage of the system is important.
	In my job, usage of the system is relevant.
Task-Technology fit (Yen et al., 2010)	The data that I use or would like to use is accurate enough for my purposes.
	I can get data quickly and easily when I need it.
	It is easy to get assistance when I am having trouble finding or using data.
	The computer systems that give me access to data are convenient and easy to use.
Perceived Enjoyment (Venkatesh, 2000)	I find using XXX to be enjoyable.
	The actual process of using XXX is pleasant.
	I have fun using XXX.
Perceived Enjoyment (Van der Heijen, 2004)	Enjoyable – Disgusting
	Exciting – Dull
	Pleasant – Unpleasant
	Interesting – Boring
Perceived Enjoyment (Ha & Im, 2014)	Using m-coupon services for shopping would make me feel good.
	Using m-coupon services for shopping would be exciting.
	Using m-coupon services for shopping would be enjoyable.
Note. Specific technologies in the scales are replaced by XXX. Some items were designed to address a system adoption within an organization. In consumer research, it is advised to modify the items to be applicable to shopping situations. See the scales by Ha & Im (2014) for example.	

users' tasks. A close fit suggests that a technology corresponds to an individual's task and assists him/her to perform the tasks well. Naturally, a close fit will lead to a higher chance of adopting the technology because the technology will be perceived useful. Table 2 presents scales used to measure these related constructs.

Early adopters perceive a higher level of compatibility with a new technology than late adopters (Yi et al., 2006), which suggests the importance of compatibility in adoption decisions. Conceptually, compatibility will positively influence PU because the match between the goals and the technology will make individuals perceive the technology to be useful. Previous research (e.g.

Moore & Benbasat, 1991) has also supported the positive relationships between compatibility and TAM belief variables, PEOU and PU. Also, researchers have demonstrated the direct effect of compatibility on attitude towards a technology and adoption of the technology (e.g. Agarwal & Prasad, 1997; Gopal, Bostrom, & Chin, 1992). Jackson, Yi, and Park (2013) found that compatibility, among five innovation characteristics from IDT, is the strongest predictor of intention to adopt the e-commerce systems in the healthcare industry.

Ha and Im (2014) found that consumers' perception of compatibility of mobile coupons with their shopping goals and shopping styles was the most important determinant of mobile coupon adoption. In their study, compatibility was the single most powerful belief/perception predictor of attitude towards mobile coupons and intention to adopt the technology. Thus, results suggest that retailers must fully understand consumers' shopping goals and styles when developing and designing mobile services.

Perceived Enjoyment

Although utilitarian perceptions of a new technology (e.g., perceived usefulness and ease of use) seem to be important determinants of technology adoption, they may not be sufficient to offer comprehensive understanding of consumers' adoption of the new technology (Childers, Carr, Peck, & Carson, 2001; Ha & Im, 2014). Some individuals may decide to adopt a new technology due to its usefulness and easiness while others may adopt it because it is enjoyable to use. Moreover, consumers may have different motivations to adopt a technology designed to be used for personal leisure as opposed to a technology for work (Van der Heijen, 2004). Therefore, understanding how both utilitarian and hedonic aspects of perceived characteristics of a technology influence consumers' adoption is deemed important. However, both the original TAM and IDT are unable to offer enough discussions about hedonic aspects of perceived characteristics. Researchers have suggested perceived enjoyment (PE), defined as the extent to which new technology usage is perceived to be enjoyable, as a hedonic factor determining consumers' decision to adopt or reject a new technology (Chutter, 2009).

The extended TAMs propose that PE is a major determinant of PEOU (Chutter, 2009; Venkatesh, 2000). When consumers enjoy using a technology, they may underestimate its difficulty and perceive it easy to use (Celik, 2011; Fagan, Neil, & Wooldridge, 2008) and develop positive attitudes toward it (Nysveen, Pedersen, & Thorbjornsen, 2005; Yang, 2010). Importantly, it was found that PE and PEOU outweigh PU in predicting inten-

tion to use a technology when the system itself is meant to serve a hedonic purpose (Van der Heijden, 2004). In the context of mobile coupon service adoption, a recent study (Ha & Im, 2014) demonstrated that PE is a critical determinant of PEOU and attitude toward using mobile coupon services. This indicates that more enjoyable mobile services would decrease perceived complexity and develop more positive attitude toward using such services. Therefore, providing intrinsically pleasant elements and functions in mobile services is critical as they influence consumers' attitude formation and increase the adoption of new mobile services.

Subjective Norm

Subjective norm is "the perceived social pressure to perform or not to perform the behavior (Ajzen, 1991, p. 188)." As an established behavioral pattern, the norm serves as a guide for the behavior of individuals within the social system and tells individuals what behaviors are permissible or not permissible (Rogers, 2003). If a new technology is inconsistent with the norm of a social system (behaviors expected by friends, family and the society), its adoption will take longer than the one that is consistent with the norm (Rogers, 2003). Subjective norm is related to Image from TAM2 because individuals often comply with the norms to maintain a positive image of themselves (Venkatesh & Davis, 2000). When adoption of a technology is identified with a desirable image, subjective norm can influence the image an individual projects and, therefore, positively affects PU because technology usage heightens their social image (Yi et al., 2006).

Originally, subjective norm was not included in TAM because the conceptualization and the available measure of subjective norm did not allow researchers to model the exact underlying process of subjective norm effects on behavioral intention (Davis et al., 1989). Three different social influence processes can drive subjective

Table 3. Scales related to social influence

		Item
Subjective Norm	David et al. (1989)	XXX (referent) thinks that I should(1) – should not(7) [do the behavior]
Subjective Norm	Karahanna et al. (1999)	Most people who are important to me think I should adopt XXX.
Subjective Norm	Venkatesh & Davis (2000)	People who influence my behavior think that I should use XXX.
		People who are important to me think that I should use XXX.
Subjective Norm	Yi et al. (2006)	People whose opinions I value prefer me to use XXX in my work.
		At work, my colleagues who are important to me think that I should use XXX.
		At work, my superiors think that I should use XXX.
		At work, my subordinates think that I should use XXX.
Image	Karahanna et al. (1999)	If I were to adopt XXX, it would give me high status in the organization.
		If I were to adopt XXX, I would have more prestige in the organization than people who have not yet adopted it.
		Having XXX is a status symbol in my organization.
Image	Venkatesh & Davis (2000)	People in my organization who use XXX have more prestige than those who do not.
		People in my organization who use XXX have a high profile.
		Having XXX is a status symbol in my organization.

Note. Specific technologies in the scales are replaced by XXX. Some items were designed to address a system adoption within an organization. In consumer research, it is advised to modify the items to be applicable to shopping situations.

norm effects: internalization, identification, and compliance (Karahanna et al., 1999). One may feel the pressure from the manager to adopt a technology at work (i.e., compliance), but one may also internalize the expectation from others and change their beliefs about the technology (i.e., internalization). Or one may feel some connection with others and work to make those likable others happy (i.e., identification). The readily available subjective norm measures do not differentiate these different kinds of social influences (see Table 3). Davis and colleagues (1989) failed to find a direct effect of subjective norm on behavioral intention in their study and reasoned that the study context (i.e., adoption of word processing software) and the weakness of subjective norm measurement might have been the reasons why the social influence was not supported.

However, researchers continued to investigate the influence of subjective norm in technology adoption due to its conceptual importance in the process. Many researchers were interested in a technology adoption scenario where individual employees were forced to adopt a new information system for their work (e.g., Karahanna et al., 1999; Venkatesh & Davis, 2000). In this mandatory adoption situation, subjective norm seems to be an obvious direct antecedent of adoption intention. These researchers provided additional insights on the matter. Karahanna et al. (1999) proposed subjective norm as a direct predictor of behavioral intention, and found that subjective norm was a very important antecedent of behavioral intention (even greater than attitude towards adoption) among those who had not adopted the technology yet. On the other hand, those who had already adopted the technology did not intend to continue using the technology due to social influence at all. Once they experienced the technology, behavioral intention was solely dependent on their attitude towards using the technology. Furthermore, when TAM was extended to include personal innovativeness and image, subjective norm was found to have both direct and indirect (via PU) effects on behavioral intention (Yi et al., 2006). Also, Venkatesh and Davis (2000) found the direct effect of subjective norm on behavioral intention only in mandatory settings but not in voluntary adoption settings. Their results also illustrate the importance of subjective norm as its indirect effect through PU is significant in both mandatory and voluntary settings. Noticeably, the strength of subjective norm effects weakened as individuals use the technology more. Therefore, subjective norm seems to be an important antecedents of technology adoption when predicting non-users' intention to adopt a technology. Also, the subjective norm effect is likely to be the strongest when the technology is first introduced.

In the context of mobile coupon adoption, subjective norm can be understood as a subjective belief that important others expect an individual to adopt and use mobile coupons. The individuals may perceive mobile coupons to be more relevant and useful when his/her significant others think it is adequate to use. Indeed, it was found that significant others such as family and friends tend to have a significant impact on consumers' decision to adopt and use mobile coupons (Hsu, Wang, & Wen, 2006). Moreover, due to the newness of various mobile services available today, consumers may be uncertain of suitability of such services and depend on significant others' perceptions about the adoption. Thus, for consumers who have not adopted mobile coupons, subjective norm can be an important predictor of adoption intention. Researchers (Ha & Im, 2014; Khalifa & Shen, 2008; Yang, 2010) have demonstrated that subjective norm increases the intention to adopt mobile technology. Also, subjective norm was found to have a significant impact on perceived ease of use and perceived risk in a mobile coupon adoption context (Im & Ha, 2013). Consumers tend to believe that mobile coupon service is easy and safe to use when there is a social pressure to adopt such technology. In this study, authors reasoned

that subjective norm would influence PEOU and perceived risk because the context of adopting mobile coupons is voluntary and casual. When friends use mobile coupons and recommend the services, consumers may lower their barrier to a new technology and perceive them as less risky and easy enough to use for themselves as well. Therefore, it is obvious that recommendations and encouragements from friends and other connections within the social system play a major role in establishing positive perceptions about mobile coupon services and in increasing consumers' intention to disclose their personal information in the mobile context.

Individual Characteristics

Personal Innovativeness

Individuals accept an innovation at different times. Depending on when they adopt the innovation, Rogers (2003) categorized people into five adopter groups: innovators, early adopters, early majority, late majority, and laggards. Individuals in each adopter group are similar in their personal characteristics such as personal innovativeness and willingness to take risks. Particularly for high-tech products, differences in these distinctive personal characteristics are major barriers of innovation diffusion (Moore, 1999).

Personal innovativeness has been discussed as the most important factor to determine when an individual adopts an innovation (Lopez-Bonilla & Lopez-Bonilla, 2014; Rogers, 2003; Yi et al., 2006). Each person has an enduring level of innovativeness, and innovative individuals constantly seek novelty (Hirschman, 1980) and are willing to change (Agarwal & Prasad, 1998). In a context of technology acceptance, individuals' predisposition to any new information technology is often captured with personal innovation in the domain of information technology (PIIT), "the willingness of an individual to try out any new information technology (Agarwal & Prasad, 1998)". Agarwal

Table 4. PIIT scale

	Item
PIIT1	If I heard about a new information technology, I would look for ways to experiment with it.
PIIT2	Among my peers, I am usually the first to try out new information technologies
PIIT3	In general, I am hesitant to try out new information technologies.*
PIIT4	I like to experiment with new information technologies.

(Agarwal & Prasad, 1998).

and Prasad (1998) conceptualized PIIT as a key personality variable that shapes perceptions and beliefs of as well as behavioral intention towards any new information technology. They developed a 4-item measurement for PIIT and validated the measurement with empirical data (Table 4). Their measurement has been repeatedly used in numerous studies in information technology adoption and found to be reliable and valid.

PIIT is proposed to be useful in understanding technology acceptance and researchers are interested in learning the role of PIIT in technology adoption. In relation to TAM, Agarwal and Prasad (1998) theorized that PIIT moderate the relationship between beliefs and behavioral intention of TAM and partially supported their argument with empirical data by showing that PIIT moderates the relationship between compatibility and behavioral intention. However, many others conceptualized PIIT as an antecedent of beliefs/perceptions because individuals' innovative tendency should correlate with innovativeness-related behaviors directly or indirectly through beliefs/perceptions. Highly innovative people tend to have more positive perceptions about a new technology. Also, it is likely that individual characteristics related to the level of competence in using technology would affect technology adoption. Yi et al. (2006) investigated this issue by comparing two alternative models (PIIT as a moderator vs. determinant) in two different technology adoption settings and

confirmed that the determinant model performs better invariably. Likewise, in a study that compares PIIT influence on mediators, Jackson and colleagues (2013) concluded that PIIT exerts a significant influence on social and personal control factors. In their study of e-commerce system adoption of 196 hospitals in South Korea, PIIT was proven to be an important predictor of beliefs about the information technology system. However, influence of PIIT was fully mediated by proposed mediators drawn from TAM and IDT. Among seven mediators (2 beliefs from TAM and 5 innovation characteristics), only perceived usefulness, image, subjective norm, and perceived behavioral control mediated PIIT effects on behavioral intention. In a mobile coupon adoption context, Ha and Im (2014) also confirmed positive influences of PIIT on behavioral intention both directly and indirectly through perception variables such as perceived usefulness, perceived enjoyment, and compatibility. Thus, the general consensus is that PIIT serves as an antecedent of perceptions and behavioral intention towards adopting a new technology.

Perceived Risk

Consumer behavior researchers have studied risk as a part of consumer problem solving because consumers always face some degree of uncertainty when making choices (Chaudhuri, 2000). Perceived risk is an individual's perception of potential loss or expectation of getting unfavorable outcome from the decision he/she makes, particularly in purchase situations. Because perceived risk is a subjective assessment, the actual level of risk does not always correspond to the level of perceived risk. In consumer research, perceived risk is typically studied in relation to the uncertainty throughout the purchasing process (Shen & Chiou, 2010). Although the overall definition of perceived risk is shared by many researchers, previous literature does not produce a single clear way to operationalize the construct (Mitchell, 1999).

Most researchers theorize perceived risk with multiple dimensions identifying as many as eight kinds of risks – financial (i.e., potential financial loss), performance (i.e., uncertainty of products/ services not performing as expected), physical (i.e., physical injury risk), psychological (i.e., psychological tension and stress), social (i.e., risk involving others' perception of the user as a result of the decision), time-loss (i.e., time and effort lost due to the shopping process), source credibility (i.e., uncertainty related to the vendor or the other business partner), and privacy (i.e., risk of losing private and sensitive information) (Hassan, Kunz, Pearson, & Mohamed, 2006). Many others also identify distinct kinds of risks while using a smaller number of risk types. For example, Im, Kim, and Han (2008) used five types of risks in their study – financial, performance, social, psychological, and physical while Mitchell (1999) identified four – time loss, physical loss, financial loss, and psycho-social loss. Sherma, Alford, Bhuian, and Pelton (2009) measured three types of risk, performance, physical, and psychological. Some researchers treat perceived risk as a single dimension by measuring the overall and global perception of risk without clarifying the specifics (Mitchell, 1999). Moreover, the scales used in the previous studies tend to be a multi-item scale with each type of risk represented as one item (see Table 5 for some examples). This difficulty in operationalizing the construct might have risen due to the broad nature of the concept of risk. As previous research suggests, perceived risk can include many different aspects and only a small subset of risks is pertinent in a specific situation (e.g., product type). Therefore, researchers argue that the perceived risk construct should be defined and measured within a particular context of a study (Dowling & Staelin, 1994; Derbaix, 1983; Dowling, 1986; Mitchell, 1999). Researchers should evaluate the setting of a study to properly define and measure perceived risk.

With the increasing popularity of digital channels in retailing, perceived risk has become even more critical in consumer decision making. Because personal information is recorded and transmitted in a digital format, concerns for misuse of personal information are heightened (Malhotra, Kim, & Agarwal, 2004). In this context, risk perception is particularly salient when consumers make decisions to release their personal information to a company via digital channels (e.g., entering the credit card information online, agreeing to release the current location information via mobile phones). Although many types of previously discussed risks can be found in digital retailing, most relevant risks are financial loss, product performance risk (i.e., the product ordered does not perform as it was promised online) and privacy risk (i.e., personal information can be misused) (Biswas & Burman, 2009; Kim, Ferrin, & Rao, 2008). Particularly in mobile coupon adoption, because the decision is not to purchase goods but to receive mobile coupons, the risk is almost solely related to personal information security (Im & Ha, 2003).

Indeed, researchers who studied perceived risk in a digital retailing context often focused on privacy risk. Malhotra and colleagues (2004) defined perceived risk very narrowly to address Internet users' privacy concerns. Internet users' information privacy concern (IUIPC) (Malhotra et al., 2004) was conceptualized and developed in response to the heightened concerns of consumers who shop and conduct business online. Grounded on social contract theory, the authors theorized information privacy concern as a second-order latent construct with three dimensions (collection, control, and awareness) which captures consumers' perception of fairness and justice in treating privacy information. In their study, privacy concerns contribute to privacy risk beliefs, which subsequently negatively predict behavioral intention (Malhotra et al., 2004).

As perceived risk seems to be an important factor in determining consumers' technology

Table 5. Perceived risk measures used in previous studies

Authors	Type of Risk	Item
Chaudhuri (2000) Adopted from Jacoby & Kaplan (1975)	Financial	What are the chances that you stand to lose money if you try an unfamiliar brand of XXX, either because it won't work at all, or because it costs more than it should to keep it in good shape?
	Performance	What are the chances that there will be something wrong with an unfamiliar brand of XXX or that it will not work properly?
	Safety	What are the chances that an unfamiliar brand of XXX may not be safe; that is, it may be harmful or injurious to your health?
	Psychological	What are the chances that an unfamiliar brand of XXX will not fit in well with your self-image or self-concept or the way you think about yourself?
	Social	What are the chances an unfamiliar brand of XXX will affect the way others think of you?
Malhotra et al. (2004)	Privacy	In general, it would be risky to give (the information) to online companies.
	Privacy	There would be high potential for loss associated with giving (the information) to online firms.
	Privacy	There would be too much uncertainty associated with giving (the information) to online firms.
	Privacy	Providing online firms with (the information) would involve many unexpected problems.
	Privacy	I would feel safe giving (the information) to online companies.*
Im et al. (2008)	Financial	It is probable that XXX would be worth its cost.
	Performance	It is probable that XXX would frustrate me because of its poor performance.
	Opportunity cost	Comparing with other technologies, using XXX has more uncertainties.
	Performance	It is uncertain whether XXX would be as effective as I think.
Kim et al. (2008)	Performance	Purchasing from this website would involve more product risk when compared with more traditional ways of shopping
	Financial	Purchasing from this website would involve more financial risk when compared with more traditional ways of shopping
	Overall	How would you rate your overall perception of risk from this site?
Sherma et al. (2009)	Performance	Purchase of unfamiliar brand/product leading to performance loss
	Physical	Purchase of unfamiliar brand/product leading to physical loss
	Psychological	Purchase of unfamiliar brand/product leading to psychological loss

adoption, researchers have also investigated the role of perceived risk in relation to TAM. Im, Kim, and Han (2008) showed that perceived risk moderates the relationships among TAM variables. For people who perceive a higher level of risk as opposed to people who perceive a lower level of risk, PEOU has a stronger effect while PU has a weaker effect on behavioral intention. On the other hand, the direct negative effect of perceived risk was confirmed in a mobile coupon adoption study. Im and Ha (2013) focused on the importance of perceived risk due to the nature of mobile coupon services and conceptualized that perceived risk significantly affect consumers' intention to use mobile coupons. By incorporating perceived risk and TAM, the authors presented that consumers evaluate both positive antecedents (e.g., PU, PEOU) and negative antecedents to make mobile coupon adoption decisions. The significance of perceived risk was even greater among the consumers who never used mobile coupons than those who had previous experience.

In sum, perceived risk is an important individual characteristic that affects consumers' technology adoption. In mobile coupon adoption, it is reasonable to consider privacy risk more than any other types of risk because of its relevance. Some researchers present that perceived risk can be an independent contributor of adoption while others show it moderates the impact of belief variables on behavioral intention. Future research that investigates the relationships among these variables is necessary to fully understand the role of perceived risk in technology adoption.

Gender Difference

Today, although the gender gap in technology adoption appears to be minimal, how various mobile technologies are utilized and adopted by different genders may vary. Recent research found that men and women use social networking sites (SNS) such as Twitter and Facebook, and mobile devices in different ways (Browne, 2014). Although both genders are actively using mobile devises, women are likely to use their mobile devices for a broader range of purposes than men do. For example, women dominate men in terms of many different mobile activities including SNS usage, website visits, downloading apps, texting, and camera use (Browne, 2014; Lewis, 2013). Related to mobile promotion, men are more likely to seek deals and prefer quick access to information such as QR codes than women (Browne, 2014). While women are more likely to use mobile coupons (eMarketer, 2012) and follow a brand in SNS for deals than men (Browne, 2014). Another noticeable difference between genders are found in actual use of mobile devices for shopping and purchasing. Men outnumber women in actual mobile purchases for many product categories (e.g., electronics, digital contents, movie tickets, etc.) (eMarketer, 2012). Moreover, it was found that men are more likely to use location-related services (Brenner & Smith, 2013). Related to privacy concerns, women mobile users are more

likely to turn off location-tracking options due to fear of others' accessing their private information than men users (Zickuhr, 2013). Therefore, the impact of perceived privacy risk on willingness to grant permission for location tracking services may vary by gender.

In the process of technology adoption, research has also emphasized the important role of various perceived characteristics (e.g., usefulness, easiness, compatibility, enjoyment) of a target technology in anticipating its adoption by different gender groups (Ha & Im, 2014; Ilie, Van Slyke, Green, & Lou, 2005; Nysveen et al., 2005; Wang & Wang, 2010). Regarding PEOU and PU, previous research showed inconsistent findings. In the case of information retrieval systems (Venkatesh & Morris, 2000) and communication technologies (Ilie et al., 2005), PEOU tends to be more important for women while PU is more important for men. However, conflicting results were found in the context of electronic learning (Chinyamurindi & Louw, 2010), online video sharing (Yang, Hsu, & Tan, 2010), and mobile service adoption (Nysyeen et al., 2005). In the context of mobile coupon adoption, perceived shopping efficiency (i.e., usefulness of mobile coupons) seems to play more important role for female consumers than male consumers. Resent study confirmed that PU is a more significant determinant of mobile coupon service adoption for women than men (Ha & Im, 2014). Regarding the influence of PEOU, research demonstrated that PEOU is a stronger determinant of attitude toward mobile service adoption for male users than for female users (Ha & Im, 2014; Nysveen et al., 2005). In sum, it is assumed that while adopting mobile coupon services, perceived usefulness may have a stronger influence on women than men, while PEOU seems more salient for men.

Compatibility is another noticeable perceived characteristic that may affect technology adoption for different genders. Compatibility is found to play more important role in technology adoption for females, indicating that lack of compatibility can be a greater barrier to adopt a new technology for females (Van Slyke, Comunale, & Belanger, 2002). In the context of ecommerce adoption, Van Slyke, Belanger, Johnson, and Hightower (2010) confirmed that compatibility is a more important determinant of e-commerce adoption for females than males. However, in the case of mobile technology adoption, the resent study (Ha & Im, 2014) found no gender difference for compatibility. Future research needs to be conducted to test and confirm how compatibility of mobile service technology influences both males and females in the context of mobile service adoption.

In addition to above mentioned determinants measuring more utilitarian characteristics of a technology, research has emphasized that women value hedonic characteristic of the technology (e.g., perceived enjoyment of the technology) as well when considering adoption of the technology (Venkatesh, Morris, & Ackerman, 2000; Wang & Wang, 2010). Recent study (Padilla-Melendez, Aguila-Obra, & Garrido-Moreno, 2013) found that in the context of e-learning, perceived enjoyment influences attitude toward its adoption more strongly for women than for men. Similarly, perceived enjoyment appears to be a stronger determinant of mobile service adoption for female users than male users (Nysveen et al., 2005). Ha and Im (2014) proved that enjoyment of mobile coupon technology is a critical determinant of mobile coupon service adoption for female consumers but not for male counterparts.

LIMITATIONS AND FUTURE RESEARCH DIRECTIONS

Technology adoption research provides a great amount of insights for any new technology. However, technology adoption research also poses some limitations. TAM is an efficient, parsimonious model and has proven to be extremely versatile in its applicability in diverse technology adoption contexts including mobile coupons. However, the very strength also poses challenges.

TAM was replicated and extended in many technology adoption studies. Once the two predictors from the original TAM, PU and PEOU, are tested and found effective, no evident new knowledge is provided by simply replicating and applying the model to a different context (Benbasat & Barki, 2007). Moreover, PU and PEOU are unable to provide any practical implications as the perceptions can be a result of any number of different factors. Therefore, in order to generate new insights in the technology adoption and usage, researchers need to divert their attentions to factors that affect PU and PEOU, which can produce actionable implications. It is advised that future researchers investigate what exact characteristics of a technology and what kind of situational, social, individual factors influence a user's perception of usefulness and ease of use. More interesting research avenues will include understanding individual differences in technology adoption, investigations of situational factors that facilitate or deter technology adoption, and evaluating effects of mobile marketing message design on consumer intentions to adopt mobile coupons. For example, experiment studies that systematically examine effects of different features of mobile coupons (e.g., coupon design features, timing of the coupons, location-based features) on beliefs and perceptions can be extremely useful.

It was also noted that the technology adoption approaches are more fruitful at the beginning stage of innovation diffusion (Laroche, 2010). People with prior experience with a technology, compared to those who do not have experience with it, rely on different factors when making decisions to use (or continue to use) the technology (Karahanna et al., 1999; Rogers, 2003; Im & Ha, 2013). In other words, as mobile technology becomes ingrained into daily lives of consumers, researchers and practitioners will need to expand their consideration beyond perceived usefulness and perceived ease of use. It also suggests that researchers may need to shift their focus from adoption to usage as time goes on. Two different research approaches are implied. The first approach is to examine the technology adoption in a longitudinal manner. This approach will show changes in importance of certain variables in technology adoption models. The second approach is to expand one's conceptualization of the behaviors as a dependent variable. Currently, the majority of studies focus on acceptance or adoption (i.e., use). After the first use of the technology, an interesting question will be the quantity and quality of usage. Models to explain different usage behaviors will be informative.

Technology adoption research attends almost exclusively to the adoption. Although some recent works show some evidence of incorporating cost-and-benefit calculations in the model (e.g., Im & Ha, 2013), the majority of studies only address the simple proposition that positive beliefs about a technology leads to adoption. These research models are almost too simplistic because it does not reflect the complex calculation of individuals' decision making. Current technology adoption research mostly utilizes adoption intention or actual adoption behavior as the final dependent variable, and measure the degree of adoption. However, the decision to reject an option is qualitatively different from a low intention to adopt the option. For example, if a consumer decided to reject a technology after an evaluation, it may be take a greater amount of effort and time to revert the decision and adopt the technology in the future than when the person never considered it. The current technology adoption models fail to capture this critical difference, and future research that shows the different decision options and their implications on retailers will be beneficial.

tegration into workplace sparked a vast amount of interest among the researchers and TAM was introduced as one of the most influential frameworks to develop plans to encourage employees to use the technology for improving productivity. Likewise, in consumer research, TAM and IDT have provided interesting discussions regarding how consumers deal with a new technology in shopping and what marketers and retailers need to consider when a new technology is integrated into their businesses. In this chapter, a review of TAM and IDT is provided as the theoretical underpinning of technology adoption research. Based on the theories and previous literature, several determinants of technology adoption that could be most pertinent to the context of mobile coupon adoption are identified. The review of literature provides critical discussions on findings in different adoption contexts as well as inconsistencies in conceptualization and results. The authors intend to offer insights for researchers interested in mobile technology adoption by this critical review. The discussed determinants, although they may not be an exhaustive list, have been found to be most influential in explaining mobile technology and mobile coupon adoption. Even though the current review presents contributions technology adoption research made to our understanding of consumer behavior in the retailing context, it is also noted that research using TAM/IDT might have reached a saturation point. Thus, researchers are advised to address the shortcomings of technology adoption research and deepen our understanding of the matter.

CONCLUSION

Technology adoption research has informed both scholars and practitioners particularly in a circumstance where a new innovative technology is introduced to a workplace and retail industry. The boom of information technology and its in-

REFERENCES

Agarwal, R., & Prasad, J. (1998). A conceptual and operational definition of personal innovativeness in the domain of information technology. *Information Systems Research*, 9(2), 204–215. doi:10.1287/isre.9.2.204

Ajzen, I. (1991). The theory of planned behavior. *Organizational Behavior and Human Decision Processes*, *50*(2), 179–211. doi:10.1016/0749-5978(91)90020-T

Benbasat, I., & Barki, H. (2007). Quo vadis, TAM? *Journal of the Association for Information Systems*, *8*(4), 211–218.

Biswas, D., & Burman, B. (2009). The effects of product digitalization and price dispersion on search intentions in offline versus online settings: The mediating effects of perceived risks. *Journal of Product and Brand Management*, *18*(7), 477–486. doi:10.1108/10610420910998208

Brenner, J., & Smith, A. (2013). *72% of online adults are social networking site users.* Retrieved June 2, 2014, from http://pewinternet.org/~/media//Files/Reports/2013/PIP_Social_networking_sites_update_PDF.pdf

Browne, C. (2014). *Facebook Inc (FB) mobile usage patterns show interesting gender splits.* Retrieved July 3, 2014, from http://www.valuewalk.com

Bruner, G. C. II, & Kumar, A. (2005). Explaining consumer acceptance of handheld internet devices. *Journal of Business Research*, *58*(5), 553–558. doi:10.1016/j.jbusres.2003.08.002

Celik, H. (2011). Influence of social norms, perceived playfulness and online shopping anxiety on customers' adoption of online retail shopping. *International Journal of Retail & Distribution Management*, *39*(6), 390–413. doi:10.1108/09590551111137967

Chaudhuri, A. (2000). A macro analysis of the relationship of product involvement and information search: The role of risk. *Journal of Marketing Theory and Practice*, *80*(1), 1–15.

Cheung, R., & Vogel, D. (2013). Predicting user acceptance of collaborative technologies: An extension of the technology acceptance model for e-learning. *Computers & Education*, *63*(April), 160–175. doi:10.1016/j.compedu.2012.12.003

Childers, T. L., Carr, C. L., Peck, J., & Carson, S. (2001). Hedonic and utilitarian motivations for online retail shopping behavior. *Journal of Retailing*, *77*(4), 511–535. doi:10.1016/S0022-4359(01)00056-2

Chinyamurindi, W. T., & Louw, G. J. (2010). Gender differences in technology acceptance in selected South African companies: Implications for electronic learning. *SA Journal of Human Resource Management*, *8*(1), 2–7. doi:10.4102/sajhrm.v8i1.204

Chuttur, M. (2009). Overview of the technology acceptance model: Origins, developments and future directions, Indiana University, USA. *Sprouts: Working Papers on Information Systems, 9*(37).

Davis, F. D. (1985). *A technology acceptance model for empirically testing new end-user information systems: theory and results.* (Unpublished Doctoral Dissertation). MIT Sloan School of Management, Cambridge, MA.

Davis, F. D. (1989). Perceived usefulness, perceived ease of use, and user acceptance of information technology. *Management Information Systems Quarterly*, *13*(3), 319–340. doi:10.2307/249008

Davis, F. D., Bagozzi, R. P., & Warshaw, P. R. (1989). User acceptance of computer technology: A comparison of two theoretical models. *Management Science*, *35*(8), 982–1003. doi:10.1287/mnsc.35.8.982

Derbaix, C. (1983). Perceived risk and risk relievers: An empirical investigation. *Journal of Economic Psychology*, *3*(March), 19–38. doi:10.1016/0167-4870(83)90056-9

Dickinger, A., & Kleijnen, M. (2008). Coupons going wireless: Determinants of consumer intentions to redeem mobile coupons. *Journal of Interactive Marketing, 22*(3), 23–39. doi:10.1002/dir.20115

Dowling, G. R. (1986). Perceived risk: The concept and its measurement. *Psychology and Marketing, 3*(3), 193–210. doi:10.1002/mar.4220030307

Dowling, G. R., & Staelin, R. (1994). A model of perceived risk and intended risk-handling activity. *The Journal of Consumer Research, 21*(1), 119–134. doi:10.1086/209386

eMarketer. (2012). *Men top women in mobile buying*. Retrieved July 4 2014, from http://www.emarketer.com/Article/Men-Top-Women-Mobile-Buying/1009374

eMarketer. (2013). *How does wi-fi affect mobile shoppers?* Retrieved from http://www.emarketer.com/Article/How-Wi-Fi-Affect-Mobile-Shoppers/1009728

eMarketer. (2014). *Smartphone users worldwide will total 1.75 billion in 2014*. Retrieved July 7, 2014, from http://www.emarketer.com/Article/Smartphone-Users-Worldwide-Will-Total-175-Billion-2014/1010536

Fagan, M. H., Neill, S., & Wooldridge, B. R. (2008). Exploring the intention to use computers: An empirical investigation of the role of intrinsic motivation, extrinsic motivation, and perceived ease of use. *Journal of Computer Information Systems, 48*(3), 405–426.

Fishbein, M., & Azjen, I. (1975). *Belief, attitude, intention and behavior: An introduction to theory and research*. Reading, MA: Addison-Wesley.

Gopal, A., Bostrom, R. P., & Chin, W. W. (1992). Applying adaptive structuration theory to investigate the process of group support systems use. *Journal of Management Information Systems, 9*(3), 45–69.

Ha, Y., & Im, H. (2014). Determinants of mobile coupon adoption among US consumers: Assessment of gender difference. *International Journal of Retail & Distribution Management, 42*(5), 441–459. doi:10.1108/IJRDM-08-2012-0074

Hassan, A. M., Kunz, M. B., Pearson, A. W., & Mohamed, F. A. (2006). Conceptualization and measurement of perceived risk in online shopping. *Marketing Management Journal, 16*(1), 138–147.

Hirschman, E. C. (1980). Innovativeness, novelty seeking, and consumer creativity. *The Journal of Consumer Research, 7*(3), 283–295. doi:10.1086/208816

Hsu, T., Wang, Y., & Wen, S. (2006). Using the decomposed theory of planned behavior to analyze consumer behavioral intention towards mobile text message coupons. *Journal of Targeting, Measurement, and Analysis for Marketing, 14*(4), 309–324. doi:10.1057/palgrave.jt.5740191

Ilie, V., Van Slyke, C., Green, G., & Lou, H. (2005). Gender differences in perceptions and use of communication technologies: A diffusion of innovation approach. *Information Researches Management Journal, 18*(3), 13–31. doi:10.4018/irmj.2005070102

Im, H., & Ha, Y. (2013). A model of permission-based marketing: Enablers and inhibitors of mobile coupon adoption. *Journal of Retailing and Consumer Services, 20*(5), 495–503. doi:10.1016/j.jretconser.2013.05.002

Im, I., Kim, Y., & Han, H.-J. (2008). The effects of perceived risk and technology type on users' acceptance of technologies. *Information & Management, 45*(1), 1–9. doi:10.1016/j.im.2007.03.005

Jackson, J. D., Yi, M. Y., & Park, J. S. (2013). An empirical test of three mediation models for the relationship between personal innovativeness and user acceptance of technology. *Information & Management, 50*(4), 154–161. doi:10.1016/j.im.2013.02.006

Juniper Research. (2012). *Press release: Ten billion mobile coupons to be redeemed this year, up 50% on 2012, Juniper report finds*. Retrieved June 16, 2014 from http://www.juniperresearch.com/viewpressrelease.php?pr=361

Karahanna, E., Straun, D. W., & Chervany, N. (1999). Information technology adoption across time: A cross-sectional comparison of pre-adoption and post-adoption beliefs. *Management Information Systems Quarterly, 23*(2), 183–213. doi:10.2307/249751

Karjaluoto, H., Jayawardhena, C., Kuckertz, A., & Kautonen, T. (2008). Sources of trust in permission-based mobile marketing: a cross-country comparison. In T. Kautonen & H. Karjaluoto (Eds.), *Trust and new technologies: Marketing and management on the internet and mobile media* (pp. 165–181). Northampton, MA: Edward Elgar. doi:10.4337/9781848445086.00019

Khalifa, M., & Shen, K. (2008). Drivers for transactional b2c m-commerce adoption: Extended theory of planned behavior. *Journal of Computer Information Systems, 48*(3), 111–117.

Kim, D. J., Ferrin, D. L., & Rao, H. R. (2008). A trust-based consumer decision-making model in electronic commerce: The role of trust, perceived risk, and their antecedents. *Decision Support Systems, 44*(2), 544–564. doi:10.1016/j.dss.2007.07.001

Laroche, M. (2010). New developments in modeling internet consumer behavior: Introduction to the special issue. *Journal of Business Research, 63*(9/10), 915–918. doi:10.1016/j.jbusres.2008.12.013

Lewis, D. (2013). *The gender divide as seen through phones, games and apps*. Retrieved July 4, 2014, from http://www.verizonwireless.com/news/article/2013/06/the-mobile-gender-divide.html

Lopez-Bonilla, J. M., & Lopez-Bonilla, L. M. (2014). Sensation-seeking profiles and personal innovativeness in information technology. *Social Science Computer Review, 30*(4), 434–447. doi:10.1177/0894439311427246

Malhotra, N. K., Kim, S. S., & Agarwal, J. (2004). Internet users' information privacy concerns (IUIPC): The construct, the scale, and a causal model. *Information Systems Research, 15*(4), 336–355. doi:10.1287/isre.1040.0032

Mitchell, V.-W. (1999). Consumer perceived risk: Conceptualisations and models. *European Journal of Marketing, 33*(1/2), 163–195. doi:10.1108/03090569910249229

MMA. (2007). *Introduction to mobile coupons*. Retrieved June 14, 2014, from http://www.mma-global.com/files/mobilecoupons.pdf

Moore, G. A. (1999). *Crossing the chasm: Marketing and selling high-tech products to mainstream customers* (2nd ed.). New York, NY: Harper Business.

Moore, G. C., & Benbasat, I. (1991). Development of an instrument to measure perceptions of adopting an information technology innovation. *Information Systems Research, 2*(3), 192–222. doi:10.1287/isre.2.3.192

Nysveen, H., Pedersen, P. E., & Thorbjornsen, H. (2005). Intentions to use mobile services. *Journal of the Academy of Marketing Science, 33*(3), 330–346. doi:10.1177/0092070305276149

Okazaki, S., & Taylor, C. R. (2008). What is SMS advertising and why do multinationals adopt it? Answers from an empirical study in European markets. *Journal of Business Research, 61*(1), 4–12. doi:10.1016/j.jbusres.2006.05.003

Olenski, S. (2013). Is location based advertising the future of mobile marketing and mobile advertising? *Forbes.com*. Retrieved July 11, 2014, from http://www.forbes.com/sites/marketshare/2013/01/17/is-location-based-advertising-the-future-of-mobile-marketing-and-mobile-advertising/

Padilla-Melendez, A., Aguila-Obra, A. R., & Garrido-Moreno, A. (2013). Perceived playfulness, gender differences and technology acceptance model in a blended learning scenario. *Computers & Education, 63*(April), 306–317. doi:10.1016/j.compedu.2012.12.014

Park, S. Y. (2009). An analysis of the technology acceptance model in understanding university students' behavioral intention to use e-learning. *Journal of Educational Technology & Society, 12*(3), 150–162.

Rogers, E. M. (2003). *Diffusion of innovations* (5th ed.). New York, NY: Free Press.

Rohm, A. J., Gao, T., Sultan, F., & Pagani, M. (2012). Brand in the hand: A cross-market investigation of consumer acceptance of mobile marketing. *Business Horizons, 55*(5), 485–493. doi:10.1016/j.bushor.2012.05.004

ROI Research Inc., & Microsoft. (2011). *Mobile advertising research study: Consumer and industry insights – United Kingdom*. Retrieved June 21, 2014, from https://advertising.microsoft.com/WWDocs/User/en-us/ForAdvertisers/2011-Microsoft-UK-MoAd-Insights-Study.pdf

Scharl, A., Dickinger, A., & Murphy, J. (2005). Diffusion and success factors of mobile marketing. *Electronic Commerce Research and Applications, 4*(2), 159–173. doi:10.1016/j.elerap.2004.10.006

Shankar, V., Venkatesh, A., Hofacker, C., & Naik, P. (2010). Mobile marketing in the retailing environment: Current insights and future research avenues. *Journal of Interactive Marketing, 24*(2), 111–120. doi:10.1016/j.intmar.2010.02.006

Shen, C.-C., & Chiou, J.-S. (2010). The impact of perceived ease of use on Internet service adoption: The moderating effects of temporal distance and perceived risk. *Computers in Human Behavior, 26*(1), 42–50. doi:10.1016/j.chb.2009.07.003

Sherma, D., Alford, B., Bhuian, S. N., & Pelton, L. E. (2009). A higher-order model of risk propensity. *Journal of Business Research, 62*(7), 741–744. doi:10.1016/j.jbusres.2008.06.005

Smith, A. (2013). *Smartphone ownership 2013*. Retrieved May 25, 2014, from http://www.pewinternet.org/2013/06/05/smartphone-ownership-2013/

Stern, B. B., Royne, M. B., Stafford, T. F., & Beinstock, C. C. (2008). Consumer acceptance of online auctions: An extension and revision of the TAM. *Psychology and Marketing, 25*(7), 619–636. doi:10.1002/mar.20228

Terzis, V., & Economides, A. A. (2011). Computer based assessment: Gender differences in perceptions and acceptance. *Computers in Human Behavior, 27*(6), 2108–2122. doi:10.1016/j.chb.2011.06.005

Tornatzky, L. G., & Klein, K. J. (1982). Innovation characteristics and innovation adoption implementation: A meta analysis of findings. *IEEE Transactions on Engineering Management, 29*(1), 28–45. doi:10.1109/TEM.1982.6447463

Van der Heijden, H. (2004). User acceptance of hedonic information systems. *Management Information Systems Quarterly, 28*(4), 695–704.

Van Slyke, C., Belanger, F., Johnson, R. D., & Hightower, R. (2010). Gender-based differences in factors influencing consumer e-commerce adoption. *Communications of the Association for Information Systems, 26*(2), 17–34.

Van Slyke, C., Comunale, C., & Belanger, F. (2002). Gender differences in perceptions of web-based shopping. *Communications of the ACM*, *45*(7), 82–86. doi:10.1145/545151.545155

Venkatesh, V. (2000). Determinants of perceived ease of use: Integrating control, intrinsic motivation, and emotion into the technology acceptance model. *Information Systems Research*, *11*(4), 342–365. doi:10.1287/isre.11.4.342.11872

Venkatesh, V., & Davis, F. D. (1996). A model of the antecedents of perceived ease of use: Development and test. *Decision Sciences*, *27*(3), 451–481. doi:10.1111/j.1540-5915.1996.tb01822.x

Venkatesh, V., & Davis, F. D. (2000). A theoretical extension of the technology acceptance model: Four longitudinal field studies. *Management Science*, *45*(2), 186–204. doi:10.1287/mnsc.46.2.186.11926

Venkatesh, V., Morris, M. G., & Ackerman, P. L. (2000). A longitudinal field investigation of gender differences in individual technology adoption decision making processes. *Organizational Behavior and Human Decision Processes*, *83*(1), 33–60. doi:10.1006/obhd.2000.2896 PMID:10973782

Wachs, D. (2013). *Five reasons you should be using SMS based marketing*. Retrieved July 11, 2014, from http://venturebeat.com/2013/05/08/five-reasons-you-should-be-using-sms-based-marketing/

Wang, H., & Wang, S. (2010). User acceptance of mobile internet based on the unified theory of acceptance and use of technology: Investigating the determinants and gender differences. *Social Behavior and Personality*, *38*(3), 415–426. doi:10.2224/sbp.2010.38.3.415

Yang, C., Hsu, Y., & Tan, S. (2010). Predicting the determinants of users' intentions for using You-Tube to share video: Moderating gender effects. *Cyberpsychology, Behavior, and Social Networking*, *13*(2), 141–152. doi:10.1089/cyber.2009.0105 PMID:20528269

Yang, K. (2010). Determinants of US consumer mobile shopping services adoption: Implications for designing mobile shopping services. *Journal of Consumer Marketing*, *27*(3), 262–270. doi:10.1108/07363761011038338

Yen, D. C., Wu, C.-S., Cheng, F.-F., & Huang, Y.-W. (2010). Determinants of users' intention to adopt wireless technology: An empirical study by integrating TTF with TAM. *Computers in Human Behavior*, *26*(5), 906–915. doi:10.1016/j.chb.2010.02.005

Yi, M. Y., Fiedler, K. D., & Park, J. S. (2006). Understanding the role of individual innovativeness in the acceptance of IT-based innovations: Comparative analyses of models and measures. *Decision Sciences*, *37*(3), 393–426. doi:10.1111/j.1540-5414.2006.00132.x

Yi, M. Y., Jackson, J., Park, J. S., & Probst, J. C. (2006). Understanding information technology acceptance by individual professionals: Toward an integrative view. *Information & Management*, *43*(3), 350–363. doi:10.1016/j.im.2005.08.006

Zickuhr, K. (2013). *Location-based services*. Retrieved June 8, 2014, from http://www.pewinternet.org/Reports/2013/Location.aspx

ADDITIONAL READING

Karjalouto, H., Lehto, H., Leppaniema, M., & Jayawardhena, C. (2008). Exploring gender influence on customer's intention to engage permission-based mobile marketing. *Electronic Markets*, *18*(3), 242–259. doi:10.1080/10196780802265793

Khajehzadeh, S., Oppewal, H., & Tojib, D. (2014). Consumer responses to mobile coupons: The roles of shopping motivation and regulatory fit..10.1016/j.jbusres.2014.02.012

Kumar, V., Zhang, X., & Luo, A. (2014). Modeling customer opt-in and opt-out in a permission-based marketing context. *JMR, Journal of Marketing Research*, *51*(4), 403–419. doi:10.1509/jmr.13.0169

Reichhart, P., Pescher, C., & Spann, M. (2013). A comparison of the effectiveness of e-mail coupons and mobile text message coupons for digital products. *Electronic Markets*, *23*(3), 217–225. doi:10.1007/s12525-013-0129-3

KEY TERMS AND DEFINITIONS

Compatibility: Subjective perception of a technology regarding how much the technology is matched with one's value and goals (e.g., shopping).

Decision Making Process (DMP): The five stages of technology adoption described in Innovation Diffusion Theory. The five stages are knowledge, persuasion, decision, implementation, and confirmation.

Image: Subjective perception of the possibility that one's social status can be heightened by adopting a technology or perception of the users of a technology in a social system.

Location-Based Services: The mobile services provided based on the current location of a GPS-enabled mobile device.

Mobile Coupon Services: Mobile services that send digital coupons to mobile devices of consumers for financial benefits when purchasing a product or service.

Perceived Risk: An individual's assessment of possible loss or expectation of getting unfavorable outcome from the adoption decision one makes.

Perceived Usefulness: Subjective belief that using the target technology (e.g., mobile coupons) would be beneficial to successful completion of a given task (e.g., shopping).

Personal Innovativeness in the Domain of Information Technology: The willingness of an individual to seek and try out any new information technology.

Subjective Norm: A perceived social pressure that an individual feels to adopt of a technology from important others.

Technology Acceptance Model (TAM): A model that predicts individuals' adoption of a technology based on perceived usefulness and perceived ease of use of the technology.

Chapter 6

Adoption of Emerging In-Store Technology Interfaces for the Apparel Retail Employee

Tasha L. Lewis
Cornell University, USA

Suzanne Loker
Cornell University, USA

ABSTRACT

Technology use in apparel retail stores is on the rise and changing the way that employees work and customers shop. In spite of increased use, advanced technology deployed within apparel retail stores has yet to match the rapid pace of growth for technologies adopted by apparel consumers enabled by mobile devices and sophisticated digital applications. Apparel retail employees are the first line of contact for customers and are often engaged with them at several points in the service interaction, including assisting with the initial selection of apparel based on customers' desired product features, the try-on of clothing, and unique in-store services like personal shopping. In this chapter, the authors examine employee usage intent for technologies supportive of these various points of service interaction. The likelihood of employee usage of technology as well as employee characteristics that influenced the extent of technology adoption were also measured.

INTRODUCTION

With increased use of personal mobile technology by consumers, such as smart phones and tablet computers, services traditionally provided by store employees have become available outside the retail store to shoppers via web-based digital formats. For example, the RedLaser software application[1] enables smart phones to read barcodes for price checking items; and, another application, MySizeFinder[2], matches customer measurements with clothing from different brands in its database. As consumers take advantage of these self-service technologies as part of their shopping

DOI: 10.4018/978-1-4666-8297-9.ch006

experience, store employees could benefit from access to advanced digital tools beyond point-of-sale (POS) technologies in order to increase work effectiveness. In fact, Kilcourse and Rosenblum (2009) have observed that:

Because of the fundamental power shift to the consumer in the past decade, retailers have had to rethink their most valuable assets: their people and their stores. When a customer potentially knows more about products and prices than the store employee does, the retailer needs to excel at value-adding services that draw the consumer to the store.... And retailers need to analyze not only what sells, but what doesn't. Their best chance of capturing that information is by engaging in a digital dialogue with the consumer as she browses the store. (p. 20)

The Occupational Information Network (2011) listed the current tools and technologies associated with work done by retail salespersons; these include barcode scanners, calculators, computerized cash registers, credit card readers, and software—each supporting accounting, human resources, and point of sale functions. Such technologies are capable of supporting traditional service interactions with customers, but they do not enable the "digital dialogue" proposed by Kilcourse and Rosenblum (2009), nor the more innovative design and customization activities that also interest apparel consumers. These activities include: designing apparel within the store with the help of an employee (Lee, Kunz, Fiore, & Campbell, 2002); the integrated use of virtual communication, body scanning, and databases for apparel customization (Wood, 2002); and the creation of digital product information (Fiore, 2008). According to Pollack, Maxwell, and Feigan Dugal (2007), the use of technology for customization and new shopping experiences was predicted to increase and become more pervasive by the year 2015, enabled by technologies like body scanning, social networking, interactive digital media, and

virtual try-on. This same report predicted that retailers would have to meet the demands of their digital generation consumers who seek to create their own products using technological tools. These tools are presently available but have not yet been widely adopted by apparel retailers as an essential part of their store operations. In this chapter, we examined existing advanced technologies that have been used by apparel retailers to explore how the technologies may provide unique service functions for consumers and some non-traditional job roles for apparel retail employees.

BACKGROUND

The Nature of Retail Work

Service

As the first contacts with retail customers, store employees play an important role in customer service, but need to be engaged and interested. This research explored how apparel retail employees reacted to three emerging technologies – body scanner, product configurator and social networking. It analyzed whether these technologies offered a strategic opportunity to support employees in their work as service providers.

Problems with store service were the main causes of customer dissatisfaction in a 2007 study by the Wharton Business School and included such customer complaints as not being able to find anyone for help, insensitivity to long lines, feeling as if one was intruding on a sales associate's time or conversation and lack of politeness. Hochschild (1983) referred to service jobs as emotional labor, implying the requirement of service workers to not only perform some physical tasks but also possess the ability to adjust their attitudes and personalities for the purposes of interacting with customers. Albrecht and Zemke (2002) offered some insight into why good service is such an issue in retail by pointing out that many service workers lack the "temperament, maturity, social skills, and tolerance for frequent human contact" and that after repeated interactions with customers and the accompanying pressures and stress, service workers' interactions with customers turn "toxic" (p.148). As a solution to avoid these toxic encounters, Albrecht and Zemke (2002) recommended that service workers should be hired based on their ability to perform not just generic service functions (found in a company's policy manual) but on their ability to address the specific demands and complaints of the company's customers.

Schlesinger and Zornitsky (1996) found that 80% of employees who were satisfied with their ability to provide customer service were also more satisfied with their jobs. The same study also revealed that efforts aimed at improving employees' ability to provide service also increased job satisfaction, which the researchers predicted would lead to customer satisfaction (Schlesinger & Zornitsky, 1996). Linkages between positive employee attitudes about their employer and customer satisfaction were found by Tornow and Willey (1991). Customer satisfaction with service quality has been inversely related to employee turnover rates (Ulrich, Halbrook, Meder, Stuchlik, & Thorpe, 1991). These studies suggested that introducing strategies to improve retail employees' customer service skills could ultimately lead to both job satisfaction and customer satisfaction.

From Service to Experience

Baron, Harris and Harris (2001), discussed the idea of "Retail Theater" as a way to introduce newness into retailing for fun and excitement for the customer. Four theatrical movements described the roles of the customer in this new environment, along with corresponding employee responsibilities. The roles of the customer were 'voyeur', 'spect-actor', 'sense-ceptor' and 'connoisseur'. For voyeurs, merchandise is presented in a realistic setting and there is a distance between the actors (employees) and the audience (customer) with

very little interaction between the two groups since employees are either busy getting products or being a character. Spect-actor customers are expected to know that they are in an environment where selling is taking place and they are able to critique the merchandise and its presentation. There is also high interaction of customers with employees as well as with other customers regarding product information. Employees working in the spect-actor setting were described as having non-traditional retail positions since they "are primarily facilitators of information exchange between customers rather than necessarily being experts in the field" (Baron et al., 2001, p.107). The sense-ceptor customer is expected to have physiological responses to in-store stimuli and this customer is presented with opportunities to physically interact with the product or experience simulations, while employees are both behind the scenes creating the experience and out front helping the customer with interactions or simulations. The connoisseur customer is left to his or her own interpretations of the abstractly presented product with no assistance from employees, who serve as "human exhibits" or as movers of merchandise displays. The four customer movements, while highly engaging and informative for customers, were also presented as a means of transforming the retail employee (actor) toward enhanced job roles, training and reduction of "boredom costs" (Baron et al., 2001).

Store types that best captured the concept of retail as theater were themed flagship brand stores. Kozinets, Sherry, DeBerry-Spence,Duhachek, Nuttavuthisit and Storm (2002), described these stores as places where consumers go to both purchase a retailer's branded products and to engage in an entertaining experience. The goal of these stores was primarily to build the company's brand image, and examples included flagship stores for apparel retailers like Levi's and Nike (Niketown) where customers were able to create custom products or use interactive displays (Solomon & Rabolt, 2004; Peñaloza, 1999). Kozinets et al. (2002) also predicted that these stores would most successfully capture the in-store and online shopping experience for customers in what they call "brick-and-click hybrids" and become the future model of retail stores (Kozinets et al., 2002):

Through the use of lavish décor, sleek finishes, and attention to the smallest of details, consumers are presented with a stage behind the storefront. Interactive displays and other engaging edifices evoke emotions and other sensations that make an experience unique and individual. For the retailer, successful brand building comes in the form of consumer experiences that entice, entrance and enrapture. (p.20)

This prediction regarding retail's future model corresponded to a larger shift in the manner in which service would be provided in many industries according to Pine and Gilmore (1999) in what they called the *Experience Economy*. The *Experience Economy* described a shift occurring in developed nations from economies based on providing services to those based on providing experiences. This shift has moved these countries from economies based on commodities, to those based on goods, to services and ultimately to experiences. The introduction of automation in the service economy (similar to automation for production of goods) with technologies like self-serve checkouts was an indicator to Pine and Gilmore (1999) that the service economy sector had peaked and was giving way to experiences. An *Experience Economy* uses goods as props and services as a stage to engage customers in memorable experiences. They described work in this economy as follows:

In the emerging Experience Economy, any work observed directly by a customer must be recognized as an act of theatre. Indeed flight attendants and hotel staff routinely perform acts of theatre when they direct patrons to the nearest exit or rented room. The work of a retail store associate is theatre

when he straightens merchandise on a shelf...All this work is theatre, even when the audience isn't paying customers, because internal acts make impressions on customers who do not pay. In the Experience Economy, businesses must figure out how to make work, whether performed on stage or off, more engaging. (p. 106-107).

Job Satisfaction

Retail store jobs suffer from a societal image of low pay and/or lack of career growth potential that discourages many people from considering retail as a long-term career (Swinyard, 1981; Swinyard, Langrehr, & Smith,1991; Broadbridge, 2003). According to the US Department of Labor (2008), retail jobs in clothing stores were the lowest paying retail positions at $8.53 per hour. Research done by Knight, Crustinger and Kim (2006) showed that apparel merchandising students already working in retail stores were more interested in other potential retail career areas than careers in store management. In another study, retail store managers who were college graduates were found to be more dissatisfied than retail corporate office workers and they indicated that they had less autonomy and variety in their jobs and showed higher turnover intentions (Rhoads, Swinyard, Geurts, & Price, 2002). Broadbridge (2003) found that students saw a retail career as having opportunities for training and development, but they also viewed retail careers as having limited career advancement. Dickerson (2003) noted that store management positions typically did not lead to other positions within a retail company (such as a merchandise buyer) beyond other in-store positions.

Career ladders developed by apparel retailers also described limited options for different career options by new workers. Macy's listed their store management career path as follows: store management executive development program →Sales Manager/Group Sales Manager → Assistant Store Manager or Merchandise

Team Manager → Regional Merchandise Manager or Store General Manager (macyscollege. com, 2008). Kohl's listed a similar path for its employees; from store associate → Assistant Store Manager → Store Manager → District Manager. JC Penney provided a path for their Sales Manager Trainees to obtain other positions at the company's home office, but this was the last position on the career ladder.

Knight et al. (2006) found that students working in retail jobs who had high career goals and job satisfaction were more likely to pursue a retail career. Retail employees often fill entry-level jobs, placing them at the lowest job positions within the store hierarchy. Entry-level employees who become satisfied with their jobs may decide to remain in that job and even decide to pursue a career, which involves setting a career goal and engaging in development activities to reach that goal. If retail employees were also given opportunities to engage in development activities while working in the store that would prepare them for future positions within a retail organization outside of the limited retail store career paths, they might also be more satisfied with their jobs and remain in store positions. Spanish retailer, Zara, was an example of a company that had a training and development program for its store employees that had served to fill apparel design positions – the company reported that in 2005 39% of its designers had come from store positions (Inditex, 2005).

The use of technology for improving customer service can be considered a part of a development activity. London (1989) noted that development programs "may be guided by corporate initiatives to prepare people for advancement or to ensure that employees have the opportunities needed to maintain and expand their skills" (p.2). By using certain technologies employees may be provided with training in the area of customer service, maintaining and expanding skills that will support career development for the digitally integrated store.

MAIN FOCUS OF THE CHAPTER

The use of technology as part of the employee-customer service encounter in apparel retail stores required some special considerations in terms of suitable technology formats for facilitating, rather than preventing, interaction and in terms of technology self-efficacy -- how comfortable retail employees feel using new technology in general as part of their work. Apparel retail work is a "high touch" environment in terms of customer interaction and technology that supports and enhances this aspect of the job can be more valuable to the interaction of employees and customers than technology that places a distance between the two groups (i.e. self-service technologies). Apparel retail employees' reactions to using a new technology based on how comfortable they would feel using it are also important so that retailers are able anticipate how much training might be necessary for a new technology and if the investment in new technology would be worthwhile for their employees. 'Employee sabotage', which involved refusal to use new technology, could result if employees have low technology self-efficacy and developed negative attitudes towards using the technology (Bickers, 2008).

Hybrid Technology Interfaces

Hybrid interfaces referred to the use of both human and technological capabilities to complete work (Rayport & Jaworski, 2005). Depending on the type of work, either the person or the technology could be dominant in the interface – for example, a retail employee using a hand-held scanner to help a customer locate an item would be considered a people-dominant interface while an employee responding to a customer e-mail using a computer would be considered a technology-dominant interface. Froehle and Roth (2004) conceptualized how both employees and customers might interact with technology in service situations and described five modes of interactions or interfaces. These interfaces of customer contact were further organized into *'face-to-face'* and *'face-to-screen'* contact. Face-to-face interfaces involved interpersonal contact between the customer and a service representative including:

1. **Technology-Free Interface:** No use of technology during service encounter,
2. **Technology-Assisted Interface:** Technology aided the service representative to improve customer interaction, and
3. **Technology-Facilitated Customer Contact Interface:** Service representative and customer both used technology to enhance the interaction.

In face-to-screen contact interfaces, technology was the only point of contact, and included:

1. **Technology-Mediated Interface:** Technology was used as the only means of interaction between customer and service representative, and
2. **Technology-Generated Customer Contact Interface:** Technology substituted for service representative.

Impact of Technology Self-Efficacy

According to Compeau and Higgins (1995), technology self-efficacy "refers to a judgment of one's capability to use a computer [and] is not concerned with what one has done in the past, but rather with judgments of what could be done in the future" (p. 192). Venkatesh and Davis (1996) found that technology self-efficacy was a determinant of a person's perceived ease of use of computer technologies and that when given information on how to use a technology beforehand, users based their ease of use ratings of computer technology solely on their technology self-efficacy and not the procedural information that was provided. A measure of technology self-efficacy considers the influence of lack of confidence in using technology in general, but it could influence a user's confidence in using a specific technology especially one that had not been used before. Technology used by employees could be influenced by technology self-efficacy -- if they did not feel confident using a new technology, in spite of its ability to support customer service, they might be less likely to want to use it as part of their work.

Technology-Enabled Consumers

The authors of a number of studies have evaluated consumer perceptions and intentions to use technology as part of their shopping experience. Burke (2002) found that interest in in-store technology among consumer respondents included electronic shelf labels, electronic signs, kiosks, and handheld scanners. Participants in Kamali and Loker's (2002) study used a web-based product configurator to design t-shirts. Results showed that interest in the design process increased as participants were able to customize more options for the t-shirt; and 88% of the participants indicated a willingness to purchase the t-shirt they had designed. Positive consumer interest in body scanning technology was reported by people who had experienced the scanning process (Loker, Cowie, Ashdown & Lewis, 2004; Lewis & Loker, 2007); and Lee et al. (2002) found that female respondents were willing to use body scanning technology for design of customized apparel. The same respondents also wanted to be able to view the customized garment on a virtual image of themselves and to receive assistance from a store employee with a specialized fashion design background (Lee et al., 2002). These desired in-store apparel design experiences extend beyond traditional retail shopping, suggesting that apparel consumers have clear expectations when it comes to service interactions with technology and employees.

Technology-Enabled Employees

Swinyard (1997) contended that, in the increasingly competitive retail environment, technology use would determine retailer success and require a technologically educated retail management workforce. Currently, most large-scale retail chains do not demand a high level of technological skill or initiative from their employees; most responsibilities like merchandising, pricing, or visual displays are controlled and disseminated to the store management by corporate headquarters or regional offices (Rayport & Jaworski, 2005). This structuring down of employee job tasks at the retail store level reduced training needs and also led to employee dissatisfaction and high turnover rates (Heskett, Sasser, & Schlesinger, 2003). In a study of technology use among sales personnel, Senecal, Pullins, and Buehrer (2007) reported that an increase in technology use resulted in better customer service and job performance.

Apparel retailers have made efforts to introduce technologies beyond the checkout counter, primarily in self-service formats for customer use. Price verification kiosks are placed throughout retail stores to allow consumers to check the accuracy of price tag information. Digital mirrors have been tested as a self-service technology inside fitting rooms (Bickers, 2008; Fleenor, 2007). Mishukoshi's Intelligent Fitting Room introduced in 2006 and powered by Cisco's mobile technologies; and TheBigSpace's Magic Mirror™ used since 2009 in select Levi's stores, are examples of self-service technology that relied on information stored in radio-frequency identification (RFID) tags to display product information on an interactive touch screen surface. In 2002, Prada introduced a similar technology in its stores called the Smart Dressing Room (Bickers, 2008) that also allowed customers to save information into their own profile. The Smart Dressing Room was not as successful as Prada expected and this was due in part to "employee sabotage" or the store employees' bad attitudes towards the technology (Bickers, 2008).

Froehle (2006) recorded customer satisfaction with employees after using technologies such as online chat and email. Results indicated that the personal characteristics of the employee, such as being knowledgeable and prepared, influenced customer satisfaction but the type of technology used by the employee during the technology-mediated service encounter did not. No evaluations of employees or their reactions to the use of technology were measured; however, the results suggest that the best customer experience is provided by complementing employee service skills with technology use.

Even if a retail company determines that a technology will be valuable for its customers, there is no guarantee that employees will use it, as in the case of Prada's "employee sabotage". For this reason, the study presented in this chapter focused on employee intent to actually use technologies that have significance for the apparel store but have not been studied before in this context. The study focused on three of the five modes that required the employee to use technology (Froehle & Roth, 2004), namely 'technology-assisted', 'technology-facilitated', and 'technology-mediated' formats. Each technology type was chosen to represent a specific mode as follows:

1. The technology-assisted mode was represented by a 3-D body scanner, where the employee operates the technology to help a customer with sizing information;
2. The technology-facilitated mode was represented by a digital product configurator, where the employee and customer interact around the technology in order to customize clothing; and
3. The technology-mediated mode was represented by social networking, where the use of this technology would be the only means of communication between employees and customers.

A Study of Apparel Retail Technologies

Three technologies were selected for a study of apparel retail employee's attitudes towards technology adoption. The technologies for this study represent recent advances in technology that were specifically adapted to the apparel retail store environment: a 3D body scanner, product configurator, and social networking. It is important to note that these technologies were not yet widely used and were not merely updates of conventional retail technologies but offered strategic opportunities through their hybrid interfaces.

Body Scanner

Body scanners have been in existence since the late 1990s; and, since that time, various scanner models have become globally available to retailers from companies like Cyberware, Human Solutions, Styku, " [TC]² ", and Unique Solutions. Both Levi's and Brooks Brothers have offered customized products enabled by body scanning technology. The scanner provides information to retail employees that can help them find products that will best fit the customer. The scanning process takes place by having the customer enter an enclosed booth where white light, lasers or radio waves are used to establish the shape and dimensions of the body. After this process the scanner can provide a visual image of customers and/ or their body measurements. By applying scan measurement data to what is called 'size selection', the scanner records customer body measurements in order to recommend clothing sizes and styles. The body scanner was considered a 'technology-assisted interface' since the employee uses this technology, for the scanning process or for size selection, to support the task of finding the right size for the customer while customer involvement is relatively inactive.

Product Configurator

The product configurator is a digital tool that enables a user to customize apparel by style or color or any other design features the retailer chooses to offer within the software and to then view the changes virtually. This technology has largely been adopted by small niche apparel businesses and by sportswear retailers to allow for the creation of customized footwear. Nike was one of the first companies to offer an online customization tool for its footwear in 1999 called NikeiD, and in 2007 they introduced the NIKEiD studio in the company's New York City store. The Nike customer was able to interact with employees known as design consultants to create their own footwear or apparel (Nike, 2007). The configurator provided an opportunity for both the employee and the customer to creatively interact around the product as a 'technology facilitated service interface'. It also has potential for providing desirable in-store experiences to shoppers for customization and consultation (Lee et al., 2002; Wood, 2002).

Social Networking

Social networking is a web-based technology that allows subscribers to communicate with others in their same geographic area, specific group or network of acquaintances using a variety of social media platforms. Currently, Facebook and Twitter are the dominant platforms used by apparel customers and retailers (Lockwood, 2012). Apparel retailers like JCPenney and Express both enabled their online catalogs on Facebook in an effort to reach more of their customers (Chaney 2010, Martinez 2011). The use of in-store social networking by retailers has not been as pervasive as their use of social networking to connect with customers outside of brick-and-mortar stores via the internet and mobile devices. One exception has been the in-store technology called 'social retailing', which was developed by the digital agency Icon Nicholson, and introduced for testing in retail stores in 2007. Social retailing allowed customers to connect to their own network of acquaintances via email or instant messaging for immediate feedback on styles that are being tried on in the store (IconNicholson, 2007). This form of social sharing has since evolved into other digital applications available for consumers use (e.g. snapette.com, gotryiton.com) and they do not require apparel retailer buy-in or employee engagement for use. For this study, social networking was considered a 'technology-mediated interface' where technology would be used by employees and would be the only point of contact for employees and customers.

As the previous descriptions illustrate, the technologies selected for this study are non-traditional formats found in retail stores and may not be readily accepted by employees. As retailers gradually adopt these and other new technologies, employee response should be measured in order to determine if employees are prepared, interested, and willing to use these advanced technologies as part of their work. Benefits of use for employees include new job roles associated with the technology as in the case of the product configurator and design consultant roles at Nike. Employees may also realize the benefits of increased customer interaction supported by technology, such as designing products, or receiving real-time feedback regarding the store's products and/or services.

Technology Acceptance Model

Willingness to use new technologies in the workplace was researched by Davis, Bagozzi and Warshaw (1992) as they developed and applied the Technology Acceptance Model (or TAM). Under the TAM, perceptions of a technology's usefulness, ease of use, and enjoyment are expected to impact user attitude and overall intent to use a new technology (Davis, Bagozzi, & Warshaw, 1989, 1992). Usefulness was defined as the degree to which users perceive that a technology would improve job performance, and was considered an *extrinsic motivation* to use technology since it provided a valuable outcome as a result of use (Davis et al., 1989, 1992). Ease of use referred to how much users felt that using a technology would be free of effort (Davis et al., 1989). And perceived enjoyment was defined as the user's determination of how much fun would be derived from using the technology, regardless of its functionality or expected output. Enjoyment was considered an intrinsic motivation since a technology was used based solely on the degree of fun derived from its operation (Davis et al., 1992). While both usefulness and enjoyment were found to have a significant impact on intended use of technology, usefulness had a greater influence on intent (Davis et al., 1992). The mediating effects of usefulness and enjoyment on behavioral intention were also found in a study of consumer perceptions of online retailer sites by Lee, Fiore, and Kim (2006). Davis et al. (1992) also evaluated task importance, or how important technology was to one's specific job responsibilities, as a moderating variable of the influence of ease of use on usefulness. In a study of how tasks and technology fit with business students, Mathieson and Keil (1998) found a significant interaction between database type and task on perceived ease of use. Task importance is a variable that would figure greatly into technology use related to work; therefore, it was included along with the other variables tested by Davis et al. (1992) for use in this study.

The TAM has been applied widely and specifically among salespeople to measure the factors influencing their adoption of technology used for daily activities such as email, instant messaging, and electronic organizing (Robinson, Marshall, & Stamps, 2005). Results support the TAM. A field setting was used by Lucas and Spitler (1999) to test use of computer work stations among brokers and sales assistants in an investment bank using the TAM. The participants used computer software that was directly related to their jobs, but the study results did not support the TAM. Szajna (1996) used the TAM to conduct a longitudinal study of email usage by employees. This study confirmed that the TAM was able to predict actual usage behavior of technology based on measures of behavioral intention.

How confident employees feel towards using technology, or their self-efficacy, can influence how they perceive a technology's ease of use (Venkatesh & Davis, 1996). Employees need to feel confident using technology first in order to view it as free of effort, able to improve job performance, or even fun to use. A measure of technology self-efficacy was used for this study since the technologies evaluated were newer, more advanced (i.e., body scanner, product configurator, and social networking), and different from those used in previous TAM studies. The scarce availability of these technologies in retail stores, along with different levels of complexity required for use, may also challenge the confidence of retail employees.

The body scanner, product configurator, and social networking technologies evaluated for this study were distinct and more advanced than the technology types used in previous TAM studies. In addition, since the selected technologies were not widely used in the context of apparel retail, this study can provide beneficial information regarding the likelihood of technology adoption as well as strategies for implementation in the retail store setting. The evaluation of TAM variables from the employee perspective is a significant contribution to the research regarding technology use for work related purposes. This evaluation can also help define areas where current job roles might be enhanced using specific technology types.

HYPOTHESES

This study used TAM variables—perceived ease of use, perceived usefulness, perceived enjoyment and behavioral intention (Davis et al.,1992)—to evaluate motivations to use tech-

nology. The workplace context for this study is advanced technology for apparel retail, as opposed to the business software used in the Davis et al. (1992) study. That study also included a measure of participants' usage intentions or how often they intended to use the technology. A measure of usage behavior, or actual technology use, was not possible in this study since the technologies tested were not widely available at retail stores for observation and not likely to be familiar to participants. However, it has been found that behavioral intention is a strong predictor of actual technology usage (Szajna, 1996; Turner, Kitchenham, Brereton, Charters, & Budgen, 2010). Based on the Davis et al. (1992) TAM, the following relationships were hypothesized:

H1: Perceived usefulness will have a significant effect on employee behavioral intention to use technology;

H2: Perceived enjoyment will also have a significant effect on employee behavioral intention to use technology;

H3: The effect of perceived ease of use on employee behavioral intention to use technology will be mediated by both perceived usefulness and perceived enjoyment;

H4: Task importance will moderate the effect of perceived ease of use on perceived usefulness;

H5: Task importance will not moderate the effect of perceived ease of use on perceived enjoyment.

In addition, the following relationship was expected based on retail employee confidence with using the new technologies:

H6: Employees with high technology self-efficacy will indicate higher perceived ease of use, usefulness, and enjoyment of technologies than those with low technology self-efficacy.

METHOD

Within Subjects Design

Participants were asked to use all three technologies in order to control for the variability in personal characteristics, particularly in terms of retail work experience and job positions. The within subjects design (also called repeated measures) is recommended whenever participant variability may significantly influence responses. For within subjects design, participant characteristics are held constant, thereby reducing the amount of error variance that might occur if individual participants used one technology. Because of increased statistical power resulting from less variability in participants, within subjects designs also allow for a smaller number of participants than required for a between subjects design (Bordens & Abbott, 2002; Kuchl, 2000). To account for participant fatigue or carryover effects that may have resulted from systematic use of the three technologies, the order of technology use was counterbalanced and treatment order combinations randomly assigned to participants.

Participants were asked to complete a set of demographic questions and technology self-efficacy measurements before being introduced to the three technologies. Demographic information also included a measure of service orientation and career aspirations for each participant. For each technology, an oral description of how the technology worked was presented by the researcher, who also demonstrated how to use the technology; then, each participant used the technology independently. When this treatment was completed, participants completed a set of printed questions for that technology, and were then introduced to the next technology.

Variables

The TAM variables were measured with scales developed and validated by Davis et al. (1992); these were modified by adding the specific name of each technology used for this study. Variables related to the TAM were measured using six 7-point items for perceived usefulness ($\alpha = .98$) and six 7-point items for perceived ease of use ($\alpha = .94$), both developed and validated by Davis (1989). From Davis et al. (1992), three 7-point items for perceived enjoyment ($\alpha = .81$), one 7-point item for task importance and two 7-point items for behavioral intention ($\alpha = .88$) were used. The single task importance item was modified from the Davis et al. (1992) questionnaire to describe the specific task that each technology would support for a retail employee: size selection (body scanner), customization of clothing (product configurator), and gathering and reviewing feedback from customers about products (social networking). The ten item 10-point computer self-efficacy measurement ($\alpha = .95$) developed by Compeau and Higgins (1995) was used to measure employee technology self-efficacy (see Figure 1). Service orientation items consisted of those taken from the five 5-point customer orientation items ($\alpha = .91$) developed by Susskind, Kacmar and Borchgrevink (2003) to measure customer service attitude. Current job position and highest desired future job position were measured with two separate items developed using job labels taken from the National Retail Federation's career ladder (nrf.com). Job labels included: sales associate, assistant manager, store manager, senior store manager, assistant district manager, district manager, regional manager, and regional vice president. Additional demographic information measured included participant job title, type of store, hours worked, gender, age, and education.

Pilot Study

A pilot study was conducted to test the clarity of questionnaire items, the procedures for using each technology, as well as any issues with their functionality or usability. Three graduate students (one male and two females) in the field of apparel and textiles along with five female

Figure 1. Service orientation means

		N^a	Service Orientation	SD	Range	Variance
Sample Description		71	4.68	.43	1.80	.18
Current job	**Not working**	30	4.56	.49	1.80	.25
	Sales Associate	18	4.69	.40	1.40	.16
	Manager	23	4.83	.31	1.00	.10
	Total	71				
Store type	**Specialty**	32	4.80*	.34	1.40	.12
	All	34	4.55*	.49	1.80	.24
	Total	66				
Gender	**Male**	15	4.46*	.54	1.80	.30
	Female	56	4.74*	.38	1.40	.14
	Total	71				
Age	**16 to 21**	42	4.60	.48	1.80	.23
	22 to 29	19	4.76	.32	1.00	.11
	30+	10	4.86	.33	1.00	.11
	Total	71				
Education	**College degree**	26	4.81*	.29	1.00	.09
	No degree	45	4.60*	.48	1.80	.23
	Total	71				

Note:*means significantly different at $p<.05$, based on 1-5 Likert-Type Scale; $^a N$ totals vary due to missing cases

participants enrolled in a local community-based retail training program took part in the pilot study. The results of the pilot study determined that it would take a total of 20 to 30 minutes for completion of the study; it also revealed problems with Internet connectivity and use of interactive web-based programs. Since the Internet connection was not consistently available at the research site and participants would be able to view comments entered by previous participants on the social networking site, the technologies were formatted so that participants did not need to connect to the Internet for interactivity. This limited the potential confounding effects of the Internet on the treatments.

Data Collection

Data were collected from a convenience sample of both apparel retail store employees and people with work experience in apparel retail but who were not currently working in a store. To assure that participants were familiar with the nature of service and work in a retail setting, retail work experience was required for participation. All participants were pre-screened for work experience during the scheduling of their research session. Data were collected in a rented space at a large mall, where retail employees had access to the technologies and sufficient time to complete the study, and in a research space near a local university. Both locations were in Central New York. Participants recruited for the mall study were employees of retail mall stores and all were offered a $5 gift card for the study and a chance to win a raffle for one of three $50 gift cards. Participants for the research space were recruited via university email listservs, the research recruitment website of the university's psychology department, social media, and recruitment by the researcher at local retail stores. The mall location was the first location for the study; and as employee participation rates were very low, the incentive was increased to $20 to encourage participation and travel to the lab location.

Both locations were set up with the same technologies: a [TC]² NX-12 body scanner and two laptop computers. The body scanner was operated by a desktop computer loaded with specific software for producing an image of the scanned person and extracting measurements that could be used for size selection. The participants were shown the inside of the body scanner and how to operate the scanner from the computer station. One laptop was used for the product configurator and another for social networking. Participants were able to select prints and style features for three garments (children's shirt, overalls and jacket) using a product configurator developed for research studies (Lee, Damhorst, Campbell, Loker, & Parsons, 2011). The social networking site was developed specifically for this study; it included a customer message board as well as customer profiles for both men's and women's clothing that participants could navigate as if they were contacting a customer regarding a store's products.

RESULTS

Sample Profile

A total of 71 participants completed the study between the two sites – 10 at the mall site and 61 at the laboratory site. The sample included 56 females (78.1%) and 15 males (21.1%). Ages of participants were from 16 years to 66 years with the most participants being ages 16 to 21 (59.2%). Thirty-nine participants had received some post-secondary education (54.4%). Fifty-two participants worked part-time (73%). There were 41 participants (57.8%) who were currently working in a retail store and 18 were employed as a sales associate (25.4%), 9 were assistant managers (12.7%), and 14 (19.7%) were store managers. Those working in stores with one product category, which could include men's, women's or children's clothing were placed into a group called *Specialty* and those working in stores with more than one product category were placed into a group called *All*. There were 32 (51%) participants in *Specialty* stores and 34 (48%) in *All* stores. Thirty participants (42.3%) had retail work experience but were not currently working in retail. Overall, the sample was aware of the importance of customer service, with a mean service orientation of 4.7 ($SD = .4$, *range* = 1.8), based on 1 – 5 Likert-type scale where *1 = Strongly Disagree* and *5 = Strongly Agree* (see Figure 1). Mean comparisons using one-way ANOVA and t-tests were used to test for significant differences between participants' service orientation based on the variables of age, gender, education, current job, and store type (see Figure 3). Gender ($t_{69}=2.3$, $p<.05$), education level ($t_{69}= -2.3$, $p<.05$) and store type ($t_{64}= 2.5$, $p<.05$) showed significant differences, with women having a higher average service orientation ($M = 4.7$) than men ($M = 4.5$); those with a college degree having a significantly higher service orientation ($M = 4.8$) than those without a college degree ($M =4.6$); and those working in specialty stores with one apparel product category ($M =4.8$) significantly higher than those working in stores with two or more different apparel categories ($M =4.5$). Career goals were determined by measuring the difference between the participant's current job and the highest job position he or she desired in the future and a new variable called *delta job* was created, where higher values indicated a larger distance from one's goal. For this sample, most people wanted to remain in their current job (*n*=24) or advance one position (*n*=29), while those with aspirations beyond one position were fewer (*n*=17).

Technology Acceptance Model (TAM)

The overall mean ratings of TAM variables for each of the technologies were high, ranging from 4.6 to 6.4 on a scale of 1-7 (see Figure 2). Mean comparisons were made among the technologies for each variable using one-way ANOVA. Significant differences were found for all variables except perceived ease of use. Post-hoc analysis with Tukey's HSD showed that means for usefulness

were different between the product configurator and body scanner, with the product configurator measuring significantly lower (see Figure 2). The product configurator also measured significantly lower than the other two technologies on task importance, receiving its lowest overall mean rating on this variable (M = 4.58). The body scanner showed significantly higher means than the other two technologies for enjoyment (M = 6.38) and behavioral intention (M = 6.16), receiving its highest overall mean for enjoyment.

The TAM hypotheses were tested using multiple regression analysis, following the hierarchical regression method used by Davis et al. (1992) to evaluate relationships among the TAM variables (see Figure 3). Since participants completed sepa-

Figure 2. Mean comparisons of TAM variables

Variable	Technology Type	N	Mean	F	p	Std Dev	Std Error
EASE	Body Scanner	71	6.33	.47	.63	.65	.08
	Product Config	71	6.36			.74	.09
	Social Netwk	70	6.43			.76	.09
USEFUL	Body Scanner	71	5.86^a	3.62	.00*	1.21	.14
	Product Config	70	4.84^{b,c}			1.67	.20
	Social Netwk	70	5.39^{a,c}			1.20	14
ENJOY	Body Scanner	70	6.38^a	9.06	.00*	.78	.09
	Product Config	70	5.96^b			1.03	.12
	Social Netwk	71	5.85^b			1.03	.12
TASK IMP	Body Scanner	66	6.20^a	32.34	.00*	1.26	.16
	Product Config	64	4.58^b			1.96	.25
	Social Netwk	68	6.10^a			.92	.11
BHV INTENT	Body Scanner	71	6.16^a	13.16	.00*	.90	.11
	Product Config	71	5.08^b			1.77	.21
	Social Netwk	71	5.48^b			1.44	.16

Note: Superscripts within each group represent pairwise comparisons. Means showing at least one letter in common are not significantly different at p <.05; * p <.05; all measured on a 1-7 Likert-type scale. Ns vary due to missing cases. ** EASE = perceived ease of use; USEFUL = perceived usefulness; ENJOY = perceived enjoyment; TASK IMP = task importance; BHV INTENT = behavioral intention.

Figure 3. Regression results for technology acceptance and technology self-efficacy

	TECHNOLOGY TYPE															
	Body Scanner (a)					**Product Configurator (b)**					**Social Networking (c)**					
	DV	R²	Independent Variable	β	SEβ	DV	R²	Independent Variable	β	SEβ	DV	R²	Independent Variable	β	SEβ	
H1	BI	.44	USF	.67*	.02	BI	.53	USF	.73*	.03	BI	.50	USF	.71*	.03	
H2	BI	.19	ENJ	.44*	.08	BI	.12	ENJ	.35*	.13	BI	.11	ENJ	.34*	.10	
H3	*Mediation Effects*					*Mediation Effects*					*Mediation Effects*					
Step 1	BI	.11	EOU	.33*	.05	BI	.19	EOU	.44*	.13	BI	.02	EOU	.16	.07	
Step 2	BI	.51	USF	.61*	.02	BI	.53	USF	.72*	.03	BI	.50	USF	.73*	.04	
			ENJ	.22*	.07			ENJ	.03	.11			ENJ	-.05	.09	
Step 3	BI	.52	USF	.64*	.03	BI	.53	USF	.72*	.04	BI	.54	USF	.74*	.04	
			ENJ	.24*	.07			ENJ	.02	.12			ENJ	.03	.09	
			EOU	-.90	.05			EOU	.01	.13			EOU	-.08	.05	
H4	*Moderating Effects*					*Moderating Effects*					*Moderating Effects*					
Step1	USF	.31	EOU	.39*	.21	USF	.53	EOU	.44*	.30	USF	.30	EOU	.25*	.16	
			TASK	.29*	.65			TASK	.48*	.46			TASK	.45*	.78	
Step2	USF	.31	EOU	.11	.83	USF	.54	EOU	.24	.72	USF	.30	EOU	.81	1.59	
			TASK	-.26	4.99			TASK	-.38	4.44			TASK	1.21	10.73	
			EOUxTASK	.69	.14			EOUxTASK	.94	.12			EOUxTASK	-1.03	.27	
H5	*Step1*															
	ENJ	.15	EOU	.35*	.08	ENJ	.29	EOU	.44*	.12	ENJ	.14	EOU	.22	.07	
			TASK	.10	.24			TASK	.21	.18			TASK	.27*	.36	
Step2	ENJ	.18	EOU	-.33	.30	ENJ	.29	EOU	.59*	.28	ENJ	.14	EOU	.57	.75	
			TASK	-1.23	1.79			TASK	.86	1.73			TASK	.74	5.04	
			EOUxTASK	1.69	.50			EOUxTASK	-.71	.05			EOUxTASK	.63	.13	
H6	*Technology Self-Efficacy*					*Technology Self-Efficacy*					*Technology Self-Efficacy*					
	ENJ	.04	TECH SEFF	.20	.02	ENJ	.06	TECH SEFF	.24*	.02	ENJ	.18	TECH SEFF	.42*	.02	
	EOU	.09	TECH SEFF	.31*	.03	EOU	.11	TECH SEFF	.32*	.02	EOU	.01	TECH SEFF	.10	.04	
	USF	.21	TECH SEFF	.46*	.05	USF	.15	TECH SEFF	.38*	.07	USF	.15	TECH SEFF	.39*	.05	

Note: DV (dependent variable); BI (behavioral intention); USF (perceived usefulness); ENJ (perceived enjoyment); EOU (perceived ease of use); TASK (task importance); TECH SEFF (technology self-efficacy); * $p < .05$.

rate questionnaires for each technology, separate analyses were conducted for each technology and results in Figure 3 are designated for each hypothesis with a corresponding letter (a = body scanner, b = product configurator, or c = social network). Independent variables were also evaluated for multicollinearity, and the collinearity statistics showed that multicollinearity did not present a problem for the data since tolerances were above .40 and the variance inflation factors were low (< 3.0).

Effects of Perceived Usefulness and Perceived Enjoyment

Hypothesis 1 stated that perceived usefulness would have a significant effect on behavioral intent to use technology, and Hypothesis 2 stated that perceived enjoyment would also have a significant effect on behavioral intent. For all three technolo-gies, results indicated that both usefulness (H1) and enjoyment (H2) influenced behavioral intention. Therefore, hypotheses 1 and 2 were supported for all technologies studied (see Figure 3).

It was also hypothesized that the effect of perceived ease of use on behavioral intention would be mediated by both perceived usefulness and perceived enjoyment (H3). For the body scanner, Hypothesis 3 was supported since both perceived usefulness and perceived enjoyment were found to mediate the influence of perceived ease of use on behavioral intention (see Figure 3). For the product configurator, the effect of perceived ease of use on behavioral intention was significant when usefulness and enjoyment were not accounted for in the model. However, when usefulness and enjoyment were added to the model, only usefulness and not enjoyment was significant as a mediating variable. Hypothesis 3 was rejected for the product configurator. For social networking, perceived ease of use was not found to have main effect on behavioral intention. When the variables of perceived usefulness and perceived enjoyment were added to the regression model, only usefulness had a significant effect on intent to use this technology. However, Hypothesis 3 was rejected for social networking since ease of use did not have a main effect that was then mediated by either usefulness or enjoyment (see Table 3).

Moderation of Task Importance

Task importance was predicted to moderate the effect of perceived ease of use on perceived usefulness (H4) but not the effect of perceived ease of use on enjoyment (H5). The importance of the technology supporting one's work (task importance) was expected to strengthen the influence of ease of use on usefulness. For all three technologies, ease of use and task importance had significant main effects on usefulness (see Figure 3). Controlling for the main effect of task importance, the interaction effect of task importance and ease of use on perceived usefulness was not significant for any of the technologies; therefore, Hypothesis 4 was rejected. The interaction effect of task importance and enjoyment on perceived usefulness was also not significant for the three technologies; as a result, Hypothesis 5 was supported. These results were partially consistent with research by Davis et al. (1992), which also did not show a significant interaction between ease of use and task importance as an influence on enjoyment, as they predicted. However, in contrast to the findings in this study, Davis et al. (1992) did find a significant interaction effect of ease of use and task importance on usefulness.

Technology Self-Efficacy

Prior to using the technologies in the study, participants answered a set of 10 printed questions regarding technology self-efficacy. Scores from the technology self-efficacy scale were summed, as recommended by Compeau and Higgins (1995) to capture both self-efficacy magnitude and strength (see Figure 4). The median score for technology self-efficacy was 72 and the mean was 72.6 (*SD* = 15.0, *range* = 77) out of 100. Overall, scores for technology self-efficacy were towards the higher end of the scale for the sample (see Figure 4). Mean comparisons for technology self-efficacy based on demographics of the sample showed a significantly higher technology self-efficacy scores for employees in Specialty stores than employees in all stores (see Figure 4).

Hypothesis 6 proposed that higher technology self-efficacy scores would correspond with higher ratings for perceived ease of use, usefulness, and enjoyment for all three technologies. Regression analysis was used to determine if higher self-efficacy scores could predict higher ratings for the TAM variables (see Figure 3). For the body scanner, higher self-efficacy scores were associated with higher ratings for ease of use and usefulness, but not enjoyment; as a result, Hypothesis 6 was rejected. For the product configurator, higher technology self-efficacy was related to higher ratings for all three TAM variables; therefore Hypothesis 6 was accepted. Finally, for social networking, higher self-efficacy scores were associated with higher ratings for usefulness and enjoyment but not ease of use; consequently, Hypothesis 6 was rejected.

Influences on Intent to Use New Technology

Usefulness

The usefulness findings for technologies in this study concur with the mediation effects found for Davis et al. (1992). Usefulness emerged as the major mediating influence on behavioral intent for all three technologies. Measures of usefulness may provide the most reliable indicator for apparel companies evaluating the introduction of

Figure 4. Technology self-efficacy means

		N[a]	Technology Self-Efficacy	SD	Range	Variance
Sample Description		71	72.29	.43	77	225.71
Current job	**Not working**	30	67.60	17.06	76	291.15
	Sales Associate	18	74.06	11.21	40	125.70
	Manager	23	77.23	13.35	49	178.18
	Total	*71*				
Store type	**Specialty**	32	75.81*	13.79	49	190.16
	All	34	68.06*	15.78	68	248.97
	Total	*66*				
Gender	**Male**	15	64.27	20.12	68	404.92
	Female	56	74.47	12.68	49	160.70
	Total	*71*				
Age	**16 to 21**	42	70.07	15.05	76	226.41
	22 to 29	19	74.37	15.97	57	255.14
	30+	10	78.22	11.69	35	136.69
	Total	*71*				
Education	**College degree**	26	72.40	14.97	57	224.00
	No degree	45	72.22	15.22	76	231.77
	Total	*71*				

Note: * Means significantly different at p<.05; [a] N totals vary due to missing cases

new technology within the retail store since Davis et al. (1992) link significant effects of usefulness to actual usage of technology once it is introduced to the user.

Enjoyment

The mediating influence of enjoyment on behavioral intent (H3) was not consistent across the technologies with findings by Davis et al. (1992). Enjoyment mediated the effect of ease of use on behavioral intent for the body scanner only. Enjoyment represents the perceived fun that a user would have with a technology irrespective of its relation to work. The scanner results may be related to its novelty in terms of the image output (i.e., 3-D body image) or even its appearance as a technology with its own built structure, containing not only the scanning hardware but a changing room and computer station. Employees' perceptions of how they might independently operate this technology could have influenced evaluations of enjoyment for this technology-assisted interface. For the product configurator (technology-facilitated), enjoyment did not have a significant mediating effect on behavioral intent, and the same was found for social networking (technology-mediated). The product configurator only contained style content for children's wear. Such a product content limitation may have also influenced perceptions of enjoyment while using this technology since many participants worked in stores selling women's apparel (45%). Participant familiarity with existing social networks, like Facebook, and its functions may have influenced enjoyment ratings for the technology format used in this study. Participants may have already used social networking in other ways and held preconceived ideas of what would be an enjoyable application of this technology.

Technology Self-Efficacy

For the body scanner and product configurator, higher self-efficacy scores were related to significantly higher ratings for ease of use and usefulness. A measure of employee technology self-efficacy could help avoid possible issues with employee sabotage of technology as encountered by Prada (Bickers, 2008). In this study, participants responded to self-efficacy questions prior to using the technologies and a similar method could be implemented by retailers prior to introducing new technology. A gauge of overall employee technology self-efficacy could determine adoption readiness.

Task Importance

The single task importance item used in the questionnaire for each technology described three different types of tasks that could be supported by each technology: size selection (body scanner), customization of clothing (product configurator), and gathering and reviewing feedback from customers about products (social networking). Task importance did not moderate the effect of ease of use or usefulness for any of the technologies as predicted. This effect may not have been significant because the technologies presented in this study are not yet widely used at retail stores; and participants may have been unable to connect each technology's importance to the specific tasks described since the tasks do not yet exist in cur-

rent job roles. In cases where new tasks are to be performed using technology, task importance may not be a valuable measure for evaluating employee adoption, since employees are not yet familiar with tasks that are enabled by the technology.

SOLUTIONS AND RECOMMENDATIONS

Customers have already expressed their interest in technology-facilitated interfaces like the product configurator (Kamali & Loker, 2002), technology-assisted formats such as the body scanner (Lee et al., 2002; Loker et al., 2004), and the technology-mediated format is rapidly advancing as retailers engage consumers via social media (Chaney, 2010; Martinez, 2011). Retail environments could be equipped with technologies that allow for simulations with customers for trying on clothing items, co-designing, or customization. Technology-facilitated formats like the product configurator could be combined with a technology-assisted format like the body scanner to create this interactive store environment. Social networking or other social media (e.g., Twitter), could be available in-store and allow retailers to provide increased interaction with customers; it could even allow digital information exchange of body scan data or images of styles created with the product configurator.

Finally, new job roles may be created as technologies are introduced to accomplish innovative tasks that may not have traditionally been part of the apparel retail employee job description. As technology enables the possibility of employee-customer interactions beyond sales transactions, retail employees may take on more technology-based job roles. Apparel retailers may further increase their competitiveness by adding technology interfaces like social networking that allow employees to know more about customer preferences based on direct feedback from customers instead of solely on data stored in point-of-sale systems that track customer purchases. Other technology interfaces may serve not only as a means of collecting customer feedback but also to provide experiences that are enjoyed by both customers and employees in the apparel retail environment. Physical spaces in retail stores might be dedicated to retail *props* like body scanners or design stations outfitted with product configurators where services are provided for fun and not necessarily as part of a sales transaction, but rather an experience. Additionally, retailers can help customers connect their online and in-store shopping experiences through virtual technologies or visual displays that re-create the interactivity of websites with the instant gratification of purchasing an item in the store. Customers will soon require that stores to keep pace with their personal technology use, and employees, as seen with this study, already show intent to use technologies that can engage customers in a more technologically-enabled apparel store.

FUTURE RESEARCH DIRECTIONS

Observation and Behavior

The experimental design of this study with treatment and research setting helped to control extraneous effects. However, it also may have detracted from the reality of a retail store setting, where these technology formats would actually be used with customers. Future studies should be conducted in an actual retail store environment to evaluate the interaction of employees and customers with these and other complex technologies, and to examine the relationships theorized in the TAM model. Davis et al. (1989) theorized that behavioral intention will influence actual usage of a technology, and observations in a retail store setting would be necessary in order to assess this relationship. Furthermore, employees and customers could be evaluated simultaneously; and results of these evaluations could be used to provide advice to retailers regarding the potential success of technology implementation with both.

Apparel Retail Employee Sample

Statistics for the apparel retail industry show that 29% of apparel retail workers are under the age of 24, more than twice the average amount for other industries (Bureau of Labor Statistics, 2010). Yet, in this study, the proportion of employees between the ages of 16 and 21 (59.2%) is greater than that found in the population; and, given that only 10 participants were over the age of 30, the results may not accurately reflect attitudes of older retail employees. For example, the sample ranked very high in terms of service orientation but did not indicate job position aspiration that would indicate a desire to have a long-term career in apparel retail. Older participants may have possessed a different level of career goals resulting from a longer work history. Additionally, younger participants are likely to be more comfortable with new technology as members of a digital generation accustomed to a variety of technology products. The sample was also predominantly female (78.9%), with only 15 males (21.1%) participating in the study; however, this closely represents the 25% male workforce in the U.S. apparel retail industry (Bureau of Labor Statistics, 2010). Future studies should evaluate different age, gender, and ethnic populations to uncover implications for broadening the employment opportunities, job satisfaction, and overall appeal in retail store careers that could result from technology use.

Technology and Apparel Retail Employee Use

The study presented is the first to apply the TAM to advanced technology use among apparel retail employees. Specifically, it examined the use of technologies that did not relate to point-of-sale, inventory tracking or cash management functions—typical areas of focus for technology advancement in retail stores. This study provided insight as to why employees would adopt emerging technologies that could be used to improve customer service interactions and even offer increased job satisfaction, two issues that present challenges for retailers.

Apparel retailers that would like to incorporate technology into their stores might consider some of the factors found in the study. First, participants rated all technologies positively in terms of usefulness and behavioral intention (see Figure 2). Specifically, these variables measured efficiency, improvement in job performance, enhancement of job effectiveness, and the likelihood of using the technologies on a regular basis. Retailers should consider the three emerging technology types presented in this study as capable of improving and/or transforming the nature of work in their stores.

CONCLUSION

This study examined three hybrid interfaces and provides specific evaluations of innovative technology by apparel retail workers. The simultaneous benefit of improved customer service and employee job satisfaction may result from technology interaction offered by the formats examined in this chapter and other advanced hybrid technology interfaces. These technologies may provide an appealing combination for retailers searching for new strategies to compete and succeed in the current competitive retail environment. The three technologies studied here represent only a few of the possibilities apparel retailers may explore as they transition from customer service to customer experiences. Deciding to incorporate technology into the store environment may not be an option for future retailers as they continue to compete in areas of service, efficiency and profit. Recently, one of America's largest apparel brands, Gap Inc., announced that it would be raising the minimum wage for its in-store employees to $9.00 an hour and eventually to $10 an hour in order to ensure a more talented pool of employees. This was reportedly a strategic move to help support its efforts to merge the online and in-store services for its

customers (Berfield, 2014). The combination of potential new job roles and enhanced customer service as a result of technology use definitely warrants further study of technologies promoting innovation in the retail workplace. This is an encouraging sign for retailers to implement more opportunities for technology use to provide increased efficiency and new in-store experiences for both employees and customers.

REFERENCES

Albrecht, K., & Zemke, R. (2002). *Service America in the new economy*. New York: McGraw-Hill.

Baron, S., Harris, K., & Harris, R. (2002). Retail theater: The "intended effect" of the performance. *Journal of Service Research*, *4*(2), 102–117. doi:10.1177/109467050142003

Berfield, S. (2014, June 24). *Gap raises wages and – surprise—more people want to work there*. Retrieved from http://www.bloomberg.com/bw/articles/2014-06-24/gap-learns-to-get-better-job-candidates-pay-them-more

Bickers, J. (2008, July). Trying on clothes, 2.0. *Retail Customer Experience*. Retrieved from http://www.retailcustomerexperience.com/article/4071/Trying-on-Clothes-2-0

Bordens, K. S., & Abbott, B. B. (2002). *Research design and methods: A process approach*. New York, NY: McGraw-Hill.

Broadbride, A. (2003). The appeal of retailing as a career: 20 years on. *Journal of Retailing and Consumer Services*, *10*(5), 287–296. doi:10.1016/S0969-6989(02)00065-6

Bureau of Labor Statistics, US Department of Labor. (2010, May). *Career guide to industries, 2008-2009 edition: Clothing, accessory and general merchandise stores*. Retrieved from http://www.bls.gov/oco/cg/cgs022.htm

Burke, R. R. (2002). Technology and the customer interface: What consumers want in the physical and virtual store. *Journal of the Academy of Marketing Science, 30*(4), 411–432. doi:10.1177/009207002236914

Chaney, P. (2010). *J.C. Penney moves entire product catalog to Facebook.* Retrieved from http://www.practicalecommerce.com/blogs/post/788-J-C-Penney-Moves-Entire-Product-Catalog-to-Facebook

Compeau, D. R., & Higgins, C. A. (1995). Computer self-efficacy: Development of a measure and initial test. *Management Information Systems Quarterly, 19*(2), 189–211. doi:10.2307/249688

Davis, F. D., Bagozzi, R. P., & Warshaw, P. R. (1989). User acceptance of computer technology: A comparison of two theoretical models. *Management Science, 35*(8), 982–1002. doi:10.1287/mnsc.35.8.982

Davis, F. D., Bagozzi, R. P., & Warshaw, P. R. (1992). Extrinsic and intrinsic motivation to use computers in the workplace. *Journal of Applied Social Psychology, 22*(14), 1111–1132. doi:10.1111/j.1559-1816.1992.tb00945.x

Dickerson, K. G. (2003). *Inside the fashion business* (7th ed.). Upper Saddle River, NJ: Prentice Hall.

Fiore, A. M. (2008). The digital consumer: Valuable partner for product development and production. *Clothing & Textiles Research Journal, 26*(2), 177–190. doi:10.1177/0887302X07306848

Fleenor, D. G. (2007, November). Magic mirror on the wall: Fitting room tool offers LP, service benefits. *Stores,* L14-L16.

Froehle, C. M. (2006). Service personnel, technology, and their interaction in influencing customer satisfaction. *Decision Sciences, 37*(1), 5–38. doi:10.1111/j.1540-5414.2006.00108.x

Froehle, C. M., & Roth, A. V. (2004). New measurement scales for evaluating perceptions of the technology-mediated customer service experience. *Journal of Operations Management, 22*(1), 1–21. doi:10.1016/j.jom.2003.12.004

Heskett, J. L., Sasser, W. E., & Schlesinger, L. A. (2003). *The value profit chain: Treat employees like customers and customers like employees.* New York: The Free Press.

Hochschild, A. R. (1983). *The managed heart.* Los Angeles, CA: University of California Press.

IconNicholson. (2007) *The mall + Facebook: Try that on!* Retrieved from http://www.iconnicholson.com/nrf07/

Inditex. (2005). *Annual report 2005.* Retrieved from http://www.inditex.com/documents/10279/13717/Grupo_INDITEX_informe_rsc_05.pdf/7155a5ed-2ac9-4571-bc3f-c42331954316

Kamali, N., & Loker, S. (2002). Mass customization: On-line consumer involvement in product design. *Journal of Computer-Mediated Communication, 7*(4), 1–21. doi:10.1111/j.1083-6101.2002.tb00155.x

Kilcourse, B., & Rosenblum, P. (2009). *Walking the razor's edge: Managing the store experience in an economic singularity.* Miami, FL: Retail Research Systems.

Knight, D. K., Crustinger, C., & Kim, H. (2006). The impact of retail work experience, career expectations, and job satisfaction on retail career intention. *Clothing & Textiles Research Journal, 24*(1), 1–14. doi:10.1177/0887302X0602400101

Knowledge@Wharton. (2007, May 16). *Are your customers dissatisfied? Try checking out your salespeople.* Retrieved November 2, 2007 from http://knowledge.wharton.upenn.edu/article.cfm?articleid=1735

Kozinets, R. V., Sherry, J. F., DeBerry-Spence, B., Duhachek, A., Nuttavuthisit, K., & Storm, D. (2002). Themed flagship brand stores in the new millennium: Theory, practice, prospects. *Journal of Retailing*, *78*(1), 17–29. doi:10.1016/S0022-4359(01)00063-X

Kuehl, R. O. (2000). *Design of experiments: Statistical principles of research design and analysis.* Pacific Grove, CA: Brooks/Cole.

Lee, H., Damhorst, M. L., Campbell, J. R., Loker, S., & Parsons, J. L. (2011). Consumer satisfaction with a mass customized internet apparel shopping site. *International Journal of Consumer Studies*, *35*(3), 316–329. doi:10.1111/j.1470-6431.2010.00932.x

Lee, H., Fiore, A. M., & Kim, J. (2006). The role of the technology acceptance model in explaining effects of image interactivity technology on consumer responses. *International Journal of Retail & Distribution Management*, *34*(8), 621–644. doi:10.1108/09590550610675949

Lee, S.-E., Kunz, G. I., Fiore, A. M., & Campbell, J. R. (2002). Acceptance of mass customization of apparel: Merchandising issues associated with preference for product, process, and place. *Clothing & Textiles Research Journal*, *20*(3), 138–146. doi:10.1177/0887302X0202000302

Lewis, T. L., & Loker, S. (2007, November). *Customization, visualization, enjoyment and utility: Consumer preferences for existing apparel industry technology.* Paper presented at the Annual Meeting of the International Textile and Apparel Association, Los Angeles, CA.

Lockwood, L. (2012). Consumers turn to social media for customer service. *WWD*, *26*(October). Retrieved from http://www.wwd.com/media-news/digital/consumers-turn-to-social-media-for-customer-service-6455590

Loker, S., Cowie, L., Ashdown, S., & Lewis, V. D. (2004). Female consumers' reactions to body scanning. *Clothing & Textiles Research Journal*, *22*(4), 151–160. doi:10.1177/0887302X0402200401

London, M. (1989). *Managing the training enterprise.* San Francisco, CA: Jossey-Bass Inc.

Lucas, H. C., & Spitler, V. K. (1999). Technology use and performance: A field study of broker workstations. *Decision Sciences*, *30*(2), 291–311. doi:10.1111/j.1540-5915.1999.tb01611.x

Martinez, J. (2011, May). *Express to offer customers opportunity to purchase entire product catalog via Facebook.* Retrieved from http://multichannel-merchant.com/from-the-wire/express-facebook-social-shopping-0503tpp9/?cid=nl_imerch

Mathieson, K., & Keil, M. (1998). Beyond the interface: Ease of use and task/technology fit. *Information & Management*, *34*(4), 221–230. doi:10.1016/S0378-7206(98)00058-5

Nike. (2007, October 4). *Nike opens new NIKEiD studio in New York giving consumers a key to unlock the world of design.* Retrieved from http://www.nikebiz.com/media/pr/2007/10/4_nikeid_nyc.html

Occupational Information Network. (2011, June). Summary report for 41-2031.00- retail salespersons. *O*Net Online.* Retrieved from http://www.onetonline.org/link/summary/41-2031.00

Peñaloza, L. (1999). Just doing it: A visual ethnographic study of spectacular consumption at Niketown. *Consumption Markets & Culture*, *2*(4), 337–465. doi:10.1080/10253866.1998.9670322

Pine, B. J., & Gilmore, J. H. (1999). *The experience economy: Work is theatre & every business a stage.* Boston: Harvard Business School Press.

Pollack, E., Maxwell, J., & Feigen Dugal, L. (2007). *Retailing 2015: New frontiers.* New York, NY: PricewaterhouseCoppers/TNS Retail Forward.

Rayport, J. F., & Jaworski, B. J. (2005). *Best face forward: Why companies must improve their service interfaces with customers.* Boston, MA: Harvard Business School Press.

Rhoads, G. K., Swinyard, W. R., Geurts, M. D., & Price, W. D. (2002). Retailing as a career: A comparative study of marketers. *Journal of Retailing, 78*(1), 71–76. doi:10.1016/S0022-4359(01)00068-9

Robinson, L. Jr, Marshall, G. W., & Stamps, M. B. (2005). An empirical investigation of technology acceptance in a field sales force setting. *Industrial Marketing Management, 34*(4), 407–415. doi:10.1016/j.indmarman.2004.09.019

Schlesinger, L. A., & Zornitsky, J. (1996). Job satisfaction, service capability, and customer satisfaction: An examination of linkages and management implications. *Human Resource Planning, 14*(2), 141–149.

Senecal, S., Pullins, E. B., & Buehrer, R. E. (2007). The extent of technology usage and salespeople: An exploratory investigation. *Journal of Business and Industrial Marketing, 22*(1), 52–61. doi:10.1108/08858620710722824

Solomon, M. R., & Rabolt, N. J. (2004). *Consumer behavior in fashion.* Upper Saddle River, NJ: Pearson Education.

Susskind, A. M., Kacmar, K. M., & Borchgrevnik, C. P. (2003). Customer service providers' attitudes relating to customer service and customer satisfaction in the customer-server exchange. *The Journal of Applied Psychology, 88*(1), 179–187. doi:10.1037/0021-9010.88.1.179 PMID:12675405

Swinyard, W. R. (1981). The appeal of retailing as a career. *Journal of Retailing, 57*(4), 86–97.

Swinyard, W. R. (1997). Retailing trends in the USA: Competition, consumers, technology and the economy. *International Journal of Retail & Distribution Management, 25*(8), 244–255. doi:10.1108/09590559710178329

Swinyard, W. R., Langrehr, F. W., & Smith, S. M. (1991). The appeal of retailing as a career: A decade later. *Journal of Retailing, 67*(4), 451–465.

Szajna, B. (1996). Empirical evaluation of the revised technology acceptance model. *Management Science, 42*(1), 85–92. doi:10.1287/mnsc.42.1.85

Tornow, W. W., & Wiley, J. W. (1991). Service quality and management practices: A look at employee attitudes, customer satisfaction, and bottom line consequences. *Service Quality and Management Practices, 14*(2), 105–115.

Turner, M., Kitchenham, B., Brereton, P., Charters, S., & Budgen, D. (2010). Does the technology acceptance model predict actual use? A systematic literature review. *Information and Software Technology, 52*(5), 463–479. doi:10.1016/j.infsof.2009.11.005

Ulrich, D., Halbrook, R., Meder, D., Stuchlik, M., & Thorpe, S. (1991). Employee and customer attachment: Synergies for competitive advantage. *Human Resource Planning, 14*(2), 89–103.

US Department of Labor. (2008). *Occupational outlook handbook, 2008-2009 edition.* Retrieved May 15, 2008, from http://www.bls.gov/oco/ocos121.htm

Venkatesh, V., & Davis, F. (1996). A model of the antecedents of perceived ease of use: Development and test. *Decision Sciences, 27*(3), 451–481. doi:10.1111/j.1540-5915.1996.tb01822.x

Wood, S. L. (2002). Future fantasies: A social change perspective of retailing in the 21st century. *Journal of Retailing, 78*(1), 77–83. doi:10.1016/S0022-4359(01)00069-0

ADDITIONAL READING

Ahearne, M., & Rapp, A. (2010). The role of technology at the interface between salespeople and consumers. *Journal of Personal Selling & Sales Management, 30*(2), 111–120. doi:10.2753/PSS0885-3134300202

Baird, N., & Rowen, S. (2011). *Keeping up with the mobile consumer* [Benchmark Study]. Miami, FL: Retail Systems Research.

Beatty, S. E., Mayer, M., Coleman, J. E., Reynolds, K. E., & Lee, J. (1996). Customer-sales associate retail relationships. *Journal of Retailing, 72*(3), 223–247. doi:10.1016/S0022-4359(96)90028-7

Cho, H., & Fiorito, S. (2009). Acceptance of online customization for apparel shopping. *International Journal of Retail & Distribution Management, 37*(5), 389–407. doi:10.1108/09590550910954892

Danziger, P. (2006). *Shopping: Why we love it and how retailers can create the ultimate customer experience.* Chicago: Kaplan Publishing.

Darian, J. C., Tucci, L. A., & Wiman, A. R. (2001). Perceived salesperson service attributes and retail patronage intentions. *International Journal of Retail & Distribution Management, 29*(5), 205–213. doi:10.1108/09590550110390986

Davis, S. M. (1987). *Future perfect.* Reading, MA: Addison-Wesley Publishing Company.

Diamond, J., & Litt, S. (2009). *Retailing in the Twenty-First Century.* New York: Fairchild Books.

Frei, F. X., Ely, R. J., & Winig, L. (2011). Zappos.com 2009: Clothing, customer service, and company culture. Harvard Case Study, 9-610-015. Boston: Harvard Business Publishing.

Gilmore, J. H., & Pine, J. B. II, (Eds.). (2000). *Markets of one: Creating customer-unique value through mass customization.* Boston: Harvard Business Review.

Gilmore, J. H., & Pine, J. B. II. (2007). *Authenticity: What consumers really want.* Boston: Harvard Business Publishing.

Ha, S., & Stoel, L. (2009). Consumer e-shopping acceptance: Antecedents in a technology acceptance model. *Journal of Business Research, 62*(5), 565–571. doi:10.1016/j.jbusres.2008.06.016

Kang, J., & Park-Poaps, H. (2011). Motivational Antecedents of Social Shopping for Fashion and its Contribution to Shopping Satisfaction. *Clothing & Textiles Research Journal, 29*(4), 331–347. doi:10.1177/0887302X11422443

Kim, J., Ma, Y. J., & Park, J. (2009). Are US consumers ready to adopt mobile technology for fashion goods? An integrated theoretical approach. *Journal of Fashion Marketing and Management, 13*(2), 215–230. doi:10.1108/13612020910957725

Lewis, R., & Dart, M. (2010). *The New Rules of Retail: Competing in the World's Toughest Marketplace.* New York: Palgrave Macmillan.

Lewis, T. L., & Loker, S. (2014). Technology usage intent among apparel retail employees. *International Journal of Retail & Distribution Management, 42*(5), 422–440. doi:10.1108/IJRDM-07-2012-0067

O'Reilly, K., & Paper, D. (2012). CRM and retail service quality: Front-line employee perspectives. *International Journal of Retail & Distribution Management, 40*(11), 865–881. doi:10.1108/09590551211267610

Pine, J. B. II, & Korn, K. C. (2011). *Infinite possibility: Creating customer value on the digital frontier.* San Francisco: Berrett-Koehler Publishers, Inc.

Rifkin, J. (1995). *The end of work: The decline of the global labor force and the dawn of the postmarket era.* New York: Jeremer Tarcher/Penguin.

Rigby, D. (2011). The future of shopping. *Harvard Business Review*. Retrieved from http://hbr.org/2011/12/the-future-of-shopping/ar/pr

Sanders, E. B., & Stappers, P. J. (2008). Co-design and the New Landscapes of Design. *CoDesign*, *4*(1), 5–18. doi:10.1080/15710880701875068

Schumann, J. H., Wunderlich, N. V., & Wangenheim, F. (2012). Technology mediation in service delivery: A new typology and an agenda for managers and academics. *Technovation*, *32*(2), 133–143. doi:10.1016/j.technovation.2011.10.002

Smith, A. N., Fischer, E., & Yongjian, C. (2012). How does brand-related user-generated content differ across youtube, facebook, and twitter? *Journal of Interactive Marketing*, *26*(2), 102–113. doi:10.1016/j.intmar.2012.01.002

Speer, J. (2012). People + technology: getting the recipe right. Retrieved from http://apparel.edgl.com/case-studies/People---Technology--Getting-the-Recipe-Right82660

Ton, Z., Corsi, E., & Dessain, V. (2010). Zara: Managing stores for fast fashion. Harvard Case Study, 9-610-042. Boston: Harvard Business Publishing.

Ulrich, P. V., Anderson-Connell, L. J., & Wu, W. (2003). Consumer Co-Design of Apparel for Mass Customization. *Journal of Fashion Marketing and Management*, *7*(4), 398–412. doi:10.1108/13612020310496985

Verhoef, P. C., Lemon, K. N., Parasuraman, A., Roggeveen, A., Tsiros, M., & Schlesinger, L. A. (2009). Customer experience creation: Determinants, dynamics, and management strategies. *Journal of Retailing*, *85*(1), 31–41. doi:10.1016/j.jretai.2008.11.001

KEY TERMS AND DEFINITIONS

Clicks and Bricks: A retail store format that is a physical space known as "brick-and-mortar" and also offers technologically supported services to customers that engage with the retailer through an online interface or by "clicking" through a website. An example would be a customer that views and orders clothing online and then visits a store to pick up or try-on the clothing.

Co-Design: Product design activities that include the end-user or consumer in the creative design process.

Digitally Integrated Store: Reference to a store that has adopted digital technologies as part of customer service. This may or may not involve a link to a retailer's online or e-commerce offerings.

Employee Sabotage: Purposeful abandonment or misuse of in-store technologies by employees in order to prevent widespread or permanent adoption.

Experience Economy: In market-based economies, this refers to an enhancement in services provided by companies in order to provide unique experiences for consumers.

Hybrid Interfaces: A format for service delivery to customers through a combination of technology use and employee expertise.

Social Shopping: The engagement of a customer's social network during the in-store buying process via a personal smart device (phone or tablet) and/or retailer's advanced hardware (interactive mirror).

ENDNOTES

[1] RedLaser app available at http://itunes.apple.com/us/app/redlaser.
[2] MySizeApp available at www.mysizefinder.com.

Chapter 7
Omni Channel Fashion Shopping

Astrid Kemperman
Eindhoven University of Technology, The Netherlands

Lieke van Delft
Wereldhave, The Netherlands

Aloys Borgers
Eindhoven University of Technology, The Netherlands

ABSTRACT

This chapter gives insight into consumers' online and offline fashion shopping behavior, consumers' omni-channel usage during the shopping process, and consumer fashion shopper segments. Based on a literature review, omni-channel shopping behavior during the shopping process was operationalized. Subsequently, an online survey was developed to collect information of 2124 consumers living in the catchment areas of five regional Dutch shopping centers in 2013. Results of the analyses confirm previous findings and contribute additional evidence that suggests relations between consumers' omni-channel shopping behavior during the shopping process and socio-demographics and psychographics. Furthermore, results show that channel usage in the previous phase of the shopping process has a major influence on the channel usage in the following phases of the shopping process. By using the TwoStep clustering technique, six fashion shopper segments are found and described, with one of them a clear omni-channel shopper segment. The results provide information for retailers to know the type of consumers they reach through various channels to offer the right information, on the right channel, during the various phases of the shopping process.

INTRODUCTION

Consumers increasingly use a range of technologies in their lives, also affecting the way they shop (Oh, Teo & Sambamurthy, 2012). The number of purchase and orientation channels (such as magazines, advertisement leaflets/catalogues, the shop, family or friends, website/web shop, social media, and applications on mobile devices) in innovative retail environments has increased

DOI: 10.4018/978-1-4666-8297-9.ch007

(Kumar, 2010). Consumers, nowadays, have many opportunities to orientate, gain information and buy products; they can shop at any time and at any location. Consumers also increasingly use a range of online and offline channels at the same time, so called omni channel usage. Consequently, consumers are well informed through all these channels and are therefore more critical while making purchase decisions.

Many retailers have expanded their shopping channels, offline and online, to better serve their customers and to increase sales (Benedicktus, Brady & Dark, 2008; Verhoef, Neslin & Vroomen, 2007). More and more existing retailers are developing a multichannel retailing strategy for serving shoppers across all channels (Seck & Philippe, 2011). For retailers it is important to offer consumers the right mix of information sources during the different phases of the shopping process (stimulation, information search, purchase, delivery and after sales service; e.g., Engel, Blackwell & Miniard, 2001).

In recent years, an increasing number of studies has focused on online shopping behavior (e.g., Javadi, Dolatabadi, Nourbakhsh, Poursaeedi & Asadollahi, 2012; Verhoef, et al., 2007; Kim & Eastin, 2011; Jepsen, 2007). Online shopping behavior has changed consumers' decision making process. It is a challenge to understand the behavior of consumers in an environment where consumers can shop anytime and anywhere. Thereby, it is important to understand the characteristics of consumer segments, in order to target and position online and offline channels well, to be able to reach new customers and serve current customers (Konuş, Verhoef & Neslin, 2008; Wallace, Giese & Johnson, 2004).

Some studies focused on multi-channel and cross channel shopping behavior (Konuş et al., 2008; Neslin et al., 2006; Verhoef, et al., 2007). Multi-channel shopping is shopping on different channels at the same time, for instance in the brick and mortar shop and online on a website. Within multi-channel shopping every channel has its own

strategy. In cross channel shopping there is one strategy for all channels and consumers use different channels. Omni channel shopping is seen as an advanced form of cross channel shopping. Consumers use several channels during the buying process, both online and offline. In addition, consumers switch easily and continuously between these channels and they experience all channels together as one complete channel.

Moreover, new media and mobile devices have influenced shopping behavior. The new shopper is always online; has fast access to information; compares and evaluates prices actively; uses several channels, online as well as offline to search, shop and buy; shares his/her product experience through social media, and at last the new shopper has high expectations for meeting his/her needs and wants, anytime and anywhere (Keller, 2010).

At the moment, European retailers and consumers experience tough times due to the financial crises. Consumers have less confidence in the economy; as a result they are more conscious about their purchases. In addition to the dropped consumer confidence, the retail market is saturated because of the continuous expansion in the last decades, leading to an increased competition between retailers (NRW, 2011). Consumers previously came automatically to the shops, but those days are over. Nowadays, consumers need to be attracted to shops. Hence, information about consumers is needed to attract new consumers, and to increase involvement and loyalty. Eventually, this should result in more profit for the retailer.

A method to study consumers and their buying behavior is consumer segmentation (Gilboa, 2009). Consumer segmentation is the process of dividing a heterogeneous market into groups of customers which have nearly the same characteristics, wishes, needs, buying habits or reactions on marketing activities. Consumer segmentation assumes that consumers exhibit heterogeneity in product preferences and buying habits (Dibb, 1998). Through segmentation, retailers can determine the most interesting customer groups to focus on. Current studies on consumer segmentation, do not consider omni channel shopping behavior and the shopping process. While insight in omni channel shopping behavior during the shopping process can help retailers and investors in retail real estate by developing a strategy to beat the competition.

The objectives of this study are:

1. To gain insight in consumers' online and offline shopping behavior,
2. To understand consumers' omni channel usage during the shopping process, and
3. To find consumer shopping segments taking into account channel usage.

With insight in the shopping process and omni channel shopping behavior of consumers, retailers can better serve their consumers and improve their competitive advantage.

Data was collected through an online survey held among 2124 consumers living in the catchment areas of five regional shopping centers in the Netherlands in 2013. As shopping behavior depends on the product category, the fashion category is selected, as this is an important category for these shopping centers. In addition, psychographic characteristics of consumers (price consciousness, shopping enjoyment, innovativeness, motivation to conform, loyalty and time pressure) and socio-demographics were added for explaining channel usage and characterizing the shopper segments (e.g., Mcgoldrick & Collins, 2007) .

Background

This study aims to provide information to retailers about consumers (omni) channel usage during the shopping process and to find segments that differ with regard to their channel usage. In this literature review first, the shopping process will be addressed, followed by omni channel shopping behavior and finally studies on segmentation of shoppers will be described.

The Shopping Process

A considerable amount of literature has been published on the consumer decision making shopping process. Steinfield, Bouwman & Adelaar (2002) describe the purchase process in three phases. The first phase is the pre-purchase stage, followed by the purchase stage and the process ends with a post-purchase stage (Kollmann, Kuckertz, & Kayser, 2012). Suominen (2005) divides the buying process in five phases: activate, browse, configure, decide and purchase. Solomon, Bamossy, Askegaard & Hogg (2002) define the following phases: problem recognition, information search, evaluation of alternatives and last, product choice (Lihra & Graf, 2007). According to Engel et al. (2001), a consumer decision making process has seven phases: need recognition, search for information, pre-purchase alternative evaluation, purchase, consumption, post-purchase alternative evaluation and divestment.

The problem recognition phase of Solomon et al. (2002) shows similarities with the activation phase of Suominen (2005) and the need recognition of Engel et al., (2001). When consumers show significant differences between the current state and their desired state, then a problem is recognized: the consumer needs a product. Problem/need recognition is a natural process, which can be stimulated by marketing. After consumers have recognized the problem, they want to gain information. This information can be found in the consumers' memory (internal search) or it can be acquired from the environment (external search). As the purchase is more expensive, a consumer generally wants to obtain more information about the product.

The scope of information search can differ regarding the product type and consumers characteristics such as age, education level and gender (Lihra & Graf, 2007; Engel et al., 2001). When the information about possible products is obtained, the consumer can evaluate the alternatives. Consumers may carefully evaluate different products based on the expected benefit or make a routine decision depending on the product category. When relevant options are known, the consumer must choose between the product options. Consumers can be influenced in making their decision by experience, available information and attachment to the brand. There are also stages after the product purchase, as described by Engel et al. (2001): consumption, post-purchase alternative evaluation and divestment. Consumption is the phase in which the product is used. The post-purchase evaluation is the evaluation of the satisfaction about the product bought. The last phase of the consumer decision making process is the divestment phase, in which the unconsumed product or its residue is disposed.

For this research, the buying process of a consumer is called 'the shopping process'. This shopping process is more enhanced than the buying process of Steinfield et al. (2002) and comparable with the consumer decision making process of Solomon et al. (2002). The shopping process for this research consists of five phases; stimulation, search for information, purchase, delivery and after sales service. These phases are the most relevant phases for retailers. The delivery phase is added in the shopping process because consumers have (among others through online shopping) several options for the delivery of their products.

Phase 1 - Stimulation: During the first phase consumers become inspired by a product. This phase is not always visible; consumers can get stimulated to buy a product in their subconscious mind. For instance, when consumers see an advertisement of a shop on Facebook they can get attracted to buy the product.

Phase 2 - Search for Information: During the search phase, consumers know what they are looking for because they are already inspired. Consumers are searching for information about products and/or services and their providers. This process can take a long

time, but it can also be done in a short time, depending on the product category. There is a distinction between high involvement and low involvement products. Grocery is in general a low involvement product; a house for instance is a high involvement product.

Phase 3 - Purchase: When all the information is collected, a purchase decision can be made. During this phase the consumer determines which product or service is actually purchased for what price and from which supplier.

Phase 4 - Delivery: When the product is bought, there are few options depending on the channel where the product is bought; take the product home directly, delivery at home or at work, collect from a pick-up point or pick-up later in the shop.

Phase 5 - After Sales Service: Then there is the after sales service. There are several channels through which consumers can reach companies offline as well as online. The importance of after sales service should not be underestimated; companies with a good after sales program acquire consumer loyalty.

Every phase in the shopping process requires the right information in order to go to the next phase. As result of an increasing number of (digital) channels, the shopping process becomes more and more complex and it is important that retailers provide the right information through the right channel.

Omni Channel Shopping Behavior

Recently, the popularity of the concept 'omni channel shopping' has increased, but little research is conducted (yet) on omni channel shopping behavior (Dholakia, Kahn, Reves, Rindfleisch, Stewart & Taylor, 2010). However, studies have addressed multi-channel and cross channel shopping behavior (Konuş, et al., 2008; Neslin et al., 2006; Verhoef, et al., 2007). Multi-channel shopping is shopping on different channels, for instance in the brick and mortar shop and online on a website. Within multi-channel shopping every channel has its own strategy. In cross channel shopping there is one strategy for all channels and consumers use different channels.

Omni channel shopping is seen as an advanced form of cross channel shopping. Consumers use several channels during the buying process, both online and offline: channels such as websites, web shops, social media, brick and mortar shops, applications on mobile devices, catalogues, and more. In addition, consumers switch easily and continuously between these channels and they experience all channels together as one complete channel. For instance, when consumers are going to shop for groceries at Albert Heijn (a large supermarket chain in the Netherlands) they can use the 'Appie' application on their smartphone; this application can show consumers' shopping list and a personalized shopping route. Consumers experience this application and the shop as one complete channel: omni channel shopping.

Consumers consider the pros and cons of each channel before using them. Gupta, Su and Walter, 2004; Gong & Maddox, (2011) found that factors that influence consumers online and offline shopping behavior are channel-risk perceptions, price-search intentions, search effort, evaluation effort and delivery time. But research also showed that online consumer behavior is associated with demographics, channel knowledge, perceived channel utility and shopping orientation (Javadi, et al., 2012). While, Zijlmans, (2010) concluded that the choice behavior of consumers regarding channels depends on characteristics of consumers, products, shopping channels and the retailer. Based on their wants and needs at a moment, the consumer decides which channel to use to search for information or buy products.

Not all goods or services are suitable for online sales. Goods which need to be experienced personally are more suited for brick and mortar shops. On the other hand, online shopping gives consumers an anywhere anytime convenience. Consumers

search online for product features, compare prices, read reviews, select products, obtain services, place orders, payments, and much more (e.g., Kollmann, et al., 2012). There is no travelling and waiting time. Furthermore, online shops also offer useful information about products and services, which makes shopping for bargains more attractive. Also, consumers can move easily among different channels; obtaining information from one retailer's channel and then switch to another retailer's channel to complete the purchase (Chiu, Hsieh, Roan, Tseng & Hsieh, 2011; Heitz-Spahn, 2013).

Recent, new media have emerged, resulting in a closer connection between retailer and consumer. In the Netherlands, social media have integrated in daily life; almost eighty percent of the Dutch uses social media (Newcom research, 2013). Social media can be defined as media for social interaction, using highly accessible and scalable communication techniques (Markova & Petkovska-Mirčevska, 2013). Social media is, among others, accessible by personal computer, tablet and smartphone. In June 2012, twenty-three percent of the Dutch population had a tablet and forty-eight percent had a smartphone. New media and mobile devices have created a new type of shopper. The new shopper has a strong functional and emotional bond with his/her smartphone. The new shopper is always online; has fast access to information; compares and evaluates prices actively; uses several channels, online as well as offline to search, shop and buy; shares his product experience through social media, and at last the new shopper has high expectations for meeting his needs and wants, anytime and anywhere (Wagner, Schramm-Klein & Steinmann, 2013).

The challenge for omni-channel retailers is to manage shopping processes of the various consumer segments in the best possible way across all the channels that are available nowadays (Baal van, 2014). Therefore, it is important to know the shopper segments they reach through their various applications and social media channels to offer the right information on the right channel.

Segmentation Studies

A considerable amount of literature has been published on consumer segmentation. The studies are classified on subject (shopping centers yes/no), variables and whether multi-channel shopping is integrated. Omni channel buying behavior has not been implemented in segmentation research yet, multi-channel shopping was integrated in some segmentation studies.

Bloch, Ridgway & Dawson (1994) identified shopping center related shopping orientations by exploring differences in shopping center habitat activity patterns. 600 consumers were clustered based on their shopping behavior, using hierarchical as well as non-hierarchical cluster analyses. Four clusters of shopping center shoppers were formed, namely enthusiasts (higher than average value on every activity dimension), traditionalists (higher score than average on mall-focused activities and relatively high on product purchasing), grazers (high tendency to pass time in the mall browsing and eating) and minimalists (low participation in all activities). Significant clusters were found based on the intensity of mall shopping.

Jarret (1996) identified a set of variables that is relevant and appropriate for shopper segmentation. Through a telephone interview, information was collected from 931 consumers in three Australian trading areas. With cluster analysis, six shopper types were identified based on the consumers' importance of the shopping offer (variety, price, quality, comparative, shopping and value), the shopping environment (progressive, exciting, clean, attractive and interest) and the shopping service (friendly, helpful, parking and information).

Another study was conducted by Frasquet, Gil & Mollá (2001), who used choice modeling to analyze the perceived value on shopping-center selection and to investigate benefits of adopting a segmentation approach in the study of consumer preference for a shopping center in Valencia, Spain. Demographic segmentation criteria were chosen because this produces segments which are easy to identify and measure, and consumers' wants and preferences are often linked to demographic characteristics. Variables which were used to identify the segments were age, occupation and marital status.

Reynolds, Ganesh & Luckett (2002) researched differences between factory outlets and traditional malls through consumer segmentation. The importance of mall attributes, mall essentials, entertainment and convenience were rated by respondents. Through a mall intercept study, data was collected from 1097 traditional mall shoppers and 827 outlet shoppers. A multistep-cluster analysis was conducted and five shopper segments were found for the traditional mall as well as the factory outlet 'the enthusiasts', 'the basic', 'the apathetic', 'the destination' and 'the serious'. Unique for the factory outlet was the cluster 'brand seekers'.

Multi-channel shopping behavior was studied by Bhatnagar and Ghose (2004). They used a latent class modelling approach to segment online shoppers based on their purchase behavior across several product categories. Data was collected from 1330 respondents through an online survey. In the online survey, respondents had to evaluate online shops in general on 11 attributes. Consumers were segmented based on benefits they perceive from online shopping. For describing the segments, variables such as age, education, gender, income, marital status and internet experience were used.

Another study on multi-channel shopping behavior was conducted by Keen, Wetzels, Ruyter & Feiberg (2004). Their research was conducted to investigate the structure for consumer preferences in making product purchases. Three channels: shop, catalogue and the internet and two product categories were considered, CD's and personal computer. Data was collected from 281 shopping center shoppers in a suburb of Chicago with the shopping center intercept technique. Conjoint analyses was used to find the structure of the decision and the importance of attributes in the decision-making process. Clusters were formed through hierarchical as well as k-means clustering in two stages.

Interesting is the segmentation study of Ruiz, Chebat & Hansen (2004). This study is based on a methodology developed by Bloch et al. (1994). Shoppers are segmented on the basis of the activities performed during their shopping center visit. Variables such as perception, emotions and motivations were used to extend the data. The variables included in the segmentation were differences in activity patterns (do exercise, talk with other consumers, browse, take a snack, go to the bank, unplanned purchase, purchase). Descriptive variables were used to describe segments and these variables are classified into these groups: geographic (postal code), socio-demographic (age, mother tongue, sex, annual income, education level, number of children under eighteen at home and occupation), psychographic (perceptions, emotions, atmospheric variables, approach avoidance reactions, motivations, non-economic costs) and related benefits sought.

Konuş et al. (2008) analyzed the multi-channel shopping behavior of Dutch consumers through segmentation. They focused on two phases of the buying process, the search and the purchase phase. Consumers were segmented based on their attitude towards several channels as search and purchase alternatives. A survey was conducted among 364 Dutch consumers in a research panel. Three types of channels (brick and mortar shop, the internet and catalogues) were evaluated by the consumers in terms of their appropriateness for the two phases. The latent-class modelling approach was used and three segments were found. The multichannel enthusiasts, uninvolved shoppers and shop-focused consumers. Several descriptive variables (shopping enjoyment, loyalty and innovativeness) were used to predict which persons belong to which segments. The research did not find significant relationships with socio-demographics, however, consumer behavior was driven more by psychographics. The results demonstrate that segment membership is affected by hedonic and economic variables.

Finally, Gilboa (2009) identified four shopper types based on the shopping behavior of Israeli shopping center visitors. Behaviors were divided into three categories: visiting patterns, motivations for trips to the mall and activities engaged in during the visit. This segmentation study labelled four types of consumers: disloyal, family bonders, minimalists and mall enthusiasts. Research variables for shopping center visits were motivation, activities performed during the visit, visiting patterns and personal details.

DATA COLLECTION PROCEDURES

A survey is developed to collect data from respondents living in the catchment area of five Dutch regional shopping centers to explore and describe consumers' online and offline shopping behavior, to understand consumers' omni channel usage during the various phases of the shopping process and to find shopper segments based on their channel usage.

The fashion product category was chosen as it is an important category in regional shopping centers in the Netherlands. In the survey, fashion was described as clothes, shoes and accessories. The survey was divided in the following sections: the shopping process; online and offline shopping behavior; omni channel shopping behavior and personal characteristics.

Measuring the Shopping Process

For each phase of the shopping process data needed to be collected about channel usage (which channel they use and how often they use it).

Phases 1 and 2: Stimulation and Search for Information

Selected online channels for measuring stimulation and search for information were web shops/ websites, applications on mobile devices and social media. Web shops and websites are already common used channels to search for product information. Applications on mobile devices and social media are probably less often used. However, these channels were investigated because the usage of these channels for shopping is expected to increase in popularity in the near future. Offline channels in this research are brick and mortar shops, advertisement leaflets/catalogues and magazines. The category, family and friends is added to the questionnaire because of the strength of word of mouth advertisement especially in shopping centers.

Phase 3: Buy

For the third phase of the shopping process 'buy', the following channels were selected: the shop, website/web shop, catalogue, applications on mobile devices and social media. Channels most often used for buying products are the shop, catalogue and website/web shop. Another channel could be the telephone or television (tell sell), but these channels are not often used for the selected product category. The usage of applications and social media is increasing; therefore these channels are very interesting for this research.

Phase 4: Delivery

The fourth phase of the shopping process is delivery. Consumers could indicate whether they take their bought product direct home, collect them from a pick-up point, pick-up the products later in the shop, or let the bought products be delivered at home or elsewhere. The option 'take the product direct home' will most often occur when products are purchased in the shop. When products are purchased through other channels than the shop (website/web shop, catalogue, applications or social media) then the other delivery options (pick-up point, in shop, delivered) are more obvious. Especially the option pick-up point is an interesting option, because the use and number of pick-up points is increasing.

Phase 5: Service

The last phase of the shopping process is service. For this question online and offline channels for service were considered. Consumers could indicate whether they go back to the shop, contact the shop through the website/web shop, send a message through social media of the shop, call the shop, send an e-mail to the shop or contact the shop through an application on a mobile device. Sending a message through social media is very interesting for this research, because the interaction between retailers and consumers is increasing through social media. Consumers can like or criticize retailers on social media, this gives the retailers the ability to respond directly and become on top of mind of the consumer. Moreover, retailers can measure consumer satisfaction on posts on social media.

The shopping process is measured through five questions. Using a five point scale ((almost) never – (almost) always) respondents could indicate the frequency of channel usage during the five phases of the shopping process. The option 'I do not know' is also included to allow respondents to state that they do not have an opinion or that they did not think about it. This results in the following questions:

1. Do the following channels ever stimulate you to buy fashion?
    a. Magazines.
    b. Advertisement leaflets/catalogues.
    c. The shop.
    d. Family or friends.
    e. Website/web shop.
    f. Social media (Twitter, Facebook, Hyves, etc.).
    g. Applications on mobile devices.
2. To what extent are you using the below channels to search for information on fashion? (comparing prices, new products, etc.)
    a. Magazines.
    b. Advertisement leaflets/catalogues.

c.   The shop.

d.   Family or friends.

e.   Website/web shop.

f.   Social media (Twitter, Facebook, Hyves, etc.).

g.   Applications on mobile devices.

3.   How often do you buy fashion via the following channels?

a.   The shop.

b.   Website/web shop.

c.   Catalogue.

d.   Applications on mobile devices.

e.   Social media (Twitter, Facebook, Hyves, etc.).

4.   Please indicate how often you let fashion be delivered in the following way.

a.   Take home directly.

b.   Pick-up at a pick-up point.

c.   Pick-up later in the shop.

d.   Deliver to the door.

5.   If you need service for your bought fashion, how often do you contact the shop through the following channel?

a.   I go back to the shop.

b.   I contact the shop through the website/web shop.

c.   I send a message through social media of the shop.

d.   I call the shop.

e.   I send an e-mail to the shop.

f.   I contact the shop through an application on a mobile device.

Online and Offline Shopping Behavior

There are three phases in the shopping process that give a good representation of omni channel shopping behavior: stimulation, searching and buying. Stimulation and searching were merged into orientation, because we wanted to make a distinction between pre-purchase and purchase behavior. Then, for the two phases, orientation and buying, a distinction is made between online and offline shopping behavior. Respondents could indicate how often they orientate and buy online as well as offline for fashion. A 7 point scale (every day, a few times a week, weekly, a few times a month, monthly, a few times a year, (almost) never) is used for respondents to indicate their online and offline orientation and buying behavior.

Omni Channel Shopping

From the questions about the shopping process information about consumers' channel usage during the shopping process can be obtained. However, for this research also omni channel shopping behavior is required. To be able to gain extra information about omni channel shopping behavior the following question is included in the questionnaire "How often do you use the below channels while you are shopping in a brick and mortar shop?". Consumers could indicate on a five point scale, how often ((almost) never – (almost) always)) they use channels (advertisement leaflets or catalogues, magazines, social media, websites/web shops and applications on mobile devices) while shopping in a brick and mortar shop. Online and offline channels are considered because the use of two offline channels at the same time can also be classified as omni channel usage. Most interesting are the channels social media, website/web shop and applications. The usage of online channels in brick and mortar shops is expected to increase in the future because the use of smartphones and tablets is increasing.

Personal Characteristics

In the literature review it was concluded that psychographics are related to benefits consumers seek in their channel selections. Konuş et al. (2008) studied six psychographic characteristics: price consciousness, shopping enjoyment, innovativeness, motivation to conform, loyalty and time pressure.

- **Price Consciousness:** An important variable for this research because price conscious people probably use more channels to compare prices, because they want to pay the lowest price. A big advantage of omni channel shopping for consumers is finding a good deal by searching through channels. Retailers attract consumers with price-offers on their channels. Price conscious consumers will probably use many channels during their shopping process. They probably get activated by price offers and search for the lowest price on different channels, then they try the product in a physical shop, but when this shop does not offer the lowest price they will probably buy the product online.

- **Shopping Enjoyment:** This is about entertainment and benefits which are obtained by shopping. Research which was conducted by Nicholson, Clarke, and Blakemore (2002) has turned out that channel selection and social shopping are related to each other. Therefore, it seems that channel selection and shopping enjoyment are related (Konuş et al., 2008).

- **Innovativeness:** The degree to which consumers like to find out new or different products and experiences (Konuş et al., 2008). It is possible that individuals with a high degree of innovativeness show different channel behavior than individuals with a low degree of innovativeness. Innovative individuals are expected to search more extensive and at different channels during their shopping process.

- **Motivation to Conform:** An elementary component of self-expression which is a hedonic benefit of shoppers. Motivation to conform is the degree to which consumers need help or an opinion from someone else about a product during shopping decisions (Ailawadi, Neslin & Gedenk, 2001; Chandon, Wansink & Laurent, 2000; Konuş

et al. 2008). In addition, multi-channel behavior can be influenced by social norms (Keen et al. 2004) and channel selection behavior may depend on the usage of channels by reference groups (Verhoef et al. 2007). Therefore, motivation to conform is a personal characteristic which probably influences omni channel behavior.

- **Brand/Retailer Loyalty among Consumers:** This is very common. It costs lots of time to continuously switch between brands and retailers (Konuş et al., 2008). The expectation is that the more loyal consumers are, the fewer channels they use during their shopping process.

- **Time Pressure:** According to Kleijnen, De Ruyter & Wetzels (2007) when a person considers time as scarce (Konuş et al., 2008). Persons who experience time pressure plan their time well. Shopping online can offer time saving benefits for those persons. But shopping online is just one channel, the relation between omni channel shopping and time pressure is unclear yet.

In total 18 questions are implemented from the research of Konuş et al. (2008) to measure consumers' psychographics. Respondents had to response on these questions through a 5-point Likert-type scale with a range from completely disagree to completely agree.

Because of expected relations between shopping behavior and demographics in order to characterize consumer segments, demographics are added to this research as well. The following demographic characteristics of the respondents are asked in the questionnaire: age, gender, education, marital status, country of birth, average spending on grocery, work, work of partner, income. The selection of the demographic characteristics is based on the selection of Konuş et al. (2008); some extra variables are added to make the results of this research comparable with other studies as well.

Data Collection

Data is collected through an online questionnaire among consumers that live within the catchment area of five regional shopping centers in the Netherlands owned by a real estate investment company (Wereldhave). The catchment area is defined based on the travel time to the shopping center (within 17.5 minutes), and on average includes 93% of the visitors of the centers. The regional shopping centers offer a wide range of apparel and soft goods. Supermarkets, drugstores, and department stores are common anchors. Retailers in these types of shopping centers sell clothes, home improvement and furnishing, toys, electronics or sporting goods. Individuals were selected based on the postal code of their residence. These individuals are members of a research panel from a marketing research agency. The data is collected in June 2013. The total survey sample existed of 3243 persons, equally divided over the 5 shopping centers.

Table 1. Sample characteristics

Variables	Levels	%
Gender	Male	42
	Female	58
Age	16-29 years	10
	30-49 years	33
	50-64 years	38
	65+ years	19
Household Income	Low	25
	Middle	24
	High	52
Work Status	Full-time	31
	Part-time	24
	Retired	23
	Student	4
	No job	18
Education Level	Low	29
	Middle	38
	High	33

(N=2124).

ANALYSES AND RESULTS

Based on the objectives of this study the data analyses are divided into four sections: online and offline shopping behavior, channel usage during the shopping process, omni channel shopping behavior, and fashion shopper segments. First, a description of the respondents is given.

Profile of Respondents

In total, 3243 respondent were invited to participate in this research. 2124 respondents were willing to complete the questionnaire, indicating a response rate of 65%. Within the catchment area of every shopping center at least 417 respondents have completed the questionnaire; therefore the respondents are equally divided over the shopping centers. Table 1 provides an overview of the characteristics of the respondents.

Relatively many women have completed the questionnaire (58%) and thus relatively less males (42%). Ten percent of the respondents is below 30 years old, and one third of the respondents are between 30 and 49 years old. The largest group of respondents is between 50 and 64 years old (38%), and 19% of the consumers are over 65 years old. 25% of the respondents have incomes below average (less than €1600 a month), 24% have average incomes (€1600 – €2100 a month), and 52% of the consumers have above average incomes (more than €2100 a month). 31% of the respondents work full-time, 24% part-time and 23% is retired. In addition, a significant group of respondents has no job (18%). On third of the respondents within this research is high educated, the largest group is middle educated (38%) and 29% of the respondents is low educated.

Table 2. Online versus offline fashion orientation and buying behavior

	Categories	%
Online Orientate	Regularly Sometimes Never	41.4 22.1 36.5
Offline Orientate	Regularly Sometimes Never	40.6 26.4 33.0
Online Buy	Regularly Sometimes Never	16.8 35.4 47.8
Offline Buy	Regularly Sometimes Never	30.3 38.3 31.4

Consumers' Online and Offline Shopping Behavior

First online and offline buying behavior of consumers is explored, followed by relations between online and offline shopping behavior and personal characteristics.

In the questionnaire respondents could indicate how often (daily, a few times a week, weekly, a few times a month, monthly, a few times a year, (almost) never, I don't know) they orientate for fashion products and how often they buy products online as well as offline. Because of a low variance between the answers (too many categories), the data was first reorganized into three categories: regularly (daily, a few times a week, weekly, a few times a month, monthly), sometimes (a few times a year) and never (almost never). Table 2 shows that over 41% of the consumers orientate regularly online for fashion, while only 17% of

the consumers buy fashion regularly online. 35% of the respondents buy fashion online a few times a year. In general fashion is bought more often offline than online.

Cross tabs were used to describe the relationships between online orientation, offline orientation, online buying and offline buying. Specifically, in Table 3 the distribution of online orientation behavior with offline orientation, and on- and offline buying behavior is presented. Results show that consumers who regularly orientate online for fashion also regularly orientate offline for fashion. Within the consumer group who orientates regularly online for fashion 70% orientates as well regularly offline for fashion, while only 40% was expected based on independency. 62% of the respondents that never orientate online for fashion neither orientate offline for fashion. 38% of the consumers that regularly orientate online for fashion also regularly buy fashion online.

Logistic regression is used to estimate which personal characteristics of the respondents (psychographics, situation at home, work, income, gender, age and education) significantly influence their shopping behavior. The shopping behavior of respondents is considered as a categorical dichotomy, for instance; fashion orientate online; Yes=1, No=0. Nagelkerke R Square is an indication for the fit of the model. Table 4 shows a summary of the results of four logistic regression analyses. Significant results with a Nagelkerke R Square above .100 and an exp(B) value above 1.4 and below 0.600 are discussed.

Table 3. On- and offline orientation and on- and offline buying

Online Orientation %	Offline Orientation			Online Buy			Offline Buy		
	Regularly	Sometimes	Never	Regularly	Sometimes	Never	Regularly	Sometimes	Never
Regularly (n=872)	70	15	15	38	45	18	50	31	20
Sometimes (n=465)	28	53	19	4	60	37	22	54	24
Never (n=769)	15	24	62	1	10	89	13	37	50

Table 4. Summary logistic regression analyses for online and offline orientation and buying behavior and personal characteristics

Dependent Variable	Nagelkerke R Square	Predictors
Orientation Online	.244	Innovative, loyal, shopping enjoyment, income, gender, age and education
Orientation Offline	.244	Innovative, loyal, shopping enjoyment, gender, age and education
Buy Online	.202	Innovative, loyal, gender, age and education
Buy Offline	.227	Innovative, loyal, shopping enjoyment, gender, age and education

Whether consumers orientate online for fashion can be predicted by psychographics (innovation, loyalty and shopping enjoyment), income, gender, age and education. In general we can say that young respondents (<30 years old and 30-49 years old) and women are very likely to orientate and buy fashion online as well as offline. The fact that younger consumers are more involved in online orientation and buying behavior probably depends on the use of internet; the aging population is not grown up with the use of computers and the internet. In addition, the more un-innovative a consumer is, the less likely the consumer orientates online for fashion. Furthermore, interesting relationships are found between online orientation for fashion and loyalty as well as online orientation for fashion and shopping enjoyment. Un-loyal consumers are very likely to orientate online for fashion, and consumers who do not enjoy shopping are unlikely to orientate online for fashion. Also a relation is found between income and online orientation for fashion, consumers with low incomes are unlikely to orientate online for fashion.

Consumers' offline orientation behavior depends on consumers' innovativeness, loyalty, shopping enjoyment, gender, age and education. Un-innovative consumers are very unlikely to orientate offline for fashion, this is also the case for online orientation for fashion. Loyal consumers are likely to orientate offline for fashion while un-loyal consumers are very unlikely to orientate offline for fashion. In addition, a relation is found between shopping enjoyment and offline orientation for fashion. When consumers do

not enjoy shopping they are unlikely to orientate offline for fashion. This outcome was expected, because consumers who do not enjoy shopping are also unlikely to orientate online for fashion; they do not orientate for fashion online as well as offline. Women and younger respondents are more likely to orientate offline for fashion. Since the same results were found for online orientation for fashion, we can conclude that women and younger respondents are more likely to orientate online as well as offline for fashion.

Innovativeness, loyalty, gender, age and education significantly influence consumers' online buying behavior. Un-innovative consumers are very unlikely to purchase fashion online. Consumers' offline buying behavior can be predicted by innovativeness, loyalty, shopping enjoyment, gender, age and education. Consumers who do not enjoy shopping and low educated consumers are very unlikely to buy fashion offline. In addition, women and younger consumers are likely to buy fashion online.

Channel Usage during the Shopping Process

The main objective within this section is to gain insight in consumer's channel usage during the various phases of the shopping process. Respondents have indicated how often they use channels during the five phases of the shopping process. Because of a low variance between the answers, the data was recoded into three categories: regularly (regularly, often and

Table 5. Channel usage during the phases of the shopping process

Phases, Channels, Stimulation %	Applications	Social Media	Websites	Family and Friends	The Shop	Advertisement Leaflets or Catalogues	Magazines
Regularly	4.5	6.5	27.3	18.4	51.9	37.2	11.2
Sometimes	10.7	13.1	35.0	44.8	36.1	43.6	36.2
Never	84.8	80.4	37.7	36.8	12.1	19.3	52.6
Search for Information	Applications	Social Media	Websites	Family and Friends	The Shop	Advertisement Leaflets or Catalogues	Magazines
Regularly	5.6	5.0	37.0	14.1	55.9	42.0	12.5
Sometimes	10.6	9.9	30.7	40.4	30.5	36.5	32.5
Never	83.8	85.0	32.2	45.5	13.5	21.5	54.9
Buy	Applications	Social Media	Websites	The Shop	Catalogues		
Regularly	2.5	1.6	28.5	75.2	9.0		
Sometimes	5.6	4.2	34.1	20.4	33.6		
Never	91.9	94.2	37.3	4.4	57.5		
Delivery	Delivery at Home or Elsewhere	Pick-Up Later in Store	Pick-Up Point	Take Home Directly			
Regularly	35.8	4.2	5.9	85.0			
Sometimes	32.4	15.3	18.6	10.8			
Never	31.9	80.4	75.5	4.2			
Service	Application	E-Mail	Call the Shop	Social Media	Website	Back to the Shop	
Regularly	1.5	9.1	12.6	1.9	17.4	61.7	
Sometimes	3.8	19.6	29.9	3.1	27.6	29.2	
Never	94.7	71.3	57.5	95.0	55.1	9.0	

almost always), sometimes, and never (almost never). For every phase in the shopping process (stimulation, search for information, purchase, delivery and service) the frequencies are described in Table 5.

The first phase within the shopping process is stimulation. Consumers can get stimulated to buy products by different channels. Table 5 shows which channels are used by the respondents. The channel used most often for getting stimulated is the shop, followed by advertisement leaflets and catalogues. Search for information is the second phase of the shopping process. When consumers are stimulated to buy products, they go searching for information about the products. The shop is the channel most frequently used for searching for information, followed by advertisement leaflets and catalogues.

After searching for information consumers can decide to buy a product. Over 95% of the consumers buy fashion in the shop, and over sixty percent buys fashion through websites. Over forty percent buys fashion through catalogues. Only 6% of the respondents indicated that they buy fashion through social media, and 8% answered that they buy fashion through applications. Although this is only a small group, it is an interesting category (Shankar, Venkatesh, Hofacker & Naik, 2010). The shop is the most used channel for buying fashion, followed by the website/web shop and the catalogues. 68% of the respondents have indicated to buy fashion through a website/web shop.

When a product is bought consumers can take the products home directly, this is obvious. However regarding buying products online, it is

Table 6. Omni channel shopping behavior

Use of Channel While in a Brick and Mortar Shop	Advertisement Leaflets	Magazines	Social Media	Websites	Applications
Yes (%)	58	14	6	16	12

more interesting to find out how consumers get their purchases home; 68% of the consumers let their fashion products be delivered at home or elsewhere. About a quarter of the consumers collects their fashion purchases at a pick up point.

Consumers might need service after buying a product. Service is very important, because good service can increase customers' loyalty and the value for a retailer. For service, consumers go usually back to the shop. However, for fashion products they also call to the shop or contact the shop through the website of the shop.

Omni Channel Shopping Behavior

Another main objective of this study is to explore consumers' omni channel shopping behavior. Therefore, respondents were asked about their omni channel shopping behavior. They have indicated whether and how often ((almost) never, sometimes, regularly, often, (almost) always) they use advertisement leaflets, magazines, social media, websites and applications on mobile devices while shopping in a brick and mortar shop. Because of the low variance between the answers the data was recoded into two categories (yes (= sometimes + regularly + often + (almost) always), and no (= (almost) never)). Table 6 shows the frequencies of omni channel shopping behavior (=yes).

Logistic regression analyses are used to estimate which variables significantly influence omni channel shopping behavior of consumers. The omni channel shopping behavior of respondents is considered as a categorical dichotomy, for instance; using social media while shopping in a brick and mortar shop; Yes=1, No=0. Using this regression analysis we can predict to which category (Yes or No) a respondent

belongs to, given information about psychographics and demographics. Variables included in the analyses are psychographics, household situation, work, income, gender, age and education. Table 7 shows a summary of the results of five logistic regression analyses. Significant results with a Nagelkerke R Square above .100 and an exp(B) value above 1.400 and below 0.600 are discussed.

Consumers can use advertisement leaflets while shopping for instance to check which products are for sale. Whether consumers use advertisement leaflets during shopping in brick and mortar shop can be predicted by independent variables. Psychographics and personal characteristics estimate whether consumers are likely to use advertisement leaflets. Un-loyal consumers are very unlikely to use advertisement leaflets during shopping in a brick and mortar shop. Further, consumers who do not enjoy shopping are very unlikely to use advertisement leaflets while shopping. As expected, price un-conscious consumers are unlikely to use advertisement leaflets. Remarkable is the fact that low educated consumers are more likely than other consumers to use advertisement leaflets while shopping.

Consumers can also use magazines while shopping in a brick and mortar shop, for instance, when there was a jacket shown in the newest magazine distributed by a retailer, consumers can go to the shop with this magazine to buy this jacket. Un-innovative consumers are less likely to use magazines while shopping in a brick and mortar shop. Consumers that do not need motivation to conform are unlikely to use magazines while shopping, this is probably due to the fact that magazines reflect person's wishes and opinions.

Table 7. Summary logistic regression analyses for omni channel shopping behavior and personal characteristics

Dependent Variable	Nagelkerke R Square	Predictors
Omni Channel: Advertisement Leaflets	.142	innovativeness, loyalty, motivation to conform, shopping enjoyment, price consciousness, age and education
Omni Channel: Magazines	.109	innovativeness, loyalty, motivation to conform and shopping enjoyment
Omni Channel: Social Media	.265	innovativeness and age
Omni Channel: Website	.207	innovativeness, loyalty, price consciousness and work
Omni Channel: Applications	.264	innovativeness, work, and education

While shopping consumers can use social media, this channel can be used to check other persons opinions about a product or to share products bought with friends. Un-innovative consumers are very unlikely to use social media while shopping, this was to be expected because un-innovative consumers are also less likely to use social media in general. Further, young consumers (below 50 years old) and especially very young consumers (below 30 years old) are very likely to use social media while shopping. This is presumably due to the fact that social media is more often used by younger individuals.

Un-innovative consumers are unlikely to use websites while shopping in a brick and mortar shop. Interesting is the fact that consumers who (totally) disagreed on the statement 'I generally do my shopping in the same way' are more likely than other consumers to use websites while shopping.

Un-innovative consumers are very unlikely to use applications while shopping in a brick and mortar shop. Interesting is the fact that low educated consumers are less likely than high educated consumers to use applications while shopping.

Segments of Fashion Shoppers

Cluster analysis is used to find fashion shopper segments. Since information is needed about consumers' channel usage during the shopping process, variables of the shopping process and channel usage of the respondents are used as input variables. The two most interesting channels: websites and the brick and mortar shops, for three phases of the shopping process: getting stimulated, search for information, and buying are selected for the analysis. The data was recoded into three categories (never, sometimes, regularly) for all variables.

TwoStep cluster analysis was used: a method to find natural groupings within a dataset (e.g., Moiseeva, 2013; SPSS Inc., 2001). It is a convenient clustering procedure because it can handle a mixture of categorical and continuous variables, the best number of clusters is automatically selected and it can deal with large datasets. It has an auto-clustering feature using two indicators, BIC (Swarz' Bayesian Information Criterion) or AIC (Akaike's Information Criterion). For this research, the BIC indicator is used, this indicator uses a log-likelihood distance measure, which is interesting because we are handling categorical variables.

The following variables of the shopping process were used as input variables: simulate – website, stimulate – shop, search for information –website, search for information – shop, buy – website, and buy – shop. The auto-clustering procedure of the fashion shopping process resulted in six clusters with a fair quality (BIC= 14772.682; ratio of distance measures = 1.539). The smallest cluster contains 248 respondents; the largest cluster has 464 respondents. To further characterize the segments, they were related to the personal characteristics (socio-demographics and psychographics), channel usage, the shopping process, and their omni channel shopping behavior. Crosstabs and chi square tests were used to find significant differences between the various segments. Each of the six segments will be described by its specific characteristics.

Omni Channel Fashion Shoppers (Cluster 1)

Omni channel fashion shoppers get stimulated, search and buy fashion regularly online and also offline. Consumers within this group are often below 50 years old (69%), they work fulltime (40%), part-time (33%) or are students (7%). They have high incomes and are high educated. Omni channel fashion shoppers are innovative, loyal, and they often need motivation to conform. Further they enjoy shopping, feel pressured in time and are price conscious. Omni channel fashion shoppers regularly orientate online for fashion (89% orientates regularly online for fashion). They are very likely to get stimulated by social media and applications on mobile devices to buy fashion; they also search for information about fashion through applications and social media. In addition, 26% of the consumers within this shopper type buys fashion through an application. Thereby, 48% of these consumers use pick-up points to collect their fashion bought. While shopping in a brick and mortar shop, 36% of the omni channel fashion shoppers use websites, 29% use applications and 35% use social media.

Omni Channel Adopters (Cluster 2)

This shopper type represents consumers that regularly get stimulated, search for information and buy fashion online (but not as often as the omni channel fashion shoppers). They sometimes get stimulated and search for information about fashion offline but they regularly buy fashion offline. Omni channel adopters are between 30 and 49 years old and they work full-time or part-time. They have high incomes (above €2800 a month) and they are high educated. Omni channel adopters are quite innovative and loyal consumers who feel pressured in time and are price conscious. Omni channel adopters orientate online for fashion regularly and they sometimes buy fashion online. However this group gets stimulated by social media and applications on mobile devices to buy fashion and they search for information through social media and applications. 12% of the omni channel adopters buy fashion through an application and 33% use pick-up points to collect the fashion products they bought online. While shopping in a brick and mortar shop 'omni channel adopters' use websites and applications.

Online Searchers (Cluster 3)

Consumers within this group search regularly online when they need information about fashion. However, they rarely buy fashion online. Online searchers orientate online but they buy fashion in a brick and mortar shop. Online searchers are often females between 30 and 49 years old. They work (full-time or part-time) and they have above modal incomes (above €2100 a month). These consumers are innovative, they often need motivation to conform and they enjoy shopping. In addition, online searchers are price conscious. They regularly orientate online for fashion and sometimes buy fashion online. Consumers within this group do get stimulated by social media to buy fashion. Also, they use social media while shopping in a brick and mortar shop.

Targeted Offline Purchasers (Cluster 4)

Shopper type 'targeted offline purchasers' regularly buy fashion offline in a shop, they sometimes get stimulated and orientate online but not on a regular basis. They neither get stimulated nor search for information in the shop. Within this cluster there are relatively many males (49% while only 42% of the total dataset is male). Consumers above 65 years old are overrepresented within this cluster. Moreover, 'targeted offline purchasers' are often retired (28%) or they work fulltime (31%). Consumers within this cluster have modal or below modal incomes and they are in the middle educated category. Consumers within this group are not very likely to use social media and applications on mobile devices to get stimulated, search for information or buy fashion. While shopping they neither use websites, applications, nor social media.

Offline Single Channel Shoppers (Cluster 5)

Consumers within this group (almost) never get stimulated, search for information or buy fashion online. But they regularly get stimulated, search for information and buy fashion offline. These consumers often shop offline for clothes. Within this group females are overrepresented (64% is female while in the total dataset 58% is female). Consumers within this cluster are over 50 years of age and they work part-time or are retired. Offline single channel shoppers have modal incomes and are low educated. These consumers are very loyal towards brands and retailers, they often need motivation to conform and they enjoy shopping. They do neither use social media or applications during their shopping process for fashion. This group also does not use applications, websites or social media while shopping in a brick and mortar shop.

Laggards (Cluster 6)

Consumers within this cluster do not shop often for clothes, and not online at all. They probably only shop for fashion when they really need something. Consumers within this group are mainly males (58% is male while only 42% of the total dataset is male). Laggards are above 50 years old and retired; they have modal incomes and are low educated. They do not use social media nor applications during their shopping process

for fashion. Moreover, these consumers do not use applications, websites or social media while shopping in a brick and mortar shop.

CONCLUSION

The aim of this study was to gain insight in consumers' omni channel shopping behavior. When consumers shop omni channel they continuously switch between channels online as well as offline. Channels are for instance brick and mortar shops and applications on mobile devices. Omni channel retailers offer consumers a seamless shopping experience through all channels; consumers can use several channels but these channels feel as one. Within this research omni channel shopping behavior is studied during the shopping process. The shopping process consists of the following five phases: stimulation, search for information, purchase, delivery, and after sales service. Consumers can use different channels for every phase in the shopping process. Consequently, consumers are well informed through all these channels and are therefore more critical while making purchase decisions. Consumers know what they can buy, for what price and where.

Based on the literature review omni channel shopping behavior during the shopping process was operationalized into measurable variables. Consumers' omni channel shopping behavior during the shopping process is measured in three stages:

- Online and offline shopping behaviour;
- Channel usage during the shopping process;
- Omni channel shopping behaviour.

As shopping behavior depends on the product category, for this study specifically the fashion category was selected. An online survey was developed to collect information of Dutch consumers living in the catchment areas of five regional shopping centers.

Results indicated that consumers orientate more often for fashion products online than that they buy them online. It is more convenient to gather information about products online, because consumers can find online a clear overview of products, product features, alternatives and prices.

Furthermore, the present study confirms previous findings and contributes additional evidence that suggests relations between consumers' omni channel shopping behavior during the shopping process and personal characteristics (socio-demographics and psychographics). First, positive relations were found between psychographics and omni channel shopping behavior. Consumers that enjoy shopping often shop online as well as offline. Probably consumers search and shop online for fun. Hedonic shopping and online shopping are presumably related to each other. Furthermore, price un-conscious consumers are very likely to get stimulated by magazines to buy fashion.

Second, many interesting relationships were found between demographics and omni channel shopping behavior during the shopping process. Young consumers have better knowledge about online channels such as applications, websites and social media. This is clearly visible within the results. Regarding online shopping behavior, a generation gap is arisen due to the development of the internet. Offline channels investigated within this research are catalogues, advertisement leaflets and the brick and mortar shops. Whether consumers use advertisement leaflets and catalogues while shopping is often related to age and education. Low educated consumers search for information in advertisement leaflets and catalogues. Thereby low and middle educated consumers buy fashion through catalogues. Also interesting is the fact that low educated consumers use advertisement leaflets while shopping in a brick and mortar shop. The generation gap is thus also visible for buying through catalogues. Probably is buying through catalogues decreasing in popularity because it is more convenient to buy products online.

Since the number of online sales increase, the delivery of products is getting more and more important. This study indicated that socio-demographic characteristics and psychographics are related to pick-up point usage. Pick-up points are most often used by consumers below 50 years old. Furthermore, low educated consumers are unlikely to use pick-up points for collecting fashion products that were bought online.

Nowadays, consumers use online channels while shopping in a brick and mortar shop. Relations were found between online channel usage while shopping and personal characteristics. Consumers below 50 years of age are likely to use applications on mobile devices and social media while shopping (70% of the respondents use applications and are below 50 years old, 82% of the consumers that use social media while shopping is below 50 years old). Especially consumers between 30 and 49 years old use more often applications on mobile devices. In addition, consumers with high incomes are more likely to use applications while shopping than consumers with low incomes. Especially consumers below 30 year old use most often social media while shopping. Thereby, social media is most often used while shopping by high educated consumers.

Further, results showed that consumers' channel usage during a certain phase in the shopping process depends on whether consumers use the same channel in a previous phase of the shopping process. For instance, when a consumer gets stimulated to buy a product on a website than the consumer is likely to search for information about that product on a website. This indicates that it is very important for retailers to be on top of mind of consumers within every phase of the shopping process.

The findings from this study make several contributions to the current literature. First, omni channel shopping behavior during the shopping process is related to consumers' socio-demographic characteristics. Positive relations are found between several socio-demographic characteristics of respondents and their omni channel shopping behavior during the shopping process. Second, omni channel shopping behavior during the shopping process is related to psychographics. For instance, a positive relation is found between searching and buying fashion online and offline and shopping enjoyment. When consumers enjoy shopping they search and shop more often. Also, consumers that feel pressured in time are very likely to buy products online. Another contribution is the fact that channel usage in the previous phase of the shopping process is of a major influence on the channel usage in the following phases of the shopping process. For example, when consumers do not get stimulated by websites to buy fashion, they do not search for information on websites to buy fashion and also they do not buy fashion through a website.

Literature research has shown that segmenting consumers based on their channel orientation can lead to interesting typologies. For clustering consumers, both online and offline channels are selected. For this research it is assumed that consumers choose from a set of channels for every phase of the shopping process separately. By using the TwoStep clustering technique interesting shopper segments were found. Six fashion shopper types, are found and described, with one of them a clear omni channel shopper segment.

FUTURE RESEARCH DIRECTIONS

For this study, data was collected through an online questionnaire among consumers that live in the catchment areas of five regional shopping centers. For further research it would be interesting to select consumers that live in other type of areas as well.

Due to the exploratory character of this research, every phase within the shopping process is investigated at an aggregate level. Therefore, we cannot define a specific shopping process for buying products. In future research it would be interesting to investigate the shopping process of individuals for a particular purchase. Recently for example, Borgers, Baggerman and Van den Berg (2014) investigated the influence of social media on shopping and consumer behavior. Within their research respondents were asked about their last purchases for buying non-daily products and which social media channel they used during the consumer decision process. In addition, we now know which channels consumers use and how often they uses those channels, however we do not have insight in consumers spending within those channels. It would be very interesting to gain insight in consumers' spending behavior on several channels.

According to the literature research, shopping behavior depends on the product category. For this study the fashion category was selected. However, in the survey the respondents were also asked about their omni channel shopping behavior for personal care products and groceries. In future research the results of the other product categories will be addressed as well.

Current retailers are implementing online channels within brick and mortar shops in order to offer consumers the convenience of online channels and the experience of a brick and mortar shop. Further research regarding the role of online channels within brick and mortar shops would be of great help in combining the best of both worlds.

The results of this research showed a generation gap between consumers below and over 50 years of age. This generation gap will probably disappear because of the aging population. Young consumers today are the older consumers of the future. In addition, online channel usage and the number of channels will increase in the future. Therefore, it is very interesting to conduct this research again over 5 to 10 years. Developments will become visible when this research is conducted again.

SOLUTIONS AND RECOMMENDATIONS

The findings of this research suggest several courses of action for managers in retail real estate. Consumers most often buy their products offline or online through a website. Social media and applications are less often used for buying products. Consumers do get stimulated and search for information through social media and applications. In the future, the use of online channels will increase because the number of internet users also increases. Online channels can strengthen offline sales, because through online channels retailers can be visible for consumers during every step within the shopping process. Taken together, these findings suggest a role for retailers in promoting the use of online channels in brick-and-mortars shops. A few years from now, successful retailers can be found online and offline. The results of this study show that channel usage within the stimulation and search phase of the shopping process influences channel usage within the buying phase. This finding has important implications for developing strategies for retailers.

An implication of the findings of this research, is that both retailers and managers in retail should take into account their target groups when developing omni channel strategies. Online channels are clearly used by consumers with specific characteristics. Therefore, online channels must be developed in line with an omni channel strategy; otherwise online channels can harm the brick and mortar shop.

One of the issues that emerges from the findings in this research is the generation gap. Aging consumers are less likely to use online channels during their shopping process. However, the population of aging consumers is voluminous. By developing an omni channel strategy managers in retail should take into account aging consumers because they determine a significant portion of sales. For instance, it could be of in-terest to organize courses for aging consumers in order to learn how to use applications while shopping. Especially, managers in shopping centers must take their responsibility in order to serve aging consumers in the best possible way and learn them how to use online channels. Because, especially for aging consumers it can be very convenient to select products through an application while shopping and let the products be delivered at home.

For managers in shopping centers it is important to offer consumers convenience and experience. These two elements must be considered by developing online strategies for shopping centers. Thereby, it is important to strengthen the role of a shopping center by using online channels. Consumers must be attracted by online channels to visit the shopping centers. For instance, give consumers the opportunity to collect online purchases from a pick-up point at the shopping center. Or attract consumers through targeted advertising through online channels. Through targeted online advertisement, for instance Facebook, it is easy to be on top of mind of consumers. However, to be successful it is important to manage online channels and targeted advertisement on online channels well.

REFERENCES

Ailawadi, K. L., Neslin, S. A., & Gedenk, K. (2001). Pursuing the value conscious consumer: Store brands versus national brand promotions. *Journal of Marketing*, *65*(1), 71–89. doi:10.1509/jmkg.65.1.71.18132

Baal van S. (2014). Should retailers harmonize marketing variables across their distribution channels? An investigation of cross-channel effects in multi-channel retailing. *Journal of Retailing and Consumer Services*. doi:10.1016/j.jretconser.2014.04.012

Benedicktus, R. L., Brady, M. K., & Dark, P. R. (2008). Consumer trust in multiple channels: new evidence and directions for future research. In T. M. Lowrey (Ed.), Brick & mortar shopping in the 21st century (pp. 107-127). Mahwah, NJ: Lawrence Erlbaum Associates.

Bhatnagar, A., & Ghose, S. (2004). Segmenting consumers based on the benefits and risks of internet shopping. *Journal of Business Research*, *57*(12), 1352–1360. doi:10.1016/S0148-2963(03)00067-5

Bloch, P. H., Ridgway, N. M., & Dawson, S. A. (1994). The shopping mall as consumer habitat. *Journal of Retailing*, *70*(1), 23–42. doi:10.1016/0022-4359(94)90026-4

Borgers, A., Baggerman, L., & Van den Berg, P. (2014). *Shopping and the use of social media*. Paper presented at the Recent Advances in Retailing and Consumer Services Science Conference, Bucharest, Romania.

Chandon, P., Wansink, B., & Laurent, G. (2000). A benefit congruency framework of sales promotion effectiveness. *Journal of Marketing*, *64*(4), 177–183. doi:10.1509/jmkg.64.4.65.18071

Chiu, H. C., Hsieh, Y. C., Roan, J., Tseng, K. J., & Hsieh, J. K. (2011). The challenge for multichannel services: Cross-channel free-riding behavior. *Electronic Commerce Research and Applications*, *10*(2), 268–277. doi:10.1016/j.elerap.2010.07.002

Dholakia, U. M., Kahn, B. E., Reeves, R., Rindfleish, A., Stewart, D., & Taylor, E. (2010). Consumer behavior in a multichannel, multimedia retailing environment. *Journal of Interactive Marketing*, *24*(2), 86–95. doi:10.1016/j.intmar.2010.02.005

Dibb, S. (1998). Market segmentation: Strategies for success. *Marketing Intelligence & Planning*, *16*(7), 394–406. doi:10.1108/02634509810244390

Engel, J. F., Blackwell, R. D., & Miniard, P. W. (2001). *Consumer behavior* (9th ed.). The Dryden Press, Harcourt Brace College Publishers.

Frasquet, M., Gil, I., & Mollá, A. (2001). Shopping-centre selection modelling: A segmentation approach. *International Review of Retail, Distribution and Consumer Research*, *11*(1), 23–38. doi:10.1080/09593960122279

Gilboa, S. (2009). A segmentation study of Israeli mall consumers. *Journal of Retailing and Consumer Services*, *16*(2), 135–144. doi:10.1016/j.jretconser.2008.11.001

Gong, W., & Maddox, L. (2011). Online buying decisions in China. *The Journal of American Academy of Business*, *17*(1), 43–50.

Gupta, A., Su, B., & Walter, Z. (2004). Risk profile and consumer shopping behavior in electronic and traditional channels. *Decision Support Systems*, *38*(3), 347–367. doi:10.1016/j.dss.2003.08.002

Heitz-Spahn, S. (2013). Cross-channel free-riding consumer behavior in a multichannel environment: An investigation of shopping motives, sociodemographics and product categories. *Journal of Retailing and Consumer Services*, *20*(6), 570–578. doi:10.1016/j.jretconser.2013.07.006

Jarret, D. G. (1996). A shopper taxonomy for retail strategy development. *International Review of Retail, Distribution and Consumer Research*, *6*(2), 196–215. doi:10.1080/09593969600000020

Javadi, M., Dolatabadi, H., Nourbakhsh, M. Poursaeedi, A., & Asadollahi, A. (2012). An analysis of factors affecting on online shopping behavior of consumers. *International Journal of Marketing Studies*, *4*(5), 81 – 98.

Keen, C., Wetzels, M., de Ruyter, K., & Feiberg, R. (2004). E-tailers versus retailers: Which factors determine consumer preferences. *Journal of Business Research*, *57*(7), 685–695. doi:10.1016/S0148-2963(02)00360-0

Keller, K. L. (2010). Brand equity management in a multichannel, multimedia retail environment. *Journal of Interactive Marketing, 24*(2), 58–70. doi:10.1016/j.intmar.2010.03.001

Kleijnen, M., De Ruyter, K., & Wetzels, M. (2007). An assessment of value creation in mobile services delivery and the moderating role of time consciousness. *Journal of Retailing, 83*(1), 33–46. doi:10.1016/j.jretai.2006.10.004

Kollman, T., Kuckertz, A., & Kayser, I. (2012). Cannibalization or synergy? Consumers' channel selection in online-offline multichannel systems. *Journal of Retailing and Consumer Services, 19*(2), 186–194. doi:10.1016/j.jretconser.2011.11.008

Konuş, U., Verhoef, P. C., & Neslin, S. A. (2008). Multichannel shopper segments and their co-variates. *Journal of Retailing, 84*(4), 398–413. doi:10.1016/j.jretai.2008.09.002

Kumar, V. (2010). A customer lifetime value-based approach to marketing in the multichannel, multimedia retailing environment. *Journal of Interactive Marketing, 24*(2), 71–85. doi:10.1016/j.intmar.2010.02.008

Lihra, T., & Graf, R. (2007). Multi-channel communication and consumer choice in the household furniture buying process. *Direct marketing. International Journal (Toronto, Ont.), 1*(3), 146–160.

Markova, S., & Petkovska-Mirčevska, T. (2013). Social media and supply chain. *Supply Chain Management, 14*(33), 89–102.

Mcgoldrick, P. J., & Collins, N. (2007). Multichannel retailing: Profiling the multichannel shopper. *International Review of Retail, Distribution and Consumer Research, 17*(2), 139–158. doi:10.1080/09593960701189937

Moiseeva, A. V. (2013). *Experience the city: Analysis of space-time behavior and spatial learning.* Eindhoven University of Technology.

Neslin, S. A., Grewal, D., Leghorn, R., Shankar, V., Teerling, M. L., Thomas, J. S., & Verhoef, P. C. (2006). Challenges and opportunities in multichannel consumer management. *Journal of Service Research, 9*(2), 95–112. doi:10.1177/1094670506293559

Newcom Research. (2013). *Social media onderzoek 2013.* Retrieved on 26 February 2013, from http://newcomresearch.nl/socialmedia (Dutch).

Nicholson, M., Clarke, I., & Blakemore, S. M. (2002). One brand, three ways to shop: Situational variables and multi-channel consumer behavior. *International Review of Retail, Distribution and Consumer Research, 12*(2), 131–148. doi:10.1080/09593960210127691

NRW. (2011). *Consumentenbeleving in winkelgebieden.* Retrieved on 20 November 2012, from www.nrw.nl (Dutch)

Oh, L. B., Teo, H. H., & Sambamurthy, V. (2012). The effects of retail channel integration through the use of information technologies on firm performance. *Journal of Operations Management, 30*(5), 368–381. doi:10.1016/j.jom.2012.03.001

Reynolds, K. E., Ganesh, J., & Luckett, M. (2002). Traditional malls versus factory outlets: Comparing shopper typologies and implications for retail strategy. *Journal of Business Research, 55*(9), 687–696. doi:10.1016/S0148-2963(00)00213-7

Ruiz, J. P., Chebat, J. C., & Hansen, P. (2004). Another trip to the mall: A segmentation study of consumers based on their activities. *Journal of Retailing and Consumer Services, 11*(6), 333–350. doi:10.1016/j.jretconser.2003.12.002

Seck, A. M., & Philippe, J. (2011). Service encounter in multi-channel distribution context: Virtual and face-to-face interactions and consumer satisfaction. *Service Industries Journal, 33*(6), 565–579. doi:10.1080/02642069.2011.622370

Shankar, V., Venkatesh, A., Hofacker, C., & Naik, P. (2010). Mobile marketing in the retailing environment: Current insights and future research avenues. *Journal of Interactive Marketing*, *24*(2), 111–120. doi:10.1016/j.intmar.2010.02.006

Solomon, M., Bamossy, G., Askegaard, S., & Hogg, M. K. (2002). *Consumer behavior: A European perspective*. Harlow, MA: Prentice Hall.

SPSS Inc. (2001). *The SPSS TwoStep cluster component. A scalable component to segment your customers more effectively*. Retrieved from ftp://ftp.spss.com/pub/web/wp/TSCWP-0101.pdf

Steinfield, C., Bouwman, H., & Adelaar, T. (2002). The dynamics of click-and-mortar electronic commerce: Opportunities and management strategies. *International Journal of Electronic Commerce*, *7*(1), 93–119.

Suominen, J. (2005). *One experience: Optimizing consumer experience channel planning process*. Paper presented at Keynote presentation at the 3rd Interdisciplinary World Congress on Mass Customization and Personalization, Hong Kong.

Verhoef, P. C., Neslin, S. A., & Vroomen, B. (2007). Multichannel consumer management: Understanding the research-shopper phenomenon. *International Journal of Research in Marketing*, *24*(2), 129–148. doi:10.1016/j.ijresmar.2006.11.002

Wagner, G., Schramm-Klein, H., & Steinmann, S. (2013). Effects of cross-channel synergies and complementarity in a multichannel e-commerce system – An investigation of the interrelation of e-commerce, m-commerce and IETV-commerce. *International Review of Retail, Distribution and Consumer Research*, 1–11.

Wallace, D. W., Giese, J. L., & Johnson, J. L. (2004). Customer retailer loyalty in the context of multiple channel strategies. *Journal of Retailing*, *80*(4), 249–263. doi:10.1016/j.jretai.2004.10.002

Zijlmans, O. M. (2010). *De veranderende vraag naar winkelvastgoed onder invloed van online winkelen: een onderzoek naar toekomststrategieën van (r)etailers*. Eindhoven: University of Technology.

KEY TERMS AND DEFINITIONS

Consumer Segmentation: Subdividing the heterogeneous consumer market into segments of consumers, each of which tends to be homogeneous in a number of aspects.

Fashion: Fashion includes clothes, shoes, and accessories.

Omni Channel Shopping: Consumers use a range of channels at the same time during the shopping process, including both online and offline channels such as websites, web shops, social media, brick and mortar shops, applications on mobile devices, catalogues, and more.

Retail: The sale of goods and services from businesses to the end-user, a consumer.

Shopping Center: A group of retail shops, restaurants, and other businesses with a common interest in soliciting sales. The facility is developed as planned commercial location and typically offers private, off-street parking facilities or areas. In this study, the regional shopping centers offer a wide range of apparel and soft goods, and supermarkets, drugstores, and department stores are common anchors.

Shopping Process: The shopping process consists of five phases; stimulation, search for information, purchase, delivery and after sales service.

Chapter 8
Analyzing Online Reviews to Measure Augmented Reality Acceptance at the Point of Sale:
The Case of IKEA

Daniel Baier
BTU Cottbus-Senftenberg, Germany

Alexandra Rese
BTU Cottbus-Senftenberg, Germany

Stefanie Schreiber
BTU Cottbus-Senftenberg, Germany

ABSTRACT

Increasingly, brick and mortar retailers compete with their counterparts by enriching the point of sale through technological innovations that make use of customer-owned mobile devices. So, for example, IKEA, the world's largest furniture retailer, has introduced an interactive mobile app that provides the customer with additional insights in a personalized and convenient way: by scanning quick response codes in the printed catalogue, 3D objects, pictures, text, or videos are provided on the customer's smartphone or tablet. They inform about a furniture's interior or its potential usage, give planning aids, or visualize the furniture in alternative surroundings. In this chapter, the perceived usefulness, ease of use, and attitude towards such new technology-based innovations are discussed. Customers' perceptions are measured by applying a modified technology acceptance model. Traditional customer surveys as well as online customer reviews are analyzed. The results are encouraging: the mobile app is seen as an enrichment of the shopping experience but can be improved. Both data collection formats lead to similar results.

DOI: 10.4018/978-1-4666-8297-9.ch008

INTRODUCTION

For some years, augmented reality (AR) is used by retailers (see, e.g., Pantano and Servidio, 2012, Poncin and Mimoun 2014) to enrich the store atmospherics and shopping experience. Retailer-owned, stationary devices with scanning, planning, visualization, and recommendation features assist customers, e.g. to find the right hairstyle, jacket, suit, or to plan a new kitchen or cupboard.

However, today, the younger generation expects these AR services not only on a stationary device but on their personal device via a mobile app (short for application software): Surveys found out that the younger generation spends more time with their mobile devices (smartphone, tablet) than with stationary ones (PC, TV, McKinsey&Company, 2012) and that the online sales even for costly products (e.g. furniture) increase (McKinsey&Company, 2013).

So, it is not surprising that bricks and mortar retailers – especially when targeting at the younger generation – introduce mobile apps with AR features to make their offline and online buying situation more attractive. Market observers assume that – with the increasing availability of smartphones and tablets – an era of new "Retail 3.0" (Duncan et al., 2013, p.6.) is to come and that this revolution has the "potential to transform the shopping experience (both in-store and online)" completely.

Nevertheless, the use of (stationary and mobile) AR is discussed controversially in the literature in terms of its benefits for customers since, e.g., many problems are still unsolved (e.g. speed, presentation quality, ease of use). This is especially true when focusing on mobile AR with – typically – limited connectivity and additional handling problems than in the stationary case. Studies on AR acceptance are available, but they are often criticized for their small samples and their experimental setting (see, e.g. Bulearca and Tamarjan, 2010; Olsson et al., 2013). Also, the usage of student samples and the employment of self-reported item scales have been addressed (Legris et al., 2003).

This chapter aims to close this gap by investigating the acceptance of mobile AR at the point of sale using IKEA's mobile app – an AR extension of their online product catalogue – as a case. A technology acceptance model (TAM) analysis and a detailed likes/dislikes analysis (with closed and open-ended questioning) are performed. In addition to the traditional TAM analysis, the open-ended questions and the likes/dislikes are analyzed using text mining. The results are also compared to a text mining analysis of comments on the mobile app in online customer reviews. In summary, it is found out that the TAM analysis can – with some reservations – be replaced by the automated data analysis using comments gathered in the shop or in online blogs. In addition, the results point to an overestimation of the TAM constructs in the experimental setting.

The chapter is structured as follows: the next section provides background for AR at the point of sale and for TAM. In further sections a modified TAM for AR applications as well as text mining methods for analyzing customer reviews are developed and tested using IKEA's mobile app as an example. After presenting the results, the paper closes with theoretical implications, limitations, and avenues for further research. The chapter extends a discussion of the mobile app IKEA case in Rese et al. (2014). It differs insofar, that the practical aspects of AR for retailing and acceptance measurement are discussed more deeply. In Rese et al. (2014) the focus was more on technical and theoretical aspects of analyzing the word-of-mouth in online customer reviews.

Background

Augmented Reality (AR) to Improve the Shopping Experience

AR has been defined by Olsson et al. (2013, p.288) as a technique "to combine real and computer-generated digital information into the user's view of the physical real world in such a way that they appear as one environment". Digital content (e.g. 3D objects) can be tied for example to a QR (quick response) code (Yuen et al., 2011). In addition to 3D objects avatars, pictures, videos, audios or text can also be included (Güven et al., 2009). AR has been described as "enabling technology for innovative mobile applications" (Välkkynen, et al., 2011, p.1). Olssen et al. (2013) use the term mobile AR (MAR). These AR applications can be jointly referred to as mobile services offering content and transaction possibilities (see Saarijärvi et al., 2014 for more examples). According to Gartner in the next few years AR will "not be a niche technology [...] but a much more mainstream set of applications in the consumer market" (Vaughan-Nichols, 2009, p.22). With additional information but also as an enhancement of the shopping experience, AR aims "to engage and interest potential consumers" (Yuen et al., 2011, p.124).

To strengthen customer relationship and to attract (new) customers AR can assist retailers by offering virtual trial and product education. This may enhance purchasing accuracy, e.g. 3D product previews (LEGO) or virtual fitting tools (e.g. at companies like Carrefour or Deichmann). The customer is provided with additional information about products, e.g. 3D product previews (Brother, Audi) or videos (AUTO BILD, Tesco). The shopping experience is enriched, e.g. by visualization of product catalogues (IKEA, Tesco) or gamification (WarBot). In addition, AR can assist retailers in terms of brand recognition (Bulmers) and promotion (advertising campaigns, customer attraction to a store, e.g. by visualization of product catalogues). These improvements may be overlapping, for example virtual fitting tools are supposed to enhance both the shopping experience and to attract customers. Further benefits of AR, which are not here in the focus, are the localization of businesses by consumers (Valpark) or warehouse space optimization.

Using search engines and keywords such as "augmented reality applications in retail" altogether 36 AR applications could be indentified

in August 2014. These applications are listed in the Appendix of this paper. They are categorized with regard to the categories "virtual trial and product education" and "brand recognition enhancement". As an additional category "in-store customer experience enhancement" is introduced. AR applications can be used at any locations, e.g. at home, outside or in stores, and with different displays, e.g. PCs, smartphone/tablet or kiosks. Most identified AR applications focus on virtual trial and product education (83.3%) relying on mobile devices such as smartphones or tablets (77.8%). Taking a look at different retail sectors, furniture industry is on first place (22.2%), followed by fashion (13.9%), food (11.1%), eyewear and print media (8.3% respectively).

With regard to furniture, AR can enable customers to interact with often expensive products and to check visual appearance or fit in their homes (Lu and Smith, 2007; Oh et al., 2008). In their "shopping furniture" scenario which presents fictional mobile services Olsson et al. (2012) describe 3D virtualization of homes and furniture with tags to store additional information such as prices, availability or colors. Since being introduced in 2013, IKEA's mobile app allows mobile interaction by the potential buyer with the online product catalogue at home or in the shop. It extends IKEA's most important tool for market communication – the product catalogue (see, e.g., Burt et al. 2011) – as an information tool.

A QR code in the printed catalogue can be used to access additional information on a customer-owned smartphone or tablet. An "x-ray" view enables the viewer to look behind cupboard doors (www.mashable.com/2012/07/19/ikea-augmented-reality-catalog). Figure 1 gives three sample screens on a smartphone during a sample interaction. The customer gets additional information on a cupboard. Here, in Figure 1, especially the variability of the cupboard's content is of interest for the customer.

Figure 1. Screens from IKEA's mobile app on a smartphone during a sample interaction with a customer; the 3D object can be rotated, transferred, and modified according to the customer's interests.

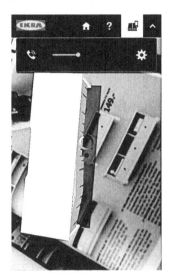  

Research examining the usage and users of AR applications has focused on the perception and usability including the development of usability guidelines (see the studies listed in Olsson et al., 2013). Studies on user acceptance and satisfaction are scarce (see Table 1). A hypothesized and explained research model – e.g. similar to TAM – is only used by few authors, e.g., Pantano and Servidio (2012) or Poncin and Mimoun (2014).

The Technology Acceptance Model (TAM)

The Technology Acceptance Model (TAM) by Davis (1989) and Davis et al. (1989) is one of the most influential measurement approaches for examining technology-based innovations (e.g. Hausman and Siepke, 2009, p. 6). Originally developed for explaining the acceptance of computer technology within an organizational context, TAM has now been applied in various areas and several meta-analyses have been conducted (e.g. refer to the overview of recent meta-analysis studies in Wu et al., 2011).

It bases essentially on Fishbein and Aijzen (1975)'s Theory of Reasoned Action (TRA), a theory that models and relates predictions of attitude with predictions of behavior. In many applications TRA as well as – especially – TAM have shown their practical value as a flexible modeling instrument. So, e.g., when analyzing the acceptance of a new information system, it helps to relate the intention to use the new system to two constructs: the perceived usefulness ("the degree to which a person believes that using a particular system would enhance his or her job performance", Davis 1989, p.320) and the perceived ease of use of the system ("the degree to which a person believes that using a particular system would be free of effort", Davis 1989, p.320). In the basic TAM these two constructs are linked to two other constructs: attitude and behavioral intention to use. For all these constructs, robust and valid questionnaire instruments have been developed. The behavioral intention to use has been used as a proxy for user acceptance (Venkatesh et al., 2003). Meta-analyses have confirmed the proposed positive relationships between the five constructs and the usefulness of TAM overall to predict usage (e.g. Legris et al., 2003).

Table 1. Studies on AR user acceptance and satisfaction

Reference	Object of Research	Investigated Research Issues	Data Collection	Kind of Data	Sample Size	User Experience
Olsson and Salo (2011)	Most used available AR application per respondent	Application usage (area, environment), reasons for adoption/usage, perceived usefulness, intention to use, strength / weakness of the application	Online survey	Quantitative (item scales), qualitative (open-ended questions)	90	Users with high technological orientation
Olsson et al. (2012)	Five scenarios with fictional mobile AR services (on the bus, jogging, shopping furniture, virtual mirror, street art)	Perceived value, perceived ease of use, intention to use the services	Online survey	Quantitative (item scales), qualitative (open-ended questions)	260	Mostly users with moderate and high technological orientation
Pantano and Servidio (2012)	Computing landscape that displays 3D virtual products, furniture, and other store components in an immersive shop	Store perception, perceived ease of use, perceived enjoyment, consumer satisfaction	Experiment in an university laboratory, survey	Quantitative (item scales)	150	Students with low online shopping experience
Poncin and Mimoun (2014)	Magic mirror and interactive game terminal in a toy-brand's flagship store	Shopping value, emotions, perceived store atmosphere, patronage intention, satisfaction	Experiment in a shop, survey using tablets	Quantitative (item scales)	165	Parents accompanied by their children

TAM FOR MOBILE APPS WITH AR: DATA COLLECTION VIA ONLINE REVIEWS

With regard to technology-based innovations in retailing and specifically concerning stationary and online points of sale, several TAM studies have been undertaken. So, e.g., electronic payment systems (Plouffe et al., 2001), online-shopping recommendation systems (Baier and Stüber, 2010, 2011), and mobile coupons (Dickinger and Kleijnen, 2008) have been investigated.

We therefore propose that TAM is useful to predict usage of mobile apps and hypothesize:

H1: The relationships of TAM are valid for mobile apps:

1. Perceived ease of use has a direct positive effect (a1) on perceived usefulness and (a2) on attitude,
2. Perceived usefulness has a direct positive effect (b1) on attitude and (b2) on behavioral intention to use, (c) attitude has a direct positive effect on behavioral intention to use.

In addition, external variables have been integrated in TAM with an effect on perceived ease of use and perceived usefulness (Legris et al., 2003). With regard to AR applications Olsson et al. (2013) mention the usefulness of given information (perceived informativeness) as well as their entertaining resp. fun providing component (perceived enjoyment) as two important factors. This is in line with research in the field of electronic and mobile commerce (Chen and Tan, 2004; Bruner and Kumar, 2005; Hausman

Figure 2. Research model for measuring acceptance of mobile apps

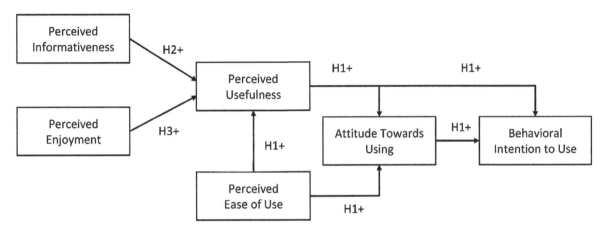

and Siepke, 2009). Both factors have been linked in empirical studies to positively influencing the attitude towards a website or a mobile device (see e.g. Hausman and Siepke, 2009, Pantano and Naccarato, 2010; Pantano and Servidio, 2012). Nevertheless they have also been proposed as having a positive effect on the perceived usefulness of an innovation in satisfying different customer needs. The product information offered by an innovative system satisfies customers' informational needs and supports them in their purchase decision (Chen and Tan, 2004). An innovative system perceived as entertaining satisfies customers' need "for escapism, diversion, aesthetic enjoyment, or emotional release" (Ducoffe, 1996, p. 23). Davis et al. (1992) found a positive interaction effect between usefulness and enjoyment of using a computer.

These considerations lead to the following research hypotheses for our mobile apps:

H2: The perceived informativeness of mobile apps has a direct positive effect on perceived usefulness.

H3: The perceived enjoyment of mobile apps has a direct positive effect on perceived usefulness.

The research model is presented in Figure 2.

Overall the TAM displays high internal consistency that explains about 40% of the variance of usage intentions (e.g. Venkatesh and Davis, 2000). Nevertheless, Turner et al. (2010, p.464) present the criticism that "the results of applying the TAM are often accepted as being accurate predictors of usage and adoption." Typically self-reported item scales are used for measurement with TAM (Turner et al., 2010). Legris et al. (2003, p.202) come to the conclusion that "[a]t best, self-reported use should serve as a relative indicator". In addition, studies often rely on students as respondents in experimental settings (Legris et al., 2003).

To address these problems, in this chapter the results of self-reported scales by students in an experimental environment are compared to a content analysis of online reviews. The online reviews are considered here as the description of critical incidents when applying the mobile app. An incident has been defined as "any observable human activity that is sufficiently complete in itself to permit inferences and predictions to be made about the person performing the act" (Flanagan, 1954, p. 327). A critical incident is described by Bitner et al. (1990, p.73) as one that is "especially satisfying or especially dissatisfying" with regard to the activity. The identification of critical incidents (critical incident technique - CIT) has been used for example in combination with focus groups to improve scales in terms of the completeness and relevance of items to the current situation (Dabholkar et al., 2000).

Despite the advantage of capturing relevant behavior Butterfield et al. (2005, p.480) describe data collection as "very labour intensive and therefore expensive". With regard to online reviews Tang and Guo (2012, p.2) mention that the evaluation of "the enormous quantity of unstructured customer information can be challenging". In contrast, TAM relies on established measurement scales (Legris et al., 2003) that allow the results to be compared. Nevertheless, the experimental settings and sample sizes are criticized (Legris et al., 2003). In a similar way to TAM scales, online reviews are retrospective and self-reporting (De Bruyn and Lilien, 2008), but Tang and Guo (2012) emphasize the "natural" situations of which online reviews result as well as the high data volume. Text mining methods are proposed to help to reduce the challenge of data processing and to produce valuable findings.

To summarize: In this chapter new ways to collect data for TAM is proposed. To compare the results with a traditional TAM data collection format, scales as well as open-ended questions and adjective semantic differential pairs are used. Overall we propose that extracting the TAM constructs out of textual content, e.g. publicly available online reviews, can replace the use of questionnaires with self-reported scales.

This leads to the following hypothesis:

H4: The results of TAM based on reviews are equivalent to the results of self-reported item scales.

For testing this hypothesis (as well as the above hypotheses) various samples and data collection formats have been applied with respect to the above described mobile app with AR extensions. Data collection, analyses, and results are described in the following.

TAM FOR MOBILE APPS WITH AR: IKEA'S MOBILE APP WITH AR EXTENSIONS

Online Ratings and Reviews

In May 2013 a total of 16,390 (online) ratings and ratings for IKEA's mobile app were retrieved from a popular app forum (Google Play, see play.google.com, see play.google.com/store/apps/details?id=com. ikea.catalogue.android for IKEA's mobile app). The users had the opportunity to give an (overall) star rating of the mobile app; 480 users also wrote (till May 2013) an (online) review in form of an additional textual comment. Interestingly, the 16,390 users rated the mobile app with an average of 3.7 stars, whereas the subsample of 480 users (that gave an additional review) rated on average with 2.3 stars indicating that the "online reviewers" were – in contrast to the whole sample of "online raters" – more often triggered by negative aspects. This result is in accordance to previous research (Anderson, 1998).

It should also be mentioned that the ratings in the offline reviewer sample (described in the next subsection) are – on average – closer to the ratings of the whole sample (see Table 2). Also interesting is that the online ratings for IKEA's mobile app are very stable over time (despite some improvements by new versions): Till June 2014, the number of online raters of the mobile app in Google Play raised to 33,323, but the average rating of 3.7 stars and even the distribution of the ratings didn't change a lot: Till June 2014, there were 16.0% (n=5,326) ratings with 1 star, 6.3% (n=2,093) with 2 stars, 12.0% (n=3,971) with 3, 21.2% (n=7,033) with 4, and 44.5% (n=14,800) with 5 (compare with the data from May 2013 in Table 2). However, to make the analyses from the

Table 2. Ratings of the mobile IKEA app using 1 to 5 stars

Sample	Online Raters (Retrieved from Google Play in May 2013)	Online Reviewers (Retrieved from Google Play in May 2013)	Participants in the Survey (Experimental Setting, Data Collected in June 2013)
Sample size	n=16,390	n=480	n=275
Share of ratings with 1 star	17.6% (n=2,891)	47.8% (n=228)	2.5% (n=7)
Share of ratings with 2 stars	6.1% (n=995)	12.3% (n=59)	14.2% (n=39)
Share of ratings with 3 stars	11.7% (n=1,917)	13.8% (n=66)	34.2% (n=94)
Share of ratings with 4 stars	22.3% (n=3,662)	10.6% (n=51)	41.1% (n=113)
Share of ratings with 5 stars	42.3% (n=6,925)	15.3% (n=73)	8.0% (n=22)
Average rating across the sample (number of stars)	3.7	2.3	3.4

Figure 3. Participants using IKEA's mobile app on a tablet in the experimental setting

different data collection formats comparable, in the following, only the samples from Table 2 are used.

Survey

In June 2013 a survey was conducted at a German university that involved 275 participants in order to test the above-mentioned TAM for mobile apps with AR (see the right column in Table 2). Most participants were German undergraduate university students. The gender distribution in the sample was 58.9% male and 41.1% female. On average the participants were 22.1 years old (18-34: 98.9%).

The sample and its quota (with respect to age and gender) were selected according to the known target segment of mobile apps. So, e.g., 60.5% of U.S. American users scanning QR codes with their mobile devices are male, 53.4% of them are 18-34 years old (comScore, 2011).

Experience with the app was not required. During the survey, the participants were briefly

Table 3. Data collection formats in the analysis

	Sample	Data from Each Person (Besides the Star Rating)	Data Analysis
Data collection format 1	Online reviewers (n=480)	Online review (title and comment)	Text pre-processing (elimination of stopwords, Porter stemming) and processing (allocation of words to TAM constructs according to a dictionary, summing positive (+1) and negative (-1) allocations as a proxy for the person's composite scores for TAM constructs), TAM modeling
Data collection format 2	Participants in the survey (n=275)	Offline review (likes and dislikes in a critical incident format)	
Data collection format 3		Up to 10 picks/selections of adjectives from a list of 16 adjective pairs that describe TAM constructs (e.g., "simple" and "complicated" as a positive and a negative aspect for the TAM construct "perceived ease of use")	Text processing (allocation of words to TAM constructs according to a dictionary, summing positive (+1) and negative (-1) allocations as a proxy for the person's composite scores for TAM constructs), TAM modeling
Data collection format 4		Ratings with respect to traditional TAM item scales	Analysis of item quality, calculation of composite scores for TAM constructs, TAM modeling

introduced to the functionality and use of the mobile app. The participants became acquainted with the mobile app and its AR features through the task of searching for particular products using IKEA's printed catalogue in interaction with the mobile app (see Figure 3). They all also received the same (standard) tablet with the mobile app installed.

In order to test different data collection formats, a questionnaire was developed based on both the TAM literature with tested item batteries and the online reviews (see third column of Table 2) for understanding the wording of the users.

In total three additional data collection formats (besides the online reviews, which we refer to as data collection format 1) were implemented into the questionnaire (see Table 3 for a summary): An offline review, a picking/selecting of adjectives from a list of pairs, and ratings with respect to traditional TAM item scales.

- For the offline reviews (data collection format 2), a similar response format as with the online reviews was offered to the participants: They could rate the mobile app on a five stars scale and give additional comments in an open-ended questioning format to reflect likes/dislikes respectively critical incidents.

- For the picking/selecting of up to 10 adjectives (data collection format 3) a list of 16 adjective pairs was developed taking the TAM literature and the online reviews as a basis. They represent a simple operationalization of the TAM constructs as the different adjective pairs can be easily allocated to a TAM construct (e.g., "simple" and "complicated" as a positive and a negative aspect for the TAM construct "perceived ease of use", or "superfluous" and "useful" for the TAM construct "perceived usefulness"). For finding these frequent words, text pre-processing and processing was applied to the online reviews using the text mining packages 'tm' and 'snowball' (Feinerer and Hornik, 2013; Hornik et al., 2013) in the programming language R (see www.r-project.org). With these packages, so-called stopwords like "and", "or", "but", or "now" can be eliminated. Also, words are reduced to so-called stems by removing morphological and inflexional endings

Table 4. Frequency of positive and negative adjectives in the survey (data collection format 3)

Negative Adjective	%	Positive Adjective	%	Negative Adjective	%	Positive Adjective	%
Poor	3.6	Good	60.7	Absurd	14.2	Meaningful	17.1
Not informative	13.8	Informative	36.4	Impractical	16.4	Practical	34.5
Superfluous	24.7	Useful	37.5	Unhelpful	9.8	Helpful	29.1
Not worth recommending	5.5	Worth recommending	20.7	Not interactive	1.8	Interactive	35.3
Immature	37.8	Mature	3.6	Complicated	8.4	Simple	47.6
Confusing	9.5	Clear	31.3	Unexciting	6.2	Exciting	30.5
Slow	22.2	Fast	35.3	Not innovative	4.0	Innovative	52.4
Inadequate	12.7	Perfect	5.1	Weak	6.5	Great	5.1

(by, e.g., Porter stemming). Afterwards "frequent" words in the comments can be easily identified and checked according to the TAM constructs (as described above). Here, a "dictionary" for TAM constructs is helpful, which means that for each construct related positive and negative words are available (e.g. "simple", "easy", "complicated" and so on for "perceived ease of use"). The related words were derived from the TAM literature by analyzing questionnaires. The generation of the dictionary relied on the CIT approach (Bitner et al., 1990; Keaveney, 1995, for details see Rese et al. 2014).

- The item scales for the last part of the questionnaire (data collection format 4) were also – as the dictionary base – taken from the literature (see, e.g., Rese et al. 2014 for more details, a list of these items is given in Table 4). A pre-test study was used to ensure that a comprehensive list of measures was included. All item scales were measured on a seven point Likert scale (with "1" = "strongly disagree" to "7" = "strongly agree").

DATA ANALYSIS

For analyzing the online (data collection format 1) and offline reviews (data collection format 2) with respect to the TAM constructs and the model, again, text pre-processing and processing was applied in connection with the above mentioned TAM dictionary: For each person's review, the stop words had to be eliminated and the words had to be reduced to its stem. Both data collection formats involved a similar number of words: the online reviews had 1,429 words, the offline reviews 1,278 words. Then, the words in the comments were checked for allocations to TAM constructs according to the dictionary. Finally, for each person and each TAM construct "scores" could be calculated by summing up the positive (+1) and negative (-1) allocations. While 403 words of data collection format 1 could be assigned to a TAM construct, this was the case for 371 words of data collection format 2.

In a similar way, the picking/selecting of up to 10 adjectives (data collection format 3) can be aggregated to person-specific TAM construct scores. The app was described as being good (60.7%), innovative (52.4%) and simple/not complicated (47.6%) (see Table 4).

For analyzing the item scales (data collection format 4), the usual TAM analysis was applied:

Table 5. Summary of construct scales and scores

Construct	Mean [a]	Std. Dev.	Com-ponent	Cron-bach's Alpha	Varian-ce Ex-plained	CR [b]	AVE [c]	Reference
Perceived Enjoyment	5.39	1.37		0.892	75.718			Online reviews
Using the mobile app is really fun.	4.97	1.55	0.857					
The scan function is a nice gimmick.	5.77	1.41	0.818					
It is fun to discover the scan function.	5.45	1.64	0.932					
The mobile app invites you to discover the cat.	4.97	1.55	0.870					
Perceived Informativeness	4.66	1.28		0.870	66.063			Ahn et al. (2004); Hausman and Siepke (2009)
The mobile app showed the information I expected.	4.63	1.50	0.731					
The mobile app provides detailed information.	4.88	1.52	0.878					
The mobile app provides the complete information.	4.44	1.56	0.846					
The mobile app helps me in my decision.	4.85	1.68	0.835					
The mobile app provides information to compares.	4.49	1.65	0.764					
Perceived Ease Of Use	5.73	1.19		0.892	76.078			Venkatesh and Davis (2000); Gefen et al. (2003)
I found the mobile app to be very easy to use.	5.65	1.36	0.889					
The mobile app was intuitive to use.	5.56	1.43	0.903					
It was easy to learn how to use the mobile app.	6.04	1.20	0.874					
Handling the scan function was easy.	5.65	1.46	0.820					
Perceived Usefulness	4.82	1.46		0.917	80.241			Online reviews
For me, the mobile app has great value.	4.06	1.64	0.855					
The mobile app provides interior design ideas.	5.24	1.63	0.921					
The mobile app is very for interior design.	5.21	1.56	0.932					
The mobile app is perfect for keeping overview.	4.76	1.69	0.873					
Attitude Towards Using	4.48	1.49		0.942	81.538			Ahn et al. (2004); Porter and Donthu (2006)
I am positive about the mobile app.	4.91	1.46	0.894					
So interesting that you want to learn more about.	4.28	1.72	0.865					
It just makes sense to use the mobile app.	4.00	1.74	0.901					
The use of the mobile app is a good idea.	4.71	1.72	0.922					
Other people should also use the mobile app.	4.51	1.63	0.931					
Behavioral Intention to Use If I were to buy furniture in the future, I would…	3.72	1.72		0.912	74.666			Ahn et al. (2004)
…download or use the mobile app immediately.	3.78	1.98	0.887					
…give the mobile app priority over the printed cat.	3.78	2.11	0.766					
…give the mobile app priority over other cat.s.	3.97	2.06	0.833					
I will recommend the mobile app to my friends.	3.97	2.03	0.925					
I will use the mobile app regularly in the future.	3.09	1.80	0.901					

[a]: Scale/Score: 1 = strongly disagree, 7 = strongly agree. [b]: Average variance extracted. [c]: Composite Reliability.

In the IKEA case, exploratory and confirmatory factor analysis resulted in satisfactory results (Gerbing and Hamilton, 1996); a composite score was therefore calculated for all item scales (see Table 5).

RESULTS

When comparing the scores for the six TAM constructs (see Table 6) important similarities and dissimilarities are obvious: In nearly all data collection formats, the behavioral intention to use is low (rank 5 or 6) whereas the attitude is high (with the exception of the traditional data collection format, rank 1 or 2). The weakness of the mobile app is – at least according to the "new" data collection formats in the perceived ease of use (rank 5 or 6). It seems that here again the observation from Table 2 is relevant that reviews are typically written by dissatisfied persons.

Additionally, to test the other hypotheses, PLS (partial least squares) analysis was used to calculate the TAM model for each of the four data collection formats (see Figure 4).

While the items of the respective latent constructs were used as indicators in the traditional TAM model (here: sample 4), the combined value was used as a single indicator of the respective latent construct in the other three data collection formats (here: sample 1 to 3). A comparison of the traditional TAM model of sample 4 to the other three samples shows that the online reviews (sample 1), the adjective pairs (sample 3) and the item scales (sample 4) reflect the basic TAM model best. Hypothesis 1 is completely confirmed for sample 3, and for the most part for sample 1 and 4. For sample 4 the relationship perceived ease of use and perceived usefulness is insignificant, as is the relationship perceived usefulness and behavioral intention to use for sample 1. The relationship between the two external variables perceived enjoyment and perceived informativeness on perceived usefulness is not confirmed by the critical incidents (sample 1 and 2), but rather by the item-based questions (sample 3 and 4). Overall the results show that online reviews can be used instead of self-reported questionnaires in experimental settings to confirm important relationships in the TAM model. Hypothesis 3 is therefore supported. Nevertheless text samples are not in general suitable as demonstrated by sample 2 where none of the relationships were confirmed.

RECOMMENDATIONS

This chapter provides several insights when measuring customer acceptance and collecting data at the point of sale. Firstly, it was possible to confirm the usability of online reviews to model the basic TAM constructs. Nevertheless there seems to be a threshold with regard to the number of words which should be included in a sample. Otherwise, as in the case of perceived informativeness and perceived enjoyment, no significant relationships can be found. Secondly, experiments seem to overestimate the TAM constructs. For IKEA's mobile app the online reviews give a more realistic picture of the difficulties and problems than the laboratory conditions. Therefore experimental settings should be as close to reality as possible. In addition to the analysis of online reviews, the approach of identifying important adjective pairs out of the online reviews seems to be a promising alternative. Nevertheless, similar to the item scales, there is the problem of overestimation due to the experimental conditions. The collection of free text in experimental conditions appears not to be a useful approach since none of the proposed relationships of the TAM model could be confirmed. In contrast, for IKEA's mobile app negative incidents in a larger sample of online reviews seem to be a valuable source of information for constructing TAM constructs or identifying important words. Nevertheless, with regard to statistical significance the higher R^2 seems to be more in favor of the traditional measurement model.

Table 6. Mean values (standard deviation) of the TAM constructs in the different data collection formats

	Perceived In-Formativeness	Perceived Enjoyment	Perceived Ease of Use	Perceived Usefulness	Attitude	Behavioral In-Tention to Use
Data collection format 1 *(Rank)*	4.01 (0.31) *(3)*	4.06 (0.40) *(2)*	3.63 (0.52) *(6)*	3.94 (0.35) *(4)*	4.12 (0.98) *(1)*	3.81 (0.52) *(5)*
Data collection format 2 *(Rank)*	4.07 (0.70) *(4)*	4.16 (0.38) *(3)*	3.97 (0.89) *(5)*	4.50 (0.69) *(2)*	4.70 (0.68) *(1)*	3.82 (0.60) *(6)*
Data collection format 3 *(Rank)*	4.98 (1.63) *(1)*	4.73 (1.63) *(3)*	4.24 (1.25) *(6)*	4.71 (1.18) *(4)*	4.83 (1.00) *(2)*	4.40 (1.38) *(5)*
Data collection format 4 *(Rank)*	4.66 (1.28) *(4)*	5.39 (1.37) *(2)*	5.73 (1.19) *(1)*	4.82 (1.46) *(3)*	4.48 (1.49) *(5)*	3.72 (1.72) *(6)*

Scale: 1 = strongly disagree, 7 = strongly agree.

FUTURE RESEARCH DIRECTIONS

Besides offering several interesting research issues, the research in this chapter (and in the related paper Rese et al. 2014) is also confronted with several research limitations. Firstly, only one innovation at the point of sale, i.e. IKEA' mobile app, was investigated. The approach should be employed in follow-up studies to confirm the results. With regard to external variables of the TAM model it should be investigated in further studies whether they are reflected by important incidents and if a threshold value of incidents/words exists. Nevertheless, there is the problem of faked online reviews which must be taken into account. The results are predominantly useful for available systems with a critical mass of feedback volume. Overall online reviews offer rich data. However, the data preparation is not without effort. The comments have to be controlled for words which actually reflect a positive content, but are answered together with a negation in the

Figure 4. TAM model with results using PLS with respect to the four data collection formats (Here: samples as in Rese et al. 2014).

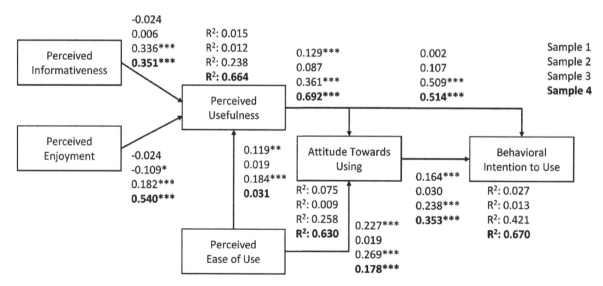

*: p<0.5, **: p<0.01, ***: p<0.001, in bold: traditional TAM model

negative. Automating the processing of the textual data, e.g. develop an ontology of linguistic indicators for constructs, to evaluate online reviews appears to be promising, especially with regard to the TAM model.

CONCLUSION

From a theoretical point of view our findings demonstrate that online reviews basing on the critical incident technique (Bitner et al., 1990; Keaveney, 1995) can be used to model the important relationships of the TAM model. With regard to AR at the point of sale the results confirm the importance of the basic TAM model (Davis et al., 1989) for customer acceptance. Nevertheless, the non-significant results of the two external variables of perceived informativeness and perceived enjoyment indicate that for the use of online reviews a certain number of positive or negative critical incidents must be present. In addition, our results confirm the criticism towards the external validity of the TAM model, which relies on experimental settings and student samples (Legris et al., 2003). From a practical point of view, online reviews can contribute valuable ideas for (technical) improvements to IKEA's mobile app. When collecting feedback in pilot/early stages of a system the setting should be as realistic as possible. Otherwise the words used in the comments differ too much from those used in an authentic setting.

REFERENCES

Ahn, T., Seewon, R., & Han, I. (2004). The impact of the online and offline features on the user acceptance of Internet shopping malls. *Electronic Commerce Research and Applications*, *3*(4), 405–420. doi:10.1016/j.elerap.2004.05.001

Anderson, E. W. (1998). Customer satisfaction and word of mouth. *Journal of Service Research*, *1*(1), 5–17. doi:10.1177/109467059800100102

Baier, D., & Stüber, E. (2010). Acceptance of recommendations to buy in online retailing. *Journal of Retailing and Consumer Services*, *17*(3), 3–180. doi:10.1016/j.jretconser.2010.03.005

Baier, D., & Stüber, E. (2011). Recommendations to buy in online retailing and their acceptance. In E. Pantano & H. Timmermans (Eds.), *Advanced technology management for retailing: Framework and cases* (pp. 237–252). Hershey, PA: IGI Global. doi:10.4018/978-1-60960-738-8.ch012

Bitner, M. J., Booms, B., & Tetreault, M. (1990). The service encounter: Diagnosing favorable and unfavorable incidents. *Journal of Marketing*, *54*(1), 71–84. doi:10.2307/1252174

Bruner, G. C. II, & Kumar, A. (2005). Explaining consumer acceptance of handheld Internet devices. *Journal of Business Research*, *58*(5), 553–558. doi:10.1016/j.jbusres.2003.08.002

Bulearca, M., & Tamarjan, D. (2010). Augmented reality: A sustainable marketing tool? *Global Business and Management Research: An International Journal*, *2*(2 & 3), 237–252.

Burt, S., Johansson, U., & Thelander, Å. (2011). Standardized marketing strategies in retailing? IKEA's marketing strategies in Sweden, the UK and China. *Journal of Retailing and Consumer Services*, *18*(3), 183–193. doi:10.1016/j.jretconser.2010.09.007

Butterfield, L. D., Borgen, W. A., Amundson, N. E., & Maglio, A.-S. T. (2005). Fifty years of the critical incident technique: 1954-2004 and beyond. *Qualitative Research*, *5*(4), 475–497. doi:10.1177/1468794105056924

Chen, L.-D., & Tan, J. (2004). Technology adaptation in e-commerce: Key determinants of virtual stores acceptance. *European Management Journal, 22*(1), 74–86. doi:10.1016/j.emj.2003.11.014

comScore. (2011). *14 million Americans scanned QR codes on their mobile phones in June 2011.* Retrieved from: http://www.comscore.com/ger/Insights/Press_Releases/2011/8/14_Million_Ameri-cans_Scanned_QR_or_Bar_Codes_on_their_Mobile_Phones_in_June_2011

Dabholkar, P. A., Shepherd, C. D., & Thorpe, D. I. (2000). A comprehensive framework for service quality: An investigation of critical conceptual and measurement issues through a longitudinal study. *Journal of Retailing, 76*(2), 139–173. doi:10.1016/S0022-4359(00)00029-4

Davis, F. D. (1989). Perceived usefulness, perceived-ease-of-use and user acceptance of information technology. *Management Information Systems Quarterly, 13*(3), 319–340. doi:10.2307/249008

Davis, F. D., Bagozzi, P. R., & Warshaw, P. R. (1989). User acceptance of computer technology: A comparison of two theoretical models. *Management Science, 35*(8), 982–1002. doi:10.1287/mnsc.35.8.982

Davis, F. D., Bagozzi, R. P., & Warshaw, P. R. (1992). Extrinsic and intrinsic motivation to use computers in the workplace. *Journal of Applied Social Psychology, 22*(14), 1111–1132. doi:10.1111/j.1559-1816.1992.tb00945.x

De Bruyn, A., & Lilien, G. L. (2008). A multistage model of word-of-mouth influence through viral marketing. *International Journal of Research in Marketing, 25*(3), 151–163. doi:10.1016/j.ijresmar.2008.03.004

Dickinger, A., & Kleijnen, M. (2008). Coupons going wireless: Determinants of consumer intentions to redeem mobile coupons. *Journal of Interactive Marketing, 22*(3), 23–39. doi:10.1002/dir.20115

Ducoffe, R. H. (1996). Advertising value and advertising on the web. *Journal of Advertising Research, 36*(5), 21–35.

Duncan, E., Hazan, E., & Roche, K. (2013). *IConsumer: Digital consumers altering the value chain.* Retrieved from www.mckinsey.com

Feinerer, I., & Hornik, K. (2013). Text mining package tm for R. *CRAN Repository.* Retrieved from: http://tm.r-forge.r-project.org

Fishbein, M., & Ajzen, I. (1975). *Belief, attitude, intention, and behavior: An introduction to theory and research.* Reading, MA: Addison-Wesley.

Flanagan, J. C. (1954). The critical incident technique. *Psychological Bulletin, 51*(4), 327–358. doi:10.1037/h0061470 PMID:13177800

Gefen, D., Karahanna, E., & Straub, D. W. (2003). Trust and TAM in online shopping: An integrated model. *Management Information Systems Quarterly, 27*(1), 51–90.

Gerbing, D. W., & Hamilton, J. G. (1996). Viability of exploratory factor analysis as a precursor to confirmatory factor analysis. *Structural Equation Modeling, 3*(1), 62–72. doi:10.1080/10705519609540030

Güven, S., Oda, O., Podlaseck, M., Stavropoulos, H., Kolluri, S., & Pingali, G. (2009). Social mobile augmented reality for retail. In *Proceedings of the Conference of Pervasive Computing and Communications (PerCom 2009).* Academic Press.

Hausman, A. V., & Siepke, J. S. (2009). The effect of web interface features on consumer online purchase intentions. *Journal of Business Venturing, 62*(1), 5–13.

Hornik, K., Porter, M., & Boulton, R. (2013). Snowball: Snowball stemmers. *CRAN Repository.* Retrieved from http://CRAN.R-project.org/package=Snowball

Keaveney, S. M. (1995). Customer switching behavior in service industry: An exploratory study. *Journal of Marketing*, *59*(2), 71–82. doi:10.2307/1252074

Legris, P., Ingham, J., & Collerette, P. (2003). Why do people use information technology? A critical review of the technology acceptance model. *Information & Management*, *40*(3), 191–204. doi:10.1016/S0378-7206(01)00143-4

Lu, Y., & Smith, S. (2007). Augmented reality e-commerce assistant system: Trying while shopping. *Lecture Notes in Computer Science*, *4551*, 643–652. doi:10.1007/978-3-540-73107-8_72

McKinsey & Company. (2012). *The young and the digital: a glimpse into future market evolution*. Retrieved from: http://www.mckinsey.com/client_service/high_tech/iconsumer

McKinsey & Company. (2013). *IConsumers: Life online*. Retrieved from: https://tmt.mckinsey.com/

Oh, H., Yoon, S.-Y., & Shyu, C.-R. (2008). How can virtual reality reshape furniture retailing? *Clothing & Textiles Research Journal*, *26*(2), 143–163. doi:10.1177/0887302X08314789

Olsson, T., Kärkkäinen, T., Lagerstam, E., & Ventä-Olkkonen, L. (2012). User evaluation of mobile augmented reality scenarios. *Journal of Ambient Intelligence and Smart Environments*, *4*(1), 29–47.

Olsson, T., Lagerstam, E., Kärkkäinen, T., & Väänänen-Vainio-Mattila, K. (2013). Expected user experience of mobile augmented reality services: A user study in the context of shopping centres. *Personal and Ubiquitous Computing*, *17*(2), 287–304. doi:10.1007/s00779-011-0494-x

Olsson, T., & Salo, M. (2011). Online user survey on current mobile augmented reality applications. In *Proceedings of the 10th IEEE International Symposium on Mixed and Augmented Reality (ISMAR)* (pp. 75-84). IEEE. doi:10.1109/ISMAR.2011.6092372

Pantano, E., & Naccarato, G. (2010). Entertainment in retailing: The influences of advanced technologies. *Journal of Retailing and Consumer Services*, *17*(3), 200–204. doi:10.1016/j.jretconser.2010.03.010

Pantano, E., & Servidio, R. (2012). Modeling innovative points of sales through virtual and immersive technologies. *Journal of Retailing and Consumer Services*, *19*(3), 279–286. doi:10.1016/j.jretconser.2012.02.002

Plouffe, C. R., Vandenbosch, M., & Hulland, J. (2001). Intermediating technologies and multigroup adoption: A comparison of consumer and merchant adoption intentions toward a new electronic payment system. *Journal of Product Innovation Management*, *18*(2), 65–81. doi:10.1016/S0737-6782(00)00072-2

Poncin, I., & Mimoun, M. S. B. (2014). The impact of "e-atmospherics" on physical stores. *Journal of Retailing and Consumer Services*, *21*(5), 851–859. doi:10.1016/j.jretconser.2014.02.013

Porter, C. E., & Donthu, N. (2006). Using the technology acceptance model to explain how attitudes determine Internet usage: The role of perceived access barriers and demographics. *Journal of Business Research*, *59*(9), 999–1007. doi:10.1016/j.jbusres.2006.06.003

Rese, A., Schreiber, S., & Baier, D. (2014). Technology acceptance modeling of augmented reality at the point of sale: Can surveys be replaced by an analysis of online reviews? *Journal of Retailing and Consumer Services*, *21*(5), 869–876. doi:10.1016/j.jretconser.2014.02.011

Saarijärvi, H., Mitronen, L., & Yrjölä, M. (2014). From selling to supporting – Leveraging mobile services in the context of food retailing. *Journal of Retailing and Consumer Services, 21*(1), 26–36. doi:10.1016/j.jretconser.2013.06.009

Tang, C., & Guo, L. (2013). Digging for gold with a simple tool: Validating text mining in studying electronic word-of-mouth (eWOM) communication. *Marketing Letters*, 1–14. doi:10.1007/s11002-013-9268-8

Turner, M., Kitchenham, B., Brereton, P., Charters, S., & Budgen, D. (2010). Does the technology acceptance model predict actual use? A systematic literature review. *Information and Software Technology, 52*(5), 463–479. doi:10.1016/j.infsof.2009.11.005

Välkkynen, P., Boyer, A., Urhemaa, T., & Nieminen, R. (2011). Mobile augmented reality for retail environments. In *Proceedings of Workshop on Mobile Interaction in Retail Environments in Conjunction with MobileHCI*. ACM.

Vaughan-Nichols, S. J. (2009). Augmented reality: No longer a novelty? *Computer, 42*(12), 19–22. doi:10.1109/MC.2009.380

Venkatesh, V., & Davis, F. D. (2000). A theoretical extension of the technological acceptance model: Four longitudinal field studies. *Management Science, 46*(2), 186–204. doi:10.1287/mnsc.46.2.186.11926

Venkatesh, V., Morris, M., Davis, G., & Davis, F. (2003). User acceptance of information technology: Toward a unified view. *Management Information Systems Quarterly, 27*(3), 425–478.

Wu, K., Zhao, X., Zhu, Q., Tan, X., & Zheng, H. (2011). A meta-analysis of the impact of trust on technology acceptance model: Investigation of moderating influence of subject and context type. *International Journal of Information Management, 31*(6), 572–581. doi:10.1016/j.ijinfomgt.2011.03.004

Yuen, S., Yaoyuneyong, G., & Johnson, E. (2011). Augmented reality: An overview and five directions for AR in education. *Journal of Educational Technology Development and Exchange, 4*(1), 119–140.

ADDITIONAL READING

Ajzen, I. (1985). From intentions to actions: a theory of planned behavior. In J. Kuhl & J. Beckmann (Eds.), *Action control: from cognition to behavior* (pp. 11–39). Berlin, Heidelberg: Springer. doi:10.1007/978-3-642-69746-3_2

Ajzen, I. (1991). The theory of planned behavior. *Organizational Behavior and Human Decision Processes, 50*(2), 179–211. doi:10.1016/0749-5978(91)90020-T

Ajzen, I., & Fishbein, M. (1980). *Understanding attitudes and predicting social behavior*. Englewood Cliffs, NJ: Prentice-Hall.

Bagozzi, R. P. (2007). The legacy of the technology acceptance model and a proposal for a paradigm shift. *Journal of the Association for Information Systems, 8*(4), 244–254.

Benbasat, I., & Barki, H. (2007). Quo vadis, TAM? *Journal of the Association for Information Systems, 8*(4), 211–218.

Bickart, B., & Schindler, R. M. (2001). Internet forums as influential sources of consumer information. *Journal of Interactive Marketing, 15*(3), 31–40. doi:10.1002/dir.1014

Chuttur, M. Y. (2009). *Overview of the technology acceptance model: Origins, developments and future directions. All Sprouts Content.* Paper 290. http://aisel.aisnet.org/sprouts_all/290

Dijkstra, T. (1983). Some comments on maximum likelihood and partial least squares methods. *Journal of Econometrics, 22*(1-2), 67–90. doi:10.1016/0304-4076(83)90094-5

Fornell, C., & Larcker, D. F. (1981). Evaluating structural equation models with unobservable variables and measurement error. *JMR, Journal of Marketing Research, 18*(1), 39–50. doi:10.2307/3151312

Henseler, J., Ringle, C. M., & Sinkovics, R. R. (2009). The use of partial least squares path modeling in international marketing. *Advances in International Marketing, 20*, 277–319.

Königstorfer, J., & Gröppel-Klein, A. (2007). Experiences of failure and anger when using the mobile and wired Internet: The interference of acceptance- and resistance-driving factors. *Marketing Journal of Resource Management, 29*(1e), 34–47.

Lee, Y., Kozar, K. A., & Larsen, K. R. (2003). The technology acceptance model: Past, present, and future. *Communications of AIS, 12*, 752–780.

Tenenhaus, M., Esposito Vinzi, V., Chatelin, Y.-M., & Lauro, C. (2005). PLS path modeling. *Computational Statistics & Data Analysis, 48*(1), 159–205. doi:10.1016/j.csda.2004.03.005

Venkatesh, V., & Davis, F. D. (2000). A theoretical extension of the technology acceptance model: Four longitudinal field studies. *Management Science, 46*(2), 186–204. doi:10.1287/mnsc.46.2.186.11926

Wold, H. O. (1974). Causal flows with latent variables: Partings of the ways in the light of NIPALS modeling. *European Economic Review, 5*(1), 67–86. doi:10.1016/0014-2921(74)90008-7

Wold, H. O. (1982). Soft modeling: The basic design and some extensions. In K. G. Jöreskog & H. O. Wold (Eds.), *Systems under indirect observations, part II* (pp. 1–54). Amsterdam: North Holland.

Wold, H. O. (1985). Partial least squares. In S. Kotz & N. L. Johnson (Eds.), *Encyclopedia of statistical sciences, 6* (pp. 581–591). New York, NY: Wiley.

KEY TERMS AND DEFINITIONS

Augmented Reality: A technique to combine real and computer-generated digital information into the user's view of the physical real world in such a way that they appear as one environment.

Mobile App: Computer program designed to run on a smartphone, tablet, or other mobile devices. Apps (short for application software) are available through application distribution platforms, e.g. Apple App Store, Google Play, or Windows Phone Store. Some apps are free of charge, others must be bought.

Online Customer Reviews: A customer review is a review of a product (e.g. PCs, cameras, TVs, books, films) or a service (hotels, restaurants, bars, destinations, leisure parks, sellers, retailers) made by a customer who has used it. Since – nowadays – the upload of and access to such reviews is very easy and other customers are assumed to be more trustworthy than sellers, other customers use them for making their buying decisions. They can easily be found and used on websites of online shops (e.g. Amazon, HRS, Booking) or on specific review sites (e.g. tripadvisor, epinions). However, often the reliability of such customer reviews is questioned due to no or few control with respect to favorable reviews by sellers and their friends or whether the reviewing customer really has used the product or service.

Perceived Ease of Use: Perceived ease of use is defined as the degree to which a person believes that using a particular new information technology or system would be free of effort. According to TAM perceived ease of use is a major factor that influences the decision of a person about how and when to use the new information technology or system.

Perceived Enjoyment: Perceived enjoyment is defined as the entertaining / fun providing component of a particular new information technology or system (Olsson et al., 2013). According to the modified TAM in this chapter perceived enjoyment is a major factor that influences the perceived usefulness of the new information technology or system.

Perceived Informativeness: Perceived informativeness is defined as the usefulness of given information of a particular new information technology or system (Olsson et al., 2013). According to the modified TAM in this chapter perceived informativeness is a major factor that influences the perceived usefulness of the new information technology or system.

Perceived Usefulness: Perceived usefulness is defined as the degree to which a person believes that a particular new information technology or system would enhance his or her performance in a specific application setting. According to TAM perceived usefulness is a major factor that influences the decision of a person about how and when to use the new information technology or system.

APPENDIX

Table 7. AR applications in retailing grouped into different categories

Case	Display	Context	Description	Source/Website
Virtual Trial and Product Education				
Artelia 3D - Augmented Reality	Smartphone/ tablet	Furniture	Visualizes 3D furniture at true size in a real setting.	https://itunes.apple.com/app/artelia-viewar/ id543137431?mt=8
Atelier Pfister	Smartphone/ tablet	Furniture	Visualizes 3D furniture at true size in a real setting.	https://itunes.apple.com/app/atelier-pfister/ id385703066?mt=8 https://play.google.com/store/apps/details?id=ch. vanija.pfisterapp&hl=de
Audi eKurzinfo	Smartphone/ tablet	Cars	Enhances customers' experience through additional information.	https://itunes.apple.com/de/app/audi-ekurzinfo/ id436341817 https://play.google.com/store/apps/ details?id=com.audi.a1ekurzinfo
AUTO BILD Augmented Reality	Smartphone/ tablet	Print media	Enhances customers' experience through additional information, audio details, sound effects, videos and interactive images. Works with the printed Auto Bild magazine.	https://play.google.com/store/apps/details?id=de. autobild.augmentedreality
Bellaluce Virtual Try-on	Desktop application with webcams	Jewelry	Offers a virtual try-on experience for jewelry.	http://www.bellaluce.de/jewelry/current-news/ experience-bellaluce-virtually/
Brille24	Desktop application with webcams	Eyewear	Offers a virtual try-on experience for eyewear.	http://www.brille24.de/beratung/brillenanprobe. html
Brother AR	Smartphone/ tablet	Consumer electronics	Visualizes the products in 3D. Enhances customers' experience through additional information.	http://welcome.brother.com/ae-en/support-downloads/augmented-reality_PC.html
Butlers-Augmented Reality App	Smartphone/ tablet	Furniture	Visualizes 3D furniture at true size in a real setting.	http://www.butlers.de/viewar_LP.html
Deichmann Mobile App	Smartphone/ tablet	Fashion	Offers a virtual try-on experience for footwear.	https://itunes.apple.com/de/app/deichmann/ id634957574 https://play.google.com/store/apps/ details?id=com.deichmann.deichmannapp
IKEA Catalogue	Smartphone/ tablet	Furniture	Visualizes 3D furniture at true size in a real setting. Enhances customers' experience through additional information, videos, x-ray views, 3D animations, 360° product views and interactive images. Works with IKEA's printed catalogue.	http://www.ikea.com/ms/en_GB/virtual_ catalogue/online_catalogues.html

continued on following page

Table 7. Continued

Case	Display	Context	Description	Source/Website
KARE Room Designer	Smartphone/ tablet	Furniture	Visualizes 3D furniture at true size in a real setting.	https://itunes.apple.com/app/kare-room-designer/id578687611?mt=8
LEGO 3D Catalogue	Smartphone/ tablet	Toys	Visualizes toys at true size in a real setting. Enhances customers' experience with 3D animations, additional information, sound effects and 360° views of the models. Works with LEGO's printed catalogue.	https://itunes.apple.com/de/app/lego-3d-katalog/id768629920?mt=8 https://play.google.com/store/apps/details?id=com.lego.catalogue.nbb
Mister Spex Online Fitting	Desktop application with webcams	Eyewear	Offers a virtual try-on experience for eyewear.	http://www.misterspex.co.uk/service/try-on-glasses.html
My Forevermark Fitting	Desktop application with webcams	Jewelry	Offers a virtual try-on experience for jewelry.	http://www.forevermark.com/hi-in/Collections/Millemoi/The-Story/My-Forevermark-Fitting/
Moosejaw X-RAY	Smartphone/ tablet	Fashion	Enhances customers' experience: X-ray scanner allows to see outerwear models in their underwear. Works with the Moosejaw catalogue.	https://play.google.com/store/apps/details?id=com.marxentlabs.moosejaw.XRay&feature=search_result
NicArt Augmented Reality ViewAR	Smartphone/ tablet	Artwork	Visualizes artwork in a real setting.	https://itunes.apple.com/app/nicart-augmented-reality-viewar/id525689318?mt=8
OBI 3D Kamin-Viewer	Smartphone/ tablet	Furniture (fireplaces)	Visualizes fireplaces at true size in a real setting.	http://www.obi.de/de/services/online-services/mobil/obi-3d-kamin-viewer/index.html
Ottobock Augmented Reality	Smartphone/ tablet	Orthopaedic technology	Visualizes orthopaedic equipment at true size in a real setting.	http://professionals.ottobock.de/cps/rde/xchg/ob_de_de/hs.xsl/7615.html
Popular Science+	Desktop application with webcams	Print media	Visualizes 3D images by holding the magazine cover up to a webcam.	http://www.metaio.com/customers/case-studies/popular-science-3d-magazine-cover/
Ravensburger Augmented Reality Puzzles	Smartphone/ tablet	Toys	Enhances customers' experience through additional information, audio details, sound effects, videos and 360° images.	https://itunes.apple.com/app/ar-puzzle/id502524775?mt=8
Ray-Ban Virtual Mirror	Desktop application with webcams	Eyewear	Offers a virtual try-on experience for eyewear.	http://www.ray-ban.com/international/virtual-mirror
Sharp Augmented Reality App	Smartphone/ tablet	Consumer electronics	Visualizes television sets at true size in a real setting.	https://itunes.apple.com/app/sharp-ar-tv/id610411242?mt=8 https://play.google.com/store/apps/details?id=com.sharp_eu.ste.tvar
SnapShop Showroom	Smartphone/ tablet	Furniture	Visualizes 3D furniture at true size in a real setting.	https://itunes.apple.com/app/snapshop-showroom/id373144101?mt=8

continued on following page

Table 7. Continued

Case	Display	Context	Description	Source/Website
Soli Kiani ViewAR	Smartphone/ tablet	Artwork	Visualizes artwork in a real setting.	https://itunes.apple.com/app/soli-kiani-viewar/ id534515717?mt=8
Steinway Augmented Reality ViewAR	Smartphone/ tablet	Musical instruments	Visualizes musical instruments at true size in a real setting.	https://itunes.apple.com/app/steinway-augmented-reality/id600058288?mt=8
Stern AR App	Smartphone/ tablet	Print media	Enhances customers' experience through animated cartoons, 3D animations and video. Works with the printed Stern magazine.	https://play.google.com/store/apps/ details?id=com.metaio.junaio.plugin.stern_ar
Tesco Discover App	Smartphone/ tablet	Food, general retail	Enhances customers' experience through 3D animations, additional information (e.g. provenance of Tesco products), videos, exclusive offers, competitions. Works with Tesco recipe cards, the Gift Guide, Tesco Magazine and Wine Magazine.	http://www.tesco.com/apps/ https://play.google.com/store/apps/ details?id=com.aurasma.skinned.tesco_discover https://itunes.apple.com/de/app/tesco-discover/ id544347167?mt=8
The Sampler by Converse	Smartphone/ tablet	Fashion (footwear)	Offers a virtual try-on experience for footwear.	https://itunes.apple.com/app/the-sampler-by-converse/id392276032?mt=8
Vauni ViewAR	Smartphone/ tablet	Furniture (fireplaces)	Visualizes fireplaces at true size in a real setting.	https://itunes.apple.com/app/vauni-viewar/ id600035019?mt=8
Viking Footwear AR	Smartphone/ tablet	Fashion (footwear)	Offers a virtual try-on experience for footwear.	https://itunes.apple.com/app/viking-footwear-ar/ id466632818?mt=8 https://play.google.com/store/apps/ details?id=com.Labrat.VikingShoe01&hl=de
In-Store Customer Experience Enhancement				
Carrefour	In-store information kiosk (virtual fitting room)	Fashion	Offers a virtual try-on experience for fashion.	http://www.carrefour.com/current-news/carrefour-breaking-new-ground-first-virtual-fitting-rooms-created-partnership-clear
LEGO Digital Box	In-store information kiosk	Toys	Visualizes the 3D animations to the corresponding LEGO model. Enhances customers' experience through sound effects.	http://www.metaio.com/customers/case-studies/ lego/
WarBot	Smartphone/ tablet	Toys	Enhances customers' experience through games. Customer can win discounts. Works by scanning toys.	https://itunes.apple.com/app/warbot/ id714980838?mt=8
Brand Recognition Enhancement				
Bulmers deCider	Smartphone/ tablet	Food	Enhances customers' experience through 3D animations and missions to complete. Customer can win prizes. Works by scanning a promotional Bulmers pint bottle.	https://itunes.apple.com/app/bulmers-decider/ id514568580?mt=8 https://play.google.com/store/apps/ details?id=com.eightytwenty.decider&hl=de

Section 3
Innovation Management and Innovative Strategies

This section offers a collection of recent studies proposing some promising strategies for the successful adoption of innovations in retail settings. Findings contribute to the body of literature on innovation and technology management for retailing and broaden the understanding of adoption dynamics in general. In particular, they offer a management perspective of the innovative force characterizing retail sector, and the possible strategies for creating new services within the financial sustainability standpoint.

Chapter 9
Differentiation through Service Excellence:
Empirical Findings on the Role of Self–Service Technology in Retail

Philipp Spreer
University of Gottingen, Germany

Katrin Kallweit
University of Gottingen, Germany

ABSTRACT

Service excellence is one of the key differentiators for retailers in the digital environment. To ensure a high level of service quality at the point of sale, retailers contemplate the implementation of Self-Service Information Technologies (SSITs). This chapter 1) examines the mediation effect of service quality within the technology acceptance model and 2) identifies relevant segments based on the level of acceptance and the perception of the service quality provided by an SSIT. Building on data from a laboratory experiment using a fully functional application for Tablet PCs, the partial least squares approach and a combined hierarchical and non-hierarchical cluster analysis were used. The findings reveal that the perceived service quality partially mediates the effect of the attitude towards using on the intention to reuse. Moreover, two distinct segments are identified: the "occasional handymen" and the "enthusiastic experts," who differ significantly in terms of SSIT acceptance.

INTRODUCTION

Service Quality as a Key Differentiator in Retail

In recent years, bricks-and-mortar retailers came under tremendous pressure as online competitors to continuously gain market shares (Weitz, 2010).

Due to superior cost structures resulting from the absence of expensive retail stores and well-educated salespeople, these competitors can act very price-aggressively and undercut the prices of traditional retailers (Balasubramanian, Raghunathan, & Mahajan, 2005). This is compounded by the fact that the evolution of technology provides perfect price transparency as customers are able to

DOI: 10.4018/978-1-4666-8297-9.ch009

compare product prices using their smartphones regardless of the time or place. As a result, consumers become more sophisticated shoppers and can instantly switch to an alternative competitor when large price differences are not justified by any additional value provided by the retailer (Weitz & Whitfield, 2010).

As a consequence, a rising number of retailers moved away from competing with the prices of e-commerce companies and identified service quality (SQ) as a possible differentiator. Retailers such as Build-A-Bear, Trader Joe's, Best Buy, or Lowe's who provide great customer service can distinguish themselves from competitors by adding significant value to what they offer (Grewal, Krishnan, & Munger, 2010). These retailers meet the customer requirement of maximum convenience, including a cross-channel buying experience. Combined with the advantage of a haptic product experience representing one of the few competitive factors which cannot be imitated by online retailers, a high SQ increases the probability of choosing a bricks-and-mortar retailer (Laroche, Yang, McDougall, & Bergeron, 2005; Chiu, Hsieh, Roan, Tseng, & Hsieh, 2011).

Hence, given the time and money that retailers invest to attract customers, it is surprising that so little attention is paid to customer service (Grewal et al., 2010) although a high SQ strengthens the competitive position of traditional retailers and reduces the dependence on a continuously successful acquisition of new customers. This low level of engagement in SQ might be explained through a lack of state-of-the-art knowhow.

Usually, SQ improvement requires large investments in additional personnel and trainings, but many retailers do not consider additional salespeople as the most efficient solution. A prominent example is the European do-it-yourself (DIY) retail industry: While the selling spaces keep growing (Datamonitor, 2010; Rincker, 2011), the number of salespeople remains stable. The result is a decreasing staff density in the stores, which leads to a lack of service, negatively af-

fecting customer satisfaction and ultimately the economic success of the retailer. Thus, the decision not to invest in additional salespeople even exacerbates the challenge of keeping the SQ at a high level or improving it. Hence, many retailers ask themselves how SQ excellence can be realized without affecting profitability. Instead of hiring additional sales staff, a rising number of innovative retailers aim to defend their competitive position using technology-based service-delivery options that fulfill the standardizable tasks of salespeople (Weijters, Rangarajan, Falk, & Schillewaert, 2007; Berry et al., 2010) in order to increase the SQ without rising personnel costs.

The interest in such technologies is still growing, but currently the scale-economy effects remain unexplored (Pantano & Viassone, 2014). A latent uncertainty and existing gaps in knowledge impede the broad implementation of SSITs in retail and other scopes of application, such as e-government, education, health or public transportation. Among other things, it is unclear how important the SQ provided by a technology is for its adoption.

Chapter Objectives

Hence, the present chapter aims at shedding some light onto the hotly debated question of the role of SQ in the use of SSITs. Building on this, we try to characterize the typical users of retail technologies in order to provide the basis for a customer-oriented implementation of SSITs.

Technology Acceptance has been broadly researched in the past. Most studies come to the conclusion that the attitude towards using technology has a strong influence on the behavioral intentions, but no empirical work can be found that answers the question of how this strong effect between the predictor and the criterion variable can be explained. Because the customer benefit plays a crucial role in technology acceptance and as this benefit consists in a SQ improvement in the context of SSITs, one can assume that SQ provides explanatory potential for the relationship between the attitude towards using technology and the intention to use. The evaluation of SQ is especially important in the context of retail SSITs as the outcome directly redounds upon the evaluation of the retailer (Meuter, Bitner, Ostrom, & Brown, 2000; Wang, 2012). Recent studies, for example, have shown its huge relevance e.g. for retail patronage (Lee & Yang, 2013; Lee, Fairhurst, & Lee, 2009) and customer satisfaction (Dabholkar & Spaid, 2012; Demirci Orel & Kara, 2014).

Hence, the study attempts to improve our understanding of technology acceptance in the context of retail SSITs by analyzing the mediating effect of SQ between the attitude towards using a technology and the intention to use it.

For a successful implementation, however, more insights on the specification of these drivers is necessary as SSITs will neither provide the same benefit nor be used by all customers. The existing literature reveals that customers vary in their perception of the technology delivered value (Cooil, Aksoy, Keiningham, & Maryott, 2007) and in the acceptance of technology-based services (Berry et al., 2010). Accordingly, Bolton and Saxena-Iyer (2009) state, that in the case of interactive services retailers need to develop new ways to manage customer heterogeneity.

In order to assess heterogeneous groups of customers or users of a technology, segmentations are usually applied. Past research focused on building customer segments based on socio-demographic variables (e.g. Browning & Zabriskie, 1985) or buying behavior (e.g. Reutterer, Mild, Natter, & Taudes, 2006). However, the question remains as to which customer groups can be addressed by SSITs and how the systems can be tailored to increase their service quality perception. This question requires the assessment of behavioral variables linked to the future use of a technology. Thus, in the present chapter, we aim at contributing to theory and practice by identifying and describing segments among the users' SSIT acceptance in retail and at deducing possible implications for its conceptualization and implementation.

The remainder of this paper is organized as follows: Firstly, we present the theoretical background, focusing on SSITs acceptance and SQ research. Building on that, the conceptual framework is presented and hypotheses are developed. Concerning the empirical analysis, the research setting is described first. Afterwards, the principles of our data collection, a sample description and our methodology are highlighted before the findings from the analyses are outlined and discussed. Academic and managerial implications as well as limitations of the study conclude the paper.

THEORETICAL BACKGROUND

Self-Service Technologies in Retail

The increasing diffusion of information technology is on the brink of revolutionizing the way people shop. This development does not only affect digital distribution channels, but also bricks-and-mortar stores: Retailers progressively substitute or enlarge traditional modes of service delivery by sales clerks through the implementation of technology (Colby & Parasuraman, 2003; Lee & Yang, 2013) in order to build up a customer-friendly service landscape and differentiate in terms of shopping experience. These self-service technologies (SST) are defined as technological interfaces that enable customers to produce a service independent of direct service employee involvement (Chen, 2005; Meuter et al., 2000). In recent years, they were implemented most often to cut costs and raise productivity by turning customers into co-producers of services (Hilton, Hughes, Little, & Marandi, 2013; Meuter, Bitner, Ostrom, & Brown, 2005; Weijters et al., 2007) or simply to keep up with technological advancements (Demirci Orel & Kara, 2014). Hence, SSTs address the three big challenges and trends for bricks-and-mortar retail identified by Grewal et al. (2010): Value through service as a key differentiator, being permanently innovative and cost control through the use of technology.

Figure 1. Different types of SSTs

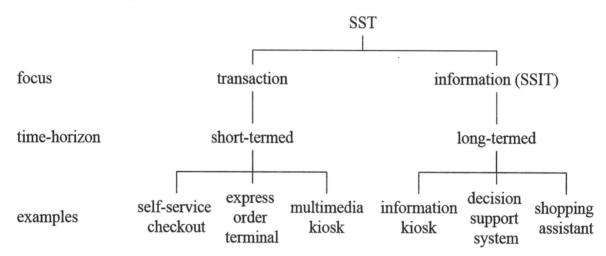

Two types of SSTs can be distinguished addressing these challenges: transaction-related technologies and customer-service or information-related technologies (Meuter et al., 2000). Early SSTs mainly focused on the first category of "technology-facilitated transactions" (Meuter et al., 2000), such as placing an order, scanning or paying. As in recent years, the SQ has become increasingly important for retailers, the role of SSTs in retail also changed: Today, transaction-related retail technologies tend to be regarded as a measure with a short-term impact (Berry et al., 2010). Current approaches are increasingly aimed at delivering information to the user and allow for the provision of customized services instead of executing transactions (Wang, 2012; Hilton et al., 2013). Such technologies build on convenience as one of the most important drivers of SQ: Customers appreciate being provided with the appropriate information for making a good buying decision without waiting or a major search effort. Examples are information kiosks (Zielke, Toporowski, & Kniza, 2011), decision support systems (Kallweit, Spreer, & Toporowski, 2014), interactive service terminals (Sha & Guo-Liang, 2012), mobile shopping assistants (Spreer & Kallweit, 2014) and multimedia kiosks (Wang, 2012).

Customer-service or information-related technologies (Meuter et al., 2000) from the second category of SSTs are referred to as self-service information technologies (SSITs, see Figure 1). Customers are enabled to collect detailed product information, check inventories or identify suitable accessories independent of the availability and knowhow of sales clerks. In return, the search cost can be reduced by pooling all the relevant information available and providing it in a much more customized way (Pantano & Viassone, 2013). This is especially important in the case of complex products which require explanation and subsequently have a higher buying risk (Chaudhuri, 2000).

Hence, SSITs are particularly attractive for customers who are looking for a high level of individual control and want to avoid interpersonal interactions to form an opinion without being influenced by sales clerks (Meuter, Ostrom, Bitner, & Roundtree, 2003) or for those who have a low need for personal interaction (Gelderman, Ghijsen, & van Diemen, 2011), e.g. due to the habit of self-information on the internet. Moreover, waiting times can be reduced for customers who are searching for specific information while sales clerks are engaged in customer talks (Dabholkar, 1994; Meuter et al., 2000). Therefore, many researchers and retailers try to identify the technology capable of best satisfying customer requests (Pantano, 2010), which is basically a question of technology acceptance. Understanding customer acceptance is highly crucial due to the huge monetary investments and late returns on investment involved in the implementation process (Pantano & Viassone, 2013).

Acceptance of Service Technology

Research on the acceptance of SSTs and SSITs has been conducted in a broad range of different contexts, using many different designs and examining a great variety of different technologies. Despite this methodological diversity, the majority of quantitative studies use the technology acceptance model (TAM; Davis, 1989) or related models, such as the

theory of reasoned action (TRA; Fishbein & Ajzen, 1975), as a theoretical basis, as demonstrated in a broad overview presented in Table 1.

According to TAM, the acceptance of a technology is reflected in the strength of the attitude towards using (ATU) and the intention to use it (ITU; Davis, Bagozzi, & Warshaw, 1989), which in turn are fundamentally influenced by the constructs of perceived usefulness (PU) and perceived ease of use (PEOU), as depicted in Figure 2.

PU is defined as "the degree to which a person believes that using a particular system would enhance his or her job performance" (Davis, 1989, p. 320). PEOU in turn is defined by the user's subjective evaluations on how much cognitive effort she or he must expend when using the system (Davis, 1989, p. 320).

Table 1. Overview of relevant literature on retail service technology

Study	SST/SSIT	Retail Context	Focus on SQ	Theory	Research Design	Analysis	N
Meuter et al. (2000)	diverse	no	no		online panel survey	qualitative/ quantitative	1,000
Dabholkar & Bagozzi (2002)	self-service terminal	yes	no	TAM	laboratory experiment	quantitative	392
Weijters et al. (2007)	mobile self-scanning	yes	no	TAM, Diffusion Theory	field study	quantitative	497
Kowatsch & Maass (2010)	mobile recommendation agent	yes	no	TAM, Diffusion Theory	laboratory experiment	quantitative	46
Lee et al. (2010)	self-service checkout	yes	no		online survey	quantitative	285
Corvello et al. (2011)	virtual shopping assistant	yes	no	Adaptive Structuration Theory	conceptual paper		
Zielke et al. (2011)	interactive terminal for cooking receipts	yes	no	TAM	field study	quantitative	216
Wang (2012)	multimedia kiosk	yes	no	Expectation-Confirmation Model	online panel survey	quantitative	424
Hilton et al. (2013)	diverse	no	(yes)		in-depth interviews	qualitative	24
Demirci Orel & Kara (2014)	self-service checkout	yes	(yes)		field study	quantitative	275
Lee & Yang (2013)	self-service checkout	yes	yes	TRA	online panel survey	quantitative	300

Figure 2. Technology acceptance model (Davis, 1989).

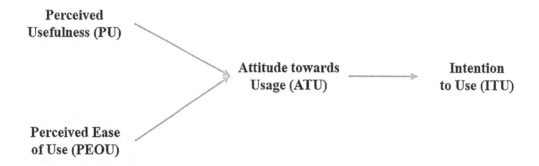

TAM is widely understood to be particularly useful to predict the social acceptance and use of technologies while they are still being developed and provide trustworthy estimates for both users that are very familiar and users that have (almost) no experience in using the technology (Davis, 1989). As both suits the context of our study, we decided to consult the model as a basis for our research.

Service Quality

The retail environment changes rapidly: Intensified competition due to a spate of mergers and acquisitions and the rise of e-commerce companies' challenges retailers to differentiate themselves by meeting the needs of their customers better than their competitors (Dabholkar, Thorpe, & Rentz, 1996). In the introduction to this chapter, we identified SQ delivered by SSITs as a possible key differentiator. However, an SSIT will only improve SQ when it is actively used. Thus, the customers' acceptance is a necessary prerequisite. Hence, variations in the TAM including the SQ are of particular interest for both researchers and practitioners (Dabholkar, 1996; Weijters et al., 2007).

Although some may say that TAM research has reached its saturation point with regard to the multiplicity of studies (Benbasat & Barki, 2007), we identified gaps in the present literature that require further examination. Table 1 outlined that

SSTs geared towards improvements SQ surprisingly are still an underrepresented research field. Moreover, previous research specifically called for research to extend the TAM with regard to the relationship between ATU and IR in the context of technology-based self-services (Oghazi, Mostaghel, Hultman, & Parida, 2012).

An important stream of research investigates the concept of SQ and argues that the customer is in the focal point of service delivery. Therefore, only his perception of quality is regarded as critical (Grönroos, 1993; Anitsal & Paige, 2006). We follow this argumentation and consider the perceived service quality (PSQ) instead of SQ in the following. PSQ can be defined as the evaluation of the result of the comparison that customers make between the expectations for a service and the perception of the way the service has been performed (Parasuraman, Zeithaml, & Berry, 1985; Lehtinen & Lehtinen, 1991). In recent decades, SQ has predominantly been understood as a global measure for a company's offering (Parasuraman, Zeithaml, & Berry, 1988). Nowadays, however, researchers argue that the assessment of SQ should have a narrower focus on every different service offering because of its unique nature (Demirci Orel & Kara, 2014). Thus, when we consider PSQ in this context we mean the quality perception of the SSIT rather than the total quality perception of the retailer.

CONCEPTUAL FRAMEWORK

The TAM offers numerous benefits to researchers, such as making reliable predictions also for technologies under development and users with low experience in using the technology, and therefore serves as a basis for the conceptual framework of this study.

However, the TAM has been also the object of some criticism. One point for questioning the model is the limitation to PU and PEOU as independent variables. Heijden (2004) claims that this conceptualization makes the TAM inappropriate for hedonic information systems. However, Kallweit et al. (2014) tested one possible influence of perceived enjoyment on ATU in the context of retail SSITs and did not find any significant relations. As the use of retail SSITs is assumed to be highly goal or utility-oriented, we consider hedonic aspects to be not particularly crucial in the present research context. Moreover, Benbasat & Barki (2007) criticize that PU has been treated as a "black box" in recent TAM research without investigating what actually makes a technology useful. Indeed, this point is critical in the SSIT context: It is not the technology itself that constitutes the usefulness for a user but rather the information that is accessed through the technology and that satisfies the user's particular need. Thus, we agree with Dabholkar and Bagozzi (2002), who suggest that PU is not strictly relevant for SSTs that are not owned by the customer. In the present research model, we replace PU by the perceived information quality (PIQ) that refers to the additional value customer's associate with the SSIT (Childers, Carr, Peck, & Carson, 2001; Weijters et al., 2007). Studies from SST research suppose that PIQ is mainly influenced by the quality and quantity of information: Yang et al. (2005) conceptualize PIQ as a construct consisting of the adequacy of information (AI, referring to the quantity of information) and the usefulness of content (UC, referring to the

quality of information). In the context of retail SSITs, AI concerns the number of product data sheets stored in the application for example. UC in turn indicates how well the generated product recommendation suits the needs of the user, for instance. Because the buying decision is based on the quantity and quality of the available information about a product, we hypothesize:

H1: The adequacy of information has a positive impact on the attitude towards using the SSIT.

H2: The usefulness of content has a positive impact on the attitude towards using the SSIT.

Based on the underlying assumptions of the TAM, PEOU represents the second important acceptance predictor (Davis, 1989). As mentioned above, it concerns the user friendliness or convenience of the SSIT. Research has advocated that retailers need to advertise a technology's ease of use to ensure that customers develop a positive attitude towards the system (Dabholkar & Bagozzi, 2002). Moreover, if customers find a technology easy to use, they consider the self-service as an attractive alternative as it reduces the effort and the risk involved in using the service (Shamdasani, Mukherjee, & Malhotra, 2008). Thus, we assume:

H3: The perceived ease of use has a positive impact on the attitude towards using the SSIT.

The ATU of novel technologies is widely believed to have an impact on the behavioral intention to use (IU) a system (Fishbein & Ajzen, 1975; Curran & Meuter, 2005). Hence, we also assume this relation to be significant and merely replace IU with the intention to reuse (IR) as a dependent variable as the participants already got involved with the SSIT during the data collection.

H4: The attitude towards using the SSIT has a positive impact on the intention to reuse the SSIT.

Services above the adequate level are considered capable of creating a competitive advantage for a retailer (Dabholkar et al., 1996). In the case of SSITs, the implementation leads to a perception of enhanced service when customers are able to obtain high quality information more conveniently and quickly (Demirci Orel & Kara, 2014). Bitner (1992) also claims that PSQ is closely related to ATU. Thus, the positive evaluation of using a technology is a prerequisite for a favorable perception of SQ. Consequently, there might be a positive relationship between ATU and PSQ in the context of SSITs (Dabholkar, 1996). Therefore, it is postulated:

H5: The attitude towards using the SSIT has a positive impact on the perceived service quality.

Boulding et al. (1993) reveal that there is a positive correlation between PSQ and behavioral intentions. Moreover, PSQ has been considered as a direct antecedent of IR within the technology acceptance paradigm (Shamdasani et al., 2008), also in the context of SSITs (Lee, Fairhurst, & Cho, 2013). Zeithaml et al. (1996) and Dabholkar (1996) support these findings. If customers

evaluate the output delivered by a high-quality SSIT, they will intend to use it again. Thus, one can assume as follows:

H6: The perceived service quality has a positive impact on the intention to reuse the SSIT.

In the behavioral literature, it is widely presumed that processes that link attitudes towards an object and behavior exist (Snyder & Ickes, 1985; Sherman & Fazio, 1983). However, there is little agreement about the concrete way the TAM constructs are related to behavioral intentions (Brady et al., 2005). Especially the strong relationship between ATU and IR is rarely examined. Baron and Kenny (1986) recommend the introduction of a mediator when such a strong relation between the predictor and criterion variable exist. Further studies examined several mediation effects of external variables within the TAM and found significant effects (Burton-Jones & Hubona, 2006). With regard to the major importance of SQ in the context of retail service technologies, it seems reasonable to analyze the possibility that PSQ intervenes between ATU and IR as illustrated in Figure 3 to gain a deeper understanding of how the effect is produced (Preacher & Hayes, 2004).

Figure 3. Proposed model and hypotheses

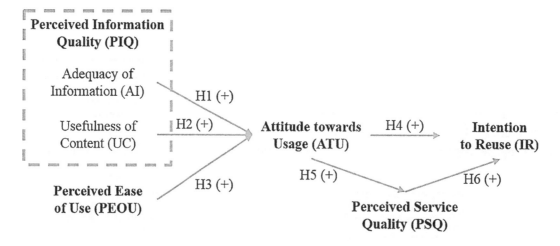

STUDY SETTING

For the empirical analysis, we sought an exemplary retail sector that was particularly convenient for the implementation of interactive information systems. The choice fell on DIY for three reasons: Firstly, the sector is characterized by a low staff density at the point of sale, which leads to a poor reachability of the employees and enhances the benefit of an SSIT. A prominent example is the German DIY retail: Since 2009, the selling space has grown by almost 10% while the number of employees has remained stable for reasons of cost efficiency (Gemaba, 2013). Secondly, there is high standardization potential as the questions salespeople are confronted with basically remain the same: Which product satisfies my needs best? What are characteristics of product X? How do the products X and Y differ? And thirdly, many product categories, such as drilling machines, are complex and not self-explanatory, which makes customers look for an aggregated source of information. Moreover, building centers and home improvement stores look back on a long history of self-service systems as this was one of the first retail segments to introduce digital point-of-sale media, which also makes it particularly suitable for this research.

The empirical work started with a series of pre-studies to verify the relevance of the constructs identified in the literature review. In expert interviews, employees from DIY markets described a typical sales conversation, including the most frequently asked questions. Using data from unstructured interviews, these insights were compared with the customers' perspective to understand the information process in DIY retail. It became obvious that the familiarity with the product category (FPC) influences the information behavior. Moreover, differences in the need for interaction (NFI) seem to shape the information process. Additionally, the information was enriched by observations of people buying

drilling machines, which served as an exemplary product category.

In cooperation with the leading provider of intelligent product filter systems we then developed software for a touch-sensitive SSIT as a stimulus for the subsequent experiment. The application enabled customers to retrieve information such as product details, high resolution images, customer reviews, and test results without asking an employee. Moreover, it identified the best-fitting product based on a structured needs assessment and offered the possibility of comparing two or more products directly. In addition, a smart filter system was implemented to offer quick access to product information for customers with a very clear idea of their needs. These functionalities referred to the most relevant customer demands raised in the prestudy. For the main study, an artificial shopping environment was created in the room where the laboratory experiment took place. The experiment started with a brief introduction into using the technology. Afterwards, the participants were allowed to orientate themselves before using the application in a similar manner to how they would in a store. Following to the experiment, the participants answered a structured online questionnaire regarding their evaluation of the use of the SSIT. Figure 4 summarizes the organization of the study.

We recruited a total of 229 potential DIY shoppers for the experiment. The data was collected in the center of a medium-sized German city. 48.5% of the participants were female. As a high proportion of students participated in the experiment, 62.0% of the participants were between 18 and 25 years of age. We decided to continue the analysis with this relatively heterogeneous sample in terms of age for three reasons: Firstly, King and He (2006) show that there are no great differences in the construct relationships across different categories of participants in 88 TAM studies: "Professionals", "students" and "general users" led to very similar results. Secondly, the young sample represents the potential users of

Figure 4. Structure of the study

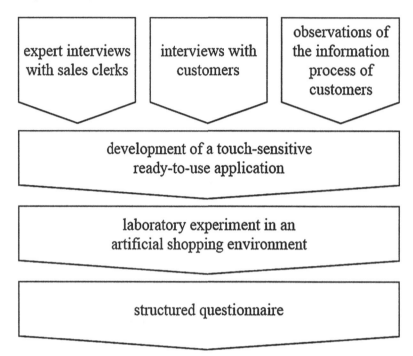

the SSIT fairly well as it has a high technology affinity and a significant need for tools such as drilling machines, having left the parental home. And thirdly, this enabled us to minimize the influence of age as a possible acceptance factor.

First, we conducted several descriptive analyses to obtain an overview of the dataset. 83.8% of the participants used the smart filtering function, whereas only 20.0% made use of the option to compare two or more products directly. It became apparent that the price (69.4%), the surface to be treated (66.4%) and the intended purpose (e.g. drilling and screwing; 64.2%) were the most frequently used filter criteria. Customer reviews also played an important role (45.0%), while criteria such as the weight, frequency of use, battery capacity, brand, and type of drilling machine (e.g. drill hammer, impact drill, cordless drill) were only rarely applied. Regarding the future use of SSITs, 81.2% of the participants stated that they would use a similar system at the next convenient opportunity (Table 2 shows the functionalities of the application used in the experiment).

METHODOLOGY

Analysis Strategy

To assess the role of PSQ in the TAM as the first research focus, this chapter employs the partial least squares (PLS) approach to estimate the measurement and structural parameters in the structural equation model (SEM). PLS is an iterative combination of principal component analysis and ordinary least squares path analysis. Its purpose is to maximize the prediction quality of endogenous constructs (Yi, Gong, & Lee, 2013). In contrast to covariance-based approaches of SEM, PLS does not require a multivariate normal dataset (Jain, Malhotra, & Guan, 2012) and it is recommended for small sample sizes. Referring to Jarvis et al. (2003), the relations in both the measurement models and the structural model were supposed to be reflective. Following the recommendation of Baron and Kenny (1986) to avoid unreliability, the mediation path from ATU via PSQ to IR was

Table 2. Functionalities of the application used in the experiment

Functionality	Frequency of Usage
Comparative tool	45%
Product finder (filter)	84%
Price range	69%
Drilling substrate	66%
Reason for usage	64%
Customer reviews	45%
Weight	16%
Frequency of use	13%
Battery life	9%
Brand	8%
Type of drilling machine	7%

also estimated by SEM. As a specialized *t*-test, the Sobel test examines if the postulated mediation effect is significant (Sobel, 1982). This test was calculated with the "Sobel Test Calculator for the Significance of Mediation" (Soper, 2013).

Regarding customer segmentation as the second research focus, the study conducts a cluster analysis to identify different clusters of SSIT users. The clustering algorithm attempts to identify groups in a set of objects by maximizing the homogeneity of the objects within the clusters while maximizing the heterogeneity between the clusters (Hair, Black, Babin, Anderson, & Tatham, 2006). We decided to apply a combined approach of hierarchical and non-hierarchical (single-level) algorithms as proposed by Milligan and Cooper (1985).

Construct Measurement

Based on the insights from the literature review and the prestudies, a questionnaire consisting of 30 items was developed. An initial draft of the questionnaire was compiled in English based on the established constructs before it was translated into the local language (German). Occasionally, the formulations had to be changed slightly in order

to suit the current research context and accommodate linguistic peculiarities. Two researchers back-translated the wording independently to ensure a high-quality translation. For AI and UC, a scale consisting of five and four items borrowed from the work of Yang et al. (2005) was used. PEOU was measured using a four-item scale based on the work of Davis (1989). To measure ATU and IR, scales consisting of four items adapted from Venkatesh et al. (2003) were used. Finally, PSQ was measured with two items borrowed from Brady and Cronin (2001).

Based on the insights from the prestudies, the constructs NFI and FPC were added to contribute to the second research focus. While the constructs mentioned above are related to the technology, these two refer to personal attributes of the user. NFI was measured based on a three-item scale developed by Dabholkar (1996). FPC in turn consists of four items identified by Raju (1977). Apart from the demographic criteria, all items were measured using a five-point Likert scale ranging from 1 (meaning "strongly disagree") to 5 (meaning "strongly agree").

Measurement Validation

The internal reliability of the scale items was tested by calculating Cronbach's coefficient alpha. All constructs were proved to have a good level of reliability. All loadings of the constructs tested were greater than 0.7 (Nunally, 1978, p. 245), except for PSQ, which was slightly lower (0.665) due to the small number of measurement items. One item of the UC construct was dropped due to low and insignificant loadings (SL = 0.21) and two items of the AI construct due to limited applicability to the research context. The results of all remaining items are presented in Table 3. Furthermore, the composite reliability was assessed, typically referring to measurements of true reliability using SEM. Composite reliability is supposed to produce better estimates of true reliability than Cronbach's coefficient alpha as it includes the number of indicators used (Chin, 1998; Hair et al., 2006, p. 777). All constructs achieved values much greater than 0.7 (Hulland, 1999). Moreover, the average variance extracted (AVE) was analyzed as an additional measure for evaluating the set of indicators. The AVE should be higher than 0.5, meaning that at least 50% of the total variance of all indicators can be explained by the construct (Fornell & Larcker, 1981). In this study, each construct fulfills this criterion as shown in Table 3.

Subsequently, the discriminant validity of the measures was assessed and item cross-loadings for all constructs inspected (Chin, 1998). As no item loads were higher on another construct than the construct it is intended to measure, it can be concluded that all constructs exhibit satisfactory discriminant validity and can be deemed unrelated.

Additionally, the average variance detected for each construct exceeds the intercorrelations among the constructs as demanded by Fornell and

Table 3. Measure and items

Construct	Item	Standard Loadings		Cronbach's Coefficient Alpha	Composite Reliability	Average Variance Extracted
Adequacy of Information	AI1	0.685	(6.517)	0.739	0.847	0.651
	AI2	0.862	(23.612)			
	AI3	0.861	(21.632)			
Usefulness of Content	UC1	0.792	(9.191)	0.749	0.851	0.655
	UC2	0.806	(10.596)			
	UC3	0.829	(20.695)			
Perceived Ease of Use	PEOU1	0.771	(14.095)	0.779	0.858	0.602
	PEOU2	0.826	(18.673)			
	PEOU3	0.797	(14.212)			
	PEOU4	0.705	(9.213)			
Attitude towards Usage	ATU1	0.878	(28.075)	0.891	0.925	0.754
	ATU2	0.861	(25.330)			
	ATU3	0.894	(35.221)			
	ATU4	0.839	(24.012)			
Perceived Service Quality	PSQ1	0.879	(30.260)	0.665	0.856	0.749
	PSQ2	0.852	(19.660)			
Intention to Reuse	IR1	0.897	(39.708)	0.858	0.904	0.703
	IR2	0.753	(17.184)			
	IR3	0.849	(20.356)			
	IR4	0.848	(24.272)			
Familiarity with the Product Category	FPC1	0.911	(7.993)	0.894	0.925	0.755
	FPC2	0.917	(8.888)			
	FPC3	0.825	(7.480)			
	FPC4	0.818	(6.160)			
Need for Interaction	NFI1	0.717	(3.012)	0.804	0.849	0.657
	NFI2	0.733	(3.015)			
	NFI3	0.960	(4.015)			

Table 4. Shared variance and average variance extracted

SV/AVE	AI	ATU	IR	FPC	NFI	PEOU	PSQ	UC
AI	0,651	0	0	0	0	0	0	0
ATU	0.395	0.754	0	0	0	0	0	0
IR	0.290	0.639	0.703	0	0	0	0	0
FPC	0.108	0.106	0.131	0.657	0	0	0	0
NFI	0.048	0.043	0.032	0.002	0.755	0	0	0
PEOU	0.163	0.250	0.155	0.020	0.001	0,602	0	0
PSQ	0.383	0.448	0.393	0.150	0.067	0.116	0,749	0
UC	0.398	0.360	0.337	0.010	0.042	0.198	0.317	0,655

Note: ATU = Attitude towards Usage; IR = Intention to Reuse; PEOU = Perceived Ease of Use; UC = Usefulness of Content; AI = Adequacy of Information; PSQ = Perceived Service Quality; FPC = Familiarity with the Product Category; NFI = Need for Interaction. On the diagonal, average variance extracted of each construct is displayed; the other values display r^2 (shared variance) between the constructs (Fornell and Larcker, 1981).

Larcker (1981) to make sure that a construct shares more variance with its measures than with other model constructs (Chin, 1998). Table 4 provides a detailed summary of all the results regarding the shared variance (SV) and the AVE, showing that the criterion is fulfilled by all constructs.

RESULTS

Structural Equation Modeling

The hypotheses postulate that the AI, UC, and PEOU have a positive influence on the ATU (H1, H2, and H3). Also, the ATU should increase the IR (H4) and the PSQ (H5). Moreover, the IR is influenced by the PSQ (H6). To test the proposed model and establish the significance of parameter estimates, t-values using 1,000 bootstrap samples were calculated (Henseler, Ringle, & Sinkovics, 2009). As directional hypotheses were postulated, one-tailed significance tests were conducted.

Table 5 presents the path coefficients β and t-values for the model along with the R^2 for ATU, PSQ and IR and indicates the results of the hypothesis test for a level of significance of 0.5%.

All postulated hypotheses are confirmed except for H1 (AI → ATU). The results reveal that the UC ($\beta1$ = 0.374; $p < 0.01$) and the PEOU ($\beta3$ = 0.276; $p < 0.001$) have a significant effect on the ATU, supporting H2 and H3 whereas AI ($\beta2$ = 0.209; $p <$ n.s.) does not exhibit a significant influence on ATU. Consistent with H4, the effect of the ATU ($\beta5$ = 0.689; $p < 0.001$) on the IR is significant and positive. As H5 predicted, the effect of the ATU ($\beta4$ = 0.669; $p < 0.001$) on the PSQ is also significant and positive. In addition, the effect of PSQ on IR ($\beta6$ = 0.166; $p < 0.01$) supports H6.

The relationship between the ATU and the IR is assumed to be a mediation effect that exists due to the influence of the PSQ, in addition to the direct effect. The results are shown in Table 6.

By including the PSQ as a mediator, the effect of the ATU on IR is reduced while the effect of the PSQ remains significant. Thus, a partial mediation is proven (Preacher & Hayes, 2004). The Sobel test examines a significant effect (z = 2.046, p < 0.01) of the postulated mediation (Sobel, 1982).

The model has great explanatory power for the dependent variables: As shown in Table 5, more than 66% of the variance of the IR is explained by the exogenous factors. Obviously, the integration of the PSQ improves the prediction quality

Table 5. Hypotheses testing

Hypothesis	Relationship	Direction	Standardized Coefficient (β)	t-Value	Result
H1	AI → ATU	Positive	0.209	1.700	Not Supported
H2	UC → ATU	Positive	0.374	2.900	Supported
H3	PEOU → ATU	Positive	0.276	3.321	Supported
H4	ATU → IR	Positive	0.689	9.357	Supported
H5	ATU → PSQ	Positive	0.669	11.452	Supported
H6	PSQ → IR	Positive	0.166	2.086	Supported
Fit Measures	Endogenous Construct	Model			
R^2	ATU	0.467			
	IR	0.665			
	PSQ	0.448			

Table 6. Mediation effect of perceived service quality

Direct Effect with no mediator	**0.801**
Direct Effect with mediator	**0.689**
ATU → PSQ (Beta)	0.669
PSQ → IR (Beta)	0.166
ATU → PSQ (SE)	0.059
PSQ → IR (SE)	0.080
Sobel test statistic:	**2.046 > 1.96**
One-tailed probability:	0.020 < 0.05
Two-tailed probability:	0.041 < 0.05

Note: SE = Standardized Error

of the TAM. Also, the explanatory power for the PSQ with almost 45% and for the ATU with more than 46% is high, suggesting that UC and PEOU are predictors of ATU. As mentioned above, all suggested relationships were confirmed except one (AI → ATU). Most of them were shown to be significant on a level of 0.1% as pictured in Figure 5.

To assess the problem of a possible omitted variable bias, which can occur when a model incorrectly leaves out one or more important causal factors, several control variables (i.e. customer age and gender, customer education, technology readiness, product experience and need for interaction) were included in the structural model. This inclusion did not alter the substantive findings, indicating the absence of an omitted variable bias (Chamberlain, 1979).

Cluster Analysis

In addition to the constructs analyzed in the SEM, NFI and FPC were included in the cluster analysis in order to describe the user segments based on both technology and personality-related constructs. The analysis started with the identification of outliers using the single-linkage procedure, which tends to fuse extreme values at the end of the clustering process due to its so-called chaining phenomenon (Griffiths, Robinson, & Willett, 1984). We found one case that did not fit any of the clusters and removed it from the data set. Afterwards, a hierarchical cluster analysis was conducted using Ward's algorithm, which has proved to be very effective in finding the optimal number of clusters when outliers are removed (Punj & Stewart, 1983). Some researchers criticize the calculation of a cluster analysis based on factor scores, claiming that it implies a loss of information and leads to less accurate segments (Ketchen & Shook, 1996). To address this criti-

Figure 5. Empirical results

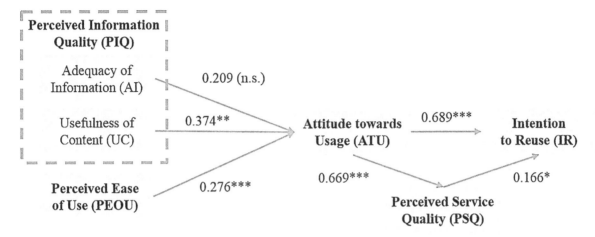

Notes: ***p < 0.001, ** p < 0.01, * p < 0.05

cism, we followed the suggestions of Ketchen and Shook (1996) and calculated cluster analyses for both the factor scores and the raw items. The results display a high degree of similarity. Due to the large number of raw items, these clusters were difficult to interpret. Hence, we followed the factor-cluster approach, which is characterized by a clearly comprehensible outcome due to the use of well-established constructs, the meanings of which were clearly defined in extant studies (Frochot & Morrison, 2001). A dendrogram and a screeplot indicated that two clusters are convenient for the data. To confirm the assumption, solutions with two, three, and four clusters were tested. The three and four-cluster solutions each yielded one cluster that contained only one case. Moreover, we calculated the Mojena stopping rule (Mojena, 1977), which is among the best statistical criteria to define the optimal number of clusters according to the comparative simulation study of Milligan and Cooper (1985). The results also supported our finding that a two-cluster solution is most suited to the data (Appendix 1). The classification split the sample into clusters comprising 137 and 92 cases respectively (Table 7).

Table 7. Cluster overview

Cluster	Frequency	%
Cluster 1	137	59.8%
Cluster 2	92	40.2%
Total	229	100.0%

Afterwards, a non-hierarchical cluster analysis using k-means was conducted to obtain the final cluster solution. This statistical procedure is restricted to continuous data and requires a determination of the number of clusters (Burns & Burns, 2008), both criteria which are fulfilled. The mean values from the preceding hierarchical analysis were used as initial cluster centers and distances were calculated using the simple Euclidean distance. The iteratively calculated final solution of the cluster centers and the other profile characteristics for the two clusters are shown in Table 8.

To assess the statistical significance of the cluster analysis, a one-way analysis of variance (ANOVA) was calculated, the results of which are shown in Table 9. The differences between the objects should be as small as possible within

Table 8. Cluster centers and user characteristics of the final solution

	Cluster 1 (n=137)	Cluster 2 (n=92)
User Traits		
Familiarity with the Product Category	2.7	3.4
Need for Interaction	3.4	4.0
Usefulness of Content	4.2	3.6
Adequacy of Information	3.8	3.1
Perceived Ease of Use	4.4	3.9
Attitude towards Usage	4.3	3.3
Perceived Service Quality	4.0	2.9
Intention to Use	4.2	3.1
User Characteristics		
Percent men	44.5%	62.0%
Percent women	55.5%	38.0%
Percent using price filter	72.3%	65.2%
Percent compared products	12.4%	28.3%

one cluster and as large as possible for objects from different clusters (Hair et al., 2006). Thus, the magnitude of the F-values and the statistical significance values for each factor are evidence of how well the respective factor distinguishes between groups. The factors ATU, PSQ, ITU, AI, and UC display the highest F-statistics and appropriate mean square errors, which suggests that they are most appropriate to differentiate the clusters. The factors PEOU, NFI, and I exhibit smaller F-values. Nevertheless, the inter-group differences are proved to be highly significant on a level of 0.1% for all factors considered.

The examination of the cluster analysis results reveals that the first cluster is considered to be representative for people with a lower familiarity in the DIY sector and a lower need for interaction, whereas the second cluster consists of highly involved SSIT users who appreciate personal interaction with a salesperson. As far as the TAM constructs are concerned, the first cluster stands out due to a higher level of SSIT acceptance.

In particular, the AI, UC, and PEOU of such a technology seem to be assessed better by people from the first cluster who face a buying decision. A perceptible difference can also be seen concerning ATU and ITU: Both are assessed better by the first segment, which is thus more likely to use the SSIT again. Furthermore, in the case of cluster 1 the SSIT provides a higher level of PSQ than in cases from cluster 2.

DISCUSSION

Despite the fact that a significant amount of research has been conducted in recent years, understanding the customer acceptance of interactive self-service technologies remains a challenge for researchers (Venkatesh, 2006). Whereas transaction-related technologies have already been intensively researched, this holds particularly true for customer-service and information-related technologies in retail. Especially the relationship between ATU and IR regarding the role of SQ is rarely examined. To gain a deeper understanding of this relationship, we used a touch-sensitive application for SST including a sophisticated product finder and comparison tool. By bundling all the product-related information available and displaying them in a highly customized way the application supports the customer's solution-oriented information process.

The empirical results provide strong evidence to support the proposed model as almost all of the postulated relations were shown to be highly significant. Consistent with previous research in the field of technology acceptance, PEOU has a positive influence on the ATU. While the UC has a positive impact on the ATU, the effect of AI on ATU is not significant. This suggests that the quality but not the quantity of information is important for the evaluation of an SSIT. However, the influence of the PEOU was weaker. Therefore, the results are in line with other studies from similar research contexts.

Table 9. Results of the ANOVA

Factor	Mean Difference	Mean Square Cluster	Mean Square Error	F	Sign.
Attitude towards Usage	1.01	56.31	0.30	189.56	0.000***
Perceived Service Quality	1.22	82.06	0.45	183.70	0.000***
Intention to Use	1.07	62.68	0.36	173.37	0.000***
Adequacy of Information	0.74	30.24	0.27	113.45	0.000***
Usefulness of Content	0.66	33.68	0.30	80.99	0.000***
Perceived Ease of Use	0.54	15.90	0.33	47.83	0.000***
Need for Interaction	-0.57	17.71	0.63	28.19	0.000***
Familiarity with the Product Category	-0.63	21.64	0.90	23.93	0.000***

Note: *** $p < 0.001$.

Special emphasis has been placed on the effect of the ATU on the IR. Firstly, we confirmed the expected strong relationship between these two constructs. Secondly, it was shown that the PSQ partially mediates the effect between the ATU and IR. Thus, with regard to the findings of Lee and Yang (2013), who found PSQ to have a high relevance for retail patronage and customer satisfaction, we can add that PSQ is also relevant for technology acceptance as it mediates the relationship between the attitude and behavioral intentions.

Furthermore, we show that distinct and meaningful customer segments can be established based on technology acceptance. The existence of two clearly separated clusters is especially remarkable as the sample used in the empirical analysis was proportionally homogenous in terms of demographic characteristics. Consequently, the results are in line with the findings of Lee et al. (2010), who discovered that demographic factors only have an indirect effect on the acceptance of SSITs.

The first cluster can be named "occasional shoppers" and is characterized by people who only consider products as relevant when they are in a concrete need situation. In contrast, the second segment consists of "enthusiastic experts" who exhibit high familiarity with the particular retail segment. More specifically, we found that people from the "enthusiastic expert" cluster did not rec-ognize the benefit of information provided by the SSIT for their individual buying decision to the same degree as "occasional shoppers" (AI cluster 1 = 3.8; AI cluster 2 = 3.1 and UC cluster 1 = 4.2; UC cluster 2 = 3.6). With regard to the filter usage during the experiment, the price filter seems to be more relevant for the "occasional shoppers" segment whereas the product comparison tool is used more often by the "enthusiastic experts". Moreover, the usage of filter applications within the two clusters indicates a different relevance of information. For example, the "occasional shoppers" make a product choice based on the price rather than on quality features, which fits the low familiarity values of this cluster.

The findings suggest that SSITs mainly address non-expert users, i.e. customers with a low familiarity and limited knowledge of the retail segment. This can be explained as follows: People who believe they have a high level of knowledge of the relevant product category due to their high familiarity also believe that additional information will not create any additional value. In principle, customers need information to identify a suitable product and make a well-founded buying decision (Berry et al., 2010). This information can be acquired from two different sources: Firstly, prior knowledge which refers to experiences from former buying decisions and examinations with similar products stored in the memory (Srinivasan & Agrawal, 1988). And secondly, external searches, such as point-of-sale media (Chaney, 2000). Especially for people without considerable prior knowledge, the buying process is characterized by a high level of perceived risk (Moorthy, Ratchford, & Talukdar, 1997), which customers tend to minimize by collecting external information (Bennett & Harrell, 1975). This especially holds true when it comes to complex products, which can be found in many product categories in DIY, which served as an exemplary retail segment in this study. Therefore, our findings are consistent with the work of Schmidt and Spreng (1996), who demonstrate that additional information offers greater value to customers with a low level of product knowledge and a high degree of uncertainty.

Thus, it is not surprising that both the ATU and the PSQ is assessed better by "occasional shoppers" who have a higher need for general information. Accordingly, 93.4% of them felt able to make a buying decision for one of the 40 drilling machines offered in the virtual shelf after using the SSIT ("enthusiastic experts": 59.8%). This results in a better evaluation (ATU "occasional shoppers" = 4.3; ATU "enthusiastic experts" = 3.3) and stronger intention to use the SSIT again (ITU "occasional shoppers" = 4.2; ITU "enthusiastic experts" = 3.1).

Regarding DIY as a representative retail segment, the findings match the predominant motivations for purchasing behavior identified by Wolf and McQuitty (2011): The "occasional shoppers" are motivated through economic benefits and have a pragmatic view on DIY. Thus, these customers are more likely to use an SSIT to find the right product more easily. On the other hand, the "enthusiastic experts" are motivated by identity enhancement and consider DIY as part of their lifestyle. Therefore, they exhibit a lower willingness to use non-personal forms of interaction. In turn, the greater need for personal interaction among the "enthusiastic experts" can

be explained with the low potential for standardization regarding their questions resulting in a lower pertinence of the information provided As Wolf and McQuitty (2011) state, encounters of expert customers go far beyond finding a certain item, e.g. exchanging ideas with the store personnel or developing customized projects ideas. In contrast, the importance of the presence of a salesperson is rather low for "occasional shoppers".

IMPLICATIONS AND LIMITATIONS

Managerial Implications

SSITs are becoming increasingly relevant for retailers to improve customer satisfaction and create a competitive advantage by offering information-related services. SSITs are especially useful for retail segments with a poor availability of sales clerks and substantial need for information like the DIY branch. Managers who wish to use SSITs should gain a profound understanding of the factors that drive customer acceptance and usage intentions first. The PSQ accounts for the relationship between ATU and IR and serves as a mediator through which the stressor affects the outcome variable. This implies that if the information service delivered by the SSIT is not well evaluated by users, the intention to use the SSIT will decrease again. This supports the assumption that the ATU is related to the evaluation process of the SQ after using the SSIT. Therefore, retailers have to emphasize the service-related value of the SSIT in their point-of-sale communication to support continuous usage.

As a critical element of the TAM the perceived usefulness was replaced by PIQ. Referring to the aspects of quality and quantity of information and in line with previous research (Yang et al., 2005) PIQ was represented through AI and UC. While UC has a strong effect on ATU, AI does not exhibit a significant influence. This can be explained through the use of a product finder that does not display all available but only relevant information selected by the user himself. Moreover, only a limited number of information is used when making a buying decision. In our study the price, the drilling substrate, the reason for usage or the customer reviews were the most commonly demanded information. To recap, it is not important to provide a high variety of information, but information with a high relevance for the needs of the customer. Therefore, SSITs should be designed with regard to the requirements of the target audience (e.g. a product finder with different filter options and a product-comparing tool) to avoid overstimulation. It can be deduced that once the quantity of information is substantial enough to avoid search queries without results, no significant positive effect on the attitude towards the SSIT can be expected anymore.

Customers consider SSITs as an attractive alternative if it is believed to be easy to use. The high share of smartphone users in the sample (83%) indicates a high affinity towards technology, which matches the appreciation of the SSIT and the positive evaluation of its ease of use. Thus, the convenience should be advertised by the retailer to increase the willingness for the first use. However, the influence of PEOU on ATU was weaker than the influence of the content quality. Obviously, the SSIT is mainly evaluated with regard to its problem-solving capacities, as opposed to the cognitive effort involved in its use. One explanation might be that people have learned how to use touchscreen terminals over time. Therefore, it is even more important to employ well-known control elements and gestures. Moreover, we included the perceived enjoyment as a control variable in the model to assess the importance of hedonic aspects with regard to Heijden (2004). As assumed above, these were shown not to be particularly relevant in the present research-context.

The application used in this study provided both an interactive product finder and a comparative feature. Most users focused on the product finder (84%) based on their personal needs instead of comparing relevant products directly (45%). Thus, the design of a digital advisor should be geared towards the practice of sales clerks starting with the assessment of customer needs. Moreover, care should be taken to meet high technical standards regarding up to date content, advanced search algorithms and high quality images.

With regard to the heterogeneous customer groups in DIY, however, the results of the empirical investigation show that SSITs do not provide the same benefit to all customers. Retailers need to tailor such technologies to the specific needs of the target group. The use of the product-comparing tool is much greater in the group of "enthusiastic experts" (28.3% vs. 12.4% in the "occasional shoppers" cluster), which indicates that sophisticated features of an SSIT can also be considered a concrete benefit and even more so for expert users. For "enthusiastic experts", the SSIT should focus on advanced functionalities such as interactive project planners (e.g. for bathrooms or gardens) to enable its use also for ambitious projects. This holds true all the more in the project planning phase, where the readiness to use media is particularly high (Wolf & McQuitty, 2011). When implementing an SSIT for "occasional shoppers", retailers should in turn provide highly specific information (e.g. one concrete product recommendation instead of ten products matching the applied filter criteria) to reduce complexity as the familiarity with the product category is rather low while AI exhibits high values.

Despite the promising results, salespeople should not be replaced by technology as a large portion of customers has highly specific needs that cannot be satisfied adequately through the use of an interactive information system. Hence, it should be implemented permeably, e.g. by including a "call a salesperson" option. Regarding the high NFI among "enthusiastic experts", salespeople might use a portable version of the SSIT as a support system in sales conversations in order to enrich their didactic competence and flexibility through a technology's depth of information. To sum up,

SSITs can be seen as a supplementary tool that relieves salespeople of repetitive tasks and enables them to focus on more complex customer requests.

LIMITATIONS AND RESEARCH DIRECTIONS

Although the findings contribute to the academic literature, there are certain limitations that require further examination. First of all, the study has a rather explorative character using a scenario-based laboratory experiment as a method of collecting data and should be replicated in a field setting to confirm the proposed research model. A self-selection bias cannot be excluded as the test subjects participated in the experiment voluntarily. As the data was obtained near the university campus, the sample contains a high proportion of students and is not fully representative. Moreover, the development of the application focused on functionality and was aimed at reducing the influence of interface design. As a result, one factor that potentially affects the adoption was eliminated (Meuter et al., 2000).

Many respondents declared that they could imagine using similar SSITs in different retail segments, such as consumer electronics or sports equipment. Hence, future research is encouraged to expand the findings of this study across various industries to provide greater generalizability. Further representative studies might analyze the moderating effects of individual characteristics and predispositions such as age, technology anxiety or need for interaction (Lee & Yang, 2013). Also, the insights into the targeted customer groups should be deepened to improve the usability of the software and the communication in the closer surrounding of the digital system. The experiment was conducted using a Tablet PC as hardware. Although the participants were free to try the application in a mobile manner, almost no test subjects took the Tablet PC with them. This begs the question as to whether the mobility of the system is a relevant influencing factor for usage and adoption. Furthermore, the behavioral intentions of non-users should be compared with the intentions of the SSIT users investigated in this research (Proença & Rodrigues, 2011). Finally, we already underlined the importance of salespeople for successful selling. The comparison between SSIT and mobile technologies supporting salespeople could shed some light on the much discussed question as to how important the human is in retailing.

ACKNOWLEDGMENT

Special thanks go to Peter Habit, former chairman of the Rid Foundation, and Michaela Pichlbauer, chairwoman of the Rid Foundation, for funding this research as well as to Waldemar Toporowski for his conceptual input.

REFERENCES

Anitsal, I., & Paige, R. C. (2006). An exploratory study on consumer perceptions of service quality in technology-based self-service. *Services Marketing Quarterly*, *27*(3), 53–67. doi:10.1300/J396v27n03_04

Balasubramanian, S., Raghunathan, R., & Mahajan, V. (2005). Consumers in a multichannel environment: Product utility, process utility, and channel choice. *Journal of Interactive Marketing*, *19*(2), 12–30. doi:10.1002/dir.20032

Baron, R. M., & Kenny, D. A. (1986). The moderator–mediator variable distinction in social psychological research: Conceptual, strategic, and statistical considerations. *Journal of Personality and Social Psychology*, *51*(6), 1173–1182. doi:10.1037/0022-3514.51.6.1173 PMID:3806354

Benbasat, I., & Barki, H. (2007). Quo vadis, TAM. *Journal of the Association for Information Systems, 8*(4), 211–218.

Bennett, P. D., & Harrell, G. D. (1975). The role of confidence in understanding and predicting buyers' attitudes and purchase intentions. *The Journal of Consumer Research, 2*(2), 110–117. doi:10.1086/208622

Berry, L. L., Bolton, R. N., Bridges, C. H., Meyer, J., Parasuraman, A., & Seiders, K. (2010). Opportunities for innovation in the delivery of interactive retail services. *Journal of Interactive Marketing, 24*(2), 155–167. doi:10.1016/j.intmar.2010.02.001

Bitner, M. J. (1992). Servicescapes: The impact of physical surroundings on customers and employees. *Journal of Marketing, 56*(2), 57–71. doi:10.2307/1252042

Bolton, R., & Saxena-Iyer, S. (2009). Interactive services: A framework, synthesis and research directions. *Journal of Interactive Marketing, 23*(1), 91–104. doi:10.1016/j.intmar.2008.11.002

Boulding, W., Kalra, A., Staelin, R., & Zeithaml, V. A. (1993). A dynamic process model of service quality: From expectations to behavioral intentions. *JMR, Journal of Marketing Research, 30*(1), 7–27. doi:10.2307/3172510

Brady, M. K., & Cronin, J. J. Jr. (2001). Some new thoughts on conceptualizing perceived service quality: A hierarchical approach. *Journal of Marketing, 65*(3), 34–49. doi:10.1509/jmkg.65.3.34.18334

Brady, M. K., Knight, G. A., Cronin, J. J. Jr, Tomas, G., Hult, M., & Keillor, B. D. (2005). Removing the contextual lens: A multinational, multi-setting comparison of service evaluation models. *Journal of Retailing, 81*(3), 215–230. doi:10.1016/j.jretai.2005.07.005

Browning, J. M., & Zabriskie, N. B. (1985). Do-it yourself consumer: Segmentation insights for retailers. *Journal of Consumer Marketing, 2*(3), 5–15. doi:10.1108/eb008128

Burns, R. B., & Burns, R. A. (2008). *Business research methods and statistics using SPSS.* London: SAGE Publications.

Burton-Jones, A., & Hubona, G. (2006). The mediation of external variables in the technology acceptance model. *Information & Management, 43*(6), 706–717. doi:10.1016/j.im.2006.03.007

Chamberlain, G. (1979). *Heterogeneity, omitted variable bias, and duration dependence.* Cambridge, MA: Harvard Institute of Economic Research.

Chaney, I. M. (2000). External search effort for wine. *International Journal of Wine Marketing, 12*(2), 5–21. doi:10.1108/eb008706

Chaudhuri, A. (2000). A macro analysis of the relationship of product involvement and information search: The role of risk. *Journal of Marketing Theory and Practice, 8*(1), 1–15.

Chen, K.-J. (2005). Technology-based service and customer satisfaction in developing countries international. *Journal of Management, 22*(2), 307–318.

Childers, T. L., Carr, C. L., Peck, J., & Carson, S. (2001). Hedonic and utilitarian motivations for online retail shopping behavior. *Journal of Retailing, 77*(4), 511–535. doi:10.1016/S0022-4359(01)00056-2

Chin, W. W. (1998). The partial least squares approach to structural equation modeling. In G. A. Marcoulides (Ed.), *Modern methods for business research* (pp. 295–336). Mahwah, NJ: Lawrence Erlbaum Associates.

Chiu, H. C., Hsieh, Y. C., Roan, J., Tseng, K. J., & Hsieh, J. K. (2011). The challenge for multichannel services: Cross-channel free-riding behavior. *Electronic Commerce Research and Applications*, *10*(2), 268–277. doi:10.1016/j.elerap.2010.07.002

Colby, C. L., & Parasuraman, A. (2003). Technology still matters - Never mind the doomsayers. E-services are alive, well, and positioned for growth. *Marketing Management*, *12*(4), 28–33.

Cooil, B., Aksoy, L., Keiningham, T. L., & Maryott, K. M. (2009). The relationship of employee perceptions of organizational climate to business-unit outcomes: An MPLS approach. *Journal of Service Research*, *11*(3), 277–294. doi:10.1177/1094670508328984

Corvello, V., Pantano, E., & Tavernise, A. (2011). The design of an advanced virtual shopping assistant for improving consumer experience. In E. Pantano & H. Timmermans (Eds.), *Advanced technologies management for retailing* (pp. 70–86). Hershey, PA: Business Science Reference.

Curran, J. M., & Meuter, M. L. (2005). Self-service technology adoption: Comparing three technologies. *Journal of Services Marketing*, *19*(2), 103–113. doi:10.1108/08876040510591411

Dabholkar, P. A. (1994). Technology-based service delivery: A classification scheme for developing marketing strategies. In T. A. Swartz, D. A. Bowen, & S. W. Brown (Eds.), *Advances in services marketing and management* (Vol. 3, pp. 241–271). Bingley: Emerald Group Publishing. doi:10.1016/S1067-5671(94)03021-9

Dabholkar, P. A. (1996). Consumer evaluations of new technology-based self-service options: An investigation of alternative models of service quality. *International Journal of Research in Marketing*, *13*(1), 29–51. doi:10.1016/0167-8116(95)00027-5

Dabholkar, P. A., & Bagozzi, R. P. (2002). An attitudinal model of technology-based self-service: Moderating effects of consumer traits and situational factors. *Journal of the Academy of Marketing Science*, *30*(3), 184–201. doi:10.1177/0092070302303001

Dabholkar, P. A., & Spaid, B. I. (2012). Service failure and recovery in using technology-based self-service: Effects on user attributions and satisfaction. *Service Industries Journal*, *32*(9), 1415–1432. doi:10.1080/02642069.2011.600518

Dabholkar, P. A., Thorpe, D. I., & Rentz, J. O. (1996). A measure of service quality for retail stores: Scale development and validation. *Journal of the Academy of Marketing Science*, *24*(1), 3–16. doi:10.1007/BF02893933

Datamonitor. (2010). *DIY and home improvement retail in Europe: Market size, retailer strategies and competitor performance*. Retrieved December 23, 2013 from http://www.datamonitor.com/store/Product/diy_and_home_improvement_retail_in_europe_market_size_retailer_strategies_and_competitor_performance?productid=DMVT0563

Davis, F. D. (1989). Perceived usefulness, perceived ease of use, and user acceptance of information technology. *Management Information Systems Quarterly*, *13*(3), 319–340. doi:10.2307/249008

Davis, F. D., Bagozzi, R. P., & Warshaw, P. R. (1989). User acceptance of computer technology: A comparison of two theoretical models. *Management Science*, *35*(8), 982–1004. doi:10.1287/mnsc.35.8.982

Demirci Orel, F., & Kara, A. (2014). Supermarket self-checkout service quality, customer satisfaction, and loyalty: Empirical evidence from an emerging market. *Journal of Retailing and Consumer Services*, *21*(2), 118–129. doi:10.1016/j.jretconser.2013.07.002

Fishbein, M., & Ajzen, I. (1975). *Belief, attitude, intention, and behavior: An introduction to theory and research.* Reading, MA: Addison-Wesley.

Fornell, C., & Larcker, D. F. (1981). Evaluating structural equation models with unobservable variables and measurement errors. *JMR, Journal of Marketing Research, 18*(1), 39–50. doi:10.2307/3151312

Frochot, I., & Morrison, A. M. (2001). Benefit segmentation: A review of its applications to travel and tourism research. *Journal of Travel & Tourism Marketing, 9*(4), 21–45. doi:10.1300/J073v09n04_02

Gelderman, C. J., Ghijsen, P. W. T., & van Diemen, R. (2011). Choosing self-service technologies or interpersonal services - The impact of situational factors and technology-related attitudes. *Journal of Retailing and Consumer Services, 18*(5), 414–421. doi:10.1016/j.jretconser.2011.06.003

Gemaba - Gesellschaft für Stuktur- und Betriebsanalyse. (2013). *Baumarkt-Strukturuntersuchung 2013.* Retrieved December 16, 2013 from http://www.gemaba.de/Baumarkte2013.pdf

Grewal, D., Krishnan, R., Levy, M., & Munger, J. (2010). Retail success and key drivers. In M. Krafft & M. K. Mantrala (Eds.), *Retailing in the 21st century* (pp. 15–30). Berlin: Springer. doi:10.1007/978-3-540-72003-4_2

Griffiths, A., Robinson, L. A., & Willett, P. (1984). Hierarchic agglomerative clustering methods for automatic document classification. *The Journal of Documentation, 40*(3), 175–205. doi:10.1108/eb026764

Grönroos, C. (1993). Quality comes to service. In E. E. Scheuing & W. F. Christopher (Eds.), *Service quality handbook* (pp. 17–24). New York, NY: American Management Association.

Hair, J. F., Black, W. C., Babin, B. J., Anderson, R. E., & Tatham, R. L. (2006). *Multivariate data analysis* (6th ed.). Upper Saddle River, NJ: Prentice Hall.

Heijden, H. d. (2004). User acceptance of hedonic information systems. *Management Information Systems Quarterly, 28*(4), 695–704.

Henseler, J., Ringle, C. M., & Sinkovics, R. R. (2009). The use of partial least squares path modeling in international marketing. In R. R. Sinkovics & P. N. Ghauri (Eds.), *Advances in international marketing* (Vol. 20, pp. 277–319). Bingley: Emerald Group Publishing. doi:10.1108/S1474-7979(2009)0000020014

Hilton, T., Hughes, T., Little, E., & Marandi, E. (2013). Adopting self-service technology to do more with less. *Journal of Services Marketing, 27*(1), 3–12. doi:10.1108/08876041311296338

Hulland, J. (1999). Use of partial least squares (PLS) in strategic management research: A review of four recent studies. *Strategic Management Journal, 20*(2), 195–204. doi:10.1002/(SICI)1097-0266(199902)20:2<195::AID-SMJ13>3.0.CO;2-7

Jain, A. K., Malhotra, N. K., & Guan, C. (2012). Positive and negative affectivity as mediators of volunteerism and service-oriented citizenship behavior and customer loyalty. *Psychology and Marketing, 29*(12), 1004–1017. doi:10.1002/mar.20582

Jarvis, C., MacKenzie, S. B., & Podsakoff, P. M. (2003). A critical review of construct indicators and measurement model misspecification in marketing and consumer research. *The Journal of Consumer Research, 30*(2), 199–218. doi:10.1086/376806

Kallweit, K., Spreer, P., & Toporowski, W. (2014). Why do customers use self-service information technologies in retail? The mediating effect of perceived service quality. *Journal of Retailing and Consumer Services*, *21*(3), 268–276. doi:10.1016/j.jretconser.2014.02.002

Ketchen, D. J. Jr., & Shook, C. L. (1996). The application of cluster analysis in strategic management research: An analysis and critique. *Strategic Management Journal*, *17*(6), 441–458. doi:10.1002/(SICI)1097-0266(199606)17:6<441::AID-SMJ819>3.0.CO;2-G

King, W. R., & He, J. (2006). A meta-analysis of the technology acceptance model. *Information & Management*, *43*(6), 740–755. doi:10.1016/j.im.2006.05.003

Kowatsch, T., & Maass, W. (2010). In-store consumer behavior: How mobile recommendation agents influence usage intentions, product purchases, and store preferences. *Computers in Human Behavior*, *26*(4), 697–704. doi:10.1016/j.chb.2010.01.006

Laroche, M., Yang, Z., McDougall, G. H., & Bergeron, J. (2005). Internet versus bricks-and-mortar retailers: An investigation into intangibility and its consequences. *Journal of Retailing*, *81*(4), 251–267. doi:10.1016/j.jretai.2004.11.002

Lee, H. J., Cho, H. J., Xu, W., & Fairhurst, A. (2010). The influence of consumer traits and demographics on intention to use retail self-service checkouts. *Marketing Intelligence & Planning*, *28*(1), 46–58. doi:10.1108/02634501011014606

Lee, H. J., Fairhurst, A., & Cho, H. J. (2013). Gender differences in consumer evaluations of service quality: Self-service kiosks in retail. *Service Industries Journal*, *33*(2), 248–265. doi:10.1080/02642069.2011.614346

Lee, H. J., Fairhurst, A. E., & Lee, M. Y. (2009). The importance of self-service kiosks in developing consumers' retail patronage intentions. *Managing Service Quality*, *19*(6), 687–701. doi:10.1108/09604520911005071

Lee, H. J., & Yang, K. (2013). Interpersonal service quality, self-service technology (SST) service quality, and retail patronage. *Journal of Retailing and Consumer Services*, *20*(1), 51–57. doi:10.1016/j.jretconser.2012.10.005

Lehtinen, U., & Lehtinen, J. R. (1991). Two approaches to service quality dimensions. *Service Industries Journal*, *11*(3), 287–303. doi:10.1080/02642069100000047

Meuter, M. L., Bitner, M. J., Ostrom, A. L., & Brown, S. W. (2005). Choosing among alternative service delivery modes: An investigation of customer trial of self-service technologies. *Journal of Marketing*, *69*(2), 61–83. doi:10.1509/jmkg.69.2.61.60759

Meuter, M. L., Ostrom, A. L., Bitner, M. J., & Roundtree, R. (2003). The influence of technology anxiety on consumer use and experiences with self-service technologies. *Journal of Business Research*, *56*(11), 899–906. doi:10.1016/S0148-2963(01)00276-4

Meuter, M. L., Ostrom, A. L., Roundtree, R. I., & Bitner, M. J. (2000). Self-service technologies: Understanding customer satisfaction with technology-based service encounters. *Journal of Marketing*, *64*(3), 50–64. doi:10.1509/jmkg.64.3.50.18024

Milligan, G. W., & Cooper, M. C. (1985). An examination of procedures for determining the number of clusters in a data set. *Psychometrika*, *50*(2), 159–179. doi:10.1007/BF02294245

Mojena, R. (1977). Hierarchical grouping methods and stopping rules: An evaluation. *The Computer Journal, 20*(4), 359–363. doi:10.1093/comjnl/20.4.359

Moorthy, S., Ratchford, B. T., & Talukdar, D. (1997). Consumer information search revisited: Theory and empirical analysis. *The Journal of Consumer Research, 23*(4), 263–277. doi:10.1086/209482

Nunnally, J. C. (1978). *Psychometric theory* (2nd ed.). New York, NY: McGraw-Hill.

Oghazi, P., Mostaghel, R., Hultman, M., & Parida, V. (2012). Antecedents of technology-based self-service acceptance: A proposed model. *Services Marketing Quarterly, 33*(3), 195–210. doi:10.1080/15332969.2012.689937

Pantano, E. (2010). New technologies and retailing: Trends and directions. *Journal of Retailing and Consumer Services, 17*(3), 171–172. doi:10.1016/j.jretconser.2010.03.004

Pantano, E., & Viassone, M. (2014). Demand pull and technology push perspective in technology-based innovations for the points of sale: The retailers evaluation. *Journal of Retailing and Consumer Services, 21*(1), 43–47. doi:10.1016/j.jretconser.2013.06.007

Parasuraman, A., Zeithaml, V. A., & Berry, L. L. (1985). A conceptual model of service quality and its implications for future research. *Journal of Marketing, 49*(4), 41–50. doi:10.2307/1251430

Parasuraman, A., Zeithaml, V. A., & Berry, L. L. (1988). Servqual. *Journal of Retailing, 64*(1), 12–40.

Preacher, K. J., & Hayes, A. F. (2004). SPSS and SAS procedures for estimating indirect effects in simple mediation models. *Behavior Research Methods, Instruments, & Computers, 36*(4), 717–731. doi:10.3758/BF03206553 PMID:15641418

Proença, J. F., & Rodrigues, M. A. (2011). A comparison of users and non-users of banking self-service technology in Portugal. *Managing Service Quality, 21*(2), 192–210. doi:10.1108/09604521111113465

Punj, G., & Stewart, D. W. (1983). Cluster analysis in marketing research: Review and suggestions for application. *JMR, Journal of Marketing Research, 20*(2), 134–148. doi:10.2307/3151680

Raju, P. S. (1977). Product familiarity, brand name and price influences on product evaluation. *Advances in Consumer Research. Association for Consumer Research (U. S.), 4*(1), 64–71.

Reutterer, T., Mild, A., Natter, M., & Taudes, A. (2006). A dynamic segmentation approach for targeting and customizing direct marketing campaigns. *Journal of Interactive Marketing, 20*(3/4), 43–57. doi:10.1002/dir.20066

Rincker, N. (2011). *Industry briefing: Germany's DIY market: Consumer and shopper insights, June 2011*. Retrieved December 1, 2014 from http://csi.mckinsey.com/Home/Knowledge_by_region/Europe_Africa_Middle_East/GermanyDIY.aspx

Schmidt, J. B., & Spreng, R. A. (1996). A proposed model of external consumer information search. *Journal of the Academy of Marketing Science, 24*(3), 246–256. doi:10.1177/0092070396243005

Sha, D. Y., & Guo-Liang, L. (2012). Improving service quality of retail store by innovative digital content technology. In *Proceedings of IEEE 3rd International Conference on Software Engineering and Service Science (ICSESS)* (pp. 655-660). Beijing: IEEE. doi:10.1109/ICSESS.2012.6269552

Shamdasani, P., Mukherjee, A., & Malhotra, N. (2008). Antecedents and consequences of service quality in consumer evaluation of self-service internet technologies. *Service Industries Journal, 28*(1), 117–138. doi:10.1080/02642060701725669

Sherman, S. J., & Fazio, R. H. (1983). Parallels between attitudes and traits as predictors of behavior. *Journal of Personality, 51*(3), 308–345. doi:10.1111/j.1467-6494.1983.tb00336.x

Snyder, M., & Ickes, W. (1985). Personality and social behavior. In G. Lindzey & E. Aronson (Eds.), *Handbook of social psychology* (Vol. 2, pp. 883–947). New York, NY: Random House.

Sobel, M. E. (1982). Asymptotic confidence intervals for indirect effects in structural equation models. *Sociological Methodology, 13,* 290–312. doi:10.2307/270723

Soper, D. S. (2013). *Sobel test calculator for the significance of mediation* [Software]. Retrieved December 16, 2013 from http://www.danielsoper.com/statcalc

Spreer, P., & Kallweit, K. (2014). Augmented reality in retail: Assessing the acceptance and the potential for multimedia product presentation at the PoS. *SOP Transactions on Marketing Research, 1*(1), 20–25. doi:10.15764/MR.2014.01002

Srinivasan, N., & Agrawal, J. (1988). The relationship between prior knowledge and external search. *Advances in Consumer Research. Association for Consumer Research (U. S.), 15*(1), 27–31.

Venkatesh, V. (2006). Where to go from here? Thoughts on future directions for research on individual-level technology adoption with a focus on decision making. *Decision Sciences, 37*(4), 497–518. doi:10.1111/j.1540-5414.2006.00136.x

Venkatesh, V., Morris, M. G., Davis, G. B., & Davis, F. D. (2003). User acceptance of information technology: Toward a unified view. *Management Information Systems Quarterly, 27*(3), 425–478.

Wang, M. C. H. (2012). Determinants and consequences of consumer satisfaction with self-service technology in a retail setting. *Managing Service Quality, 22*(2), 128–144. doi:10.1108/09604521211218945

Weijters, B., Rangarajan, D., Falk, T., & Schillewaert, N. (2007). Determinants and outcomes of customers' use of self-service technology in a retail setting. *Journal of Service Research, 10*(1), 3–21. doi:10.1177/1094670507302990

Weitz, B. A. (2010). Electronic retailing. In M. Krafft & M. K. Mantrala (Eds.), *Retailing in the 21ˢᵗ century* (pp. 357–371). Berlin: Springer. doi:10.1007/978-3-540-72003-4_22

Weitz, B. A., & Whitfield, M. B. (2010). Trends in US retailing. In M. Krafft & M. K. Mantrala (Eds.), *Retailing in the 21ˢᵗ century* (pp. 83–99). Berlin: Springer. doi:10.1007/978-3-540-72003-4_6

Wolf, M., & McQuitty, S. (2011). Understanding the do-it-yourself consumer: DIY motivations and outcomes. *AMS Review, 1*(3-4), 154-170.

Yang, Z., Cai, C., Zhou, Z., & Zhou, N. (2005). Development and validation of an instrument to measure user perceived service quality of information presenting web portals. *Information & Management, 42*(4), 575–589. doi:10.1016/j.im.2004.03.001

Yi, Y., Gong, T., & Lee, H. (2013). The impact of other customers on customer citizenship behavior. *Psychology and Marketing, 30*(4), 341–356. doi:10.1002/mar.20610

Zeithaml, V. A., Berry, L. L., & Parasuraman, A. (1996). The behavioral consequences of service quality. *Journal of Marketing, 60*(2), 31–46. doi:10.2307/1251929

Zielke, S., Toporowski, W., & Kniza, B. (2011). Customer acceptance of a new interactive information terminal in grocery retailing. In E. Pantano & H. Timmermans (Eds.), *Advanced technologies management for retailing* (pp. 289–305). Hershey, PA: Business Science Reference. doi:10.4018/978-1-60960-738-8.ch015

ADDITIONAL READING

Baron, R. M., & Kenny, D. A. (1986). The moderator–mediator variable distinction in social psychological research: Conceptual, strategic, and statistical considerations. *Journal of Personality and Social Psychology, 51*(6), 1173–1182. doi:10.1037/0022-3514.51.6.1173 PMID:3806354

Berry, L. L., Bolton, R. N., Bridges, C. H., Meyer, J., Parasuraman, A., & Seiders, K. (2010). Opportunities for innovation in the delivery of interactive retail services. *Journal of Interactive Marketing, 24*(2), 155–167. doi:10.1016/j.intmar.2010.02.001

Browning, J. M., & Zabriskie, N. B. (1985). Do-it yourself consumer: Segmentation insights for retailers. *Journal of Consumer Marketing, 2*(3), 5–15. doi:10.1108/eb008128

Chiu, H. C., Hsieh, Y. C., Roan, J., Tseng, K. J., & Hsieh, J. K. (2011). The challenge for multichannel services: Cross-channel free-riding behavior. *Electronic Commerce Research and Applications, 10*(2), 268–277. doi:10.1016/j.elerap.2010.07.002

Corvello, V., Pantano, E., & Tavernise, A. (2011). The design of an advanced virtual shopping assistant for improving consumer experience. In E. Pantano & H. Timmermans (Eds.), *Advanced Technologies Management for Retailing* (pp. 70–86). Hershey, PA: Business Science Reference. doi:10.4018/978-1-60960-738-8.ch004

Dabholkar, P. A., & Bagozzi, R. P. (2002). An attitudinal model of technology-based self-service: Moderating effects of consumer traits and situational factors. *Journal of the Academy of Marketing Science, 30*(3), 184–201. doi:10.1177/0092070302303001

Grewal, D., Krishnan, R., Levy, M., & Munger, J. (2010). Retail success and key drivers. In M. Krafft & M. K. Mantrala (Eds.), *Retailing in the 21st Century* (pp. 15–30). Berlin: Springer. doi:10.1007/978-3-540-72003-4_2

Kallweit, K., Spreer, P., & Toporowski, W. (2014). Why do customers use self-service information technologies in retail? The mediating effect of perceived service quality. *Journal of Retailing and Consumer Services, 21*(3), 268–276. doi:10.1016/j.jretconser.2014.02.002

King, W. R., & He, J. (2006). A meta-analysis of the technology acceptance model. *Information & Management, 43*(6), 740–755. doi:10.1016/j.im.2006.05.003

Kowatsch, T., & Maass, W. (2011). Mobile purchase decision support systems for in-store shopping environments. In E. Pantano & H. Timmermans (Eds.), *Advanced Technologies Management for Retailing* (pp. 270–288). Hershey, PA: Business Science Reference. doi:10.4018/978-1-60960-738-8.ch014

Meuter, M. L., Bitner, M. J., Ostrom, A. L., & Brown, S. W. (2005). Choosing among alternative service delivery modes: An investigation of customer trial of self-service technologies. *Journal of Marketing, 69*(2), 61–83. doi:10.1509/jmkg.69.2.61.60759

Pantano, E. (2010). New technologies and retailing: Trends and directions. *Journal of Retailing and Consumer Services, 17*(3), 171–172. doi:10.1016/j.jretconser.2010.03.004

Pantano, E., & Viassone, M. (2014). Demand pull and technology push perspective in technology-based innovations for the points of sale: The retailers evaluation. *Journal of Retailing and Consumer Services, 21*(1), 43–47. doi:10.1016/j.jretconser.2013.06.007

Rudolph, T., Schröder, T., & Böttger, T. (2012). Improving retailer profitability with selfsService technologies throughout all sales phases – the role of the business model. In T. Rudolph et al. (Eds.), *European Retail Research* (pp. 95–122). Wiesbaden: Springer. doi:10.1007/978-3-8349-4237-1_5

Shamdasani, P., Mukherjee, A., & Malhotra, N. (2008). Antecedents and consequences of service quality in consumer evaluation of self-service internet technologies. *Service Industries Journal*, *28*(1), 117–138. doi:10.1080/02642060701725669

Zeithaml, V. A., Berry, L. L., & Parasuraman, A. (1996). The behavioral consequences of service quality. *Journal of Marketing*, *60*(2), 31–46. doi:10.2307/1251929

KEY TERMS AND DEFINITIONS

Customer Segment: A homogeneous group of customers that is built based on a set of characteristics. Different customer segments should be heterogeneous among themselves.

Do-It-Yourself (DIY) Retail: The retail segment that markets raw and semi-raw materials and component parts to produce, transform, or reconstruct material possessions, including those drawn from the natural environment. Also referred to as the home improvement industry.

Mediation Effect: A relationship between an exogenous variable and an endogenous variable is explained through the inclusion of a third explanatory variable, also referred to as mediator variable. The mediator variable can either account for all (full mediation) or some (partial mediation) of the observed relationship between the two variables.

Service Quality: The degree to which the needs and expectations of a retailer's customers are met through the (product and service) offering.

Self-Service Technology (SST): A technological interface that enables customers to produce a service independent of direct service employee involvement.

Self-Service Information Technology (SSIT): Self-service technology that delivers information to the user and allows the provision of customized services instead of executing transactions.

Technology Acceptance: The degree to which a technology is adopted, used or intended to be used in the future by its users.

APPENDIX

Table 10. Application of the Mojena stopping rule

Number of Fusions	Number of Clusters	Fusion Coefficient Q_i	Standardized Fusion Coefficient
1	9	34.094	-2.525
2	8	83.548	-2.182
3	7	143.283	-1.768
4	6	230.500	-1.163
5	5	325.020	-0.507
6	4	488.886	0.629
7	3	723.831	2.258
8	2	1156.388	5.257

The standardized fusion coefficient exceeds the critical threshold of 2.75 in a two-cluster-solution (5.257). Consequently, the results support the findings of the analysis of the dendogram and the screeplot.

Chapter 10
Towards a Benchmark in the Innovation of the Retail Channel

Milena Viassone
University of Turin, Italy

ABSTRACT

In recent years, the issue of innovation in marketing channels has assumed an increasing importance, but this topic has been considered in reference to specific areas of innovation or to single categories of subjects within channels. Despite this, there is a lack of contributions that provide guidelines to excel in innovative retail channels. This chapter aims at describing the set of features of benchmark firms awarded for the innovation in retail channels and proposing an illustrative framework to be followed by retailers who choose the path of innovation. This objective is carried out throughout a systematic analysis of related literature both on innovation and benchmark in retail channels and throughout the analysis of 127 benchmark retailers awarded with two important prizes for innovation in the period 2011-2014. Results allow the creation of a set of best practices for innovative retailers, thus providing an important contribution to this topic.

INTRODUCTION

In the last decade, the issue of innovation has assumed a higher and higher importance in marketing studies by providing tools for increasing consumers' experience (Pantano & Viassone, 2013), by quickly replying to environmental changes in market trends, by developing new strategies for increasing market shares and by successfully exploiting the existing resources (Hauser, Tellis, & Griffin, 2006).

Along the way retailing has become a huge part of the global economy: in fact in the US consumer spending on it represents 70 percent of gross domestic product (GDP). Today it is possible to assist to a most profound change that the retail industry has ever gone through and to significant changes in the way consumers shop, where they shop and when they shop. All these facts have entailed deep changes in the retailing landscape (IBM, 2012).

DOI: 10.4018/978-1-4666-8297-9.ch010

Several multichannel firms offer customers the possibility to visit the retailer through different channels for different purposes, such as making purchases offline or getting information online, etc. Retailer practice is increasingly encompassing a broader range of activities as retailers expand the boundaries of their target markets and develop new ways of interaction with customers and channel partners (Sorescu, Frambach, Singh, Rangaswamyd, & Bridges, 2011).

In particular, innovation in marketing channels is a topic that has been considered in reference to specific areas of innovation or to single categories of subjects within channels.

In recent years, the evolution of the Internet as a new important distribution channel has obtained much attention; indeed, e-commerce has become an essential channel of distribution in the retail sector. Many products like clothing, tools, books and electronics are increasingly purchased online by customers (Seitz, 2013). Multichannel retailing is challenging because it requires retailers to have functional integration across areas such as marketing, inventory, order fulfillment, and product returns so that the operations and logistical efforts are streamlined with the frontend marketing activities (Mollenkopf, Rabinovich, Laseter, & Boyer, 2007). It consists of an extensive use of information technologies to digitize and integrate resources and operations from physical and online retail channels (Oh, Teo, & Sambamurthy, 2012).

Main innovations in retailing consist prevalently of: changes in business models, store formats and technologies, fundamentally new ideas and concepts for pursuing growth opportunities in global markets (Shankar & Yadav, 2011).

Starting from them, important questions could be asked: What are the main drivers of innovation in retail channels? What are the features characterizing benchmark firms in innovation in retail channels? Are there guidelines to be followed in order to become the best firm in this field? And, finally, more generally, what are the strategic implications for retailers? Exploring answers to these and related questions is the focus of this special issue.

Fewer studies have been conducted with a perspective referring to the channel as a whole (Musso, 2010). A higher number of papers have investigated innovation in retailing as 'product innovation' for distribution companies (Dawson, 2001; Castaldo, 2001) with a particular focus on communication technologies (Tardivo, Viasssone, & Scilla, 2013) and their implications for marketing channels (Kim, Cavusgil, & Calantone, 2006; Hausmana & Stockb, 2003).

If the studies concerning innovations in retail channels are limited, it is registered a real lack of contributions that provide guidelines to excel in innovative retail channels.

This chapter contributes to literature on this topic by describing the set of features of benchmark firms awarded for the innovation in retail channels and proposing, in this way, an illustrative framework to be followed by retailers who choose the path of innovation.

This objective is carried out throughout a systematic analysis of related literature and throughout the analysis of 127 benchmark retailers awarded with two of the most important prizes for innovation in the period 2011-2014. The heterogeneity of sectors considered in our sample is useful to determine the main common characteristics that make them excellent; in this way, the sample is representative for our exploratory research, which aims at deeply drawing up paths of innovation for retailers.

The qualitative research is based on an analysis of different characteristics of the several factors affecting innovation in retail channels.

Results show how most winners are selling their products via both brick-and-mortar and e-Commerce web sites, in addition to mobile web sites and other channels.

These results in the creation of a set of best practices for innovative retailers, thus providing an important contribution to the literature and practice on this topic. The chapter is structured in four main parts: the background, where contributions of literature on innovation in retail channels and benchmarking are analyzed; "Towards a Framework of Excellence in Innovation in Retail Channels", where the perspective on this issue, controversies and problems are described, together with the methodological framework. Finally, solutions and future strategies for innovation in retail channels are drawn and conclusions are developed.

Background

Innovation in Retail Channels

In the last decade multichannel retailing has grown tremendously; customers are more and more accustomed to use several channels when making a purchase and this aspect has attracted an increasing attention in literature (Konus, Verhoef, & Neslin, 2008; Neslin & Shankar, 2009). World have assisted to the development of the best technology for improving the traditional points of sale such as interactive displays and smart mirrors, new systems for searching and purchasing products, etc. (Pantano & Di Pietro, 2012; Bodhani, 2012).

Musso (2010) analyzes innovation in marketing channels following three perspectives: a technological perspective (what are the fronts of technological innovation for the optimization of interactions among channel members and with the final demand); a relational perspective (with respect to vertical relationships between firms in a marketing channel); a structural perspective (focused on which new channel configurations may occur).

The integration of these new different channels raises the question of how to redefine the operations and the strategic marketing elements because they have different constraints and require different competencies (Lang & Bressoles, 2013). Literature on this topic focuses mainly on customer behavior on the one side (Belvaux & Labbé-Pinlon, 2009) and the relations and conflicts between channels on the other (Avery, Steenburgh, Deighton, & Caravella, 2009; Falk, Schepers, Hammerschmidt, & Bauer, 2007).

According to Sorescu et al. (2011) there are several ways to carry out Retail Business Model innovations:

- Fast fashion model (i.e. that adopted by the retailer Zara), that consists of using a smaller assortment with faster turning inventory: this creates an atmosphere of exclusivity and cuts down on the need for excessive markdowns;
- Self-service model used by Redbox, the chain of kiosks dispensing DVD rentals for $1 per day: it re-invented self-service model that, in this case, consists of an automated kiosk placed in convenient locations such as McDonald's or grocery stores with assortment and prices significantly lower than those of competitors and of the absence of any employees in the retail process;
- "Name your own price" model typical of Priceline that allows customers' input into pricing decisions, thus resulting in a minimization of unused products which increases efficiency;
- Leveraging complementaries, characteristic of Apple stores where customers experience the products and get one-on-one tutorials on a wide range of technical issues, get their computer repaired at the Genius Bar and participate in workshops improving their know-how on the products;
- Adjacency model consisting of the capitalization on seemingly unrelated demand that has a physical proximity to the retailer's current products/services just like in the case Ikea vs. Mega Mall in Russia;
- Leverage exclusive products: product assortment has been leveraged but product assortment has not a so high potential to become a driver of competitive advantage; for this motivation some retailers have created an assortment of products that have characteristics of uniqueness;

- Enduring customer engagement via multichannel processes throughout a continuous experimentation in order to identify appropriate assortments and customer experiences;
- Innovative format which facilitates the shopping experience (stores within stores);
- Relying on stakeholders to determine the optimal depth of assortment and supporting services; this allows to involve customers in a co-creation process where, for example, they can create their sport shoes online using the NikeID system;
- Relying on added value tie-ins (i.e. Walmart with its emphasis on sustainability or the America Girl Place, symbol of a retail brand ideology able to immerse the customer in a complex experience including socialization, co-creation and embedding of the brand).

Several technological innovations have allowed retailers the ability to create and offer these new business models. For example, with regard to dynamic pricing, newer technologies are electronic price tags and mobile applications that have made it easier to implement marketplace offers (Grewal, Ailawadi, Gauri, Hall, Kopalle, & Robertson, 2011).

Also online channels are more and more explored by literature and of increasing importance to business and academia (Klaus & Maklan, 2011; Verhoef et al., 2009). In particular, previous studies indicate how the creation of compelling online experiences for web users will have numerous positive impacts for retailers (Dholakia, Bagozzi, & Pearo, 2004).

A very important solution is also offered by the introduction of self-service technologies (SSTs) that is "a technological interface that enables customers to produce a service independent of direct service employee involvement" (Meuter, Ostrom, Roundtree, & Bitner, p. 50). They consist of "on-site" options, such as touch screens in department stores, automated teller machines (ATMs) and ticket machines and "off-site" options,

such as telephone and online banking and shopping (Dabholkar & Bagozzi, 2002). In addition, among the SSTs introductions it is possible to emphasize: self-service checkouts in supermarkets, self-check-in at airports and self-service petrol pumps. An important technologic innovation is given by the intelligent shopping trolleys, that is traditional shopping trolleys enriched with systems able to interact with consumers through interfaces, providing more information, localizing the consumer's position and proposing the best path for reaching the selected items, etc. (Black, Clemmenses, & Skov., 2009).

Pantano and Viassone (2014) classify the most recent technologies in three main categories:

- Touch screen displays/in-store totems, focused on technologies belonging to the point of sale, i.e. the virtual garment fitting systems or the Self-Service Technologies (SSTs) such as the automatic cash desk systems for mobile (mobile applications) hybrid systems;
- Systems for mobile, that is systems for consumers' own mobile phones, able to provide interactive contents and services for enriching consumers' in-store shopping experience (i.e. automatic payment modality, automatic item searching according to the own wish list, etc.) (Rudolph & Emrich, 2009; Bennet & Savani, 2011);
- Hybrid systems, based on retailers' own technologies that users can move around the store, generally based on RFID (Radio Frequency IDeintification) systems.

Given these important innovations, with regard to marketing channels, the concept of innovation can be viewed on the one hand as a strategic activity for both industrial and distribution firms to acquire a competitive advantage along the distribution channel and, on the other hand, as a changing process of the economic function of the distribution systems (Musso, 2010)

In the future these tools should be increasingly developed and firms will need more and more a guideline to follow in order to improve on their innovation paths.

BENCHMARK IN INNOVATIVE RETAIL CHANNELS

A study that benchmarks cross channel capabilities among leading retailers across different countries could represent a suitable way to help retailers as they determine their cross channel future.

There are several firms such as Chevron, Xerox and IBM that use the benchmarking concept to excel in their respective fields (Camp, 1998). Given the extensive attention of practitioners and the importance of benchmarking performance, managers and researchers have a great deal of interest in understanding the factors at the base of benchmarking in the innovation of the retail channels.

Aberdeen Group (2005) supports the idea that best-in-class multi-channel leaders result particularly vulnerable to some laggards who take aggressive steps to get their houses in order:

- **Laggard Steps to Success:** In case of the lack of a multi-channel strategy in place, it is important to implement it and it is essential to assure that the organization is aligned by product, not by channel, and to establish performance metrics by brand rather than by channel;
- **Industry Norm Steps to Success:** It is necessary to consider outsourcing programming in order to improve system integration and escalate timing of initiatives to implement management systems of distributed order;
- **Best in Class Steps to Success:** It is of extreme importance to be prepared for continued growth by automating critical functions and to develop collaboration among internal stakeholders.

According to Elliott et al. (2012) a culture of innovation in retail channels should come from the top of the business but, in the same way, not stop there. Innovative ideas must bubble up from many layers of the enterprise and should involve every stakeholder. In particular omni-channel is a new buzzword that has emerged: in this case the customer experience is integrated across stores, websites, direct mail and catalogues, mobile platforms, social networks, home shopping and gaming. In fact, according to a December 2011 report in the Harvard Business Review, digital retailing now accounts for about 10 percent of sales in the UK and 9 percent in the United States.

There is a great need of guidelines and benchmark to be followed: in fact Accenture's recent benchmark survey of retailer's readiness to deliver a seamless customer experience found 74% of the surveyed retailers ranked at or below "underdeveloped". 72.5% showed absent or underdeveloped capabilities in making the end-to-end shopping experience feel connected across channels and 81% declared absent or underdeveloped capabilities in tailoring assortment, pricing and shopping occasion to customer expectations across channels (Accenture, 2012).

In order to improve performances in innovation in retail channels, it is considered important to look at those firms that excel in this field. An objective parameter for choosing these firms could be given by the awards they obtained. Although that there are several prizes awarded for innovation in retail channels, the most famous are:

- Channel Innovation Award (2011-2014), an award program designed to honor retailers who are achieving cross-channel success in today's challenging retail environment;
- Innov@ Retail Award (since 2012), award destined to enterprises that have distinguished themselves for the realization of innovative projects in the light of service quality, customer retention and brand awareness in different sectors such as re-

tail, fashion and telecommunications; this award is structured in five main categories: best E-tailer, best store, best marketing campaign, best technology innovation, best outsourcing project;

- BT Retail Week Technology Award, an award that supports and celebrates the best innovators in retail technology;
- Retail Innovation Award (companies that provide outstanding technologies, products and services to support the booming Asia retail sector), the Asian only recognition for excellence in retailing; the award consists of 17 categories, covering three areas:
  - **Store Front Solutions:** Providers, services and products that bring outstanding customer services and memorable shopping experiences;
  - **Backend Operations:** Providers, services and products that optimize and automate retailers' operations to speed up business process, reduce costs and enhance success;
  - **Innovative Marketing:** This category awards retailers that are outstanding at using technologies to develop omni-channel retailing and marketing strategies.

In particular the first two awards offer the possibility to consider firms awarded in a period of time relatively long (since 2011 for the Channel Innovation Award and since 2012 for Innov@ Retail Award) and provide a large number of awarded firms coming from different countries. These prizes are preferred with respect to the last two ones also because they are focused on innovation with reference to the different retail channels.

Investigating the common drivers of benchmark firms awarded for innovation in retail channels with Channel Innovation Award and Innov@ Retail Award will be very useful to draw paths of development for all those firms that want to improve themselves in this field.

Towards a Framework of Excellence in Innovation in Retail Channels

Despite the increasing importance assumed by innovation in retailing in the last decades (Pantano & Viassone, 2013; Bennet & Savani, 2011; Black et al., 2009), a lot needs to be done in this research area.

In particular, several academics have focused on the evolution of internet and e-commerce as important channels of distribution in the retail sector (Seitz, 2013) or have analyzed innovative products in retailing (K. Keeling, D. Keeling, & McGoldrick, 2013; Pantano, Iazzolino, & Migliano, 2013; Vrontis & Thrassou, 2013; Kim et al., 2006; Hausmana & Stockb, 2003; Dawson, 2001; Castaldo, 2001).

A very large literature has been produced with regard to the perception of these new technological innovations in retail channels by customers with particular reference to different topics like trust (Pantano & Di Pietro, 2012; Chattaraman, Known, & Gilbert, 2012), enjoyment in the use of these innovations (Venkatesh, 2000; Wang, 2012) or expectations towards the introduction of innovative (technological) solutions (Pantano & Viassone, 2012; Tardivo & Viassone, 2011). On the other side, the point of view of retailers on these tools has been less considered in the academic debate (Pantano & Viassone, 2014; Pantano et al., 2013; Alkemade & Suurs, 2012).

All these contributions offer suggestions to implement or to apply these innovations with reference to a particular perspective (that of the customer, retailer, employees, etc.) but it does not exist a systematic research that analyzes the common characteristics of benchmark destinations for innovation in retail channels, able to sketch a sort of guideline useful to those firms aiming at becoming excellent in this field.

For this reason, the present study aims at identifying the set of common features of benchmark firms awarded (with Channel Innovation Award or Innov@ Retail Award) for innovation in retail channels in the period 2011-2014 in order to propose an illustrative framework to be followed by enterprises which choose the path of innovation. These two awards result particularly suitable for the purpose of the study because they exist since 2011 (Channel Innovation Award) and 2012 (Innov@ Retail Award) and this allows to analyze the existence of possible patterns in this time range. Furthermore, they involve a large number of firms awarded and settled in different countries; anyway, the most important characteristic of these awards consist of the fact that they are particularly focused on innovation and creativity of firms with regard to the use of different channels. In addition, these two awards use several variables (also justified in literature) for the individuation of winners.

The analysis involves 38 benchmark firms awarded with Channel Innovation Award (Table 1) and 89 firms awarded with Innov@ Retail Award (Table 2), all belonging to different sectors (food and beverage, clothing, toys, telephones, entertainment, bank, etc.). In the tables 1 and 2 names and size/sector of the winners are indicated, in addition to the main channels awarded. The heterogeneity of world firms considered in our sample is useful to determine the main common characteristics that make them excellent.

Even if circumscribed to the period 2011-2014, this sample is representative for our exploratory research, which aims at deeply drawing up paths of innovation in retail for enterprises.

Table 1. Description of the firms awarded with the Channel Innovation Award

Firms				Channels Awarded	Firms Size/Sector
Stage stores	Indigo books & music	Republic	Guess jeans	Award winners have demonstrated achievements in some or all of the following areas: sales gains, meeting consumer demands with convenient cross-channel shopping opportunities, cross-channel marketing, customer recognition, technology innovations. Winners focus their channel efforts around a variety of strategies (i.e. personalization, social media and mobile technology and integrate the benefits of cross-channel marketing and services to their customers). Main channels used: brick-and-mortar and e-Commerce web sites, in addition to mobile web sites and other channels.	The award winners operate in different industry segments and they are both U.S.- and internationally-based retail companies.
Clarks footwear	Heels.com	Tesco	Domino's pizza		
Bebe	Famous footwear	S group and foodie.fm	Moosejaw		
Build.com	Tabcorp	Envelopes.com	Target corp.		
Toys r us canada	Fast lane wireless	David's bridal	Macy's		
Kidrobot	Telnet mobile	Marks & spencer	Starbucks		
Sears holdings	Soccerpro.com	Target	Advance auto parts		
B&H photo	Verizon wireless	Step2	Jcpenney		
Wine enthusiast	National wholesale liquidators	Stop & shop	Home shopping network		
Country club prep	Title nine				

Source: personal elaboration

Table 2. Description of the firms awarded with the Innov@ Retail Award

Firms			Channels Awarded	Firms Size/Sector
R.T.I. Gruppo Mediaset	Zara	Webank	This award is structured in 5 sections: Best E-tailer (Best pure online player and Best omnichannel player), Best Store (Best format innovation and Best customer experience), Best Marketing Campaign (Best omnichannel marketing campaign and Best social media project), Best Technology Innovation (Best big data technology and Best customer application), Best Outsourcing Project (Best customer insight and Best social analytics program).	This award involves the Italian firms with annual sales higher or equal to Euros 40.000.000, operating in the following sectors: retail, banks, fashion, TLC and that have distinguished themselves for innovative services relating to the quality of service, customer loyalty and brand awareness.
Hellobank! By BNL	Media World	Blomming		
Spazioitaly	Yoox Group	Groupon		
Gruppo Coin	Marcopolo Expert	Mediamarket		
Banco Popolare	Fujitsu	Prénatal		
Totalerg	Zalando	Tramezzino itì		
Metro Iitalia C&C	Decathlon	Luxottica		
BNP Banca Paribas Cardif	Eurostar	Essere Benessere		
H3G	t.riciclo	Intesa Sanpaolo		
Autogrill	Kiko	Unicoop		
Fashion District Group	Sapori&Dintorni	Carlsberg		
laRinascente	Quality Living	Carrefour Banque		
The Walt Disney Company Italia	Coop.fi	Galimberti		
Thun	Coop Italia	Ikea		
Illycaffè	Simply	Carrefour		
Swarovski Internazionale d'Italia	Unes	Unicredit		
Telekom Italia	Gruppo Poli	laRinascente		
Unes Centro Soc. Coop	Gruppo Sait	Enel Green Power		
Zurich Insurance	Gabrielli	Ikea		
BNL	Ergon	Bricocenter		
LVMH Italia divisione Sephora	Coop Italia	Conad		
Unicredit	Unes	Sephora		
Eni	A&O	I Buoni Motıvı		
Auchan		Risparmio Super		
Vodafone Omnitel		Banca MPS		
Day Ristoservice		UBI Banca		
UBI Banca		Vodafone		
U-Hopper		Octo Telematics		
Amplifon		Banca MPS		
DHL Supply Chain Italy		Cariparma		
Intesa Sanpaolo		Certilogo		
Postemobile		BeMyEye		

Source: Personal elaboration.

The qualitative research is based on an analysis of several factors affecting the innovation in retail channels shown by benchmark firms in this field.

In particular, retailer current attention is focused on two important factors. The first is the economic downturn: in fact, nowadays retailers are charged with finding innovative and creative ways to increase the bottom line while decreasing costs. The second is the new age of multi-channel retailing: retailers' efforts are focused on finding ways to incorporate social media and mobile strategies into their portfolio of multi-channel business processes because customers expect the best products when and where they want them and at the price they desire. In order to remain competitive, retailers must join the mobile and social revolution and develop the system in order to facilitate cohesive and consistent cross-channel strategies (Oracle, 2011).

In order to face these important challenges, retailers must understand the key drivers of retail success: starting from this research and from a review of the various features of benchmark retail firms, it is possible to offer an illustrative framework able to describe strategic innovative drivers that retailers must consider as they deliver value to their customers and defend their competitive advantage (Grewal, Krishnan, Levy, & Munger 2006).

Main drivers analyzed for each firm are those suggested by literature and considered as the most important in the assignment of these awards:

- Channel growth statistics, that details on sales performances either overall or via specific channels, considered very important by Oh et al (2012); every awarded firms registered an increase of sales, or E-commerce or online and multichannel sales, or in kiosk usage, or in self-service orders and some of their activities of Search Engine Optimization; cross channel marketing - in-store promotions or external marketing and promotion (unique cam-

paigns that promotes cross-channel offerings): one of the few works that analyzes the topic of innovation in marketing channels with a perspective focused on the entire channel - with reference to its structure and flows that drive the operations and link all the subjects - is that by Musso (2010) while the other paper (Dawson, 2001; Castaldo, 2001) focused on innovation in retailing as "product innovation" for distribution companies or as innovation in the supply chain. Cross channel marketing consists of mobile marketing solutions, personalized promotions, multichannel communications technology, increased promotional activity online (in-store coupons), cable TV ads, distribution of pamphlets, charitable donations, promo codes, semi-annual collection preview events, digital marketing strategy that focuses on selling products via comparison shopping engines, in-store kiosks, tablets for in-store associates, eCommerce and digital marketing manager, consumer websites, daily effort to synchronize catalogue offering with the company website, marketing promotions synchronization, presence on Facebook, Google+, Pinterest, Tumblr, Twitter and YouTube, specialized campaign, QR codes on in-store signage, multi-channel campaign, a personalized Web presence with in-store, call center, social and mobile channels.

- Satisfaction of customer demands with convenient cross-channel shopping opportunities (unique shopping offerings): it is more and more important to understand what customer expects, to design the service that fits the expectations and to deliver the service; this allows retailers to fulfil the gap between clients' expectations and effective perception of the service with benefits for satisfaction and loyalty (Ryding, 2011); in this study, customer satisfaction is increased through access to merchandise with the help of associates using tablets, unique shopping offerings across all channels (e.g. coupons redeemability), inventory lookup via mobile app integrated with Apple Passbook, flexible delivery options (order online, pickup in-store), Cloud-based e-commerce, returns and exchanges (online and in-store) in less than 5 minutes, in-vehicle Pickup (pick up online purchases within five minutes of arrival, without ever leaving the car) in the case of Sears Holding, a large satisfaction with regard to the "easy use" of the kiosks. Furthermore, in the case of Telnet Mobile, customers can be assisted by various technical devises during the decision-making process (Scala-powered Elo touch screens, analysis of preferences, screens, detailed examination of shown devices, information about other products, holographic projection for specialist assistance). In most cases customers receive a personalized shopping experience, in-store services, the possibility to purchase online without registering, a better sale assistance and personalized marketing based on shopping patterns.

- Customer tracking (background into the retailers approach to CRM, customer data): among the different expectation of customers it must be remembered also customer support and order tracking (Yong, Gruca, & Klemz., 2003); generally, customers would like to use different retail channels, sometimes simultaneously, to buy a product or a service and benefit from services such as rapid home deliveries or online tracking of orders (Lang, 2012). In order to develop this aspect, the benchmark enterprises under inspection have adopted the following strategies: new loyalty card, multichannel communications platform and expertise to develop relationships with new and existing customers, increasing in-

teractions with the customers by adding an additional communications channel – text – to its voice communications, loyalty program integrated also via mobile, geo-fencing (targeted offers for customers via push notification when they are near a store), tracking metrics, multi-touch attribution and optimization solution that tracks the path to purchase for customers across all touch points and pulls actionable insights from that customer data, tracking through user accounts and behaviours and actions on the web site, determination of the number of in-store customers who entered the store after an online campaign, methods of customer tracking provided by CrossView: customer sales data, reviews, browsing behaviours and business analytics, loyalty cards.

- Integration (any new technology implementations or processes that improve fulfillment or other key performance areas): nowadays the imperative for traditional retailers is to integrate across channels with the scope of providing their customers the same experience online as in their stores (Heckmann, Huisman, Kesteloo, & Schmaus, 2012). The integration could be realized in different ways: through a new e-Commerce site integrated with the company system of order management, by reporting and monitoring tools across channels, by means of an integrated cross-channel business model and through an integration between online and offline experience. Other example of integration could be a new mobile site where the entire purchase history can be seen on the basis of the times the password of the loyalty card has been used, daily synchronization with full price transparency.

- Key competitive products (Dawson, 2001; Castaldo, 2001). These vary from make-up and accessories to toy and baby products, smartphones, cell phones, tablets, MP3 players, hot and cold beverages, television production and distribution on different platforms, services of wireless and internet television mobile, advanced technology for the mobile marketing, totally integrated and seamless telematic solutions for insurance companies, car rental and fleet management, motor manufacturers and governmental authorities, services of crowdsourcing for firms that desire to perform operations on shops, check shops for product, merchandising and customers, mystery shopping on the base of the sector of reference.

- Innovative merchandising displays and techniques: J. Diamond and E. Diamond (2007) maintain how in the current world of visual merchandising, artistic talents play a major role in creating an atmosphere that motivates shoppers to become customers. Main merchandising techniques adopted by our sample are: websites for each of its retail banners, themed window, possibility to switch from the magazine site to a retail site with a single click, cross-promotion between the channels, specific channel strategies to improve business (like, in-store kiosks to increase sales, mobile technology, product fulfillment), investments in the development of a real-time customer rewards platform and the expansion of the customer loyalty strategy, partnering with third-party marketplaces, selling via online marketplaces, as well as through web store, digital technology to showcase the fashion trends offered, new store layouts and store formats, more interactive banks accessible via e-mail, chat, twitter or telephone almost 6 out of 7 days.
- Competition: this aspect is particularly emphasized by Bolt (2013) who analyzes competition and innovation in retail pay-

ments and their relation to payment pricing and payment efficiency. Our sample shows different levels of competition: some of them work in a clime of low competition or in a monopoly situation, some other competes with many companies in single product categories but the most of them is in a leader position with regard to the sector of reference.

- Quality of customer service, given that customers may be willing to pay a higher price for substantially better quality service or choose a service-oriented provider at the same price (Deloitte, 2013). The qualitative level of the service offered to customers by benchmark firms is high. They show excellent performance and customer satisfaction on this aspect.

This analysis represents a first attempt to investigate the current efforts made by firms in the innovation in retail channels and it is a starting point to draw guidelines on this topic.

SOLUTIONS AND RECOMMENDATIONS

Starting from the drivers characterizing the benchmark firms, this study offers an important framework for those companies that would like to follow the path of innovation. Anyway it represents only a starting point to perform better.

This study allows to integrate the existent literature about innovation in retail channels concerning the evolution of internet and e-commerce as channels of distribution in the retail sector (Seitz, 2013), innovative products in retailing (Keeling et al., 2013; Pantano et al., 2013; Vrontis & Thrassou, 2013) and the new technological innovation in this field (Pantano & Viassone, 2014; Pantano & Di Pietro, 2012; Chattaram et al., 2012) with a new point of view starting from the features of firms of excellence in innovative marketing channels.

Results show how benchmark firms in this field are very performing with regard to channel growth statistics with an important growth in main variables like sales (Oh et al., 2012), cross channel marketing like mobile marketing solutions or personalized promotions, etc. Also with reference to the attention towards customers, benchmark firms devote extreme importance to the satisfaction of customers' demands with convenient cross-channel shopping opportunities (Ryding, 2011) and providing them with a personalized shopping experience also by means of innovative solutions. Still with reference to customer attention, very important are also the efforts in terms of customer tracking throughout different tools like new loyalty card, multichannel communications platform, geo-fencing, multi-touch attribution and optimization solution, etc. A strong attention is also dedicated to the quality of customer service that results high in all the cases.

Every benchmark firm should also integrate across channels in order to offer the same experience both online and in the store (Heckmann et al., 2012) throughout mobile site, daily synchronization with full price transparency and so on and propose key competitive products (Dawson, 2001; Castaldo, 2001). In addition, they have to adopt innovative merchandising displays and techniques (J. Diamond & E. Diamond, 2007) throughout websites, in-store kiosks, selling via online marketplaces, etc. and they show a favorite competitive position (Bolt, 2013).

These nine drivers should constitute a real identity card of excellent innovative firms in retail channels that every enterprise should be inspired to, but this study proposes a further effort and in this phase it also aims at emphasizing the points of strengths of the best firms with regard to innovation in retail channels. They can be provided in three different activities:

- Merchandising, in terms of merchandising mix and development of the in-house one;

- Website, in terms of improvements in site search function and store and mobile site integrated by 'browse & order' feature;
- Platforms, in particular social shopping platform supporting business growth and traditional store-based segment transformed by e-Commerce platform.

Starting from these results, these firms suggest three key pillars of strategy:

1. Creating lasting relationships with members by allowing them to manage their lives;
2. Attaining best-in-class productivity and efficiency;
3. Building the brands and reinventing the company continuously through technology and innovation

These findings open important perspectives for future researches directions that will be explained in detail in the following paragraph.

FUTURE RESEARCH DIRECTIONS

The analysis of progresses and the description of the features of benchmark firms described in the present study represent a base to open a debate on the future of these important tools in the retailing activity.

Nowadays retailers face four important challenges (Grewal et al., 2006):

- Consolidation in the retailing industry: given that several retailers are unable to deliver high levels of value relative to their more astute competitors, it is possible to assist to meaningful consolidation by big retailers (i.e. the acquisition of Sears by Kmart);
- The creation and sustaining of value throughout the creation of centers of excellence or concentrating their efforts in order to become leaders in terms of the merchandise they provide;

- **The Focus on Innovation:** Several efforts are done with regard to the experimentation with their store formats in order to be perceived as "innovative retailers" by customers: this is possible by introducing always innovative retail formats and implementing new ideas;
- **Cost Controls:** Leader in retailing are those that are efficient and effective in integrating their suppliers, manufacturers, warehouses, stores, and transportation intermediaries into a seamless value chain; this allows to minimize system-wide costs and, at the same time, to satisfy the service levels required by its customers.

In this scenario several proposals come directly from the sample that hypothesizes future directions in this field: first, they assume an improvement of the existent tools like, for example, the personalization and service on the site for private-label credit card users. Second, other efforts could be done in the integration: a possible goal could consist of the integration of digital content and in displaying with RFID technology. Third, important improvement could also been done with regard to customers' satisfaction: it would be possible to gain insights into long-term customer behaviors by developing reliable customer segments, integrating customer data into testing strategies and increasing conversion and recreating an atmosphere where it is fun to shop for both children and adults. Fourth, several firms declare their intention to expand their retail presence by opening up to 20 more brick-and-mortar Kidrobot stores and widening/deepening their product lines; in this way they would increase the percentage of stores where customers can pick up their orders. Then some of these firms reduce cost-to-serve (shifting transactions from the branch to different channels). Finally, almost all firms forecast to launch new products/services such as a new business-to-business voucher scheme with unique codes for each voucher to ensure reimbursements can be tracked and verified at the PoS.

However, this explorative study shows important limitations: it only considers retailers awarded for innovation in channels in the period 2011-2014, it does not supply a distinction between different sectors and, finally, as the unique parameter of benchmark of innovation it employs two awards assigned to different retailers. Although these firms are reasonable representatives of the phenomenon, they represent a convenience sample.

In the future, this research could be focused on particular sectors and it could be proposed a comparison between a benchmark retailer and one that aims at becoming it, thus individuating gaps and development strategies.

CONCLUSION

Integrating ideas from innovation management, technology management, retail channels and marketing research, this study attempts to examine the secrets of success of firms that distinguish themselves for innovation in retail channels. In fact, despite the large diffusion of innovative retail channels (Pantano & Viassone, 2013), there are not clear trajectories assessed by literature. For this reason, our results provide a sort of guideline that can constitute a very important aid for retailers interested in improving their performances in terms of innovation of their channels.

Suggestions come from benchmark firms with regard to important drivers like channel growth statistics (Oh et al., 2012), cross channel marketing (Musso, 2010), satisfaction of customer demands (Ryding, 2011), customer tracking (Yong et al., 2003), integration (Heckmann et al., 2012), key competitive products (Dawson, 2001; Castaldo, 2001), innovative merchandising displays and techniques (J. Diamond & E. Diamond (2007), competition (Bolt, 2013) and quality of customer service (Deloitte, 2013).

The profile of an excellent firm in innovation is that of a firm that registers increase of sales, E-commerce or online and multichannel sales and developments in cross channel marketing.

It is generally able to increase customers' satisfaction through different tools such as access to merchandise with the help of associates using tablets, unique shopping offerings across all channels, flexible delivery options, etc. It develops sophisticated techniques to track customers like new loyalty card, multichannel communications platform, loyalty program integrated also via mobile, tracking metrics and so on.

Furthermore, it is very sensitive to the integration, the constant launch of key competitive products and innovative merchandising displays and techniques. A very peculiar feature is given by the fact that almost all benchmark firms operate with low competition or in a monopoly situation and show a high qualitative level of the service offered to customers.

This analysis represents a first attempt to investigate the current efforts made by firms in the innovation in retail channels and it is a starting point to draw guidelines on this topic.

ACKNOWLEDGMENT

A special thanks goes to Tina Kuhlmann for the cooperation in the collection of data.

REFERENCES

Aberdeen Group. (2005). *The multi-channel retail benchmark report*. Boston: Aberdeen Group.

Accenture. (2012). *A new era for retail. Cloud computing changes the game*. Accenture.

Alkemade, F., & Suurs, R. A. A. (2012). Patterns of expectations for emerging sustainable technologies. *Technological Forecasting and Social Change*, *79*(3), 448–456. doi:10.1016/j.techfore.2011.08.014

Avery, J., Steenburgh, T. J., Deighton, J., & Caravella, M. (2009). *Adding bricks to clicks: The contingencies driving cannibalization and complementarity in multichannel retailing*. Harvard Business School, Working Paper 07-043, February 2009. Cambridge, MA: Harvard.

Bennet, R., & Savani, S. (2011). Retailers' preparedness for the introduction of third wave (ubiquitous) computing applications: A survey of UK companies. *International Journal of Retail & Distribution Management*, *39*(5), 306–325. doi:10.1108/09590551111130748

Black, D., Clemmenses, N. J., & Skov, M. B. (2009). Supporting the supermarket shopping experience through a context-aware shopping trolley. In *Proceedings of the 21st Annual Conference of the Australian Computer-Human Interaction*. New York: ACM. doi:10.1145/1738826.1738833

Bodhani, A. (2012). Shops offer the e-tail experience. *Engineering and Technology*, *7*(5), 46–49. doi:10.1049/et.2012.0512

Bolt, W. (2013). Pricing, competition and innovation in retail payment systems: A brief overview. *Journal of Financial Market Infrastructures*, *1*(3), 73–90.

Camp, R. C. (1998). *Global cases in benchmarking*. Milwaukee, WI: ASQ Quality Press.

Castaldo, S. (Ed.). (2001). *Retailing & innovazione*. Milano: Egea.

Chattaraman, V., Known, W.-S., & Gilbert, J. E. (2012). Virtual agents in retail web sites: Benefits of simulated social interaction for older users. *Computers in Human Behavior, 28*(6), 2055–2066. doi:10.1016/j.chb.2012.06.009

Dabholkar, P. A., & Bagozzi, R. P. (2002). An attitudinal model of technology-based self-service: Moderating effects of consumer traits and situational factors. *Journal of the Academy of Marketing Science, 30*(3), 184–201. doi:10.1177/0092070302303001

Dawson, J. A. (2001). Is there a new commerce in Europe? *International Review of Retail, Distribution and Consumer Research, 11*(3), 287–299. doi:10.1080/713770598

Deloitte. (2013). *Keeping promises putting customers at the heart of retail financial services.* London, UK: Deloitte.

Dholakia, U. M., Bagozzi, R. P., & Pearo, L. K. (2004). A social influence model of consumer participation in network- and small-group-based virtual communities. *International Journal of Research in Marketing, 21*(3), 241–263. doi:10.1016/j.ijresmar.2003.12.004

Diamond, J., & Diamond, E. (2007). *Contemporary visual merchandising and environmental design.* Prentice Hall.

Elliott, S., Twynam, B., & Connell, S. (2012). *Building for breakthroughs: The leadership of innovation in UK retail.* Los Angeles, CA: Korn/Ferry Institute.

Falk, T., Schepers, J., Hammerschmidt, M., & Bauer, H. (2007). Identifying cross-channel dissynergies for multichannel service providers. *Journal of Service Research, 10*(2), 143–160. doi:10.1177/1094670507306683

Grewal, D., Ailawadi, K. L., Gauri, D., Hall, K., Kopalle, P., & Robertson, J. R. (2011). Innovations in retail pricing and promotions. *Journal of Retailing, 87S*, S43–S52. doi:10.1016/j.jretai.2011.04.008

Grewal, D., Krishnan, R., Levy, M., & Munger, J. (2006). Retail success and key drivers: Current and future trends. In M. Kraft & M. K. Mantrala (Eds.), *Retailing in the 21st century* (pp. 13–25). Heidelberg, Germany: Springer Berlin. doi:10.1007/3-540-28433-8_2

Hausmana, A., & Stockb, J. R. (2003). Adoption and implementation of technological innovations within long-term relationships. *Journal of Business Research, 56*(8), 681–686. doi:10.1016/S0148-2963(01)00313-7

Heckmann, P., Huisman, R., Kesteloo, M., & Schmaus, B. (2012). *Cross-channel integration in retail: creating a seamless customer experience.* Booz & Company.

IBM. (2012). *Retail 2020: Reinventing retailing once again.* Armonk, NY: IBM Corporation.

Keeling, K., Keeling, D., & McGoldrick, P. (2013). Retail relationships in a digital age. *Journal of Business Research, 66*(7), 847–855. doi:10.1016/j.jbusres.2011.06.010

Kim, D., Cavusgil, S. T., & Calantone, R. J. (2006). Information system innovations and supply chain management: Channel relationships and firm performance. *Journal of the Academy of Marketing Science, 34*(1), 40–54. doi:10.1177/0092070305281619

Klaus, P., & Maklan, S. (2011). Bridging the gap for destination extreme sports – a model of sports tourism customer experience. *Journal of Marketing Management, 27*(13–14), 1341–1365. doi:10.1080/0267257X.2011.624534

Konuş, U., Verhoef, P. C., & Neslin, S. A. (2008). Multichannel shopper segments and their antecedents. *Journal of Retailing, 84*(4), 398–413. doi:10.1016/j.jretai.2008.09.002

Lang, G. (2012). Multi-channel retail. Position Paper. BEM Bordeaux Management School Centre de Recherche en Gestion de l'Ecole polytechnique (PREG CRG) – CNRS Chaire Orange Innovation et regulation des services numériques.

Lang, G., & Bressoles, G. (2013). Economic performance and customer expectation in e-fulfillment systems: A multi-channel retailer perspective. *Supply Chain Forum: International Journal (Toronto, Ont.), 14*(1), 16–26.

Meuter, M. L., Ostrom, A. L., Roundtree, R. I., & Bitner, M. J. (2000). Self-service technologies: Understanding customer satisfaction with technology-based service encounters. *Journal of Marketing, 64*(3), 50–64. doi:10.1509/jmkg.64.3.50.18024

Mollenkopf, D. A., Rabinovich, E., Laseter, T. M., & Boyer, K. K. (2007). Managing internet product returns: A focus on effective service operations. *Decision Sciences, 38*(2), 215–250. doi:10.1111/j.1540-5915.2007.00157.x

Musso, F. (2010). Innovation in marketing channels: relationships, technology, channel structure. *Symphonya: Emerging Issues in Management*, (1), 23-42.

Neslin, S., & Shankar, V. (2009). Key issues in multichannel customer management: Current knowledge and future directions. *Journal of Interactive Marketing, 23*(1), 70–81. doi:10.1016/j.intmar.2008.10.005

Nielsen. (2014). *Continual innovation: The key to stand out and win in retail*. Retrieved from http://www.nielsen.com/us/en/newswire/2014/continual-innovation-the-key-to-stand-out-and-win-in-retail.html

Oh, L.-B., Teo, H.-H., & Sambamurthy, V. (2012). The effect of retail channel integration through the use of information technologies on firm performance. *Journal of Operations Management, 30*(5), 368–381. doi:10.1016/j.jom.2012.03.001

Oracle. (2011). *The new growth imperative how innovative companies are using unique strategies & channels to drive margin expansion*. Oracle Retail.

Pantano, E., & Di Pietro, L. (2012). Understanding consumer's acceptance of technology-based innovations in retailing. *Journal of Technology Management & Innovation, 7*(4), 1–19. doi:10.4067/S0718-27242012000400001

Pantano, E., Iazzolino, G., & Migliano, G. (2013). Obsolescence risk in advanced technologies for retailing: A management perspective. *Journal of Retailing and Consumer Services, 20*(1), 225–233. doi:10.1016/j.jretconser.2013.01.002

Pantano, E., & Viassone, M. (2012). Consumers' expectation of innovation: shift retail strategies for more attractive points of sale. *International Journal of Digital Content Technology and its Applications, 6*(21), 455-461.

Pantano, E., & Viassone, M. (2014). Demand pull and technology push perspective in technology-based innovations for the points of sale: The retailers evaluation. *Journal of Retailing and Consumer Services, 21*(1), 43–47. doi:10.1016/j.jretconser.2013.06.007

Rudolph, T., & Emrich, O. (2009). Situation-related tasks for mobile services in retailing. *International Review of Retail, Distribution and Consumer Research, 19*(5), 483–503. doi:10.1080/09593960903445285

Ryding, D. (2011). A comparative analysis of the relative importance of service quality for two UK grocery retailers. *Journal of Food Products Marketing, 17*(5), 503–517. doi:10.1080/10454446.2011.618788

Shankar, V., & Yadav, M. (2011). Innovations in retailing. *Journal of Retailing, 87*(July), S1–S2. doi:10.1016/j.jretai.2011.04.004

Sorescu, A., Frambach, R. T., Singh, J., Rangaswamyd, A., & Bridges, C. (2011). Innovations in retail business models. *Journal of Retailing, 87*(1), S3–S16. doi:10.1016/j.jretai.2011.04.005

Tardivo, G., Scilla, A., & Viassone, M. (2013). "Codice QR": Una risposta innovativa per la comunicazione e la soddisfazione del cliente. In *Proceedings of Referred Electronic Conference Proceeding XXV Annual Sinergie Conference* (430-444). Verona: Sinergie.

Tardivo, G., & Viassone, M. (2011). Creating an innovative social assistential performance management system. beyond the economic financial perspective: Empirical research findings. *Journal of Financial Management and Analysis, 23*(2), 99–110.

Venkatesh, V. (2000). Determinants of perceived ease of use: Integrating control, intrinsic motivation, and emotion into the technology acceptance model. *Information Systems Research, 11*(4), 342–365. doi:10.1287/isre.11.4.342.11872

Verhoef, P. C., Lemon, K. N., Parasuraman, A., Roggeveen, A., Tsiros, M., & Schlessinger, L. A. (2009). Customer experience creation: Determinants, dynamics and management strategies. *Journal of Retailing, 85*(March), 31–41. doi:10.1016/j.jretai.2008.11.001

Vrontis, D., & Thrassou, A. (2013). *Innovative business practices: Prevailing a turbolent era.* Newcastle, UK: Cambridge Scholar Publishing.

Wang, M. C.-H. (2012). Determinants and consequences of consumer satisfaction with self-service technology in a retail setting. *Managing Service Quality, 22*(2), 128–144. doi:10.1108/09604521211218945

Yong, C., Gruca, T. S., & Klemz, B. R. (2003). Internet pricing, price satisfaction and customer satisfaction. *International Journal of Electronic Commerce, 8*(2), 31–50.

ADDITIONAL READING

Bandarian, R. (2007). Evaluation of commercial potential of a new technology at the early stage of development with fuzzy logic. *Journal of Technology Management & Innovation, 2*(4), 73–85.

Bhattacherjee, A. (2001). Understanding information systems continuance: An expectation-confirmation model. *Management Information Systems Quarterly, 25*(3), 351–370. doi:10.2307/3250921

Bodhani, A. (2012). Shops offer the e-tail experience. *Engineering and Technology, 7*(5), 46–49. doi:10.1049/et.2012.0512

Chang, H. H., Tsai, Y., & Hsu, C. (2013). Eprocurement and supply chain performance. *Supply Chain Management:An International Journal, 18*(1), 34–51. doi:10.1108/13598541311293168

Chatterjee, P. (2010). Multiple-channel and cross-channel shopping behaviour. *Marketing Intelligence & Planning, 28*(1), 9–24. doi:10.1108/02634501011014589

Chen, Q., Griffith, D., & Wan, F. (2004). The behavioural implications of consumer trust across brick-and-mortar and online retail channels. *Journal of Marketing Channels, 11*(4), 61–87. doi:10.1300/J049v11n04_05

Chiu, Y.-T. H., Fang, S.-C., & Tseng, C.-C. (2010). Early versus potential adopters. Exploring the antecedents of use intention in the context of retail service innovations. *International Journal of Retail & Distribution Management, 38*(6), 443–459. doi:10.1108/09590551011045357

Di Stefano, G., Bambardella, A., & Verona, G. (2012). Technology push and demand pull perspectives in innovation studies: Current findings and future research directions. *Research Policy, 41*(8), 1283–1295. doi:10.1016/j.respol.2012.03.021

Ghosh, A. (1984). Parameter non-stationarity in retail choice models. *Journal of Business Research, 19*(4), 425–436. doi:10.1016/0148-2963(84)90023-7

Hauser, J., Tellis, G. J., & Griffin, A. (2006). Research on innovation: A review and agenda for marketing science. *Informs, 25*(6), 687–717.

Kopalle, P. K. (2010). Modeling retail phenomenon [editorial]. *Journal of Retailing, 86*(June), 117–124. doi:10.1016/j.jretai.2010.04.001

Liu, C., & Forsythe, S. (2011). Examining drivers of online purchase intensity: Moderating role of adoption duration in sustaining post-adoption online shopping. *Journal of Retailing and Consumer Services, 18*(1), 101–109. doi:10.1016/j.jretconser.2010.10.004

Meuter, M. L., Ostrom, A. L., Roundtree, R. I., & Bitner, M. J. (2000). Self-service technologies: Understanding customer satisfaction with technology-based service encounters. *Journal of Marketing, 64*(3), 50–64. doi:10.1509/jmkg.64.3.50.18024

Montoya-Weiss, M., & Grewal, D. (2003). Determinants of online channel use and overall satisfaction

Montoya-Weiss, M. M., Voss, G. B., & Grewal, D. (2003, September 1). with a relational, multichannel service provider. *Journal of the Academy of Marketing Science, 31*(4), 448–458. doi:10.1177/0092070303254408

Nysveen, H., Pedersen, P. E., & Thorbjørnsen, H. (2005). Intentions to use mobile services: Antecedents and cross-service comparisons. *Journal of the Academy of Marketing Science, 33*(3), 330–346. doi:10.1177/0092070305276149

Ohazi, P., Mostaghel, R., Hultamn, M., & Parida, V. (2012). Antecedents of technology-based self-service acceptance: A proposed model. *Services Marketing Quarterly, 33*(3), 195–210. doi:10.10 80/15332969.2012.689937

Park, J., Gunn, F., & Han, S. L. (2012). Multidimensional trust building in e-retailing: Cross-cultural differences in trust formation and implications for perceived risk. *Journal of Retailing and Consumer Services, 19*(3), 304–312. doi:10.1016/j.jretconser.2012.03.003

Rangaswamy, A., & van Bruggen, G. H. (2005). Opportunities and challenges in multichannel marketing. *Journal of Interactive Marketing, 19*(2), 5–12. doi:10.1002/dir.20037

Rosenbloom, B. (2007). Multi-channel strategy in business-to-business markets: Prospects and problems. *Industrial Marketing Management, 36*(January), 4–9. doi:10.1016/j.indmarman.2006.06.010

Saleem, Z., & Rashid, K. (2011). Relationship between customer satisfaction and mobile banking adoption in Pakistan. *International Journal of Trade. Economics and Finance, 2*(6), 537–544.

Schierz, P. G., Schilke, O., & Wirtz, B. W. (2010). Understanding consumer acceptance of mobile payment services: An empirical analysis. *Electronic Commerce Research and Applications, 9*(3), 209–216. doi:10.1016/j.elerap.2009.07.005

Wang, M. C.-H. (2012). Determinants and consequences of consumer satisfaction with self-service technology in a retail setting. *Managing Service Quality, 22*(2), 128–144. doi:10.1108/09604521211218945

Wood, S., & Reynolds, J. (2013). Knowledge management, organisational learning and memory in UK retail network planning. *Service Industries Journal*, *33*(2), 150–170. doi:10.1080/02642069.2011.614340

Yan, R. L., & Pei, Z. (2009). Retail services and firm profit in a dual-channel market. *Journal of Retailing and Consumer Services*, *16*(4), 306–314. doi:10.1016/j.jretconser.2009.02.006

Yao, D. Q., Yue, X., Mukhopadhyay, S., & Wang, Z. P. (2009). Strategic inventory deployment for retail and E-tail stores. *Omega*, *37*(3), 646–658. doi:10.1016/j.omega.2008.04.001

KEY TERMS AND DEFINITIONS

Benchmark: The process of comparing one's business processes to industry bests or best practices from other industries.

E-Commerce: The act of buying and selling products/services by customers throughout electronic medium without the use of paper documents.

Hybrid Systems: Systems based on retailers' own technologies that users can move around the store, generally based on RFID.

Intelligent Shopping Trolleys: Traditional shopping trolleys enriched with systems able to interact with consumers through ease of use interfaces, provide more information, localize the consumer's position and propose the best path for reaching the selected items.

Multichannel Retailing: A marketing strategy that offers customers a choice of ways to buy products; it consists in the use of a variety of channels in a customer shopping experience including research before a purchase.

Self-Service Technologies: Technological interfaces allowing customers to produce services independent of involvement of direct service employee.

Systems for Mobile: Systems for consumers' own mobile phones, able to provide interactive contents and services for enriching consumers' in-store shopping experience.

Chapter 11
Radical and Incremental Innovation Effectiveness in Relation to Market Orientation in the Retail Industry:
Triggers, Drivers, and Supporters

Michael Lewrick
University Ulm, Germany

Robert Williams Jr.
Susquehanna University, USA

Maktoba Omar
Edinburgh Napier University, UK

Nathalia C. Tjandra
Edinburgh Napier University, UK

Zui-Chih Lee
Susquehanna University, USA

ABSTRACT

The retail industry market environment is very competitive; thus, in order to maintain their competitive advantage retailers are required to continuously come up with innovative offerings and systems. This chapter aims to provide useful insights for the retailers regarding the correlation between market orientation and innovation. The chapter illustrates the differences in start-up and mature companies, and reveals new insights with regard to market orientation and its constituent elements, and its relationship with both incremental and radical innovations. Readers learn that strong competitor orientation, a key ingredient of market orientation, has a positive relationship to incremental innovation for start-up companies, but it is counterproductive for mature companies, where a strong customer orientation is associated with radical innovation. The focus is to understand the dynamics of the entrepreneur versus manager during the transition process as a company grows.

INTRODUCTION

The business demands of a decentralized, networked, globalized, post-industrial environment forces enterprises to respond dynamically, and to continuously adapt their innovation style to not only prosper, but to survive. The first objective of this chapter is to evaluate the current level of technology innovation and the components of market orientation in general, and within the

DOI: 10.4018/978-1-4666-8297-9.ch011

retail sector specifically. The second objective is to empirically investigate and discuss the link between market orientation and innovation within the context of start-up and mature companies. The final objective is to provide solutions and recommendations as to how retail companies can enhance their performance and encourage innovation. The chapter acknowledges that innovators improve competitive advantage, foster growth, and create opportunities in new markets, thus it investigates the transformation process in the growth of innovative companies by analyzing the effects of different parameters of market orientation on radical and incremental innovation. Finally, it looks at the influencing factors that change during implementation of different innovation styles.

Background

This study investigates the effects of different parameters of market orientation on radical and incremental innovation in both start-up and mature companies. This contrasts to other research in this area, as distinguishing between start-up and mature companies yields new insights about the transformation process in the growth of innovative companies. Market orientation is generally recognized as part of the business strategy of companies and it is considered as an important strategic orientation in literature (Gatignon & Xuereb, 1997; Hunt & Lambe, 2000). Studies identify that market orientation is an important determinant of firm performance and positively affects retail performance (Chung, 2013; Liu & Davies, 1997; Panigyrakis & Theodoridis, 2007; Theodoridis & Panigyrakis, 2011). The concept of market orientation as a business strategy includes the collection of market relevant information. The information is distributed within the organisation with the aim to align products and services to customer needs. The foundation of this is based on the "marketing concept" (Drucker, 1954; Levitt, 1960). However,

market orientation goes beyond the concept and it is associated with the implementation of this approach (Wren, 1997).

To be market orientated implies that the firm embraces a strategy to obtain and use information about the environment and to disseminate this information throughout the firm. As mentioned before, the foundation of the marketing discipline is the "marketing concept" and the origin of this concept is in the focus by the firm on the customer and their needs (Drucker, 1954; Levitt, 1960).

In the context of this study innovation is measured by three categories: counts of incremental, radical and overall innovation. Incremental innovations are the improvements/expansions of existing products, services, processes, technical or administrative conditions. Incremental innovation does not cause a significant departure from the status-quo. In contrast, radical innovations in products, services, processes, etc. are breakthroughs that fundamentally change a product or service or process. Overall innovativeness is the total of all innovations put into practice, both radical and incremental in all typologies. These categories have been clearly identified as measures of innovatory activity by a number of authors (Garcia & Calantone, 2002; Gatignon et al., 2002; Tidd et al., 2003; Utterback, 1996).

Market orientation can be defined as the organizational culture that most effectively and efficiently creates the necessary behaviors for the creation of superior value for customers and, thus, superior performance for the business (Narver & Slater, 1990). The term market orientation has been used in many directions and often the terms customer focused, market driven, and customer centric have become terms associated with market orientation (Deshpande, 1999). Within this study market orientation is considered to consist of four pillars (a) customer centric, (b) customer intelligence, (c) competitor orientation, and (d) market dynamism. A more comprehensive definition of each dimension of market orientation is outlined later.

In the following section a short literature review is given, first to assess the current level of technology innovation, and then to tease out the definition of the components of market orientation. Afterwards the key questions of the research instrument and research design with two key hypotheses to test in this study are outlined. The link between market orientation and innovation is demonstrated and from this the variation between start-up and mature companies is discussed. Recommendations as to how performance of a firm can be enhanced are then made, within the context of the retail marketplace.

Retail Industry

The two key retail industry drivers are to foster customer loyalty, and drive sales and growth. Innovation can have a critical impact on these drivers. One base-line indication of technological innovation in the retail industry, albeit somewhat dated, can be gleaned from the Community Innovation Survey (CIS) which examines service industries in Europe. In work done by Miles (2008) we see that in the UK when plotting technology innovation (product & process) versus organizational innovation (including marketing change), the retail industry ranked basically as the smallest share of firms implementing technology innovation. More recent research indicates the emphasis on technology implementation to provide consumers with information and services in a way they can customize (Puccinelli et al., 2009; Reinders et al., 2008) as well as providing managers with consumers' behavior and preference data (C. M. Chiu, Huang, & Yen, 2010; P. H. Chiu, Kao, & Lo, 2010). The importance of the Technology Acceptance Model (Davis, 1989) for the retail sector was identified by numerous authors and was grouped into 10 variables in four main areas: consumer's perception of technology safety and cost, consumer's personal traits, social pressure, and hedonic value (Pantano & Di Pietro, 2012).

The retail industry sector can be categorized into six areas of innovation having the greatest impact today (European Commission, 2014): (1) Reducing effort for customers; (2) Consumers as innovation drivers; (3) Business Model innovation; (4) Brand Development; (5) Education and training; (6) Technology.

To reduce effort for customers and/or utilizing consumers as innovation drivers, retailers are increasingly turning toward self-service technologies (SSTs) aimed at improving productivity and service quality while cutting costs. Weijters et al. (2007) identify a process model to understand the antecedents and consequences of SST from the customers' perspective toward an in-store retail setting. Retailers' efforts to increase perceived usefulness, perceived ease of use, reliability, and fun were identified as key drivers of customer attitude toward innovation of SST. Customer attitude toward the SST also predicted their actual time usage of technology in the store. The positive impact of self-service technologies (SST) usage actually help customers' perceptions of waiting time and, consequently, on their level of satisfaction. Higher satisfaction, intentions to use the self-service technologies (SST) and the likelihood of participating in positive word-of-mouth happened in consumers' retailing experience when they feel lower technology anxiety (TA) (Meuter et al., 2003). Seeking to utilize SST innovation to fit the customers' expectation of service, the theory advanced by Dabholker et al. (2003) suggests the factors driving customer preference or avoidance of self-scanning checkouts include the attributes of self-scanners; consumer differences; and situational influences.

SST of self-scanning is being tested by major supermarket chains as well as other types of retailers across the world. Other examples include researching items online before 'brick & mortar' purchases, or showrooming – where customers browse in the physical store first and then purchase it online at a lower price. One solution to this online/offline activity can include real-time price matching, which negates any pricing advantages.

When looking at innovations in Retail Business Models themselves, Sorescu et al. (2011) highlight the need to stay abreast of and incorporate new consumer-facing product and/or process innovations (Shankar et al., 2011) as well as technologies themselves that could "disrupt" a retailer's product offering. The extensive use of social media by today's consumers necessitates that retailers use this technology both as an advertising communication channel medium, but also as *exchange media* (Sorescu et al. 2011).

An example of brand development (product innovation) is seen in Isfi Spices, Inc., an SME which specializes in retail own (private label) brand development of herbs & spices. They take only three weeks to develop and introduce a new brand (product) for major retailers, versus the 6 months the retailer needs to do it in-house.

Education and training is necessary to develop creative and entrepreneurial knowledge and skills in the retail industry. The Institute of Retail Management of St. Gallen University offers a program in Cross-Channel Management for retail managers, while the Oxford Institute of Retail Management provides Loyalty Marketing Workshops to enhance purchasing by consumers, by focusing on creating loyalty programs that manage customer relationships.

Four aspects of Technology to consider in the retail environment include eCommerce, data analytics, inter-firm technology functions, and software platforms. For example, Amazon's acquisition of Twitch gives them a technology platform for a new segment of video game advertising and sales. Software from Oracle (Retail version 14) utilizes channel-synthesizing technology to support processes that assist customers to buy, pickup, or return items via any retail multichannel without constraints. H&M is experimenting with virtual reality applied to clothes purchasing, while the Virtual Makeover product offering from EZface Inc. applies virtual technology on any platform for makeup, coloring, and accessories. METRO Group uses online reverse auctions; ASOS Inc.

offers live mapping to track deliveries real-time, and one of the world's largest retailers, Tesco, introduced their own 7-inch tablet for in-store shopping. Indeed, many CIOs and CMOs refer to CX – the Customer eXperience – to include a wide range of cloud and technology solutions such as loyalty apps, to complement existing CRM strategies (Foley, 2014).

With increasing competition and a growing need for operational efficiencies and customer orientation, retailers are looking beyond their organizational limitations to develop the resources and capabilities of their chain partners to create superior value and competitive advantages in the marketplace. Recent trends such as global sourcing, multichannel markets, and relationship-based innovation are transforming the retail landscape in regards to brand image, reputation, sales and profits, and relationships (Ganesan et al., 2009)

Dedrick et al. (2010) analyzes the distribution of financial value from innovation in the global supply chains of iPods and notebook computers and finds that Apple has captured a great deal of value from the innovation embodied in the iPod, while notebook makers capture a better share of the value from PC innovation. This growing attention to seek important factors in determining whether a company competes effectively in its chosen markets reveals a concern with technology application of customer communication and product delivery in banking service (James, 1995). Thus, technology formulated its critical role as a convenient, cheap, and efficient retailing service (e.g., mobile banking service, Kiosk distribution). Studies further focus on innovation's impact on a company's performance between internet-enabled and non-internet-enabled product/process innovations, and it is positively associated with turnover and employment growth (Koellinger, 2008).

Different from product innovation, companies also seek ways to optimize their shipping processes such as radio frequency identification (RFID) adoption and the electronic product code (EPC) which impacts their mobile B2B, eCommerce and supply chain projects. Technology fosters a higher level of information sharing/synchronization between supply chain members and provides an integration perspective of the benefits of innovation (Wamba et al., 2008). Indeed, due to the penetration of the Internet and information accessibility into the shopping process, Amazon.com, the world's largest online retailer, uses a wide range of customer data metrics to predict which products will be popular in different areas of the country, and then ship them to its hubs in that area. This "anticipatory shipping" enables greater 'same-day-delivery' services, and forces all retailers to increase their use of technology.

Innovation and Market Orientation

The deliberate management of a climate supportive of innovation is a key challenge for those who lead and manage organizations (Isaksen & Ekvall, 2010). The last decade was driven by globalization, the transformation from the industrial society into the service-, information- and knowledge-society, and the development from central, hierarchical organizational structures towards decentralised and connected organizational structures (Brink & Holmén, 2009; Hopfenbeck et al., 2001). As a result, enterprises have to respond dynamically and change their innovation style continuously to survive in such an environment. It becomes essential to know which kind of innovation pattern leads to success while a business grows in revenue, corporate size and functional complexity. The question is not of whether or not to innovate, but rather what are the influencing factors that change as innovation styles are implemented? Is it the customer, the social network, R&D, experience, organization learning or merely knowledge applied at the right time and place?

The positive influence of market orientation to business success has been addressed in several studies (Cano et al., 2004; Gainer & Padanyi, 2002; Hult et al., 2005; Kara et al., 2005; Zhou et al., 2005). The relationship between market ori-

entation and innovations has been also addressed (Gatignon & Xuereb, 1997; Lewrick et al. 2011; Ruekert, 1992; Slater & Narver, 1994). Kohli and Jaworksi suggest that, "market orientation entails: (1) one or more departments engaging in activities geared toward developing an understanding of customers' current and future needs and the factors affecting them; (2) sharing of this understanding across departments; and (3) the various departments engaging in activities designed to meet select customers' needs" (1990 p.3).

The cross-functional share of information and knowledge might trigger invention and streamline the innovation process leading to market success. However, the negative influence of market orientation, especially on radical innovations, has been detected (Bennett & Cooper, 1979; Lawton & Parasuraman, 1980). Lawton and Parasuraman (1980) revealed in a study that the adoption of the marketing concept did not affect the success of new product ideas in the market or the innovativeness of new product offerings. Other scholars concluded that a strong customer orientation has a negative impact on market success of new products and services (Christensen & Bower, 1996; Leonard-Barton et al., 1996), while others claim that customer orientation leads to more innovations (Von Hippel, 2005). Market and business opportunities might arise from extensive research and will reach the market via the push effect, or the market has the need for something different or new – the pull effect. Both approaches (push and pull) might be essential to be innovative and Tidd et al. (2003) comment that: "sometimes the "push" will dominate, sometimes the "pull", but successful innovations require interaction between the two" (p.43).

A broad literature review reveals various approaches towards innovation management. The research spectrum ranges from multidimensional to one-dimensional typologies which results in the creation of multidimensional and one-dimensional scales and validations. Common typologies are: product/services, organization/processes, strategy/

business and administrative/technical, extended by the degree of novelty, which distinguishes radical from incremental innovations. Most research focused on a single sector, R&D project or merely one typology, e.g. product/service innovations. With regard to the organizational variables on innovation it seems that there is a discrepancy in the outcomes. A good example of such discrepancy is the correlation between the age of a company and innovativeness – in some cases age is positively related to innovation (Sorensen & Stuart, 2000), while the opposite can also be found (Boeker, 1997). The same conflicting results can be recognized on the influence of diversification (Ahuja & Lampert, 2001; Ahuja, 2000; Boeker, 1997), centralization (Cardinal, 2001; Sivadas & Dwyer, 2000), size of the organization (Koberg et al., 2003; Landry et al., 2002; Stringer, 2000; Thether, 2002), management styles (Williams & Omar, 2009) and resource levels/resource-based-view on innovation. This theory of dynamic capabilities is built on the influencing factors of the firm's environment (Eisenhardt & Martin, 2000; Teece et al., 1997). While some scholars see dynamic capabilities as the key success factor for competitive advantage, other argues that such capabilities do not exist (Winter, 2003). Still others focus on the tenure level of management without finding a clear correlation to innovativeness (Kimberly & Evanisko, 1981; Meyer & Goes, 1988; Rao & Drazin, 2002).

On the other hand, some variables seem proven from various research. For example, it holds common wisdom that an external factor such as a dynamic environment forces companies to innovate and adapt (Meyer & Goes, 1988; Nohria & Gulati, 1996). In such a dynamic environment firms more often seek risks and innovate (Kahneman & Tversky, 1979). The strong influence and correlation of individuals to the innovation process has been addressed by many scholars (Keister, 2002; Rao & Drazin, 2002; Sivadas & Dwyer, 2000). Other scholars analyzed the influence of an integrated product development process on in-

novation (Gerwin & Barrowman, 2002) or focused solely on the development of new products (Brown & Eisenhardt, 1995; Krishnan & Ulrich, 2000). The list could be expanded endlessly, reviewing the different dimensions tested with the various outcomes.

Some studies investigate the market orientation and innovation of new ventures or small firms and their success (Audretsch, 2001; Cohen & Klepper, 1992; Hyvonen & Tuominen, 2006; Lewrick et al. 2010; Verbees, Matthew, & Meulenberg, 2004). Lewrick et al. (2011, p.48) has analyzed the differences between start-up and mature companies and the change in their behavior over time i.e. their transition, and found that "strong competitor orientation (market orientation) has a positive relationship to incremental innovation for start-up companies but it is contra productive for mature companies [where] a strong customer orientation is associated with radical innovation". It can be summarized that most of the empirical studies on innovation are mainly focused on specific industries or in a specific project analyzed over the time perspective. Holistic cross sector analyses have not obtained the attention of researchers to identify the change in capabilities applied in growing companies. In addition, the transition process from a start-up phase to a more mature phase of business cannot be found in this connection at all.

Customer Centricity and Customer Intelligence

The customer has become recognized as a dominant influence on company strategy and can be defined as a co-creator of value. The extent of the company's interaction with customers can be quantified and qualified by the amount of data collected, analysis of customer needs and information relevant to realize innovations. However, the customer as co-developer for new products and services differ in start-up and mature companies (Lewrick, 2004). Kohli and Jaworski (1990) recognized the importance of customer focus, but in their definition market intelligence is at the centre of market orientation. In this conjunction, market intelligence includes ascertaining current and future customer needs, dissemination of the intelligence across departments, and organisation-wide responsiveness to customer needs. They introduce market intelligence instead of customer focus since in their view market intelligence is much broader than customer focus. However, within this study customer centricity includes the integration of customer needs and strategies as well as the processes of an organisation. Customer intelligence is the knowledge about the customer which might be collected e.g. by focus groups, surveys and observation. Previous research suggests that understanding customers increases the value of innovation created in the product and service development process. In addition, it was suggested that intelligence dissemination in a retail system would influence its overall market orientation (Elg, 2003). Von Hippel (2005) pointed out that some customers of products might be ahead of the trend and can drive the development of new products. Lukas and Ferrell (2000) also found that customer orientation increases the introduction of new-to-the world products and reduces the launching of "me-too products". Hence, it can be hypothesized that market needs drive innovations.

Competitor Orientation

Organizations that are focused on their competitors are less likely to come up with radical innovations. A strong competitor orientation causes *"me-too"* products and incremental innovations (Lukas and Ferrell, 2000). According to Narver and Slater (1990) competitor orientation, an element of market orientation, means that "a seller understands the short-term strengths and weaknesses and long-term capabilities and strategies of both the key current and potential competitors" (p.21-22). Previous studies highlight the short term thinking of new ventures and argued the need for more long-term thinking and strategic competitive positioning (Amer & Bain, 1990; Robinson & Pearce, 1984).

Market Dynamism

Competition is seen as a key influencing factor for innovativeness (Kimberly & Evanisko, 1981; Utterback, 1974). Start-up and mature companies operating in environments characterized by dynamic competition are forced to create innovative products and services and innovations are correlated to risky actions to create superior performance (Barney, 1991). More recent research explored a positive relationship between market orientation and innovation integrated in the amount of innovations implemented (Lukas & Ferrell, 2000). It seems that entrepreneurs and managers must scan the market more carefully in a highly competitive environment. However, market orientation by itself does not help to create value from market dynamism: it needs both management and knowledge creation capabilities (Lewrick, 2007). Essential drivers might be management experience, management tenure, inter-organizational networks as well as the ability of organizational learning. Within this study market dynamism is defined as the change of technology, customer needs, and the actions of competitors. It is assumed that dynamic markets are unpredictable with regard to the competitive conditions.

MAIN FOCUS OF THE CHAPTER

The focus of this chapter is to understand the dynamics of the entrepreneur versus manager during the transition process as a company grows, and to suggest beneficial applications in the retail industry context. The transition process of a company from start-up phase to a more mature phase seeks to first explore the settings of the entrepreneur. Schumpeter (1934) defines the entrepreneur as an innovator, implementing change within markets, by carrying out new combinations. The new combinations are seen in different ways:

1. The introduction of a new good or quality thereof,
2. The introduction of a new method of production,
3. The opening of a new market,
4. The conquest of a new source of supply of new materials or parts,
5. The carrying out of the new organization of any industry.

Schumpeter associated entrepreneurship with the thought of innovation applied to a wide business context. As a result, the entrepreneur shifts the market away from equilibrium. Schumpter's definition also highlights the combination of various resources. However, the managers of already established business are not entrepreneurs according to Schumpeter. Penrose (1963) agrees with Schumpeter and suggests that managerial capacities are different from entrepreneurial capacities. He characterizes entrepreneurial activities as an activity of identifying opportunities within the economic system. However, to come up with radical innovations the common characteristics of entrepreneurs which mainly consist of behaviours, personal attributes and skills, must somehow exist in innovative mature companies. Gibb, (2000) summarizes such behaviour as:

1. Opportunity seeking and grasping,
2. Taking the initiatives to make things happen,
3. Solving problems creatively,
4. Managing autonomously,
5. Taking responsibility for, and ownership of, things;
6. Seeing things through,
7. Networking effectively to manage interdependence;
8. Putting things together creatively, and
9. Using judgment to take calculated risks.

In addition to the individualities of the entrepreneur, he/she needs strength to influence the growth and to undergo strategic decisions. The skills needed to successfully start a business are often not those essential for growth and even more often not those required to manage it once it grows to any size (Di-Masi, 2000). To manage the transition, time-honored change management approaches (e.g. the three stage change model "unfreezing", "change", and "refreezing") are not adequate in turbulent, flexible and uncertain organizational and environmental conditions (Brink & Holmén, 2009; Orlikowski & Baroudi, 1991). Hence, the entrepreneur in the "transition" is more challenged to manage the *anticipated* changes (changes planned ahead of time and occur as intended) and *emergent* changes (changes that arise unexpectedly out of new opportunities, local innovations and which are originally not intended) (Mintzberg, 1987). The complexity of the system and influencing factors are increasing over the time perspective. Other factors might become the drives for change; like economic policies, social norms, ties and networks.

Research Question, Framework, and Hypotheses

The following research question can be formulated: What are the influencing factors that impact changes in innovation styles? How do firms change their innovation styles over the time perspective? Is it possible to identify a general pattern of when and how changes in innovation styles occur?

The development of the two research instruments (for start-up and mature companies) was based on literature review to identify the critical factors and constraints with regard to innovativeness, knowledge management, entrepreneurship, and social networks. The two research instruments are built on various capabilities and influencing factors in the categories:

1. **Environment:** Competition, turbulences, legislation, government policy, etc.,
2. **Organization:** Age, size, centralization, competitor orientation, customer orientation, complexity, diversification and learning, past innovation, interfunctional coordination,

organizational networks, interorganizational networks, resources, knowledge skills, risk awareness, technology influence, business strategy, etc.,

3. **Management:** Education, tenure, openness to change, professionalism, etc., and

4. **Outcome:** Financial performance, efficiency.

Such an approach aims to create the big picture. As mentioned earlier, the dynamic business environment makes it mandatory to combine different business resources to achieve innovation. It is habitually agreed to categorize business resources into tangible (physical, financial), intangible (technology, reputation, and culture) and human (skills/ know-how, capacity for communication and collaboration, and motivation) (Gram, 2002).

The research instrument addresses diverse innovation typologies by exploring incremental and radical innovations in processes, products, services, administration, and technology. For each element the research instruments ask for the number of innovations in a typical year to understand the effects of both incremental and radical innovation for each of the typologies.

In the end of each block of questions the research instrument (mature) asks about the past to understand how the company changed the operational practice and how it affected their innovativeness. In contrast the research instrument (start-up) asks in the end of each block of questions about the future, how companies strategize to act in two years' time. Such an approach allows us to identify various gaps between the present situation and the desired end, compared to the reality of mature companies and their original inspirations

The hypotheses tested in this analysis are built on the central question: what are the influencing factors and capabilities for radical innovations and incremental innovations. This is based on the assumption that radical innovations improve competitive advantage, foster growth and create opportunities in new markets (Lynn, Morone, & Paulson, 1996; C. McDermott & Handfield, 2000;

McDermott & O'Connor, 2002). On a macro perspective, start-ups in general, and innovative start-ups in particular are seen as an important factor for economic growth and job creation (Birch, 1979; Brüderl & Preisendörfer, 1998; Dejardin, 2002; Kirchhoff, 1994; Storey & Tether, 1996). The hypotheses have developed around the following 12 capabilities: customer orientation, competitor orientation, market and competitive environment, centralisation vs. decentralisation, diversification and learning, management of knowledge, education level of management, management tenure, organisational social network, interorganizational social network, performance outcomes, and efficiency outcomes. The hypotheses are outlined below.

Customer Orientation: Understanding customers increases the value of innovation created in the product development process. Some customers of products might be ahead of the trend and develop really new products (Von Hippel, 2005). Lukas and Ferrell (2000) also that customer orientation increases the introduction of new-to-the world products and reduces the launching of me-too products. It seems that market needs drive innovations. Based on this, the following is hypothesized:

Hypothesis H1 (radical innovations):

$H_{0(r)}$: There is no relation of customer orientation to radical innovation.

$H_{a(r)}$: Customer orientation is related to radical innovations.

Hypothesis H1 (incremental innovations):

$H_{0(i)}$: There is no relation of customer orientation to incremental innovation.

$H_{a(i)}$: Customer orientation is related to incremental innovations.

- **Competitor Orientation:** Organisations that are focused on their competitors are less likely to come up with radical innovations. A strong competitor orientation causes "me-too" products and incremental innovations (Lukas & Ferrell, 2000). Based on this, the following is hypothesized:

Hypothesis H2 (radical innovations):

$H_{0(r)}$: There is no relation of competitor orientation to radical innovation.
$H_{a(r)}$: Competitor orientation is related to radical innovations.

Hypothesis H2 (incremental innovations):

$H_{0(i)}$: There is no relation of competitor orientation to incremental innovation.
$H_{a(i)}$: Competitor orientation is related to incremental innovations.

- **Market and Competitive Environment:** Common wisdom holds that competition is an influencing factor and driver for innovativeness (Kimberly & Evanisko, 1981). More recent research explored a positive relationship between market orientation and the amount of innovations implemented (Hurley & Hult, 1998; Lukas & Ferrell, 2000). Entrepreneurs and managers must scan the market more carefully in a highly competitive environment. Consequently, innovation is necessary to survive and grow. Based on this, the following is hypothesized:

Hypothesis H3 (radical innovations):

$H_{0(r)}$: There is no relation of the competitive environment to radical innovation.
$H_{a(r)}$: Competitor Environment is related to radical innovations.

Hypothesis H3 (incremental innovations):

$H_{0(i)}$: There is no relation of the competitive environment to incremental innovation.

$H_{a(i)}$: Competitor Environment is related to incremental innovations.

- **Company Characteristic-Centralisation:** There is agreement that centralisation supports the process to discover innovations. However, centralisation in larger and more mature companies does not allow involvement of lower level employees. Consequently, they do not feel involved in the innovation process. Centralisation does not support communication and knowledge transfer but it is obviously necessary to be innovative (Khan & Manopichetwattana, 1989). On the other side, the concentration of power is necessary for the successful change process and associated with the capability to be innovative (Dewer and Dutton, 1986). Based on this, the following is hypothesized:

Hypothesis H4 (radical innovations):

$H_{0(r)}$: There is no relation of centralised inter-functional coordination to radical innovation.
$H_{a(r)}$: Centralised inter-functional coordination is related to radical innovations.

Hypothesis H4 (incremental innovations):

$H_{0(i)}$: There is no relation of centralised inter-functional coordination to incremental innovation.
$H_{a(i)}$: Centralized inter-functional coordination is related to incremental innovations.

- **Diversification and Learning:** A diverse portfolio of products and services has an impact on R&D because resources have to be split between several R&D activities. Consequently, the number of resources allocated to R&D has an impact to innovativeness (Boeker, 1997; Hoskisson et al., 2001). However, diversification causes more knowledge that can be used for inventions and promotes the dissemination of diverse ideas (Day, 1994; Hitt et al., 1996).

Hypothesis H5 (radical innovations):

$H_{0(r)}$: There is no relation of diversification/exploration to radical innovation.

$H_{a(r)}$: Diversification/exploration is related to radical innovations.

Hypothesis H5 (incremental innovations):

$H_{0(i)}$: There is no relation of diversification/exploration to incremental innovation.

$H_{a(i)}$: Diversification/exploration is related to incremental innovations.

- **Innovation Capabilities - Knowledge:** There is common understanding that knowledge/skills are essential to explore tomorrow's capabilities (Leonard, 1998). The challenge is that some knowledge becomes redundant or is not available at certain time and therefore it has to be acquired.

Hypothesis H6 (radical innovations):

$H_{0(r)}$: There is no relation of active knowledge/skills seeking to radical innovation.

$H_{a(r)}$: Active knowledge/skills seeking is related to radical innovations.

Hypothesis H6 (incremental innovations):

$H_{0(i)}$: There is no relation of active knowledge/skills seeking to incremental innovation.

$H_{a(i)}$: Active knowledge/skills seeking is related to incremental innovations.

- **Innovation Capabilities - Management (Education):** Common wisdom holds that managers/entrepreneurs with higher education tend to be more open minded with regard to organisational change. In general, education is also thought to support the better understanding of diverse information that in turn enables innovativeness (Blind & Grupp, 1999; Faber & Hesen, 2004).

Hypothesis H7 (radical innovations):

$H_{0(r)}$: There is no relation of higher education of the manager/entrepreneur to radical innovation.

$H_{a(r)}$: Higher education of the manager/entrepreneur is related to radical innovations.

Hypothesis H7 (incremental innovations):

$H_{0(i)}$: There is no relation of higher education of the manager/entrepreneur to incremental innovation.

$H_{a(i)}$: Higher education of the manager/entrepreneur is related to incremental innovations.

- **Management (Tenure):** Changes in innovation styles occur over time. Generally it is assumed that managers with longer tenure have the knowledge and experience to accomplish objectives, manage office politics, and accomplish organisation targets. However, managers with higher levels of tenure are less open for new ideas or radical changes caused by a fear of losing the status quo, and strategic persistence (Ancona & Caldwell, 1992; Boeker, 1997; Finkelstein & Hambrick, 1990; Grimm & Smith, 1991; Katz, 1982; Wiersema & Bantel, 1992).

Hypothesis H8 (radical innovations):

$H_{0(r)}$: There is no relation of high tenure to radical innovation.

$H_{a(r)}$: High tenure is related to radical innovations.

Hypothesis H8 (incremental innovations):

$H_{0(i)}$: There is no relation of high tenure to incremental innovation.

$H_{a(i)}$: High tenure is related to incremental innovations.

- **Social Network (Organisational):** Innovations occur within collaborative activities between R&D, marketing, manufacturing and other functions (Hagedoorn, 2002; Zahra et al., 2000). Common wisdom holds that collaborative activities foster company's capabilities to be innovative. Within the start-up activities the entrepreneur utilizes his personal networks of peers and family which can play a crucial part (Rosenblatt et al., 1985).

Hypothesis H9 (radical innovations):

$H_{0(r)}$: There is no relation of collaborative activities to radical innovation.

$H_{a(r)}$: Collaborative activities are related to radical innovations.

Hypothesis H9 (incremental innovations):

$H_{0(i)}$: There is no relation of collaborative activities to incremental innovation.

$H_{a(i)}$: Collaborative activities are related to incremental innovations.

- **Social Network (Inter-Organisational):** Innovation is often linked to the inter-organisational networks between companies. Start-ups and less established companies especially benefit from inter-organisational networks (Baum et al., 2000; Shan, Walker, & Kogut, 1994; Stuart, 2000). Some scholars incorporate a broader view on social capital and include elements of friendship, trust, and reciprocity (Coleman, 1988; Nahapiet & Ghoshal, 1998). Common wisdom holds that

innovative companies have a greater readiness to cooperate and establish themselves in a central position within the alliance network.

Hypothesis H10 (radical innovations):

$H_{0(r)}$: There is no relation of a central position in a network to radical innovation.

$H_{a(i)}$: A central position in the network is related to radical innovations.

Hypothesis H10 (incremental innovations):

$H_{0(i)}$: There is no relation of a central position in a network to incremental innovation.

$H_{a(i)}$: A central position in the network is related to incremental innovations.

- **Outcomes (Performance):** Innovations are essential to gain competitive advantage (Ahuja, 2000; Stephens et al., 1999). In addition, innovations deliver more value for customers and customers are more likely to purchase the innovations that can strengthen financial performance. However, an innovation needs a great amount of resources and is linked to internal risks. In case the market is not ready for the innovation, financial performance decreases (Markham & Griffin, 1998).

Hypothesis H11 (radical innovations):

$H_{0(r)}$: There is no relation of financial performance to radical innovation.

$H_{a(r)}$: Financial Performance is related to radical innovations.

Hypothesis H11 (incremental innovations):

$H_{0(i)}$: There is no relation of financial performance to incremental innovation.

$H_{a(i)}$: Financial Performance is related to incremental innovations.

- **Outcome (Efficiency):** In some cases, especially in process innovations, organisational efficiency is crucial. Organisations are able to improve efficiency through innovation. However, innovation requires resources, set-up costs and investment that might cause inefficiency in the short run. For example, inefficiency occurs when companies do not minimize the cost of producing the outputs (Leibenstein, 1966). Inefficiency might also occur due to a lack of competition or incentive to minimize cost within a company. Implementing significant new ideas involves the ability to manage risk, including minimizing harmful consequences while maximizing opportunities.

Hypothesis II12 (radical innovations):

$H_{0(r)}$: There is no relation of efficiency to radical innovation.

$H_{a(r)}$: Efficiency is related to radical innovations.

Hypothesis H12 (incremental innovations):

$H_{0(i)}$: There is no relation of efficiency to incremental innovation.

$H_{a(i)}$: Efficiency is related to incremental innovations.

The categories of innovation are context-dependent and influenced by antecedents clustered in basic company data and characteristics, product/service development (including customer orientation, competitor orientation, market and competitive environment, diversification and learning); innovativeness (including amount of incremental and radical innovations realized in the typologies: processes, products, services, administration, technology; incremental, and radical innovation performance; resources for innovations); innovation capability (including knowledge and management); social networks (including organisational networks and inter-organisational networks); and outcomes (e.g. measurement tools for innovations) (see (Russell, 1990). The hypotheses are tested on two surveys, a) start-up companies – b) mature companies, and on three major performance levels,

1. Low performer (LP),
2. Average performer (AP), and
3. High Performer (HP).

The comparison of these profiles is the central point of analysis to identify the changes over the time perspective.

Both research instruments start with general questions about the company and biographical information. Within the first part it is asked which sector the company belongs to? What are the core competences? How long has the company existed? How many employees work for the company? Which position does the respondent hold and his/her tenure of managing innovations? How was the company founded (e.g. start-up, incubator, spin-off, MBO, etc.)? The second part of the research instrument is followed by four question blocks about Customer Orientation; Competitor Orientation; Market and Competitive Environment; Diversification and Learning. In the third part, for each typology (process, product, service, administration, and technology) the number of realized innovations in a typical year is prompted. With the overall emphasis to explore more about radical innovations an additional block of questions explores what constrains and promotes radical innovations; namely Finance, Legislation, Government Policy, and Supply Chain (obtaining materials). "Innovation Capabilities" has two major blocks of questions, Knowledge and Management; "Social Networks" asks about the organizational network (within the company) and about the interorganizational network (between companies), while "Outcomes" is structured to obtain insights about internal risk awareness and evolution of innovations.

A total of 171 companies have been analysed out of 216 participants from a population of 530 companies. Out of the realisable 171, 55 (32.2%) of the companies that participated in the survey were start-ups, and 116 (67.8%) were mature companies. To explore the change in innovation capabilities two major characteristics are of importance. Firstly, the identification of a location with a high amount of technology driven start-up as well as mature companies. Secondly, related platforms on which all of these companies have been founded. The combination of both was particularly available in the innovative region around Munich, in combination with the incumbent regional *Munich Business Plan Competition*. The Munich region offers outstanding innovative companies, active in the fields of Information and Telecommunication, BioTech, Aerospace, Software, Electronic Components, as well other centre of competencies of various sectors. Moreover, Munich is one of the world's five most interesting high-tech locations alongside Silicon Valley, Boston, Tel Aviv and Austin, Texas. The second condition (unitary platform) is enabled by utilizing the Munich Business Plan Competition. Since 1996, this platform "produced" over 400 companies. The competition is derived from the MIT idea to establish a platform for universities, entrepreneurs, and venture capitalists to set-up innovative companies to foster growth in the region.

SOLUTIONS AND RECOMMENDATIONS

After a deep exploration of the correlations between different influencing factors and capabilities in comparison with innovativeness (amount of incremental and radical innovations implemented) for start-ups, and different performance levels of mature companies, the hypotheses H1-H12 ($H_{0(r)}$ V $H_{a(r)}$ and $H_{0(i)}$ V $H_{a(i)}$) are tested. To test the hypotheses a significance level p value < 0.1 is applied, marked as (O) in comparison to the p value < 0.05 level marked as (✓). Remaining relation-

ships are marked as (x). In the end of each table "Overall" summarises all p value < 0.1 aiming to focus merely on the significant subject matter. A second row marks if the hypotheses holds true regarding positive/negative relations.

H1 is designed to explore the customer orientation related to innovativeness. The hypothesis $H_{a(r)}$ *customer orientation is positively related to radical innovations* is accepted for start-ups and mature companies (LP, AvP, HP) within the data analysed. In addition, the same applies for incremental innovations and therefore hypothesis $H_{a(i)}$ is also accepted. Consequently, the use of research techniques such as focus groups, surveys, and observations to gather customer orientation is related to radical innovations for all start-ups and mature companies.

The next hypotheses (H2) developed from the literature review asks for validation to the statement that competitor orientation is related to innovativeness. The hypothesis $H_{a(r)}$ and $H_{a(i)}$ *competitor orientation is positively related to radical innovations* is accepted for start-ups but it has no effect ($H_{o(r)}$ and $H_{o(i)}$) for all mature companies. It seems that start-ups use different information about their competitors to put mainly incremental innovations in place.

H3 reconsiders the external driving forces by putting emphasis on the validation of the statement that the competitive environment is related to innovativeness. A positive direction of association is seen for all mature companies with regard to radical innovations. However, the fact that actions of foreign competitors change quite rapidly is mostly related to innovativeness. However, there is no effect $H_{o(r)}$ for Start-ups, LPs, AvPs and HPs. $H_{o(i)}$ has no effect for Start-ups, AvPs and HPs. The alternative hypothesis $H_{a(i)}$ is accepted for LPs.

H4 asked for validation about the distinct organisational characteristics: centralised vs. decentralised and their correlation to innovativeness. *Centralized inter-functional coordination* is positively related to radical innovations. However, a negative correlation is recognised between centralisation and incremental innovations for start-ups. There is no effect $H_{o(r)}$ for Start-ups, LPs, AvPs and HPs. $H_{o(i)}$ has no effect for Start-ups, LPs and HPs. The alternative hypothesis $H_{a(i)}$ accepted for AvPs.

H5 states that diversification/exploration is positively related to innovativeness. Diversification/exploration is positively related to radical innovations and incremental innovations. Especially start-ups exploit the entire portfolio of diversification and learning possibilities to realize mainly incremental innovations. However, there is no effect $H_{o(r)}$ for Start-ups, LPs and HPs. $H_{o(i)}$ has no effect for HPs. The alternative hypothesis $H_{a(i)}$ is accepted for Start-ups LPs and AvPs. Subsequently, H6 is validating the assumption that active knowledge/skills seeking is positively related to innovativeness. There is a positive relationship between active knowledge/skills seeking and innovativeness. Again, start-ups are applying the whole portfolio of knowledge management elements to implement incremental innovations. For radical innovations, the relation is strong between the improvement of development processes and improvements of efficiency of existing innovation activities leading to radical innovations. There is no effect $H_{o(r)}$ for LPs, AvPs and HPs. $H_{o(i)}$ has no effect for AvPs and HPs. The alternative hypothesis $H_{a(i)}$ is accepted for Start-ups and LPs. The alternative hypotheses $H_{a(r)}$ is accepted for Start-ups.

H7 states that the education level of manager/entrepreneurs is positively related to innovativeness. The analysis validates that the education level is positively related to radical and incremental innovations, however leading merely to incremental innovations. There is no effect $H_{o(r)}$ for Start-ups, LPs, AvPs and HPs. $H_{o(i)}$ has no effect for Start-ups and HPs. The alternative hypothesis $H_{a(i)}$ is accepted for LPs and AvPs.

H8 states that management tenure is negatively related to innovativeness. H8 shows only a negative relation between management tenure and radical innovations in the cluster start-ups. All the others are positively related. There is no effect $H_{o(r)}$ for Start-up and HPs. $H_{o(i)}$ has no effect for LPs and AvPs. The alternative hypothesis $H_{a(i)}$

is accepted for Start-ups and HPs. The alternative hypotheses $H_{a(r)}$ is accepted for LPs and AvPs. H9 states that collaborative activities are related to innovativeness. H9 is validated (positively related) for radical innovations. HPs concentrate on the larger organisational network, while start-ups are more influenced by family and friends. There is no effect $H_{o(r)}$ for Start-ups, LPs, AvPs and HPs. $H_{o(i)}$ has no effect for Start-ups, AvPs and HPs. The alternative hypothesis $H_{a(i)}$ is accepted for LPs.

H10 states that a central position in a network is positively related to innovativeness. The following table lists the entire dimensions related to the inter-organisational network. H10 holds true as it is positively related to both radical and incremental innovations. However, correlation on a significant level for "Central Position" is recognised for incremental innovations for start-ups and for radical and incremental innovations for LPs and AvPs. For HPs inter-organisational network relates to incremental innovations in the categories "markets complementary products with other companies" and "establishment of cooperative R&D agreements" with other companies. There is no effect $H_{o(r)}$ for LPs and HPs. $H_{o(i)}$ has no effect for LPs and HPs. The alternative hypothesis $H_{a(i)}$ and $H_{a(r)}$ are accepted for Start-ups and AvPs.

The next hypothesis, H11, is based on the assumption that innovations in general are positively related to innovativeness. As start-ups naturally do not have a track record of financial performance, the hypothesis is tested merely on mature companies. H11 holds true, because first of all it is positively related and secondly significantly relevant. This assumption is essential because it is assumed that financial performance (followed by clustering in sales increase) has a strong relation to the ability of implementing innovations. The alternative hypotheses $Ha_{(r)}$ and $Ha_{(i)}$ are accepted for all mature companies. H12 states that innovativeness is negatively related to efficiency. Efficiency is outlined in different dimensions ranging from the comparison to competitors to R&D expenditures for innovations and so forth.

H12 holds not true, because all of the statements related to efficiency with regard to the innovativeness are positively correlated. There is no effect $H_{o(r)}$ for Start-ups, LPs, and AvPs. $H_{o(i)}$ has no effect for LPs and HPs. The alternative hypothesis $H_{a(i)}$ is accepted for Start-ups and AvPs. The alternative hypothesis $H_{a(r)}$ is accepted for HPs.

In relation to the retail industry, in particular we looked more closely at two sets of findings: (1) Market variables & innovation, and (2) Differences between innovativeness of start-up and mature companies (see Tables 1 and 3) The correlation between the market orientation variables and the number and type of innovation score, representing the number and type of innovations, is laid out in Table 1. There are a number of significant correlations between specific customer orientation variables and the incremental, radical and total innovation score. In particular, all the customer orientation variables, but one, have a strong correlation with radical innovation. Some dimensions of competitor orientation were significantly positively correlated with the number of incremental innovations in areas, such as, competitor orientation strategy and competitor orientation information. In contrast, there appeared to be little evidence of a correlation between competitor orientation and radical innovation. The correlations between the market and competitive environment variables and innovativeness were also mainly significantly positively correlated.

It should be noted that the correlations in Table 1 are relatively low. However, it is possible to suggest some implications arising from these results. The strong correlations between customer orientation and radical innovation indicates that a highly customer centric approach is necessary to create radical innovations. This gives some support to Von Hippel (as cited in Kronberger, 2005) who highlights the fact that although approximately 75 per cent of all commercial innovations fail they still follow the traditional ways of R&D. He emphasized that many innovations are triggered from outside a company. Customers of products often are ahead of the trend and are able to develop radical product and service innovations.

Kim and Mauborgne (2005, p.42) described a strong competitor orientation occurring when "the value curve converges with its competitors [...] this signals slow growth". They argue that value innovation occurs when an organization avoids direct competition with their competitors, which they term a red ocean strategy, but aims instead at creating new and uncontested market space, which they term a blue ocean strategy. The correlations between competitor orientation strategy and competitor orientation knowledge with incremental innovation support the argument that competitor orientation leads to a "red ocean" strategy. Within the market and competitive environment, both the correlation between changes action and customer preferences indicate a strong relationship to radical innovation.

Factor analysis with varimax rotation was used to create factor scores from the sixteen questions. Four factors were formed which have been labeled customer centric, competitor orientation, market dynamism and customer intelligence (see Table 2). Both customer centric and customer intelligence were proxies for customer orientation. These variables accounted for 21.6%, 17.7%, 16.4% and 11.1% respectively, (see the rotated component matrix displayed in Table 2). The Kaiser-Meyer-Olkin Measure of Sampling Adequacy was 0.73 and Bartlett's test of Sphericity was statistically significant ($P < 0.001$) indicating that the application of factor analysis was successful. The differences between innovativeness of start-up and mature companies and their respective factor scores are shown in Table 2.

The second set of findings related to the implementation of technology in the retail industry involves the age of the company. From Table 3 it is clear that start-up companies have more radical innovations but fewer incremental innovations than mature companies (these differences are significant at the 5% level). Total innovative activity is fairly similar. Starts-up companies appear more

Table 1. Correlations of market variables and innovativeness

Correlations / n=171	Incremental Innovation Score	Radical Innovation Score	Total Innovation Score
Customer Orientation Potential Needs	0.056	0.200(**)	0.151(*)
Customer Orientation Monitoring	0.138	0.224(**)	0.213(**)
Customer Orientation Knowledge	0.274(**)	0.260(**)	0.313(**)
Customer Orientation Strategy	0.125	0.210(**)	0.197(**)
Customer Orientation Research Techniques	0.330(**)	0.290(**)	0.363(**)
Customer Orientation Relationships	0.296(**)	0.372(**)	0.392(**)
Customer Orientation Information	0.182(*)	0.189(*)	0.218(**)
Competitor Orientation Strategy	0.154(*)	0.041	0.114
Competitor Orientation Potential	0.107	-0.037	0.040
Competitor Orientation Information	0.065	0.054	0.069
Competitor Orientation Knowledge	0.230(**)	0.051	0.164(*)
Market & Competitive Environment: Changes Action	0.131	0.194(**)	0.190 (**)
Market & Competitive Environment: Changes Technology	0.224(**)	0.162(*)	0.226(**)
Market & Competitive Environment: Conditions	0.140	0.125	0.155(*)
Market & Competitive Environment: Customer Preferences	0.054	0.249(**)	0.178(*)
Market & Competitive E Environment: Changes Customer Needs	0.060	0.116	0.103

** Correlation is significant at the 0.01 level (2-tailed). * Correlation is significant at the 0.05 level (2-tailed).

Table 2. Rotated component matrix (component 1 – customer centric, component 2 – competitor orientation, component 3 – market dynamism, component 4 – customer intelligence)

Rotated Component Matrix(a)	Component			
	1	2	3	4
Customer Orientation Knowledge	0.857			
Customer Orientation Strategy	0.829			
Customer Orientation Relationships	0.776			
Customer Orientation Potential Needs	0.762			
Customer Orientation Monitoring	0.721			
Competitor Orientation Potential		0.889		
Competitor Orientation Strategy		0.817		
Competitor Orientation Information		0.779		
Competitor Orientation Knowledge		0.748		
Market & Competitive Environment Changes Technology			0.812	
Market & Competitive Environment Changes Customer Needs			0.796	
Market & Competitive Environment Conditions			0.790	
Market & Competitive Environment Customer Preferences			0.662	0.366
Market & Competitive Environment Changes Action		0.342	0.456	0.391
Customer Orientation Research Techniques				0.791
Customer Orientation Information	0.350			0.754

Extraction Method: Principal Component Analysis. Rotation Method: Varimax with Kaiser Normalization. (a) Rotation converged in 5 iterations.

Table 3. Startup and mature companies compared

		Incremental Innovation	Radical Innovation	Total Innovation	Customer Centric	Competitor Orientation	Market Dynamism	Customer Intelligence
Start-up	Mean	1.745	1.909	1.836	0.147	0.140	0.172	-0.187
	Std. Dev.	0.751	0.752	0.714	0.722	1.004	1.134	0.744
Mature	Mean	2.026	1.672	1.897	-0.070	-0.067	-0.081	0.088
	Std. Dev.	0.625	0.682	0.664	1.104	0.996	0.924	1.093
Total	Mean	1.936	1.749	1.877	0.000	0.000	0.000	0.000
	Std. Dev.	0.679	0.712	0.679	1	1	1	1

customer centric and customer orientated and seem more concerned about market dynamism than mature companies. However, the reverse is the case for customer intelligence.

To determine the degree to which the constructed variables, of customer centric, market dynamism, customer intelligence and competitor orientation, make to fostering innovative activity, ordinary least square regression models were constructed for all companies, start-up and mature. The natural logarithm of total, incremental and radical innovation was taken as the distributions of these were skewed toward zero and taking

natural logarithms successfully transformed these dependent variables to more normal distributions. These models are displayed in Table 4.

In Table 5 the correlation of customer satisfaction with radical and incremental innovations is confirmed. This suggests that innovations have a positive impact on customer satisfaction and retention. In addition, where there is radical innovation, there is a positive correlation with customer satisfaction for both radical and incremental innovations. It may be that customers recognize the radical innovations of a company and this influences their propensity to buy other products by the same com-

Table 4. Coefficients of regression models with standard errors in parenthesis

Variable	All Companies (N = 171)			Start-Up Companies (N = 55)			Mature Companies (N = 116)		
	Log of Total Innovations	Log of Total Incremental Innovations	Log of Total Radical Innovations	Log of Total Innovations	Log of Total Incremental Innovations	Log of Total Radical Innovations	Log of Total Innovations	Log of Total Incremental Innovations	Log of Total Radical Innovations
Constant	3.034** (0.020)	2.383** (0.025)	2.259** (0.024)	2.990** (0.038)	2.248** (0.043)	2.319** (0.047)	3.050** (0.023)	2.447** (0.029)	2.225** (0.028)
Customer Centric	0.078** (0.020)	0.073** (0.025)	0.099** (0.024)	0.069 (0.053)	0.0121** (0.059)	0.018 (0.065)	0.068** (0.021)	0.059** (0.026)	0.091** (0.026)
Market Dynamism	0.054** (0.020)	0.047* (0.025)	0.064** (0.024)	0.018 (0.034)	0.029 (0.039)	-0.004 (0.042)	0.075** (0.025)	0.086** (0.031)	0.074** (0.031)
Customer Intelligence	0.069** (0.020)	0.041 (0.025)	0.089** (0.024)	0.059 (0.056)	0.069 (0.063)	0.035 (0.067)	0.044** (0.021)	0.001 (0.027)	0.080** (0.026)
Competitor Orientation	0.012 (0.020)	0.034 (0.025)	-0.018 (0.024)	0.114** (0.041)	0.102** (0.047)	0.131** (0.051)	-0.032 (0.023)	0.002 (0.029)	-0.078** (0.029)
Adjusted R^2	15.7%	7.9%	16.4%	23.9%	22.9%	12.9%	19.0%	7.9%	25.5%

** Correlation is significant at the 0.01 level (2-tailed). * Correlation is significant at the 0.05 level (2-tailed).

Table 5. Correlations of innovation performance

Correlations / All Companies / n=171	Incremental Innovation Score	Radical Innovation Score	Total Innovation Score
Innovation Performance (Incremental) % Sales	0.199(**)	0.030	0.134
Innovation Performance (Radical) % Sales	0.257(**)	0.540(**)	0.468(**)
Innovation Performance (Incremental) Customer Satisfaction	0.246(**)	0.081	0.191(**)
Innovation Performance (Radical) Customer Satisfaction	0.218(**)	0.354(**)	0.336(**)

** Correlation is significant at the 0.01 level (2-tailed). * Correlation is significant at the 0.05 level (2-tailed).

pany which only provide incremental improvements to existing offerings. As a result, the enhancement to reputation gained from the company offering innovative breakthrough products also improves the sales volume of the less innovative products.

Exploring both start-up and mature companies, this research focused on market orientation and its impact on producing either incremental or radical innovations. The paper contributes to knowledge in a number of areas. The study identifies a generally positive relationship between a number facets of customer orientation and across innovation types. We will explore two hypotheses specifically, given their greater applicability to the retail industry. In particular, all elements of customer orientation apart from one have a strong relationship with radical innovation. However, the component customer centric derived from the factor analysis only demonstrated a strong relationship with radical innovation in mature companies. As a result, the hypothesis (H1) that Customer orientation is related positively to racial innovations can be accepted for mature companies but has to be rejected for start-up companies.

The research results suggest that for mature companies a strong competitor orientation leads to imitation and does not foster more fundamental invention and innovation. For start-up companies the competitor orientation appears to help identify competitive opportunities that facilitate the launching of new products or services. As a result the hypothesis (H2) competitor orientation is related positively to incremental innovations can be accepted for start-up companies and must be rejected for mature companies.

The results of this study reveal that there are differences between start-up and mature companies with respect to market orientation and innovations. A number of recommendations and observations flow from these results. Start-up companies should observe and analyze competitor's activities in the process of bringing ideas to market. This might be already included in the development of the initial business plan and it should help to bring incremental innovations to market success. In contrast, to stay innovative and to continuously generate the new ideas that bring market success an orientation towards competitors might be not the ideal strategic focus for mature companies. Knowing the strategy of competitors might enhance the market intelligence of a mature organization but it does not lead to innovation success, and appears to mitigate against the development of radical innovations.

The findings identify the Triggers (capabilities with a strong impact in a start-up phase), Supporters (capabilities necessary over the entire company life), and Drivers (capabilities relevant for high business performance in mature companies) for innovation and business success. Figure 1 provides a simplified view with some examples of Trigger, Driver and Supporter for innovation and business success. Some capabilities are important in almost every phase of the company life cycle. For example, it seems that higher education is a relevant trigger for starting a venture but also a driver for high performing companies.

Figure 1. Changes of innovation capabilities while companies grow

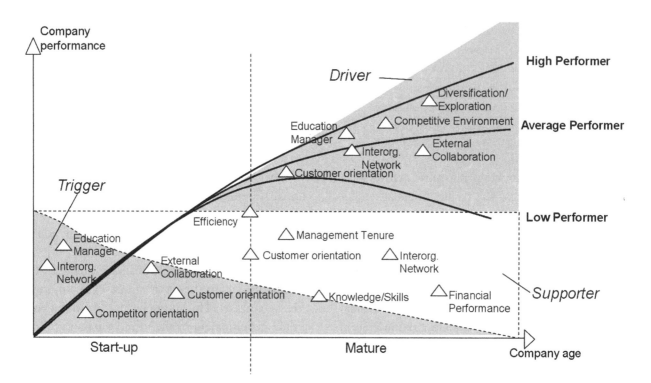

Applying the conclusions revealed in Figure 1 (Trigger, Supporter, Driver) to the 6 categories having impact in today's retail industry, we find many examples where the industry can develop and grow. Reducing effort for customers and Utilizing them as innovation drivers are reflected in the Trigger, and Driver quadrants. Business Model innovations (example Zara in fast fashion; Square in online purchase processing; Groupon in mobile apps) often are rolled out first by Start-ups (Trigger) or "entrepreneurial" factions within Mature companies (Drivers). Brand Development in the retail industry would seem to be more competition-focused early as a start-up (Trigger), yet later in mature companies (Driver); perhaps reflecting the effects of the product life cycle or a combination of both organizations' external collaboration innovation capabilities (as with Isfi Spices). Similarly, the category of the value of education falls both as a Trigger as well as a Driver. Certainly as the speed of technology innovation increases (see following category), the demand for constant education

and training increases, which also may be addressed through external collaboration. Finally, the impact of the implementation of technology is reflected in numerous Trigger and Driver capabilities, along with some limited Supporter capabilities. This suggests they will be relevant for high business performance in the retail industry.

The illustration depicts the importance of interorganizational networks for start-up and mature companies. It proves that a strong relationship exists between the interorganizational network and innovativeness. Some scholars state that start-ups especially benefit from such networks (Baum et al., 2000; Stuart, 2000). Similarly, they benefit from the organizational network, because of a strong correlation and positive impact between collaborative activities and a companies' capabilities to be innovative (Hagedoorn, 2002). External collaboration becomes especially important to start-up companies as this study proves. Knowledge and skills are essential supports for innovativeness and they become a central point. Knowledge about customers, competitor, suppliers, processes, and so forth provide the information and insight to manage uncertainty and risk. Diverse skills and continuous learning are paramount for knowledge gathering and knowledge transfer. Davenport (1998, p.7) condenses and describes knowledge as a "fluid mix of framed experience, values, contextual information and insight". Again, functional complexity and size of firms might become constraints of knowledge transfer and sharing. The education of the management has also an effect on the innovativeness and company success, whereas management tenure can only be classified as an supporter for innovation. Therefore, successful mature companies with the ability to develop manifold radical innovations utilize various factors best to strengthen their competitive advantage.

FUTURE RESEARCH DIRECTIONS

Having identified some significant differences between start-up and mature companies with respect to market orientation and its effect on innovation, and discussion regarding its impact on the retail industry, we suggest that further research is required to explore the transformation process of growing companies. Observing the actual changes and influencing factors might help to foster a deeper understanding of the different perceptions around market orientation and its relationship to successful innovation. The two research instruments have been designed to explore more profoundly *how* and *why* changes in innovation styles occur and what the outcomes are. Further explorations are necessary to understand more precisely the impact and correlations of different capabilities and innovation success. Further analysis of the results and model (Figure 1) should be directly investigated in the retail industry. In-depth understanding of the acquisition and manipulation of customer data can be a rich source of new research, as would enhanced methods to develop retail consumer behaviour preferences.

CONCLUSION

The retail industry started from a poor technology innovation base (Miles, 2008), although given the advantages of the Internet, and especially social media, it becomes clearer that the retail industry acknowledges the potential of applying technology not just in "the back room", but at the customer interface as well. While this study's data did not specifically test for changes in innovation capabilities of technology in the retail industry, we can make some observations.

The findings depict a snapshot of the complexity of the correlation of capabilities and innovation success. It is possible to depict a pattern for innovation and business success, and suggest its relevance if applied to the retail industry. Some capabilities are crucial in a start-up phase, but turn out to be less important in the long term, while others are crucial to maintain innovation success. A strong discrepancy is detected in the innovation style applied in low-performing mature and average-performing mature companies. It seems that some organizational capabilities, skills and behaviors lead to innovation success.

Retail executives must consider the impact on their operations due to innovations such as consumer effort, business models, brand development, education, and technology. As technology applications increase in the retail sector it will begin to separate 'winners' from 'losers', and provide the environment for innovation to impact new market entrants and established players. Understanding how the innovation capabilities of companies change as they grow (Triggers, Drivers, and Supporters) and how the individual variables involved with innovation and market orientation impact the organization, a retail company can take advantage of technologies, innovations and new developments in the retail sector to make positive critical strategic decisions.

REFERENCES

Acs, Z. J., & Audretsch, D. B. (1990). *Innovation and small firms*. Cambridge, MA: MIT Press.

Ahuja, G. (2000). The duality of collaboration: Inducements and opportunities in the formation of interfirm linkages. *Strategic Management Journal*, *21*(3), 317–343. doi:10.1002/(SICI)1097-0266(200003)21:3<317::AID-SMJ90>3.0.CO;2-B

Ahuja, G., & Lampert, C. (2001). Entrepreneurship in the large corporation: A longitudinal study of how established firms create breakthrough inventions. *Strategic Management Journal*, *22*(6-7), 521–543. doi:10.1002/smj.176

Amer, T. S., & Bain, C. E. (1990). Making small business planning easier: Microcomputers facilitate the process. *Journal of Accountancy*, *170*(1), 53–58.

Ancona, D., & Caldwell, D. (1992). Demography and design: Predictors of new product team performance. *Organization Science*, *3*(3), 321–341. doi:10.1287/orsc.3.3.321

Audretsch, D. B. (2001). Research issues relating to structure, competition, and performance of small technology-based firms. *Small Business Economics*, *16*(1), 37–51. doi:10.1023/A:1011124607332

Barney, J. (1991). Firm resources and sustained competitive advantage. *Journal of Management*, *17*(1), 99–120. doi:10.1177/014920639101700108

Baum, J., Calabrese, T., & Silverman, B. (2000). Don't go it alone: Alliance network composition and start-ups' performance in Canadian biotechnology. *Strategic Management Journal*, *21*(3), 267–294. doi:10.1002/(SICI)1097-0266(200003)21:3<267::AID-SMJ89>3.0.CO;2-8

Bennett, R. C., & Cooper, R. G. (1979). Beyond the marketing concept. *Business Horizons*, *22*(3), 76–83. doi:10.1016/0007-6813(79)90088-0

Birch, D. G. W. (1979). *The job generation process*. Washington, DC: US Department of Commerce.

Blind, K., & Grupp, H. (1999). Interdependencies between the science and technology infrastructure and innovation activities in German regions: Empirical findings and policy consequences. *Research Policy*, *28*(5), 451–468. doi:10.1016/S0048-7333(99)00007-4

Boeker, W. (1997). Executive migration and strategic change: The effect of top manager movement on product-market entry. *Administrative Science Quarterly*, *42*(2), 213–236. doi:10.2307/2393919

Brink, J., & Holmén, M. (2009). Capabilities and radical changes of the business models of new bioscience firms. *Creativity and Innovation Management*, *18*(2), 109–120. doi:10.1111/j.1467-8691.2009.00519.x

Brown, S., & Eisenhardt, K. (1995). Product development: Past research, present findings, and future directions. *Academy of Management Review*, *20*(2), 343–378.

Brüderl, J., & Preisendörfer, P. (1998). Network support and the success of newly founded businesses. *Small Business Economics*, *10*(3), 213–225. doi:10.1023/A:1007997102930

Cano, C. R., Carrillat, F. A., & Jaramillo, F. (2004). A meta-analysis of the relationship between market orientation and business performance: Evidence from five continents. *International Journal of Research in Marketing*, *21*(2), 179–200. doi:10.1016/j.ijresmar.2003.07.001

Cardinal, L. (2001). Technological innovation in the pharmaceutical industry: The use of organizational control in managing research and development. *Organization Science*, *12*(1), 19–36. doi:10.1287/orsc.12.1.19.10119

Chiu, C. M., Huang, H. Y., & Yen, C. H. (2010). Antecedents of trust in online auctions. *Electronic Commerce Research and Applications*, *9*(2), 148–159. doi:10.1016/j.elerap.2009.04.003

Chiu, P. H., Kao, G. Y. M., & Lo, C. C. (2010). Personalized blog content recommender system for mobile phone users. *International Journal of Human-Computer Studies*, *68*(8), 496–507. doi:10.1016/j.ijhcs.2010.03.005

Christensen, C. M., & Bower, J. L. (1996). Customer power, strategic investment, and the failure of leading firms. *Strategic Management Journal*, *17*(3), 197–218. doi:10.1002/(SICI)1097-0266(199603)17:3<197::AID-SMJ804>3.0.CO;2-U

Chung, J.-E. (2013). Does small retailer market orientation matter for long-term oriented relationships with suppliers? *Journal of Small Business Management*. doi:10.1111/jsbm.12061

Cohen, W. M., & Klepper, S. (1992). The trade off between firm size and diversity in the pursuit of technological progress. *Small Business Economics*, *4*(1), 1–14.

Coleman, J. (1988). Social capital in the creation of human capital. *American Journal of Sociology*, *94*(s1), 95–120. doi:10.1086/228943

Dabholkar, P. A., Bobbitt, L. M., & Lee, E. J. (2003). Understanding consumer motivation and behavior related to self-scanning in retailing: Implications for strategy and research on technology-based self-service. *International Journal of Service Industry Management*, *14*(1), 59–95. doi:10.1108/09564230310465994

Davenport, T. (1998). *Working knowledge: How organizations manage what they know*. Boston: Harvard Business Review Press.

Davis, F. D. (1989). Perceived usefulness, perceived ease of use, and user acceptance of information technology. *Management Information Systems Quarterly*, *13*(3), 319–340. doi:10.2307/249008

Day, G. (1994). The capabilities of market-driven organizations. *Journal of Marketing*, *58*(4), 37–52. doi:10.2307/1251915

Dedrick, J., Kraemer, K., & Linden, G. (2010). Who profits from innovation in global value chains?: A study of the iPod and notebook PCs. *Industrial and Corporate Change*, *19*(1), 81–16. doi:10.1093/icc/dtp032

Dejardin, M. (2002). Dejardin, Marcus. In *ERSA conference papers*. European Regional Science Association.

Deshpande, R. (1999). *Developing a market orientation*. Thousand Oaks, CA: SAGE.

Di-Masi, P. (2000). *Defining entrepreneurship*. Global Development Research Centre. Retrieved June 06, 2014, from http://www.gdrc.org/icm/micro/define-micro.html

Drucker, P. (1954). *The practice of management*. New York: Harper.

Eisenhardt, K., & Martin, J. (2000). Dynamic capabilities: What are they? *Strategic Management Journal*, *21*(10-11), 1105–1121. doi:10.1002/1097-0266(200010/11)21:10/11<1105::AID-SMJ133>3.0.CO;2-E

Elg, U. (2003). Retail market orientation: A preliminary framework. *International Journal of Retail & Distribution Management*, *31*(2), 107–117. doi:10.1108/09590550310462001

European Commission. (2014). *Six perspectives on retail innovation*. Retrieved August 08, 2014, from http://ec.europa.eu/research/innovation-union/pdf/Six_perspectives_on_Retail_Innovation_EG_on%20Retail_Sector_Innovation_web.pdf

Faber, J., & Hesen, A. (2004). Innovation capabilities of European nations: Cross-national analyses of patents and sales of product innovations. *Research Policy, 33*(2), 193–207. doi:10.1016/S0048-7333(03)00122-7

Finkelstein, S., & Hambrick, D. (1990). Top management team tenure and organizational outcomes: The moderating role of managerial discretion. *Administrative Science Quarterly, 35*(3), 484–503. doi:10.2307/2393314

Foley, J. (2014). *10 technology trends that will revolutionize retail.* Retrieved August 08, 2014, from at http://www.forbes.com/sites/oracle/2014/01/13/10-technology-trends-that-will-revolutionize-retail/

Gainer, B., & Padanyi, P. (2002). Applying the marketing concept to cultural organisations: Non-profit, empirical study of the relationship between market orientation and performance. *Journal of and Voluntary Sector Marketing, 7*(2), 182–193. doi:10.1002/nvsm.178

Ganesan, S., George, M., Jap, S., Palmatier, R. W., & Weitz, B. (2009). Supply chain management and retailer performance: Emerging trends, issues, and implications for research and practice. *Journal of Retailing, 85*(1), 84–94. doi:10.1016/j.jretai.2008.12.001

Garcia, R., & Calantone, R. (2002). A critical look at technological innovation typology and innovation terminology: A literature review. *Journal of Product Innovation Management, 19*(2), 110–132. doi:10.1016/S0737-6782(01)00132-1

Gatignon, H., Tushman, M. L., Smith, W., & Anderson, P. (2002). A structural approach to assessing innovation: Construct development of innovation locus, type, and characteristics. *Management Science, 48*(September), 1103–1122. doi:10.1287/mnsc.48.9.1103.174

Gatignon, H., & Xuereb, J. (1997). Strategic orientation of the firm and new product performance. *JMR, Journal of Marketing Research, 34*(February), 77–90. doi:10.2307/3152066

Gerwin, D., & Barrowman, N. (2002). An evaluation of research on integrated product development. *Management Science, 48*(June), 938–953. doi:10.1287/mnsc.48.7.938.2818

Gibb, A. (2000). Corporate restructuring and entrepreneurship: What can large organisations learn from small? *Enterprise and Innovation Management Studies, 1*(1), 19–35. doi:10.1080/146324400363509

Gram, R. (2002). *Contemporary strategy analysis* (4th ed.). Oxford, UK: Blackwell.

Grimm, C., & Smith, K. (1991). Management and organizational change: A note on the railroad industry. *Strategic Management Journal, 12*(7), 557–562. doi:10.1002/smj.4250120708

Hagedoorn, J. (2002). Interfirm R&D partnerships: An overview of major trends and patterns since 1960. *Research Policy, 31*(4), 477–492. doi:10.1016/S0048-7333(01)00120-2

Han, J. K., Kim, N., & Srivastava, R. K. (1998). Market orientation and organizational performance: Is innovation a missing link? *Journal of Marketing, 62*(4), 30–45. doi:10.2307/1252285

Hitt, M., Hoskisson, R., Johnson, R., & Moesel, D. (1996). The market for corporate control and firm innovation. *Academy of Management Journal, 39*(October), 1048–1119.

Hopfenbeck, W., Müller, M., & Peisl, T. (2001). *Wissensbasiertes management: Ansätze und strategien zur unter-nehmensführung in der internet ökonomie* (1. Auflage.). Landsberg/Lech: Moderne Industrie.

Hoskisson, R., Johnson, R., Yiu, D., & Wan, W. (2001). Restructuring strategies of diversified business groups: Differences associated with country institutional environments. In M. A. Hitt, E. Freeman, & J. Harrison (Eds.), *The Blackwell handbook of strategy* (pp. 433–463). Oxford, UK: Blackwell Publishers.

Hult, G., Tomas, M., Ketchen, D. J., & Slater, S. F. (2005). Market orientation and performance: An integration of disparate approaches, strategic management. *Strategic Management Journal*, *26*(12), 1173–1181. doi:10.1002/smj.494

Hunt, S., & Lambe, C. J. (2000). Marketing's contribution to business strategy: Market orientation, relationship marketing and resource-advantage theory. *International Journal of Management Reviews*, *2*(1), 17–43. doi:10.1111/1468-2370.00029

Hurley, R. F., & Hult, T. M. (1998). Innovation, market orientation and organizational learning: An integration and empirical examination. *Journal of Marketing*, *62*(July), 42–54. doi:10.2307/1251742

Hyvonen, S., & Tuominen, M. (2006). Entrepreneurial innovations, market-driven intangibles and learning orientation: Critical indicators for performance advantages in SMEs. *International Journal of Management and Decision Making*, *7*(6), 643–660. doi:10.1504/IJMDM.2006.011074

Isaksen, G., & Ekvall, G. (2010). Managing for innovation: The two faces of tension in creative climates. *Creativity and Innovation Management*, *19*(2), 73–88. doi:10.1111/j.1467-8691.2010.00558.x

James, F. D. (1995). Technology and innovation in retail banking distribution. *International Journal of Bank Marketing*, *13*(4), 19–25. doi:10.1108/02652329510082915

Kahneman, D., & Tversky, A. (1979). Prospect theory: An analysis of decisions under risk. *Econometrica*, *47*(2), 263–291. doi:10.2307/1914185

Kara, A., Spillan, J. E., & DeShields, O. W. Jr. (2005). The effect of a market orientation on business performance: A study of smalls sized service retailers using MARKOR scale. *Journal of Small Business Management*, *43*(2), 105–118. doi:10.1111/j.1540-627x.2005.00128.x

Katz, R. (1982). The effects of team longevity of project commitment and performance. *Administrative Science Quarterly*, *27*(1), 81–104. doi:10.2307/2392547

Keister, L. (2002). Adapting to radical change: Strategy and environment in piece rate adaption during China's transition. *Organization Science*, *13*(5), 459–474. doi:10.1287/orsc.13.5.459.7811

Khan, A., & Manopichetwattana, V. (1989). Innovative and noninnovative small firms: Types and characteristics. *Management Science*, *35*(May), 597–606. doi:10.1287/mnsc.35.5.597

Kim, W. C., & Mauborgne, R. (2005). *Blue ocean strategy: How to create uncontested market space and make competition irrelevant*. Boston: Harvard Business School Press.

Kimberly, J., & Evanisko, M. (1981). Organizational innovation: The influence of individual, organizational, and contextual factors on hospital adoption of technological and administrative innovations. *Academy of Management Journal*, *24*(4), 689–713. doi:10.2307/256170 PMID:10253688

Kirchhoff, B. A. (1994). *Entrepreneurship and dynamic capitalism: The economics of business firm formation and growth*. Westport, CT: Praeger.

Koberg, C., Detienne, D., & Heppard, K. (2003). An empirical test of environmental, organizational, and process factors affecting incremental and radical innovation. *The Journal of High Technology Management Research*, *14*(1), 21–45. doi:10.1016/S1047-8310(03)00003-8

Koellinger, P. (2008). The relationship between technology, innovation, and firm performance-empirical evidence from e-business in Europe. *Research Policy, 37*(8), 1317–1328. doi:10.1016/j.respol.2008.04.024

Kohli, A. K., & Jaworsky, B. J. (1990). Market orientation: The construct, research propositions, and managerial implications. *Journal of Marketing, 54*(April), 1–8. doi:10.2307/1251866

Krishnan, V., & Ulrich, K. (2000). Product development decisions: A review of the literature. *Management Science, 47*(1), 1–21. doi:10.1287/mnsc.47.1.1.10668

Kronberger, M. (2005). Another good idea from Eric. *Australian Financial Review, 34*, 38–41.

Landry, R., Amara, N., & Lamari, M. (2002). Does social capital determine innovation? *Technological Forecasting and Social Change, 69*(7), 681–701. doi:10.1016/S0040-1625(01)00170-6

Lawton, L., & Parasuraman, A. (1980). The impact of the marketing concept on new product planning. *Journal of Marketing, 44*(1), 19–25. doi:10.2307/1250030

Leibenstein, H. (1966). Allocative efficiency vs. x-efficiency. *The American Economic Review, 56*(3), 392–415.

Leonard, D. (1998). *Wellspring of knowledge: Building and sustaining the sources of innovation*. Boston, MA: Harvard Business School Press.

Leonard-Barton, D., Wilson, E., & Doyle, J. (1996). Commercializing technology: Imaginative understanding of user needs. In Engines of innovation (pp. 177–208). Boston: Harvard Business.

Levitt, T. (1960). Marketing myopia. *Harvard Business Review, 38*(4), 45–57. PMID:15252891

Lewrick, M. (2004). *Customer relationship management: Applying relationship management to deliver more value to clients and partners of the automotive industry development centre in South Africa*. Bristol Business School, University of the West of England.

Lewrick, M. (2007). *Changes in innovation styles: Comprehensive study of the changes in innovation styles to identify the causes and effects of different influencing factors and capabilities to create a general innovation pattern*. Edinburgh Napier University.

Lewrick, M., Omar, M., & Williams, R. Jr. (2011). Market orientation and innovators' success: An exploration of the influence of customer and competitor orientation. *Journal of Technology Management & Innovation, 6*(3), 48–61. doi:10.4067/S0718-27242011000300004

Lewrick, M., Omar, M., & Williams, R. (2010). Management of Innovations in Growth SMEs. In S. Nwankwo & T. Gbadamosi (Eds.), *Entrepreneurship marketing: Principles and practice of SME marketing*. London: Routledge.

Liu, H., & Davies, G. (1997). Market orientation in UK multiple retail companies: Nature and pattern. *International Journal of Service Industry Management, 8*(2), 170–187. doi:10.1108/09564239710166281

Lukas, B. A., & Ferrell, O. C. (2000). The effect of market orientation on product innovation. *Journal of the Academy of Marketing Science, 28*(2), 239–247. doi:10.1177/0092070300282005

Lynn, G., Morone, J. G., & Paulson, A. S. (1996). Marketing and discontinuous innovation: The probe and learn process. *California Management Review, 38*(3), 8–37. doi:10.2307/41165841

Markham, S., & Griffin, A. (1998). The breakfast of champions: Associations between champions and product development environments, practices and performance. *Journal of Product Innovation Management, 15*(5), 436–454. doi:10.1016/S0737-6782(98)00010-1

McDermott, C., & Handfield, R. (2000). Concurrent development and strategic outsourcing: Do the rules change in breakthrough innovation? *The Journal of High Technology Management Research, 11*(1), 35–57. doi:10.1016/S1047-8310(00)00020-1

McDermott, C. M., & O'Connor, G. C. (2002). Managing radical innovation: An overview of emergent strategy issues. *Journal of Product Innovation Management, 19*(6), 424–438. doi:10.1016/S0737-6782(02)00174-1

Meuter, M. L., Ostrom, A. L., Bitner, M. J., & Roundtree, R. (2003). The influence of technology anxiety on consumer use and experiences with self-service technologies. *Journal of Business Research, 56*(11), 899–906. doi:10.1016/S0148-2963(01)00276-4

Meyer, A., & Goes, J. (1988). Assimilation of innovation: A multilevel contextual analysis. *Organizational Academy of Management Journal, 31*(December), 897–923.

Miles, I. (2008). Patterns of innovation in service industries. *IBM Systems Journal, 47*(1), 115–128. doi:10.1147/sj.471.0115

Mintzberg, H. (1987). Crafting strategy. *Harvard Business Review, 65*(Jul-Aug), 66–75.

Nahapiet, J., & Ghoshal, S. (1998). Social capital, intellectual capital, and the organizational advantage. *Academy of Management Review, 22*(2), 242–266.

Narver, J. C., & Slater, S. F. (1990). The effect of a market orientation on business profitability. *Journal of Marketing, 54*(October), 20–35. doi:10.2307/1251757

Nohria, K., & Gulati, S. (1996). Is slack good or bad for innovation. *Academy of Management Journal, 39*(5), 799–825. doi:10.2307/256998

Orlikowski, W. J., & Baroudi, J. J. (1991). Studying information technology in organization: Research approaches and assumptions. *Information Systems Research, 2*(1), 1–14. doi:10.1287/isre.2.1.1

Panigyrakis, G., & Theodoridis, P. K. (2007). Market orientation and performance: An empirical investigation in the retail industry in Greece. *Journal of Retailing and Consumer Services, 14*(2), 137–149. doi:10.1016/j.jretconser.2006.05.003

Pantano, E., & Di Pietro, L. (2012). Understanding consumer's acceptance of technology-based innovations in retailing. *Journal of Technology Management and Innovation, 7*(4), 1–19. doi:10.4067/S0718-27242012000400001

Penrose, E. (1963). *The theory of the growth of the firm*. Oxford, UK: Blackwell.

Puccinelli, N. M., Goodstein, R., Grewal, D., Price, R., Raghubir, P., & Stewart, D. (2009). Customer experience management in retailing: Understanding the buying process. *Journal of Retailing, 85*(Spring), 15–30. doi:10.1016/j.jretai.2008.11.003

Rao, H., & Drazin, R. (2002). Overcoming resource constraints on product innovation by recruiting talent from rivals: A study of the mutual fund industry. *Academy of Management Journal, 45*(June), 491–507. doi:10.2307/3069377

Reinders, M. J., Dabholkar, P. A., & Frambach, R. T. (2008). Consequences of forcing customers to use technology-based self-service. *Journal of Service Research, 11*(2), 107–123. doi:10.1177/1094670508324297

Robinson, R. B. Jr, & Pearce, J. A. II. (1984). Research thrusts in small firm strategic planning. *Academy of Management Review, 9*(1), 128–137.

Rosenblatt, P. C., de Mik, L., Anderson, R. M., & Johnson, P. A. (1985). *The family in business.* San Francisco: Jossey-Bass.

Ruekert, R. W. (1992). Developing a market orientation: An organizational strategy perspective. *International Journal of Research in Marketing, 9*(3), 225–245. doi:10.1016/0167-8116(92)90019-H

Russell, R. (1990). Innovation in organizations: Toward an integrated model. *Review of Business, 12*(2), 19–25.

Schumpeter, J. A. (1934). *The theory of economic development: An inquiry into profits, capital, credit, interest, and the business cycle.* Cambridge, MA: Harvard University Press.

Shan, W., Walker, G., & Kogut, B. (1994). Interfirm cooperation and startup innovation in the biotechnology industry. *Strategic Management Journal, 15*(5), 387–394. doi:10.1002/smj.4250150505

Shankar, V., Inman, J. J., Mantrala, M., Kelley, E., & Rizley, R. (2011). Innovations in shopper marketing: Current insights and future research issues. *Journal of Retailing, 87*, 29–42. doi:10.1016/j.jretai.2011.04.007

Sivadas, E., & Dwyer, F. (2000). An examination of organizational factors influencing new product success in internal and alliance based processes. *Journal of Marketing, 64*(1), 31–49. doi:10.1509/jmkg.64.1.31.17985

Slater, S. F., & Narver, J. C. (1994). Marketing orientation, customer value and superior performance. *Business Horizons, 37*(2), 22–28. doi:10.1016/0007-6813(94)90029-9

Sorensen, J., & Stuart, T. (2000). Aging, obsolescence, and organizational innovation. *Administrative Science Quarterly, 45*(March), 81–112. doi:10.2307/2666980

Sorescu, A., Frambach, R. T., Singh, J., Rangaswamy, A., & Bridges, C. (2011). Innovations in retail business models. *Journal of Retailing, 87*(1), S3–S16. doi:10.1016/j.jretai.2011.04.005

Stephens, J., Huber, E., & Ray, L. (1999). The welfare state in hard times. In H. Kitschelt, P. Lange, G. Marks, & J. D. Stephens (Eds.), *Continuity and change in contemporary capitalism.* Cambridge, UK: Cambridge University Press. doi:10.1017/CBO9781139175050.008

Storey, D. J., & Tether, B. (1996). *Review of the empirical knowledge and an assessment of statistical data on the economic importance of new technology-based firms in Europe.* Coventry.

Stringer, R. (2000). How to manage radical innovation. *California Management Review, 42*(4), 70–88. doi:10.2307/41166054

Stuart, T. (2000). Inter-organizational alliances and the performance of firms: A study of growth and innovation rates in a high-technology industry. *Strategic Management Journal, 21*(8), 791–811. doi:10.1002/1097-0266(200008)21:8<791::AID-SMJ121>3.0.CO;2-K

Teece, D. J., Pisano, G., & Shuen, A. (1997). Dynamic capabilities and strategic management. *Strategic Management Journal, 18*(7), 509–533. doi:10.1002/(SICI)1097-0266(199708)18:7<509::AID-SMJ882>3.0.CO;2-Z

Theodoridis, P. K., & Panigyrakis, G. G. (2011). Internal marketing, market orientation and organisational performance: The mythological triangle in a retail context. European Retail Research, 24, 33–67.

Thether, B. (2002). Who co-operates for innovation, and why, an empirical analysis. *Research Policy, 31*(6), 947–967. doi:10.1016/S0048-7333(01)00172-X

Tidd, J., Bessant, J., & Pavitt, K. (2003). *Managing innovation.* Chichester, UK: John Wiley and Sons.

Utterback, J. M. (1974). Innovation in industry and the diffusion of technology. *Science, 183*(4125), 620–626. doi:10.1126/science.183.4125.620 PMID:17778831

Utterback, J. M. (1996). *Mastering the dynamics of innovation: Mastering the dynamics of innovation.* Boston, MA: Harvard Business School Press.

Verbees, F., Matthew, J. H. M., & Meulenberg, T. G. (2004). Market orientation, innovativeness, product innovation, and performance in small firms. *Journal of Small Business Management, 42*(2), 134–154. doi:10.1111/j.1540-627X.2004.00102.x

Von Hippel, E. (2005). *Democratizing innovation.* Cambridge, MA: The MIT Press.

Wamba, S. F., Lefebvre, L. A., Bendavid, Y., & Lefebvre, E. (2008). Exploring the impact of RFID technology and the EPC network on mobile B2B eCommerce: A case study in the retail industry. *International Journal of Production Economics, 112*(2).

Weijters, B., Rangarajan, D., Falk, T., & Schillewaert, N. (2007). Determinants and outcomes of customers' use of self-service technology in a retail setting. *Journal of Service Research, 10*(1), 3–21. doi:10.1177/1094670507302990

Wiersema, M., & Bantel, K. (1992). Top management team demography and corporate change. *Academy of Management Journal, 35*(1), 91–121. doi:10.2307/256474

Williams, R., & Omar, M. (2009). Renaming services organizations for growth. In *Proceedings of Academy of Marketing Conference.* Leeds, UK: Leeds Metropolitan University.

Winter, S. (2003). Understanding dynamic capabilities. *Strategic Management Journal, 24*(10), 991–995. doi:10.1002/smj.318

Wren, B. M. (1997). The market orientation construct: Measurement and scaling issues. *Journal of Marketing Theory and Practice, 15*(3), 31–54.

Zahra, S., Ireland, R., & Hitt, M. (2000). International expansion by new venture firms: International diversity, mode of market entry, technological learning and performance. *Academy of Management Journal, 43*(5), 925–950. doi:10.2307/1556420

Zhou, K. Z., Yim, C. K., & Tse, D. K. (2005). The effects of strategic orientations on technology- and market-based breakthrough innovations. *Journal of Marketing, 69*(2), 42–60. doi:10.1509/jmkg.69.2.42.60756

ADDITIONAL READING

Hortinha, P., Lages, C., & Lages, L. F. (2011). The trade-off between customer and technology orientations: Impact on innovation capabilities and export performance. *Journal of International Marketing, 19*(3), 36–58. doi:10.1509/jimk.19.3.36

Ju, M., & Zheng, Z. K. (2013). Technological capability growth and performance outcome: Foreign versus local firms in China. *Journal of International Marketing, 21*(2), 1–16. doi:10.1509/jim.12.0171

Rubera, G., & Kirca, A. H. (2012). Firm innovativeness and its performance outcomes: A meta-analytic review and theoretical integration. *Journal of Marketing, 76*(3), 130–147. doi:10.1509/jm.10.0494

Sorescu, A. B., & Spanjol, J. (2008). Innovation's effect on firm value and risk: Insights from consumer packaged goods. *Journal of Marketing, 72*(2), 114–132. doi:10.1509/jmkg.72.2.114

Tellis, G. J., Prabhu, J. C., & Chandy, R. K. (2009). Radical innovation across nations: The preeminence of corporate culture. *Journal of Marketing, 73*(1), 3–23. doi:10.1509/jmkg.73.1.3

Zhang, J., Benedetto, C. A. D., & Hoenig, S. (2009). Product development strategy, product innovation performance, and the mediating role of knowledge utilization: Evidence from subsidiaries in China. *Journal of International Marketing, 17*(2), 42–58. doi:10.1509/jimk.17.2.42

KEY TERMS AND DEFINITIONS

Competitor Orientation: An element of market orientation, it means that a seller understands the short-term strengths and weaknesses and long-term capabilities and strategies of both the key current and potential competitors.

Customer Intelligence: The knowledge about the customer which might be collected e.g. by focus groups, surveys and observation.

Customer Orientation: The integration of customer needs and strategies as well as the processes of an organisation.

Incremental Innovation: The improvements/expansions of existing products, services, processes, technical or administrative conditions. Incremental innovation does not cause a significant departure from the status-quo.

Innovation: In the context of this study innovation is measured by three categories: counts of incremental, radical and overall innovation. Innovativeness is the total of all innovations put into practice, both radical and incremental, in all typologies.

Innovation Drivers: Capabilities relevant for high business performance in mature companies.

Innovation Supporters: Capabilities necessary over the entire company life.

Innovation Triggers: Capabilities with a strong impact in a start-up phase.

Market Dynamism: The change of technology, customer needs, and the actions of competitors. It is assumed that dynamic markets are unpredictable with regard to the competitive conditions.

Market Orientation: The organizational culture that most effectively and efficiently creates the necessary behaviors for the creation of superior value for customers and, thus, superior performance for the business.

Radical Innovation: Radical innovations in products, services, processes, etc. are breakthroughs that fundamentally change a product or service or process.

Chapter 12
Fashion Retail Innovation:
About Context, Antecedents, and Outcome in Technological Change Projects

Torben Tambo
Aarhus University, Denmark

ABSTRACT

Fashion retail is recognised for its strong capabilities in product innovation, while also having the potential to improve the governance of technology-based process innovation. This chapter proposes a model perspective in management of technology and innovation, including special requirements of fashion retailing. In particular, this chapter discusses the context of fashion retailing understood as product and brand-based characteristics. A case study-based methodology is then used to guide an analysis of antecedents and (expected) outcome of fashion retail innovation. IT-based innovation dominates, but innovation is suggested to include a broader scope of technologies. Contrary to innovation maturity models, this chapter proposes to consider innovation as a continuous refinement between dynamic capabilities and absorptive capacity where technologies must be adapted to the special characteristics of the fashion retail industry.

INTRODUCTION

Fashion retail holds a dominant position in many of the physical retail environments in the industrialised societies, no matter if we look at high streets, malls, department stores or outlet centres (Zentes, Morschett, & Schramm-Klein, 2007; Aastrup, Bjerre, Kornum, & Kotzab, 2010). Fashion remains a megatrend where consumers are attracted and the "magic" remains strong despite criticisms of waste, lack of sustainability and un-

necessary consumption (Pomodoro, 2013). Also in emerging economies, malls are dominated by fashion being constructed at an unprecedented pace (Sinha & Kar, 2010). With 15 years of proliferation of e-commerce, it is remarkable that fashion retailing persists while newsstands, music shops, bookstores, ticket agencies, etc. have vanished from physical retailing or declined into obscurity (Caro & Martinez-de-Albéniz, 2014). The change from physical retailing to e-tail/retail to multichannel and now to omni-channel retailing

DOI: 10.4018/978-1-4666-8297-9.ch012

has been a journey during which brand owners, consumers and retailers have tested and tried a great many technologies, have experienced a lot of success and failure (Brynjolfson, Hu, & Rahman, 2013; Grewal & Levy, 2009).

Technology, especially information technology (IT) and, to some extent, supply chain technologies (Purvis, Naim, & Towill, 2013), has been the fulcrum of the retail innovation with retailers paradoxically adopting the roles of both eager technology adopters and sceptic spectators to their own businesses lacking deep technological insight (Pantano & Timmermans, 2010; De Felice, Petrillo, & Autorino, 2013; Cillo & Verona, 2008). The literature is divided over the level of technology investments in retailing with claims of retailing being on par with comparable industries (Doms, Jarmin, & Klimek, 2004) as well as claims of retailing being laggards (Reynolds & Hristov, 2009; Reynolds, Howard, Cuthbertson, & Hristov, 2007). As the fashion retail industry has traditionally been focusing on product innovation and partially on service or customer service innovation (EU Commission, 2014), there is a schism between the orientation towards brand expression, consumer experience and technology. The underlying assumption of this chapter is that the retail industry, at least at store level, is somewhat distant to innovation in areas of technology-supported business processes, enabling technologies and in-store technologies. At the same time, the retail industry is quite technology savvy in terms of investments, focus on the data-driven business and with a booming marketplace for retail technologies (Stern & Verweij, 2014; Galloway, 2013; Gartner, 2014; Platt Retail Institute, 2012).

E-commerce serves as an exemplary case, where the fashion industry has acted as a rapid adopter (Bruce & Daly, 2010; Heinemann & Schwartzl, 2010; Tambo, 2014a). It has so far avoided several of the downsides of online commerce experienced in other retail segments, for instance store closures and a one-eyed price-only focus (Suryandari & Paswan, 2014; Caro & Martinez-de-Albeniz, 2014; Klena, 2013). The e-commerce introduction has changed many fashion companies in a more technological direction (McColl & Moore, 2013). This is furthermore motivating studies in efficient planning and assessment of technological innovation in the (fashion) retail industry (Pantano & Viassone, 2013).

This chapter aims at analysing selected technological development projects in the space between brand owners and retailers in fashion chains to get closer to an understanding of what drives projects forward in respect to technological design and implementation, what makes the initiative fit with the business requirements and what the outcome is. The chapter suggests a review model for innovation capability assessment in selected areas of retailing, namely the technological innovation taking place between the brand owner and the stores in the chain of the brand.

THEORETICAL BACKGROUND

In considering a theoretical perspective for innovation and technology in retailing, a distinction must be made between centralised technologies and decentralised technologies (Zentes et al., 2007). Centralised technologies are driven from chain headquarters and impact the full retail operation; e.g. when prices in webshops are lower than in stores, it will immediately affect all stores. Decentralised technologies are distinctive to retailing, as retailing involves a larger geographical dispersion of people, knowledge, equipment and real estate. Centralised and decentralised technologies will typically interact, making technological changes complex and risky. Third parties will normally be deeply engaged in the technological development and the subsequent implementation and operation. Innovation will thus normally start from triads and exercise a trend towards an actual, multi-actor network.

Retail Theory

Retailing is the organised endpoints in most supply chains, and organisational design is highly determinative for the function and meaning of the individual organisational entity (Castelli & Brun, 2010; De Brito, Carbone, & Blanquart, 2008; Brun et al., 2008). The assumption of this chapter is that retailing is mostly, or as a major trend, organised as branded chains (Zentes et al., 2007). The branding can relate to the chain (e.g. "Walmart") or the merchandise (e.g. "H&M" or "Gap"). Occasionally, stores can operate with both own brands, aka private labels (e.g. "Debenhams", "Peek & Cloppenburg"), and general brands (e.g. "Diesel", "Levis").

Ownership, governance and chain coherence is a contributing factor for the formation of the retail chain. Chains may involve multiple ownership structures pertaining to varying degrees of local influence on store profiling and operations (Berman & Evans, 2007; Zentes et al., 2007). Franchise is commonly used in chains to ensure local operational responsibility while retaining a corporate (global) look-and-feel of the store (Lu, Karpova, & Fiore, 2011). Various countries mandate local co-ownership of stores. The simplest form of ownership is when the chain and the stores have the same owner (e.g. "H&M").

Special for retailing is the involvement of large amounts of real estate and physical processes that point to location, transportation, convenience, attraction and human resources as key issues (Lu et al., 2011; Arrigo, 2010). Its physical nature makes retail investment intensive and means that, although brands can be dynamic in the marketplace, the retailing as such is rather static.

Logistics and supply chain management are integrated with a general theory of retailing, and any fashion retailing organisation needs to keep a strong focus on these disciplines as a management framework or associated with the IT systems of the organisation (Battista & Schiraldi, 2013; De Brito et al., 2008; Brun et al., 2008; Brun & Castelli, 2008; Caniato et al., 2014; Castelli & Brun, 2010; Christopher & Peck, 1997). Also associated with this field, corporate social responsibility (CSR) (Lueg et al., 2013) has increasingly evolved as a theoretical position within fashion retailing (Caro & Martinez-de-Albeniz, 2014).

In fashion retailing, a number of particular issues add to the operational practices. Seasonality is determining for product life cycles (Wong, Arlbjørn, Hvolby, & Johansen, 2006) and tends to shorten down to the level of fast fashion where new products can be introduced on a weekly basis (Zhenxiang & Lijie, 2011; Arrigo, 2010). Assortments and assortment planning also add to the operational practices (Rajaram, 2001). Pricing is an independent area of both price setting, bundle prices, discount approaches and markdowns (Choi, 2007); price structures relate both to consumer prices and price and promotional schemes between the central brand organisation and the retailer (Vaagen & Wallace, 2008; Kurata & Yue, 2008; Lee & Rhee, 2008; Gereffi, 2008; Choi et al., 2013).

E-commerce and internet-driven marketing impact most retail operations directly or indirectly (Bruce & Daly, 2010; Song, Hwang, Kim, & Kwak, 2013; Blazquez, 2014; Piotrowicz & Cuthbertson, 2014). In multi-channel environments, products can be sold in parallel; typically across both physical retail and e-commerce. In omni-channel retailing, any combination of channels can promote, sell, deliver and service products (Tambo, 2014b); such channels may include mobile platforms, games, social media, bloggers and cross-branding.

Innovation Management and Assessment

Innovation is colloquially related to some kind of breakthrough in technologies and processes. Garcia and Calantone (2002) term this as "newness", which can relate to, among others, the world, the industry, the firm, the customer, etc.

(Christensen, 2013). Innovation must be rightfully defined and understood to provide sense and transcend from colloquialism into appropriate contexts of change, improvement, solutions and new systems (Kusunoki & Aoshima, 2010). Innovation must emerge from the organisation's ability to manage and utilise the innovation, often referred to as the dynamic capability (Caniato et al., 2013; Hemphälä & Magnusson, 2012; Cillo & Verona, 2008). The organisation's ability to cope with larger changes, complex changes and several changes in converting innovation into business would be called its absorptive capacity (Enkel & Heil, 2014; Hervas-Oliver & Sempere-Ripoll, 2014).

Armbruster et al. (2008) consider organisational innovation to be the ability create and sustain organisational change and to enable the organisation to perform differently and provide a higher level of innovation. Several scholars point to the need for a Technological Innovation System (TIS) (Bergek et al., 2008) extended to include understandings of Organisational Innovation Systems (OIS), too.

In recent years, there has been a strong focus on open innovation, where perspectives of interorganisational collaboration within innovation (Ganter & Hecker, 2014; Kennard, 2012) are highlighted, particularly innovation in business communities, industry initiatives, company-supplier-university collaborations and global networks (Guercini & Runfola, 2010; Tambo, 2014a).

Two of the studies of innovation management are also related to of assessment of innovation (de Jesus-Hitzschky, 2007; Stern & Verweij, 2014). Innovation assessment is the assessment of innovation through the stages of innovation; from early innovation, through phases of maturing, to implementation and further life-cycle management. Assessment must follow the argument above on capability in the early phases and capacity in the implementation phase. Assessment relates to the overall ability to go from pre-stage to post-stage

of the innovation process (Cerne et al., 2013). This also means that innovation is not necessarily about the individual company's ability to develop technological artefacts, but about how to manage the network in which these artefacts are developed. In Tambo (2011), it is described how a company manages the development of point-of-sale systems in a retail organisation without having hardware or software skills by coordinating the network between retailers and vendors.

The fashion industry is generally very successful in product innovation, including the development of new and advanced fabrics, trimmings, printing and finishings (Bandinelli et al., 2013), particularly when considering that most "time-to-market" product life-cycles are less than nine months. "Green" manufacturing and advanced supply chain development are also areas where the fashion industry has demonstrated a high level of maturity of innovation. When it comes to management and assessment of innovation of process and enabling technologies, it is necessary to approach the relationship between the actual technological artefacts and the context of use – be it organisationally, culturally or technologically.

Within innovation management, it is critical to manage activities not meeting expectations on an ongoing basis. Cost overrun is also typical and a reason to redefine or terminate a project. Loss of scope, scope creep and technological obsolescence (Pantano et al., 2013) are other reasons to halt or redefine activities at any point in their life cycle.

Retail Technology

For years, retail technologies at store level consisted of the point-of-sale (POS) system (Shaw & Leeming, 1998). At the brand headquarter, the most dominant technology would most likely be the enterprise resource planning (ERP) system and some supply chain management (SCM) technologies, unless this was outsourced (Brun et al., 2008). Over the past 10 years, retail technologies have grown in number and complexity (Tambo,

2011). As a dominant technology provider, Cisco has suggested the following categories of in-store, networked technologies:

- *Connected retail solutions,*
- *Digital media systems,*
- *Remote expert assistance,*
- *Video surveillance,*
- *Payment systems/EFT,*
- *Workforce optimisation/WFO,*
- *Lean store inventory management/SCM. (Cisco, from Tambo, 2011)*

The literature on new in-store services is growing (Pantano & Viassone, 2013; Blazquez, 2014). Ayanso et al. (2010) discuss technologies where e-commerce supported at store level is viewed as retail technologies, which is in line with other studies pointing to the increasingly closer integration between physical and online retail and the impact of this on the technologies of the store (Heinemann & Schwartzl, 2010). Jørgensen et al. (2010) describe the case of a smartphone-based system for visual merchandising (Wu et al., 2013). Klena (2013) points to issues of the data accumulated across platforms and channels being part of the information available in-store for servicing the customer. The mobile devices of the consumers are increasingly in focus as technological artefacts within the store (Magrath & McCormick, 2013; Mangiaracina et al., 2012). In addition to traditional media systems, there are also interactive media systems that might influence the store; Pantano (2014) mentions an interactive mirror and a game simulator.

Systems for data collection, data enrichment, operational reporting, metrics and visualisation and similar technologies related to business intelligence form part of the overall technological orientation of retailing (Tambo et al., 2012; Iannone et al., 2013). The portfolio of analytics can furthermore comprise technologies for planning, forecasting, prediction and strategic analysis (Lui et al., 2013; Xia et al., 2012; Hübner, 2011; SAS, 2014; Wong & Guo, 2010).

Stern and Verweij (2014) describe retail technology innovation as broad and integrated, normally encompassing complex elements of both digital and physical technologies with an emphasis on issues such as sales displays, store layout, product merchandising and associated off-site or in-store digital services. Gartner (2014) characterises the current technological development in retail to be "disruptive, pervasive and irreversible" with issues such as mobile technologies outpacing computers in digital commerce, consumerisation, consumer-to-consumer support and sales processes that are "continuous, contiguous, convenient and consistent".

Retail Technology Innovation

The Oslo Manual describes four basic types of innovation (OECD, 2005): product innovation, process innovation, marketing innovation and organisational innovation. All types are relevant to fashion retail, although product innovation is already at a high level.

Reynolds and Hristov (2009) discuss the fact that, in retailing, innovation is generally perceived to be low, but that the picture, when appropriately and adequately defining the concept, might be more positive: In particular, it is necessary to consider barriers to innovation such as lack of skilled personnel, risks, costs and non-compliance with regulations.

Technological development is not attributed to single actants or drivers, but could beneficially be analysed from the push-pull perspective (Brem & Voigt, 2009; Pantano & Viassone, 2013). Gartner (2014) and Ebeltoft Group (Stern & Verweij, 2014) observe consumer behaviour, competitive landscapes and technological opportunities as drivers of the innovation momentum. Consumers' shift in online commerce from computers to smartphones, for instance, is creating a host of technological opportunities, "push", but is also calling for a "pull", where innovators must address the phone to reach out to the consumers.

In developing an overall framework for theorising on retail technology innovation, and in particular fashion retail innovation, it is necessary to pinpoint the fundamentals of innovation in an environment with these characteristics:

- What kind of organisational environment is the innovation intended for? Environment is broadly seen as commercial, social, physical, geographical and cultural. This is the *context* of innovation.

- Why has the innovation activity at all started and been conceptualised? Is there a certain issue that needs to be improved? Or do we want to explore or exploit a certain technology or business opportunity? Or is it all about keeping pace with competition and stay abreast of the industry? Here we are looking at the *antecedents* of the innovation.

- What is the result? Or anticipated result of the innovation? At all levels and broadly understood. Even the results of individual phases of the innovation could be interesting to review and analyse. Here it is a matter of identifying relevant, direct or indirect, *outcomes* of the innovation activity.

The triad of context, antedecent and outcome has relevance to the activity on an overall basis, but could be applied to parts of the activity as well. It is also worthwhile to consider that most activities would involve a degree of organisational learning, potentially resulting in smaller or larger adjustments to the planned innovation. Larger adjustments could range from termination, merger, reduction and increase in scope.

METHOD

This chapter will use a qualitative, case-based methodology (Ellram, 1996) in the analysis of context, antecedents and outcome of the in-novation activities. This study is qualitative, cross-disciplinary and inspired by interpretivism (Walsham, 1998; Lee, 1989). The basic platform of retail technologies is viewed as an innovation system (Bergek et al., 2008). Information conveyed by the technological platform includes disciplines such as sales, customer relationship management, branding and an array of socio-technical issues, which each has research traditions of its own (Klein & Myers, 1989). This paper stretches beyond business strategy into strategy of technology (Brem & Voigt, 2009), but keeps the scope of technology broad and open.

A critical issue within retail technology innovation is that various technologies relate to different foci: social commerce, mobile commerce, affiliate marketing and gaming. Thus, the research agenda must follow an agenda of diversity (Taylor et al., 2009). Communication is always prevalent in innovation studies, and communication conveys social constructs, i.e. aims at retaining the view on the techno-social construct around the technologies; the context of the system, more than the system itself, is critical (Avgerou, 2001). Smithson & Hirschheim (1998) have in their seminal contribution(s) underlined especially information systems as a research discipline of comprehension through evaluation of technological and business factors.

To avoid studying past technologies, this chapter is based on cases with a strong empirical foundation and studied in close collaboration with practitioners (Benbasat & Zmud, 1999) emphasising relevance in practice. In designing the research agenda, reason must be in focus, and it should provide practitioners as well as research communities with insights from the matured use of retail technologies.

This study is based on data collected from a number of fashion companies pursuing a commercial interest in technological development in keeping with Klein & Myers (1999). The data have been collected by means of unstructured

Figure 1. Research model

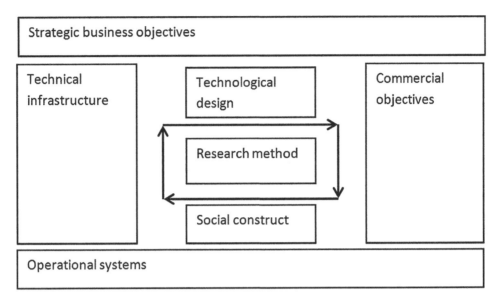

and open-ended interviews with managers, technology suppliers and business partners. The data collection identified strategic, tactical and operational approaches to technological innovation in each case. The method can be conceived as revolving between two main pillars of *technical infrastructure* (enablers) and a set of *commercial objectives* (promoters) with two beams of *technological design* and the *social construct*.

The social construct includes the branding organisation and the retail operation as well as relevant partners typically within the supply chain but, in this case, also within actors in the innovation network.

Technological design includes decision-making about technology life cycles along with the functional design of the technology. The boundaries of the method are made by the business strategy and the existing operational systems – with organisational and temporal limitations inspired by Ahleman et al. (2013) and their suggestions of focusing on theoretical and empirical rooting of the project management research contrary to dominant prescriptive and conceptual research.

MAIN FOCUS OF THE CHAPTER

Innovation practices are the representations of intentions related to an overall direction of innovation and the field of realisation, implementation and operations. In retailing, technological innovation must spring very direct from the creation of increased attractiveness for the consumer. This applies to "back office", enabling, technologies as well as direct consumer-oriented technologies, such as in-store entertainment, internet-based services, mobile functionalities or cross-branding initiatives.

Fashion retailers might be sceptical of general technological innovation, as many innovations continuously fail to prove their economic viability. The above-mentioned approach of being haphazard and opportunistic (Reynolds & Hristov, 2009) is most likely not related to bad intent but to intrinsic characteristics of the industry, such as

- Brand expression comes before operational effectiveness,
- Brand expression is to ensure high margins again lowering the pressure for effectiveness,

- High geographical dispersion in different retail environments: Mall, high street, shop-in-shop, e-commerce penetration,
- Seasonality and short product life cycles as adverse to long-term planning and investments,
- Education and skills of the personnel,
- Cultural phenomena.

I the following, a number of cases will be presented to highlight technological innovation, innovation planning, change management and impact considerations.

Case: SportStar

The key interaction lying behind the chapter's assumptions is the dyadic relationship between the fashion chain headquarters and the stores. This can beneficially be extended into a triadic relationship with an external party specialised in the actual technology as innovator or vendor or within research and implementation. In the following case, an external party plays an interesting role in creating innovation between the central and decentral level.

The global fashion and recreational equipment chain of SportStar determined a need to automate and digitise its corporate central lookbooks for visual merchandising. In collaboration with the Dutch technology vendor Visual Retailing, SportStar converted its seasonal lookbooks into a digital mobile platform that could enable fast and accurate global communication with visual merchandisers.

SportStar has several thousand stores operated by themselves or as franchises. Motivations for the initiative were practically founded in the potential of the digital technology combined with the perceived and actual low usage of expensive printed paper documentation. After some time, SportStar realised that there were some issues with the digital solution. Visual Retailing started to analyse usage and effect of the digital system

and found a certain degree of resistance to the technology at store level. Some stores felt that the system overruled the creativeness of the store and merchandisers and overlooked local and short-term adaptations of store decoration normally done on an ongoing basis. At the local level, store operators have a good sense of appropriateness and the focal consumer's tastes and desires.

Consequently, Visual Retailing decided to accept that full local control was infeasible and should be replaced by a more collaborative approach. The mobile visual merchandising was then modified to enable photos to be taken locally and uploaded and exposed centrally to display deviations between the lookbooks and the actual merchandising. Furthermore, the idea was formed that similar stores could share pictures and issue comments and other information to highlight good and bad merchandising. The mobile system was thus turned into a collaborative approach aiming at understanding and supporting local needs and traditions. The outcome of the implementation was in this sense an innovation effort focused on the needs at store level and the ability to collaborate between stores.

In the longer term, Visual Retailing will be extending the system to enable business intelligence data from the stores to be integrated with the various conducts of the local merchandising teams. Thereby the economic impact of compliance/non-compliance with the corporate guidelines can be quantified, or at least, the evaluation of the merchandising approach can be supported by quantitative information, given that stores are sufficiently comparable. Examples quoted are store locations in recreational areas, where the weather might be more determining for the consumers' behaviour. For instance, in sunny weather, more swimsuits will be sold, and in rainy weather less; however, raincoat sales will increase.

Visual Retailing's motivation for creating online mobile technologies is based on several years of experience with offline fashion store planning technologies. The offline technologies then "feed" data into the online system.

SportStar's initial motivation for working with Visual Retailing was the idea of increasing the effectiveness of its communication. The issue of avoiding print and shipping is less important for pursuing a stronger brand adherence among its stores. As responsible for the brand expression and the values of the brand, SportStar must also consider how to protect, "enforce" and manage the brand at store level.

Case: ICC

ICC is a premium brand fashion company based in Northern Europe. ICC operates 200+ stores directly or as franchises. ICC wants to provide the same service to high-end consumers in stores and on e-commerce platforms. Whatever preferences and behaviour exercised by the consumer on e-commerce platforms should reflect past store or e-commerce buying patterns and should also be utilised in stores to support the consumer seamlessly between platforms and channels. This is in line with the concept of omni-channel retailing; however, the actual implementation is similar to that of multichannel retailing with "weak" (offline) links between the online and the in-store systems.

A unique customer ID will provide a lot of advantages primarily in the customer service experience. However, several back-office functions will also be able to benefit from such an initiative:

- Marketing and campaigns can be much better targeted and customised to the specific customer segments, even down to the individual customer.
- The impact of marketing can be traced and evaluated. An actual "return-of-investment" of marketing expenditures can be introduced.
- The online services can be qualified at the shop assistant level with data on past purchases and taste.

- Return rates on e-commerce might be reduced by providing the consumer with better advice with respect to appropriate choices given data from prior purchasing activities.
- Generally consider the unique ID as an extended loyalty programme covering both benefits, bonuses, previews and added services.

IT vendors, e-commerce providers, department stores, retail management and equipment suppliers all need to collaborate. A common data exchange platform constitutes the "workhorse", but customer relationship management (CRM) needs to be introduced at both store and consumer level. This pushes the limits of CRM and requires that a broad network of vendors and consultants contributes. Retailers will have a particular role in interacting with consumers who both use stores and e-commerce, and retailers will have to utilise their technological and business network in creating the desired services.

Actual tasks involved are:

- Exchange of customer data back and forth between ICC's head office and the external e-commerce service provider.
- The stores of ICC use different POS. Adaptations of each POS must be made to ensure registration of customer data, use of customer data in sales situations and exchange of data with head office systems.
- Some stores are shop-in-shop concepts operated by ICC but with POS hosted by the department store operator. Data exchange must be set up with the IT service provider of the department stores.
- Marketing systems are operated by third parties and are different from brand to brand and occasionally from country to country. System operatives must be engaged in using data.

- The merchandising and retail planning operatives of ICC must, through the CRM system, monitor the process and consider engagement and functionalities at brand and store level.
- In addition to the CRM system, ICC is running a range of IT platforms; some are to be terminated, some will be continuing. Many business processes rely on more than one IT system. Data must be disseminated across relevant platforms with a robust technology.

Initially, approximately 10 suppliers are needed to implement Unique ID. Some suppliers have several roles and can therefore take on more of the assignments above. Within the internal IT systems, a so-called Enterprise Service Bus (ESB) has been established as a means to securely transport data between systems.

Unique ID is justified by the increased level of service to upscale/premium customers. The project is included in the long-term IT/business strategy and is expected to be implemented over several years.

Case: Bumble

The Bumble Company is a European sport/fashion company. The company name and the brand are identical; the company has existed for more than 40 years, and the brand is well-known and admired especially among handball fans. The main markets are Eastern and Western Europe and East Asia. Bumble does not operate stores or have full store concepts. Instead, Bumble works closely with large chains and department stores on well-established shop-in-shop systems.

Bumble's brand appeals to a wide range of consumers in the leisure segment: men, boys and younger women. Its brand and logo are highly recognised and closely associated with an active lifestyle.

Bumble's central office manages the brand, develops new products, carries out procurement and serves selected markets. Bumble's sales organisation is distributed between 15 country offices with a high degree of autonomy. Some sales offices also issue purchase orders directly to the manufacturers.

Due to its dependence on relatively few large chain store customers, Bumble has been hesitant to initiate B2C e-commerce. Motivators for establishing a B2C e-commerce initiative are, among others:

- Lack of clear digital presence and identity related to Bumble's products.
- Lack of a fast platform for displaying products and prices formerly only printed in catalogues.
- The desire to use a sales platform for strengthening the brand and support storytelling.
- Opportunity to support the community of brand followers, the brand value and the activity of handball.

After a while, the e-commerce project team wanted to investigate the general presence of the brand on the internet. Contrary to the common belief in the headquarters, the team found more and more websites already selling the Bumble brand. In a total of 12 countries, it was found that 49 retailers had established e-commerce platforms and had added Bumble's products to these. Furthermore, 25 specialised webshops had been set up with more or less awkward names – all with references to Bumble, however. In total, 74 e-commerce sites were dedicated to Bumble or selling Bumble on a multi-brand basis.

Some of the sites were created or condoned by local sales offices impatient to have an online sale without the knowledge or consent from the headquarters. Others were unknown to Bumble, even as wholesale customers. Bumble "suspected" that some trade agents with exclusive rights in certain countries systematically re-exported goods. Basically, the sites should figure as regular customers, which is largely the case with the segment "retailers with e-commerce", but not with the segment "specialised e-commerce". For the "retailers with e-commerce", the e-commerce activity was not included in or guided by the general sales terms and conditions between Bumble and the retailers.

It is assumed that given the relative anonymity of customers, the turnover in most of these 74 stores is very low. Many of the sites did not follow any kind of corporate branding schemes and used, for instance, 5-8-year-old logos and design. In the worst cases, logos were badly scanned and of very low quality.

At an international sales meeting, Bumble decided to start up a management framework for the Independent Online Retailer (IOR) segment. Above all, the management framework consisted of the ability to recognise B2B customers as having e-commerce activities. Within a period of time, IORs not adhering to corporate guidelines would be asked to end their activities. The intention of the management framework was to avoid brand degradation and to support brand integrity. This is assumed to be a risk if:

1. The visual presentation of the brand is outdated, unprofessional or not aligned with the authorised look.
2. Product presentations are wrong, misleading, not aesthetically pleasing or out of line with corporate intentions.
3. Consumers' rights are undermined or violated regarding mainly shipping policies, payment terms, return policies and warranties.
4. The context of the products is inappropriate, e.g. connected to fraudulent products, irrelevant products (e.g. food, tobacco, alcohol) or highly differently appealing products not related to the active lifestyle.

These risks are assumed to affect Bumble's core values of honesty, active lifestyle and "mental balance". Bumble decided to take the following initiatives to ensure and manage online presence as a whole:

1. Notify the sales organisation of the need to be aware of the existence and potential consequences of the IOR segment.
2. Set up digital corporate design guidelines available to all sales offices, salespersons and customers.
3. Establish an electronic repository from which IORs can retrieve graphics and pictures, including a Digital Asset Management (DAM) database closely linked to Bumble's Master Data Management (MDM) system of names, numbers, properties, prices and markets.
4. Insist on making the IORs sales and delivery terms as good as or better than Bumble's general conditions, e.g. providing a returned goods policy, payment terms and warranty.
5. Sustain central activities aiming at making the corporate brand site work.
6. Seek to close webshops not following the stipulated rules by tracking the supply chain.

Bumble is well aware that the 74 identified IOR shops are just a limited subset of all online resellers. Generally, the large chain and department store customers are already online or about to become online. This means that most of the customer portfolio per default will implement online sales channels alongside the physical stores. Bumble considers initiatives sufficient to protect the digital branding for the next while. The implemented technological solutions will to a large extent support both the "grey" online retailers and the large "white" retailers that already make up the majority of Bumble customers.

Case: TexBrand

TexBrand is a leading European company in fashion wholesale and retail. TexBrand is privately held and operates around 2,000 stores under five primary brands and several specialisations or affiliations of these brands. The stores are partially operated and owned by TexBrand and partially by a network of partners. About 50% of the turnover is generated from wholesale activities to department stores, general chain stores and online retailers. Common to the stores is that they exclusively sell TexBrand's brands and that they use point-of-sales (POS) systems supplied by TexBrand. The POS system provides fast and concise data to the stores and facilitates retrieval of data for the central data warehouse reporting system. TexBrand has since 2007 had increasing success with online retailing. Originally, online retailing was organised in a separate entity. Gradually, some multi-channel retailing features have been introduced, but full-fletched omni-channel retailing has only been present at an experimental basis.

The organisational separation of the online activities and the organisational distance to some retail partners have led to the identification of insufficiencies in the current master data model. The model was designed to support seasonality, product creation, purchasing and supply chain management from the manufacturers to the stores. The model was not designed to support high quality marketing material, photos, multimedia, a post-warehouse product life cycle and a multi-channel retail business model. Furthermore, the different primary brands have different cultures of data management, ranging from loosely structured processes to processes with a high level of governance. Adding to this, the existing data model has been tree-structured from brands to seasons and categories. Now, the business considers aiming for a more dynamic structure of products combined across seasons and categories to suit the need for more specialised retailers, wholesalers and e-commerce operators.

TexBrand has now decided to redesign the operating master data model.

Important positions in the redesign are:

- Extending the data model from supply chain management into marketing, adding characteristics of PDM/PLM.
- Recognising the dynamic character of the sales process ranging from one-off orders for short seasons and up to never-of-out-stock concepts.
- Improved support of mixed channel structures.
- More distinctive preservation of product history in the in-store phases.
- Late phases of the product life cycle are seen as ideal for increasing the sales to wholesale customers, online retailers and partner-owned stores.

The case highlights the shortcomings of the traditional ERP-inspired master data model mostly servicing the supply chain management needs and to a lesser extent the commercial needs. Commercial needs require a broader understanding, especially considering the rapid growth in the digital channels and the expected slow decline of physical retailing. Products are distributed and sold differently on the different platforms, and this business model must be embedded into the MDM. Images, marketing material, rich media, references to external product referrals and localisations (country/language adaptations) in the MDM will improve the overall efficiency of the sales process.

The stores are to benefit from the new data model in having data better adapted to the store operations. A typology of nine different store formats has been developed. Formats range from "company owner, company operated, single-brand store, small" to "multi-brand, partner-owned, partner-operated, multi-brand, large". By having the opportunity to group and "package" products more dynamically, stores may experience better correspondence between offered products and the store format. Furthermore, the improved data model will enable a more logical connection between physical retail and digital channels as data is founded on the same central model.

As an effort of innovation, the master data project will integrate business functions better, integrate retailers with online activities and better meet the needs of internal and external e-commerce operations. The data model is specified on a conceptual level by TexBrand's internal personnel. A range of suppliers are needed to ensure full value of the model throughout the system landscape: Suppliers of POS systems, data producing systems in general (e.g. photo automates, freight costing, currency rates), data integration services, service providers of the customers and hosting providers. All of these noted as parties that have identifiable responsibilities of producing, using and integrating data.

Case Summary

Within the overall objective of this chapter, the cases can be summarised using considerations of context, antecedent and outcome with emphasis on the cross-cutting matters and transitional character of each case as illustrated in Table 1.

In terms of outcomes, there are specifics influencing each project. The SportStar project is vendor-driven, and the vendor, Visual Retailing, is assumed to continue the development of the technology. ICC has, since the data collection, reduced its organisation significantly and is no longer pursuing the project. Bumble has implemented the framework and been operating it since 2013. TexBrand will be using the developed technological framework in technological transition activities from 2014-2018.

SOLUTIONS AND RECOMMENDATIONS

The four cases represent a variety of contemporary innovative efforts associated with fashion retailing. The activities are unique within each case company and are assumed important within the actual contexts, thereby meeting the definition of innovation of OECD (2005) as: "An innovation is the implementation of a new or significantly improved product (good or service), or process, a new marketing method, or a new organisational method in business practices, workplace organisation or external relations."

Table 1. Case summary

	Context	Antecedents	Outcome
SportStar	Communication of visual merchandising. Global brand expression.	Lacking lookbook interest.	A new context of collaborative store decoration.
ICC	Add value to the service of premium customers. Alignment of IT development with commercial objectives.	Lacking use of consumer insight. Improved consumer service and impact measurement.	A problematic, costly solution to a complex value proposition.
Bumble	A global context of "self-organisation", and the attempt to organise behaviour via technology.	Free internet retailers not following standards.	Greater control of independent e-commerce. Improved brand expression.
TexBrand	In search of the next stage of multi-channel retailing through a common foundation of data.	Data not supporting multi-channel retailing, and "a gap" between supply chain and sales/marketing.	Technical and commercial alignment.

Figure 2. Impact matrix
(de Jesus-Hitzschky, 2007).

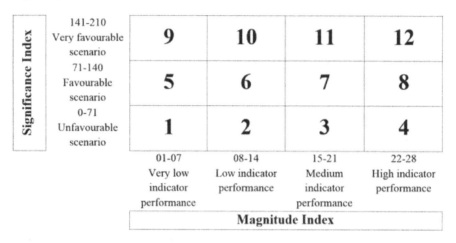

Often, theory requires strategic alignment, but except for ICC, none of the cases have been condoned by a CEO. The cases rather represent a tactically driven effort to improve business via technology and continuously optimise functionality as incremental innovation (Ünay & Zehir, 2012). Despite the radical potential of each innovation, the implementation effort, maturing, "roll-out", communication and harvesting of business value will take 2-5 years. The strategic potential, but tactical reality, seems to be a paradox of the innovation management. Each innovation can be questioned for strategic alignment and might fail to answer, even if it contributes to the overall business objectives. This again adds to the concern of the fashion industry about its ability to manage technological process innovation.

Innovation Assessment

Innovation assessment is complex and multifactorial. Following de Jesus-Hitzschky (2007), assessment must include the broadest of business, human, social, societal and global aspects. This holds true for certain innovations, but must be limited in the current discussion. Although inspiration can be found in de Jesus-Hitzschky's coupling of the broad parameterised assessment with an impact metric following this as depicted in Figure 2.

De Jesus-Hitzschky (2007) furthermore suggests a weighting based on Extent, Scope and Influence. This weighting is a 360-degree view of the innovation and its impact in its realm of application locally and "globally". Objectives might differ in fashion retailing between the brand and the store, but largely it must be assumed that the dyad has a symbiosis. Innovation assessment is suggested to follow the dominant strands of activity with the overall fashion retail supply chain outlined in Table 2.

Financial flow covers issues of flow of goods and funds and costs of production and brand management. Information flow refers to all data in all respects. Brand expression is the intangible values of the brand, not only design, but issues that can incite affection in the consumer. Retail opportunities are the structure of the retail and goods distribution environment. CSR is social impact. The global business environment is always a factor, whether it is social unrest, commodity prices or real estate speculation. In Table 3, de Jesus-Hitzschky's assessment framework translated into fashion retailing is illustrated.

Scholars often develop the assessment of corporate capability into a maturity model. In this case, this would have been an "innovation maturity model" or "technology maturity model".

Table 2. Simplified fashion retail supply chain and cross-cutting flows

(Global) Business Environment											
Design	Raw Material	Cut-Sew-Trim	Dye	Transport	Warehouse	Transport	In-Store	Purchase	Use	Re-use	Waste or Recycle
Financial Flow											
Information Flow											
Brand Expression											
Retail Opportunities											
CSR											

Battista & Schiraldi (2013) discuss a logistics maturity model and its application within the fashion industry. In the cases, there are indications of the processes to be on a relatively low level of maturity prior to project execution. Each activity of innovation seems to have its individual context set by employees, technologies, business environments and a range of other factors. The "maturity" lies in the ability to match technological opportunities with business objectives and drive the process onwards from this.

Rather, a maturity model would be a model guiding change related to technology-based business transformation and, in this respect,

it would take as its starting point the dynamic capabilities (Caniato et al., 2013; Hemphälä & Magnusson, 2012) of the company but need to rely on its absorptive capacity (Enkel & Heil, 2014; Hervas-Oliver & Sempere-Ripoll, 2014) in the transformation from innovation to business. Noteworthy is the non-linearity of the process: SportStar started to use one innovation, but found that it failed to produce the intended outcome, for which reason the innovation scope was refined and recontextualised with a clearer outcome. ICC realised that the innovation would require many iterations and substantial initiatives throughout its partner network. Bumble

Table 3. Weighted assessment model

Weight	Factor	Data of Assessment	Factor's Weight Range	Correctional Factor
Supply Chain Management				
2	More effective purchasing		0..2	
2	Improved collaboration with both retailers and wholesale customers		0..2	
Brand Expression				
Improve operational effectiveness at store level				
Criteria, weights and data for each item of the supply chain and its cross-cutting flows.				

realised early on that its innovativeness relies on recurring reviews of the behaviour of independent online retailers. TexBrand is also not currently aware of where the ongoing activities will lead, but sees this as an opportunity to redefine marketplaces.

Issues of the dynamic capability may include:

- Possession of sufficient infrastructure and ability to make this work.
- Ability to establish and govern adequate networks of inter- and intra-organisational actors.
- Ability to learn from other/similar industries.
- Competencies in converting innovation into operational technologies.

Issues of the absorptive capacity may include:

- Infrastructural development, e.g. availability of the same digital tools at store level as the consumers have and physical realignment of the store to reflect changes.
- Frameworks for rewarding the store for engagement.
- Reduction of distance between the store and the brand.
- Training.
- Metrics and analytics that ensure a transparent outcome.

To summarise innovation assessment, the companies benefit from being able to co-think business and technology; not as business should be ahead and technology should be adapted, but in the sense that technologies can both meet existing requirements and create new opportunities.

Fashion Considerations

Fundamental to fashion is the ability to balance brand expression with supply chain management. The brand's expression is the value proposition in the form of design, storytelling, quality, price and CSR. In fashion retail, additional factors play a role, such as store location, customer demography, store decoration, staff attitude and customer service profile. Supply chain management must ensure the flow of products, as suggested in Figure 2.

It is important to consider if the described technological innovation differs between fashion and any other commercial organisation, and fashion retail and any other retailer. Examples of issues are suggested in Table 4.

Technological development in fashion retail must reflect the intrinsic characteristics but obviously "borrows" from general retailing and general commercial organisations. In the examples of Bumble and ICC, suppliers were not particularly associated with the fashion industry. The urgency of understanding and supporting fashion retail is clearly highlighted in the European Commission's

Table 4. Exemplary fashion and fashion retail characteristics

General Commercial Organisations	Fashion, Brand Organisations	Technological Responses
Seasonality bound to purpose. Products have objective values. Objective values remain over time. Existing designs are continuously refined.	Seasonality bound to desire. Products also have subjective values. Subjective values decline. Designs start from scratch at the beginning of each season.	Integrated PLM and SCM. Brand value assessment. Support stock realisation. Improve SCM efficiency.
General and Specialty Retail	**Fashion Retail**	**Technological Adaptation**
Long product life cycle. Space management. General, continuous replenishment. Low margins. High predictability of consumer behaviour.	Short product life cycle. Visual retailing. Selective replenishment. High margins. Low predictability.	High and managed throughput. Qualitative support tools. Ensure relevant models. More holistic approach. Big data-inspired methods.

(2014) recommendations, in which the fashion industry and fashion retail's economic impact is described and the potential of technological innovation is determined as critical for the European economies.

In the case of TexBrand, suppliers are selected specifically to support the fashion retail issues, but also to bring in common knowledge of solutions from general industrial contexts in, for instance, data integration, image/picture databases and specific technological competencies. In the case of SportStar, the supplier, Visual Retailing, has created a suite of applications specifically targeted at fashion retail.

Furthermore, the studies indicate that innovation must interact in synergy with the core values of the fashion industry in terms of brand values, design orientation and support of the consumer's lifestyle. Core values can, for example, be affordability – requirement operational effectiveness – and fast fashion – the ability to maintain different paces in the supply chain. Innovation must therefore be able to encompass fashion characteristics: Short-to-very-short product life cycles, seasonality, trend and category.

Innovation must thus have an outlook for current consumerism and support conversion hereof into new business tendencies, e.g. in-store used items, recommenders/fashion bloggers, new forms of corporate social responsibility (CSR), selling via games, social media and similar new platforms.

Critical Evaluation

This chapter uses a case-based methodology (Ellram, 1996) in order to reach a deeper understanding of the positions and elements involved in the described area of technological innovation. The cases demonstrate the relevance of a mixed-method paradigm with a clear orientation towards the qualitative multi-factor and multi-actor drivers of the innovation in scope.

Reservations as to the cases include the fact that they come from the same area in Northern Europe; however, at least two of the companies are global actors. In other geographies, different, more system-oriented approaches might have been taken. As with Klein & Myers (1989), the cases demonstrate technology as found within theory of socio-technical systems. A critique of this might be "where is the technology" and "where is the economy". For the companies, the technology does not make sense without a business context. Here, the technological scepticism can prove itself to be an advantage for the companies, as effort rather than cost has to be justified. The objectives of the innovation are more important than the specific costs and benefits at a monetary level. For instance, with TexBrand, the costs could amount to anything between one and 50 million EUR, but the benefit could be to achieve a leading position in Europe within its field.

In learning from the companies, TexBrand is the most "regular" fashion company with several brands primarily targeted at demographic segments of the low-to-midrange markets. Bumble and SportStar are both in the fashion-sport segment. During the research, ICC has divested all low-to-midrange brands and only retained premium, high-end brands. However, the challenges seem to remain the same across the fashion sector, which followingly suggests that obtained learnings knowledge could be generalisable. More complex is the degree of technology applied within the respective organisations. Bumble had a "simple" Microsoft Dynamics NAV ERP system prior to the process and outsourced services within marketing, logistics and customer relationships. TexBrand and SportStar have large complex technological infrastructures covering a wide range of corporate processes.

The knowledge contribution of the chapter has the limitations as mentioned above, but it also has opportunities when considering analysing the object of innovation. When thinking context, the cases can provide evidence of a combined technological and business perspective making an inseparable socio-technical construct (Hervas-Oliver & Sempere-Ripoll, 2014). This is also interesting given the methodological inspiration of e.g. Benbasat & Zmud (1999); learning from practitioners to develop theoretical positions suggests relevance to practice.

The cases suggest much diversity in the motivations and expectations of technological innovation. A diversity also found in the contemporary examples of Ebeltoft Group (Stern & Verweij, 2014), as retail technologies range from cutting-edge technologies to impressive brand-oriented physical and online presence.

FUTURE RESEARCH DIRECTIONS

There is every indication that technology is expected to play an increasing role in retailing. Many of these technologies do not exist today. Technological innovation projects are thus assumed to be decisive for existing actors in defending their markets, but also for technological newcomers as well as the chains' abilities to exploit technological innovation and market opportunities.

Amazon's patent of shipment of goods in advance of the customer's decision and based solely on behaviour and correlations with assumed patterns of consumption, eventually shipping with drones, is a case of a potential game changer leaving actual implementation and business impact unexplored (Amazon.com, 2013).

In future studies, it would be interesting to investigate if fashion retailing is able to incorporate technological innovation as firmly in its organisational innovation system as the industry has done with product innovation. The perception of concrete technological artefacts as assets of active management relates to this process; for instance, can geolocation of customers be used for more than offering products in one store – that is, can it also serve to recognise general attitudes of the customer? Or can the past 5 years of sales

history better qualify future purchase than the last 24 months of sales? Research themes of "the exploitation of the unknown" and "surprisingly radical" are thus far more a reality nowadays than in the less technological store with only one POS system, also considering the cases of Ebeltoft Group (Stern & Verweij, 2014), where future and flagship stores are game changers in established fields of retailing.

CONCLUSION

Fashion retail is converging to a far more technological basis than 10 or just 5 years ago; retail management is generally positive towards technology in its early stages, but struggle with integrating innovation management and technology management into the overall fashion management. The high rate of change and receptiveness to innovation is obviously creating some degree of scepticism towards important issues of cost (overrun), technological obsolescence and lack of absorptive capacity, especially at the store level. This chapter has presented four cases that highlight the degree of complexity fashion retailers are facing and need to manage. The cases also indicate a high degree of dynamic capability in scope, impact and level of advanced technologies that fashion retail management must take into account. The cases are a snapshot of an ongoing, seemingly endless development in the respective companies. Gartner (2014) states that "multichannel retailing is not an endgame … (as we) indicated in 2007". Fashion retail has thus started a transition into technology very much inspired by e-commerce.

Basic requirements in innovation management are the ability to identify a context of relevance and importance within the relation between the brand and the store and eventually the consumer. The necessary antecedents of innovation must furthermore be specified as well, as they can form the basis of the technological design process. Outcome is a matter of ability to enact organisational learning from commercial assessment of the technologies in scope. Ongoing redefinition of innovation is not wrong or negative, but a simple activity of innovation management. With this chapter's suggestion of thinking innovation in terms of its "corporate life-cycle" of context, antecedents and outcome assessment, the innovation management of fashion retail is properly guided to move innovation into the inner circle of corporate management attention. In conclusion, this study points to the fact that technological innovation is deeply rooted in and intertwined with business innovation; neither can stand alone, but together they form a dynamic mutuality.

ACKNOWLEDGMENT

Thanks to the following for contributing to the data collection: Per Andersen, Anders Patrick Jørgensen, Tom van Soest, Harald Hovmøller and Rina Hansen.

REFERENCES

Aastrup, J., Bjerre, M., Kornum, N., & Kotzab, H. (2010). The Danish retail market: Overview and highlights. *European Retail Research*, *24*(1), 195–222. doi:10.1007/978-3-8349-8938-3_9

Ahlemann, F., El Arbi, F., Kaiser, M. G., & Heck, A. (2013). A process framework for theoretically grounded prescriptive research in the project management field. *International Journal of Project Management*, *31*(1), 43–56. doi:10.1016/j.ijproman.2012.03.008

Amazon.com. (2013). *Method and system for anticipatory package shipping, US Patent 8,615,473*. Washington, DC: U.S. Patent and Trademark Office.

Armbruster, H., Bikfalvi, A., Kinkel, S., & Lay, G. (2008). Organizational innovation: The challenge of measuring non-technical innovation in large-scale surveys. *Technovation*, *28*(10), 644–657. doi:10.1016/j.technovation.2008.03.003

Arrigo, E. (2010). Innovation and market-driven management in fast fashion -companies. *Symphonya: Emerging Issues in Management*, *2*, 67–85. doi:10.4468/2010.2.06arrigo

Avgerou, C. (2001). The significance of context in information systems and organizational change. *Information Systems Journal*, *11*(1), 43–63. doi:10.1046/j.1365-2575.2001.00095.x

Ayanso, A., Lertwachara, K., & Thongpapanl, N. (2010). Technology-enabled retail services and online sales performance. *Journal of Computer Information Systems*, *50*(3), 102–111.

Bandinelli, R., Rinaldi, R., Rossi, M., & Terzi, S. (2013). New product development in the fashion industry: An empirical investigation of Italian firms. *International Journal of Engineering Business Management*, *5*, 1–9. doi:10.5772/56841

Battista, C., & Schiraldi, M. M. (2013). The logistic maturity model: Application to a fashion company. *International Journal of Engineering Business Management*, *5*, 1–11. doi:10.5772/56838

Benbasat, I., & Zmud, R. W. (1999). Empirical research in information systems. *Management Information Systems Quarterly*, *23*(1), 3–16. doi:10.2307/249403

Bergek, A., Jacobsson, S., Carlsson, B., Lindmark, S., & Rickne, A. (2008). Analyzing the functional dynamics of technological innovation systems: A scheme of analysis. *Research Policy*, *37*(3), 407–429. doi:10.1016/j.respol.2007.12.003

Berman, B., & Evans, J. R. (2007). *Retail management: A strategic approach* (11th ed.). Upper Saddle River, NJ: Prentice Hall.

Blázquez, M. (2014). Fashion shopping in multichannel retail: The role of technology in enhancing the customer experience. *International Journal of Electronic Commerce, 18*(4), 97–116. doi:10.2753/JEC1086-4415180404

Brem, A., & Voigt, K. I. (2009). Integration of market pull and technology push in the corporate front end and innovation management—Insights from the German software industry. *Technovation, 29*(5), 351–367. doi:10.1016/j.technovation.2008.06.003

Bruce, M., & Daly, L. (2010). Innovative process in e-commerce fashion supply chains. In T. C. E. Cheng & T.-M. Choi (Eds.), *Innovative quick response programs in logistics and supply chain management* (pp. 227–242). Heidelberg, Germany: Springer Verlag. doi:10.1007/978-3-642-04313-0_11

Brun, A., Caniato, F., Caridi, M., Castelli, C., Miragliotta, G., Ronchi, S., & Spina, G. (2008). Logistics and supply chain management in luxury fashion retail: Empirical investigation of Italian firms. *International Journal of Production Economics, 114*(2), 554–570. doi:10.1016/j.ijpe.2008.02.003

Brun, A., & Castelli, C. (2008). Supply chain strategy in the fashion industry: Developing a portfolio model depending on product, retail channel and brand. *International Journal of Production Economics, 116*(2), 169–181. doi:10.1016/j.ijpe.2008.09.011

Brynjolfsson, E., Hu, Y. J., & Rahman, M. S. (2013). Competing in the age of omnichannel retailing. *MIT Sloan Management Review, 54*(4).

Caniato, F., Caridi, M., & Moretto, A. (2013). Dynamic capabilities for fashion-luxury supply chain innovation. *International Journal of Retail & Distribution Management, 41*(11/12), 9–9.

Caniato, F., Caridi, M., Moretto, A., Sianesi, A., & Spina, G. (2014). Integrating international fashion retail into new product development. *International Journal of Production Economics, 147*, 294–306. doi:10.1016/j.ijpe.2013.04.005

Caro, F., & Martınez-de-Albéniz, V. (2015in press). Fast fashion: Business model overview and research opportunities. In N. Agrawal & S. A. Smith (Eds.), *Retail supply chain management: Quantitative models and empirical studies* (2nd ed.). New York, NY: Springer.

Castelli, C. M., & Brun, A. (2010). Alignment of retail channels in the fashion supply chain: An empirical study of Italian fashion retailers. *International Journal of Retail & Distribution Management, 38*(1), 24–44. doi:10.1108/09590551011016313

Černe, M., Jaklič, M., & Škerlavaj, M. (2013). Decoupling management and technological innovations: Resolving the individualism–collectivism controversy. *Journal of International Management, 19*(2), 103–117. doi:10.1016/j.intman.2013.03.004

Choi, T. M. (2007). Pre-season stocking and pricing decisions for fashion retailers with multiple information updating. *International Journal of Production Economics, 106*(1), 146–170. doi:10.1016/j.ijpe.2006.05.009

Choi, T. M., Hui, C. L., Liu, N., Ng, S. F., & Yu, Y. (2013). Fast fashion sales forecasting with limited data and time. *Decision Support Systems, 59*(March), 84–92.

Christensen, C. (2013). *The innovator's dilemma: When new technologies cause great firms to fail.* Boston, MA: Harvard Business Review Press.

Christopher, M., & Peck, H. (1997). Managing logistics in fashion markets. *International Journal of Logistics Management. The, 8*(2), 63–74.

Cillo, P., & Verona, G. (2008). Search styles in style searching: Exploring innovation strategies in fashion firms. *Long Range Planning, 41*(6), 650–671. doi:10.1016/j.lrp.2008.08.001

Commission, E. U. (2014). *Final report from the expert group on retail sector innovation.* Brussels: Directorate General for Research and Innovation.

De Brito, M. P., Carbone, V., & Blanquart, C. M. (2008). Towards a sustainable fashion retail supply chain in Europe: Organisation and performance. *International Journal of Production Economics, 114*(2), 534–553. doi:10.1016/j.ijpe.2007.06.012

De Felice, F., Petrillo, A., & Autorino, C. (2013). Key success factors for organizational innovation in the fashion industry. *International Journal of Engineering Business Management, 5*(27), 1–11.

de Jesus-Hitzschky, K. R. E. (2007). Impact assessment system for technological innovation: Inova-tec System. *Journal of Technology Management & Innovation, 2*(2), 67–81.

Doms, M. E., Jarmin, R. S., & Klimek, S. D. (2004). Information technology investment and firm performance in US retail trade. *Economics of Innovation and New Technology, 13*(7), 595–613. doi:10.1080/1043859042000201911

Ellram, L. M. (1996). The use of the case study method in logistics research. *Journal of Business Logistics, 17*(2), 93-138.

Enkel, E., & Heil, S. (2014). Preparing for distant collaboration: Antecedents to potential absorptive capacity in cross-industry innovation. *Technovation, 34*(4), 242–260. doi:10.1016/j.technovation.2014.01.010

Galloway, S. (2013). *L2 digital IQ index: Fashion.* Retrieved July 24, 2014 from http://www.l2thinktank.com/research/fashion-2013

Ganter, A., & Hecker, A. (2014). Configurational paths to organizational innovation: Qualitative comparative analyses of antecedents and contingencies. *Journal of Business Research, 67*(6), 1285–1292. doi:10.1016/j.jbusres.2013.03.004

Garcia, R., & Calantone, R. (2002). A critical look at technological innovation typology and innovativeness terminology: A literature review. *Journal of Product Innovation Management, 19*(2), 110–132. doi:10.1016/S0737-6782(01)00132-1

Gartner. (2014). *Agenda overview for retail 2014.* Retrieved July 20, 2014 from https://www.gartner.com/doc/2643719?ref=clientFriendlyURL

Gereffi, G. (1999). International trade and industrial upgrading in the apparel commodity chain. *Journal of International Economics, 48*(1), 37–70. doi:10.1016/S0022-1996(98)00075-0

Grewal, D., & Levy, M. (2009). Emerging issues in retailing research. *Journal of Retailing, 85*(4), 522–526. doi:10.1016/j.jretai.2009.09.007

Guercini, S., & Runfola, A. (2010). Business networks and retail internationalization: A case analysis in the fashion industry. *Industrial Marketing Management, 39*(6), 908–916. doi:10.1016/j.indmarman.2010.06.010

Heinemann, G., & Schwarzl, C. (2010). *New online retailing* (1st ed.). Wiesbaden: GWV Fachverlage. doi:10.1007/978-3-8349-6378-9

Hemphälä, J., & Magnusson, M. (2012). Networks for innovation–but what networks and what innovation? *Creativity and Innovation Management, 21*(1), 3–16. doi:10.1111/j.1467-8691.2012.00625.x

Hervas-Oliver, J. L., & Sempere-Ripoll, F. (2014). Disentangling the influence of technological process and product innovations. *Journal of Business Research, 68*(1), 109–118. doi:10.1016/j.jbusres.2014.04.010

Hübner, A. (2011). Framework for retail demand and supply chain planning. In A. Hübner (Ed.), *Retail category management* (pp. 15–41). Berlin: Springer Verlag. doi:10.1007/978-3-642-22477-5_2

Iannone, R., Ingenito, A., Martino, G., Miranda, S., Pepe, C., & Riemma, S. (2013). Merchandise and replenishment planning optimization for fashion retail. *International Journal of Engineering Business Management*, 5, 1–14.

Jørgensen, A. P., Collard, M., & Koch, C. (2010). Prototyping iPhone apps: Realistic experieces on the device. In HvannbergE.LarusdottirM.BlandfordA.GulliksenJ. (Eds.), *Proc. of 6th Nordic Conference on Human-Computer Interaction* (pp. 687-690). New York, NY: ACM Press. doi:10.1145/1868914.1869005

Kennard, M. J. (2012). Open innovation in a retail driven business environment. In *Proceedings of The XXIII ISPIM Conference 2012*. Barcelona, Spain: Academic Press.

Klein, H. K., & Myers, M. D. (1999). A set of principles for conducting and evaluating interpretive field studies in information systems. *Management Information Systems Quarterly*, *23*(1), 67–93. doi:10.2307/249410

Klena, K. (2013). *From transactions to relationships - Connecting with a transitioning shopper*. IBM.

Kurata, H., & Yue, X. (2008). Trade promotion mode choice and information sharing in fashion retail supply chains. *International Journal of Production Economics*, *114*(2), 507–519. doi:10.1016/j.ijpe.2007.05.021

Kusunoki, K., & Aoshima, Y. (2010). Redefining innovation as system re-definition. In H. Itami, K. Kusunoki, T. Numagami, & A. Takeishi (Eds.), *Dynamics of knowledge, corporate systems and innovation* (pp. 43–75). London: Springer. doi:10.1007/978-3-642-04480-9_3

Lee, A. S. (1989). A scientific methodology for MIS case studies. *Management Information Systems Quarterly*, *13*(1), 33–50. doi:10.2307/248698

Lee, C. H., & Rhee, B. D. (2008). Optimal guaranteed profit margins for both vendors and retailers in the fashion apparel industry. *Journal of Retailing*, *84*(3), 325–333. doi:10.1016/j.jretai.2008.07.002

Liu, N., Ren, S., Choi, T. M., Hui, C. L., & Ng, S. F. (2013). Sales forecasting for fashion retailing service industry: A review. *Mathematical Problems in Engineering*, *2013*. doi:10.1155/2013/738675

Lu, Y., Karpova, E. E., & Fiore, A. M. (2011). Factors influencing international fashion retailers' entry mode choice. *Journal of Fashion Marketing and Management*, *15*(1), 58–75. doi:10.1108/13612021111112340

Lueg, R., Pedersen, M. M., & Clemmensen, S. N. (2013). *The role of corporate sustainability in a low-cost business model–A case study in the Scandinavian fashion industry*. New York, NY: Wiley.

Magrath, V., & McCormick, H. (2013). Marketing design elements of mobile fashion retail apps. *Journal of Fashion Marketing and Management*, *17*(1), 115–134. doi:10.1108/13612021311305173

Mangiaracina, R., Perego, A., & Tumino, A. (2012). Re-designing retail stores with mobile and wireless technologies. *International Journal of Engineering Business Management*, 4, 1–11. doi:10.5772/51642

McColl, J., & Moore, C. (2013). Developing and testing a value chain for fashion retailers: Activities for competitive success. *Journal of the Textile Institute*, *105*(2), 136–149. doi:10.1080/00405000.2013.829934

OECD. (2005). *Oslo manual: Guidelines for collecting and interpreting innovation data*. Paris: OECD Publishing.

Pantano, E. (2014). Innovation management in retailing: From consumer perspective to corporate strategy. *Journal of Retailing and Consumer Services, 21*(5), 825–826. doi:10.1016/j.jretconser.2014.02.017

Pantano, E., Iazzolino, G., & Migliano, G. (2013). Obsolescence risk in advanced technologies for retailing: A management perspective. *Journal of Retailing and Consumer Services, 20*(2), 225–233. doi:10.1016/j.jretconser.2013.01.002

Pantano, E., & Timmermans, H. (Eds.). (2010). *Advanced technologies management for retailing – Frameworks and cases*. Hershey, PA: IGI Global.

Pantano, E., & Viassone, M. (2013). Demand pull and technology push perspective in technology-based innovations for the points of sale: The retailers evaluation. *Journal of Retailing and Consumer Services, 21*(1), 43–47. doi:10.1016/j.jretconser.2013.06.007

Piotrowicz, W., & Cuthbertson, R. (2014). Introduction to the special issue information technology in retail: Toward omnichannel retailing. *International Journal of Electronic Commerce, 18*(4), 5–16. doi:10.2753/JEC1086-4415180400

Platt Retail Institute. (2012). *Retailers' investment in technology: An industry perspective*. Retrieved February 2, 2014 from http://www.plattretailinstitute.org/documents/free/download.phx?navid=366&itemid=419

Pomodoro, S. (2013). Temporary retail in fashion system: An explorative study. *Journal of Fashion Marketing and Management, 17*(3), 341–352. doi:10.1108/JFMM-07-2012-0033

Purvis, L., Naim, M. M., & Towill, D. (2013). Intermediation in agile global fashion supply chains. *International Journal of Engineering Science and Technology, 5*(2), 38–48.

Rajaram, K. (2001). Assortment planning in fashion retailing: Methodology, application and analysis. *European Journal of Operational Research, 129*(1), 186–208. doi:10.1016/S0377-2217(99)00406-3

Reynolds, J., Howard, E., Cuthbertson, C., & Hristov, L. (2007). Perspectives on retail format innovation: Relating theory and practice. *International Journal of Retail & Distribution Management, 35*(8), 647–660. doi:10.1108/09590550710758630

Reynolds, J., & Hristov, L. (2009). Are there barriers to innovation in retailing? *International Review of Retail, Distribution and Consumer Research, 19*(4), 317–330. doi:10.1080/09593960903331295

SAS. (2014). *Digital marketing drives the omnichannel experience*. Retrieved August 14, 2013 from http://www.sas.com/da_dk/whitepapers/digital-marketing-drives-omnichannel-experience-106652.html

Shaw, D., & Leeming, A. (1998). The retail industry and information technology. In *Modelling for added value* (pp. 139–154). London: Springer Verlag. doi:10.1007/978-1-4471-0601-2_14

Sinha, P. K., & Kar, S. K. (2010). Insights into the growth of new retail formats in India. In M. Kraft & M. K. Mantrala (Eds.), *Retailing in the 21st century* (pp. 119–140). Heidelberg, Germany: Springer Verlag. doi:10.1007/978-3-540-72003-4_8

Smithson, S., & Hirschheim, R. (1998). Analysing information systems evaluation: Another look at an old problem. *European Journal of Information Systems, 7*(3), 158–174. doi:10.1057/palgrave.ejis.3000304

Song, K., Hwang, S., Kim, Y., & Kwak, Y. (2013). The effects of social network properties on the acceleration of fashion information on the web. *Multimedia Tools and Applications, 64*(2), 455–474. doi:10.1007/s11042-012-1068-2

Stern, N., & Verweij, L. (2014). *Retail innovations 9: The pace of change accelerates.* Ebeltoft Group. Retrieved July 31, 2014 from http://www.ebeltoftgroup.com/retail-innovations-9----the-pace-of-change-accelerates.html

Suryandari, R. T., & Paswan, A. K. (2014). Online customer service and retail type-product congruence. *Journal of Retailing and Consumer Services*, *21*(1), 69–76. doi:10.1016/j.jretconser.2013.08.004

Tambo, T. (2011). International fashion retailing from an enterprise architecture perspective. In E. Pantano & H. Timmermanns (Eds.), *Advanced technologies management for retailing: Frameworks and cases* (pp. 105–120). Hershey, PA: IGI global. doi:10.4018/978-1-60960-738-8.ch006

Tambo, T. (2014a). Collaboration on technological innovation in Danish fashion chains: A network perspective. *Journal of Retailing and Consumer Services*, *21*(5), 827–835. doi:10.1016/j.jretconser.2014.02.016

Tambo, T. (2014b). Omni-channel retail information systems. In M. Khosrow-Pour (Ed.), *Encyclopedia of information science and technology* (3rd ed.). Hershey, PA: Idea Group Publishing.

Tambo, T., Gabel, O. D., Olsen, M., & Bækgaard, L. (2012). Organisational dynamics and ambiguity of business intelligence in context of enterprise information systems – A case study. In *Proceedings of the 6th International Conference on Research and Practical Issues of Enterprise Information Systems (CONFENIS): Enterprise Information Systems of the Future - Evolving towards More Performance through Transparency and Agility.* Gent: CONFENIS.

Taylor, H., Dillon, S., & Van Wingen, M. (2010). Focus and diversity in information systems research: Meeting the dual demands of a healthy applied discipline. *Management Information Systems Quarterly*, *34*(4), 647–667.

Ünay, F. G., & Zehir, C. (2012). Innovation intelligence and entrepreneurship in the fashion industry. *Procedia: Social and Behavioral Sciences*, *41*, 315–321. doi:10.1016/j.sbspro.2012.04.036

Vaagen, H., & Wallace, S. W. (2008). Product variety arising from hedging in the fashion supply chains. *International Journal of Production Economics*, *114*(2), 431–455. doi:10.1016/j.ijpe.2007.11.013

Walsham, G. (1989). Interpretive case studies in IS research: Nature and method. *European Journal of Information Systems*, *4*(2), 74–81. doi:10.1057/ejis.1995.9

Wong, C. Y., Arlbjørn, J. S., Hvolby, H. H., & Johansen, J. (2006). Assessing responsiveness of a volatile and seasonal supply chain: A case study. *International Journal of Production Economics*, *104*(2), 709–721. doi:10.1016/j.ijpe.2004.12.021

Wong, W. K., & Guo, Z. X. (2010). A hybrid intelligent model for medium-term sales forecasting in fashion retail supply chains using extreme learning machine and harmony search algorithm. *International Journal of Production Economics*, *128*(2), 614–624. doi:10.1016/j.ijpe.2010.07.008

Wu, J., Ju, H. W., Kim, J., Damminga, C., Kim, H. Y., & Johnson, K. K. (2013). Fashion product display: An experiment with Mockshop investigating colour, visual texture, and style coordination. *International Journal of Retail & Distribution Management*, *41*(10), 765–789. doi:10.1108/IJRDM-08-2012-0072

Xia, M., Zhang, Y., Weng, L., & Ye, X. (2012). Fashion retailing forecasting based on extreme learning machine with adaptive metrics of inputs. *Knowledge-Based Systems*, *36*, 253–259. doi:10.1016/j.knosys.2012.07.002

Zentes, J., Morschett, D., & Schramm-Klein, H. (2007). *Strategic retail management – Text and international cases.* Wiesbaden: Betriebswirtschaftlicher Verlag Dr. Th. Gabler.

Zhenxiang, W., & Lijie, Z. (2011). Case study of online retailing fast fashion industry. *International Journal of e-Education, e-Business, e- Management Learning, 1*(3), 195–200.

ADDITIONAL READING

Averwater, C. (2012). *Retail Truths: The Unconventional Wisdom of Retailing*. ABB Press.

Dunne, P., Lusch, R., & Carver, J. (2013). *Retailing*. Mason, OH: Cengage Learning.

Fisher, M., & Raman, A. (2010). *The new science of retailing: how analytics are transforming the supply chain and improving performance*. Harvard Business Review Press.

Harder, F. (2010). *Fashion For Profit: A Professional's Complete Guide to Designing, Manufacturing, & Marketing a Successful Line and Retailing*. Harder Publications.

Janda, S., Trocchia, P. J., & Gwinner, K. P. (2002). Consumer perceptions of Internet retail service quality. *International Journal of Service Industry Management, 13*(5), 412–431. doi:10.1108/09564230210447913

Keeling, K., Keeling, D., & McGoldrick, P. (2013). Retail relationships in a digital age. *Journal of Business Research, 66*(7), 847–855. doi:10.1016/j.jbusres.2011.06.010

Lewis, R., & Dart, M. (2010). *The New Rules of Retail: Competing in the World's Toughest Marketplace*. Basingstoke: Palgrave Macmillan.

Sonninen, A. (2013). *Digitalization strategies for retailers–a consumer research approach*. Espoo: Aalto University.

Sorensen, H. (2009). *Inside the mind of the shopper: the science of retailing*. Upper Saddle River, NJ: Pearson Education.

Stolz, A. (2011). *Multi-Channel-Strategien als strategische Herausforderung für den stationären Einzelhandel in Deutschland*. Norderstedt: GRIN Verlag.

Xie, Y., & Allen, C. (2013). Information technologies in retail supply chains: A comparison of Tesco and Asda. *International Journal of Business Performance and Supply Chain Modelling, 5*(1), 46–62. doi:10.1504/IJBPSCM.2013.051648

KEY TERMS AND DEFINITIONS

Area Management: The distributed management in retailing. As retail is geographic in nature, it is often necessary to introduce one or more management layers between central management and the store. Purchasing and human resource management can reside within the area management as well as other cross-store functions given that the store size cannot justify these responsibilities within the single store.

Bricks and Mortar: The physical store where the customers can approach staff as well as merchandise. The bricks and mortar can exist as a dedicated building, a defined area within a mall, as areas within department stores, shop-in-shops or in-stores and in an array of other physical and permanent locations.

Chain: A multiple location-based retail operation based on a selected set of commonalities or the fullest adaptation of identical artefacts and services at the local level. Chains can be voluntary as well as capital-based. Voluntary chains are recognised by local ownership, occasionally also of the central level. Capital chains are recognised by a strong central ownership, potentially ownership of all retail activities.

Comparable Store: In retail reporting, comparable stores are stores that by size, placement, brand and category composition and stability of environment statistically can be compared on a year-to-year basis. Comparable store indices are important to create trustworthy data on economic and commercial outlooks for a chain, where statistical "noise" is filtered out of data.

Fashion: In retail, an overarching term for apparel, clothing, garment and similar wearables and accessories. The term reflects a shift from clothing as a fundamental necessity to a choice of desire often characterised by a relative short product life cycle. Therefore, to some extent, the term excludes work wear, religious dressing and similar situational products.

Fixture: The most fundament parts of a store except building components. Fixtures cover shelves, tables, hangers, partitions, functional walls and similar hardware aimed at exposing products to consumers and ensuring simplicity in product retrieval and stockage for both consumers and store associates.

Merchandising (Product): The process of forecasting, planning, selecting and buying an appropriate set of categories and products to a store at any given season.

Merchandising (Visual): The process of ensuring the desired visual impression of a store. Decoration guidelines and seasonal lookbooks might be supportive in the process. The overall rationale is to adhere to the chosen styling and outline of the chain and thereby benefit from corporate learning and corporate identity. Furthermore, the uniformity of the stores provided by visual merchandising contributes to the clarity and protection of the brand and prevents depletion of brand equity.

Omni-Channel Retailing: Omni-channel retailing designates retailing on an arbitrary set of channels, which work more or less seamlessly together, support each other and ensure a positive customer experience across the channels.

Replenishment: In retailing, replenishment is the adding of products to designated fixtures at the same pace as the products are sold. For short life cycle products, e.g. in the fashion industry, replenishment can probably not happen with the major amount of products once delivered to the store. In more general retailing, and with never-out-of-stock products, replenishment is a part of the daily operations of the store. Replenishment will often need computerised support, either to retrieve actual information of sales and subsequent replenishment demands or to develop prognoses for estimation of required deliveries.

Space Management: The discipline of, by manual or computerised work processes, allocating the space of the store in the financially and commercially most optimal way. This relates to increasing the space allocated to high earning products, ordering of products that create traffic of consumers through the store and contributing to the overall goals of expression and effectiveness of the store as an economical phenomenon.

Chapter 13
Financial Sustainability of Innovative Technology in Retailing

Sanda Renko
University of Zagreb, Croatia

Ivan Kovac
University of Zagreb, Croatia

ABSTRACT

The main purpose of this chapter is to address two important areas for successfully managing retail businesses—financial sustainability and innovative technology—in order to find out in which ways they affect each other. In order to clarify the financial sustainability of innovative technologies and the ways innovative technologies contribute in achieving financial sustainability in a retail company as a whole, it has been explored in grocery retailing in the Republic of Croatia. The results of a study among the top retail companies operating in the Croatian market suggest that innovative technology has the highest priority in their strategic and financial planning as one of the four fundamental pillars of financial sustainability. However, the results also indicated a long payback period after the implementation of new technological solutions.

INTRODUCTION

The reporting of sustainability matters has progressed as stakeholders are increasingly seeking disclosures, not just on companies' financial matters but also on environmental and social practices (Milne & Gray, 2007). Cremers (2013) points out that sustainability-related issues, such as financial sustainability or energy efficiency, can be part of the board's strategic planning tasks. The issue of sustainability is multifaceted, because it involves the avoidance of imposing an excessive burden on future generations and ensuring the country's capacity to appropriately adjust budgetary policy in the medium and long run (European Commission, 2006).

The word 'sustainable' has gained common usage in a variety of areas since the 1990's (LGA, 2012), and it is most often used in the context of environmental management in seeking alternative

DOI: 10.4018/978-1-4666-8297-9.ch013

renewable energy resources, along with energy-saving practices and technologies, to try to make energy consumption practices sustainable. Financial sustainability is a similar concept relating to the capacity to cover all expenses with revenues.

This quest for sustainability has already started to transform the retail environment, and forced companies to change the way they think about customers, competitors, products, technologies, processes, etc. Retailers place an emphasis on activities designed to cut costs, to make shopping more exciting for their consumers, and to manage their environmental and social responsibility as well. Among them, innovative technologies play important role in improving the sustainability of retail businesses. They improve services to customers, management operations and reduce retailer`s distribution costs. However, investments in technologies do not always provide the expected returns. If the implementation of new technologies allows retailers to offer their products and services to the market at prices that cover their expenses and generate a profit, as well as improve their communication with suppliers and other members of the supply chain, then we can say that financial sustainability has been achieved.

The objective of this chapter is to identify the determining factors of financial sustainability in retailing. However, induced by a suggestion in the literature that a retailer`s ability to build and defend competitive position on the market depends, to a large extent, on the willingness and capacity of the company to invest in and use technology, we aimed to investigate whether innovative technology could help retailers secure their long term sustainability.

The fact is that there is an interaction between sustainability and innovative technology in retailing. Retailers have become more than passive intermediaries between producers and manufacturers on the one hand and customers on the other. They have to be involved in the implementation of innovative business practices provided by technological innovations as retailing technologies are constantly emerging.

Following this introduction, the chapter begins with the theoretical background and the definition of the term financial sustainability, basic principles and key elements of financial sustainability, etc. As there is a vast body of literature that is not harmonized regarding the benefits and limitations of new technologies, the main purpose of next chapter is to shed light on the opportunities of innovative technologies in retailing. In order to clarify the financial sustainability of innovative technologies and the ways how innovative technologies contribute in achieving financial sustainability of the retail company as a whole, it has been explored in grocery retailing in the Republic of Croatia. The chapter concludes with a summary of the major findings of the study, where managerial implications are also discussed.

THEORETICAL BACKGROUND

To understand the connection between financial sustainability and innovative technology for retailers, it is first important to define the terminology that will be used. As there is no literature with an extant definition for financial sustainability, this chapter will draw upon broad literature within sustainability, sustainable development, financial management, etc.

The literature mostly deals with sustainability and sustainable development, as a measure or a process of change in which the resources consumed are not depleted to the extent that they cannot be replicated (Renko, 2008). Hasna (2007) considers it as a process which tells of the development of all aspects of human life affecting sustenance. „It means resolving the conflict between various competing goals, and involves the simultaneous pursuit of economic prosperity, environmental quality and social equity famously known as the three dimensions with the resultant vector being technology,…". The way some companies are defining the term sustainability has cast doubt on their commitment to protecting the planet for future generations (Adams & Larrinaga-González, 2007, p. 337).

There are three commonly cited pillars of the sustainability area - economic, ecological and social dimensions – that should be in (Durieu, 2003). Kuisma (2003, p. 10) explains the relationship between the three key sustainable issues as follows: "In any company good economic results and financial resources are essential to developing environmental and social responsibilities". Namely, if a company must be reorganized for financial reasons, then some projects in the area of environmental management will definitely be postponed. On the other hand, acting in a responsible way has to be profitable, either directly or indirectly, or sparing no effort will decrease. Parallel to the growth of interest in sustainability and sustainable development, is increasing interest in another aspect of sustainability - financial sustainability. Namely, companies have become aware that a business that is not financially sustainable will only be able to survive in the market for so long.

CONCEPT OF FINANCIAL SUSTAINABILITY

When making decisions that will affect the financial situation of a company`s business, the focus should be on achieving the company`s long term goals. Although incorporated in every organisation, there is no common definition of the concept of financial sustainability. Theoretically, financial sustainability relates to covering the company`s administrative costs and prioritizing activities so as to accomplish its mission (Leon, 2001).

Financial sustainability is a common feature used by scholars in various areas, from finance, accounting, the construction industry, education, government, personal lives, etc. In the area of finance, authors (Ayayi & Sene, 2010) use this concept to describe the institution`s capacity to cover all of its expenses by its revenue and to generate a margin to finance its growth. Due to the high cost of providing financial products and services, Brau and Woller (2004), and Hermes and Lensink (2007) doubt the financial sustainability of financial institutions. Morduch (2000) underlines the importance of innovations for obtaining financial sustainability. He points out the need to continue to serve the "poor" through financially sustainable microfinance institutions, by developing the institutional capacity and management of these institutions and by encouraging new innovations and experimentation in the field of microfinance.

The literature on financial sustainability in the construction industry mostly considers the topic of sustainable construction and sustainable buildings (Feige, Wallbaum, Janser, & Windlinger, 2013). However, there is the general lack of information on the topic of sustainability (Feige et al., 2011), and such sustainable construction projects are often presumed as costly (Langdon, 2007; Siew, Balatbat, & Carmichael, 2013). Those additional investment costs for sustainable buildings seem to present an obstacle for the wider development of sustainable construction. On the other hand, Wargocki, et al. (2008) outlined the importance of taking into consideration employee needs and their effect on financial aspects, because there is a link between building design, comfort and productivity.

Due to increasing environmental challenges and rising concern for cutting costs in institutions of higher education, Dahle and Neumayer (2001) consider financial sustainability important, but complex and a relatively new field of research. The authors investigate how the implementation of renewable energy technology can reduce financial costs, increase possibilities for saving money, and reduce environmental impact. However, their survey carried out on a sample of higher educational institutions within London showed that due to its long payback period, such innovations are not widespread among HE institutions today, and that initiatives with short financial payback periods are mainly preferred.

The concept of financial sustainability that most people use in their personal and business lives is probably thought of as whether they can afford their current lifestyle: whether they can pay for rent, food and other expenses with the income they receive each year (LGA, 2012). For those who own homes, farms or businesses, they may think in longer terms as to whether they will be in a position to repay debts by the time they retire. For local governments, financial sustainability presents (LGA, 2013, p.3) "...a government's ability to manage its finances so it can meet its spending commitments, both now and in the future. It ensures future generations of taxpayers do not face an unmanageable bill for government services provided to the current generation." In his explanation of the factors affecting sustainability disclosures by a local coastal shire council in Australia Sciulli's study (2011) points out the community demand for information on sustainability in managing population growth, planning for land use, climate change and community engagement, and the way the information is communicated to stakeholders.

BASIC PRINCIPLES AND KEY ELEMENTS OF FINANCIAL SUSTAINABILITY

Research (Ayayi & Sene, 2010) on financial sustainability dictates that companies should have modern and efficient employee management and should integrate new information technologies in their management that allow them to control operating costs and by extension their personnel costs, which are currently exorbitant. The integration of new information technologies in management can allow companies to monitor, analyse and control operations. In addition, in the quest for efficiency, cost reduction and optimization of means to attain financial sustainability, companies should increasingly adopt good business practices and to develop long term goals that outline where they want their business to stand financially in the future.

Financial sustainability is achieved when a business is able to deliver products and services to the market at a price that covers their expenses and generates a profit. In investigating financial sustainability in the healthcare industry, Chandra et al. (2013) point out that though profitability was never the driving force in ensuring availability of all supplies, it is imperative for any system to be financially sustainable to achieve its mission statement. In general, companies should make a lot of effort to achieve financial sustainability and provide (Leon, 2001, p. 21):

- **Long-Term Commitment:** Companies require a long-term commitment to generate income and achieve success,
- **Leadership:** It is nearly impossible to achieve financial sustainability without the commitment of the organization's leadership and directors,
- **Investment of Time and Money:** Resources are necessary to achieve financial sustainability, and companies have to make decisions whether to spend money or to invest it in business operations,
- **Business Plan:** A business plan enables a company to identify essential factors for evaluating whether the effort involved in the initiative is worthwhile,
- **Effective Management Team:** A business cannot function without a leader with the vision to implement the initiative,
- **Team Work:** It is essential to train staff members and communicate with them in order to increase their capacity and motivation.

Leon (2001, p. 15) suggests that there are four key elements of financial sustainability:

1. **Strategic Planning:** The mechanism to help clarify an organization's mission and objectives as well as prioritize the actions needed to accomplish them. In searching

for growth, every company takes on an increasing number of activities. However, it runs the risk of focusing on day to day management issues and losing sight of long range objectives. In order to convert the actions described in the strategic plan into figures, it is important to start with a parallel financial planning process. The purpose of the financial plan is to determine if the company is going to have sufficient resources available in the medium term to meet the objectives described in the strategic plan.

2. **Income Diversification:** Relates not only to internal income generation, but also to the number of income sources that provide main funding. In the case of non-profit organizations, at least 60% of the organization's overall budget must come from five different sources (Leon, 2001, p. 16).

3. **Manage Resources to Achieve Financial Sustainability:** It is important to know how to manage resources to achieve financial sustainability as well as to know how to generate income. There are some financial statements that the organization's management must review periodically (balance sheet, inventory control, investments, etc.). Companies need to maintain incoming cash flow requirements to cover outgoing expenses. The balance sheet is one of the important financial statements that should be used to monitor the financial stability and sustainability of a company`s business in the medium to long term. In other words, financial sustainability means ensuring the longevity of the organization.

4. **Income Generation:** Relates to a way for an organization to diversify its sources of revenue. Many companies offer products or services as an income-generating strategy while non-profit organizations can generate income through public contributions or through corporate alliances.

OPPORTUNITIES OF INNOVATIVE TECHNOLOGIES IN RETAILING

Innovation can be considered as an investment that helps companies secure long term sustainability. Namely, the resources and effort that companies put into the innovation process now will continue to repay them in the future. Innovations involve new ideas, products and solutions that meet the needs on the market, and can help companies remain up to date and competitive in the marketplace.

As the retail sector is one of the fastest growing and most competitive sectors of the economy, we witness a large body of literature on new technologies in retailing. The literature confirmed that retailing can benefit from the implementation of new technologies (Gil-Saura, Berenguer-Congri, & Ruiz-Molina, 2009; Pantano & Naccarato, 2010; Pantano & Viassone, 2014; Timmor & Rymon, 2007) and that innovative technologies offer new opportunities for retailers to better manage their companies and enhance the shopping experience for their customers (Clodfelter, 2011).

The review of the available literature suggests that there are two streams of research related to innovative technology in retailing. Both streams strongly look at innovation technology as an investment that provides cutting and covering expenses and generating a profit in the long term. However, the first one (Dabholkar, Bobbitt, & Lee, 2003; De Moerloose, Antioco, Lindgreen, & Palmer, 2005; Eckefeld, 2005; Lee, Park, Yoon, & Yeon, 2007; Reda, 2005; Visich, Li, Khumawala, & Reyes, 2009; Wang, 2012; etc.) showed growing interest for innovative technologies in the supply chain and retail formats, while the other one focused on environmental initiatives in retailing (Dobler & Sollbach, 2003; Durieu, 2003; Jones, Comfort, & Hiller, 2007; Kuisma, 2003; etc.).

Technological innovations in the supply chain and retail formats include barcode scanners at retail POS (point-of-sale) checkouts, electronic shelf labels, self-checkouts, RFID, fingerprint authentication, interactive information terminals, and web portals and e-tailing. Such technologies provide benefits to retailers through improved sales and inventory data analysis, the ability to exchange information with suppliers, quick feedback to suppliers, the display of various information, reducing labour costs and delays, more automated and up-to-date inventory management, conducting a retail business in a cost-efficient manner, etc. On the other hand, retailers` environmental initiatives embracing their product range, packaging, waste disposal, recycling, energy consumption, etc.

SUSTAINABLE ASPECTS OF INNOVATIVE TECHNOLOGY IN RETAILING

Taking into consideration that financial sustainability of innovative technology means that retailers offer their products and services at prices that cover their expenses and generate a profit, the attention is placed on innovations in areas of supply chain management, customer management, customer satisfaction and environmental issues. There are enormous opportunities for reducing the carbon footprint and operating costs by implementing innovative technologies, such as long life and low power consumption POS terminals, double-sided receipt printing printers, and advanced LED lighting systems that have nearly one-third the operating costs compared to other systems (Kusunoki, 2009).

Watson, Klingenberg, Polito and Geurts (2004) discuss technologies that, on one hand, emphasize the reduction of waste and process/product redesign in the quest of reducing the environmental impact and improving environmental performance. On the other hand, the authors suggest that the perceived cost of the implementation of such innovations should not negatively affect financial performance. Feige et al. (2013) point out higher planning and material costs for sustainable constructions as a major factor in the low share of sustainable retailers` buildings. Namely, although

life-cycle analysis may show financial paybacks, the time span until these buildings break-even is often too far in the future and outside the investors' considered timescales (Meins, Wallbaum, Hardziewski, & Feige, 2010). Wallbaum and Meins (2009) also argued whether the widely used argument of cost savings for sustainable buildings related to energy savings is relevant enough since energy costs are currently too low to really pay back the additional investments.

A slightly different approach is found in the work of Wargocki et al. (2008) who specifically addressed the connection between innovations in building criteria, comfort parameters and performance parameters like work performance, work engagement, etc. The authors outlined the importance of the consideration of employee needs and their effect on the financial aspects as better work environments with enhanced indoor environment quality leads to higher user satisfaction and thus increased financial paybacks. Features such as operable windows and the absence of air conditioning have a positive impact on the comfort and health of employees, and on productivity as well. Finally, it can hence hold financial importance for the institutional investor (Feige et al., 2013).

METHODOLOGY

To increase knowledge and understanding of the concept of financial sustainability and its interaction with innovative technology in retailing, a review of the literature was conducted. First, relevant key words concerning the investigated topic were identified. The key words used for the selection of relevant literature were: sustainability, financial sustainability, innovative technology, and retailing. Then, several information sources and scholarly databases Emerald, Ebsco and ProQuest were consulted.

For the purpose of this chapter - to clarify financial sustainability of innovative technologies and the ways how innovative technologies contribute in achieving financial sustainability of retail companies - the qualitative approach was implemented as Boyce and Neale (2006, p. 3) considered it as particularly suitable for exploring phenomena in-depth. The qualitative approach of the study included in-depth interviews with the senior managers of ten retail grocery companies operating in Croatia. Similar to Dahle and Neumayer (2001), the interviewees were people chosen by the criteria used and whether they would have the knowledge necessary to be able to answer and elaborate on the questions in the interview guide. Therefore we interviewed retail managers who dealt with operational activities on a daily basis.

In making decisions about which retail companies to include in the sample our major assumption was that large retailers were more interested to invest in innovative technology than small ones. Thus, retail companies which hold more than 50% of the Croatian retail market were included in the interviewing sample. For a more complete understanding of the situation in the Croatian retail market, Table 1 (Appendix) with the Croatian retail market structure is presented.

The motivation for including Croatia in the research has been led by the conclusion of Roztocki and Weistroffer (2014; 2009) that the models and theories developed in highly developed countries may be of limited use in transition economies. Accordingly, there is a great need for research on the awareness of the importance of innovative technology in retail environments, as well as the financial and environmental impact of its implementation.

In order to be sure and to identify whether the selected retail companies would be prepared to participate in this survey, we made pre-survey telephone calls. All the necessary contact phone numbers were obtained using the information available on companies` corporate web pages. The participants were assured anonymity and confidentiality. Moreover, similar to Coltman (2007), in order to avoid any unnecessary wasting of time, the research instruments were sent to

each company a few days before interviewing. On average, the interviews lasted about 25 minutes and were transcribed. The research was carried out during April 2014.

The research instrument – a questionnaire consisting of two sections (See Table 2 in the Appendix for the interview guide). The first section was created in accordance with Indicators of Financial Sustainability researched by Leon (2000), and investigates the role of innovative technology in strategic planning and its link to financial sustainability. This part of the research instrument comprises questions on the importance of the innovative technology in retailers' strategic planning, the effects and benefits of the implementation of innovative technology on their business success and the payback period of the implemented innovative technology.

The second section consists of a set of questions adapted from UNEP (2008) and Dahle and Neumayer (2001), on the implementation of innovative technology in Croatian retail companies, renewable energy resources and energy-saving technologies, etc. Moreover, in this section retail companies were asked questions related to the concrete implementation of innovative technology and retailers' usage of renewable energy resources. Respondents were asked "green questions" related to the benefits of the usage of energy-saving technology of air-conditioning and heating, the usage of solar water heaters, the usage of timers/motion sensors that turn the lights on or off in unfrequented places and the installing of self-closing faucets in the lavatories.

Results of the interviews were analysed by categorising the responses into major conceptual areas. Using a „scissors and paste'' method (Ryan & Russell Bernard, 2003) responses were grouped by their contents to create larger categories. For example, various statements concerning the importance of innovative technology in retailers' strategic planning were gathered together in the discussion section.

RESULTS AND DISCUSSION

The findings of the interview among the ten Croatian retail companies revealed that all of them were highly aware of the importance and benefits of innovative technology. Innovative technology has the highest priority in their strategic plans. This is in line with Leon (2001), who considers strategic planning as the mechanism which helps to clarify an organization's mission and objectives, as well as prioritizes the actions needed to accomplish them. The same author defines strategic and financial planning as one of the four fundamental pillars of financial sustainability (the four components of financial sustainability are: strategic and financial planning, income diversification, sound administration and finance, personal income generation). Due to this fact, Croatian retail companies were asked about the priority of innovative technology in their strategic plans in order to determine an interaction between sustainability and innovative technology in the Croatian retail industry.

Like Morduh (2000), all respondents agreed that financial sustainability and innovative technology were closely linked to each other and that innovative technology played an important role in improving the financial sustainability of their companies: "In the beginning, the majority of our employees are afraid of introducing innovative technologies, fearing for their jobs. Today, they all understand the extreme importance of the introduction of new technologies significant to the success and survival of our companies, as well as to the survival of their working positions", and "We succeeded in convincing our owners and employees to introduce innovative technologies into our business and it was immediately recognized by our customers."

As the literature suggests that financial sustainability is obtained when a company's expenses are covered by its revenue, respondents were asked about the payback period of implemented innovative technology. For the majority of the investigated Croatian retail companies, this period was more than five years. This long payback period is in line with the findings of the research conducted by Dahle and Neumayer (2001).

Taking into consideration the economic situation in Croatia, it is logical to expect that kind of viewpoint and the respondents' explanations such as: "Today, investing in innovative technologies in the retail business is considered a sign of success, due to the recession in Croatia and long periods of return on these investments."

However, due to an increasing number of international retail chains on the Croatian market, there are also suggestions: "We are a foreign company in the Croatian market and our management has decided to introduce new technology in our retail formats, regardless of our current business results and long payback periods."

In accordance with the relevant research (Dabholkar et al., 2003; De Moerloos et al., 2005; Eckefeld, 2005; Dobler & Sollbach, 2003; Durieu, 2003; Jones et al., 2007; etc.), the results of this study also show that innovative technology in Croatian retail companies can be found in two main directions, namely the supply chain and retail formats as the first one, and environmental areas as the second one.

The findings of this research indicate that innovative technology in Croatian retail companies is more implemented in supply chains compared to its implementation in retail formats. In the area of supply chain, implemented innovative technology is related to the improvement of inventory flow and logistics. Retailers implement innovative technology in order to speed up operations and reduce inventory and logistics costs, which is evident from such answers: "In the last few years we have mainly introduced the latest technology into our distribution and logistics centres in order to make them run faster and more cost-effective", or "In the past we had only introduced innovative technology at our outlets, but in the last three years, we have largely been modernizing our distribution."

They also concluded that the greatest value for consumers derived from innovative technology includes its use in retail formats: "Since we introduced innovative technology in all of our retail outlets, there have been no more long lines in our stores and, according to our information, our customers are happier and more satisfied."

All respondents said that they had introduced the Electronic data interchange system (EDI) and point-of-sale scanners (POS) more than fifteen years ago, which is in line with the findings of Pantano and Viassone (2014). Additionally, they have all pointed out that their companies have already been using loyalty cards programmes for eight years. Moreover, the findings of this research suggest that all of them have websites, but only one retail company offers online shopping.

There are interesting differences in the length of usage of innovative technology among the investigated companies. Namely, in the area of the supply chain and retail formats, only a few Croatian retailers have implemented self-service checkouts in the last five years. However, none of retail companies, including foreign retail companies operating in Croatia, have introduced new technological solutions related to electronic shelf labels, fingerprint authentication and RFID. They gave answers like: "Unfortunately, we have not yet introduced electronic shelf labels but they are included in our future plans and will be introduced soon, namely, our company has such systems in Europe."

The findings of the interview have revealed that only a few of the investigated retail companies use renewable energy (solar water heaters). Half of the sample uses energy-saving technology of air-conditioners and heating. Their explanations were simple:

We are aware of the importance of energy-saving technology and we have already been using it for three years.

We have already forgotten when we had self-closing faucets installed in all our lavatories.

Four years ago we installed timers/motion sensors that turn the lights on or off in unfrequented places in all our new and old buildings and, according to our calculations, we saved money.

Almost all of the companies use timers/motion sensors that turn the lights on or off in unfrequented places. All of them have installed self-closing faucets.

FUTURE RESEARCH DIRECTIONS

Given the complex nature of the study phenomenon, there are many opportunities that lay ahead for new research. On the one hand, future research could expand completely into the financial aspect of the implementation of innovative technology in retailing, outlining where the retailer wants its business to stand financially in the future. The areas of investigation will also include the profit the retailer wants to make, its level of debt and its cash flow requirements. On the other hand, attention of researchers could be placed on innovations in the areas of environmental issues in retailing. There is growing potential for the retail industry to implement technological solutions directed towards resources and environmental systems such as water, land and air, including reducing energy consumption, waste management and recycling, carbon dioxide emissions, ethical trading, training, healthy and safe living, community support initiatives, humanitarian campaigns, etc. Acting in such a way retailers could make decisions that will affect the financial situation of their business, and to achieve long term goals, too. As resource degradation and pollution impact increase, future studies should encompass the economic, environmental and social sustainability of finance (Wilson, 2010). An additional starting point for future research could be to extend the qualitative approach by incorporating the key elements of financial sustainability and more convenient data collection that could allow generalization of the findings across the entire retail industry.

CONCLUSION AND MANAGERIAL IMPLICATIONS

As discussed in this chapter, the concept of financial sustainability of innovative technologies has become important for retailers as investments are increasingly required to prove sustainability credentials. Financial sustainability is a popular phrase, and it implicitly assumes that "finance", corporate or otherwise, should be used in a manner to generate economic activity that does not compromise the future ability to produce the same level of economic activity (Wilson, 2010, p. 269). It has been incorporated in every organisation, as businesses that are not financially sustainable cannot survive in the market for very long. This chapter points out greater awareness about the environment and innovations in todays` retail business. The results of the literature review suggest that there is an interaction between sustainability and innovative technology in retailing. Namely, retailing can benefit from the implementation of new technologies and innovative technologies offer new opportunities for retailers to better manage their companies and enhance the shopping experience for their customers. On the other hand, the literature emphasizes the technological solutions that provide the reduction of waste and process/product redesign in the quest of reducing environmental impact and improving environmental performance. The study conducted among retail companies operating on the Croatian market shows that they are highly aware of the importance and benefits of innovative technology, and that there are two streams of innovative technology usage in Croatian retail companies: i) the supply chain and retail formats; and ii) the

environmental area. However, it is also obvious that retailers have considered the perceived costs of the implementation of such innovations and the payback period as the main obstacles of their financial sustainability.

The results of the study allow us to extract some managerial implications. First of all, from the retailer`s point of view, it is desirable to involve innovation technology in a financially sustainable manner because innovations could improve the sustainability of your business. This means that a retailer will come up with new ideas, products and solutions that meet the changing and sophisticated needs of the market. Additionally, retailers may facilitate an environmentally friendly corporate image which has been shown to increase sales and a long-lasting relationship with their customers (Rudawska, 2008). Secondly, innovative technology allows retailers to decrease their costs and thus to offer more competitive pricing strategies to their targeted market segments.

REFERENCES

Ayayi, A. G., & Sene, M. (2010). What drives microfinance institution`s financial sustainability. *Journal of Developing Areas*, *44*(1), 303–323. doi:10.1353/jda.0.0093

Boyce, C., & Neale, P. (2006). Conducting in-depth interviews: A guide for designing and conducting in-depth interviews for evaluation input. *Pathfinder International Tool Series. Monitoring and Evaluation, 2.* Retrieved August 30, 2014, from http://www.cpc.unc.edu/measure/training/materials/data-quality-portuguese/m_e_tool_series_indepth_interviews.pdf

Chandra, H., Vashishta Rinko, A., Kumar Verma, J., Verma, S., Kapoor, R., & Sharma, R. K. (2013). Supply chain management with cost containment & financial sustainability in a tertiary care hospital. *Journal of Health and Human Services Administration*, *36*(1), 3–23. PMID:24010261

Cremers, J. (2013). Non-financial reporting and reference to workers` representatives. *Contemporary Readings in Law and Social Justice, 5*(2), 2013, 50–89.

Croatia, G. F. K. Research Agency. (2012). *Consumer tracking presentation.* Retrieved June 01, 2014, from http://www.gfk.hr/public_relations/press/press_articles/009459/index.hr.html

Dabholkar, P. A., Bobbitt, L. M., & Lee, E.-J. (2003). Understanding consumer motivation and behavior related to self-scanning in retailing: Implications for strategy and research on technology-based self-service. *International Journal of Service Industry Management, 14*(1), 59–95. doi:10.1108/09564230310465994

Dahle, M., & Neumayer, E. (2001). Overcoming barriers to campus greening: A survey among higher educational institutions in London. *International Journal of Sustainability in Higher Education, 2*(2), 139–160. doi:10.1108/14676370110388363

De Moerloose, C., Antioco, M., Lindgreen, A., & Palmer, R. (2005). Information kiosks: The case of the Belgian retail sector. *International Journal of Retail & Distribution Management, 33*(6), 472–490. doi:10.1108/09590550510603651

Dobler, C. & Sollbach, M., (2003). The metro group takes responsibility for sustainable development: Examples of good practice. *UNEP Industry and Environment, 26*(1), 20-22.

Durieu, X. (2003). How Europe's retail sector helps promote sustainable production and consumption. *UNEP Industry and Environment, 26*(1), 7–9.

Eckefeld, B. (2005). What does RFID do for the consumer? *Communications of the ACM, 48*(9), 77–79. doi:10.1145/1081992.1082024

European Commission. (2006). The long-term sustainability of public finances in the European Union. *European Economy, 4.* Retrieved August 30, 2014, from http://ec.europa.eu/economy_finance/publications/publication7903_en.pdf

Feige, A., Wallbaum, H., Janser, M., & Windlinger, L. (2013). Impact of sustainable office buildings on occupant's comfort and productivity. *Journal of Corporate Real Estate, 15*(1), 7–34. doi:10.1108/JCRE-01-2013-0004

Feige, A., Wallbaum, H., & Krank, S. (2011). Harnessing stakeholder motivation: Towards a Swiss sustainable building sector. *Building Research and Information, 39*(5), 504–517. doi:10.1080/09613218.2011.589788

Forum for the Future. (2009). *Sustainability trends in European retail.* Retrieved June 30, 2014, from https://www.forumforthefuture.org/sites/default/files/images/Forum/Documents/Sustainability_trends_in_European_retail_Sept09.pdf

Gil-Saura, I., Berenguer-Congri, G., & Ruiz-Molina, M. (2009). Information and communication technology in retailing: A cross-industry comparison. *Journal of Retailing and Consumer Services, 16*(3), 232–238. doi:10.1016/j.jretconser.2008.11.018

Hasna, A. M. (2007). Dimensions of sustainability. *Journal of Engineering for Sustainable Development: Energy Environmental Health, 2*(1), 47–57. doi:10.1016/j.jbusvent.2010.01.002

Jones, P., Comfort, D., & Hiller, D. (2007). What's in store? Retail marketing and corporate social responsibility. *Marketing Intelligence & Planning, 25*(1), 17–30. doi:10.1108/02634500710722371

Kuisma, J. (2003). Practical steps towards sustainability in the retail trade: The case of Finland's Kesko. *UNEP Industry and Environment, 26*(1), 10–12.

Kusunoki, M. (2009). *Sustainable technology in the retail environment*. TOSHIBA TEC Europe Retail Information Systems. Retrieved June 01, 2014, from http://www.toshibatec-eu.com/upl/1/default/doc/Sustainability_15.pdf

Langdon, D. (2007). *The costs & benefits of achieving green buildings*. Info Data. Retrieved June 30, 2014, from http://www.aecom.com/deployedfiles/Internet/Geographies/Australia-New%20Zealand/PCC%20General%20content/InfoData_Green_Buildings.pdf

Lee, S. M., Park, S.-H., Yoon, S. N., & Yeon, S.-J. (2007). RFID based ubiquitous commerce and consumer trust. *Industrial Management & Data Systems, 107*(5), 605–617. doi:10.1108/02635570710750381

León, P. (2001). *Four pillars of financial sustainability*. Arlington, VA: The Nature Conservancy.

LGA. (2012). *Financial sustainability*. Information Paper No 1. Retrieved June 01, 2014, from http://www.lga.sa.gov.au/

Meins, E., Wallbaum, H., Hardziewski, R., & Feige, A. (2010). Sustainability and property valuation: A risk-based approach. *Building Research and Information, 38*(3), 280–300. doi:10.1080/09613211003693879

Milne, M. J., & Gray, R. (2007). Future prospects for corporate sustainability reporting. In B. O'Dwyer, J. Bebbington, & J. Unerman (Eds.), *Sustainability accounting and accountability* (pp. 184–207). Abingdon, UK: Routledge.

Pantano, E., & Naccarato, G. (2010). Entertainment in retailing: The influences of advanced technologies. *Journal of Retailing and Consumer Services, 17*(3), 200–204. doi:10.1016/j.jretconser.2010.03.010

Pantano, E., & Viassone, M. (2014). Demand pull and technology push perspective in technology-based innovations for the points of sale: The retailers evaluation. *Journal of Retailing and Consumer Services, 21*(1), 43–47. doi:10.1016/j.jretconser.2013.06.007

Reda, S. (2005, September). What you don't know about RFID. *Stores,* 26-34.

Renko, S. (2008). How the process of internationalization enhances the sustainability of the Croatian retailing. *World Journal of Retail Business Management, 2*(4), 3–10.

Richardson, N. (2008). To what extent have key retail and generic marketing texts adopted sustainability? *World Journal of Retail Business Management, 2*(4), 47–55.

Roztocki, N., & Weistroffer, H. R. (2009). Research trends in information and communications technology in developing, emerging and transition economies. *Roczniki Kolegium Analiz Ekonomicznych Zeszyt, 20,* 113–127.

Roztocki, N., & Weistroffer, H. R. (2014). Information and communication technology in transition economies: An assessment of research trends. *Information Technology for Development,* 1–35. doi:10.1080/02681102.2014.891498

Rudawska, I. (2008). Towards sustainability in the retail services markets. *World Journal of Retail Business Management, 2*(4), 56–64.

Ryan, G. W., & Russell Bernard, H. (2003). Techniques to identify themes in qualitative data. *Field Methods, 15*(1), 85-109. doi:10.1177/1525822X02239569

Sciulli, N. (2011). The views of managers from a local coastal council on sustainability reporting issues: An Australian-based case study. *Qualitative Research in Accounting & Management, 8*(2), 139–160. doi:10.1108/11766091111137555

Siew, R. Y. J., Balatbat, M. C. A., & Carmichael, D. G. (2013). The relationship between sustainability practices and financial performance of construction companies. *Smart and Sustainable Built Environment*, *2*(1), 6–27. doi:10.1108/20466091311325827

Timmor, Y., & Rymon, T. (2007). To do or not to do: The dilemma of technology-based service improvement. *Journal of Services Marketing*, *21*(2), 99–111. doi:10.1108/08876040710737868

UNEP/Wuppertal Institute Collaborating Centre on Sustainable Consumption and Production. (2008). *A guidelines manual for retailers towards sustainable consumption & production*. Retrieved August 30, 2014, from http://www.unep.org/Documents.Multilingual/Default.asp?DocumentID=321&ArticleID=4019&l=en

Visich, J., Li, S., Khumawala, B., & Reyes, P. (2009). Empirical evidence of RFID impacts on supply chain performance. *International Journal of Operations & Production Management*, *29*(12), 1290–1315. doi:10.1108/01443570911006009

Wallbaum, H., & Meins, E. (2009). Nichtnachhaltiges Planen, Bauen und Betrieben – Aus guten Gründen (noch) die Praxis in der Bauwirtschaft? *Bauingenieur*, *84*(7/8), 291–304.

Wang, M. C.-H. (2012). Determinants and consequences of consumer satisfaction with self-service technology in a retail setting. *Managing Service Quality*, *22*(2), 128–144. doi:10.1108/09604521211218945

Wargocki, P., Seppanen, O., Andersson, J., Boestra, A., Clements-Croome, D., Fitzner, K., & Hanssen, S. O. (2008). *Indoor climate and productivity in offices: How to integrate productivity in life cycle costs analysis of building services*. Brussels: REHVA.

Watson, K., Klingenberg, B., Polito, P., & Geurts, T. G. (2004). Impact of environmental management system implementation on financial performance: A comparison of two corporate strategies. *Management of Environmental Quality: An International Journal*, *15*(6), 622–628. doi:10.1108/14777830410560700

Wilson, C. (2010). Why should sustainable finance be given priority? Lesson from pollution and biodiversity degradation. *Accounting Research Journal*, *23*(3), 267–280. doi:10.1108/10309611011092592

ADDITIONAL READING

Bingham, T., & Walters, G. (2013). Financial Sustainability Within UK Charities: Community Sport Trusts and Corporate Social Responsibility Partnerships. *Voluntas: International Journal of Voluntary & Nonprofit Organizations*, *24*(3), 606–629. doi:10.1007/s11266-012-9275-z

Lützkendorf, T., & Lorenz, D. (2007). Integrating sustainability into property risk assessments for market transformation. *Building Research and Information*, *35*(6), 644–661. doi:10.1080/09613210701446374

Nidumolu, R., Prahalad, C. K., & Rangaswami, M. R. (2009). Why Sustainability Is Now the Key Driver of Innovation. *Harvard Business Review*, *87*(9), 57–64.

Robinson, M. S. (1996). Addressing some key questions on finance and poverty. *Journal of International Development*, *8*(2), 153–163. doi:10.1002/(SICI)1099-1328(199603)8:2<153::AID-JID372>3.0.CO;2-6

Watson, K., Polito, T., Klingenberg, B., & Geurts, T. (2003). Financial evidence on the impact of environmental management systems, In *Proceedings of the 33rd Annual Meeting of the Southeast Decision Sciences Institute*, Williamsburg, VA.

KEY TERMS AND DEFINITIONS

Financial Sustainability: Covering company's administrative costs and prioritizing activities so as to accomplish its missions.

Innovation: A process that involves coming up with new ideas, products and solutions that meet the needs of the market.

Innovative Technology: New technological solutions for improving service quality and decreasing costs at the same time, such as the Internet, handheld and wireless devices, touchscreen kiosks, electronic signage and shelf labels, virtual reality displays, body scanning, smart cards, robotics, etc.

Retailing: A set of activities that result in the offering for sale of merchandise to consumers for their own use.

Strategic Planning: The process of identifying actions needed to accomplish companies' goals.

Supply Chain: Is a complex system which involves multiple entities encompassing activities of moving goods and adding value from the raw material stage to the final delivery stage.

Sustainability: A process of change in which the resources consumed (both social and ecological) are not depleted to the extent that they cannot be replicated.

Sustainable Development: The development which meets the needs of the present without comprising the ability of future generations to meet their own needs.

APPENDIX

Table 1. Croatian retail market structure

Retailer	2009	2010	2011
Konzum	25.80	27.80	29.00
Kaufland	7.70	7.60	8.90
Lidl	5.30	6.70	7.60
Plodine	5.40	6.80	7.00
Mercator	4.90	5.90	5.70
Billa	5.20	5.00	4.70
Drogerie Markt	3.90	4.30	4.50
Spar	1.90	2.60	3.60
Tommy	2.00	2.40	2.20
Diona	2.40	2.40	2.70
KTC	2.90	2.90	2.50
Total top 10	67.40	*74.40*	*78.40*
Others	32.60	25.60	21.60

Source: GFK, Consumer tracking presentation, 2012.

Table 2. Research instrument - interview guide

1. Innovative technology- strategic planning – financial sustainability
a. Does your organization have a strategic plan?
b. What is the importance of the innovative technology in your strategic planning?
c. What are the effects and benefits of implementing innovative technology on your business success?
d. Can you specify the payback period of the implemented innovative technology?
2. Implementation of innovative technology
a. Which initiatives have been carried out to conserve energy and to increase energy efficiency at your company?
b. Explain in which parts of your organization such initiatives are implemented.
c. Has your company implemented innovative technology in air-conditioning and heating? If so, what are the benefits of it?
d. Has your company used solar water heaters? If so, what are the benefits of it?
e. 5. Has your company used timers/motion sensors that turn the lights on or off in unfrequented places? If so, what are the benefits of it?

Source: Own table according to UNEP (2008), Dahle and Neumayer (2001), Leon (2000).

Chapter 14
The Roles of Corporate Marketing Strategies and Brand Management in the Global Retail Industry

Kijpokin Kasemsap
Suan Sunandha Rajabhat University, Thailand

ABSTRACT

This chapter explores the roles of corporate marketing strategies and brand management in the global retail industry, thus describing the concepts of marketing strategy, international retail marketing strategy, retail marketing mix, and internationalization; the relationship between corporate marketing strategies and internationalization; the challenges of retail marketing mix in the fashion retail industry; the overview of brand management; and the significance of brand management in the global retail industry. The implementation of corporate marketing strategies and brand management is critical for modern organizations that seek to serve suppliers and customers, increase business performance, strengthen competitiveness, and achieve continuous success in global business. Therefore, it is necessary for modern organizations to examine their corporate marketing strategies and brand management applications, create a strategic plan to regularly check their practical advancements, and rapidly respond to the corporate marketing strategies and brand management needs of customers in the global retail industry.

INTRODUCTION

The rapidly evolving consumer needs and habits are bringing radical change to the world's retail industry (Manasseh, Muller-Sarmiento, Reuter, von Faber-Castell, & Pallua, 2012). The ability to internationalize has become a competitive necessity for many small and medium-sized enterprises (SMEs), enabling their survival and access to larger markets (Dutot, Bergeron, & Raymond, 2014). Marketing must be elevated to a higher level of consciousness. An important step in the internationalization process of emerging economy firms is the shift from exports to foreign direct investment (Gaur, Kumar, & Singh, 2014). Retail internationalization is measured in terms of

DOI: 10.4018/978-1-4666-8297-9.ch014

both exporting and foreign purchasing (Hessels & Parker, 2013). Concerning the international nature of retailing (Bianchi & Ostale, 2006), and corporate and consumer responses toward the issue of globalization (Alden, Steenkamp, & Batra, 2006), there has been little consideration of how international retailers may implement retail marketing strategies abroad, or of how these may compare with those domestically implemented.

Creating and maintaining a good brand relationship is necessary for brand management in emerging markets (Kasemsap, 2014a). From the retailer's perspective, retail brands represent equity that can have a significant impact on a retailer's differentiation and competitive superiority (Lymperopoulos, Chaniotakis, & Rigopoulou, 2010). Brand management function needs a partial rethinking since brand managers have to perform the traditional tasks while addressing new challenges (Brexendorf & Daecke, 2012). Corporate brands are strategic assets for organizations, but it is difficult to understand the value added by corporate brand name changes because they often occur simultaneously with business restructuring initiatives (Kalaignanam & Bahadir, 2013).

Business practitioners and researchers have struggled for many years to understand the role of marketing in describing business performance differences between firms (Morgan, 2012). Organizations strive to establish a relationship between brands and consumers (Neudecker, Hupp, Stein, & Schuster, 2012). Strong brand names facilitate competitive advantage (Lee & Back, 2010), increase organizational cash flow (Miller & Muir, 2004), and provide premium price, profitability, and loyalty for customers (Madden, Fehle, & Fournier, 2006).

The strength of this chapter is on the thorough literature consolidation of corporate marketing strategies and brand management in the global retail industry. The extant literatures of corporate marketing strategies and brand management in the global retail industry provide a contribution to practitioners and researchers by describing a comprehensive view of the functional applications of corporate marketing strategies and brand management in the global retail industry to appeal to different segments of corporate marketing strategies and brand management in the global retail industry in order to maximize the business impact of corporate marketing strategies and brand management in the global retail industry.

Background

In the late 1980s, a new wave of international retail activity had begun to build (Alexander & Doherty, 2010). The consumer society that had emerged in the 1980s increasingly generated retailers capable of addressing the challenge of international marketing activity either because of their increasing market orientation (Piercy & Alexander, 1988), their operational size (Treadgold, 1988) or their brand strength (Alexander, 1990; Williams, 1992). It is widely recognized that today's retail environment is highly competitive and that it is essential for retailers to gain some form of differential advantage (Swoboda, Haelsig, Morschett, & Schramm-Klein, 2007).

Regarding corporate marketing strategies, the retailers try to position their stores in such a way that they obtain a defendable and sustainable market position (Oppewal & Timmermans, 1997). Morschett, Swoboda, and Schramm-Klein (2006) applied Porter's framework to develop competitive strategies in retailing (i.e., cost leadership strategy, product differentiation strategies, and focus strategy). The aims of cost leadership strategy are to minimize investment in store design and reduce customer service (Skallerud & Grønhaug, 2010). Other marketing strategies are the economy of scale and the negotiation power over suppliers of products (Ellis & Kelly, 1992). Large firms possess more financial and human resources and higher economy of scale levels (Sun & Lee, 2013). A differentiation strategy implies differentiating the retail offer from its competitors (Davis, 1992). The purpose of differentiation strategy is to adjust certain features more directly to the specific needs of the chosen customer segments (Skallerud & Grønhaug, 2010).

Brands are the sources of organizational value (Brexendorf & Daecke, 2012). Branding is recognized as a key component of marketing strategy (Kent, 2003; Ailawadi & Keller, 2004; Burt & Davies, 2010). Branding within retail settings has been associated with private label brand produced by retailers (Burt & Davies, 2010), thus enabling competitive advantage in the form of superior profit margins, economy of scale, market segmentation, and differentiation. Competing retail brand perspectives have emerged in the retail literature, which embrace the combinations of tangible and intangible service, product, and multi-sensory brand elements as an organized brand strategy (Kent, 2003; Burt & Davies, 2010).

CORPORATE MARKETING STRATEGIES AND BRAND MANAGEMENT IN THE GLOBAL RETAIL INDUSTRY

This section describes the concepts of marketing strategy, international retail marketing strategy, retail marketing mix, and internationalization; the relationship between corporate marketing strategies and internationalization; the challenges of retail marketing mix in the fashion retail industry; the overview of brand management; and the significance of brand management in the global retail industry.

Concept of Marketing Strategy

Global conditions challenge traditional views of management, marketing, and economics (Maglio, Nusser, & Bishop, 2010). Formulating consistent marketing strategies is a difficult task, but successfully implementing them is more challenging (Prange & Schlegelmilch, 2009). Ethical corporate marketing transcends the domains of corporate

social responsibility, business ethics, stakeholder theory and corporate marketing (Balmer, Powell, & Greyser, 2011). A vast majority of marketing theory and research has focused on relativism and idealism in order to understand ethical behavior (Rawwas, Arjoon, & Sidani, 2013). Organizations with a large customer base earn higher profits in global marketing (Schmidt, 2013). Organizational culture has a positive impact on marketing-related decision making (Yarbrough, Morgan, & Vorhies, 2011).

Marketing strategy can be defined as an organization's integrated pattern of decisions that specify its crucial choices concerning products, markets, marketing activities and marketing resources in the creation, communication, and delivery of products that offer value to customers in exchanges with the organization and enables organization to achieve specific objectives (Varadarajan, 2010). Marketing strategists should create, maintain, and arrest the decrease of ambiguous resource competences that lead to competitiveness and performance (Hansen, McDonald, & Mitchell, 2013). Marketing segmentation and positioning have been at the essence of marketing management (Cornelius, Wagner, & Natter, 2010). The consideration of strategic customers, who can delay a purchase to take advantage of a future discount, has dramatically increased (Gonsch, Klein, Neugebauer, & Steinhardt, 2013).

Information technology has altered the growth of retail trade sector in the affluent economies (Watson, 2011). Technology has the ability to influence marketing and supply chain practice (Richey, Tokman, & Dalela, 2010). Kasemsap (2014b) suggested that the emergence of social media has a strong and positive influence on the development of modern communication and business growth. Social media utilization contributes to brand performance, retailer performance, and consumer–retailer loyalty (Rapp, Beitelspacher, Grewal, & Hughes, 2013). Social media has transformed the traditional marketing communication, resulting in organizations evolving their customer approach and integrating social media into their marketing strategies (Cvijikj, Spiegler, & Michahelles, 2013). Together with regular retail channels, firms can distribute products through Internet (Hu & Li, 2012). Retail channels need to reallocate their shelf spaces while keeping up their total profit margins (Fadıloğlu, Karaşan, & Pınar, 2010). In information-intensive environments, many firms send their customers to other affiliates' websites in order to generate additional sales for their marketing affiliates (Akcura, 2010).

Considerable research explores advertising's role in influencing consumer perceptions and behavior (Hughes, 2013). A consciousness that grows beyond solving small, immediate problems to addressing long-term, large problems that goes beyond individual customer satisfaction and short-term financial performance to encompass total value creation system (Webster & Lusch, 2013). Both managers and investors are increasingly concerned with the impact of advertising spending on shareholder returns (Luo & de Jong, 2012). Marketing communication tools can play a major role in conveying an organization's corporate social responsibility (CSR) messages and communicating a socially responsible image (Jahdi & Acikdilli, 2010). CSR and corporate reputation have positive effects on industrial brand equity and brand performance (Lai, Chiu, Yang, & Pai, 2010). Many organizations utilize online brand communities to support the launch of their new products (Gruner, Homburg, & Lukas, 2014).

Marketing capabilities are the significant drivers of organizational performance (Vorhies, Orr, & Bush, 2011). In terms of business challenges, intense competition, complexity of managing multiple markets and coordinating marketing strategy, a host of risk elements, and the sheer difficulty of managing geographic, cultural, and political barriers are among factors which obstruct organizational success in global marketplace (Cavusgil & Cavusgil, 2012). Marketing strategy decisions are informed by the characteristics of organization, product offering, target customers, industry, and macro environment, among other factors (Varadarajan, 2011). The natures of business disciplines of marketing, strategic management, and operations are recognized as controllable functions within an organization from which strategies can be enacted to affect an organization's stakeholders (Cronin, Smith, Gleim, Ramirez, & Martinez, 2011).

Concept of International Retail Marketing Strategy

Retail internationalization research has been concerned primarily with understanding its scope, scale and its motivations and directions at a strategic level (Doherty, 2000). Economies also benefit from foreign operations of domestic firms because these activities promote socio-economic development, increase employment, and generate spillover effects such as societal prosperity and assistance for local industries to boost productivity (Pinho & Martins, 2010). Treadgold (1991) described how retailers progress through a process of retail internationalization. Treadgold's (1991) model has been criticized in the context of technological, economic and political developments to enhance retail internationalization in modern business (Alexander & Myers, 2000; Hutchinson, Quinn, & Alexander, 2006).

Salmon and Tordjman (1989) identified the three strategic approaches for internationalization dependent on a retailer's trading characteristics and internal capabilities; the international investment, global and multi-national models. Each of the three strategies is defined by the essence of goods sold by the retailer, the degree of market involvement it desires, the extent and nature of operational control demanded, and the retailer's corporate experience. Each of the three strategies is characterized by the international retailer's foreign market entry method, its organization and management of non-domestic businesses, the store formats they operate from, their branding and consumer communications, and the product ranges they sell (Salmon & Tordjman, 1989; Dawson, 1994).

Literature on the internationalization of SMEs identifies location in a geographic cluster of networked firms as a source of competitive advantage (Brown, McNaughton, & Bell, 2010). Marketing concept and strategic marketing management are recognized as corporate management philosophies driven by the needs and capabilities of larger organizations (Gilmore, Kraus, O'Dwyer, & Miles, 2012). Marketers experience high distribution costs in distributing rural market with widely dispersed population (Velayudhan, 2014). Retail strategy and consumer behavior influence the coexistence of local stores and central retail locations (Velayudhan, 2014). In the global retail industry, the distance between retail stores and the distance between customers and retail stores influence the shopping behavior (Lee & Pace, 2005). Retailers locate close to each other to take advantage of agglomeration factors and certain retailers locate close to consumers to profit from proximity advantage (Mejia & Benjamin, 2002).

Levy and Weitz (2012) defined retail positioning as the decision and implementation of a retail marketing mix to create an image of the retailer in customer's mind related to its competitors. Achieving differentiation is one of the main objectives of retail marketing and is central to the marketing and branding concept, with the assumption that higher levels of differentiation from the competitor lead to the higher marketing profitability (Buzzell & Gale, 1987; Davies, 1992). Differentiating the product is considered important in firms' strategies and productivity growth (Kato, 2012). Differentiation and successful positioning of retailers are the results of the overall image of the retail store and the personality of the store in the consumer's mind (Davies, 1992). Retailers should distinguish themselves from their competitors in order to be successful in the global retail industry (Dennis, Murphy, Marsland, Cockett, & Patel, 2002).

Retailers' entry timing is jointly influenced by the economic conditions of foreign markets, cultural distance, and entry mode (Cai & Wang, 2010). Dynamic processes of interaction and knowledge exchange are shaped by vendor mobility as well as collaborative and competitive forces (Beckie, Kennedy, & Wittman, 2012). The strategic alliance between manufacturer and retailer can effectively achieve desired channel coordination (Hong, Wang, Wang, & Zhang, 2013). Retailers and suppliers must work to integrate marketing activities and supply chain processes both within and across organizations to effectively serve consumer at retail shelf and increase market share (Waller, Williams, Tangari, & Burton, 2010).

Concept of Retail Marketing Mix

Many franchise-based retail outlets offer both the franchisor-owned brand and brands of competitors or independent suppliers (Rajab, Kraus, & Wieseke, 2013). Retailers seek to develop products and brands, promote them and distribute them by adopting a retail marketing strategy. Retail marketing exists as a distinctive off-shoot of the wider marketing strategy literature and shares many of the same antecedents (McGoldrick, 2002). The origins of the term marketing mix may be traced to Culliton (1948), defined by McCarthy (1964) as the classic 4P framework (i.e., product, price, place, and promotion) which remains one of the keystones of marketing theory and practice (Smith & Taylor, 2004; Kotler & Armstrong, 2006). In addition, the 4P model has to be adapted according to the nature of the industry and the factors contingent to the activity of the business (Gronroos, 1994; Rafiq & Ahmed, 1995).

The retailers simultaneously determine purchase time (i.e., lead time) and order quantity (Wang, Wang, Ye, Xu, & Yu, 2013). The price of products and the manufacturing firms' profits are affected by the competition style established in retail market (Ishikawa, 2010). Producers' pricing policies tend to be influenced more by the level of market concentration in retail industries than by competitors' price movements (Michis & Markidou, 2013). Retailers gain bargaining power through lower wholesale prices on imitated national brands (Meza & Sudhir, 2010).

Managers need to understand how customers view commercial relationships with retail staff or other social actors in retailing (Keeling, Keeling, & McGoldrick, 2013). Retailers reserve the right to verify the availability at competitor location (Nalca, Boyaci, & Ray, 2010). Consumers rely on consumer reviews when making decisions about which products and services to purchase online (Malbon, 2013). Marketing competitors seek to match or exceed the price cuts of their marketing rivals while responding to promotions (Volpe, 2013). Online video is a famous form of marketing promotion (Hsieh, Hsieh, & Tang, 2012). However, price promotions cause the significant amounts of waste in packaged goods retailing (Breiter & Huchzermeier, 2010).

The market is progressively saturated, price sensitive, and commoditized (Deloitte, 2013). An effective innovation regarding demand pull and technology push should focus on both the final users/consumers' needs and expectations and the retailers/employees' needs and expectations (Pantano & Viassone, 2014). Marketing innovations make product and process innovations more successful (Schubert, 2010). The presence of a larger quantity of retail goods considerably attracts customers (Parthasarathi, Sarmah, & Jenamani, 2011). Product complexity affects competition and consumers in retail markets (Sitzia & Zizzo, 2011). Competent management of marketing activity is required to create a retail offer that fits with the expectations of the targeted customer segments (Darling, 2001). By combining the retail mix activities, an overall positioning of retail offer may be achieved (Skallerud & Grønhaug, 2010).

Walters and Laffy (1996) identified the four marketing activities that are integrated and parts of the retail mix. The first marketing activity is related to merchandise decisions (i.e., the core merchandise policy, branding, assortment profiles, and merchandise extension). The second marketing activity is related to store format and environment (i.e., profile of the outlet, space allocation, visual merchandising, design, and atmosphere). The third marketing activity is related to customer service (i.e., product services, service products, and personnel services). The fourth and last marketing activity is related to customer communications (i.e., advertising, in-store displays, and visual merchandising). Contributing to brand image is advertising, the purpose of which is to sell the establishment, attract customers to the premises, and sell goods (Jefkins & Yadin, 2000). Cooperative advertising is a key incentive offered by a manufacturer to influence retailers' promotional decisions (Chutani & Sethi, 2012).

The 4P framework has been considered inappropriate for retail industries on account of its production-orientated as opposed to marketing-orientated view (Gronroos, 1994). Below are the characteristics of marketing mix framework regarding retail settings.

1. **Product Quantity:** Retailers sell small quantities of items on a frequent basis (Dibb, Simkin, Pride, & Ferrell, 2006).
2. **Product Assortment:** Retailers offer a greater range of products than do manufacturers (Kent & Omar, 2003).
3. **Convenience:** Retailers provide superior services in terms of location, payment and credit facilities, merchandise range and after-sales support (Levy & Weitz, 2012).
4. **Product Sourcing:** Retailers buy products from often varied and geographically distant suppliers (Kent & Omar, 2003).
5. **Variety of Sales Channels:** Retailers may sell products through stores, mobile shops, mail-order or electronic channels (Levy & Weitz, 2012).
6. **Additional Selling:** Retailers can sell additional services and goods to compliment their prime activities (Fernie, Fernie, & Moore, 2003).
7. **Target Customers:** Retailers should adapt different marketing types of consumer to gain competitive advantage (Kent & Omar, 2003).

Marketing value creation is the core purpose of economic exchange in retail sector (Dean & Rolland, 2012). The importance of managing product categories effectively is increasing (Liu & McGoldrick, 1996). Adding value for the consumer is brand image, the perception of the brand identity as interpreted by consumers (Keller, 1993). This is of value to a retailer as it assures the organization of sales and on-going customer loyalty (Kent & Omar, 2003) and enables them to justify higher selling prices (Levy & Weitz, 2012).

Concept of Internationalization

Internationalization refers to the mobilization of human, material, technological, and organizational resources for international markets (Spowart & Wickramasekera, 2012). Internationalization brings about greater uncertainty and complexity in the environmental and strategic context of SMEs (Westhead, Wright, & Ucbasaran, 2004). Internationalization is considered as a learning strategy (Calza, Aliane, & Cannavale, 2013). The internationalization of a firm is the outward movement of its operations and the process of mobilization, accumulation, and development of a specific set of resources in order to achieve greater performance (Dutot et al., 2014). Knowledge is not only a key influence on foreign operations, but also an important outcome of the internationalization process (Aulakh, 2009).

Internationalization process can vary related to research and development (R&D) innovation, network, technology, and human resources (Raymond & St-Pierre, 2013). Internationalization is jointly linked to globalization and growth (Ruzzier, Hisrich, & Antoncic, 2006). Internationalization is a successful strategy for firms in emerging economies to access and explore vast opportunities at the global level and to build their competitive advantage (Luo & Tung, 2007; Guillen & Garcia-Canal, 2009). Expanding sales to different markets offers learning opportunities that cut across industry or geography and are independent of the actions of foreign firms (Ellis, Davies, & Wong, 2011). As firms extend their scope of international activities or enter diverse foreign markets, they encounter different consumer needs, rival practices, new testing grounds for their products, and engage in exploratory learning (Aulakh, 2009). However, internationalization tends to be a double-edged sword because the theory-based predictions of the effect of internationalization on organizational performance are not unilaterally positive or negative (Chung, Lee, Beamish, Southam, & Nam, 2013).

Relationship between Corporate Marketing Strategies and Internationalization

In a globalized and hypercompetitive world, organizations have to internationalize in order to enlarge their potential markets, and to reach higher levels of efficiency (Calza et al., 2013). Rapid change in the global business environment during the last few decades has had a strong impact on the internationalization process of many firms around the world (Uner, Kocak, Cavusgil, & Cavusgil, 2013). Global and regional retailers should realize that consumers' perceptions are country specific (To, Tam, & Cheung, 2013). Recent cases in retailing reflect that ethics have a major impact on brands and performance, in turn, demonstrating that brand owners, employees, and consumers focus on ethical values (Biong, Nygaard, & Silkoset, 2010). In today's retail markets, products display opaque pricing that provides no information about the allocation of retail proceeds among marketing agents who bring the products to market (Carter & Curry, 2010). Organizations have to learn new resources and systematic ways to combine the new and existing marketing resources (Calza et al., 2013).

There exist various forms of internationalization strategies for SMEs (Kotabe & Helsen, 2010). Six basic forms of partnership can be identified: exportation, subcontracting, outsourcing, offshoring, strategic alliance, and joint venture (Dutot et al., 2014). Root (1994) indicated that these strategies can be classified into three categories: the first one is called export entry mode (i.e., exportation only). The second one is the contractual entry mode (i.e., transfer of technological or human skills, strategic alliances, subcontracting). The third one is the investment entry mode (i.e., joint-venture, sole venture or foreign direct investment which includes wholly owned subsidiary). Organization chooses the strategy based on its requirements, its resources, the complexity of operation, and its profitability (Ruzzier & Konecnik, 2006). The international activities of SMEs have different levels of complexity (Dutot et al., 2014).

Marketing concepts apply to all forms of exchange concerning goods, services, places, and ideas (Achrol & Kotler, 2012). Marketing capabilities improve customer satisfaction and employee fulfillment which may increase financial indicators (Cruz-Ros, Cruz, & Perez-Cabanero, 2010). Marketing activity refers to the pervasiveness of promotion expenditures and number of retail outlets per capita in a country (Sirgy, Yu, Lee, Wei, & Huang, 2012). Cooperative advertising plays a strategically important role in marketing programs (Yan, 2010). Marketing channel structure is critical in determining both who benefits and the mechanism by which this benefit occurs (Xiao, Palekar, & Liu, 2011). All marketing channel members achieve higher advertising efforts and profit level in the cooperative case rather than in the non-cooperative case (Zhou & Lin, 2014). A higher compatibility of a product with online marketing leads to a higher advertising effort for online channel by manufacturer, an enhanced steady state for demand of brand as well as greater sales in the steady state through online channel (Sayadi & Makui, 2014).

The growing numbers of large retailers have internationalized to emerging markets (Moser, Schaefers, & Meise, 2012). Retail internationalization is important in global business (Doherty, 2007; Wigley & Moore, 2007). When organizations invest abroad, they have to employ new people,

integrate new organizational units within their structure, enlarge their stakeholders, and adapt to different environments. Internationalization poses the big marketing challenges in modern organizations. Entering a new market implies the necessity to work within a different culture context. The practical internationalization has been confined to the food-retailing sector (Palmer & Quinn, 2003). The different rules, different behaviors, and different social norms can make coordination difficult, and can significantly impact on communication and organizational image (House, Hanges, Javidan, Dorfman, & Gupta, 2004).

Brouthers and Xu (2002) stated that pursuing a low-price strategy to compete at the international level weakens a firm's performance because profits tend to be smaller under extremely fierce price-based competition. Excessive internationalization increases governance and coordination costs associated with managing export operations, spread management resources across various markets, and increase management's information-processing needs (Aulakh, Kotabe, & Teegen, 2000; Chung, Lu, & Beamish, 2008), which can induce challenges for managers (Xiao, Jeong, Moon, Chung, & Chung, 2013). Managers need to develop a well-rounded appreciation of international expansion that views internationalization not only as a source of additional income, but also an important platform for marketing learning, capability enhancement and organizational renewal (Ibeh & Kasem, 2014).

Salesperson learning has the potential to contribute to the competitive advantage of the organization by increasing its capacity for organizational learning (Bell, Menguc, & Widing, 2010). Learning about new marketplace allows organizations to use their resources, to discover new ones, and to combine them in order to improve their competitiveness (Tung, 1998; Jun, Gentry, & Hyun, 2001). Organizations have to acquire market-knowledge both to coordinate the activity well, and to attract new customers in the global marketplace (Calza et al., 2013).

Learning motivation leads to the learning transfer in modern organizations (Kasemsap, 2013a). Organizational learning, knowledge management, and knowledge-sharing behavior positively affect organizational performance in global business (Kasemsap, 2013b). Kasemsap (2013c) explained that knowledge management practically leads to better job performance. Empowering leadership, team cohesion, and knowledge-sharing behavior are effectively correlated with team performance (Kasemsap, 2013d). Kasemsap (2014c) stated that perception of learning is favorably related to perceived training transfer in the digital age. Academic efforts to create new social networks should be implemented in order to minimize the lack of knowledge (Kasemsap, 2014d). Leaders of global businesses should provide training and provide the necessary information and communication technology skills for all employees to enhance their knowledge in modern business (Kasemsap, 2014e).

Organizations capture new knowledge generated by frontline employees in addressing productivity-quality tradeoffs during customer interactions and transform it into updated knowledge for frontline use (Ye, Marinova, & Singh, 2012). Organizations can internalize service experience knowledge by aggregating learned rules from organization's retail stores (Lin, Po, & Orellan, 2011). Information sharing shifts power upstream which enhances the manufacturer's incentive to bear costs to increase retail demand (Mittendorf, Shin, & Yoon, 2013). Knowledge is a key aspect of internationalization: organizations need to learn how to be competitive in different markets, as well as how to transfer their technology and practical application in order to delocalize their activities in the cheaper marketplace.

Challenges of Retail Marketing Mix in the Fashion Retail Industry

A change in product preference due to fashion trends is the main reason why the demand of fashion industry shows more variations than other industries (Wang, Gou, Sun, & Yue, 2012). Many retailers are in the process of adjusting their logistics operations to their specific requirements against the backdrop of raising pressure in a highly competitive environment (Kuhn & Sternbeck, 2013). Consumption is a central component of many peoples' lives (Ganglmair-Wooliscroft & Lawson, 2012). Consumption is deeply intertwined with social relations and norms (Carrigan, Moraes, & Leek, 2011). The increasing diversity of consumers' demand represents a challenge for retail stores (Walter, Battiston, Yildirim, & Schweitzer, 2012). Firms from different sectors can be expected to differ in philanthropic approach due to differences in public relations exposure (Amato & Amato, 2012). As luxury goods are more than any other products bought for what they mean, beyond what they are, multi-sensory experiences of luxury brands gain more and more relevance in creating superior customer-perceived value (Wiedmann, Hennigs, Klarmann, & Behrens, 2013).

The retail distribution sector is facing a difficult time as the current landscape is characterized by ever-increasing competition (Roig-Tierno, Baviera-Puig, & Buitrago-Vera, 2013). Regulation in retail sector has a considerable influence on firms' efficiency (Suarez & de Jorge, 2010). Retailers' competition drives retail prices lower (Mills, 2013). Prices tend to rise faster when costs rise, relative to the rate at which prices drop when costs fall (Hofstetter & Tovar, 2010). The pricing strategy is considered as one of the five most important priorities in retail management (Fassnacht & Husseini, 2013). Extant pricing strategies assume that all brands in the market are included while setting prices (Pancras, 2010). Coordination beyond simple knowledge of price will be beneficial for improving overall profits (Li, Nukala, & Mohebbi, 2013). The low-priced and medium-priced store brands are able to build individual store brand loyalty and store loyalty among customers (Yang & Wang, 2010).

Product design is defined as important to fashion retailers according to the relationship between fashion products and consumers' need for utility and self-image (Wigley, Moore, & Birtwistle, 2005). Retail shelf space allocation problem is recognized in marketing literature (Gajjar & Adil, 2010). A product's shelf location has a significant impact on sales for retail perspectives (Russell & Urban, 2010). To expand market and financial performance, firms should seek to generate meaningful product innovations through a moderate level of relative R&D power, particularly when their environments are characterized by high competitive intensity (Stock & Reiferscheid, 2014).

Fashion firms are recognized among the successful international retailers (Doherty, 2007; Wigley & Moore, 2007), reflecting in the marketing literature, with various studies focusing on the examples of fashion retailer internationalization (Wigley & Moore, 2007), and emphasizing internationalization among fashion retailers (Hutchinson et al., 2006). Fashion firms focus on the importance of branding (Moore, Fernie, & Burt, 2000), the range and ease of market entry methods (Dawson, 1994), and the potential for off-shore manufacturing (Sparks, 1996). The seasonal sales periods require the mark-down and promotions in order to shift slow-selling goods, but these must be managed toward better marketing profitability (Jackson & Shaw, 2006). The seasonality of fashion retailing and the sensitivity to customer demand require quick turnover of product ranges (Christopher & Peck, 2004).

Fashion retailers manage their pricing strategy, brand image, and market performance. When making order decisions the retailer only examines the price ratio and the fluctuation size of random demand, rather than the channel cost and the retailer's marketing efficiency (Liu, Lei, & Liu, 2014). The retailers operate in the same consumer market in which they compete in prices for consumer demand (Ouardighi, Jørgensen, & Pasin, 2013). Fashion retailers should expand product ranges in order to generate sales revenue, and gain competitive advantage through market attendance. Fashion retailers should improve and maintain the positive relationships with their customers in global retail markets (Sheridan, Moore, & Nobbs, 2006). Fashion retailers should develop the highly sophisticated, distinctive and focused brand identities in retail settings (Harrow, Lea-Greenwood, & Otieno, 2005).

Overview of Brand Management

The concept of brand can be traced back to product marketing where the role of brand and brand management has been primarily to create differentiation and preference for a product or service in the mind of the customer (Knox & Bickerton, 2003). Marketing lacks comprehension on the increasingly important segment of mature consumers concerning their behavior and respective reasons for certain behavior (Helm & Landschulze, 2013). The strong brand influences consumers' perception and brand loyalty focuses on the variables of marketing mix (Yoo, Donthu, & Lee, 2000). Consumers' perceptions of other consumers' product reviews affect brand buying intentions through two intervening variables: product-related attitudes and brand-related attitudes (Bartikowski & Walsh, 2014). Branding is a powerful mean of distinction (Pappu, Quester, & Cooksey, 2005). Brands play a central role in marketing, thus attracting the attention of academicians and practitioners (Brodie, Glynn, & Little, 2006; Erdem, Swait, & Valenzuela, 2006).

One of the major challenges for brand managers in the twenty-first century is to comprehend the relations between loyalty and its antecedents (Taylor, Celuch, & Goodwin, 2004). Business managers increasingly seek to develop brand loyalty through sponsorship activities (Masodier & Merunka, 2012). Staff behavior has an effective impact on brand success (Engel, Tran, Pavlek, Blankenberg, & Meyer, 2013). Branding supports the opportunity of brand extension (Yasin, Nasser

Noor, & Mohamad, 2007). Building brand equity is considered as an important part of brand building (Pappu et al., 2005). Brand equity refers to the incremental utility or added value which brand adds to the product (Chen & Chang, 2008). Brand equity is an appropriate metric for evaluating the long-run impact of marketing decision (Atilgan, Aksoy, & Akinci, 2005).

Kasemsap (2014f) indicated that the dimensions of customer value, customer satisfaction, and brand loyalty have mediated positive effect on customer relationship management (CRM) performance in the social media age. Corporate brands are exposed to a wide variety of corporate publicity, which may elicit unexpected consumer responses and requires more academic attention (Xi & Peng, 2010). Brand trust is positively correlated with brand loyalty (Singh, Iglesias, & Batista-Foguet, 2012). Brand attitudes are determined by advertising content for innovative brands (Barone & Jewell, 2014). A favorable online brand experience is important for strengthening the consumers' brand relationship in a digital world (Simon, Brexendorf, & Fassnacht, 2013). The success of new product extension is an increasing function of parent brand's quality and the degree of fit between parent brand and new product extension (Carter & Curry, 2013).

Significance of Brand Management in the Global Retail Industry

In the global retail industry, branding can be especially important in influencing customer perceptions, as well as in motivating store choice and loyalty (Ailawadi & Keller, 2004; Hartman & Spiro, 2005). Customer loyalty has become a major concern for retail stores across the globe (Thomas, 2013). Retail brand can be perceived as an emotional connection between customer and organization (Kozinets, Sherry, DeBerry-Spence, Duhachek, Nuttavuthisit, & Storm, 2002). A better understanding of retail brand management techniques is required from the perspectives of consumers and practitioners (Ailawadi & Keller, 2004). Retail branding has moved beyond product-based explanations of retail brand distinctiveness to a more corporate store-based level (Burt & Davies, 2010). The development of retail brand thinking persists in line with the wider debate presented within the brand management field (Louro & Cunha, 2001).

Brand valuation has a significant positive effect on consumers' perceived value (Lin, 2013). As the retailers have continued to develop and promote such brands, consumers' perceptions of such brands have steadily improved and retail brands have become part of the accepted repertoire of consumer choice (Baltas, 2003). Appropriate management of brand equity leads to the increase in loyalty, to decrease the risk of marketing activity and marketing crisis, flexible response to price fluctuations, more business support and cooperation, high effectiveness of marketing communications, licensing opportunities, additional opportunities for brand extension, more attraction and support from investors (VanAuken, 2005), greater profit margins (Kim & Kim, 2005), increasing the ability to attract good employees (DelVecchio, Jarvis, Klink, & Dineen, 2007), protecting of potential competitors which enter during outsourcing (Lim & Tan, 2009).

Brand equity is the result of consumers' perception (Yasin et al., 2007). Brand equity sources include consumers' brand awareness and strong, favorable and unique brand associations. The first step in creating brand equity is to develop a brand identity (Aaker, 1996; Keller, 2003), achieved through a unique set of brand associations that a firm aspires to create or maintain (Aaker, 1996). There are many empirical researches about the dimensions of brand equity (i.e., brand awareness, brand association, perceived brand quality and brand loyalty) and overall brand equity (Yasin et al., 2007). High brand awareness is a signal of brand quality that assists consumers in making purchase decisions in the global retail industry (Yoo et al., 2000).

Brand awareness can be viewed as an antecedent of brand loyalty (Yoo et al., 2000). Brand awareness plays a special role in driving brand equity in business markets (Davis, Golicic, & Marquardt, 2008). Brand name and brand awareness explain a significant amount of the variation in brand equity in industrial firms (Davis et al., 2008). Consumer's satisfaction has positively influenced loyalty (Ismail, Hasnah, Ibrahim, & Mohd Isa, 2006). When consumers are satisfied with brand, they are more likely to recommend the product to others, are less likely to switch to other alternative brands (Bennett & Rundle-Thiele, 2004). Brand loyalty is considered as a desired outcome of publishing a brand, or brand equity (Van Riel, De Mortanges, & Streukens, 2005; Cater & Cater, 2009). Van Riel et al. (2005) stated that there is a positive relationship between industrial brand equity and brand loyalty.

The importance of brand associations is highlighted in several studies as the brand association can positively influence consumer choice, preferences, purchase intention, and brand extensions' acceptance (Yoo et al., 2000). Perceived brand quality has significant impact on customer satisfaction and brand loyalty (Nguyen, Barrett, & Miller, 2011). Hong-Youl and Kang-Hee (2012) stated that perceived quality have direct impact on brand loyalty and satisfaction. Yoo et al. (2000) showed the perceived brand quality has a positive relationship with a brand that is distributed with a good brand image. Branding enables organizations to achieve competitive advantage through building higher value perception of customers to get a higher price premium (Hsiao & Chen, 2013).

Brand equity is an antecedent of brand loyalty (Taylor et al., 2004). A brand that receives high attention from customers will have a competitive advantage (Nguyen et al., 2011). Managers of international brands design the marketing programs able to communicate distinctive associations with their brands in order to create high brand awareness in building high consumer perception of the brand's perceived value, thus leading to

an increase in brand loyalty in the global retail industry (Nguyen et al., 2011). Keller (2003) stated that a positive brand equity can lead to more revenue, lower costs and higher profits, tending customer to seek new distribution channels, marketing communications effectiveness, and success in developing brand and selling licensing opportunities (Atilgan et al., 2005).

FUTURE RESEARCH DIRECTIONS

The strength of this chapter is on the thorough literature consolidation of corporate marketing strategies and brand management in the global retail industry. The extant literatures of corporate marketing strategies and brand management in the global retail industry provide a contribution to practitioners and researchers by describing a comprehensive view of the functional applications of corporate marketing strategies and brand management in the global retail industry to appeal to different segments of corporate marketing strategies and brand management in the global retail industry in order to maximize the business impact of corporate marketing strategies and brand management in the global retail industry. The classification of the prevailing literature in the domains of corporate marketing strategies and brand management will provide the potential opportunities for future research. Future research direction should broaden the perspectives in the implementation of corporate marketing strategies and brand management to be utilized in the knowledge-based organizations.

Practitioners and researchers should recognize the applicability of a more multidisciplinary approach toward research activities in implementing corporate marketing strategies and brand management in terms of knowledge management-related variables (i.e., knowledge-sharing behavior, knowledge creation, organizational learning, learning orientation, and motivation to learn). It will be useful to bring additional disciplines together (i.e., strategic management, marketing, finance, and human resources) to support a more holistic examination of corporate marketing strategies and brand management in order to combine or transfer existing theories and approaches to inquiry in this area.

CONCLUSION

This chapter explored the roles of corporate marketing strategies and brand management in the global retail industry, thus describing the concepts of marketing strategy, international retail marketing strategy, retail marketing mix, and internationalization; the relationship between corporate marketing strategies and internationalization; the challenges of retail marketing mix in the fashion retail industry; the overview of brand management; and the significance of brand management in the global retail industry. To be the successful global retailers, the ability to apply and adjust the retail marketing mix elements and retail brand strategy concerning specific target-market conditions and a wider global marketing strategy, is functionally important in retail settings. The successful global retailing requires both strategic and tactical initiatives, both taking into account company capabilities.

The global retailers should manage retail marketing mix elements and retail brand strategy in order to achieve better marketing outcomes within actionable business architecture. However, the level of manipulation of each in specific markets may be varied within the bounds set by the company's wider strategy. While some retail marketing mix elements and retail brand strategy should be maintained at a consistent level around the world, specific retail marketing mix elements and retail brand strategy may be adapted to suit the local market conditions. Product design and brand image in the retail brand strategy are attributed as being the most important factors, with variables tangible to consumers (i.e., pricing, advertising, product range, shelf space, and customer relationships), supporting these marketing factors in the global marketplace.

Retail marketing mix elements and the associated responsibility for their management tasks should be delegated to foreign markets management. Concerning retail internationalization literature, in order to be successful in the global retail industry, the global retailers should adopt a multinational approach. The overall brand image and product design in retail brand strategy should globally remain consistent and be supported by generally uniform store environment. Corporate marketing strategies should adapt pricing, advertising and product range in each local market, thus performing in the development of managerial structures and roles in retail settings.

The implementation of corporate marketing strategies and brand management is critical for modern organizations that seek to serve suppliers and customers, increase business performance, strengthen competitiveness, and achieve continuous success in global business. Therefore, it is necessary for modern organizations to examine their corporate marketing strategies and brand management applications, create a strategic plan to regularly check their practical advancements, and rapidly respond to the corporate marketing strategies and brand management needs of customers in the global retail industry. Applying corporate marketing strategies and brand management will greatly improve market performance and reach business goals in retail settings.

REFERENCES

Aaker, D. A. (1996). Measuring brand equity across products and markets. *California Management Review*, *38*(3), 102–120. doi:10.2307/41165845

Achrol, R. S., & Kotler, P. (2012). Frontiers of the marketing paradigm in the third millennium. *Journal of the Academy of Marketing Science, 40*(1), 35–52. doi:10.1007/s11747-011-0255-4

Ailawadi, K. L., & Keller, K. L. (2004). Understanding retail branding: Conceptual insights and research priorities. *Journal of Retailing, 80*(4), 331–342. doi:10.1016/j.jretai.2004.10.008

Akcura, M. T. (2010). Affiliated marketing. *Information Systems and e-Business Management, 8*(4), 379-394.

Alexander, N. (1990). Retailers and international markets: Motives for expansion. *International Marketing Review, 7*(4), 75–85. doi:10.1108/02651339010142797

Alexander, N., & Doherty, A. M. (2010). International retail research: Focus, methodology and conceptual development. *International Journal of Retail & Distribution Management, 38*(11-12), 928–942.

Alexander, N., & Myers, H. (2000). The retail internationalisation process. *International Marketing Review, 17*(4-5), 334–353. doi:10.1108/02651330010339888

Amato, L. H., & Amato, C. H. (2012). Retail philanthropy: Firm size, industry, and business cycle. *Journal of Business Ethics, 107*(4), 435–448. doi:10.1007/s10551-011-1048-x

Atilgan, E., Aksoy, S., & Akinci, S. (2005). Determinants of the brand equity: A verification approach in the beverage industry in Turkey. *Marketing Intelligence & Planning, 23*(3), 237–248. doi:10.1108/02634500510597283

Aulakh, P. S. (2009). Revisiting the internationalization—Performance relationship: Implications for emerging economy firms. *Decision, 36*(2), 25–39.

Aulakh, P. S., Kotabe, M., & Teegen, H. (2000). Export strategies and performance of firms from emerging economies: Evidence from Brazil, Chile, and Mexico. *Academy of Management Journal, 43*(3), 342–361. doi:10.2307/1556399

Balmer, J. M. T., Powell, S. M., & Greyser, S. A. (2011). Explicating ethical corporate marketing. Insights from the BP deepwater horizon catastrophe: The ethical brand that exploded and then imploded. *Journal of Business Ethics, 102*(1), 1–14. doi:10.1007/s10551-011-0902-1

Baltas, G. (2003). A combined segmentation and demand model for store brands. *European Journal of Marketing, 37*(10), 1499–1513. doi:10.1108/03090560310487211

Barone, M. J., & Jewell, R. D. (2014). How brand innovativeness creates advertising flexibility. *Journal of the Academy of Marketing Science, 42*(3), 309–321. doi:10.1007/s11747-013-0352-7

Bartikowski, B., & Walsh, G. (2014). Attitude contagion in consumer opinion platforms: Posters and lurkers. *Electronic Markets, 24*(3), 207–217. doi:10.1007/s12525-013-0149-z

Beckie, M. A., Kennedy, E. H., & Wittman, H. (2012). Scaling up alternative food networks: Farmers' markets and the role of clustering in western Canada. *Agriculture and Human Values, 29*(3), 333–345. doi:10.1007/s10460-012-9359-9

Bell, S. J., Menguc, B., & Widing, R. E. (2010). Salesperson learning, organizational learning, and retail store performance. *Journal of the Academy of Marketing Science, 38*(2), 187–201. doi:10.1007/s11747-009-0149-x

Bennett, R., & Rundle-Thiele, S. (2004). Customer satisfaction should not be the only goal. *Journal of Services Marketing, 18*(7), 514–523. doi:10.1108/08876040410561848

Bianchi, C. C., & Ostale, E. (2006). Lessons learned from unsuccessful internationalization attempts: Examples of multinational retailers in Chile. *Journal of Business Research, 59*(1), 140–147. doi:10.1016/j.jbusres.2005.01.002

Biong, H., Nygaard, A., & Silkoset, R. (2010). The influence of retail management's use of social power on corporate ethical values, employee commitment, and performance. *Journal of Business Ethics, 97*(3), 341–363. doi:10.1007/s10551-010-0523-0

Breiter, A., & Huchzermeier, A. (2010). The new logic of truly efficient retail promotions. *International Commerce Review, 9*(1-2), 36–47. doi:10.1007/s12146-010-0052-x

Brexendorf, T. O., & Daecke, N. (2012). The brand manager – Current tasks and skill requirements in FMCG companies. *Marketing Review St. Gallen, 29*(6), 32–37. doi:10.1365/s11621-012-0175-9

Brodie, R. J., Glynn, M. S., & Little, V. (2006). The service brand and the service-dominant logic: Missing fundamental premise or the need for stronger theory. *Marketing Theory, 6*(3), 363–379. doi:10.1177/1470593106066797

Brouthers, L. E., & Xu, K. (2002). Product stereotypes, strategy and performance satisfaction: The case of Chinese exporters. *Journal of International Business Studies, 33*(4), 657–677. doi:10.1057/palgrave.jibs.8491038

Brown, P., McNaughton, R. B., & Bell, J. (2010). Marketing externalities in industrial clusters: A literature review and evidence from the Christchurch, New Zealand electronics cluster. *Journal of International Entrepreneurship, 8*(2), 168–181. doi:10.1007/s10843-010-0053-y

Burt, S., & Davies, K. (2010). From the retail brand to the retailer as a brand: Themes and issues in retail branding research. *International Journal of Retail & Distribution Management, 38*(11-12), 865–878.

Buzzel, R. D., & Gale, B. T. (1987). *The PIMS principles*. New York, NY: Free Press.

Cai, R., & Wang, Y. (2010). An empirical study on the timing of big retailers' initial internationalization: Influence of the target market and entry-mode choice. *Frontiers of Business Research in China, 4*(4), 608–629. doi:10.1007/s11782-010-0113-0

Calza, F., Aliane, N., & Cannavale, C. (2013). Cross-cultural bridges in European firms' internationalization to Islamic countries: The key role of cultural competence. *EuroMed Journal of Business, 8*(2), 172–187. doi:10.1108/EMJB-07-2013-0038

Carrigan, M., Moraes, C., & Leek, S. (2011). Fostering responsible communities: A community social marketing approach to sustainable living. *Journal of Business Ethics, 100*(3), 515–534. doi:10.1007/s10551-010-0694-8

Carter, R. E., & Curry, D. J. (2010). Transparent pricing: Theory, tests, and implications for marketing practice. *Journal of the Academy of Marketing Science, 38*(6), 759–774. doi:10.1007/s11747-010-0189-2

Carter, R. E., & Curry, D. J. (2013). Perceptions versus performance when managing extensions: New evidence about the role of fit between a parent brand and an extension. *Journal of the Academy of Marketing Science, 41*(2), 253–269. doi:10.1007/s11747-011-0292-z

Cater, B., & Cater, T. (2009). Relationship-value-based antecedents of customer satisfaction and loyalty in manufacturing. *Journal of Business and Industrial Marketing, 24*(7-8), 585–597. doi:10.1108/08858620910999457

Cavusgil, S. T., & Cavusgil, E. (2012). Reflections on international marketing: Destructive regeneration and multinational firms. *Journal of the Academy of Marketing Science, 40*(2), 202–217. doi:10.1007/s11747-011-0287-9

Chen, C. F., & Chang, Y. (2008). Airline brand equity, brand preference, and purchase intentions: The moderating effects of switching costs. *Journal of Air Transport Management*, *14*(1), 40–42. doi:10.1016/j.jairtraman.2007.11.003

Christopher, M., & Peck, H. (2004). *Marketing logistics*. Oxford, UK: Butterworth-Heinemann.

Chung, C. C., Lee, S. H., Beamish, P. W., Southam, C., & Nam, D. (2013). Pitting real options theory against risk diversification theory: International diversification and joint ownership control in economic crisis. *Journal of World Business*, *48*(1), 122–136. doi:10.1016/j.jwb.2012.06.013

Chung, C. C., Lu, J., & Beamish, P. W. (2008). Multinational networks during times of economic crisis versus stability. *Management International Review*, *48*(3), 279–295. doi:10.1007/s11575-008-0016-x

Chutani, A., & Sethi, S. P. (2012). Cooperative advertising in a dynamic retail market oligopoly. *Dynamic Games and Applications*, *2*(4), 347–375. doi:10.1007/s13235-012-0053-8

Cornelius, B., Wagner, U., & Natter, M. (2010). Managerial applicability of graphical formats to support positioning decisions. *Journal für Betriebswirtschaft*, *60*(3), 167–201. doi:10.1007/s11301-010-0061-y

Cronin, J. J., Smith, J. S., Gleim, M. R., Ramirez, E., & Martinez, J. D. (2011). Green marketing strategies: An examination of stakeholders and the opportunities they present. *Journal of the Academy of Marketing Science*, *39*(1), 158–174. doi:10.1007/s11747-010-0227-0

Cruz-Ros, S., Cruz, T. F. G., & Perez-Cabanero, C. (2010). Marketing capabilities, stakeholders' satisfaction, and performance. *Service Business*, *4*(3-4), 209–223. doi:10.1007/s11628-009-0078-2

Culliton, J. W. (1948). *The management of marketing costs*. Boston, MA: Harvard University Press.

Cvijikj, I. P., Spiegler, E. D., & Michahelles, F. (2013). Evaluation framework for social media brand presence. *Social Network Analysis and Mining*, *3*(4), 1325–1349. doi:10.1007/s13278-013-0131-y

Darling, J. R. (2001). Successful competitive positioning: The key for entry into the European consumer market. *European Business Review*, *13*(4), 209–221. doi:10.1108/EUM0000000005535

Davies, G. (1992). The two ways in which retailers can be brands. *International Journal of Retail & Distribution Management*, *20*(2), 24–34. doi:10.1108/09590559210009312

Davis, D. F., Golicic, S. L., & Marquardt, A. J. (2008). Branding a B2B service: Does a brand differentiate a logistics service provider? *Industrial Marketing Management*, *37*(2), 218–227. doi:10.1016/j.indmarman.2007.02.003

Davis, G. (1992). Positioning, image and the marketing of multiple retailers. *International Review of Retail, Distribution and Consumer Research*, *2*(1), 13–34. doi:10.1080/09593969200000002

Dawson, J. (1994). The internationalisation of retailing operations. *Journal of Marketing Management*, *10*(4), 267–282. doi:10.1080/0267257X.1994.9964274

Dean, A. M., & Rolland, S. E. (2012). Using an age-based lens to test the antecedents of value in retail. *der markt. International Journal of Marketing*, *51*(2-3), 85–100.

Deloitte. (2013). *Keeping promises putting customers at the heart of retail financial services*. London, UK: Deloitte.

DelVecchio, D., Jarvis, C. B., Klink, R. R., & Dineen, B. B. (2007). Leveraging brand equity to attract human capital. *Marketing Letters*, *18*(3), 149–164. doi:10.1007/s11002-007-9012-3

Dennis, C., Murphy, J., Marsland, D., Cockett, T., & Patel, T. (2002). Measuring image: Shopping centre case studies. *International Review of Retail, Distribution and Consumer Research*, *12*(4), 355–373. doi:10.1080/09593960210151153

Dibb, S., Simkin, L., Pride, W. M., & Ferrell, O. C. (2006). *Marketing: Concepts and strategies.* Boston, MA: Houghton Mifflin.

Doherty, A. M. (2000). Factors influencing international retailers market entry mode. *Journal of Marketing Management*, *16*(1), 223–245. doi:10.1362/026725700785100514

Doherty, A. M. (2007). The internationalisation of retailing: Factors influencing the choice of franchising as a market entry method. *International Journal of Service Industry Management*, *18*(2), 184–205. doi:10.1108/09564230710737826

Dutot, V., Bergeron, F., & Raymond, L. (2014). Information management for the internationalization of SMEs: An exploratory study based on a strategic alignment perspective. *International Journal of Information Management*, *34*(5), 672–681. doi:10.1016/j.ijinfomgt.2014.06.006

Ellis, B., & Kelly, S. (1992). Competitive advantage in retailing. *International Review of Retail, Distribution and Consumer Research*, *2*(2), 381–396. doi:10.1080/09593969200000014

Ellis, P., Davies, H., & Wong, A. (2011). Export intensity and marketing in transition economies: Evidence from China. *Industrial Marketing Management*, *40*(4), 593–602. doi:10.1016/j.indmarman.2010.10.003

Engel, J., Tran, C., Pavlek, N., Blankenberg, N., & Meyer, A. (2013). The impact of friendliness on brand perception. *Marketing Review St. Gallen*, *30*(6), 82–95. doi:10.1365/s11621-013-0302-2

Erdem, T., Swait, J., & Valenzuela, A. (2006). Brands as signals: A cross country validation study. *Journal of Marketing*, *70*(1), 34–49. doi:10.1509/jmkg.2006.70.1.34

Fadılolu, M. M., Karaşan, O. E., & Pınar, M. C. (2010). A model and case study for efficient shelf usage and assortment analysis. *Annals of Operations Research*, *180*(1), 105–124. doi:10.1007/s10479-008-0497-9

Fassnacht, M., & Husseini, S. E. (2013). EDLP versus Hi–Lo pricing strategies in retailing—A state of the art article. *Journal of Business Economics*, *83*(3), 259–289. doi:10.1007/s11573-012-0648-y

Fernie, J., Fernie, S., & Moore, C. M. (2003). *Principles of retailing.* Oxford, UK: Butterworth-Heinemann.

Gajjar, H. K., & Adil, G. K. (2010). A piecewise linearization for retail shelf space allocation problem and a local search heuristic. *Annals of Operations Research*, *179*(1), 149–167. doi:10.1007/s10479-008-0455-6

Ganglmair-Wooliscroft, A., & Lawson, R. (2012). Subjective wellbeing and its influence on consumer sentiment towards marketing: A New Zealand example. *Journal of Happiness Studies*, *13*(1), 149–166. doi:10.1007/s10902-011-9255-9

Gaur, A. S., Kumar, V., & Singh, D. (2014). Institutions, resources, and internationalization of emerging economy firms. *Journal of World Business*, *49*(1), 12–20. doi:10.1016/j.jwb.2013.04.002

Gilmore, A., Kraus, S., O'Dwyer, M., & Miles, M. (2012). Editorial: Strategic marketing management in small and medium-sized enterprises. *The International Entrepreneurship and Management Journal*, *8*(2), 141–143. doi:10.1007/s11365-011-0175-2

Gonsch, J., Klein, R., Neugebauer, M., & Stein-hardt, C. (2013). Dynamic pricing with strategic customers. *Journal of Business Economics*, *83*(5), 505–549. doi:10.1007/s11573-013-0663-7

Gronroos, C. (1994). From marketing mix to relationship marketing: Towards a paradigm shift in marketing. *Journal of Management Decision*, *32*(2), 4–20. doi:10.1108/00251749410054774

Gruner, R. L., Homburg, C., & Lukas, B. A. (2014). Firm-hosted online brand communities and new product success. *Journal of the Academy of Marketing Science*, *42*(1), 29–48. doi:10.1007/s11747-013-0334-9

Guillen, M. F., & Garcia-Canal, E. (2009). The American model of the multinational firm and the "new" multinationals from emerging econo-mies. *The Academy of Management Perspectives*, *23*(2), 23–35. doi:10.5465/AMP.2009.39985538

Hansen, J. M., McDonald, R. E., & Mitchell, R. K. (2013). Competence resource specialization, causal ambiguity, and the creation and decay of competitiveness: The role of marketing strategy in new product performance and shareholder value. *Journal of the Academy of Marketing Science*, *41*(3), 300–319. doi:10.1007/s11747-012-0316-3

Harrow, C., Lea-Greenwood, G., & Otieno, R. (2005). The unhappy shopper a retail ex-perience: Exploring fashion fit and afford-ability. *International Journal of Retail & Distribution Management*, *33*(4), 298–309. doi:10.1108/09590550510593220

Hartman, K., & Spiro, R. (2005). Recapturing store image in customer-based store equity: A construct conceptualization. *Journal of Business Research*, *58*(8), 1112–1120. doi:10.1016/j.jbusres.2004.01.008

Helm, R., & Landschulze, S. (2013). How does consumer age affect the desire for new products and brands? A multi-group causal analysis. *Review of Managerial Science*, *7*(1), 29–59. doi:10.1007/s11846-011-0072-7

Hessels, J., & Parker, S. C. (2013). Constraints, internationalization and growth: A cross-country analysis of European SMEs. *Journal of World Business*, *48*(1), 137–148. doi:10.1016/j.jwb.2012.06.014

Hofstetter, M., & Tovar, J. (2010). Common knowledge reference price and asymmetric price adjustments. *Review of Industrial Organization*, *37*(2), 141–159. doi:10.1007/s11151-010-9261-9

Hong, X., Wang, J., Wang, D., & Zhang, H. (2013). Decision models of closed-loop supply chain with remanufacturing under hybrid dual-channel collection. *International Journal of Advanced Manufacturing Technology*, *68*(5-8), 1851–1865. doi:10.1007/s00170-013-4982-1

Hong-Youl, H., & Kang-Hee, P. (2012). Effects of perceived quality and satisfaction on brand loyalty in China: The moderating effect of cus-tomer orientation. *African Journal of Business Management*, *6*(22), 6745–6753.

House, R. J., Hanges, P. J., Javidan, M., Dorfman, P. W., & Gupta, V. (2004). *Culture, leadership and organizations: The GLOBE study of 62 societies*. Thousand Oaks, CA: Sage.

Hsiao, Y. C., & Chen, C. J. (2013). Branding vs. contract manufacturing: Capability, strat-egy, and performance. *Journal of Business and Industrial Marketing*, *28*(4), 317–334. doi:10.1108/08858621311313910

Hsieh, J. K., Hsieh, Y. C., & Tang, Y. C. (2012). Exploring the disseminating behaviors of eWOM marketing: Persuasion in online video. *Elec-tronic Commerce Research*, *12*(2), 201–224. doi:10.1007/s10660-012-9091-y

Hu, W., & Li, Y. (2012). Retail service for mixed retail and e-tail channels. *Annals of Operations Research, 192*(1), 151–171. doi:10.1007/s10479-010-0818-7

Hughes, D. E. (2013). This ad's for you: The indirect effect of advertising perceptions on salesperson effort and performance. *Journal of the Academy of Marketing Science, 41*(1), 1–18. doi:10.1007/s11747-011-0293-y

Hutchinson, K., Quinn, B., & Alexander, N. (2006). SME retailer internationalisation: Case study evidence from British retailers. *International Marketing Review, 23*(1), 25–53. doi:10.1108/02651330610646287

Ibeh, K., & Kasem, L. (2014). Internationalization's effect on marketing learning: A study of Syrian firms. *Journal of Business Research, 67*(5), 680–685. doi:10.1016/j.jbusres.2013.11.027

Ishikawa, T. (2010). Effects of retail market structure and production conditions on firm's location selections of fragmented production process. *Jahrbuch für Regionalwissenschaft, 30*(2), 91–103. doi:10.1007/s10037-010-0044-4

Ismail, I., Hasnah, H., Ibrahim, D. N., & Mohd Isa, S. (2006). Service quality, client satisfaction, and loyalty towards audit firms. Perceptions of Malaysian public listed companies. *Managerial Auditing Journal, 22*(7), 738–756.

Jackson, T., & Shaw, D. (2006). *The fashion handbook*. Oxon, UK: Routledge.

Jahdi, K. S., & Acikdilli, G. (2010). Marketing communications and corporate social responsibility (CSR): Marriage of convenience or shotgun wedding? *Journal of Business Ethics, 88*(1), 103–113. doi:10.1007/s10551-009-0113-1

Jefkins, F., & Yadin, D. (2000). *Advertising*. London, UK: Financial Times/Prentice-Hall.

Jun, S., Gentry, J. W., & Hyun, Y. J. (2001). Cultural adaptation of business expatriates in the host marketplace. *Journal of International Business Studies, 32*(2), 369–377. doi:10.1057/palgrave.jibs.8490958

Kalaignanam, K., & Bahadir, S. C. (2013). Corporate brand name changes and business restructuring: Is the relationship complementary or substitutive? *Journal of the Academy of Marketing Science, 41*(4), 456–472. doi:10.1007/s11747-012-0321-6

Kasemsap, K. (2013a). Practical framework: Creation of causal model of job involvement, career commitment, learning motivation, and learning transfer. *International Journal of the Computer, the Internet and Management, 21*(1), 29-35.

Kasemsap, K. (2013b). Synthesized framework: Establishing a causal model of organizational learning, knowledge management, knowledge-sharing behavior, and organizational performance. *International Journal of the Computer, the Internet and Management, 21*(2), 29-34.

Kasemsap, K. (2013c). Innovative framework: Formation of causal model of organizational culture, organizational climate, knowledge management, and job performance. *Journal of International Business Management & Research, 4*(12), 21–32.

Kasemsap, K. (2013d). Strategic business management: A practical framework and causal model of empowering leadership, team cohesion, knowledge-sharing behavior, and team performance. *Journal of Social and Development Sciences, 4*(3), 100–106.

Kasemsap, K. (2014a). The role of brand management in emerging markets. In I. Samanta (Ed.), *Strategic marketing in fragile economic conditions* (pp. 167–184). Hershey, PA: IGI Global. doi:10.4018/978-1-4666-6232-2.ch009

Kasemsap, K. (2014b). The role of social media in the knowledge-based organizations. In I. Lee (Ed.), *Integrating social media into business practice, applications, management, and models* (pp. 254–275). Hershey, PA: IGI Global. doi:10.4018/978-1-4666-6182-0.ch013

Kasemsap, K. (2014c). Constructing a unified framework and a causal model of occupational satisfaction, trainee reactions, perception of learning, and perceived training transfer. In S. Hai-Jew (Ed.), *Remote workforce training: Effective technologies and strategies* (pp. 28–52). Hershey, PA: IGI Global. doi:10.4018/978-1-4666-5137-1.ch003

Kasemsap, K. (2014d). The role of social capital in higher education institutions. In N. Baporikar (Ed.), *Handbook of research on higher education in the MENA region: Policy and practice* (pp. 119–147). Hershey, PA: IGI Global. doi:10.4018/978-1-4666-6198-1.ch007

Kasemsap, K. (2014e). The role of social networking in global business environments. In P. A. C. Smith & T. Cockburn (Eds.), *Impact of emerging digital technologies on leadership in global business* (pp. 183–201). Hershey, PA: IGI Global. doi:10.4018/978-1-4666-6134-9.ch010

Kasemsap, K. (2014f). The role of brand loyalty on CRM performance: An innovative framework for smart manufacturing. In Z. Luo (Ed.), *Smart manufacturing innovation and transformation: Interconnection and intelligence* (pp. 252–284). Hershey, PA: IGI Global. doi:10.4018/978-1-4666-5836-3.ch010

Kato, A. (2012). Productivity, returns to scale and product differentiation in the retail trade industry: An empirical analysis using Japanese firm-level data. *Journal of Productivity Analysis*, *38*(3), 345–353. doi:10.1007/s11123-011-0251-1

Keeling, K., Keeling, D., & McGoldrick, P. (2013). Retail relationships in a digital age. *Journal of Business Research*, *66*(7), 847–855. doi:10.1016/j.jbusres.2011.06.010

Keller, K. L. (1993). Conceptualizing, measuring, and managing customer-based brand equity. *Journal of Marketing*, *57*(1), 1–22. doi:10.2307/1252054

Keller, K. L. (2003). *Strategic brand management: Building, measuring, and managing brand equity*. Upper Saddle River, NJ: Pearson Education.

Kent, T. (2003). 2D3D: Management and design perspectives on retail branding. *International Journal of Retail & Distribution Management*, *31*(3), 131–421. doi:10.1108/09590550310465503

Kent, T., & Omar, O. (2003). *Retailing*. Basingstoke, UK: Palgrave Macmillan.

Kim, H. B., & Kim, W. G. (2005). The relationship between brand equity and firms' performance in luxury hotels and chain restaurants. *Tourism Management*, *26*(4), 549–560. doi:10.1016/j.tourman.2004.03.010

Knox, S., & Bickerton, D. (2003). The six conventions of corporate branding. *European Journal of Marketing*, *37*(7-8), 998–1016. doi:10.1108/03090560310477636

Kotabe, M., & Helsen, K. (2010). *Global marketing management*. New York, NY: John Wiley & Sons.

Kotler, P., & Armstrong, G. (2006). *Principles of marketing*. Englewood Cliffs, NJ: Prentice-Hall.

Kuhn, H., & Sternbeck, M. G. (2013). Integrative retail logistics: An exploratory study. *Operations Management Research*, *6*(1-2), 2–18. doi:10.1007/s12063-012-0075-9

Lai, C. S., Chiu, C. J., Yang, C. F., & Pai, D. C. (2010). The effects of corporate social responsibility on brand performance: The mediating effect of industrial brand equity and corporate reputation. *Journal of Business Ethics*, *95*(3), 457–469. doi:10.1007/s10551-010-0433-1

Lee, J. S., & Back, K. J. (2010). Reexamination of attendee-based brand equity. *Tourism Management*, *31*(3), 395–401. doi:10.1016/j.tourman.2009.04.006

Lee, M. L., & Pace, R. K. (2005). Spatial distribution of retail sales. *The Journal of Real Estate Finance and Economics*, *31*(1), 53–69. doi:10.1007/s11146-005-0993-5

Levy, M., & Weitz, B. A. (2012). *Retailing management*. New York, NY: McGraw-Hill.

Li, X., Nukala, S., & Mohebbi, S. (2013). Game theory methodology for optimizing retailers' pricing and shelf-space allocation decisions on competing substitutable products. *International Journal of Advanced Manufacturing Technology*, *68*(1-4), 375–389. doi:10.1007/s00170-013-4735-1

Lim, W. S., & Tan, S. J. (2009). Using brand equity to counter outsourcing opportunism: A game theoretic approach. *Marketing Letters*, *20*(4), 369–383. doi:10.1007/s11002-009-9071-8

Lin, F. R., Po, R. W., & Orellan, C. V. C. (2011). Mining purchasing decision rules from service encounter data of retail chain stores. *Information Systems and e-Business Management, 9*(2), 193-221.

Lin, W. B. (2013). Factors affecting high-involvement product purchasing behavior. *Quality & Quantity*, *47*(6), 3113–3133. doi:10.1007/s11135-012-9707-2

Liu, H., Lei, M., & Liu, X. (2014). Manufacturer's uniform pricing and channel choice with a retail price markup commitment strategy. *Journal of Systems Science and Systems Engineering*, *23*(1), 111–126. doi:10.1007/s11518-014-5239-8

Liu, H., & McGoldrick, P. J. (1996). International retail sourcing: Trends, nature, and processes. *Journal of International Marketing*, *4*(4), 9–33.

Louro, M., & Cunha, P. (2001). Brand management paradigms. *Journal of Marketing Management*, *17*(7-8), 849–875. doi:10.1362/026725701323366845

Luo, W., & de Jong, P. J. (2012). Does advertising spending really work? The intermediate role of analysts in the impact of advertising on firm value. *Journal of the Academy of Marketing Science*, *40*(4), 605–624. doi:10.1007/s11747-010-0240-3

Luo, Y., & Tung, R. L. (2007). International expansion of emerging market enterprises: A springboard perspective. *Journal of International Business Studies*, *38*(4), 481–498. doi:10.1057/palgrave.jibs.8400275

Lymperopoulos, C., Chaniotakis, I. E., & Rigopoulou, I. D. (2010). Acceptance of detergent-retail brands: The role of consumer confidence and trust. *International Journal of Retail & Distribution Management*, *38*(9), 719–736. doi:10.1108/09590551011062457

Madden, T. J., Fehle, F., & Fournier, S. (2006). Brands matter: An empirical demonstration of the creation of shareholder value through branding. *Journal of the Academy of Marketing Science*, *34*(2), 224–235. doi:10.1177/0092070305283356

Maglio, P. P., Nusser, S., & Bishop, K. (2010). A service perspective on IBM's brand. *Marketing Review St. Gallen*, *27*(6), 44–48. doi:10.1007/s11621-010-0098-2

Malbon, J. (2013). Taking fake online consumer reviews seriously. *Journal of Consumer Policy*, *36*(2), 139–157. doi:10.1007/s10603-012-9216-7

Manasseh, T., Muller-Sarmiento, P., Reuter, H., von Faber-Castell, C., & Pallua, C. (2012). Customer inspiration – A key lever for growth in European retail. *Marketing Review St. Gallen*, *29*(5), 16–21. doi:10.1365/s11621-012-0159-9

Masodier, M., & Merunka, D. (2012). Achieving brand loyalty through sponsorship: The role of fit and self-congruity. *Journal of the Academy of Marketing Science*, *40*(6), 807–820. doi:10.1007/s11747-011-0285-y

McCarthy, E. J. (1964). *Basic marketing*. Homewood, IL: Irwin.

McGoldrick, P. J. (2002). *Retail marketing*. London, UK: McGraw-Hill.

Mejia, L. C., & Benjamin, J. D. (2002). What do we know about the determinants of shopping center sales? Spatial vs. non-spatial factors. *Journal of Real Estate Literature*, *10*(1), 3–26.

Meza, S., & Sudhir, K. (2010). Do private labels increase retailer bargaining power? *Quantitative Marketing and Economics*, *8*(3), 333–363. doi:10.1007/s11129-010-9085-9

Michis, A. A., & Markidou, A. G. (2013). Determinants of retail wine prices: Evidence from Cyprus. *Empirical Economics*, *45*(1), 267–280. doi:10.1007/s00181-012-0616-y

Miller, J., & Muir, D. (2004). *The business of brands*. Chichester, UK: John Wiley & Sons.

Mills, D. E. (2013). Countervailing power and chain stores. *Review of Industrial Organization*, *42*(3), 281–295. doi:10.1007/s11151-012-9364-6

Mittendorf, B., Shin, J., & Yoon, D. H. (2013). Manufacturer marketing initiatives and retailer information sharing. *Quantitative Marketing and Economics*, *11*(2), 263–287. doi:10.1007/s11129-013-9132-4

Moore, C., Fernie, J., & Burt, S. (2000). Brands without boundaries: The internationalization of the designer retailer's brand. *European Journal of Marketing*, *34*(8), 919–937. doi:10.1108/03090560010331414

Morgan, N. A. (2012). Marketing and business performance. *Journal of the Academy of Marketing Science*, *40*(1), 102–119. doi:10.1007/s11747-011-0279-9

Morschett, D., Swoboda, B., & Schramm-Klein, H. (2006). Competitive strategies in retailing – An investigation of the applicability of Porter's framework for food retailers. *Journal of Retailing and Consumer Services*, *13*(4), 275–287. doi:10.1016/j.jretconser.2005.08.016

Moser, R., Schaefers, T., & Meise, J. K. (2012). Consumer preferences for product transparency in emerging markets – Lessons learned from India. *Marketing Review St. Gallen*, *29*(3), 22–27. doi:10.1365/s11621-012-0133-6

Nalca, A., Boyaci, T., & Ray, S. (2010). Competitive price-matching guarantees under imperfect store availability. *Quantitative Marketing and Economics*, *8*(3), 275–300. doi:10.1007/s11129-010-9080-1

Neudecker, N., Hupp, O., Stein, A., & Schuster, H. (2012). Is your brand a one-night stand? Managing consumer-brand relationships. *Marketing Review St. Gallen*, *30*(6), 22–33. doi:10.1365/s11621-013-0297-8

Nguyen, T. D., Barrett, N. J., & Miller, K. E. (2011). Brand loyalty in emerging markets. *Marketing Intelligence & Planning*, *29*(3), 222–232. doi:10.1108/02634501111129211

Oppewal, H., & Timmermans, H. (1997). Retailer self-perceived store image and competitive position. *International Review of Retail, Distribution and Consumer Research, 7*(1), 41–59. doi:10.1080/095939697343120

Ouardighi, F. E., Jørgensen, S., & Pasin, F. (2013). A dynamic game with monopolist manufacturer and price-competing duopolist retailers. *OR-Spektrum, 35*(4), 1059–1084. doi:10.1007/s00291-012-0300-9

Palmer, M., & Quinn, B. (2003). The strategic role of investment banks in the retailer internationalisation process: Is this venture marketing? *European Journal of Marketing, 37*(10), 1391–1408. doi:10.1108/03090560310487167

Pancras, J. (2010). A framework to determine the value of consumer consideration set information for firm pricing strategies. *Computational Economics, 35*(3), 269–300. doi:10.1007/s10614-009-9193-3

Pantano, E., & Viassone, M. (2014). Demand pull and technology push perspective in technology-based innovations for the points of sale: The retailers evaluation. *Journal of Retailing and Consumer Services, 21*(1), 43–47. doi:10.1016/j.jretconser.2013.06.007

Pappu, R., Quester, P. G., & Cooksey, R. W. (2005). Consumer-based brand equity: Improving the measurement – Empirical evidence. *Journal of Product and Brand Management, 14*(3), 143–154. doi:10.1108/10610420510601012

Parthasarathi, G., Sarmah, S. P., & Jenamani, M. (2011). Supply chain coordination under retail competition using stock dependent price-setting newsvendor framework. *Operations Research, 11*(3), 259–279. doi:10.1007/s12351-010-0077-z

Piercy, N., & Alexander, N. (1988). The status quo of marketing organisation in UK retailers: A neglected phenomenon of the 1980s. *Service Industries Journal, 8*(2), 155–175. doi:10.1080/02642068800000027

Pinho, J. C., & Martins, L. (2010). Exporting barriers: Insights from Portuguese small and medium-sized exporters and non-exporters. *Journal of International Entrepreneurship, 8*(3), 254–272. doi:10.1007/s10843-010-0046-x

Prange, C., & Schlegelmilch, B. B. (2009). The role of ambidexterity in marketing strategy implementation: Resolving the exploration-exploitation dilemma. *BuR - Business Research, 2*(2), 215-240.

Rafiq, M., & Ahmed, P. K. (1995). Using the 7Ps as a generic marketing mix: An exploratory survey of UK and European marketing academics. *Journal of Marketing Intelligence & Planning, 13*(9), 4–15. doi:10.1108/02634509510097793

Rajab, T., Kraus, F., & Wieseke, J. (2013). Resolving conflict over salespeople's brand adoption in franchised channels of distribution. *Review of Managerial Science, 7*(4), 443–473. doi:10.1007/s11846-012-0091-z

Rapp, A., Beitelspacher, L. S., Grewal, D., & Hughes, D. E. (2013). Understanding social media effects across seller, retailer, and consumer interactions. *Journal of the Academy of Marketing Science, 41*(5), 547–566. doi:10.1007/s11747-013-0326-9

Rawwas, M. Y. A., Arjoon, S., & Sidani, Y. (2013). An introduction of epistemology to business ethics: A study of marketing middle-managers. *Journal of Business Ethics, 117*(3), 525–539. doi:10.1007/s10551-012-1537-6

Raymond, L., & St-Pierre, J. (2013). Strategic capability configurations for the internationalization of SMEs: A study in equifinality. *International Small Business Journal, 31*(1), 82–102. doi:10.1177/0266242610391325

Richey, R. G., Tokman, M., & Dalela, V. (2010). Examining collaborative supply chain service technologies: A study of intensity, relationships, and resources. *Journal of the Academy of Marketing Science, 38*(1), 71–89. doi:10.1007/s11747-009-0139-z

Roig-Tierno, N., Baviera-Puig, A., & Buitrago-Vera, J. (2013). Business opportunities analysis using GIS: The retail distribution sector. *Global Business Perspectives, 1*(3), 226–238. doi:10.1007/s40196-013-0015-6

Root, F. R. (1994). *Entry strategies for international markets.* New York, NY: Lexington Books.

Russell, R. A., & Urban, T. L. (2010). The location and allocation of products and product families on retail shelves. *Annals of Operations Research, 179*(1), 131–147. doi:10.1007/s10479-008-0450-y

Ruzzier, M., Hisrich, R. D., & Antoncic, B. (2006). SME internationalization research: Past, present, and future. *Journal of Small Business and Enterprise Development, 13*(4), 476–497. doi:10.1108/14626000610705705

Ruzzier, M., & Konecnik, M. (2006). The internationalization strategies of SMEs: The case of the Slovenian hotel industry. *Journal of Contemporary Management Issues, 11*(1), 17–35.

Salmon, W., & Tordjman, A. (1989). The internationalisation of retailing. *International Journal of Retailing, 4*(2), 3–16.

Sayadi, M. K., & Makui, A. (2014). Feedback Nash Equilibrium for dynamic brand and channel advertising in dual channel supply chain. *Journal of Optimization Theory and Applications, 161*(3), 1012–1021. doi:10.1007/s10957-013-0479-1

Schmidt, R. C. (2013). Price competition and innovation in markets with brand loyalty. *Journal of Economics, 109*(2), 147–173. doi:10.1007/s00712-012-0296-2

Schubert, T. (2010). Marketing and organisational innovations in entrepreneurial innovation processes and their relation to market structure and firm characteristics. *Review of Industrial Organization, 36*(2), 189–212. doi:10.1007/s11151-010-9243-y

Sheridan, M., Moore, C. M., & Nobbs, K. (2006). Fast fashion requires fast marketing. *Journal of Fashion Marketing and Management, 10*(3), 301–315. doi:10.1108/13612020610679286

Simon, C., Brexendorf, T. O., & Fassnacht, M. (2013). Creating online brand experience on Facebook. *Marketing Review St. Gallen, 30*(6), 50–59. doi:10.1365/s11621-013-0299-6

Singh, J. J., Iglesias, O., & Batista-Foguet, J. M. (2012). Does having an ethical brand matter? The influence of consumer perceived ethicality on trust, affect and loyalty. *Journal of Business Ethics, 111*(4), 541–549. doi:10.1007/s10551-012-1216-7

Sirgy, M. J., Yu, G. B., Lee, D. J., Wei, S., & Huang, M. W. (2012). Does marketing activity contribute to a society's well-being? The role of economic efficiency. *Journal of Business Ethics, 107*(2), 91–102. doi:10.1007/s10551-011-1030-7

Sitzia, S., & Zizzo, D. J. (2011). Does product complexity matter for competition in experimental retail markets? *Theory and Decision, 70*(1), 65–82. doi:10.1007/s11238-009-9163-1

Skallerud, K., & Grønhaug, K. (2010). Chinese food retailers' positioning strategies and the influence on their buying behaviour. *Asia Pacific Journal of Marketing and Logistics, 22*(2), 196–209. doi:10.1108/13555851011026944

Smith, P. R., & Taylor, J. (2004). *Marketing communications*. London, UK: Kogan Page.

Sparks, L. (1996). Reciprocal retail internationalisation: The southland corporation, Ito-Yokado and 7-Eleven convenience stores. In G. Akehurst & N. Alexander (Eds.), *The internationalisation of retailing* (pp. 57–96). London, UK: Frank Cass.

Spowart, M., & Wickramasekera, R. (2012). Explaining internationalisation of small to medium sized enterprises within the Queensland food and beverage industry. *International Journal of Business and Management, 7*(6), 68–80. doi:10.5539/ijbm.v7n6p68

Stock, R. M., & Reiferscheid, I. (2014). Who should be in power to encourage product program innovativeness, R&D or marketing? *Journal of the Academy of Marketing Science, 42*(3), 264–276. doi:10.1007/s11747-013-0354-5

Suarez, C., & de Jorge, J. (2010). Efficiency convergence processes and effects of regulation in the nonspecialized retail sector in Spain. *The Annals of Regional Science, 44*(3), 573–597. doi:10.1007/s00168-008-0270-7

Sun, K. A., & Lee, S. (2013). Determinants of degree of internationalization for U.S. restaurant firms. *International Journal of Hospitality Management, 33*, 465–474. doi:10.1016/j.ijhm.2012.11.006

Swoboda, B., Haelsig, F., Morschett, D., & Schramm-Klein, H. (2007). An intersector analysis of the relevance of service in building a strong retail brand. *Managing Service Quality, 17*(4), 428–448. doi:10.1108/09604520710760553

Taylor, S., Celuch, K., & Goodwin, S. (2004). The importance of brand equity to customer loyalty. *Journal of Product and Brand Management, 13*(4), 217–227. doi:10.1108/10610420410546934

Thomas, S. (2013). Linking customer loyalty to customer satisfaction and store image: A structural model for retail stores. *DECISION, 40*(1-2), 15–25. doi:10.1007/s40622-013-0007-z

To, W. M., Tam, J. F. Y., & Cheung, M. F. Y. (2013). Explore how Chinese consumers evaluate retail service quality and satisfaction. *Service Business, 7*(1), 121–142. doi:10.1007/s11628-012-0149-7

Treadgold, A. (1988). Retailing without frontiers. *Retail and Distribution Management, 16*(6), 8–12. doi:10.1108/eb018382

Treadgold, A. (1991). The emerging internationalisation of retailing: Present status and future challenges. *Irish Marketing Review, 5*(2), 11–27.

Uner, M. M., Kocak, A., Cavusgil, E., & Cavusgil, S. T. (2013). Do barriers to export vary for born globals and across stages of internationalization? An empirical inquiry in the emerging market of Turkey. *International Business Review, 22*(5), 800–813. doi:10.1016/j.ibusrev.2012.12.005

Van Riel, A. C. R., De Mortanges, C. P., & Streukens, S. (2005). Marketing antecedents of industrial brand equity: An empirical investigation in specialty chemicals. *Industrial Marketing Management, 34*(8), 841–847. doi:10.1016/j.indmarman.2005.01.006

VanAuken, B. (2005). *The brand management checklist: Proven tools and techniques for creating winning brands*. London, UK: Kogan Page.

Varadarajan, R. (2010). Strategic marketing and marketing strategy: Domain, definition, fundamental issues and foundational premises. *Journal of the Academy of Marketing Science, 38*(2), 119–140. doi:10.1007/s11747-009-0176-7

Varadarajan, R. (2011). Marketing strategy: Discerning the relative influence of product and firm characteristics. *AMS Review, 1*(1), 32–43. doi:10.1007/s13162-011-0003-4

Velayudhan, S. K. (2014). Outshopping in rural periodic markets: A retailing opportunity. *International Journal of Retail & Distribution Management, 42*(2), 151–167. doi:10.1108/IJRDM-07-2013-0136

Volpe, R. J. (2013). Promotional competition between supermarket chains. *Review of Industrial Organization, 42*(1), 45–61. doi:10.1007/s11151-012-9352-x

Vorhies, D. W., Orr, L. M., & Bush, V. D. (2011). Improving customer-focused marketing capabilities and firm financial performance via marketing exploration and exploitation. *Journal of the Academy of Marketing Science, 39*(5), 736–756. doi:10.1007/s11747-010-0228-z

Waller, M. A., Williams, B. D., Tangari, A. H., & Burton, S. (2010). Marketing at the retail shelf: An examination of moderating effects of logistics on SKU market share. *Journal of the Academy of Marketing Science, 38*(1), 105–117. doi:10.1007/s11747-009-0146-0

Walter, F. E., Battiston, S., Yildirim, M., & Schweitzer, F. (2012). Moving recommender systems from on-line commerce to retail stores. *Information Systems and e-Business Management, 10*(3), 367-393.

Walters, D., & Laffy, D. (1996). *Managing retail productivity and profitability*. London, UK: Palgrave MacMillan.

Wang, J., Wang, L., Ye, F., Xu, X., & Yu, J. (2013). Order decision making based on different statement strategies under stochastic market demand. *Journal of Systems Science and Systems Engineering, 22*(2), 171–190. doi:10.1007/s11518-013-5217-6

Wang, K., Gou, Q., Sun, J., & Yue, X. (2012). Coordination of a fashion and textile supply chain with demand variations. *Journal of Systems Science and Systems Engineering, 21*(4), 461–479. doi:10.1007/s11518-012-5205-2

Watson, B. C. (2011). Barcode empires: Politics, digital technology, and comparative retail firm strategies. *Journal of Industry, Competition and Trade, 11*(3), 309–324. doi:10.1007/s10842-011-0109-2

Webster, F. E., & Lusch, R. F. (2013). Elevating marketing: Marketing is dead! Long live marketing! *Journal of the Academy of Marketing Science, 41*(4), 389–399. doi:10.1007/s11747-013-0331-z

Westhead, P., Wright, M., & Ucbasaran, D. (2004). Internationalization of private firms: Environmental turbulence and organizational strategies and resources. *Entrepreneurship & Regional Development, 16*(6), 501–522. doi:10.1080/0898562042000231929

Wiedmann, K. P., Hennigs, N., Klarmann, C., & Behrens, S. (2013). Creating multi-sensory experiences in luxury marketing. *Marketing Review St. Gallen, 30*(6), 60–69. doi:10.1365/s11621-013-0300-4

Wigley, S., & Moore, C. M. (2007). The operationalisation of international fashion retailer success. *Journal of Fashion Marketing and Management, 11*(2), 281–296. doi:10.1108/13612020710751437

Wigley, S., Moore, C. M., & Birtwistle, G. (2005). Product and brand: Critical success factors in the internationalization of a fashion retailer. *International Journal of Retail & Distribution Management, 33*(7), 531–544. doi:10.1108/09590550510605596

Williams, D. (1992). Motives for retailer internationalization: Their impact, structure, and implications. *Journal of Marketing Management, 8*(3), 269–285. doi:10.1080/0267257X.1992.9964196

Xi, Y., & Peng, S. (2010). The effects of two kinds of corporate publicity on customer-brand relationship. *Frontiers of Business Research in China, 4*(1), 73–100. doi:10.1007/s11782-010-0004-4

Xiao, S. S., Jeong, I., Moon, J. J., Chung, C. C., & Chung, J. (2013). Internationalization and performance of firms in China: Moderating effects of governance structure and the degree of centralized control. *Journal of International Management, 19*(2), 118–137. doi:10.1016/j.intman.2012.12.003

Xiao, Y., Palekar, U., & Liu, Y. (2011). Shades of gray—The impact of gray markets on authorized distribution channels. *Quantitative Marketing and Economics, 9*(2), 155–178. doi:10.1007/s11129-011-9098-z

Yan, R. (2010). Cooperative advertising, pricing strategy and firm performance in the e-marketing age. *Journal of the Academy of Marketing Science, 38*(4), 510–519. doi:10.1007/s11747-009-0171-z

Yang, D., & Wang, X. (2010). The effects of 2-tier store brands' perceived quality, perceived value, brand knowledge, and attitude on store loyalty. *Frontiers of Business Research in China, 4*(1), 1–28. doi:10.1007/s11782-010-0001-7

Yarbrough, L., Morgan, N. A., & Vorhies, D. W. (2011). The impact of product market strategy-organizational culture fit on business performance. *Journal of the Academy of Marketing Science, 39*(4), 555–573. doi:10.1007/s11747-010-0238-x

Yasin, N., Nasser Noor, M., & Mohamad, O. (2007). Does image of country-of-origin matter to brand equity? *Journal of Product and Brand Management, 16*(1), 38–48. doi:10.1108/10610420710731142

Ye, J., Marinova, D., & Singh, J. (2012). Bottom-up learning in marketing frontlines: Conceptualization, processes, and consequences. *Journal of the Academy of Marketing Science, 40*(6), 821–844. doi:10.1007/s11747-011-0289-7

Yoo, B., Donthu, N., & Lee, S. (2000). An examination of selected marketing mix elements and brand equity. *Journal of the Academy of Marketing Science, 28*(2), 195–211. doi:10.1177/0092070300282002

Zhou, M., & Lin, J. (2014). Cooperative advertising and pricing models in a dynamic marketing channel. *Journal of Systems Science and Systems Engineering, 23*(1), 94–110. doi:10.1007/s11518-013-5221-x

ADDITIONAL READING

Abratt, R., & Kleyn, N. (2011). Corporate identity, corporate branding and corporate reputations: Reconciliation and integration. *European Journal of Marketing, 46*(7-8), 1048–1063.

Aggerholm, H. K., Andersen, S. E., & Thomsen, C. (2011). Conceptualising employer branding in sustainable organizations. *Corporate Communications: An International Journal, 16*(2), 105–123. doi:10.1108/13563281111141642

Allaway, A. W., Huddleston, P., Whipple, J., & Ellinger, A. E. (2011). Customer-based brand equity, equity drivers, and customer loyalty in the supermarket industry. *Journal of Product and Brand Management, 20*(3), 190–204. doi:10.1108/10610421111134923

Batra, R., Ahuvia, A., & Bagozzi, R. P. (2012). Brand love. *Journal of Marketing, 76*(2), 1–16. doi:10.1509/jm.09.0339

Cairns, P., Quinn, B., Alexander, N., & Doherty, A. M. (2010). The role of leadership in international retail divestment. *European Business Review, 22*(1), 25–42. doi:10.1108/09555341011008990

Carpenter, J. M., & Balija, V. (2010). Retail format choice in the US consumer electronics market. *International Journal of Retail & Distribution Management*, 38(4), 258–274. doi:10.1108/09590551011032081

Chen, Y. M., & Su, Y. F. (2012). Do country-of-manufacture and country-of-design matter to industrial brand equity? *Journal of Business and Industrial Marketing*, 27(1), 57–68. doi:10.1108/08858621211188966

Choo, H. J., Moon, H., Kim, H., & Yoon, N. (2012). Luxury customer value. *Journal of Fashion Marketing and Management*, 16(1), 81–101. doi:10.1108/13612021211203041

D'Andrea, G. (2010). Latin American retail: Where modernity blends with tradition. *International Review of Retail, Distribution and Consumer Research*, 20(1), 85–101. doi:10.1080/09593960903497864

Dogerlioglu-Demir, K., & Tansuhaj, P. (2011). Global vs. local brand perceptions among Thais and Turks. *Asia Pacific Journal of Marketing and Logistics*, 23(5), 667–683. doi:10.1108/13555851111183084

Dwivedi, A., & Merrilees, B. (2013). Brand extension feedback effects: Towards a mediated framework. *Journal of Consumer Marketing*, 30(5), 450–461. doi:10.1108/JCM-01-2013-0414

French, A., & Smith, G. (2013). Measuring brand association strength: A consumer based brand equity approach. *European Journal of Marketing*, 47(8), 1356–1367. doi:10.1108/03090561311324363

Ha, H. Y., John, J., Janda, S., & Muthaly, S. (2011). The effect of advertising spending on brand loyalty in services. *European Journal of Marketing*, 45(4), 673–691. doi:10.1108/03090561111111389

Hollebeek, L. D. (2011). Demystifying customer brand engagement: Exploring the loyalty nexus. *Journal of Marketing Management*, 27(7-8), 785–807. doi:10.1080/0267257X.2010.500132

Hur, W. M., Ahn, K. H., & Kim, M. (2011). Building brand loyalty through managing brand community commitment. *Management Decision*, 49(7), 1194–1213. doi:10.1108/00251741111151217

Juntunen, M., Saraniemi, S., Halttu, M., & Tahtinen, J. (2010). Corporate brand building in different stages of small business growth. *Journal of Brand Management*, 18(2), 115–133. doi:10.1057/bm.2010.34

Kaufmann, H. R., Vrontis, D., Czinkota, M., & Hadiono, A. (2012). Corporate branding and transformational leadership in turbulent times. *Journal of Product and Brand Management*, 21(3), 192–204. doi:10.1108/10610421211228810

Konecnik Ruzzier, M. (2012). Developing brand identity for Slovenia with opinion leaders. *Baltic Journal of Management*, 7(2), 124–142. doi:10.1108/17465261211219778

Kuikka, A., & Laukkanen, T. (2012). Brand loyalty and the role of hedonic value. *Journal of Product and Brand Management*, 21(7), 529–537. doi:10.1108/10610421211276277

Kumar, R. S., Dash, S., & Purwar, P. C. (2013). The nature and antecedents of brand equity and its dimensions. *Marketing Intelligence & Planning*, 31(2), 141–159. doi:10.1108/02634501311312044

Lindgreen, A., Beverland, M., & Farrelly, F. (2010). From strategy to tactics: Building, implementing, and managing brand equity in business markets. *Industrial Marketing Management*, 39(8), 1123–1125. doi:10.1016/j.indmarman.2010.02.018

Liu, F., Li, J., Mizerski, D., & Soh, H. (2012). Self-congruity, brand attitude, and brand loyalty: A study on luxury brands. *European Journal of Marketing*, 46(7-8), 922–937.

Lloyd, S., & Woodside, A. (2013). Corporate brand-rapture theory: Antecedents, processes, and consequences. *Marketing Intelligence & Planning*, 31(5), 472–488. doi:10.1108/MIP-04-2013-0064

Mann, B. J. S., & Kaur, M. (2013). Exploring branding strategies of FMCG, services and durables brands: Evidence from India. *Journal of Product and Brand Management*, 22(1), 6–17. doi:10.1108/10610421311298650

Marzocchi, M., Morandin, G., & Bergami, M. (2013). Brand communities: Loyal to the community or the brand? *European Journal of Marketing*, 47(1-2), 93–114. doi:10.1108/03090561311285475

Mishra, A., & Ansari, J. (2013). A conceptual model for retail productivity. *International Journal of Retail & Distribution Management*, 41(5), 348–379. doi:10.1108/IJRDM-03-2013-0062

Mitchell, R., Hutchinson, K., & Bishop, S. (2012). Interpretation of the retail brand: An SME perspective. *International Journal of Retail & Distribution Management*, 40(2), 157–175. doi:10.1108/09590551211201883

Mourad, M., Ennew, C., & Kortam, W. (2011). Brand equity in higher education. *Marketing Intelligence & Planning*, 29(4), 403–420. doi:10.1108/02634501111138563

Nam, J., Ekinci, Y., & Whyatt, G. (2011). Brand equity, brand loyalty and customer satisfaction. *Annals of Tourism Research*, 38(3), 1009–1030. doi:10.1016/j.annals.2011.01.015

Paswan, A., Pineda, M. D. S., & Ramirez, F. C. S. (2010). Small versus large retail stores in an emerging market – Mexico. *Journal of Business Research*, 63(7), 667–672. doi:10.1016/j.jbusres.2009.02.020

Pike, S., Bianchi, C., Kerr, G., & Patti, C. (2010). Consumer-based brand equity for Australia as a long-haul tourism destination in an emerging market. *International Marketing Review*, 27(4), 434–449. doi:10.1108/02651331011058590

Pillai, A. (2012). Corporate branding literature: A research paradigm review. *Journal of Brand Management*, 19(4), 331–343. doi:10.1057/bm.2011.43

Prasad, C. J., & Aryasri, A. R. (2011). Effect of shopper attributes on retail format choice behaviour for food and grocery retailing in India. *International Journal of Retail & Distribution Management*, 39(1), 68–86. doi:10.1108/09590551111104486

Quintal, V., & Phau, I. (2013). Brand leaders and me-too alternatives: How do consumers choose? *Marketing Intelligence & Planning*, 31(4), 367–387. doi:10.1108/02634501311324852

Ramkrishnan, K. (2010). The competitive response of small, independent retailers to organized retail: Study in an emerging economy. *Journal of Retailing and Consumer Services*, 17(4), 251–258. doi:10.1016/j.jretconser.2010.02.002

Rindell, A., & Strandvik, T. (2010). Corporate brand evolution: Corporate brand images evolving in consumers' everyday life. *European Business Review*, 22(3), 276–286. doi:10.1108/09555341011040976

Saini, G. K., & Sahay, A. (2014). Comparing retail formats in an emerging market - Influence of credit and low price guarantee on purchase intention. *Journal of Indian Business Research*, 6(1), 48–69. doi:10.1108/JIBR-03-2013-0026

Sathish, D., & Raju, V. D. (2010). The growth of Indian retail industry. *Advances in Management*, 3(7), 15–19.

Schnittka, O., Sattler, H., & Zenker, S. (2012). Advanced brand concept maps: A new approach for evaluating the favorability of brand association networks. *International Journal of Research in Marketing*, 29(3), 265–274. doi:10.1016/j.ijresmar.2012.04.002

Spence, M., & Essoussi, L. H. (2010). SME brand building and management: An exploratory study. *European Journal of Marketing*, *44*(7-8), 1037–1054. doi:10.1108/03090561011047517

Stahl, F., Heitmann, M., Lehmann, D. R., & Neslin, S. A. (2012). The impact of brand equity on customer acquisition, retention, and profit margin. *Journal of Marketing*, *76*(4), 44–63. doi:10.1509/jm.10.0522

Valette-Florence, P., Guizani, H., & Merunka, D. (2011). The impact of brand personality and sale promotions on brand equity. *Journal of Business Research*, *64*(1), 24–28. doi:10.1016/j.jbusres.2009.09.015

KEY TERMS AND DEFINITIONS

Brand Management: The process of maintaining, improving, and promoting a brand.

Brand Strategy: The long-term marketing support for a brand, based on the definition of the characteristics of the target consumers.

Branding: The process involved in creating a unique name and image for a product in the consumers' mind, mainly through advertising campaigns with a consistent theme.

Competitive Advantage: A superiority gained by an organization when it can provide the same value as its competitors but at a lower price, or can charge higher prices by providing greater value through differentiation.

Corporate Strategy: The overall scope and direction of a corporation and the way in which its various business operations work together to achieve particular goals.

Marketing: The management process through which goods and services move from concept to the customer.

Marketing Mix: A planned mix of the controllable elements of a product's marketing plan commonly termed as 4Ps: product, price, place, and promotion.

Marketing Strategy: An organization's strategy that combines all of its marketing goals into one comprehensive plan.

Retailing: The commercial transaction in which a buyer intends to consume the good or service through personal, family, or household use.

Compilation of References

Aaker, D. A. (1996). Measuring brand equity across products and markets. *California Management Review, 38*(3), 102–120. doi:10.2307/41165845

Aastrup, J., Bjerre, M., Kornum, N., & Kotzab, H. (2010). The Danish retail market: Overview and highlights. *European Retail Research, 24*(1), 195–222. doi:10.1007/978-3-8349-8938-3_9

Aberdeen Group. (2005). *The multi-channel retail benchmark report.* Boston: Aberdeen Group.

Accenture. (2012). *A new era for retail. Cloud computing changes the game.* Accenture.

Achrol, R. S., & Kotler, P. (2012). Frontiers of the marketing paradigm in the third millennium. *Journal of the Academy of Marketing Science, 40*(1), 35–52. doi:10.1007/s11747-011-0255-4

Acs, Z. J., & Audretsch, D. B. (1990). *Innovation and small firms.* Cambridge, MA: MIT Press.

Afgan, E., Baker, D., Coraor, N., Goto, H., Paul, I. M., Makova, K. D., & Taylor, J. et al. (2011). Harnessing cloud computing with Galaxy Cloud. *Nature Biotechnology, 29*(11), 972–974. doi:10.1038/nbt.2028 PMID:22068528

Agarwal, R., & Prasad, J. (1998). A conceptual and operational definition of personal innovativeness in the domain of information technology. *Information Systems Research, 9*(2), 204–215. doi:10.1287/isre.9.2.204

Ahlemann, F., El Arbi, F., Kaiser, M. G., & Heck, A. (2013). A process framework for theoretically grounded prescriptive research in the project management field. *International Journal of Project Management, 31*(1), 43–56. doi:10.1016/j.ijproman.2012.03.008

Ahn, T., Seewon, R., & Han, I. (2004). The impact of the online and offline features on the user acceptance of Internet shopping malls. *Electronic Commerce Research and Applications, 3*(4), 405–420. doi:10.1016/j.elerap.2004.05.001

Ahuja, G. (2000). The duality of collaboration: Inducements and opportunities in the formation of interfirm linkages. *Strategic Management Journal, 21*(3), 317–343. doi:10.1002/(SICI)1097-0266(200003)21:3<317::AID-SMJ90>3.0.CO;2-B

Ahuja, G., & Lampert, C. (2001). Entrepreneurship in the large corporation: A longitudinal study of how established firms create breakthrough inventions. *Strategic Management Journal, 22*(6-7), 521–543. doi:10.1002/smj.176

Ailawadi, K. L., & Keller, K. L. (2004). Understanding retail branding: Conceptual insights and research priorities. *Journal of Retailing, 80*(4), 331–342. doi:10.1016/j.jretai.2004.10.008

Ailawadi, K. L., Neslin, S. A., & Gedenk, K. (2001). Pursuing the value conscious consumer: Store brands versus national brand promotions. *Journal of Marketing, 65*(1), 71–89. doi:10.1509/jmkg.65.1.71.18132

Ajzen, I. (1991). The theory of planned behavior. *Organizational Behavior and Human Decision Processes, 50*(2), 179–211. doi:10.1016/0749-5978(91)90020-T

Akcura, M. T. (2010). Affiliated marketing. *Information Systems and e-Business Management, 8*(4), 379-394.

Albrecht, K., & Zemke, R. (2002). *Service America in the new economy.* New York: McGraw-Hill.

Alexander, N. (1990). Retailers and international markets: Motives for expansion. *International Marketing Review, 7*(4), 75–85. doi:10.1108/02651339010142797

Alexander, N., & Doherty, A. M. (2010). International retail research: Focus, methodology and conceptual development. *International Journal of Retail & Distribution Management*, *38*(11-12), 928–942.

Alexander, N., & Myers, H. (2000). The retail internationalisation process. *International Marketing Review*, *17*(4-5), 334–353. doi:10.1108/02651330010339888

Aljukhadar, M., Senecal, S., & Daoust, C.-E. (2012). Using recommendation agents to cope with information overload. *International Journal of Electronic Commerce*, *17*(2), 41–70. doi:10.2753/JEC1086-4415170202

Aljukhadar, M., Senecal, S., & Ouellette, D. (2010). Can the media richness of a privacy disclosure enhance outcome? A multifaceted view of trust in rich media environments. *International Journal of Electronic Commerce*, *14*(4), 103–126. doi:10.2753/JEC1086-4415140404

Alkemade, F., & Suurs, R. A. A. (2012). Patterns of expectations for emerging sustainable technologies. *Technological Forecasting and Social Change*, *79*(3), 448–456. doi:10.1016/j.techfore.2011.08.014

Amato, L. H., & Amato, C. H. (2012). Retail philanthropy: Firm size, industry, and business cycle. *Journal of Business Ethics*, *107*(4), 435–448. doi:10.1007/s10551-011-1048-x

Amazon.com. (2013). *Method and system for anticipatory package shipping, US Patent 8,615,473*. Washington, DC: U.S. Patent and Trademark Office.

Amer, T. S., & Bain, C. E. (1990). Making small business planning easier: Microcomputers facilitate the process. *Journal of Accountancy*, *170*(1), 53–58.

Ancona, D., & Caldwell, D. (1992). Demography and design: Predictors of new product team performance. *Organization Science*, *3*(3), 321–341. doi:10.1287/orsc.3.3.321

Anderson, E. W. (1998). Customer satisfaction and word of mouth. *Journal of Service Research*, *1*(1), 5–17. doi:10.1177/109467059800100102

Anitsal, I., & Paige, R. C. (2006). An exploratory study on consumer perceptions of service quality in technology-based self-service. *Services Marketing Quarterly*, *27*(3), 53–67. doi:10.1300/J396v27n03_04

Ardelet, C., & Brial, B. (2011). Influence of the recommendations of Internet users: The role of social presence and expertise. *Recherche et Applications en Marketing*, *26*(3), 45–69. doi:10.1177/076737011102600303

Armbruster, H., Bikfalvi, A., Kinkel, S., & Lay, G. (2008). Organizational innovation: The challenge of measuring non-technical innovation in large-scale surveys. *Technovation*, *28*(10), 644–657. doi:10.1016/j.technovation.2008.03.003

Armbrust, M., Fox, A., Griffith, R., Joseph, A. D., Katz, R., Konwinski, A., & Zaharia, M. et al. (2010). A view of cloud computing. *Communications of the ACM*, *53*(4), 50–58. doi:10.1145/1721654.1721672

Armstrong, K. M., Fitzgerald, J. K., & Moore, T. (2006). Changes in visual receptive fields with microstimulation of frontal cortex. *Neuron*, *50*(5), 791–798. doi:10.1016/j.neuron.2006.05.010 PMID:16731516

Arnould, E. J., Price, L., & Zinkhan, G. (2002). *Consumers*. New York: McGraw-Hill.

Arrigo, E. (2010). Innovation and market-driven management in fast fashion -companies. *Symphonya: Emerging Issues in Management*, *2*, 67–85. doi:10.4468/2010.2.06arrigo

Atilgan, E., Aksoy, S., & Akinci, S. (2005). Determinants of the brand equity: A verification approach in the beverage industry in Turkey. *Marketing Intelligence & Planning*, *23*(3), 237–248. doi:10.1108/02634500510597283

Audretsch, D. B. (2001). Research issues relating to structure, competition, and performance of small technology-based firms. *Small Business Economics*, *16*(1), 37–51. doi:10.1023/A:1011124607332

Aulakh, P. S. (2009). Revisiting the internationalization—Performance relationship: Implications for emerging economy firms. *Decision*, *36*(2), 25–39.

Aulakh, P. S., Kotabe, M., & Teegen, H. (2000). Export strategies and performance of firms from emerging economies: Evidence from Brazil, Chile, and Mexico. *Academy of Management Journal*, *43*(3), 342–361. doi:10.2307/1556399

Auvray, M., & Fuchs, P. (2007). Perception, immersion et interactions sensorimotrices en environnement virtuel. Intellectica, 45(1), 23-35.

Avery, J., Steenburgh, T. J., Deighton, J., & Caravella, M. (2009). *Adding bricks to clicks: The contingencies driving cannibalization and complementarity in multichannel retailing.* Harvard Business School, Working Paper 07-043, February 2009. Cambridge, MA: Harvard.

Avgerou, C. (2001). The significance of context in information systems and organizational change. *Information Systems Journal, 11*(1), 43–63. doi:10.1046/j.1365-2575.2001.00095.x

Ayanso, A., Lertwachara, K., & Thongpapanl, N. (2010). Technology-enabled retail services and online sales performance. *Journal of Computer Information Systems, 50*(3), 102–111.

Ayayi, A. G., & Sene, M. (2010). What drives microfinance institution`s financial sustainability. *Journal of Developing Areas, 44*(1), 303–323. doi:10.1353/jda.0.0093

Baal van S. (2014). Should retailers harmonize marketing variables across their distribution channels? An investigation of cross-channel effects in multi-channel retailing. *Journal of Retailing and Consumer Services.* doi:10.1016/j.jretconser.2014.04.012

Babiloni, F., Mattia, D., Babiloni, C., Astolfi, L., Salinari, S., Basilisco, A., & Cincotti, F. et al. (2004). Multimodal integration of EEG, MEG and fMRI data for the solution of the neuroimage puzzle. *Magnetic Resonance Imaging, 22*(10), 1471–1476. doi:10.1016/j.mri.2004.10.007 PMID:15707796

Babin, B. J., & Attaway, J. S. (2000). Atmospheric affect as a tool for creating value and gaining share of customer. *Journal of Business Research, 49*(2), 91–100. doi:10.1016/S0148-2963(99)00011-9

Babin, B. J., Chebat, J. C., & Michon, R. (2004). Perceived appropriateness and its effect on quality, affect, and behavior. *Journal of Retailing and Consumer Services, 11*(5), 287–298. doi:10.1016/j.jretconser.2003.09.002

Babin, B. J., & Darden, W. R. (1996). Good and bad shopping vibes: Spending and patronage satisfaction. *Journal of Business Research, 35*(3), 201–106. doi:10.1016/0148-2963(95)00125-5

Babin, B. J., Darden, W. R., & Griffin, M. D. (1994). Work and/or fun: Measuring hedonic and shopping value. *The Journal of Consumer Research, 20*(4), 644–656. doi:10.1086/209376

Bäckström, K., & Johansson, U. (2006). Creating and consuming experiences in retail store environments: Comparing retailer and consumer perspectives. *Journal of Retailing and Consumer Services, 13*(6), 417–430. doi:10.1016/j.jretconser.2006.02.005

Badot, O., & Cova, B. (2003). Néo-marketing, 10 ans après: Pour une théorie critique de la consommation et du marketing réenchantés. *Revue Française du Marketing, 195*(5), 79–94.

Bagge, D. (2007). *Multichannel retailing: The route to customer focus.* London: IBM Global Business Services.

Baier, D., & Stüber, E. (2010). Acceptance of recommendations to buy in online retailing. *Journal of Retailing and Consumer Services, 17*(3), 3–180. doi:10.1016/j.jretconser.2010.03.005

Baier, D., & Stüber, E. (2011). Recommendations to buy in online retailing and their acceptance. In E. Pantano & H. Timmermans (Eds.), *Advanced technology management for retailing: Framework and cases* (pp. 237–252). Hershey, PA: IGI Global. doi:10.4018/978-1-60960-738-8.ch012

Bain. (2011). *Omnichannel retailing.* Retrieved November 20, 2013, from http://www.bain.com/Images/Bain%202011%20Holiday%20Series_Issue%233.pdf

Baker, J., Grewal, D., & Parasuraman, A. (2009). The influence of store environment on quality inferences and store image. *Journal of the Academy of Marketing Science, 22*(4), 328–339. doi:10.1177/0092070394224002

Balasubramanian, S., Raghunathan, R., & Mahajan, V. (2005). Consumers in a multichannel environment: Product utility, process utility, and channel choice. *Journal of Interactive Marketing, 19*(2), 12–30. doi:10.1002/dir.20032

Balconi, M., Brambilla, E., & Falbo, L. (2009). BIS/BAS, cortical oscillations and coherence in response to emotional cues. *Brain Research Bulletin, 80*(3), 151–157. doi:10.1016/j.brainresbull.2009.07.001 PMID:19591907

Ballantine, P. W., Jack, R., & Parsons, A. G. (2010). Atmospheric cues and their effect on the hedonic retail experience. *International Journal of Retail & Distribution Management*, *38*(8), 641–653. doi:10.1108/09590551011057453

Balmer, J. M. T., Powell, S. M., & Greyser, S. A. (2011). Explicating ethical corporate marketing. Insights from the BP deepwater horizon catastrophe: The ethical brand that exploded and then imploded. *Journal of Business Ethics*, *102*(1), 1–14. doi:10.1007/s10551-011-0902-1

Baltas, G. (2003). A combined segmentation and demand model for store brands. *European Journal of Marketing*, *37*(10), 1499–1513. doi:10.1108/03090560310487211

Bandinelli, R., Rinaldi, R., Rossi, M., & Terzi, S. (2013). New product development in the fashion industry: An empirical investigation of Italian firms. *International Journal of Engineering Business Management*, *5*, 1–9. doi:10.5772/56841

Barnes, S., & Mattsson, J. (2008). Brand value in virtual worlds: An axiological approach. *Journal of Electronic Commerce Research*, *9*(3), 195–206.

Barney, J. (1991). Firm resources and sustained competitive advantage. *Journal of Management*, *17*(1), 99–120. doi:10.1177/014920639101700108

Barone, M. J., & Jewell, R. D. (2014). How brand innovativeness creates advertising flexibility. *Journal of the Academy of Marketing Science*, *42*(3), 309–321. doi:10.1007/s11747-013-0352-7

Baron, R. M., & Kenny, D. A. (1986). The moderator–mediator variable distinction in social psychological research: Conceptual, strategic, and statistical considerations. *Journal of Personality and Social Psychology*, *51*(6), 1173–1182. doi:10.1037/0022-3514.51.6.1173 PMID:3806354

Baron, S., Harris, K., & Harris, R. (2002). Retail theater: The "intended effect" of the performance. *Journal of Service Research*, *4*(2), 102–117. doi:10.1177/109467050142003

Bartikowski, B., & Walsh, G. (2014). Attitude contagion in consumer opinion platforms: Posters and lurkers. *Electronic Markets*, *24*(3), 207–217. doi:10.1007/s12525-013-0149-z

Battista, C., & Schiraldi, M. M. (2013). The logistic maturity model: Application to a fashion company. *International Journal of Engineering Business Management*, *5*, 1–11. doi:10.5772/56838

Baudrillard, J. (1994). *Simulacra and simulation*. University of Michigan.

Baum, J., Calabrese, T., & Silverman, B. (2000). Don't go it alone: Alliance network composition and start-ups' performance in Canadian biotechnology. *Strategic Management Journal*, *21*(3), 267–294. doi:10.1002/(SICI)1097-0266(200003)21:3<267::AID-SMJ89>3.0.CO;2-8

Bearne, S. (2014). In-store tech, sales driver or hype. *Business of Fashion*. Retrieved November 20, 2013, from http://www.businessoffashion.com/2014/06/store-tech-sales-driver-hype.html?utm_source=Subscribers&utm_campaign=6da089d3b1-&utm_medium=email&utm_term=0_d2191372b3-6da089d3b1-417168977)

Beckie, M. A., Kennedy, E. H., & Wittman, H. (2012). Scaling up alternative food networks: Farmers' markets and the role of clustering in western Canada. *Agriculture and Human Values*, *29*(3), 333–345. doi:10.1007/s10460-012-9359-9

Bell, S. J., Menguc, B., & Widing, R. E. (2010). Salesperson learning, organizational learning, and retail store performance. *Journal of the Academy of Marketing Science*, *38*(2), 187–201. doi:10.1007/s11747-009-0149-x

Benbasat, I., & Barki, H. (2007). Quo vadis, TAM. *Journal of the Association for Information Systems*, *8*(4), 211–218.

Benbasat, I., & Zmud, R. W. (1999). Empirical research in information systems. *Management Information Systems Quarterly*, *23*(1), 3–16. doi:10.2307/249403

Benedicktus, R. L., Brady, M. K., & Dark, P. R. (2008). Consumer trust in multiple channels: new evidence and directions for future research. In T. M. Lowrey (Ed.), Brick & mortar shopping in the 21st century (pp. 107-127). Mahwah, NJ: Lawrence Erlbaum Associates.

Bennet, R., & Savani, S. (2011). Retailers' preparedness for the introduction of third wave (ubiquitous) computing applications: A survey of UK companies. *International Journal of Retail & Distribution Management*, *39*(5), 306–325. doi:10.1108/09590551111130748

Bennett, P. D., & Harrell, G. D. (1975). The role of confidence in understanding and predicting buyers' attitudes and purchase intentions. *The Journal of Consumer Research*, 2(2), 110–117. doi:10.1086/208622

Bennett, R. C., & Cooper, R. G. (1979). Beyond the marketing concept. *Business Horizons*, 22(3), 76–83. doi:10.1016/0007-6813(79)90088-0

Bennett, R., & Rundle-Thiele, S. (2004). Customer satisfaction should not be the only goal. *Journal of Services Marketing*, 18(7), 514–523. doi:10.1108/08876040410561848

Berfield, S. (2014, June 24). *Gap raises wages and – surprise—more people want to work there*. Retrieved from http://www.bloomberg.com/bw/articles/2014-06-24/gap-learns-to-get-better-job-candidates-pay-them-more

Bergek, A., Jacobsson, S., Carlsson, B., Lindmark, S., & Rickne, A. (2008). Analyzing the functional dynamics of technological innovation systems: A scheme of analysis. *Research Policy*, 37(3), 407–429. doi:10.1016/j.respol.2007.12.003

Berman, B., & Evans, J. R. (2007). *Retail management: A strategic approach* (11th ed.). Upper Saddle River, NJ: Prentice Hall.

Berridge, K. C. (1996). Food reward: Brain substrates of wanting and liking. *Neuroscience and Biobehavioral Reviews*, 20(1), 1–25. doi:10.1016/0149-7634(95)00033-B PMID:8622814

Berry, L. L., Bolton, R. N., Bridges, C. H., Meyer, J., Parasuraman, A., & Seiders, K. (2010). Opportunities for innovation in the delivery of interactive retail services. *Journal of Interactive Marketing*, 24(2), 155–167. doi:10.1016/j.intmar.2010.02.001

Bhatnagar, A., & Ghose, S. (2004). Segmenting consumers based on the benefits and risks of internet shopping. *Journal of Business Research*, 57(12), 1352–1360. doi:10.1016/S0148-2963(03)00067-5

Bhatnagar, N., & Fang, W. (2011). Is self-character similarity always beneficial? *Journal of Advertising*, 40(2), 39–50. doi:10.2753/JOA0091-3367400203

Bianchi, C. C., & Ostale, E. (2006). Lessons learned from unsuccessful internationalization attempts: Examples of multinational retailers in Chile. *Journal of Business Research*, 59(1), 140–147. doi:10.1016/j.jbusres.2005.01.002

Bickers, J. (2008, July). Trying on clothes, 2.0. *Retail Customer Experience*. Retrieved from http://www.retailcustomerexperience.com/article/4071/Trying-on-Clothes-2-0

Biehl-Missal, B., & vom Lehn, D. (2014). Aesthetic atmospheres in museums: A critical marketing perspective. In M. Henning (Ed.), *Museum media / international handbook of museum studies*. Chichester, UK: Wiley-Blackwell.

Biocca, F., & Delaney, B. (1995). Immersive virtual reality technology. In F. Biocca & M. R. Levy (Eds.), *Communication in the age of virtual reality* (pp. 57–124). Hillsdale, NJ: Lawrence Erlbaum Associates.

Biong, H., Nygaard, A., & Silkoset, R. (2010). The influence of retail management's use of social power on corporate ethical values, employee commitment, and performance. *Journal of Business Ethics*, 97(3), 341–363. doi:10.1007/s10551-010-0523-0

Birch, D. G. W. (1979). *The job generation process*. Washington, DC: US Department of Commerce.

Biswas, D., & Burman, B. (2009). The effects of product digitalization and price dispersion on search intentions in offline versus online settings: The mediating effects of perceived risks. *Journal of Product and Brand Management*, 18(7), 477–486. doi:10.1108/10610420910998208

Bitner, M. J. (1992). Servicescapes: The impact of physical surroundings on customers and employees. *Journal of Marketing*, 56(April), 57–71. doi:10.2307/1252042

Bitner, M. J., Booms, B., & Tetreault, M. (1990). The service encounter: Diagnosing favorable and unfavorable incidents. *Journal of Marketing*, 54(1), 71–84. doi:10.2307/1252174

Black, D., Clemmenses, N. J., & Skov, M. B. (2009). Supporting the supermarket shopping experience through a context-aware shopping trolley. In *Proceedings of the 21st Annual Conference of the Australian Computer-Human Interaction*. New York: ACM. doi:10.1145/1738826.1738833

Blázquez, M. (2014). Fashion shopping in multichannel retail: The role of technology in enhancing the customer experience. *International Journal of Electronic Commerce, 18*(4), 97–116. doi:10.2753/JEC1086-4415180404

Blind, K., & Grupp, H. (1999). Interdependencies between the science and technology infrastructure and innovation activities in German regions: Empirical findings and policy consequences. *Research Policy, 28*(5), 451–468. doi:10.1016/S0048-7333(99)00007-4

Bloch, P. H., Ridgway, N. M., & Dawson, S. A. (1994). The shopping mall as consumer habitat. *Journal of Retailing, 70*(1), 23–42. doi:10.1016/0022-4359(94)90026-4

Bodhani, A. (2012). Shops offer the e-tail experience. *Engineering and Technology, 7*(5), 46–49. doi:10.1049/et.2012.0512

Boeker, W. (1997). Executive migration and strategic change: The effect of top manager movement on product-market entry. *Administrative Science Quarterly, 42*(2), 213–236. doi:10.2307/2393919

Böhme, G. (1995). *Atmosphäre, Essays zur neuen Ästhetik.* Frankfurt: Suhrkamp.

Böhme, G. (2001). *Aisthetik, Vorlesung über Ästhetik als allgemeine Wahrnehmungslehre.* München: Wilhelm Fink Verlag.

Bolton, R., & Saxena-Iyer, S. (2009). Interactive services: A framework, synthesis and research directions. *Journal of Interactive Marketing, 23*(1), 91–104. doi:10.1016/j.intmar.2008.11.002

Bolt, W. (2013). Pricing, competition and innovation in retail payment systems: A brief overview. *Journal of Financial Market Infrastructures, 1*(3), 73–90.

Bonner, J. M. (2010). Customer interactivity and new product performance: Moderating effects of product newness and product embeddedness. *Industrial Marketing Management, 39*(3), 485–492. doi:10.1016/j.indmarman.2008.11.006

Bordens, K. S., & Abbott, B. B. (2002). *Research design and methods: A process approach.* New York, NY: McGraw-Hill.

Borgers, A., Baggerman, L., & Van den Berg, P. (2014). *Shopping and the use of social media.* Paper presented at the Recent Advances in Retailing and Consumer Services Science Conference, Bucharest, Romania.

Borgers, A., Brouwer, M., Kunen, T., Jessurun, J., & Janssen, I. (2010). A virtual reality tool to measure shoppers' tenant mix preferences. *Computers, Environment and Urban Systems, 34*(5), 377–388. doi:10.1016/j.compenvurbsys.2010.04.002

Bosmans, A. (2006). Scents and sensibility: When do (in)congruent ambient scents influence product evaluations? *Journal of Marketing, 70*(3), 32–43. doi:10.1509/jmkg.70.3.32

Boulding, W., Kalra, A., Staelin, R., & Zeithaml, V. A. (1993). A dynamic process model of service quality: From expectations to behavioral intentions. *JMR, Journal of Marketing Research, 30*(1), 7–27. doi:10.2307/3172510

Bowman, D. A., Kruijff, E., LaViola, J. J. Jr, & Poupyrev, I. (2004). *3D user interfaces: Theory and practice.* Redwood City, CA: Addison Wesley.

Boyce, C., & Neale, P. (2006). Conducting in-depth interviews: A guide for designing and conducting in-depth interviews for evaluation input. *Pathfinder International Tool Series. Monitoring and Evaluation, 2.* Retrieved August 30, 2014, from http://www.cpc.unc.edu/measure/training/materials/data-quality-portuguese/m_e_tool_series_indepth_interviews.pdf

Brady, M. K., & Cronin, J. J. Jr. (2001). Some new thoughts on conceptualizing perceived service quality: A hierarchical approach. *Journal of Marketing, 65*(3), 34–49. doi:10.1509/jmkg.65.3.34.18334

Brady, M. K., Knight, G. A., Cronin, J. J. Jr, Tomas, G., Hult, M., & Keillor, B. D. (2005). Removing the contextual lens: A multinational, multi-setting comparison of service evaluation models. *Journal of Retailing, 81*(3), 215–230. doi:10.1016/j.jretai.2005.07.005

Braeutigam, S., Rose, S. P., Swithenby, S. J., & Ambler, T. (2004). The distributed neuronal systems supporting choice-making in real-life situations: Differences between men and women when choosing groceries detected using magnetoencephalography. *The European Journal of Neuroscience, 20*(1), 293–302. doi:10.1111/j.1460-9568.2004.03467.x PMID:15245501

Brakus, J. J., Schmitt, B. H., & Zarantonello, L. (2009). Brand experience: What is it? How do we measure it? And does it affect loyalty? *Journal of Marketing*, *73*(3), 52–68. doi:10.1509/jmkg.73.3.52

Breiter, A., & Huchzermeier, A. (2010). The new logic of truly efficient retail promotions. *International Commerce Review*, *9*(1-2), 36–47. doi:10.1007/s12146-010-0052-x

Brem, A., & Voigt, K. I. (2009). Integration of market pull and technology push in the corporate front end and innovation management—Insights from the German software industry. *Technovation*, *29*(5), 351–367. doi:10.1016/j.technovation.2008.06.003

Brenner, J., & Smith, A. (2013). *72% of online adults are social networking site users*. Retrieved June 2, 2014, from http://pewinternet.org/~/media//Files/Reports/2013/PIP_Social_networking_sites_update_PDF.pdf

Bretonès, D. D., Quinio, B., & Réveillon, G. (2010). Bridging virtual and real worlds: Enhancing outlying clustered value creations. *Journal of Strategic Marketing*, *18*(7), 613–625. doi:10.1080/0965254X.2010.529157

Brexendorf, T. O., & Daecke, N. (2012). The brand manager – Current tasks and skill requirements in FMCG companies. *Marketing Review St. Gallen*, *29*(6), 32–37. doi:10.1365/s11621-012-0175-9

Brink, J., & Holmén, M. (2009). Capabilities and radical changes of the business models of new bioscience firms. *Creativity and Innovation Management*, *18*(2), 109–120. doi:10.1111/j.1467-8691.2009.00519.x

Broadbride, A. (2003). The appeal of retailing as a career: 20 years on. *Journal of Retailing and Consumer Services*, *10*(5), 287–296. doi:10.1016/S0969-6989(02)00065-6

Brodie, R. J., Glynn, M. S., & Little, V. (2006). The service brand and the service-dominant logic: Missing fundamental premise or the need for stronger theory. *Marketing Theory*, *6*(3), 363–379. doi:10.1177/1470593106066797

Brouthers, L. E., & Xu, K. (2002). Product stereotypes, strategy and performance satisfaction: The case of Chinese exporters. *Journal of International Business Studies*, *33*(4), 657–677. doi:10.1057/palgrave.jibs.8491038

Browne, C. (2014). *Facebook Inc (FB) mobile usage patterns show interesting gender splits*. Retrieved July 3, 2014, from http://www.valuewalk.com

Browning, J. M., & Zabriskie, N. B. (1985). Do-it yourself consumer: Segmentation insights for retailers. *Journal of Consumer Marketing*, *2*(3), 5–15. doi:10.1108/eb008128

Brown, P., McNaughton, R. B., & Bell, J. (2010). Marketing externalities in industrial clusters: A literature review and evidence from the Christchurch, New Zealand electronics cluster. *Journal of International Entrepreneurship*, *8*(2), 168–181. doi:10.1007/s10843-010-0053-y

Brown, S., & Eisenhardt, K. (1995). Product development: Past research, present findings, and future directions. *Academy of Management Review*, *20*(2), 343–378.

Bruce, M., & Daly, L. (2010). Innovative process in e-commerce fashion supply chains. In T. C. E. Cheng & T.-M. Choi (Eds.), *Innovative quick response programs in logistics and supply chain management* (pp. 227–242). Heidelberg, Germany: Springer Verlag. doi:10.1007/978-3-642-04313-0_11

Brüderl, J., & Preisendörfer, P. (1998). Network support and the success of newly founded businesses. *Small Business Economics*, *10*(3), 213–225. doi:10.1023/A:1007997102930

Brun, A., Caniato, F., Caridi, M., Castelli, C., Miragliotta, G., Ronchi, S., & Spina, G. (2008). Logistics and supply chain management in luxury fashion retail: Empirical investigation of Italian firms. *International Journal of Production Economics*, *114*(2), 554–570. doi:10.1016/j.ijpe.2008.02.003

Brun, A., & Castelli, C. (2008). Supply chain strategy in the fashion industry: Developing a portfolio model depending on product, retail channel and brand. *International Journal of Production Economics*, *116*(2), 169–181. doi:10.1016/j.ijpe.2008.09.011

Bruner, G. C. II, & Kumar, A. (2005). Explaining consumer acceptance of handheld internet devices. *Journal of Business Research*, *58*(5), 553–558. doi:10.1016/j.jbusres.2003.08.002

Brynjolfsson, E., Hu, Y. J., & Rahman, M. S. (2013). Competing in the age of omnichannel retailing. *MIT Sloan Management Review, 54*(4).

Brynjolfsson, E., Hu, Y. J., & Rahman, M. S. (2013). Competing in the age of omnichannel retailing. *MIT Sloan Management Review, 54*(4), 1–7.

Bulearca, M., & Tamarjan, D. (2010). Augmented reality: A sustainable marketing tool? *Global Business and Management Research: An International Journal, 2*(2 & 3), 237–252.

Bullinger, H.-J., Bauer, W., Wenzel, G., & Blach, R. (2010). Towards user centred design (UCD) in architecture based on immersive virtual environments. *Computers in Industry, 61*(4), 372–379. doi:10.1016/j.compind.2009.12.003

Bureau of Labor Statistics, US Department of Labor. (2010, May). *Career guide to industries, 2008-2009 edition: Clothing, accessory and general merchandise stores.* Retrieved from http://www.bls.gov/oco/cg/cgs022.htm

Burke, R. R. (2002). Technology and the customer interface: What consumers want in the physical and virtual store. *Journal of the Academy of Marketing Science, 30*(4), 411–432. doi:10.1177/009207002236914

Burke, R. R. (2009). Behavioral effects of digital signage. *Journal of Advertising Research, 49*(2), 180–185. doi:10.2501/S0021849909090254

Burns, R. B., & Burns, R. A. (2008). *Business research methods and statistics using SPSS.* London: SAGE Publications.

Burton-Jones, A., & Hubona, G. (2006). The mediation of external variables in the technology acceptance model. *Information & Management, 43*(6), 706–717. doi:10.1016/j.im.2006.03.007

Burt, S., & Davies, K. (2010). From the retail brand to the retailer as a brand: Themes and issues in retail branding research. *International Journal of Retail & Distribution Management, 38*(11-12), 865–878.

Burt, S., Johansson, U., & Thelander, Å. (2011). Standardized marketing strategies in retailing? IKEA's marketing strategies in Sweden, the UK and China. *Journal of Retailing and Consumer Services, 18*(3), 183–193. doi:10.1016/j.jretconser.2010.09.007

Bush, G., Luu, P., & Posner, M. I. (2000). Cognitive and emotional influences in anterior cingulate cortex. *Trends in Cognitive Sciences, 4*(6), 215–222. doi:10.1016/S1364-6613(00)01483-2 PMID:10827444

Butterfield, L. D., Borgen, W. A., Amundson, N. E., & Maglio, A.-S. T. (2005). Fifty years of the critical incident technique: 1954-2004 and beyond. *Qualitative Research, 5*(4), 475–497. doi:10.1177/1468794105056924

Buzzel, R. D., & Gale, B. T. (1987). *The PIMS principles.* New York, NY: Free Press.

Cacioppo, J. T. (2002). Social neuroscience: Understanding the pieces fosters understanding the whole and vice versa. *The American Psychologist, 57*(11), 819–831. doi:10.1037/0003-066X.57.11.819 PMID:12564179

Cadoz, C. (1994). *Les réalites virtuelles.* Paris: Dominos Flammarion.

Cai, R., & Wang, Y. (2010). An empirical study on the timing of big retailers' initial internationalization: Influence of the target market and entry-mode choice. *Frontiers of Business Research in China, 4*(4), 608–629. doi:10.1007/s11782-010-0113-0

Calza, F., Aliane, N., & Cannavale, C. (2013). Cross-cultural bridges in European firms' internationalization to Islamic countries: The key role of cultural competence. *EuroMed Journal of Business, 8*(2), 172–187. doi:10.1108/EMJB-07-2013-0038

Camp, R. C. (1998). *Global cases in benchmarking.* Milwaukee, WI: ASQ Quality Press.

Caniato, F., Caridi, M., & Moretto, A. (2013). Dynamic capabilities for fashion-luxury supply chain innovation. *International Journal of Retail & Distribution Management, 41*(11/12), 9–9.

Caniato, F., Caridi, M., Moretto, A., Sianesi, A., & Spina, G. (2014). Integrating international fashion retail into new product development. *International Journal of Production Economics, 147,* 294–306. doi:10.1016/j.ijpe.2013.04.005

Cano, C. R., Carrillat, F. A., & Jaramillo, F. (2004). A meta-analysis of the relationship between market orientation and business performance: Evidence from five continents. *International Journal of Research in Marketing, 21*(2), 179–200. doi:10.1016/j.ijresmar.2003.07.001

Cardinal, L. (2001). Technological innovation in the pharmaceutical industry: The use of organizational control in managing research and development. *Organization Science, 12*(1), 19–36. doi:10.1287/orsc.12.1.19.10119

Carlin, A. S., Hoffman, H. G., & Weghorst, S. (1997). Virtual reality and tactile augmentation in the treatment of spider phobia: A case report. *Behaviour Research and Therapy*, *35*(2), 153–158. doi:10.1016/S0005-7967(96)00085-X PMID:9046678

Caro, F., & Martınez-de-Albéniz, V. (2015in press). Fast fashion: Business model overview and research opportunities. In N. Agrawal & S. A. Smith (Eds.), *Retail supply chain management: Quantitative models and empirical studies* (2nd ed.). New York, NY: Springer.

Carrigan, M., Moraes, C., & Leek, S. (2011). Fostering responsible communities: A community social marketing approach to sustainable living. *Journal of Business Ethics*, *100*(3), 515–534. doi:10.1007/s10551-010-0694-8

Carter, R. E., & Curry, D. J. (2010). Transparent pricing: Theory, tests, and implications for marketing practice. *Journal of the Academy of Marketing Science*, *38*(6), 759–774. doi:10.1007/s11747-010-0189-2

Carter, R. E., & Curry, D. J. (2013). Perceptions versus performance when managing extensions: New evidence about the role of fit between a parent brand and an extension. *Journal of the Academy of Marketing Science*, *41*(2), 253–269. doi:10.1007/s11747-011-0292-z

Carù, A., & Cova, B. (2006a). Expériences de marque: Comment favoriser l'immersion du consommateur? *Décisions Marketing*, *41*(1), 43–52.

Carù, A., & Cova, B. (2006b). How to facilitate immersion in a consumption experience: Appropriation operations and service elements. *Journal of Consumer Behaviour*, *5*(1), 4–14. doi:10.1002/cb.30

Castaldo, S. (Ed.). (2001). *Retailing & innovazione*. Milano: Egea.

Castelli, C. M., & Brun, A. (2010). Alignment of retail channels in the fashion supply chain: An empirical study of Italian fashion retailers. *International Journal of Retail & Distribution Management*, *38*(1), 24–44. doi:10.1108/09590551011016313

Cater, B., & Cater, T. (2009). Relationship-value-based antecedents of customer satisfaction and loyalty in manufacturing. *Journal of Business and Industrial Marketing*, *24*(7-8), 585–597. doi:10.1108/08858620910999457

Cavusgil, S. T., & Cavusgil, E. (2012). Reflections on international marketing: Destructive regeneration and multinational firms. *Journal of the Academy of Marketing Science*, *40*(2), 202–217. doi:10.1007/s11747-011-0287-9

Celik, H. (2011). Influence of social norms, perceived playfulness and online shopping anxiety on customers' adoption of online retail shopping. *International Journal of Retail & Distribution Management*, *39*(6), 390–413. doi:10.1108/09590551111137967

Černe, M., Jaklič, M., & Škerlavaj, M. (2013). Decoupling management and technological innovations: Resolving the individualism–collectivism controversy. *Journal of International Management*, *19*(2), 103–117. doi:10.1016/j.intman.2013.03.004

Chamberlain, G. (1979). *Heterogeneity, omitted variable bias, and duration dependence*. Cambridge, MA: Harvard Institute of Economic Research.

Chandon, P., Wansink, B., & Laurent, G. (2000). A benefit congruency framework of sales promotion effectiveness. *Journal of Marketing*, *64*(4), 177–183. doi:10.1509/jmkg.64.4.65.18071

Chandra, H., Vashishta Rinko, A., Kumar Verma, J., Verma, S., Kapoor, R., & Sharma, R. K. (2013). Supply chain management with cost containment & financial sustainability in a tertiary care hospital. *Journal of Health and Human Services Administration*, *36*(1), 3–23. PMID:24010261

Chaney, P. (2010). *J.C. Penney moves entire product catalog to Facebook*. Retrieved from http://www.practicalecommerce.com/blogs/post/788-J-C-Penney-Moves-Entire-Product-Catalog-to-Facebook

Chaney, I. M. (2000). External search effort for wine. *International Journal of Wine Marketing*, *12*(2), 5–21. doi:10.1108/eb008706

Chang, P. L., & Chieng, M. H. (2006). Building consumer-brand relationship: A cross-cultural experiential view. *Psychology and Marketing*, *23*(11), 927–959. doi:10.1002/mar.20140

Chartrand, T. L., & Bargh, J. A. (1999). The chameleon effect: The perception-behavior link and social interaction. *Journal of Personality and Social Psychology*, *76*(6), 893–910. doi:10.1037/0022-3514.76.6.893 PMID:10402679

Chattaraman, V., Known, W.-S., & Gilbert, J. E. (2012). Virtual agents in retail web sites: Benefits of simulated social interaction for older users. *Computers in Human Behavior, 28*(6), 2055–2066. doi:10.1016/j.chb.2012.06.009

Chaudhuri, A. (2000). A macro analysis of the relationship of product involvement and information search: The role of risk. *Journal of Marketing Theory and Practice, 80*(1), 1–15.

Chebat, J. C., & Michon, R. (2003). Impact of ambient odors on mall shoppers' emotions, cognition and spending: A test of competitive causal theories. *Journal of Business Research, 56*(7), 529–539. doi:10.1016/S0148-2963(01)00247-8

Chen, B., & Wu, W. V. (2007). Extolling the virtues of language immersion in whole-family camps. *The Business Review, Cambridge, 7*(2), 77–83.

Chen, C. F., & Chang, Y. (2008). Airline brand equity, brand preference, and purchase intentions: The moderating effects of switching costs. *Journal of Air Transport Management, 14*(1), 40–42. doi:10.1016/j.jairtraman.2007.11.003

Chen, K.-J. (2005). Technology-based service and customer satisfaction in developing countries international. *Journal of Management, 22*(2), 307–318.

Chen, L.-D., & Tan, J. (2004). Technology adaptation in e-commerce: Key determinants of virtual stores acceptance. *European Management Journal, 22*(1), 74–86. doi:10.1016/j.emj.2003.11.014

Cheung, R., & Vogel, D. (2013). Predicting user acceptance of collaborative technologies: An extension of the technology acceptance model for e-learning. *Computers & Education, 63*(April), 160–175. doi:10.1016/j.compedu.2012.12.003

Childers, T., Carr, C., Peck, J. C., & Carson, S. (2001). Hedonic and utilitarian motivations for online retail shopping behavior. *Journal of Retailing, 77*(4), 511–535. doi:10.1016/S0022-4359(01)00056-2

Chin, W. W. (1998). The partial least squares approach to structural equation modeling. In G. A. Marcoulides (Ed.), *Modern methods for business research* (pp. 295–336). Mahwah, NJ: Lawrence Erlbaum Associates.

Chinyamurindi, W. T., & Louw, G. J. (2010). Gender differences in technology acceptance in selected South African companies: Implications for electronic learning. *SA Journal of Human Resource Management, 8*(1), 2–7. doi:10.4102/sajhrm.v8i1.204

Chiu, C. M., Huang, H. Y., & Yen, C. H. (2010). Antecedents of trust in online auctions. *Electronic Commerce Research and Applications, 9*(2), 148–159. doi:10.1016/j.elerap.2009.04.003

Chiu, H. C., Hsieh, Y. C., Roan, J., Tseng, K. J., & Hsieh, J. K. (2011). The challenge for multichannel services: Cross-channel free-riding behavior. *Electronic Commerce Research and Applications, 10*(2), 268–277. doi:10.1016/j.elerap.2010.07.002

Chiu, P. H., Kao, G. Y. M., & Lo, C. C. (2010). Personalized blog content recommender system for mobile phone users. *International Journal of Human-Computer Studies, 68*(8), 496–507. doi:10.1016/j.ijhcs.2010.03.005

Choi, J., Lee, H. J., & Kim, Y. C. (2011). The influence of social presence on customer intention to reuse online recommender systems: The roles of personalization and product type. *International Journal of Electronic Commerce, 16*(1), 129–153. doi:10.2753/JEC1086-4415160105

Choi, T. M. (2007). Pre-season stocking and pricing decisions for fashion retailers with multiple information updating. *International Journal of Production Economics, 106*(1), 146–170. doi:10.1016/j.ijpe.2006.05.009

Choi, T. M., Hui, C. L., Liu, N., Ng, S. F., & Yu, Y. (2013). Fast fashion sales forecasting with limited data and time. *Decision Support Systems, 59*(March), 84–92.

Christensen, C. (2013). *The innovator's dilemma: When new technologies cause great firms to fail.* Boston, MA: Harvard Business Review Press.

Christensen, C. M., & Bower, J. L. (1996). Customer power, strategic investment, and the failure of leading firms. *Strategic Management Journal, 17*(3), 197–218. doi:10.1002/(SICI)1097-0266(199603)17:3<197::AID-SMJ804>3.0.CO;2-U

Christopher, M., & Peck, H. (2004). *Marketing logistics.* Oxford, UK: Butterworth-Heinemann.

Chu, A., & Lam, M. C. (2007). Store environment of fashion retailers: a Hong Kong perspective. In T. Hines & M. Bruce (Eds.), Fashion marketing (2nd ed.; pp. 151-167). Oxford, UK: Elsevier.

Chu, J., & Paglucia, G. (2002). *Enhancing the customer shopping experience.* London: IBM Institute for Business Value.

Chung, C. C., Lee, S. H., Beamish, P. W., Southam, C., & Nam, D. (2013). Pitting real options theory against risk diversification theory: International diversification and joint ownership control in economic crisis. *Journal of World Business*, 48(1), 122–136. doi:10.1016/j.jwb.2012.06.013

Chung, C. C., Lu, J., & Beamish, P. W. (2008). Multinational networks during times of economic crisis versus stability. *Management International Review*, 48(3), 279–295. doi:10.1007/s11575-008-0016-x

Chung, J.-E. (2013). Does small retailer market orientation matter for long-term oriented relationships with suppliers? *Journal of Small Business Management.* doi:10.1111/jsbm.12061

Chutani, A., & Sethi, S. P. (2012). Cooperative advertising in a dynamic retail market oligopoly. *Dynamic Games and Applications*, 2(4), 347–375. doi:10.1007/s13235-012-0053-8

Chuttur, M. (2009). Overview of the technology acceptance model: Origins, developments and future directions, Indiana University, USA. *Sprouts: Working Papers on Information Systems, 9*(37).

Cillo, P., & Verona, G. (2008). Search styles in style searching: Exploring innovation strategies in fashion firms. *Long Range Planning*, 41(6), 650–671. doi:10.1016/j.lrp.2008.08.001

Citrin, A. V., Stem, D. E. Jr, Spangenberg, E. R., & Clark, M. J. (2003). Consumer need for tactile input: An internet retailing challenge. *Journal of Business Research*, 56(11), 915–922. doi:10.1016/S0148-2963(01)00278-8

Clifford, E. (2012). *Fashion online.* Mintel.

Cohen, W. M., & Klepper, S. (1992). The trade off between firm size and diversity in the pursuit of technological progress. *Small Business Economics*, 4(1), 1–14.

Colby, C. L., & Parasuraman, A. (2003). Technology still matters - Never mind the doomsayers. E-services are alive, well, and positioned for growth. *Marketing Management*, 12(4), 28–33.

Coleman, J. (1988). Social capital in the creation of human capital. *American Journal of Sociology*, 94(s1), 95–120. doi:10.1086/228943

Colley, R. H. (1961). *Defining advertising goals for measured advertising results.* New York, NY: Association of National Advertisers.

Commission, E. U. (2014). *Final report from the expert group on retail sector innovation.* Brussels: Directorate General for Research and Innovation.

Compeau, D. R., & Higgins, C. A. (1995). Computer self-efficacy: Development of a measure and initial test. *Management Information Systems Quarterly*, 19(2), 189–211. doi:10.2307/249688

comScore. (2011). *14 million Americans scanned QR codes on their mobile phones in June 2011.* Retrieved from: http://www.comscore.com/ger/Insights/Press_Releases/2011/8/14_Million_Ameri-cans_Scanned_QR_or_Bar_Codes_on_their_Mobile_Phones_in_June_2011

Cooil, B., Aksoy, L., Keiningham, T. L., & Maryott, K. M. (2009). The relationship of employee perceptions of organizational climate to business-unit outcomes: An MPLS approach. *Journal of Service Research*, 11(3), 277–294. doi:10.1177/1094670508328984

Corbató, F. J., Merwin-Daggett, M., & Daley, R. C. (1962). An experimental time-sharing system. In *Proceedings of Spring Joint Computer Conference* (pp. 335-344). New York, NY: ACM.

Coricelli, G., Critchley, H. D., Joffily, M., O'Doherty, J. P., Sirigu, A., & Dolan, R. J. (2005). Regret and its avoidance: A neuroimaging study of choice behavior. *Nature Neuroscience*, 8(9), 1255–1262. doi:10.1038/nn1514 PMID:16116457

Cornelius, B., Wagner, U., & Natter, M. (2010). Managerial applicability of graphical formats to support positioning decisions. *Journal für Betriebswirtschaft*, 60(3), 167–201. doi:10.1007/s11301-010-0061-y

Corvello, V., Pantano, E., & Tavernise, A. (2011). The design of an advanced virtual shopping assistant for improving consumer experience. In E. Pantano & H. Timmermans (Eds.), *Advanced technologies management for retailing* (pp. 70–86). Hershey, PA: Business Science Reference.

Cremers, J. (2013). Non-financial reporting and reference to workers' representatives. *Contemporary Readings in Law and Social Justice, 5*(2), 2013, 50–89.

Croatia, G. F. K. Research Agency. (2012). *Consumer tracking presentation*. Retrieved June 01, 2014, from http://www.gfk.hr/public_relations/press/press_articles/009459/index.hr.html

Cronin, J. J., Smith, J. S., Gleim, M. R., Ramirez, E., & Martinez, J. D. (2011). Green marketing strategies: An examination of stakeholders and the opportunities they present. *Journal of the Academy of Marketing Science, 39*(1), 158–174. doi:10.1007/s11747-010-0227-0

Cruz-Ros, S., Cruz, T. F. G., & Perez-Cabanero, C. (2010). Marketing capabilities, stakeholders' satisfaction, and performance. *Service Business, 4*(3-4), 209–223. doi:10.1007/s11628-009-0078-2

Culliton, J. W. (1948). *The management of marketing costs*. Boston, MA: Harvard University Press.

Curran, J. M., & Meuter, M. L. (2005). Self-service technology adoption: Comparing three technologies. *Journal of Services Marketing, 19*(2), 103–113. doi:10.1108/08876040510591411

Cvijikj, I. P., Spiegler, E. D., & Michahelles, F. (2013). Evaluation framework for social media brand presence. *Social Network Analysis and Mining, 3*(4), 1325–1349. doi:10.1007/s13278-013-0131-y

Dabholkar, P. A. (1994). Technology-based service delivery: A classification scheme for developing marketing strategies. In T. A. Swartz, D. A. Bowen, & S. W. Brown (Eds.), *Advances in services marketing and management* (Vol. 3, pp. 241–271). Bingley: Emerald Group Publishing. doi:10.1016/S1067-5671(94)03021-9

Dabholkar, P. A. (1996). Consumer evaluations of new technology-based self-service options: An investigation of alternative models of service quality. *International Journal of Research in Marketing, 13*(1), 29–51. doi:10.1016/0167-8116(95)00027-5

Dabholkar, P. A., & Bagozzi, R. P. (2002). An attitudinal model of technology-based self-service: Moderating effects of consumer traits and situational factors. *Journal of the Academy of Marketing Science, 30*(3), 184–201. doi:10.1177/0092070302303001

Dabholkar, P. A., Bobbitt, L. M., & Lee, E. J. (2003). Understanding consumer motivation and behavior related to self-scanning in retailing: Implications for strategy and research on technology-based self-service. *International Journal of Service Industry Management, 14*(1), 59–95. doi:10.1108/09564230310465994

Dabholkar, P. A., Shepherd, C. D., & Thorpe, D. I. (2000). A comprehensive framework for service quality: An investigation of critical conceptual and measurement issues through a longitudinal study. *Journal of Retailing, 76*(2), 139–173. doi:10.1016/S0022-4359(00)00029-4

Dabholkar, P. A., & Spaid, B. I. (2012). Service failure and recovery in using technology-based self-service: Effects on user attributions and satisfaction. *Service Industries Journal, 32*(9), 1415–1432. doi:10.1080/02642069.2011.600518

Dabholkar, P. A., Thorpe, D. I., & Rentz, J. O. (1996). A measure of service quality for retail stores: Scale development and validation. *Journal of the Academy of Marketing Science, 24*(1), 3–16. doi:10.1007/BF02893933

Dahan, E., & Hauser, J. R. (2002). The virtual customer. *Journal of Product Innovation Management, 19*(5), 332–353. doi:10.1016/S0737-6782(02)00151-0

Dahle, M., & Neumayer, E. (2001). Overcoming barriers to campus greening: A survey among higher educational institutions in London. *International Journal of Sustainability in Higher Education, 2*(2), 139–160. doi:10.1108/14676370110388363

Dalgarno, B., & Lee, M. J. W. (2010). What are the learning affordances of 3-D virtual environments? *British Journal of Educational Technology, 41*(1), 10–30. doi:10.1111/j.1467-8535.2009.01038.x

Damasio, A. R., Everitt, B. J., & Bishop, D. (1996). The somatic marker hypothesis and the possible functions of the prefrontal cortex. *Philosophical Transactions of the Royal Society of London. Series B, Biological Sciences*, *351*(1346), 1413–1420. doi:10.1098/rstb.1996.0125 PMID:8941953

Darling, J. R. (2001). Successful competitive positioning: The key for entry into the European consumer market. *European Business Review*, *13*(4), 209–221. doi:10.1108/EUM0000000005535

Das, S., Agrawal, D., & Abbadi, A. E. (2010). G-Store: A scalable data store for transactional multi key access in the cloud. In *Proceedings of the 1st ACM Symposium on Cloud Computing* (pp. 163-174). New York, NY: ACM. doi:10.1145/1807128.1807157

Datamonitor. (2010). *DIY and home improvement retail in Europe: Market size, retailer strategies and competitor performance*. Retrieved December 23, 2013 from http://www.datamonitor.com/store/Product/diy_and_home_improvement_retail_in_europe_market_size_retailer_strategies_and_competitor_performance?productid=DMVT0563

Davenport, T. (1998). *Working knowledge: How organizations manage what they know*. Boston: Harvard Business Review Press.

Davidson, R. J., Ekman, P., Saron, C. D., Senulis, J. A., & Friesen, W. V. (1990). Approach-withdrawal and cerebral asymmetry: Emotional expression and brain physiology. I. *Journal of Personality and Social Psychology*, *58*(2), 330–341. doi:10.1037/0022-3514.58.2.330 PMID:2319445

Davidson, R. J., Shackman, A. J., & Maxwell, J. S. (2004). Asymmetries in face and brain related to emotion. *Trends in Cognitive Sciences*, *8*(9), 389–391. doi:10.1016/j.tics.2004.07.006 PMID:15350238

Davies, G. (1992). The two ways in which retailers can be brands. *International Journal of Retail & Distribution Management*, *20*(2), 24–34. doi:10.1108/09590559210009312

Davis, F. D. (1985). *A technology acceptance model for empirically testing new end-user information systems: theory and results*. (Unpublished Doctoral Dissertation). MIT Sloan School of Management, Cambridge, MA.

Davis, D. F., Golicic, S. L., & Marquardt, A. J. (2008). Branding a B2B service: Does a brand differentiate a logistics service provider? *Industrial Marketing Management*, *37*(2), 218–227. doi:10.1016/j.indmarman.2007.02.003

Davis, F. D. (1989). Perceived usefulness, perceived ease of use, and user acceptance of information technology. *Management Information Systems Quarterly*, *13*(3), 319–340. doi:10.2307/249008

Davis, F. D., Bagozzi, R. P., & Warshaw, P. R. (1989). User acceptance of computer technology: A comparison of two theoretical models. *Management Science*, *35*(8), 982–1003. doi:10.1287/mnsc.35.8.982

Davis, F. D., Bagozzi, R. P., & Warshaw, P. R. (1992). Extrinsic and intrinsic motivation to use computers in the workplace. *Journal of Applied Social Psychology*, *22*(14), 1111–1132. doi:10.1111/j.1559-1816.1992.tb00945.x

Davis, G. (1992). Positioning, image and the marketing of multiple retailers. *International Review of Retail, Distribution and Consumer Research*, *2*(1), 13–34. doi:10.1080/09593969200000002

Dawson, J. (1994). The internationalisation of retailing operations. *Journal of Marketing Management*, *10*(4), 267–282. doi:10.1080/0267257X.1994.9964274

Dawson, J. A. (2001). Is there a new commerce in Europe? *International Review of Retail, Distribution and Consumer Research*, *11*(3), 287–299. doi:10.1080/713770598

Day, G. (1994). The capabilities of market-driven organizations. *Journal of Marketing*, *58*(4), 37–52. doi:10.2307/1251915

De Brito, M. P., Carbone, V., & Blanquart, C. M. (2008). Towards a sustainable fashion retail supply chain in Europe: Organisation and performance. *International Journal of Production Economics*, *114*(2), 534–553. doi:10.1016/j.ijpe.2007.06.012

De Bruyn, A., & Lilien, G. L. (2008). A multi-stage model of word-of-mouth influence through viral marketing. *International Journal of Research in Marketing*, *25*(3), 151–163. doi:10.1016/j.ijresmar.2008.03.004

De Felice, F., Petrillo, A., & Autorino, C. (2013). Key success factors for organizational innovation in the fashion industry. *International Journal of Engineering Business Management*, *5*(27), 1–11.

de Jesus-Hitzschky, K. R. E. (2007). Impact assessment system for technological innovation: Inova-tec System. *Journal of Technology Management & Innovation, 2*(2), 67–81.

De Moerloose, C., Antioco, M., Lindgreen, A., & Palmer, R. (2005). Information kiosks: The case of the Belgian retail sector. *International Journal of Retail & Distribution Management, 33*(6), 472–490. doi:10.1108/09590550510603651

Dean, A. M., & Rolland, S. E. (2012). Using an age-based lens to test the antecedents of value in retail. *der markt. International Journal of Marketing, 51*(2-3), 85–100.

Dede, C. (2009). Immersive interfaces for engagement and learning. *Science, 323*(5910), 66–69. doi:10.1126/science.1167311 PMID:19119219

Dedrick, J., Kraemer, K., & Linden, G. (2010). Who profits from innovation in global value chains?: A study of the iPod and notebook PCs. *Industrial and Corporate Change, 19*(1), 81–16. doi:10.1093/icc/dtp032

Dejardin, M. (2002). Dejardin, Marcus. In *ERSA conference papers*. European Regional Science Association.

Deloitte. (2011). *Store 3.0.* Retrieved November 20, 2013, from http://www.deloitte.com/assets/Dcom-MiddleEast/Local%20Assets/Documents/Industries/Consumer%20Business/me_consumer_business_store_3.0_11.pdf

Deloitte. (2013). *Keeping promises putting customers at the heart of retail financial services.* London, UK: Deloitte.

DelVecchio, D., Jarvis, C. B., Klink, R. R., & Dineen, B. B. (2007). Leveraging brand equity to attract human capital. *Marketing Letters, 18*(3), 149–164. doi:10.1007/s11002-007-9012-3

Demery, P. (2006). As consumers flock to high bandwidth, e-retailers shake, rattle and roll. *Internet Retailer.* Retrieved July 2013 from http://www.internetretailer.com/article.asp?id=17145

Demirci Orel, F., & Kara, A. (2014). Supermarket self-checkout service quality, customer satisfaction, and loyalty: Empirical evidence from an emerging market. *Journal of Retailing and Consumer Services, 21*(2), 118–129. doi:10.1016/j.jretconser.2013.07.002

Demoulin, N. T. M. (2011). Music congruency in a service setting: The mediating role of emotional and cognitive responses. *Journal of Retailing and Consumer Services, 18*(1), 10–18. doi:10.1016/j.jretconser.2010.08.007

Dennis, C. (2005). *Objects of desire: Consumer behavior in shopping centre choices.* Basingstoke, UK: Palgrave Macmillan.

Dennis, C., Michon, R., Brakus, J., Newman, A., & Alamanos, E. (2012). New insights into the impact of digital signage as a retail atmospheric tool. *Journal of Consumer Behaviour, 11*(6), 454–466. doi:10.1002/cb.1394

Dennis, C., Murphy, J., Marsland, D., Cockett, W., & Patel, T. (2002). Measuring image: Mall case studies. *International Review of Retail, Distribution and Consumer Research, 12*(4), 353–373. doi:10.1080/09593960210151153

Dennis, C., Newman, A., Michon, R., Brakus, J., & Wright, L. T. (2010). The mediating effects of perception and emotion: Digital signage in mall atmospherics. *Journal of Retailing and Consumer Services, 17*(3), 205–215. doi:10.1016/j.jretconser.2010.03.009

Derbaix, C. (1983). Perceived risk and risk relievers: An empirical investigation. *Journal of Economic Psychology, 3*(March), 19–38. doi:10.1016/0167-4870(83)90056-9

Deshpande, R. (1999). *Developing a market orientation.* Thousand Oaks, CA: SAGE.

Dholakia, U. M., Bagozzi, R. P., & Pearo, L. K. (2004). A social influence model of consumer participation in network- and small-group-based virtual communities. *International Journal of Research in Marketing, 21*(3), 241–263. doi:10.1016/j.ijresmar.2003.12.004

Dholakia, U. M., Kahn, B. E., Reeves, R., Rindfleish, A., Stewart, D., & Taylor, E. (2010). Consumer behavior in a multichannel, multimedia retailing environment. *Journal of Interactive Marketing, 24*(2), 86–95. doi:10.1016/j.intmar.2010.02.005

Diamond, J., & Diamond, E. (2007). *Contemporary visual merchandising and environmental design.* Prentice Hall.

Dibb, S. (1998). Market segmentation: Strategies for success. *Marketing Intelligence & Planning, 16*(7), 394–406. doi:10.1108/02634509810244390

Dibb, S., Simkin, L., Pride, W. M., & Ferrell, O. C. (2006). *Marketing: Concepts and strategies*. Boston, MA: Houghton Mifflin.

Dickerson, K. G. (2003). *Inside the fashion business* (7th ed.). Upper Saddle River, NJ: Prentice Hall.

Dickinger, A., & Kleijnen, M. (2008). Coupons going wireless: Determinants of consumer intentions to redeem mobile coupons. *Journal of Interactive Marketing, 22*(3), 23–39. doi:10.1002/dir.20115

Diffina, J. (2010). Cloud collaboration - Using Microsoft SharePoint as a tool to enhance access services. *Journal of Library Administration, 50*(5-6), 570–580. doi:10.1080/01930826.2010.488619

Di-Masi, P. (2000). *Defining entrepreneurship.* Global Development Research Centre. Retrieved June 06, 2014, from http://www.gdrc.org/icm/micro/define-micro.html

Dinh, H. Q., Walker, N., & Hodges, L. (1999). Evaluating the importance of multi-sensory input on memory and the sense of presence in virtual environments. In *Proceedings of the IEEE Virtual Reality Conference 1999* (pp. 222–228). IEEE. doi:10.1109/VR.1999.756955

Dobler, C. & Sollbach, M., (2003). The metro group takes responsibility for sustainable development: Examples of good practice. *UNEP Industry and Environment, 26*(1), 20-22.

Doherty, A. M. (2000). Factors influencing international retailers market entry mode. *Journal of Marketing Management, 16*(1), 223–245. doi:10.1362/026725700785100514

Doherty, A. M. (2007). The internationalisation of retailing: Factors influencing the choice of franchising as a market entry method. *International Journal of Service Industry Management, 18*(2), 184–205. doi:10.1108/09564230710737826

Doms, M. E., Jarmin, R. S., & Klimek, S. D. (2004). Information technology investment and firm performance in US retail trade. *Economics of Innovation and New Technology, 13*(7), 595–613. doi:10.1080/1043859042000201911

Donovan, R. J., & Rossiter, J. (1982). Store atmosphere: An environmental psychology approach. *Journal of Retailing, 58*(1), 34–57.

Donovan, R. J., Rossiter, J., Marcoolyn, G., & Nesdale, A. (1994). Store atmosphere and purchasing behavior. *Journal of Retailing, 70*(3), 283–294. doi:10.1016/0022-4359(94)90037-X

Dowling, G. R. (1986). Perceived risk: The concept and its measurement. *Psychology and Marketing, 3*(3), 193–210. doi:10.1002/mar.4220030307

Dowling, G. R., & Staelin, R. (1994). A model of perceived risk and intended risk-handling activity. *The Journal of Consumer Research, 21*(1), 119–134. doi:10.1086/209386

Drapers. (2012). *Technology in fashion.* Retrieved November 20, 2013, from http://www.drapersonline.com/news/news-headlines/technology-in-fashion/

Drucker, P. (1954). *The practice of management.* New York: Harper.

Ducoffe, R. H. (1996). Advertising value and advertising on the web. *Journal of Advertising Research, 36*(5), 21–35.

Dudley, J. T., Pouliot, Y., Chen, R., Morgan, A. A., & Butte, A. J. (2010). Translational bioinformatics in the cloud - An affordable alternative. *Genome Medicine, 2*(8), 51–57. doi:10.1186/gm172 PMID:20691073

Duncan, E., Hazan, E., & Roche, K. (2013). *IConsumer: Digital consumers altering the value chain.* Retrieved from www.mckinsey.com

Duncan, T., & Moriarty, S. (2006). How integrated marketing communication's "touchpoints" can operationalize the service dominant logic. In R.F. Lusch & S.L. Vargo (Eds.), The service-dominant logic of marketing (pp. 236-244). New York: M.E. Sharpe.

Durieu, X. (2003). How Europe's retail sector helps promote sustainable production and consumption. *UNEP Industry and Environment, 26*(1), 7–9.

Dutot, V., Bergeron, F., & Raymond, L. (2014). Information management for the internationalization of SMEs: An exploratory study based on a strategic alignment perspective. *International Journal of Information Management, 34*(5), 672–681. doi:10.1016/j.ijinfomgt.2014.06.006

Eckefeld, B. (2005). What does RFID do for the consumer? *Communications of the ACM, 48*(9), 77–79. doi:10.1145/1081992.1082024

Edvardsson, B., Enquist, B., & Johnston, R. (2003). Cocreating customer value through hyperreality in the prepurchase service experience. *Journal of Service Research*, *10*(10), 1–13.

Edvardsson, B., Kristensson, P., Magnusson, P., & Sundstrom, R. (2012). Customer integration within service development - A review of methods and an analysis of insitu and exsitu contributions. *Technovation*, *32*(7-8), 419–429. doi:10.1016/j.technovation.2011.04.006

Eichenbaum, H. (2000). A cortical-hippocampal system for declarative memory. *Nature Reviews. Neuroscience*, *1*(1), 41–50. doi:10.1038/35036213 PMID:11252767

Eisenhardt, K., & Martin, J. (2000). Dynamic capabilities: What are they? *Strategic Management Journal*, *21*(10-11), 1105–1121. doi:10.1002/1097-0266(200010/11)21:10/11<1105::AID-SMJ133>3.0.CO;2-E

Eisingerich, A. B., & Rubera, G. (2010). Drivers of brand commitment: A cross-national investigation. *Journal of International Marketing*, *18*(2), 64–79. doi:10.1509/jimk.18.2.64

El Kamel, L., & Rigaux-Bricmont, B. (2011). Les apports du postmodernisme à l'analyse des univers virtuels comme expérience de consummation: Cas de Second Life. *Recherche et Applications en Marketing*, *26*(3), 71–92. doi:10.1177/076737011102600304

Elg, U. (2003). Retail market orientation: A preliminary framework. *International Journal of Retail & Distribution Management*, *31*(2), 107–117. doi:10.1108/09590550310462001

Elliott, R., Dolan, R. J., & Frith, C. D. (2000). Dissociable functions in the medial and lateral orbitofrontal cortex: Evidence from human neuroimaging studies. *Cereb Cortex*, *10*(3), 308–317. doi:10.1093/cercor/10.3.308 PMID:10731225

Elliott, S., Twynam, B., & Connell, S. (2012). *Building for breakthroughs: The leadership of innovation in UK retail*. Los Angeles, CA: Korn/Ferry Institute.

Ellis, B., & Kelly, S. (1992). Competitive advantage in retailing. *International Review of Retail, Distribution and Consumer Research*, *2*(2), 381–396. doi:10.1080/09593969200000014

Ellis, P., Davies, H., & Wong, A. (2011). Export intensity and marketing in transition economies: Evidence from China. *Industrial Marketing Management*, *40*(4), 593–602. doi:10.1016/j.indmarman.2010.10.003

Ellis, S. R. (1996). Presence of mind: A reaction to Thomas Sheridan's "Further musings on the psychophysics of presence". *Presence (Cambridge, Mass.)*, *5*(2), 247–25. PMID:11539412

Ellis, S. R., Dorighi, N. S., Menges, B. M., Adelstein, B. D., & Jacoby, R. H. (1997). In search of equivalence classes in subjective scales of reality. In M. J. Smith, G. Salvendy, & R. J. Koubek (Eds.), *Design of computing systems: Advances in human factors ergonomics* (pp. 873–876). Elsevier.

Ellram, L. M. (1996). The use of the case study method in logistics research. *Journal of Business Logistics, 17*(2), 93-138.

eMarketer. (2012). *Men top women in mobile buying*. Retrieved July 4 2014, from http://www.emarketer.com/Article/Men-Top-Women-Mobile-Buying/1009374

eMarketer. (2013). *How does wi-fi affect mobile shoppers?* Retrieved from http://www.emarketer.com/Article/How-Wi-Fi-Affect-Mobile-Shoppers/1009728

eMarketer. (2014). *Smartphone users worldwide will total 1.75 billion in 2014*. Retrieved July 7, 2014, from http://www.emarketer.com/Article/Smartphone-Users-Worldwide-Will-Total-175-Billion-2014/1010536

Engel, J. F., Blackwell, R. D., & Miniard, P. W. (2001). *Consumer behavior* (9th ed.). The Dryden Press, Harcourt Brace College Publishers.

Engel, J., Tran, C., Pavlek, N., Blankenberg, N., & Meyer, A. (2013). The impact of friendliness on brand perception. *Marketing Review St. Gallen*, *30*(6), 82–95. doi:10.1365/s11621-013-0302-2

Enkel, E., & Heil, S. (2014). Preparing for distant collaboration: Antecedents to potential absorptive capacity in cross-industry innovation. *Technovation*, *34*(4), 242–260. doi:10.1016/j.technovation.2014.01.010

Erdem, T., Swait, J., & Valenzuela, A. (2006). Brands as signals: A cross country validation study. *Journal of Marketing*, *70*(1), 34–49. doi:10.1509/jmkg.2006.70.1.34

Ernst and Young. (2001). *Global online retailing*. Retrieved November 20, 2013, from https://www2.eycom.ch/publications/items/globalonlineretailing/de.pdf

Eroglu, S., Machleit, K., & Davis, L. (2003). Empirical testing of a model of online store atmospherics and shoppers responses. *Psychology and Marketing*, *20*(2), 139–150. doi:10.1002/mar.10064

Esch, F. R., Moll, T., Schmitt, B., Elger, C. E., Neuhaus, C., & Weber, B. (2012). Brands on the brain. Do consumers use declarative information or experienced emotions to evaluate brands? *Journal of Consumer Psychology*, *22*(1), 75–85. doi:10.1016/j.jcps.2010.08.004

Euromonitor International. (2009). *Global retailing: New concepts in retailing: The thin line between success and failure*. London: Euromonitor International.

European Commission. (2006). The long-term sustainability of public finances in the European Union. *European Economy, 4*. Retrieved August 30, 2014, from http://ec.europa.eu/economy_finance/publications/publication7903_en.pdf

European Commission. (2014). *Six perspectives on retail innovation*. Retrieved August 08, 2014, from http://ec.europa.eu/research/innovation-union/pdf/Six_perspectives_on_Retail_Innovation_EG_on%20Retail_Sector_Innovation_web.pdf

Faber, J., & Hesen, A. (2004). Innovation capabilities of European nations: Cross-national analyses of patents and sales of product innovations. *Research Policy*, *33*(2), 193–207. doi:10.1016/S0048-7333(03)00122-7

Fadılolu, M. M., Karaşan, O. E., & Pınar, M. C. (2010). A model and case study for efficient shelf usage and assortment analysis. *Annals of Operations Research*, *180*(1), 105–124. doi:10.1007/s10479-008-0497-9

Fagan, M. H., Neill, S., & Wooldridge, B. R. (2008). Exploring the intention to use computers: An empirical investigation of the role of intrinsic motivation, extrinsic motivation, and perceived ease of use. *Journal of Computer Information Systems*, *48*(3), 405–426.

Falk, T., Schepers, J., Hammerschmidt, M., & Bauer, H. (2007). Identifying cross-channel dissynergies for multichannel service providers. *Journal of Service Research*, *10*(2), 143–160. doi:10.1177/1094670507306683

Fassnacht, M., & Husseini, S. E. (2013). EDLP versus Hi–Lo pricing strategies in retailing—A state of the art article. *Journal of Business Economics*, *83*(3), 259–289. doi:10.1007/s11573-012-0648-y

Feige, A., Wallbaum, H., Janser, M., & Windlinger, L. (2013). Impact of sustainable office buildings on occupant's comfort and productivity. *Journal of Corporate Real Estate*, *15*(1), 7–34. doi:10.1108/JCRE-01-2013-0004

Feige, A., Wallbaum, H., & Krank, S. (2011). Harnessing stakeholder motivation: Towards a Swiss sustainable building sector. *Building Research and Information*, *39*(5), 504–517. doi:10.1080/09613218.2011.589788

Feinerer, I., & Hornik, K. (2013). Text mining package tm for R. *CRAN Repository*. Retrieved from: http://tm.r-forge.r-project.org

Fernie, J., Fernie, S., & Moore, C. M. (2003). *Principles of retailing*. Oxford, UK: Butterworth-Heinemann.

Fields, H. L., Hjelmstad, G. O., Margolis, E. B., & Nicola, S. M. (2007). Ventral tegmental area neurons in learned appetitive behavior and positive reinforcement. *Annual Review of Neuroscience*, *30*(1), 289–316. doi:10.1146/annurev.neuro.30.051606.094341 PMID:17376009

Finkelstein, S., & Hambrick, D. (1990). Top management team tenure and organizational outcomes: The moderating role of managerial discretion. *Administrative Science Quarterly*, *35*(3), 484–503. doi:10.2307/2393314

Fiore, A. M. (2008). The digital consumer: Valuable partner for product development and production. *Clothing & Textiles Research Journal*, *26*(2), 177–190. doi:10.1177/0887302X07306848

Firat, A. F., & Venkatesh, A. (1995). Liberatory postmodernism and the reenchantment of consumption. *The Journal of Consumer Research*, *22*(3), 239–267. doi:10.1086/209448

Fishbein, M., & Azjen, I. (1975). *Belief, attitude, intention and behavior: An introduction to theory and research*. Reading, MA: Addison-Wesley.

Flach, J. M., & Holden, J. G. (1998). The reality of experience. *Presence (Cambridge, Mass.)*, *7*(1), 90–95. doi:10.1162/105474698565550

Flanagan, J. C. (1954). The critical incident technique. *Psychological Bulletin*, *51*(4), 327–358. doi:10.1037/h0061470 PMID:13177800

Fleenor, D. G. (2007, November). Magic mirror on the wall: Fitting room tool offers LP, service benefits. *Stores*, L14-L16.

Foley, J. (2014). *10 technology trends that will revolutionize retail*. Retrieved August 08, 2014, from at http://www.forbes.com/sites/oracle/2014/01/13/10-technology-trends-that-will-revolutionize-retail/

Fornell, C., & Bookstein, F. L. (1982). Two structural equation models: LISREL and PLS applied to consumer exit-voice theory. *JMR, Journal of Marketing Research*, *19*(4), 440–452. doi:10.2307/3151718

Fornell, C., & Larcker, D. (1981). Evaluating structural equation models with unobservable variables and measurement error. *JMR, Journal of Marketing Research*, *18*(1), 39–50. doi:10.2307/3151312

Fornerino, M., Helme-Guizon, A., & Gotteland, D. (2008). Movie consumption experience and immersion: Impact on satisfaction. *Recherche et Applications en Marketing*, *23*(3), 93–111. doi:10.1177/205157070802300306

Forum for the Future. (2009). *Sustainability trends in European retail*. Retrieved June 30, 2014, from https://www.forumforthefuture.org/sites/default/files/images/Forum/Documents/Sustainability_trends_in_European_retail_Sept09.pdf

Frasquet, M., Gil, I., & Mollá, A. (2001). Shopping-centre selection modelling: A segmentation approach. *International Review of Retail, Distribution and Consumer Research*, *11*(1), 23–38. doi:10.1080/09593960122279

Frochot, I., & Morrison, A. M. (2001). Benefit segmentation: A review of its applications to travel and tourism research. *Journal of Travel & Tourism Marketing*, *9*(4), 21–45. doi:10.1300/J073v09n04_02

Froehle, C. M. (2006). Service personnel, technology, and their interaction in influencing customer satisfaction. *Decision Sciences*, *37*(1), 5–38. doi:10.1111/j.1540-5414.2006.00108.x

Froehle, C. M., & Roth, A. V. (2004). New measurement scales for evaluating perceptions of the technology-mediated customer service experience. *Journal of Operations Management*, *22*(1), 1–21. doi:10.1016/j.jom.2003.12.004

Fuller, J., Hutter, K., & Faullant, R. (2011). Why cocreation experience matters? Creative experience and its impact on the quantity and quality of creative contributions. *R & D Management*, *41*(3), 259–273. doi:10.1111/j.1467-9310.2011.00640.x

Gainer, B., & Padanyi, P. (2002). Applying the marketing concept to cultural organisations: Nonprofit, empirical study of the relationship between market orientation and performance. *Journal of and Voluntary Sector Marketing*, *7*(2), 182–193. doi:10.1002/nvsm.178

Gajjar, H. K., & Adil, G. K. (2010). A piecewise linearization for retail shelf space allocation problem and a local search heuristic. *Annals of Operations Research*, *179*(1), 149–167. doi:10.1007/s10479-008-0455-6

Galloway, S. (2013). *L2 digital IQ index: Fashion*. Retrieved July 24, 2014 from http://www.l2thinktank.com/research/fashion-2013

Ganesan, S., George, M., Jap, S., Palmatier, R. W., & Weitz, B. (2009). Supply chain management and retailer performance: Emerging trends, issues, and implications for research and practice. *Journal of Retailing*, *85*(1), 84–94. doi:10.1016/j.jretai.2008.12.001

Ganglmair-Wooliscroft, A., & Lawson, R. (2012). Subjective wellbeing and its influence on consumer sentiment towards marketing: A New Zealand example. *Journal of Happiness Studies*, *13*(1), 149–166. doi:10.1007/s10902-011-9255-9

Ganter, A., & Hecker, A. (2014). Configurational paths to organizational innovation: Qualitative comparative analyses of antecedents and contingencies. *Journal of Business Research*, *67*(6), 1285–1292. doi:10.1016/j.jbusres.2013.03.004

Garau, M., Friedman, D., Ritter Weidenfeld, H., Antley, A., Brogni, A., & Slater, M. (2008). Temporal and spatial variations in presence: Qualitative analysis in interviews from an experiment on breaks in presence. *Presence (Cambridge, Mass.)*, *17*(3), 293–309. doi:10.1162/pres.17.3.293

Garcia, R., & Calantone, R. (2002). A critical look at technological innovation typology and innovation terminology: A literature review. *Journal of Product Innovation Management, 19*(2), 110–132. doi:10.1016/S0737-6782(01)00132-1

Garnier, M., & Poncin, I. (2013). *Identification to the avatar in a commercial 3D virtual world: A dynamic perspective.* Lille, France: SKEMA Research Center.

Gartner. (2014). *Agenda overview for retail 2014.* Retrieved July 20, 2014 from https://www.gartner.com/doc/2643719?ref=clientFriendlyURL

Gatignon, H., Tushman, M. L., Smith, W., & Anderson, P. (2002). A structural approach to assessing innovation: Construct development of innovation locus, type, and characteristics. *Management Science, 48*(September), 1103–1122. doi:10.1287/mnsc.48.9.1103.174

Gatignon, H., & Xuereb, J. (1997). Strategic orientation of the firm and new product performance. *JMR, Journal of Marketing Research, 34*(February), 77–90. doi:10.2307/3152066

Gaur, A. S., Kumar, V., & Singh, D. (2014). Institutions, resources, and internationalization of emerging economy firms. *Journal of World Business, 49*(1), 12–20. doi:10.1016/j.jwb.2013.04.002

Gefen, D., Karahanna, E., & Straub, D. W. (2003). Trust and TAM in online shopping: An integrated model. *Management Information Systems Quarterly, 27*(1), 51–90.

Gelderman, C. J., Ghijsen, P. W. T., & van Diemen, R. (2011). Choosing self-service technologies or interpersonal services - The impact of situational factors and technology-related attitudes. *Journal of Retailing and Consumer Services, 18*(5), 414–421. doi:10.1016/j.jretconser.2011.06.003

Gemaba - Gesellschaft für Stuktur- und Betriebsanalyse. (2013). *Baumarkt-Strukturuntersuchung 2013.* Retrieved December 16, 2013 from http://www.gemaba.de/Baumarkte2013.pdf

Gerbing, D. W., & Hamilton, J. G. (1996). Viability of exploratory factor analysis as a precursor to confirmatory factor analysis. *Structural Equation Modeling, 3*(1), 62–72. doi:10.1080/10705519609540030

Gereffi, G. (1999). International trade and industrial upgrading in the apparel commodity chain. *Journal of International Economics, 48*(1), 37–70. doi:10.1016/S0022-1996(98)00075-0

Gerwin, D., & Barrowman, N. (2002). An evaluation of research on integrated product development. *Management Science, 48*(June), 938–953. doi:10.1287/mnsc.48.7.938.2818

Gibb, A. (2000). Corporate restructuring and entrepreneurship: What can large organisations learn from small? *Enterprise and Innovation Management Studies, 1*(1), 19–35. doi:10.1080/146324400363509

Gilboa, S. (2009). A segmentation study of Israeli mall consumers. *Journal of Retailing and Consumer Services, 16*(2), 135–144. doi:10.1016/j.jretconser.2008.11.001

Gilmore, A., Kraus, S., O'Dwyer, M., & Miles, M. (2012). Editorial: Strategic marketing management in small and medium-sized enterprises. *The International Entrepreneurship and Management Journal, 8*(2), 141–143. doi:10.1007/s11365-011-0175-2

Gil-Saura, I., Berenguer-Congri, G., & Ruiz-Molina, M. (2009). Information and communication technology in retailing: A cross-industry comparison. *Journal of Retailing and Consumer Services, 16*(3), 232–238. doi:10.1016/j.jretconser.2008.11.018

Gong, W., & Maddox, L. (2011). Online buying decisions in China. *The Journal of American Academy of Business, 17*(1), 43–50.

Gonsch, J., Klein, R., Neugebauer, M., & Steinhardt, C. (2013). Dynamic pricing with strategic customers. *Journal of Business Economics, 83*(5), 505–549. doi:10.1007/s11573-013-0663-7

Gopal, A., Bostrom, R. P., & Chin, W. W. (1992). Applying adaptive structuration theory to investigate the process of group support systems use. *Journal of Management Information Systems, 9*(3), 45–69.

Graham, M. (2011). Cloud collaboration - Peer-production and the engineering of the internet. In S. Brunn (Ed.), *Engineering earth* (pp. 67–83). Berlin: Springer. doi:10.1007/978-90-481-9920-4_5

Graillot, L. (2005). Réalités (ou apparences?) de l'hyper-réalité: Une application au cas du tourisme de loisirs. *Recherche et Applications en Marketing, 20*(1), 43–63. doi:10.1177/076737010502000103

Gram, R. (2002). *Contemporary strategy analysis* (4th ed.). Oxford, UK: Blackwell.

Grantcharov, T. P., Kristiansen, V. B., Bendix, J., Bardram, L., Rosenberg, J., & Funch-Jensen, P. (2004). Randomized clinical trial of virtual reality simulation for laparoscopic skills training. *British Journal of Surgery, 91*(2), 146–150. doi:10.1002/bjs.4407 PMID:14760660

Grewal, D., Ailawadi, K. L., Gauri, D., Hall, K., Kopalle, P., & Robertson, J. R. (2011). Innovations in retail pricing and promotions. *Journal of Retailing, 87S*, S43–S52. doi:10.1016/j.jretai.2011.04.008

Grewal, D., Krishnan, R., Levy, M., & Munger, J. (2010). Retail success and key drivers. In M. Krafft & M. K. Mantrala (Eds.), *Retailing in the 21st century* (pp. 15–30). Berlin: Springer. doi:10.1007/978-3-540-72003-4_2

Grewal, D., & Levy, M. (2009). Emerging issues in retailing research. *Journal of Retailing, 85*(4), 522–526. doi:10.1016/j.jretai.2009.09.007

Griffiths, A., Robinson, L. A., & Willett, P. (1984). Hierarchic agglomerative clustering methods for automatic document classification. *The Journal of Documentation, 40*(3), 175–205. doi:10.1108/eb026764

Grimm, C., & Smith, K. (1991). Management and organizational change: A note on the railroad industry. *Strategic Management Journal, 12*(7), 557–562. doi:10.1002/smj.4250120708

Grönroos, C. (1993). Quality comes to service. In E. E. Scheuing & W. F. Christopher (Eds.), *Service quality handbook* (pp. 17–24). New York, NY: American Management Association.

Gronroos, C. (1994). From marketing mix to relationship marketing: Towards a paradigm shift in marketing. *Journal of Management Decision, 32*(2), 4–20. doi:10.1108/00251749410054774

Gruner, R. L., Homburg, C., & Lukas, B. A. (2014). Firm-hosted online brand communities and new product success. *Journal of the Academy of Marketing Science, 42*(1), 29–48. doi:10.1007/s11747-013-0334-9

Guercini, S., & Runfola, A. (2010). Business networks and retail internationalization: A case analysis in the fashion industry. *Industrial Marketing Management, 39*(6), 908–916. doi:10.1016/j.indmarman.2010.06.010

Guillen, M. F., & Garcia-Canal, E. (2009). The American model of the multinational firm and the "new" multinationals from emerging economies. *The Academy of Management Perspectives, 23*(2), 23–35. doi:10.5465/AMP.2009.39985538

Gupta, A., Su, B., & Walter, Z. (2004). Risk profile and consumer shopping behavior in electronic and traditional channels. *Decision Support Systems, 38*(3), 347–367. doi:10.1016/j.dss.2003.08.002

Gurusamy, K. S., Aggarwal, R., Palanivelu, L., & Davidson, B. R. (2009). Virtual reality training for surgical trainees in laparoscopic surgery. *Cochrane Database of Systematic Reviews, 1*, 1–74. PMID:19160288

Güven, S., Oda, O., Podlaseck, M., Stavropoulos, H., Kolluri, S., & Pingali, G. (2009). Social mobile augmented reality for retail. In *Proceedings of the Conference of Pervasive Computing and Communications (PerCom 2009)*. Academic Press.

Habib, R., Nyberg, L., & Tulving, E. (2003). Hemispheric asymmetries of memory: The HERA model revisited. *Trends in Cognitive Sciences, 7*(6), 241–245. doi:10.1016/S1364-6613(03)00110-4 PMID:12804689

Haenlein, M., & Kaplan, A. M. (2009). Flagship brand stores within virtual worlds: The impact of virtual store exposure on real-life attitude toward the brand and purchase intent. *Recherche et Applications en Marketing, 24*(3), 57–79. doi:10.1177/076737010902400304

Hagedoorn, J. (2002). Interfirm R&D partnerships: An overview of major trends and patterns since 1960. *Research Policy, 31*(4), 477–492. doi:10.1016/S0048-7333(01)00120-2

Hair, J. F., Black, W. C., Babin, B. J., Anderson, R. E., & Tatham, R. L. (2006). *Multivariate data analysis* (6th ed.). Upper Saddle River, NJ: Prentice Hall.

Han, B. J., Jung, I. Y., Kim, K. H., Lee, D. K., Rho, S., & Jeong, C. S. (2013). Cloud-based active content collaboration platform using multimedia processing. *EURASIP Journal on Wireless Communications and Networking*, *2013*(63), 63–76. doi:10.1186/1687-1499-2013-63

Han, J. K., Kim, N., & Srivastava, R. K. (1998). Market orientation and organizational performance: Is innovation a missing link? *Journal of Marketing*, *62*(4), 30–45. doi:10.2307/1252285

Hansen, J. M., McDonald, R. E., & Mitchell, R. K. (2013). Competence resource specialization, causal ambiguity, and the creation and decay of competitiveness: The role of marketing strategy in new product performance and shareholder value. *Journal of the Academy of Marketing Science*, *41*(3), 300–319. doi:10.1007/s11747-012-0316-3

Harmon-Jones, E. (2003). Early career award. Clarifying the emotive functions of asymmetrical frontal cortical activity. *Psychophysiology*, *40*(6), 838–848. doi:10.1111/1469-8986.00121 PMID:14986837

Harrow, C., Lea-Greenwood, G., & Otieno, R. (2005). The unhappy shopper a retail experience: Exploring fashion fit and affordability. *International Journal of Retail & Distribution Management*, *33*(4), 298–309. doi:10.1108/09590550510593220

Hartman, K., & Spiro, R. (2005). Recapturing store image in customer-based store equity: A construct conceptualization. *Journal of Business Research*, *58*(8), 1112–1120. doi:10.1016/j.jbusres.2004.01.008

Hasna, A. M. (2007). Dimensions of sustainability. *Journal of Engineering for Sustainable Development: Energy Environmental Health*, *2*(1), 47–57. doi:10.1016/j.jbusvent.2010.01.002

Hassan, A. M., Kunz, M. B., Pearson, A. W., & Mohamed, F. A. (2006). Conceptualization and measurement of perceived risk in online shopping. *Marketing Management Journal*, *16*(1), 138–147.

Hausman, A. V., & Siepke, J. S. (2009). The effect of web interface features on consumer online purchase intentions. *Journal of Business Venturing*, *62*(1), 5–13.

Hausmana, A., & Stockb, J. R. (2003). Adoption and implementation of technological innovations within long-term relationships. *Journal of Business Research*, *56*(8), 681–686. doi:10.1016/S0148-2963(01)00313-7

Ha, Y., & Im, H. (2014). Determinants of mobile coupon adoption among US consumers: Assessment of gender difference. *International Journal of Retail & Distribution Management*, *42*(5), 441–459. doi:10.1108/IJRDM-08-2012-0074

Heckmann, P., Huisman, R., Kesteloo, M., & Schmaus, B. (2012). *Cross-channel integration in retail: creating a seamless customer experience*. Booz & Company.

Heinemann, G., & Schwarzl, C. (2010). *New online retailing* (1st ed.). Wiesbaden: GWV Fachverlage. doi:10.1007/978-3-8349-6378-9

Heitz-Spahn, S. (2013). Cross-channel free-riding consumer behavior in a multichannel environment: An investigation of shopping motives, sociodemographics and product categories. *Journal of Retailing and Consumer Services*, *20*(6), 570–578. doi:10.1016/j.jretconser.2013.07.006

Held, R. M., & Durlach, N. I. (1992). Telepresence. *Presence (Cambridge, Mass.)*, *1*(1), 109–112.

Helm, R., & Landschulze, S. (2013). How does consumer age affect the desire for new products and brands? A multigroup causal analysis. *Review of Managerial Science*, *7*(1), 29–59. doi:10.1007/s11846-011-0072-7

Hemphälä, J., & Magnusson, M. (2012). Networks for innovation–but what networks and what innovation? *Creativity and Innovation Management*, *21*(1), 3–16. doi:10.1111/j.1467-8691.2012.00625.x

Henseler, J., Ringle, C. M., & Sinkovics, R. R. (2009). The use of partial least squares path modeling in international marketing. In R. R. Sinkovics & P. N. Ghauri (Eds.), *Advances in international marketing* (Vol. 20, pp. 277–319). Bingley: Emerald Group Publishing. doi:10.1108/S1474-7979(2009)0000020014

Hervas-Oliver, J. L., & Sempere-Ripoll, F. (2014). Disentangling the influence of technological process and product innovations. *Journal of Business Research*, *68*(1), 109–118. doi:10.1016/j.jbusres.2014.04.010

Heskett, J. L., Sasser, W. E., & Schlesinger, L. A. (2003). *The value profit chain: Treat employees like customers and customers like employees*. New York: The Free Press.

Hessels, J., & Parker, S. C. (2013). Constraints, internationalization and growth: A cross-country analysis of European SMEs. *Journal of World Business*, *48*(1), 137–148. doi:10.1016/j.jwb.2012.06.014

Hilton, T., Hughes, T., Little, E., & Marandi, E. (2013). Adopting self-service technology to do more with less. *Journal of Services Marketing*, *27*(1), 3–12. doi:10.1108/08876041311296338

Hirschman, E. C. (1980). Innovativeness, novelty seeking, and consumer creativity. *The Journal of Consumer Research*, *7*(3), 283–295. doi:10.1086/208816

Hitt, M., Hoskisson, R., Johnson, R., & Moesel, D. (1996). The market for corporate control and firm innovation. *Academy of Management Journal*, *39*(October), 1048–1119.

Hochschild, A. R. (1983). *The managed heart*. Los Angeles, CA: University of California Press.

Hoffman, D. L., & Novak, T. P. (2009). Flow online: Lessons learned and future prospects. *Journal of Interactive Marketing*, *23*(1), 23–34. doi:10.1016/j.intmar.2008.10.003

Hoffman, D., & Novak, T. (1996). Marketing in hypermedia computer-mediated environments: Conceptual foundations. *Journal of Marketing*, *60*(3), 50–68. doi:10.2307/1251841

Hofstetter, M., & Tovar, J. (2010). Common knowledge reference price and asymmetric price adjustments. *Review of Industrial Organization*, *37*(2), 141–159. doi:10.1007/s11151-010-9261-9

Holbrook, M. B., & Hirschman, E. C. (1982). The experiential aspects of consumption: Consumer fantasies, feelings and fun. *The Journal of Consumer Research*, *9*(2), 132–140. doi:10.1086/208906

Hong, X., Wang, J., Wang, D., & Zhang, H. (2013). Decision models of closed-loop supply chain with remanufacturing under hybrid dual-channel collection. *International Journal of Advanced Manufacturing Technology*, *68*(5-8), 1851–1865. doi:10.1007/s00170-013-4982-1

Hong-Youl, H., & Kang-Hee, P. (2012). Effects of perceived quality and satisfaction on brand loyalty in China: The moderating effect of customer orientation. *African Journal of Business Management*, *6*(22), 6745–6753.

Hopfenbeck, W., Müller, M., & Peisl, T. (2001). *Wissensbasiertes management: Ansätze and strategien zur unternehmensführung in der internet ökonomie* (1. Auflage.). Landsberg/Lech: Moderne Industrie.

Hornik, K., Porter, M., & Boulton, R. (2013). Snowball: Snowball stemmers. *CRAN Repository*. Retrieved from http://CRAN.R-project.org/package=Snowball

Hoskisson, R., Johnson, R., Yiu, D., & Wan, W. (2001). Restructuring strategies of diversified business groups: Differences associated with country institutional environments. In M. A. Hitt, E. Freeman, & J. Harrison (Eds.), *The Blackwell handbook of strategy* (pp. 433–463). Oxford, UK: Blackwell Publishers.

House, R. J., Hanges, P. J., Javidan, M., Dorfman, P. W., & Gupta, V. (2004). *Culture, leadership and organizations: The GLOBE study of 62 societies*. Thousand Oaks, CA: Sage.

Hsiao, Y. C., & Chen, C. J. (2013). Branding vs. contract manufacturing: Capability, strategy, and performance. *Journal of Business and Industrial Marketing*, *28*(4), 317–334. doi:10.1108/08858621311313910

Hsieh, J. K., Hsieh, Y. C., & Tang, Y. C. (2012). Exploring the disseminating behaviors of eWOM marketing: Persuasion in online video. *Electronic Commerce Research*, *12*(2), 201–224. doi:10.1007/s10660-012-9091-y

Hsu, T., Wang, Y., & Wen, S. (2006). Using the decomposed theory of planned behavior to analyze consumer behavioral intention towards mobile text message coupons. *Journal of Targeting, Measurement, and Analysis for Marketing*, *14*(4), 309–324. doi:10.1057/palgrave.jt.5740191

Hübner, A. (2011). Framework for retail demand and supply chain planning. In A. Hübner (Ed.), *Retail category management* (pp. 15–41). Berlin: Springer Verlag. doi:10.1007/978-3-642-22477-5_2

Hughes, D. E. (2013). This ad's for you: The indirect effect of advertising perceptions on salesperson effort and performance. *Journal of the Academy of Marketing Science*, *41*(1), 1–18. doi:10.1007/s11747-011-0293-y

Hulland, J. (1999). Use of partial least squares (PLS) in strategic management research: A review of four recent studies. *Strategic Management Journal*, *20*(2), 195–204. doi:10.1002/(SICI)1097-0266(199902)20:2<195::AID-SMJ13>3.0.CO;2-7

Hult, G., Tomas, M., Ketchen, D. J., & Slater, S. F. (2005). Market orientation and performance: An integration of disparate approaches, strategic management. *Strategic Management Journal*, *26*(12), 1173–1181. doi:10.1002/smj.494

Hunt, S., & Lambe, C. J. (2000). Marketing's contribution to business strategy: Market orientation, relationship marketing and resource-advantage theory. *International Journal of Management Reviews*, *2*(1), 17–43. doi:10.1111/1468-2370.00029

Hurley, R. F., & Hult, T. M. (1998). Innovation, market orientation and organizational learning: An integration and empirical examination. *Journal of Marketing*, *62*(July), 42–54. doi:10.2307/1251742

Hutchinson, K., Quinn, B., & Alexander, N. (2006). SME retailer internationalisation: Case study evidence from British retailers. *International Marketing Review*, *23*(1), 25–53. doi:10.1108/02651330610646287

Hu, W., & Li, Y. (2012). Retail service for mixed retail and e-tail channels. *Annals of Operations Research*, *192*(1), 151–171. doi:10.1007/s10479-010-0818-7

Hyvonen, S., & Tuominen, M. (2006). Entrepreneurial innovations, market-driven intangibles and learning orientation: Critical indicators for performance advantages in SMEs. *International Journal of Management and Decision Making*, *7*(6), 643–660. doi:10.1504/IJMDM.2006.011074

Iannone, R., Ingenito, A., Martino, G., Miranda, S., Pepe, C., & Riemma, S. (2013). Merchandise and replenishment planning optimization for fashion retail. *International Journal of Engineering Business Management*, *5*, 1–14.

Ibeh, K., & Kasem, L. (2014). Internationalization's effect on marketing learning: A study of Syrian firms. *Journal of Business Research*, *67*(5), 680–685. doi:10.1016/j.jbusres.2013.11.027

IBM. (2012). *Retail 2020: Reinventing retailing-once again*. Armonk, NY: IBM Corporation.

IconNicholson. (2007) *The mall + Facebook: Try that on!* Retrieved from http://www.iconnicholson.com/nrf07/

Iglesias, O., Singh, J. J., & Batista-Foguet, J. M. (2011). The role of brand experience and affective commitment in determining brand loyalty. *Journal of Brand Management*, *18*(8), 570–582. doi:10.1057/bm.2010.58

IJsselsteijn, W. A., & de Ridder, H. (1998). *Measuring temporal variations in presence*. Ipswich, UK: British Telecom Laboratories.

Ilie, V., Van Slyke, C., Green, G., & Lou, H. (2005). Gender differences in perceptions and use of communication technologies: A diffusion of innovation approach. *Information Researches Management Journal*, *18*(3), 13–31. doi:10.4018/irmj.2005070102

Im, H., & Ha, Y. (2013). A model of permission-based marketing: Enablers and inhibitors of mobile coupon adoption. *Journal of Retailing and Consumer Services*, *20*(5), 495–503. doi:10.1016/j.jretconser.2013.05.002

Im, I., Kim, Y., & Han, H.-J. (2008). The effects of perceived risk and technology type on users' acceptance of technologies. *Information & Management*, *45*(1), 1–9. doi:10.1016/j.im.2007.03.005

Inditex. (2005). *Annual report 2005*. Retrieved from http://www.inditex.com/documents/10279/13717/Grupo_INDITEX_informe_rsc_05.pdf/7155a5ed-2ac9-4571-bc3f-c42331954316

Interbrand. (2012). *What's in store for 2012?* London: Interbrand.

Isaksen, G., & Ekvall, G. (2010). Managing for innovation: The two faces of tension in creative climates. *Creativity and Innovation Management*, *19*(2), 73–88. doi:10.1111/j.1467-8691.2010.00558.x

Ishikawa, T. (2010). Effects of retail market structure and production conditions on firm's location selections of fragmented production process. *Jahrbuch für Regionalwissenschaft*, *30*(2), 91–103. doi:10.1007/s10037-010-0044-4

Ismail, I., Hasnah, H., Ibrahim, D. N., & Mohd Isa, S. (2006). Service quality, client satisfaction, and loyalty towards audit firms. Perceptions of Malaysian public listed companies. *Managerial Auditing Journal*, *22*(7), 738–756.

Iversen, O. S., Leong, T. W., Wright, P., Gregory, J., & Bowker, G. (2012). Working with human values in design. In *Proceedings of the 12th Participatory Design Conference* (pp. 143-144). New York, NY: ACM. doi:10.1145/2348144.2348191

Jackson, J. D., Yi, M. Y., & Park, J. S. (2013). An empirical test of three mediation models for the relationship between personal innovativeness and user acceptance of technology. *Information & Management, 50*(4), 154–161. doi:10.1016/j.im.2013.02.006

Jackson, T., & Shaw, D. (2006). *The fashion handbook.* Oxon, UK: Routledge.

Jahdi, K. S., & Acikdilli, G. (2010). Marketing communications and corporate social responsibility (CSR): Marriage of convenience or shotgun wedding? *Journal of Business Ethics, 88*(1), 103–113. doi:10.1007/s10551-009-0113-1

Jain, A. K., Malhotra, N. K., & Guan, C. (2012). Positive and negative affectivity as mediators of volunteerism and service-oriented citizenship behavior and customer loyalty. *Psychology and Marketing, 29*(12), 1004–1017. doi:10.1002/mar.20582

James, F. D. (1995). Technology and innovation in retail banking distribution. *International Journal of Bank Marketing, 13*(4), 19–25. doi:10.1108/02652329510082915

Jang, S. S., & Namkung, Y. (2009). Perceived quality, emotions, and behavioral intentions: Application of an extended Mehrabian-Russell model to restaurants. *Journal of Business Research, 62*(4), 451–460. doi:10.1016/j.jbusres.2008.01.038

Jantzen, C. (2013). Experiencing and experiences: A psychological framework. In J. Sundbo & F. Sørensen (Eds.), *Handbook on the experience economy* (pp. 146–170). Cheltenham, UK: Edward Elgar. doi:10.4337/9781781004227.00013

Jarret, D. G. (1996). A shopper taxonomy for retail strategy development. *International Review of Retail, Distribution and Consumer Research, 6*(2), 196–215. doi:10.1080/09593969600000020

Jarvis, C., MacKenzie, S. B., & Podsakoff, P. M. (2003). A critical review of construct indicators and measurement model misspecification in marketing and consumer research. *The Journal of Consumer Research, 30*(2), 199–218. doi:10.1086/376806

Javadi, M., Dolatabadi, H., Nourbakhsh, M. Poursaeedi, A., & Asadollahi, A. (2012). An analysis of factors affecting on online shopping behavior of consumers. *International Journal of Marketing Studies, 4*(5), 81–98.

Jefkins, F., & Yadin, D. (2000). *Advertising.* London, UK: Financial Times/Prentice-Hall.

Jones, P., Comfort, D., & Hiller, D. (2007). What's in store? Retail marketing and corporate social responsibility. *Marketing Intelligence & Planning, 25*(1), 17–30. doi:10.1108/02634500710722371

Jørgensen, A. P., Collard, M., & Koch, C. (2010). Prototyping iPhone apps: Realistic experieces on the device. In HvannbergE.LarusdottirM.BlandfordA.GulliksenJ. (Eds.), *Proc. of 6th Nordic Conference on Human-Computer Interaction* (pp. 687-690). New York, NY: ACM Press. doi:10.1145/1868914.1869005

Joy, A., & Sherry, J. Jr. (2003). Speaking of art as embodied imaginations: A multisensory approach to understanding aesthetic experience. *The Journal of Consumer Research, 30*(2), 259–282. doi:10.1086/376802

Juniper Research. (2012). *Press release: Ten billion mobile coupons to be redeemed this year, up 50% on 2012, Juniper report finds.* Retrieved June 16, 2014 from http://www.juniperresearch.com/viewpressrelease.php?pr=361

Jun, S., Gentry, J. W., & Hyun, Y. J. (2001). Cultural adaptation of business expatriates in the host marketplace. *Journal of International Business Studies, 32*(2), 369–377. doi:10.1057/palgrave.jibs.8490958

Kahneman, D., & Tversky, A. (1979). Prospect theory: An analysis of decisions under risk. *Econometrica, 47*(2), 263–291. doi:10.2307/1914185

Kalaignanam, K., & Bahadir, S. C. (2013). Corporate brand name changes and business restructuring: Is the relationship complementary or substitutive? *Journal of the Academy of Marketing Science, 41*(4), 456–472. doi:10.1007/s11747-012-0321-6

Kallweit, K., Spreer, P., & Toporowski, W. (2014). Why do customers use self-service information technologies in retail? The mediating effect of perceived service quality. *Journal of Retailing and Consumer Services, 21*(3), 268–276. doi:10.1016/j.jretconser.2014.02.002

Kaltcheva, V., & Weitz, B. (2006). When should a retailer create an exciting store environment? *Journal of Marketing, 70*(1), 107–118. doi:10.1509/jmkg.2006.70.1.107

Kamali, N., & Loker, S. (2002). Mass customization: On-line consumer involvement in product design. *Journal of Computer-Mediated Communication, 7*(4), 1–21. doi:10.1111/j.1083-6101.2002.tb00155.x

Kara, A., Spillan, J. E., & DeShields, O. W. Jr. (2005). The effect of a market orientation on business performance: A study of smalls sized service retailers using MARKOR scale. *Journal of Small Business Management, 43*(2), 105–118. doi:10.1111/j.1540-627x.2005.00128.x

Karahanna, E., Straun, D. W., & Chervany, N. (1999). Information technology adoption across time: A cross-sectional comparison of pre-adoption and post-adoption beliefs. *Management Information Systems Quarterly, 23*(2), 183–213. doi:10.2307/249751

Karjaluoto, H., Jayawardhena, C., Kuckertz, A., & Kautonen, T. (2008). Sources of trust in permission-based mobile marketing: a cross-country comparison. In T. Kautonen & H. Karjaluoto (Eds.), *Trust and new technologies: Marketing and management on the internet and mobile media* (pp. 165–181). Northampton, MA: Edward Elgar. doi:10.4337/9781848445086.00019

Karoulis, A., Sylaiou, S., & White, M. (2006). Usability evaluation of a virtual museum interface. *Informatica, 17*(3), 363–380.

Kasemsap, K. (2013a). Practical framework: Creation of causal model of job involvement, career commitment, learning motivation, and learning transfer. *International Journal of the Computer, the Internet and Management, 21*(1), 29-35.

Kasemsap, K. (2013b). Synthesized framework: Establishing a causal model of organizational learning, knowledge management, knowledge-sharing behavior, and organizational performance. *International Journal of the Computer, the Internet and Management, 21*(2), 29-34.

Kasemsap, K. (2013c). Innovative framework: Formation of causal model of organizational culture, organizational climate, knowledge management, and job performance. *Journal of International Business Management & Research, 4*(12), 21–32.

Kasemsap, K. (2013d). Strategic business management: A practical framework and causal model of empowering leadership, team cohesion, knowledge-sharing behavior, and team performance. *Journal of Social and Development Sciences, 4*(3), 100–106.

Kasemsap, K. (2014a). The role of brand management in emerging markets. In I. Samanta (Ed.), *Strategic marketing in fragile economic conditions* (pp. 167–184). Hershey, PA: IGI Global. doi:10.4018/978-1-4666-6232-2.ch009

Kasemsap, K. (2014b). The role of social media in the knowledge-based organizations. In I. Lee (Ed.), *Integrating social media into business practice, applications, management, and models* (pp. 254–275). Hershey, PA: IGI Global. doi:10.4018/978-1-4666-6182-0.ch013

Kasemsap, K. (2014c). Constructing a unified framework and a causal model of occupational satisfaction, trainee reactions, perception of learning, and perceived training transfer. In S. Hai-Jew (Ed.), *Remote workforce training: Effective technologies and strategies* (pp. 28–52). Hershey, PA: IGI Global. doi:10.4018/978-1-4666-5137-1.ch003

Kasemsap, K. (2014d). The role of social capital in higher education institutions. In N. Baporikar (Ed.), *Handbook of research on higher education in the MENA region: Policy and practice* (pp. 119–147). Hershey, PA: IGI Global. doi:10.4018/978-1-4666-6198-1.ch007

Kasemsap, K. (2014e). The role of social networking in global business environments. In P. A. C. Smith & T. Cockburn (Eds.), *Impact of emerging digital technologies on leadership in global business* (pp. 183–201). Hershey, PA: IGI Global. doi:10.4018/978-1-4666-6134-9.ch010

Kasemsap, K. (2014f). The role of brand loyalty on CRM performance: An innovative framework for smart manufacturing. In Z. Luo (Ed.), *Smart manufacturing innovation and transformation: Interconnection and intelligence* (pp. 252–284). Hershey, PA: IGI Global. doi:10.4018/978-1-4666-5836-3.ch010

Kato, A. (2012). Productivity, returns to scale and product differentiation in the retail trade industry: An empirical analysis using Japanese firm-level data. *Journal of Productivity Analysis*, *38*(3), 345–353. doi:10.1007/s11123-011-0251-1

Katz, R. (1982). The effects of team longevity of project commitment and performance. *Administrative Science Quarterly*, *27*(1), 81–104. doi:10.2307/2392547

Keaveney, S. M. (1995). Customer switching behavior in service industry: An exploratory study. *Journal of Marketing*, *59*(2), 71–82. doi:10.2307/1252074

Keeling, K., Keeling, D., & McGoldrick, P. (2013). Retail relationships in a digital age. *Journal of Business Research*, *66*(7), 847–855. doi:10.1016/j.jbusres.2011.06.010

Keen, C., Wetzels, M., de Ruyter, K., & Feiberg, R. (2004). E-tailers versus retailers: Which factors determine consumer preferences. *Journal of Business Research*, *57*(7), 685–695. doi:10.1016/S0148-2963(02)00360-0

Keister, L. (2002). Adapting to radical change: Strategy and environment in piece rate adaption during China's transition. *Organization Science*, *13*(5), 459–474. doi:10.1287/orsc.13.5.459.7811

Keller, K. L. (1993). Conceptualizing, measuring, and managing customer-based brand equity. *Journal of Marketing*, *57*(1), 1–22. doi:10.2307/1252054

Keller, K. L. (2003). Brand synthesis: The multidimensionality of brand knowledge. *The Journal of Consumer Research*, *29*(4), 595–600. doi:10.1086/346254

Keller, K. L. (2003). *Strategic brand management: Building, measuring, and managing brand equity.* Upper Saddle River, NJ: Pearson Education.

Keller, K. L. (2010). Brand equity management in a multichannel, multimedia retail environment. *Journal of Interactive Marketing*, *24*(2), 58–70. doi:10.1016/j.intmar.2010.03.001

Kennard, M. J. (2012). Open innovation in a retail driven business environment. In *Proceedings of The XXIII ISPIM Conference 2012*. Barcelona, Spain: Academic Press.

Kent, A. M., & Brown, R. (2009). *Flagship marketing, concepts and places.* Abingdon, UK: Routledge.

Kent, T. (2003). 2D3D: Management and design perspectives on retail branding. *International Journal of Retail & Distribution Management*, *31*(3), 131–421. doi:10.1108/09590550310465503

Kent, T., & Omar, O. (2003). *Retailing.* Basingstoke, UK: Palgrave Macmillan.

Ketchen, D. J. Jr, & Shook, C. L. (1996). The application of cluster analysis in strategic management research: An analysis and critique. *Strategic Management Journal*, *17*(6), 441–458. doi:10.1002/(SICI)1097-0266(199606)17:6<441::AID-SMJ819>3.0.CO;2-G

Khalifa, M., & Shen, K. (2008). Drivers for transactional b2c m-commerce adoption: Extended theory of planned behavior. *Journal of Computer Information Systems*, *48*(3), 111–117.

Khan, A., & Manopichetwattana, V. (1989). Innovative and noninnovative small firms: Types and characteristics. *Management Science*, *35*(May), 597–606. doi:10.1287/mnsc.35.5.597

Kilcourse, B., & Rosenblum, P. (2009). *Walking the razor's edge: Managing the store experience in an economic singularity.* Miami, FL: Retail Research Systems.

Kimberly, J., & Evanisko, M. (1981). Organizational innovation: The influence of individual, organizational, and contextual factors on hospital adoption of technological and administrative innovations. *Academy of Management Journal*, *24*(4), 689–713. doi:10.2307/256170 PMID:10253688

Kim, D. J., Ferrin, D. L., & Rao, H. R. (2008). A trust-based consumer decision-making model in electronic commerce: The role of trust, perceived risk, and their antecedents. *Decision Support Systems*, *44*(2), 544–564. doi:10.1016/j.dss.2007.07.001

Kim, D., Cavusgil, S. T., & Calantone, R. J. (2006). Information system innovations and supply chain management: Channel relationships and firm performance. *Journal of the Academy of Marketing Science*, *34*(1), 40–54. doi:10.1177/0092070305281619

Kim, H. B., & Kim, W. G. (2005). The relationship between brand equity and firms' performance in luxury hotels and chain restaurants. *Tourism Management*, *26*(4), 549–560. doi:10.1016/j.tourman.2004.03.010

Kim, J., Fiore, A. M., & Lee, H.-H. (2007). Influences of online store perception, shopping enjoyment, and shopping involvement on consumer patronage behaviour towards an online retailer. *Journal of Retailing and Consumer Services*, *14*(2), 95–107. doi:10.1016/j.jretconser.2006.05.001

Kim, W. C., & Mauborgne, R. (2005). *Blue ocean strategy: How to create uncontested market space and make competition irrelevant*. Boston: Harvard Business School Press.

King, W. R., & He, J. (2006). A meta-analysis of the technology acceptance model. *Information & Management*, *43*(6), 740–755. doi:10.1016/j.im.2006.05.003

Kirchhoff, B. A. (1994). *Entrepreneurship and dynamic capitalism: The economics of business firm formation and growth*. Westport, CT: Praeger.

Kjeldskov, J., & Stage, J. (2012). Combining ethnography and object-orientation for mobile interaction design: Contextual richness and abstract models. *International Journal of Human-Computer Studies*, *70*(3), 197–217. doi:10.1016/j.ijhcs.2011.10.004

Klaus, P., & Maklan, S. (2011). Bridging the gap for destination extreme sports – a model of sports tourism customer experience. *Journal of Marketing Management*, *27*(13–14), 1341–1365. doi:10.1080/0267257X.2011.624534

Kleijnen, M., De Ruyter, K., & Wetzels, M. (2007). An assessment of value creation in mobile services delivery and the moderating role of time consciousness. *Journal of Retailing*, *83*(1), 33–46. doi:10.1016/j.jretai.2006.10.004

Klein, H. K., & Myers, M. D. (1999). A set of principles for conducting and evaluating interpretive field studies in information systems. *Management Information Systems Quarterly*, *23*(1), 67–93. doi:10.2307/249410

Klena, K. (2013). *From transactions to relationships - Connecting with a transitioning shopper*. IBM.

Klimesch, W. (1999). EEG alpha and theta oscillations reflect cognitive and memory performance: A review and analysis. *Brain Research. Brain Research Reviews*, *29*(2-3), 169–195. doi:10.1016/S0165-0173(98)00056-3 PMID:10209231

Klimesch, W., Doppelmayr, M., & Hanslmayr, S. (2006). Upper alpha ERD and absolute power: Their meaning for memory performance. *Progress in Brain Research*, *159*(1), 151–165. doi:10.1016/S0079-6123(06)59010-7 PMID:17071229

Knight, D. K., Crustinger, C., & Kim, H. (2006). The impact of retail work experience, career expectations, and job satisfaction on retail career intention. *Clothing & Textiles Research Journal*, *24*(1), 1–14. doi:10.1177/0887302X0602400101

Knowledge@Wharton. (2007, May 16). *Are your customers dissatisfied? Try checking out your salespeople*. Retrieved November 2, 2007 from http://knowledge.wharton.upenn.edu/article.cfm?articleid=1735

Knox, S., & Bickerton, D. (2003). The six conventions of corporate branding. *European Journal of Marketing*, *37*(7-8), 998–1016. doi:10.1108/03090560310477636

Knutson, B., & Bossaerts, P. (2007). Neural antecedents of financial decisions. *The Journal of Neuroscience*, *27*(31), 8174–8177. doi:10.1523/JNEUROSCI.1564-07.2007 PMID:17670962

Knutson, B., Fong, G. W., Adams, C. M., Varner, J. L., & Hommer, D. (2001). Dissociation of reward anticipation and outcome with event-related fMRI. *Neuroreport*, *12*(17), 3683–3687. doi:10.1097/00001756-200112040-00016 PMID:11726774

Knutson, B., Rick, S., Wimmer, G. E., Prelec, D., & Loewenstein, G. (2007). Neural predictors of purchases. *Neuron*, *53*(1), 147–156. doi:10.1016/j.neuron.2006.11.010 PMID:17196537

Knutson, B., & Wimmer, G. E. (2007). Splitting the difference: How does the brain code reward episodes? *Annals of the New York Academy of Sciences*, *1*(1104), 54–69. doi:10.1196/annals.1390.020 PMID:17416922

Koberg, C., Detienne, D., & Heppard, K. (2003). An empirical test of environmental, organizational, and process factors affecting incremental and radical innovation. *The Journal of High Technology Management Research*, *14*(1), 21–45. doi:10.1016/S1047-8310(03)00003-8

Koellinger, P. (2008). The relationship between technology, innovation, and firm performance-empirical evidence from e-business in Europe. *Research Policy*, *37*(8), 1317–1328. doi:10.1016/j.respol.2008.04.024

Kohli, A. K., & Jaworsky, B. J. (1990). Market orientation: The construct, research propositions, and managerial implications. *Journal of Marketing*, *54*(April), 1–8. doi:10.2307/1251866

Kollman, T., Kuckertz, A., & Kayser, I. (2012). Cannibalization or synergy? Consumers' channel selection in online-offline multichannel systems. *Journal of Retailing and Consumer Services*, *19*(2), 186–194. doi:10.1016/j.jretconser.2011.11.008

Konuş, U., Verhoef, P. C., & Neslin, S. A. (2008). Multichannel shopper segments and their covariates. *Journal of Retailing*, *84*(4), 398–413. doi:10.1016/j.jretai.2008.09.002

Kotabe, M., & Helsen, K. (2010). *Global marketing management*. New York, NY: John Wiley & Sons.

Kotler, P. (1973). Atmospherics as a marketing "tool". *Journal of Retailing*, *49*(4), 48–64.

Kotler, P., & Armstrong, G. (2006). *Principles of marketing*. Englewood Cliffs, NJ: Prentice-Hall.

Kourouthanassis, P. E., Giaglis, G. M., & Vrechopoulos, A. P. (2007). Enhancing user experience through pervasive information systems: The case of pervasive retailing. *International Journal of Information Management*, *27*(5), 319–335. doi:10.1016/j.ijinfomgt.2007.04.005

Kowatsch, T., & Maass, W. (2010). In-store consumer behavior: How mobile recommendation agents influence usage intentions, product purchases, and store preferences. *Computers in Human Behavior*, *26*(4), 697–704. doi:10.1016/j.chb.2010.01.006

Kozak, J. J., Hancock, P. A., Arthur, E. J., & Chrysler, S. T. (1993). Transfer of training from virtual reality. *Ergonomics*, *36*(7), 777–784. doi:10.1080/00140139308967941

Kozinets, R. V., Sherry, J. F., DeBerry-Spence, B., Duhachek, A., Nuttavuthisit, K., & Storm, D. (2002). Themed flagship brand stores in the new millennium: Theory, practice, prospects. *Journal of Retailing*, *78*(1), 17–29. doi:10.1016/S0022-4359(01)00063-X

Krishnan, V., & Ulrich, K. (2000). Product development decisions: A review of the literature. *Management Science*, *47*(1), 1–21. doi:10.1287/mnsc.47.1.1.10668

Kronberger, M. (2005). Another good idea from Eric. *Australian Financial Review*, *34*, 38–41.

Kuehl, R. O. (2000). *Design of experiments: Statistical principles of research design and analysis*. Pacific Grove, CA: Brooks/Cole.

Kuhn, H., & Sternbeck, M. G. (2013). Integrative retail logistics: An exploratory study. *Operations Management Research*, *6*(1-2), 2–18. doi:10.1007/s12063-012-0075-9

Kuisma, J. (2003). Practical steps towards sustainability in the retail trade: The case of Finland's Kesko. *UNEP Industry and Environment*, *26*(1), 10–12.

Kumar, V. (2010). A customer lifetime value-based approach to marketing in the multichannel, multimedia retailing environment. *Journal of Interactive Marketing*, *24*(2), 71–85. doi:10.1016/j.intmar.2010.02.008

Kumar, V., & Venkatesan, R. (2005). Who are the multichannel shoppers and how do they perform? Correlates of multichannel shopping behavior. *Journal of Interactive Marketing*, *19*(2), 44–62. doi:10.1002/dir.20034

Kurata, H., & Yue, X. (2008). Trade promotion mode choice and information sharing in fashion retail supply chains. *International Journal of Production Economics*, *114*(2), 507–519. doi:10.1016/j.ijpe.2007.05.021

Kusunoki, M. (2009). *Sustainable technology in the retail environment*. TOSHIBA TEC Europe Retail Information Systems. Retrieved June 01, 2014, from http://www.toshibatec-eu.com/upl/1/default/doc/Sustainability_15.pdf

Kusunoki, K., & Aoshima, Y. (2010). Redefining innovation as system re-definition. In H. Itami, K. Kusunoki, T. Numagami, & A. Takeishi (Eds.), *Dynamics of knowledge, corporate systems and innovation* (pp. 43–75). London: Springer. doi:10.1007/978-3-642-04480-9_3

Lai, C. S., Chiu, C. J., Yang, C. F., & Pai, D. C. (2010). The effects of corporate social responsibility on brand performance: The mediating effect of industrial brand equity and corporate reputation. *Journal of Business Ethics*, *95*(3), 457–469. doi:10.1007/s10551-010-0433-1

Lakoff, G. (1987). *Women, fire, and dangerous things.* Chicago: University of Chicago Press. doi:10.7208/chicago/9780226471013.001.0001

Lakoff, G., & Johnson, M. (1999). *Philosophy in the flesh: The embodied mind and its challenge to Western thought.* New York: Basic Books.

Landry, R., Amara, N., & Lamari, M. (2002). Does social capital determine innovation? *Technological Forecasting and Social Change, 69*(7), 681–701. doi:10.1016/S0040-1625(01)00170-6

Lang, G. (2012). Multi-channel retail. Position Paper. BEM Bordeaux Management School Centre de Recherche en Gestion de l'Ecole polytechnique (PREG CRG) – CNRS Chaire Orange Innovation et regulation des services numériques.

Langdon, D. (2007). *The costs & benefits of achieving green buildings.* Info Data. Retrieved June 30, 2014, from http://www.aecom.com/deployedfiles/Internet/Geographies/Australia-New%20Zealand/PCC%20General%20content/InfoData_Green_Buildings.pdf

Lang, G., & Bressoles, G. (2013). Economic performance and customer expectation in e-fulfillment systems: A multi-channel retailer perspective. *Supply Chain Forum: International Journal (Toronto, Ont.), 14*(1), 16–26.

Langleben, D.D., Loughead, J.W., Ruparel, K., Hakun, J.G., Busch-Winokur, S., Holloway, M.B., … Lerman, C. (2009). Reduced prefrontal and temporal processing and recall of high "sensation value" ads. *Neuroimage, 46*(1), 219-25.

Laroche, M. (2010). New developments in modeling internet consumer behavior: Introduction to the special issue. *Journal of Business Research, 63*(9/10), 915–918. doi:10.1016/j.jbusres.2008.12.013

Laroche, M., Yang, Z., McDougall, G. H., & Bergeron, J. (2005). Internet versus bricks-and-mortar retailers: An investigation into intangibility and its consequences. *Journal of Retailing, 81*(4), 251–267. doi:10.1016/j.jretai.2004.11.002

Lawton, L., & Parasuraman, A. (1980). The impact of the marketing concept on new product planning. *Journal of Marketing, 44*(1), 19–25. doi:10.2307/1250030

Lee, A. S. (1989). A scientific methodology for MIS case studies. *Management Information Systems Quarterly, 13*(1), 33–50. doi:10.2307/248698

Lee, C. H., & Rhee, B. D. (2008). Optimal guaranteed profit margins for both vendors and retailers in the fashion apparel industry. *Journal of Retailing, 84*(3), 325–333. doi:10.1016/j.jretai.2008.07.002

Lee, H. J., Cho, H. J., Xu, W., & Fairhurst, A. (2010). The influence of consumer traits and demographics on intention to use retail self-service checkouts. *Marketing Intelligence & Planning, 28*(1), 46–58. doi:10.1108/02634501011014606

Lee, H. J., Fairhurst, A. E., & Lee, M. Y. (2009). The importance of self-service kiosks in developing consumers' retail patronage intentions. *Managing Service Quality, 19*(6), 687–701. doi:10.1108/09604520911005071

Lee, H. J., Fairhurst, A., & Cho, H. J. (2013). Gender differences in consumer evaluations of service quality: Self-service kiosks in retail. *Service Industries Journal, 33*(2), 248–265. doi:10.1080/02642069.2011.614346

Lee, H. J., & Yang, K. (2013). Interpersonal service quality, self-service technology (SST) service quality, and retail patronage. *Journal of Retailing and Consumer Services, 20*(1), 51–57. doi:10.1016/j.jretconser.2012.10.005

Lee, H., Damhorst, M. L., Campbell, J. R., Loker, S., & Parsons, J. L. (2011). Consumer satisfaction with a mass customized internet apparel shopping site. *International Journal of Consumer Studies, 35*(3), 316–329. doi:10.1111/j.1470-6431.2010.00932.x

Lee, H., Fiore, A. M., & Kim, J. (2006). The role of the technology acceptance model in explaining effects of image interactivity technology on consumer responses. *International Journal of Retail & Distribution Management, 34*(8), 621–644. doi:10.1108/09590550610675949

Lee, J. S., & Back, K. J. (2010). Reexamination of attendee-based brand equity. *Tourism Management, 31*(3), 395–401. doi:10.1016/j.tourman.2009.04.006

Lee, J. Y., Rhee, G. W., & Seo, D. W. (2010). Hand gesture-based tangible interactions for manipulating virtual objects in a mixed reality environment. *International Journal of Advanced Manufacturing Technology, 51*(9-12), 1069–1082. doi:10.1007/s00170-010-2671-x

Lee, K. M. (2004). Presence explicated. *Communication Theory*, *14*(1), 27–50. doi:10.1111/j.1468-2885.2004.tb00302.x

Lee, M. L., & Pace, R. K. (2005). Spatial distribution of retail sales. *The Journal of Real Estate Finance and Economics*, *31*(1), 53–69. doi:10.1007/s11146-005-0993-5

Lee, S. M., Park, S.-H., Yoon, S. N., & Yeon, S.-J. (2007). RFID based ubiquitous commerce and consumer trust. *Industrial Management & Data Systems*, *107*(5), 605–617. doi:10.1108/02635570710750381

Lee, S.-E., Kunz, G. I., Fiore, A. M., & Campbell, J. R. (2002). Acceptance of mass customization of apparel: Merchandising issues associated with preference for product, process, and place. *Clothing & Textiles Research Journal*, *20*(3), 138–146. doi:10.1177/0887302X0202000302

Legris, P., Ingham, J., & Collerette, P. (2003). Why do people use information technology? A critical review of the technology acceptance model. *Information & Management*, *40*(3), 191–204. doi:10.1016/S0378-7206(01)00143-4

Lehtinen, U., & Lehtinen, J. R. (1991). Two approaches to service quality dimensions. *Service Industries Journal*, *11*(3), 287–303. doi:10.1080/02642069100000047

Leibenstein, H. (1966). Allocative efficiency vs. x-efficiency. *The American Economic Review*, *56*(3), 392–415.

Leonard-Barton, D., Wilson, E., & Doyle, J. (1996). Commercializing technology: Imaginative understanding of user needs. In Engines of innovation (pp. 177–208). Boston: Harvard Business.

Leonard, D. (1998). *Wellspring of knowledge: Building and sustaining the sources of innovation.* Boston, MA: Harvard Business School Press.

León, P. (2001). *Four pillars of financial sustainability.* Arlington, VA: The Nature Conservancy.

Levitt, T. (1960). Marketing myopia. *Harvard Business Review*, *38*(4), 45–57. PMID:15252891

Levy, M., & Weitz, B. A. (2012). *Retailing management.* New York, NY: McGraw-Hill.

Lewis, D. (2013). *The gender divide as seen through phones, games and apps.* Retrieved July 4, 2014, from http://www.verizonwireless.com/news/article/2013/06/the-mobile-gender-divide.html

Lewis, T. L., & Loker, S. (2007, November). *Customization, visualization, enjoyment and utility: Consumer preferences for existing apparel industry technology.* Paper presented at the Annual Meeting of the International Textile and Apparel Association, Los Angeles, CA.

Lewrick, M. (2004). *Customer relationship management: Applying relationship management to deliver more value to clients and partners of the automotive industry development centre in South Africa.* Bristol Business School, University of the West of England.

Lewrick, M. (2007). *Changes in innovation styles: Comprehensive study of the changes in innovation styles to identify the causes and effects of different influencing factors and capabilities to create a general innovation pattern.* Edinburgh Napier University.

Lewrick, M., Omar, M., & Williams, R. Jr. (2011). Market orientation and innovators' success: An exploration of the influence of customer and competitor orientation. *Journal of Technology Management & Innovation*, *6*(3), 48–61. doi:10.4067/S0718-27242011000300004

Lewrick, M., Omar, O., & Williams, R. (2010). Management of Innovations in Growth SMEs. In S. Nwankwo & T. Gbadamosi (Eds.), *Entrepreneurship marketing: Principles and practice of SME marketing.* London: Routledge.

LGA. (2012). *Financial sustainability.* Information Paper No 1. Retrieved June 01, 2014, from http://www.lga.sa.gov.au/

Lian, J.-W., & Lin, T.-M. (2008). Effects of consumer characteristics on their acceptance of online shopping: Comparisons among different product types. *Computers in Human Behavior*, *24*(1), 48–65. doi:10.1016/j.chb.2007.01.002

Light, A., & Akama, Y. (2012). The human touch: participatory practice and the role of facilitation in designing with communities. In *Proceedings Series of the 12th Participatory Design Conference* (pp. 61-70). New York, NY: ACM. doi:10.1145/2347635.2347645

Li, H., Daugherty, T., & Biocca, F. (2001). Characteristics of virtual experience in electronic commerce: A protocol analysis. *Journal of Interactive Marketing, 15*(3), 13–30. doi:10.1002/dir.1013

Li, H., Daugherty, T., & Biocca, F. (2003). The role of virtual experience in consumer learning. *Journal of Consumer Psychology, 13*(4), 395–407. doi:10.1207/S15327663JCP1304_07

Lihra, T., & Graf, R. (2007). Multi-channel communication and consumer choice in the household furniture buying process. *Direct marketing. International Journal (Toronto, Ont.), 1*(3), 146–160.

Lim, W. S., & Tan, S. J. (2009). Using brand equity to counter outsourcing opportunism: A game theoretic approach. *Marketing Letters, 20*(4), 369–383. doi:10.1007/s11002-009-9071-8

Lin, F. R., Po, R. W., & Orellan, C. V. C. (2011). Mining purchasing decision rules from service encounter data of retail chain stores. *Information Systems and e-Business Management, 9*(2), 193-221.

Ling, K. C. H., Chai, L. T., & Piew, T. H. (2010). The effects of shopping orientations, online trust and prior online purchase experience towards customers' online purchase intention. *International Business Research, 3*(3), 63–76. doi:10.5539/ibr.v3n3p63

Lin, W. B. (2013). Factors affecting high-involvement product purchasing behavior. *Quality & Quantity, 47*(6), 3113–3133. doi:10.1007/s11135-012-9707-2

Liu, H., & Davies, G. (1997). Market orientation in UK multiple retail companies: Nature and pattern. *International Journal of Service Industry Management, 8*(2), 170–187. doi:10.1108/09564239710166281

Liu, H., Lei, M., & Liu, X. (2014). Manufacturer's uniform pricing and channel choice with a retail price markup commitment strategy. *Journal of Systems Science and Systems Engineering, 23*(1), 111–126. doi:10.1007/s11518-014-5239-8

Liu, H., & McGoldrick, P. J. (1996). International retail sourcing: Trends, nature, and processes. *Journal of International Marketing, 4*(4), 9–33.

Liu, N., Ren, S., Choi, T. M., Hui, C. L., & Ng, S. F. (2013). Sales forecasting for fashion retailing service industry: A review. *Mathematical Problems in Engineering, 2013*. doi:10.1155/2013/738675

Li, X., Nukala, S., & Mohebbi, S. (2013). Game theory methodology for optimizing retailers' pricing and shelf-space allocation decisions on competing substitutable products. *International Journal of Advanced Manufacturing Technology, 68*(1-4), 375–389. doi:10.1007/s00170-013-4735-1

Lockwood, L. (2012). Consumers turn to social media for customer service. *WWD, 26*(October). Retrieved from http://www.wwd.com/media-news/digital/consumers-turn-to-social-media-for-customer-service-6455590

Loke, L., & Robertson, T. (2009). Design representations of moving bodies for interactive, motion-sensing spaces. *International Journal of Human-Computer Studies, 67*(4), 394–410. doi:10.1016/j.ijhcs.2008.11.003

Loker, S., Cowie, L., Ashdown, S., & Lewis, V. D. (2004). Female consumers' reactions to body scanning. *Clothing & Textiles Research Journal, 22*(4), 151–160. doi:10.1177/0887302X0402200401

Lombard, M., & Ditton, T. (1997). At the heart of it all: The concept of presence. *Journal of Computer-Mediated Communication, 3*(2). Retrieved from http://jcmc.indiana.edu/vol3/issue2/lombard.html

London, M. (1989). *Managing the training enterprise.* San Francisco, CA: Jossey-Bass Inc.

Lopez-Bonilla, J. M., & Lopez-Bonilla, L. M. (2014). Sensation-seeking profiles and personal innovativeness in information technology. *Social Science Computer Review, 30*(4), 434–447. doi:10.1177/0894439311427246

Louro, M., & Cunha, P. (2001). Brand management paradigms. *Journal of Marketing Management, 17*(7-8), 849–875. doi:10.1362/026725701323366845

Lucas, H. C., & Spitler, V. K. (1999). Technology use and performance: A field study of broker workstations. *Decision Sciences, 30*(2), 291–311. doi:10.1111/j.1540-5915.1999.tb01611.x

Lueg, R., Pedersen, M. M., & Clemmensen, S. N. (2013). *The role of corporate sustainability in a low-cost business model–A case study in the Scandinavian fashion industry.* New York, NY: Wiley.

Lukas, B. A., & Ferrell, O. C. (2000). The effect of market orientation on product innovation. *Journal of the Academy of Marketing Science, 28*(2), 239–247. doi:10.1177/0092070300282005

Luo, W., & de Jong, P. J. (2012). Does advertising spending really work? The intermediate role of analysts in the impact of advertising on firm value. *Journal of the Academy of Marketing Science, 40*(4), 605–624. doi:10.1007/s11747-010-0240-3

Luo, Y., & Tung, R. L. (2007). International expansion of emerging market enterprises: A springboard perspective. *Journal of International Business Studies, 38*(4), 481–498. doi:10.1057/palgrave.jibs.8400275

Lu, Y., Karpova, E. E., & Fiore, A. M. (2011). Factors influencing international fashion retailers' entry mode choice. *Journal of Fashion Marketing and Management, 15*(1), 58–75. doi:10.1108/13612021111112340

Lu, Y., & Smith, S. (2007). Augmented reality e-commerce assistant system: Trying while shopping. *Lecture Notes in Computer Science, 4551,* 643–652. doi:10.1007/978-3-540-73107-8_72

Lymperopoulos, C., Chaniotakis, I. E., & Rigopoulou, I. D. (2010). Acceptance of detergent-retail brands: The role of consumer confidence and trust. *International Journal of Retail & Distribution Management, 38*(9), 719–736. doi:10.1108/09590551011062457

Lynn, G., Morone, J. G., & Paulson, A. S. (1996). Marketing and discontinuous innovation: The probe and learn process. *California Management Review, 38*(3), 8–37. doi:10.2307/41165841

Madden, T. J., Fehle, F., & Fournier, S. (2006). Brands matter: An empirical demonstration of the creation of shareholder value through branding. *Journal of the Academy of Marketing Science, 34*(2), 224–235. doi:10.1177/0092070305283356

Maglio, P. P., Nusser, S., & Bishop, K. (2010). A service perspective on IBM's brand. *Marketing Review St. Gallen, 27*(6), 44–48. doi:10.1007/s11621-010-0098-2

Magoulès, F. (2009). *Fundamentals of grid computing: Theory, algorithms and technologies.* Chapman & Hall/CRC. doi:10.1201/9781439803684

Magrath, V., & McCormick, H. (2013). Marketing design elements of mobile fashion retail apps. *Journal of Fashion Marketing and Management, 17*(1), 115–134. doi:10.1108/13612021311305173

Malbon, J. (2013). Taking fake online consumer reviews seriously. *Journal of Consumer Policy, 36*(2), 139–157. doi:10.1007/s10603-012-9216-7

Malhotra, N. K., Kim, S. S., & Agarwal, J. (2004). Internet users' information privacy concerns (IUIPC): The construct, the scale, and a causal model. *Information Systems Research, 15*(4), 336–355. doi:10.1287/isre.1040.0032

Manasseh, T., Muller-Sarmiento, P., Reuter, H., von Faber-Castell, C., & Pallua, C. (2012). Customer inspiration – A key lever for growth in European retail. *Marketing Review St. Gallen, 29*(5), 16–21. doi:10.1365/s11621-012-0159-9

Mangiaracina, R., Perego, A., & Tumino, A. (2012). Re-designing retail stores with mobile and wireless technologies. *International Journal of Engineering Business Management, 4,* 1–11. doi:10.5772/51642

Maren, S., & Quirk, G. J. (2004). Neuronal signalling of fear memory. *Nature Reviews. Neuroscience, 5*(11), 844–852. doi:10.1038/nrn1535 PMID:15496862

Markham, S., & Griffin, A. (1998). The breakfast of champions: Associations between champions and product development environments, practices and performance. *Journal of Product Innovation Management, 15*(5), 436–454. doi:10.1016/S0737-6782(98)00010-1

Markova, S., & Petkovska-Mirčevska, T. (2013). Social media and supply chain. *Supply Chain Management, 14*(33), 89–102.

Martineau, P. (1958). The personality of the retail store. *Harvard Business Review, 36*(1), 47–55.

Martinez, J. (2011, May). *Express to offer customers opportunity to purchase entire product catalog via Facebook.* Retrieved from http://multichannelmerchant.com/from-the-wire/express-facebook-social-shopping-0503tpp9/?cid=nl_imerch

Masodier, M., & Merunka, D. (2012). Achieving brand loyalty through sponsorship: The role of fit and self-congruity. *Journal of the Academy of Marketing Science, 40*(6), 807–820. doi:10.1007/s11747-011-0285-y

Mathieson, K., & Keil, M. (1998). Beyond the interface: Ease of use and task/technology fit. *Information & Management, 34*(4), 221–230. doi:10.1016/S0378-7206(98)00058-5

Mathwick, C., Malhotra, N. K., & Rigdon, E. (2002). The effect of dynamic retail experiences on experiential perceptions of value: An Internet and catalog comparison. *Journal of Retailing, 78*(1), 51–60. doi:10.1016/S0022-4359(01)00066-5

Mathwick, C., Malhotra, N., & Rigdon, E. (2001). Experiential value: Conceptualization, measurement and application in the catalog and internet shopping environment. *Journal of Retailing, 77*(1), 39–56. doi:10.1016/S0022-4359(00)00045-2

McCarthy, E. J. (1964). *Basic marketing.* Homewood, IL: Irwin.

McColl, J., & Moore, C. (2013). Developing and testing a value chain for fashion retailers: Activities for competitive success. *Journal of the Textile Institute, 105*(2), 136–149. doi:10.1080/00405000.2013.829934

McDermott, C. M., & O'Connor, G. C. (2002). Managing radical innovation: An overview of emergent strategy issues. *Journal of Product Innovation Management, 19*(6), 424–438. doi:10.1016/S0737-6782(02)00174-1

McDermott, C., & Handfield, R. (2000). Concurrent development and strategic outsourcing: Do the rules change in breakthrough innovation? *The Journal of High Technology Management Research, 11*(1), 35–57. doi:10.1016/S1047-8310(00)00020-1

McGaugh, J. L. (2000). Memory-A century of consolidation. *Science, 287*(5451), 248–251. doi:10.1126/science.287.5451.248 PMID:10634773

McGoldrick, P. J. (2002). *Retail marketing.* London, UK: McGraw-Hill.

Mcgoldrick, P. J., & Collins, N. (2007). Multichannel retailing: Profiling the multichannel shopper. *International Review of Retail, Distribution and Consumer Research, 17*(2), 139–158. doi:10.1080/09593960701189937

McKinsey & Company. (2012). *The young and the digital: a glimpse into future market evolution.* Retrieved from: http://www.mckinsey.com/client_service/high_tech/iconsumer

McKinsey & Company. (2013). *IConsumers: Life online.* Retrieved from: https://tmt.mckinsey.com/

Meins, E., Wallbaum, H., Hardziewski, R., & Feige, A. (2010). Sustainability and property valuation: A risk-based approach. *Building Research and Information, 38*(3), 280–300. doi:10.1080/09613211003693879

Mejia, L. C., & Benjamin, J. D. (2002). What do we know about the determinants of shopping center sales? Spatial vs. non-spatial factors. *Journal of Real Estate Literature, 10*(1), 3–26.

Mencarelli, R., & Pulh, M. (2012). Web 2.0 et musées. *Decisions Marketing, 65*(65), 77–82. doi:10.7193/DM.065.77.82

Mercer, J. (2013). *E-commerce-UK.* London: Mintel.

Mercier, P., Jacobsen, R., & Veitch, A. (2012). *Retail 2020, competing in a changing industry.* Boston, MA: Boston Consulting.

Merle, A., Senecal, S., & St-Onge, A. (2012). Whether and how virtual try-on influences consumer responses to an apparel web site. *International Journal of Electronic Commerce, 16*(3), 41–64. doi:10.2753/JEC1086-4415160302

Meuter, M. L., Bitner, M. J., Ostrom, A. L., & Brown, S. W. (2005). Choosing among alternative service delivery modes: An investigation of customer trial of self-service technologies. *Journal of Marketing, 69*(2), 61–83. doi:10.1509/jmkg.69.2.61.60759

Meuter, M. L., Ostrom, A. L., Bitner, M. J., & Roundtree, R. (2003). The influence of technology anxiety on consumer use and experiences with self-service technologies. *Journal of Business Research, 56*(11), 899–906. doi:10.1016/S0148-2963(01)00276-4

Meuter, M. L., Ostrom, A. L., Roundtree, R. I., & Bitner, M. J. (2000). Self-service technologies: Understanding customer satisfaction with technology-based service encounters. *Journal of Marketing, 64*(3), 50–64. doi:10.1509/jmkg.64.3.50.18024

Meyer, A., & Goes, J. (1988). Assimilation of innovation: A multilevel contextual analysis. *Organizational Academy of Management Journal, 31*(December), 897–923.

Meza, S., & Sudhir, K. (2010). Do private labels increase retailer bargaining power? *Quantitative Marketing and Economics, 8*(3), 333–363. doi:10.1007/s11129-010-9085-9

Michis, A. A., & Markidou, A. G. (2013). Determinants of retail wine prices: Evidence from Cyprus. *Empirical Economics, 45*(1), 267–280. doi:10.1007/s00181-012-0616-y

Michon, R., Yu, H., Smith, D., & Chebat, J. (2007). The shopping experience of female fashion leaders. *International Journal of Retail & Distribution Management, 35*(6), 488–501. doi:10.1108/09590550710750359

Microsoft. (2014). *Xbox official site*. Retrieved March 18, 2014 from http://www.xbox.com

Miles, I. (2008). Patterns of innovation in service industries. *IBM Systems Journal, 47*(1), 115–128. doi:10.1147/sj.471.0115

Miller, J., & Muir, D. (2004). *The business of brands*. Chichester, UK: John Wiley & Sons.

Milligan, G. W., & Cooper, M. C. (1985). An examination of procedures for determining the number of clusters in a data set. *Psychometrika, 50*(2), 159–179. doi:10.1007/BF02294245

Mills, D. E. (2013). Countervailing power and chain stores. *Review of Industrial Organization, 42*(3), 281–295. doi:10.1007/s11151-012-9364-6

Milne, M. J., & Gray, R. (2007). Future prospects for corporate sustainability reporting. In B. O'Dwyer, J. Bebbington, & J. Unerman (Eds.), *Sustainability accounting and accountability* (pp. 184–207). Abingdon, UK: Routledge.

Minsky, M. (1980). Telepresence. *Omni (New York, N.Y.), 2*(9), 45–52.

Mintel. (2012). *Clothing retailing Europe*. London: Mintel.

Mintzberg, H. (1987). Crafting strategy. *Harvard Business Review, 65*(Jul-Aug), 66–75.

Mitchell, V.-W. (1999). Consumer perceived risk: Conceptualisations and models. *European Journal of Marketing, 33*(1/2), 163–195. doi:10.1108/03090569910249229

Mittendorf, B., Shin, J., & Yoon, D. H. (2013). Manufacturer marketing initiatives and retailer information sharing. *Quantitative Marketing and Economics, 11*(2), 263–287. doi:10.1007/s11129-013-9132-4

MMA. (2007). *Introduction to mobile coupons*. Retrieved June 14, 2014, from http://www.mmaglobal.com/files/mobilecoupons.pdf

Moiseeva, A.V. (2013). *Experience the city: Analysis of space-time behavior and spatial learning*. Eindhoven University of Technology.

Mojena, R. (1977). Hierarchical grouping methods and stopping rules: An evaluation. *The Computer Journal, 20*(4), 359–363. doi:10.1093/comjnl/20.4.359

Mollen, A., & Wilson, H. (2010). Engagement, telepresence and interactivity in online consumer experience: Reconciling scholastic and managerial perspectives. *Journal of Business Research, 63*(9/10), 919–925. doi:10.1016/j.jbusres.2009.05.014

Mollenkopf, D. A., Rabinovich, E., Laseter, T. M., & Boyer, K. K. (2007). Managing internet product returns: A focus on effective service operations. *Decision Sciences, 38*(2), 215–250. doi:10.1111/j.1540-5915.2007.00157.x

Mollet, N., & Arnaldi, B. (2006). Storytelling in virtual reality for training. *Lecture Notes in Computer Science, 3942*, 334–347. doi:10.1007/11736639_45

Montano, N., Porta, A., Cogliati, C., Costantino, G., Tobaldini, E., Casali, K. R., & Iellamo, F. (2009). Heart rate variability explored in the frequency domain: A tool to investigate the link between heart and behavior. *Neuroscience and Biobehavioral Reviews, 33*(2), 71–80. doi:10.1016/j.neubiorev.2008.07.006 PMID:18706440

Moon, J. M. D., Hossain, D., Sanders, G. L., Garrity, E. J., & Jo, S. (2013). Player commitment to massively multiplayer online role-playing games (MMORPGs): An integrated model. *International Journal of Electronic Commerce, 17*(4), 7–38. doi:10.2753/JEC1086-4415170401

Moore, C., Fernie, J., & Burt, S. (2000). Brands without boundaries: The internationalization of the designer retailer's brand. *European Journal of Marketing*, *34*(8), 919–937. doi:10.1108/03090560010331414

Moore, G. A. (1999). *Crossing the chasm: Marketing and selling high-tech products to mainstream customers* (2nd ed.). New York, NY: Harper Business.

Moore, G. C., & Benbasat, I. (1991). Development of an instrument to measure perceptions of adopting an information technology innovation. *Information Systems Research*, *2*(3), 192–222. doi:10.1287/isre.2.3.192

Moorthy, S., Ratchford, B. T., & Talukdar, D. (1997). Consumer information search revisited: Theory and empirical analysis. *The Journal of Consumer Research*, *23*(4), 263–277. doi:10.1086/209482

Moreno, R. (2006). Learning in high-tech and multimedia environments. *Current Directions in Psychological Science*, *15*(2), 63–67. doi:10.1111/j.0963-7214.2006.00408.x

Morgan, N. A. (2012). Marketing and business performance. *Journal of the Academy of Marketing Science*, *40*(1), 102–119. doi:10.1007/s11747-011-0279-9

Morrin, S., & Chebat, J. C. (2005). Person-place congruency: The interactive effects of shopper style and atmospherics on consumer expenditures. *Journal of Service Research*, *8*(2), 181–191. doi:10.1177/1094670505279420

Morrison, M., Gan, S., Dubelaar, C., & Oppewal, H. (2011). In-store music and aroma influences on shopper behavior and satisfaction. *Journal of Business Research*, *64*(6), 558–564. doi:10.1016/j.jbusres.2010.06.006

Morschett, D., Swoboda, B., & Schramm-Klein, H. (2006). Competitive strategies in retailing – An investigation of the applicability of Porter's framework for food retailers. *Journal of Retailing and Consumer Services*, *13*(4), 275–287. doi:10.1016/j.jretconser.2005.08.016

Moser, R., Schaefers, T., & Meise, J. K. (2012). Consumer preferences for product transparency in emerging markets – Lessons learned from India. *Marketing Review St. Gallen*, *29*(3), 22–27. doi:10.1365/s11621-012-0133-6

Musso, F. (2010). Innovation in marketing channels: relationships, technology, channel structure. *Symphonya: Emerging Issues in Management*, (1), 23-42.

Nahapiet, J., & Ghoshal, S. (1998). Social capital, intellectual capital, and the organizational advantage. *Academy of Management Review*, *22*(2), 242–266.

Nalca, A., Boyaci, T., & Ray, S. (2010). Competitive price-matching guarantees under imperfect store availability. *Quantitative Marketing and Economics*, *8*(3), 275–300. doi:10.1007/s11129-010-9080-1

Narver, J. C., & Slater, S. F. (1990). The effect of a market orientation on business profitability. *Journal of Marketing*, *54*(October), 20–35. doi:10.2307/1251757

Neslin, S. A., Grewal, D., Leghorn, R., Shankar, V., Teerling, M. L., Thomas, J. S., & Verhoef, P. C. (2006). Challenges and opportunities in multichannel customer management. *Journal of Service Research*, *9*(2), 95–112. doi:10.1177/1094670506293559

Neslin, S., & Shankar, V. (2009). Key issues in multichannel customer management: Current knowledge and future directions. *Journal of Interactive Marketing*, *23*(1), 70–81. doi:10.1016/j.intmar.2008.10.005

Neudecker, N., Hupp, O., Stein, A., & Schuster, H. (2012). Is your brand a one-night stand? Managing consumer-brand relationships. *Marketing Review St. Gallen*, *30*(6), 22–33. doi:10.1365/s11621-013-0297-8

Newcom Research. (2013). *Social media onderzoek 2013*. Retrieved on 26 February 2013, from http://newcomresearch.nl/socialmedia (Dutch).

Newman, A., Dennis, C., & Zaman, S. (2006, Fall). Marketing images and consumers' experiences in selling environments. *Marketing Management Journal*, 515-599.

Newman, A., Dennis, C., Wright, L. T., & King, T. (2010). 'Shoppers' experiences of digital signage – A cross-national qualitative study. *Journal of Digital Contents Technology and its Applications*, *4*(7), 50-57.

Newman, A. J., & Patel, D. (2004). The marketing directions of fashion retailers. *European Journal of Marketing*, *38*(7), 770–789. doi:10.1108/03090560410539249

Nguyen, T. D., Barrett, N. J., & Miller, K. E. (2011). Brand loyalty in emerging markets. *Marketing Intelligence & Planning*, *29*(3), 222–232. doi:10.1108/02634501111129211

Nicholson, M., Clarke, I., & Blakemore, S. M. (2002). One brand, three ways to shop: Situational variables and multi-channel consumer behavior. *International Review of Retail, Distribution and Consumer Research*, *12*(2), 131–148. doi:10.1080/09593960210127691

Nielsen. (2014). *Continual innovation: The key to stand out and win in retail*. Retrieved from http://www.nielsen. com/us/en/newswire/2014/continual-innovation-the-key-to-stand-out-and-win-in-retail.html

Nike. (2007, October 4). *Nike opens new NIKEiD studio in New York giving consumers a key to unlock the world of design*. Retrieved from http://www.nikebiz.com/media/pr/2007/10/4_nikeid_nyc.html

Nohria, K., & Gulati, S. (1996). Is slack good or bad for innovation. *Academy of Management Journal*, *39*(5), 799–825. doi:10.2307/256998

NRW. (2011). *Consumentenbeleving in winkelgebieden*. Retrieved on 20 November 2012, from www.nrw.nl (Dutch)

Nunnally, J. C. (1978). *Psychometric theory* (2nd ed.). New York, NY: McGraw-Hill.

Nuttavuthisit, K. (2010). If you can't beat them, let them join: The development of strategies to foster consumers' co-creative practices. *Business Horizons*, *53*(3), 315–324. doi:10.1016/j.bushor.2010.01.005

Nysveen, H., Pedersen, P. E., & Thorbjornsen, H. (2005). Intentions to use mobile services. *Journal of the Academy of Marketing Science*, *33*(3), 330–346. doi:10.1177/0092070305276149

Occupational Information Network. (2011, June). Summary report for 41-2031.00- retail salespersons. *O*Net Online*. Retrieved from http://www.onetonline.org/link/summary/41-2031.00

O'Doherty, J., Kringelbach, M. L., Rolls, E. T., Hornak, J., & Andrews, C. (2001). Abstract reward and punishment representations in the human orbitofrontal cortex. *Nature Neuroscience*, *4*(1), 95–102. doi:10.1038/82959 PMID:11135651

OECD. (2005). *Oslo manual: Guidelines for collecting and interpreting innovation data*. Paris: OECD Publishing.

Oghazi, P., Mostaghel, R., Hultman, M., & Parida, V. (2012). Antecedents of technology-based self-service acceptance: A proposed model. *Services Marketing Quarterly*, *33*(3), 195–210. doi:10.1080/15332969.2012.689937

Oh, H., Yoon, S.-Y., & Shyu, C.-R. (2008). How can virtual reality reshape furniture retailing? *Clothing & Textiles Research Journal*, *26*(2), 143–163. doi:10.1177/0887302X08314789

Oh, L. B., Teo, H. H., & Sambamurthy, V. (2012). The effects of retail channel integration through the use of information technologies on firm performance. *Journal of Operations Management*, *30*(5), 368–381. doi:10.1016/j.jom.2012.03.001

Okazaki, S., & Taylor, C. R. (2008). What is SMS advertising and why do multinationals adopt it? Answers from an empirical study in European markets. *Journal of Business Research*, *61*(1), 4–12. doi:10.1016/j.jbusres.2006.05.003

Olenski, S. (2013). Is location based advertising the future of mobile marketing and mobile advertising? *Forbes.com*. Retrieved July 11, 2014, from http://www.forbes.com/sites/marketshare/2013/01/17/is-location-based-advertising-the-future-of-mobile-marketing-and-mobile-advertising/

Oliver, R. L. (1980). A cognitive model of the antecedents and consequences of satisfaction decisions. *JMR, Journal of Marketing Research*, *17*(4), 460–469. doi:10.2307/3150499

Olsson, T., Kärkkäinen, T., Lagerstam, E., & Ventä-Olkkonen, L. (2012). User evaluation of mobile augmented reality scenarios. *Journal of Ambient Intelligence and Smart Environments*, *4*(1), 29–47.

Olsson, T., Lagerstam, E., Kärkkäinen, T., & Väänänen-Vainio-Mattila, K. (2013). Expected user experience of mobile augmented reality services: A user study in the context of shopping centres. *Personal and Ubiquitous Computing*, *17*(2), 287–304. doi:10.1007/s00779-011-0494-x

Olsson, T., & Salo, M. (2011). Online user survey on current mobile augmented reality applications. In *Proceedings of the 10th IEEE International Symposium on Mixed and Augmented Reality (ISMAR)* (pp. 75-84). IEEE. doi:10.1109/ISMAR.2011.6092372

Omnico. (2013). *Omni-channel retailing*. London: Omnico Retail.

Oppewal, H., & Timmermans, H. (1997). Retailer self-perceived store image and competitive position. *International Review of Retail, Distribution and Consumer Research, 7*(1), 41–59. doi:10.1080/095939697343120

Oracle. (2011). *The new growth imperative how innovative companies are using unique strategies & channels to drive margin expansion*. Oracle Retail.

Orlikowski, W. J., & Baroudi, J. J. (1991). Studying information technology in organization: Research approaches and assumptions. *Information Systems Research, 2*(1), 1–14. doi:10.1287/isre.2.1.1

Ouardighi, F. E., Jørgensen, S., & Pasin, F. (2013). A dynamic game with monopolist manufacturer and price-competing duopolist retailers. *OR-Spektrum, 35*(4), 1059–1084. doi:10.1007/s00291-012-0300-9

OXIRM. (2006). *The future of retail business models*. Oxford, UK: Oxford Institute of Retail Management.

OXIRM. (2013). *The state of UK retail places*. Oxford Institute of Retail Management. Retrieved November 20, 2013, from http://oxford-institute.sbsblogs.co.uk/2013/07/19/diversity-and-the-uks-high-streets

Padilla-Melendez, A., Aguila-Obra, A. R., & Garrido-Moreno, A. (2013). Perceived playfulness, gender differences and technology acceptance model in a blended learning scenario. *Computers & Education, 63*(April), 306–317. doi:10.1016/j.compedu.2012.12.014

Palmer, M. T. (1995). Interpersonal communication and virtual reality: Mediating interpersonal relationships. In F. Biocca & M. R. Levy (Eds.), *Communication in the age of virtual reality* (pp. 277–302). Hillsdale, NJ: Lawrence Erlbaum.

Palmer, M., & Quinn, B. (2003). The strategic role of investment banks in the retailer internationalisation process: Is this venture marketing? *European Journal of Marketing, 37*(10), 1391–1408. doi:10.1108/03090560310487167

Pancras, J. (2010). A framework to determine the value of consumer consideration set information for firm pricing strategies. *Computational Economics, 35*(3), 269–300. doi:10.1007/s10614-009-9193-3

Panigyrakis, G., & Theodoridis, P. K. (2007). Market orientation and performance: An empirical investigation in the retail industry in Greece. *Journal of Retailing and Consumer Services, 14*(2), 137–149. doi:10.1016/j.jretconser.2006.05.003

Panksepp, J., Nocjar, C., Burgdorf, J., Panksepp, J. B., & Huber, R. (2004). The role of emotional systems in addiction: A neuroethological perspective. *Nebraska Symposium on Motivation, 50*(1), 85–126. PMID:15160639

Pantano, E., & Viassone, M. (2012). Consumers' expectation of innovation: shift retail strategies for more attractive points of sale. *International Journal of Digital Content Technology and its Applications, 6*(21), 455-461.

Pantano, E. (2010). New technologies and retailing: Trends and directions. *Journal of Retailing and Consumer Services, 17*(3), 171–172. doi:10.1016/j.jretconser.2010.03.004

Pantano, E. (2011). Virtual cultural heritage consumption: A 3D learning experience. *International Journal of Technology Enhanced Learning, 3*(5), 482–495. doi:10.1504/IJTEL.2011.042100

Pantano, E. (2014). Innovation management in retailing: From consumer perspective to corporate strategy. *Journal of Retailing and Consumer Services, 21*(5), 825–826. doi:10.1016/j.jretconser.2014.02.017

Pantano, E., & Di Pietro, L. (2012). Understanding consumer's acceptance of technology-based innovations in retailing. *Journal of Technology Management & Innovation, 7*(4), 1–19. doi:10.4067/S0718-27242012000400001

Pantano, E., Iazzolino, G., & Migliano, G. (2013). Obsolescence risk in advanced technologies for retailing: A management perspective. *Journal of Retailing and Consumer Services, 20*(1), 225–233. doi:10.1016/j.jretconser.2013.01.002

Pantano, E., & Naccarato, G. (2010). Entertainment in retailing: The influences of advanced technologies. *Journal of Retailing and Consumer Services, 17*(3), 200–204. doi:10.1016/j.jretconser.2010.03.010

Pantano, E., & Servidio, R. (2011). The role of pervasive environments for promotion of tourist destinations: The users' response. *Journal of Hospitality and Tourism Technology, 2*(1), 50–65. doi:10.1108/17579881111112412

Pantano, E., & Servidio, R. (2012). Modeling innovative points of sales through virtual and immersive technologies. *Journal of Retailing and Consumer Services*, *19*(3), 279–286. doi:10.1016/j.jretconser.2012.02.002

Pantano, E., & Timmermans, H. (Eds.). (2010). *Advanced technologies management for retailing – Frameworks and cases*. Hershey, PA: IGI Global.

Pantano, E., & Viassone, M. (2014). Demand pull and technology push perspective in technology-based innovations for the points of sale: The retailers evaluation. *Journal of Retailing and Consumer Services*, *21*(1), 43–47. doi:10.1016/j.jretconser.2013.06.007

Papagiannidis, S., Pantano, E., See-To, E., & Bourlakis, M. (2013). Modelling the determinants of a simulated experience in a virtual retail store and users' product purchasing intentions. *Journal of Marketing Management*, *29*(13-14), 1462–1492. doi:10.1080/0267257X.2013.821150

Pappu, R., Quester, P. G., & Cooksey, R. W. (2005). Consumer-based brand equity: Improving the measurement – Empirical evidence. *Journal of Product and Brand Management*, *14*(3), 143–154. doi:10.1108/10610420510601012

Parasuraman, A., Zeithaml, V. A., & Berry, L. L. (1985). A conceptual model of service quality and its implications for future research. *Journal of Marketing*, *49*(4), 41–50. doi:10.2307/1251430

Parasuraman, A., Zeithaml, V. A., & Berry, L. L. (1988). Servqual. *Journal of Retailing*, *64*(1), 12–40.

Park, C. W., MacInnis, D. J., Priester, J., Eisingerich, A. B., & Iacobucci, D. (2010). Brand attachment and brand attitude strength: Conceptual and empirical differentiation of two critical brand equity drivers. *Journal of Marketing*, *74*(6), 1–17. doi:10.1509/jmkg.74.6.1

Parker, J. R., & Lehmann, D. R. (2011). When shelf-based scarcity impacts consumer preferences. *Journal of Retailing*, *87*(2), 142–155. doi:10.1016/j.jretai.2011.02.001

Park, S. Y. (2009). An analysis of the technology acceptance model in understanding university students' behavioral intention to use e-learning. *Journal of Educational Technology & Society*, *12*(3), 150–162.

Parthasarathi, G., Sarmah, S. P., & Jenamani, M. (2011). Supply chain coordination under retail competition using stock dependent price-setting newsvendor framework. *Operations Research*, *11*(3), 259–279. doi:10.1007/s12351-010-0077-z

Peñaloza, L. (1999). Just doing it: A visual ethnographic study of spectacular consumption at Niketown. *Consumption Markets & Culture*, *2*(4), 337–465. doi:10.1080/10253866.1998.9670322

Penrose, E. (1963). *The theory of the growth of the firm*. Oxford, UK: Blackwell.

Petty, R. E., & Cacioppo, J. T. (1986). *The elaboration likelihood model of persuasion*. In L. Berkowitz (Ed.), Advances in experimental social psychology (pp. 123–205). New York, NY: Academic Press.

Pham, M. T. (2004). The logic of feeling. *Journal of Consumer Psychology*, *14*(4), 360–369. doi:10.1207/s15327663jcp1404_5

Phan, K. L., Wager, T., Taylor, S. F., & Liberzon, I. (2002). Functional neuroanatomy of emotion: A meta-analysis of emotion activation studies in PET and fMRI. *NeuroImage*, *16*(2), 331–348. doi:10.1006/nimg.2002.1087 PMID:12030820

Piccoli, G., Ahmad, R., & Ives, B. (2001). Web-based virtual learning environments: A research framework and preliminary assessment of effectiveness in basic it skills training. *MIS Quarterly: Management Information Systems*, *25*(4), 401–426. doi:10.2307/3250989

Piercy, N., & Alexander, N. (1988). The status quo of marketing organisation in UK retailers: A neglected phenomenon of the 1980s. *Service Industries Journal*, *8*(2), 155–175. doi:10.1080/02642068800000027

Pine, B. J., & Gilmore, J. H. (1998, July-August). Welcome to the experience economy. *Harvard Business Review*.

Pine, B. J., & Gilmore, J. H. (2011). *The experience economy*. Cambridge, MA: Harvard Business Press.

Pinho, J. C., & Martins, L. (2010). Exporting barriers: Insights from Portuguese small and medium-sized exporters and non-exporters. *Journal of International Entrepreneurship*, *8*(3), 254–272. doi:10.1007/s10843-010-0046-x

Pinker, S. (1997). *How the mind works.* New York, NY: Norton.

Piotrowicz, W., & Cuthbertson, R. (2014). Introduction to the special issue information technology in retail: Toward omnichannel retailing. *International Journal of Electronic Commerce, 18*(4), 5–16. doi:10.2753/JEC1086-4415180400

Plassmann, H., Zoëga Ramsøy, T., & Milosavljevic, M. (2012). Branding the brain: A critical review and outlook. *Journal of Consumer Psychology, 5*(1), 85–115.

Platt Retail Institute. (2012). *Retailers' investment in technology: An industry perspective.* Retrieved February 2, 2014 from http://www.plattretailinstitute.org/documents/free/download.phx?navid=366&itemid=419

Plouffe, C. R., Vandenbosch, M., & Hulland, J. (2001). Intermediating technologies and multi-group adoption: A comparison of consumer and merchant adoption intentions toward a new electronic payment system. *Journal of Product Innovation Management, 18*(2), 65–81. doi:10.1016/S0737-6782(00)00072-2

Pollack, E., Maxwell, J., & Feigen Dugal, L. (2007). *Retailing 2015: New frontiers.* New York, NY: PricewaterhouseCoppers/TNS Retail Forward.

Pomodoro, S. (2013). Temporary retail in fashion system: An explorative study. *Journal of Fashion Marketing and Management, 17*(3), 341–352. doi:10.1108/JFMM-07-2012-0033

Poncin, I., & Garnier, M. (2010). L'expérience sur un site de vente 3D. Le vrai, le faux et le virtuel: À la croisée des chemins. *Management et Avenir, 2*(32), 173–191. doi:10.3917/mav.032.0173

Poncin, I., & Garnier, M. (2012). Immersion in a new commercial virtual environment: The role of the avatar in the appropriation process. In Z. Gürhan-Canli, C. Otnes, & R. Zhu (Eds.), *Advances in consumer research.* Association for Consumer Research.

Poncin, I., & Mimoun, M. S. B. (2014). The impact of "e-atmospherics" on physical stores. *Journal of Retailing and Consumer Services, 21*(5), 851–859. doi:10.1016/j.jretconser.2014.02.013

Porter, C. E., & Donthu, N. (2006). Using the technology acceptance model to explain how attitudes determine Internet usage: The role of perceived access barriers and demographics. *Journal of Business Research, 59*(9), 999–1007. doi:10.1016/j.jbusres.2006.06.003

Potter, W. J. (1988). Developing an instrument to measure perception of reality in television content. *Journal of Broadcasting & Electronic Media, 32*, 23–41. doi:10.1080/08838158809386682

Prange, C., & Schlegelmilch, B. B. (2009). The role of ambidexterity in marketing strategy implementation: Resolving the exploration-exploitation dilemma. *BuR - Business Research, 2*(2), 215-240.

Preacher, K. J., & Hayes, A. F. (2004). SPSS and SAS procedures for estimating indirect effects in simple mediation models. *Behavior Research Methods, Instruments, & Computers, 36*(4), 717–731. doi:10.3758/BF03206553 PMID:15641418

Preuschoff, K., Quartz, S. R., & Bossaerts, P. (2008). Human insula activation reflects risk prediction errors as well as risk. *The Journal of Neuroscience, 28*(11), 2745–2752. doi:10.1523/JNEUROSCI.4286-07.2008 PMID:18337404

Proença, J. F., & Rodrigues, M. A. (2011). A comparison of users and non-users of banking self-service technology in Portugal. *Managing Service Quality, 21*(2), 192–210. doi:10.1108/09604521111113465

Puccinelli, N. M., Deshpande, R., & Isen, A. M. (2007). Should I stay or should I go? Mood congruity, self-monitoring and retail context preference. *Journal of Business Research, 60*(6), 640–648. doi:10.1016/j.jbusres.2006.06.014

Puccinelli, N. M., Goodstein, R. C., Grewal, D., Price, R., Raghubir, P., & Stewart, D. (2009). Customer experience management in retailing: Understanding the buying process. *Journal of Retailing, 85*(1), 15–30. doi:10.1016/j.jretai.2008.11.003

Punj, G., & Stewart, D. W. (1983). Cluster analysis in marketing research: Review and suggestions for application. *JMR, Journal of Marketing Research, 20*(2), 134–148. doi:10.2307/3151680

Purvis, L., Naim, M. M., & Towill, D. (2013). Intermediation in agile global fashion supply chains. *International Journal of Engineering Science and Technology*, *5*(2), 38–48.

PwC (2011). *"Pick'n'Mix": Meeting the demands of the new multichannel shopper*. London: PwC.

PwC and Kantar. (2012). *Retailing 2020: Winning in a polarized world*. Retrieved November 20, 2013, from www.pwc.com/us/retailandconsumer

Quarrick, G. (1989). *Our sweetest hours: Recreation and the mental state of absorption*. Jefferson, NC: McFarland.

Rafiq, M., & Ahmed, P. K. (1995). Using the 7Ps as a generic marketing mix: An exploratory survey of UK and European marketing academics. *Journal of Marketing Intelligence & Planning*, *13*(9), 4–15. doi:10.1108/02634509510097793

Rajab, T., Kraus, F., & Wieseke, J. (2013). Resolving conflict over salespeople's brand adoption in franchised channels of distribution. *Review of Managerial Science*, *7*(4), 443–473. doi:10.1007/s11846-012-0091-z

Rajaram, K. (2001). Assortment planning in fashion retailing: Methodology, application and analysis. *European Journal of Operational Research*, *129*(1), 186–208. doi:10.1016/S0377-2217(99)00406-3

Raju, P. S. (1977). Product familiarity, brand name and price influences on product evaluation. *Advances in Consumer Research. Association for Consumer Research (U. S.)*, *4*(1), 64–71.

Rao, H., & Drazin, R. (2002). Overcoming resource constraints on product innovation by recruiting talent from rivals: A study of the mutual fund industry. *Academy of Management Journal*, *45*(June), 491–507. doi:10.2307/3069377

Rapp, A., Beitelspacher, L. S., Grewal, D., & Hughes, D. E. (2013). Understanding social media effects across seller, retailer, and consumer interactions. *Journal of the Academy of Marketing Science*, *41*(5), 547–566. doi:10.1007/s11747-013-0326-9

Rawwas, M. Y. A., Arjoon, S., & Sidani, Y. (2013). An introduction of epistemology to business ethics: A study of marketing middle-managers. *Journal of Business Ethics*, *117*(3), 525–539. doi:10.1007/s10551-012-1537-6

Raymond, L., & St-Pierre, J. (2013). Strategic capability configurations for the internationalization of SMEs: A study in equifinality. *International Small Business Journal*, *31*(1), 82–102. doi:10.1177/0266242610391325

Rayport, J. F., & Jaworski, B. J. (2005). *Best face forward: Why companies must improve their service interfaces with customers*. Boston, MA: Harvard Business School Press.

Reda, S. (2005, September). What you don't know about RFID. *Stores*, 26-34.

Regenbrecht, H. T., Schubert, T. W., & Friedmann, F. (1998). Measuring the sense of presence and its relations to fear of heights in virtual environments. *International Journal of Human-Computer Interaction*, *10*(3), 233–249. doi:10.1207/s15327590ijhc1003_2

Reinders, M. J., Dabholkar, P. A., & Frambach, R. T. (2008). Consequences of forcing customers to use technology-based self-service. *Journal of Service Research*, *11*(2), 107–123. doi:10.1177/1094670508324297

Renko, S. (2008). How the process of internationalization enhances the sustainability of the Croatian retailing. *World Journal of Retail Business Management*, *2*(4), 3–10.

Rese, A., Schreiber, S., & Baier, D. (2014). Technology acceptance modeling of augmented reality at the point of sale: Can surveys be replaced by an analysis of online reviews? *Journal of Retailing and Consumer Services*, *21*(5), 869–876. doi:10.1016/j.jretconser.2014.02.011

Retail Week. (2012). *Ecommerce in fashion: How retailers are driving online sales*. Retrieved November 20, 2013, from http://www.retail-week.com/retail-week-ecommerce-in-fashion/5042018.article

Retail Week. (2013). *Multichannel now, 2013*. London: Retail Week.

Retail Week. (2014). *Multichannel, unraveling touchpoints*. Retrieved November 20, 2013, from http://www.retail-week.com/multichannel/analysis-tracking-shopper-journeys-across-the-multichannel-landscape/5060398.article

Reutterer, T., Mild, A., Natter, M., & Taudes, A. (2006). A dynamic segmentation approach for targeting and customizing direct marketing campaigns. *Journal of Interactive Marketing*, *20*(3/4), 43–57. doi:10.1002/dir.20066

Reychav, I., & Weisberg, J. (2009). Going beyond technology: Knowledge sharing as tool for enhancing customer-oriented attitudes. *International Journal of Information Management, 29*(5), 353–361. doi:10.1016/j.ijinfomgt.2008.11.005

Reynolds, J., Howard, E., Cuthbertson, C., & Hristov, L. (2007). Perspectives on retail format innovation: Relating theory and practice. *International Journal of Retail & Distribution Management, 35*(8), 647–660. doi:10.1108/09590550710758630

Reynolds, J., & Hristov, L. (2009). Are there barriers to innovation in retailing? *International Review of Retail, Distribution and Consumer Research, 19*(4), 317–330. doi:10.1080/09593960903331295

Reynolds, K. E., Ganesh, J., & Luckett, M. (2002). Traditional malls versus factory outlets: Comparing shopper typologies and implications for retail strategy. *Journal of Business Research, 55*(9), 687–696. doi:10.1016/S0148-2963(00)00213-7

Reznick, R. K., & MacRae, H. (2006). Teaching surgical skills- Changes in the wind. *The New England Journal of Medicine, 355*(25), 2664–2669. doi:10.1056/NEJMra054785 PMID:17182991

Rhoads, G. K., Swinyard, W. R., Geurts, M. D., & Price, W. D. (2002). Retailing as a career: A comparative study of marketers. *Journal of Retailing, 78*(1), 71–76. doi:10.1016/S0022-4359(01)00068-9

Richardson, N. (2008). To what extent have key retail and generic marketing texts adopted sustainability? *World Journal of Retail Business Management, 2*(4), 47–55.

Richey, R. G., Tokman, M., & Dalela, V. (2010). Examining collaborative supply chain service technologies: A study of intensity, relationships, and resources. *Journal of the Academy of Marketing Science, 38*(1), 71–89. doi:10.1007/s11747-009-0139-z

Rieunier, S. (1998). L'influence de la musique d'ambiance sur le comportement du client: Revue de la littérature, défis méthodologiques et voies de recherches. *Recherche et Applications en Marketing, 13*(3), 57–77. doi:10.1177/076737019801300305

Rilling, J. K., & Sanfey, A. G. (2011). The neuroscience of social decision-making. *Annual Review of Psychology, 62*(1), 23–48. doi:10.1146/annurev.psych.121208.131647 PMID:20822437

Rincker, N. (2011). *Industry briefing: Germany's DIY market: Consumer and shopper insights, June 2011.* Retrieved December 1, 2014 from http://csi.mckinsey.com/Home/Knowledge_by_region/ Europe_Africa_Middle_East/GermanyDIY.aspx

Ritzer, G. (2005). *Enchanting a disenchanted world: Revolutionizing the means of consumption.* Thousand Oaks, CA: Pine Forge Press.

Riva, G. (2009). Is presence a technology issue? Some insights from cognitive science. *Virtual Reality (Waltham Cross), 13*(3), 159–167. doi:10.1007/s10055-009-0121-6

Robinson, L. Jr, Marshall, G. W., & Stamps, M. B. (2005). An empirical investigation of technology acceptance in a field sales force setting. *Industrial Marketing Management, 34*(4), 407–415. doi:10.1016/j.indmarman.2004.09.019

Robinson, R. B. Jr, & Pearce, J. A. II. (1984). Research thrusts in small firm strategic planning. *Academy of Management Review, 9*(1), 128–137.

Rogers, E. M. (2003). *Diffusion of innovations* (5th ed.). New York, NY: Free Press.

Rohm, A. J., Gao, T., Sultan, F., & Pagani, M. (2012). Brand in the hand: A cross-market investigation of consumer acceptance of mobile marketing. *Business Horizons, 55*(5), 485–493. doi:10.1016/j.bushor.2012.05.004

Rohm, A., & Swaminatham, V. (2004). A typology of online shoppers based on shopping motivations. *Journal of Business Research, 57*(7), 748–757. doi:10.1016/S0148-2963(02)00351-X

ROI Research Inc., & Microsoft. (2011). *Mobile advertising research study: Consumer and industry insights – United Kingdom.* Retrieved June 21, 2014, from https://advertising.microsoft.com/WWDocs/User/en-us/ForAdvertisers/2011-Microsoft-UK-MoAd-Insights-Study.pdf

Roig-Tierno, N., Baviera-Puig, A., & Buitrago-Vera, J. (2013). Business opportunities analysis using GIS: The retail distribution sector. *Global Business Perspectives, 1*(3), 226–238. doi:10.1007/s40196-013-0015-6

Root, F. R. (1994). *Entry strategies for international markets*. New York, NY: Lexington Books.

Rosenblatt, P. C., de Mik, L., Anderson, R. M., & Johnson, P. A. (1985). *The family in business*. San Francisco: Jossey-Bass.

Rosenblum, P., & Rowen, S. (2012). The 2012 retail store: In transition. *Retail Systems Research*. Retrieved November 20, 2013, from http://www.rsrresearch.com/2012/05/09/the-2012-retail-store-in-transition-2/

Rose, S., Clark, M., Samouel, P., & Hair, N. (2012). Online customer experience in e-retailing: An empirical model of antecedents and outcomes. *Journal of Retailing, 88*(2), 308–322. doi:10.1016/j.jretai.2012.03.001

Rossiter, J., & Percy, L. (1997). *Advertising communications and promotion management* (2nd ed.). New York, NY: McGraw-Hill.

Rouzé, V. (2004). *Les musiques diffusées dans les lieux publics: Analyse et enjeux de pratiques communicationnelles quotidiennes*. (Doctoral Dissertation). Université Paris 8, St-Denis, France. Retrieved July, 2013 from http://tel.archives-ouvertes.fr/docs/00/63/52/96/PDF/thA_se_sans_annexe.pdf

Roy, R., Zhao, M., & Dholakia, N. (2005). Multichannel retailing: A case study of early experiences. *Journal of Interactive Marketing, 19*(2), 63–74. doi:10.1002/dir.20035

Roztocki, N., & Weistroffer, H. R. (2009). Research trends in information and communications technology in developing, emerging and transition economies. *Roczniki Kolegium Analiz Ekonomicznych Zeszyt, 20*, 113–127.

Roztocki, N., & Weistroffer, H. R. (2014). Information and communication technology in transition economies: An assessment of research trends. *Information Technology for Development*, 1–35. doi:10.1080/02681102.2014.891498

Rubio, E. M., Sanz, A., & Sebastian, M. A. (2005). Virtual reality applications for the next-generation manufacturing. *International Journal of Computer Integrated Manufacturing, 18*(7), 601–609. doi:10.1080/09511920500069259

Rudawska, I. (2008). Towards sustainability in the retail services markets. *World Journal of Retail Business Management, 2*(4), 56–64.

Rudolph, T., & Emrich, O. (2009). Situation-related tasks for mobile services in retailing. *International Review of Retail, Distribution and Consumer Research, 19*(5), 483–503. doi:10.1080/09593960903445285

Ruekert, R. W. (1992). Developing a market orientation: An organizational strategy perspective. *International Journal of Research in Marketing, 9*(3), 225–245. doi:10.1016/0167-8116(92)90019-H

Ruiz, J. P., Chebat, J. C., & Hansen, P. (2004). Another trip to the mall: A segmentation study of consumers based on their activities. *Journal of Retailing and Consumer Services, 11*(6), 333–350. doi:10.1016/j.jretconser.2003.12.002

Russell, J. A., & Barrett, L. F. (1999). Core affect, prototypical emotional episodes, and other things called emotion: Dissecting the elephant. *Journal of Personality and Social Psychology, 76*(5), 805–819. doi:10.1037/0022-3514.76.5.805 PMID:10353204

Russell, R. (1990). Innovation in organizations: Toward an integrated model. *Review of Business, 12*(2), 19–25.

Russell, R. A., & Urban, T. L. (2010). The location and allocation of products and product families on retail shelves. *Annals of Operations Research, 179*(1), 131–147. doi:10.1007/s10479-008-0450-y

Ruzzier, M., Hisrich, R. D., & Antoncic, B. (2006). SME internationalization research: Past, present, and future. *Journal of Small Business and Enterprise Development, 13*(4), 476–497. doi:10.1108/14626000610705705

Ruzzier, M., & Konecnik, M. (2006). The internationalization strategies of SMEs: The case of the Slovenian hotel industry. *Journal of Contemporary Management Issues, 11*(1), 17–35.

Ryan, G. W., & Russell Bernard, H. (2003). Techniques to identify themes in qualitative data. *Field Methods, 15*(1), 85-109. doi: 10.1177/1525822X02239569

Ryding, D. (2011). A comparative analysis of the relative importance of service quality for two UK grocery retailers. *Journal of Food Products Marketing, 17*(5), 503–517. doi:10.1080/10454446.2011.618788

Saarijärvi, H., Mitronen, L., & Yrjölä, M. (2014). From selling to supporting – Leveraging mobile services in the context of food retailing. *Journal of Retailing and Consumer Services*, *21*(1), 26–36. doi:10.1016/j.jretconser.2013.06.009

Salmon, W., & Tordjman, A. (1989). The internationalisation of retailing. *International Journal of Retailing*, *4*(2), 3–16.

Sanchez-Vives, M. V., & Slater, M. (2005). From presence to consciousness through virtual reality. *Nature Reviews. Neuroscience*, *6*(4), 332–339. doi:10.1038/nrn1651 PMID:15803164

Saramago, J. (2003). *The cave*. Harvest Books.

SAS. (2014). *Digital marketing drives the omnichannel experience*. Retrieved August 14, 2013 from http://www.sas.com/da_dk/whitepapers/digital-marketing-drives-omnichannel-experience-106652.html

Sayadi, M. K., & Makui, A. (2014). Feedback Nash Equilibrium for dynamic brand and channel advertising in dual channel supply chain. *Journal of Optimization Theory and Applications*, *161*(3), 1012–1021. doi:10.1007/s10957-013-0479-1

Scarpi, D. (2006). Fashion stores between fun and usefulness. *Journal of Fashion Marketing and Management*, *10*(1), 7–24. doi:10.1108/13612020610651097

Scharl, A., Dickinger, A., & Murphy, J. (2005). Diffusion and success factors of mobile marketing. *Electronic Commerce Research and Applications*, *4*(2), 159–173. doi:10.1016/j.elerap.2004.10.006

Schifferstein, H. N. J., & Desmet, P. M. A. (2007). The effects of sensory impairments on product experience and personal well-being. *Ergonomics*, *50*(12), 2026–2048. doi:10.1080/00140130701524056 PMID:17852370

Schlesinger, L. A., & Zornitsky, J. (1996). Job satisfaction, service capability, and customer satisfaction: An examination of linkages and management implications. *Human Resource Planning*, *14*(2), 141–149.

Schmidt, J. B., & Spreng, R. A. (1996). A proposed model of external consumer information search. *Journal of the Academy of Marketing Science*, *24*(3), 246–256. doi:10.1177/0092070396243005

Schmidt, R. C. (2013). Price competition and innovation in markets with brand loyalty. *Journal of Economics*, *109*(2), 147–173. doi:10.1007/s00712-012-0296-2

Schmitt, B. (1999). Experiential marketing. *Journal of Marketing Management*, *15*(1-3), 53–67. doi:10.1362/026725799784870496

Schmitt, B. (2012). The consumer psychology of brands. *Journal of Consumer Psychology*, *22*(1), 7–17. doi:10.1016/j.jcps.2011.09.005

Schubert, T. (2010). Marketing and organisational innovations in entrepreneurial innovation processes and their relation to market structure and firm characteristics. *Review of Industrial Organization*, *36*(2), 189–212. doi:10.1007/s11151-010-9243-y

Schubert, T. W., Friedmann, F., & Regenbrecht, H. (2001). The experience of presence: Factor analytic insights. *Presence (Cambridge, Mass.)*, *10*(3), 266–281. doi:10.1162/105474601300343603

Schultze, U. (2010). Embodiment and presence in virtual worlds: A review. *Journal of Information Technology*, *25*(4), 434–449. doi:10.1057/jit.2010.25

Schumpeter, J. A. (1934). *The theory of economic development: An inquiry into profits, capital, credit, interest, and the business cycle*. Cambridge, MA: Harvard University Press.

Sciulli, N. (2011). The views of managers from a local coastal council on sustainability reporting issues: An Australian-based case study. *Qualitative Research in Accounting & Management*, *8*(2), 139–160. doi:10.1108/11766091111137555

Seck, A. M., & Philippe, J. (2011). Service encounter in multi-channel distribution context: Virtual and face-to-face interactions and consumer satisfaction. *Service Industries Journal*, *33*(6), 565–579. doi:10.1080/02642069.2011.622370

Senecal, S., Pullins, E. B., & Buehrer, R. E. (2007). The extent of technology usage and salespeople: An exploratory investigation. *Journal of Business and Industrial Marketing*, *22*(1), 52–61. doi:10.1108/08858620710722824

Seo, D. W., & Lee, J. Y. (2013). Direct hand touchable interactions in augmented reality environments for natural and intuitive user experience. *Expert Systems with Applications, 40*(9), 3784–3793. doi:10.1016/j.eswa.2012.12.091

Seymour, N. E., Gallagher, A. G., Roman, S. A., O' Brien, M. K., Bansal, V. K., Andersen, D. K., & Blumgart, L. H. et al. (2002). Virtual reality training improves operating room performance results of a randomized, double-blinded study. *Annals of Surgery, 236*(4), 458–464. doi:10.1097/00000658-200210000-00008 PMID:12368674

Sha, D. Y., & Guo-Liang, L. (2012). Improving service quality of retail store by innovative digital content technology. In *Proceedings of IEEE 3rd International Conference on Software Engineering and Service Science (ICSESS)* (pp. 655-660). Beijing: IEEE. doi:10.1109/ICSESS.2012.6269552

Shamdasani, P., Mukherjee, A., & Malhotra, N. (2008). Antecedents and consequences of service quality in consumer evaluation of self-service internet technologies. *Service Industries Journal, 28*(1), 117–138. doi:10.1080/02642060701725669

Shankar, V., Inman, J. J., Mantrala, M., Kelley, E., & Rizley, R. (2011). Innovations in shopper marketing: Current insights and future research issues. *Journal of Retailing, 87*, 29–42. doi:10.1016/j.jretai.2011.04.007

Shankar, V., Venkatesh, A., Hofacker, C., & Naik, P. (2010). Mobile marketing in the retailing environment: Current insights and future research avenues. *Journal of Interactive Marketing, 24*(2), 111–120. doi:10.1016/j.intmar.2010.02.006

Shankar, V., & Yadav, M. (2011). Innovations in retailing. *Journal of Retailing, 87*(July), S1–S2. doi:10.1016/j.jretai.2011.04.004

Shan, W., Walker, G., & Kogut, B. (1994). Interfirm cooperation and startup innovation in the biotechnology industry. *Strategic Management Journal, 15*(5), 387–394. doi:10.1002/smj.4250150505

Shaw, D., & Leeming, A. (1998). The retail industry and information technology. In *Modelling for added value* (pp. 139–154). London: Springer Verlag. doi:10.1007/978-1-4471-0601-2_14

Shen, C.-C., & Chiou, J.-S. (2010). The impact of perceived ease of use on Internet service adoption: The moderating effects of temporal distance and perceived risk. *Computers in Human Behavior, 26*(1), 42–50. doi:10.1016/j.chb.2009.07.003

Sheridan, M., Moore, C. M., & Nobbs, K. (2006). Fast fashion requires fast marketing. *Journal of Fashion Marketing and Management, 10*(3), 301–315. doi:10.1108/13612020610679286

Sheridan, T. B. (1992). Musings on telepresence and virtual presence. *Presence (Cambridge, Mass.), 1*(1), 120–125.

Sherma, D., Alford, B., Bhuian, S. N., & Pelton, L. E. (2009). A higher-order model of risk propensity. *Journal of Business Research, 62*(7), 741–744. doi:10.1016/j.jbusres.2008.06.005

Sherman, S. J., & Fazio, R. H. (1983). Parallels between attitudes and traits as predictors of behavior. *Journal of Personality, 51*(3), 308–345. doi:10.1111/j.1467-6494.1983.tb00336.x

Shiv, B., & Fedorikhin, A. (1999). Heart and mind in conflict: The interplay of affect and cognition in consumer decision making. *The Journal of Consumer Research, 26*(3), 278–292. doi:10.1086/209563

Siew, R. Y. J., Balatbat, M. C. A., & Carmichael, D. G. (2013). The relationship between sustainability practices and financial performance of construction companies. *Smart and Sustainable Built Environment, 2*(1), 6–27. doi:10.1108/20466091311325827

Signs of the Times. (2006, November 3). *The Economist*, p. 378.

Silaiou, S., Mania, K., Karoulis, A., & White, M. (2010). Exploring the relationship between presence and enjoyment in a virtual museum. *International Journal of Human-Computer Studies, 68*(5), 243–253. doi:10.1016/j.ijhcs.2009.11.002

Simon, C., Brexendorf, T. O., & Fassnacht, M. (2013). Creating online brand experience on Facebook. *Marketing Review St. Gallen, 30*(6), 50–59. doi:10.1365/s11621-013-0299-6

Singh, J. J., Iglesias, O., & Batista-Foguet, J. M. (2012). Does having an ethical brand matter? The influence of consumer perceived ethicality on trust, affect and loyalty. *Journal of Business Ethics*, *111*(4), 541–549. doi:10.1007/s10551-012-1216-7

Sinha, P. K., & Kar, S. K. (2010). Insights into the growth of new retail formats in India. In M. Kraft & M. K. Mantrala (Eds.), *Retailing in the 21st century* (pp. 119–140). Heidelberg, Germany: Springer Verlag. doi:10.1007/978-3-540-72003-4_8

Sirgy, M. J., Yu, G. B., Lee, D. J., Wei, S., & Huang, M. W. (2012). Does marketing activity contribute to a society's well-being? The role of economic efficiency. *Journal of Business Ethics*, *107*(2), 91–102. doi:10.1007/s10551-011-1030-7

Sitzia, S., & Zizzo, D. J. (2011). Does product complexity matter for competition in experimental retail markets? *Theory and Decision*, *70*(1), 65–82. doi:10.1007/s11238-009-9163-1

Sivadas, E., & Dwyer, F. (2000). An examination of organizational factors influencing new product success in internal and alliance based processes. *Journal of Marketing*, *64*(1), 31–49. doi:10.1509/jmkg.64.1.31.17985

Skallerud, K., & Grønhaug, K. (2010). Chinese food retailers' positioning strategies and the influence on their buying behaviour. *Asia Pacific Journal of Marketing and Logistics*, *22*(2), 196–209. doi:10.1108/13555851011026944

Skard, S., Nysveen, H., & Pedersen, P. E. (2011). *Brand and customer experience in service organizations: Literature review and brand experience construct validation* (Working Paper No. 09/11). Institute for Research in Economics and Business Administration, Bergen: SNF.

Slater, M. (1999). Measuring presence: A response to the Witmer and Singer presence questionnaire. *Presence (Cambridge, Mass.)*, *8*(5), 560–565. doi:10.1162/105474699566477

Slater, M. (2002). Presence and the sixth sense. *Presence (Cambridge, Mass.)*, *11*(4), 435–439. doi:10.1162/105474602760204327

Slater, M., & Steed, A. (2000). A virtual presence counter. *Presence (Cambridge, Mass.)*, *9*(5), 413–434.

Slater, M., Usoh, M., & Steed, A. (1994). Depth of presence in virtual environments. *Presence (Cambridge, Mass.)*, *3*(2), 130–144.

Slater, M., & Wilbur, S. (1997). A framework for immersive virtual environments (five): Speculations on the role of presence in virtual environments. *Presence (Cambridge, Mass.)*, *6*, 603–617.

Slater, S. F., & Narver, J. C. (1994). Marketing orientation, customer value and superior performance. *Business Horizons*, *37*(2), 22–28. doi:10.1016/0007-6813(94)90029-9

Smith, A. (2013). *Smartphone ownership 2013*. Retrieved May 25, 2014, from http://www.pewinternet.org/2013/06/05/smartphone-ownership-2013/

Smith, P. R., & Taylor, J. (2004). *Marketing communications*. London, UK: Kogan Page.

Smithson, S., & Hirschheim, R. (1998). Analysing information systems evaluation: Another look at an old problem. *European Journal of Information Systems*, *7*(3), 158–174. doi:10.1057/palgrave.ejis.3000304

Snyder, M., & Ickes, W. (1985). Personality and social behavior. In G. Lindzey & E. Aronson (Eds.), *Handbook of social psychology* (Vol. 2, pp. 883–947). New York, NY: Random House.

Sobel, M. E. (1982). Asymptotic confidence intervals for indirect effects in structural equation models. *Sociological Methodology*, *13*, 290–312. doi:10.2307/270723

Solomon, M. R., & Rabolt, N. J. (2004). *Consumer behavior in fashion*. Upper Saddle River, NJ: Pearson Education.

Solomon, M., Bamossy, G., Askegaard, S., & Hogg, M. K. (2002). *Consumer behavior: A European perspective*. Harlow, MA: Prentice Hall.

Song, K., Hwang, S., Kim, Y., & Kwak, Y. (2013). The effects of social network properties on the acceleration of fashion information on the web. *Multimedia Tools and Applications*, *64*(2), 455–474. doi:10.1007/s11042-012-1068-2

Soper, D. S. (2013). *Sobel test calculator for the significance of mediation* [Software]. Retrieved December 16, 2013 from http://www.danielsoper.com/statcalc

Sorensen, J., & Stuart, T. (2000). Aging, obsolescence, and organizational innovation. *Administrative Science Quarterly*, *45*(March), 81–112. doi:10.2307/2666980

Sorescu, A., Frambach, R. T., Singh, J., Rangaswamyd, A., & Bridges, C. (2011). Innovations in retail business models. *Journal of Retailing*, *87*(1), S3–S16. doi:10.1016/j.jretai.2011.04.005

Sparks, L. (1996). Reciprocal retail internationalisation: The southland corporation, Ito-Yokado and 7-Eleven convenience stores. In G. Akehurst & N. Alexander (Eds.), *The internationalisation of retailing* (pp. 57–96). London, UK: Frank Cass.

Spowart, M., & Wickramasekera, R. (2012). Explaining internationalisation of small to medium sized enterprises within the Queensland food and beverage industry. *International Journal of Business and Management*, *7*(6), 68–80. doi:10.5539/ijbm.v7n6p68

Spreer, P., & Kallweit, K. (2014). Augmented reality in retail: Assessing the acceptance and the potential for multimedia product presentation at the PoS. *SOP Transactions on Marketing Research*, *1*(1), 20–25. doi:10.15764/MR.2014.01002

SPSS Inc. (2001). *The SPSS TwoStep cluster component. A scalable component to segment your customers more effectively*. Retrieved from ftp://ftp.spss.com/pub/web/wp/TSCWP-0101.pdf

Srinivasan, N., & Agrawal, J. (1988). The relationship between prior knowledge and external search. *Advances in Consumer Research. Association for Consumer Research (U. S.)*, *15*(1), 27–31.

Steinfield, C., Bouwman, H., & Adelaar, T. (2002). The dynamics of click-and-mortar electronic commerce: Opportunities and management strategies. *International Journal of Electronic Commerce*, *7*(1), 93–119.

Stephens, J., Huber, E., & Ray, L. (1999). The welfare state in hard times. In H. Kitschelt, P. Lange, G. Marks, & J. D. Stephens (Eds.), *Continuity and change in contemporary capitalism*. Cambridge, UK: Cambridge University Press. doi:10.1017/CBO9781139175050.008

Stern, N., & Verweij, L. (2014). *Retail innovations 9: The pace of change accelerates*. Ebeltoft Group. Retrieved July 31, 2014 from http://www.ebeltoftgroup.com/retail-innovations-9----the-pace-of-change-accelerates.html

Stern, B. B., Royne, M. B., Stafford, T. F., & Beinstock, C. C. (2008). Consumer acceptance of online auctions: An extension and revision of the TAM. *Psychology and Marketing*, *25*(7), 619–636. doi:10.1002/mar.20228

Steuer, J. (1992). Defining virtual reality: Dimensions determining telepresence. *Journal of Communication*, *42*(4), 73–93. doi:10.1111/j.1460-2466.1992.tb00812.x

Stock, R. M., & Reiferscheid, I. (2014). Who should be in power to encourage product program innovativeness, R&D or marketing? *Journal of the Academy of Marketing Science*, *42*(3), 264–276. doi:10.1007/s11747-013-0354-5

Storey, D. J., & Tether, B. (1996). *Review of the empirical knowledge and an assessment of statistical data on the economic importance of new technology-based firms in Europe*. Coventry.

Strachey, C. (1959). Time sharing in large fast computers. In *Proceedings of the International Conference on Information Processing* (pp. 336-341). Academic Press.

Stringer, R. (2000). How to manage radical innovation. *California Management Review*, *42*(4), 70–88. doi:10.2307/41166054

Stuart-Menteth, H., Wilson, H., & Baker, S. (2006). Escaping the channel silo: Researching the new consumer. *International Journal of Market Research*, *48*(4), 415–437.

Stuart, T. (2000). Inter-organizational alliances and the performance of firms: A study of growth and innovation rates in a high-technology industry. *Strategic Management Journal*, *21*(8), 791–811. doi:10.1002/1097-0266(200008)21:8<791::AID-SMJ121>3.0.CO;2-K

Suarez, C., & de Jorge, J. (2010). Efficiency convergence processes and effects of regulation in the nonspecialized retail sector in Spain. *The Annals of Regional Science*, *44*(3), 573–597. doi:10.1007/s00168-008-0270-7

Suh, K.-S., & Lee, Y. E. (2005). The effects of virtual reality on consumer learning: An empirical investigation. *Management Information Systems Quarterly*, *29*(4), 673–697.

Sun, K. A., & Lee, S. (2013). Determinants of degree of internationalization for U.S. restaurant firms. *International Journal of Hospitality Management, 33*, 465–474. doi:10.1016/j.ijhm.2012.11.006

Suominen, J. (2005). *One experience: Optimizing consumer experience channel planning process.* Paper presented at Keynote presentation at the 3rd Interdisciplinary World Congress on Mass Customization and Personalization, Hong Kong.

Suryandari, R. T., & Paswan, A. K. (2014). Online customer service and retail type-product congruence. *Journal of Retailing and Consumer Services, 21*(1), 69–76. doi:10.1016/j.jretconser.2013.08.004

Susskind, A. M., Kacmar, K. M., & Borchgrevnik, C. P. (2003). Customer service providers' attitudes relating to customer service and customer satisfaction in the customer-server exchange. *The Journal of Applied Psychology, 88*(1), 179–187. doi:10.1037/0021-9010.88.1.179 PMID:12675405

Sutherland, I. E. (1965). The ultimate display. In *Proceedings of the Congress of the International Federation of Information Processing* (pp. 506-508). Academic Press.

Swinyard, W. R. (1981). The appeal of retailing as a career. *Journal of Retailing, 57*(4), 86–97.

Swinyard, W. R. (1997). Retailing trends in the USA: Competition, consumers, technology and the economy. *International Journal of Retail & Distribution Management, 25*(8), 244–255. doi:10.1108/09590559710178329

Swinyard, W. R., Langrehr, F. W., & Smith, S. M. (1991). The appeal of retailing as a career: A decade later. *Journal of Retailing, 67*(4), 451–465.

Swoboda, B., Haelsig, F., Morschett, D., & Schramm-Klein, H. (2007). An intersector analysis of the relevance of service in building a strong retail brand. *Managing Service Quality, 17*(4), 428–448. doi:10.1108/09604520710760553

Szajna, B. (1996). Empirical evaluation of the revised technology acceptance model. *Management Science, 42*(1), 85–92. doi:10.1287/mnsc.42.1.85

Tajeddini, K. (2010). Effect of customer orientation and entrepreneurial orientation on innovativeness: Evidence from the hotel industry in Switzerland. *Tourism Management, 31*(2), 221–231. doi:10.1016/j.tourman.2009.02.013

Tambo, T., Gabel, O. D., Olsen, M., & Bækgaard, L. (2012). Organisational dynamics and ambiguity of business intelligence in context of enterprise information systems – A case study. In *Proceedings of the 6th International Conference on Research and Practical Issues of Enterprise Information Systems (CONFENIS): Enterprise Information Systems of the Future - Evolving towards More Performance through Transparency and Agility.* Gent: CONFENIS.

Tambo, T. (2011). International fashion retailing from an enterprise architecture perspective. In E. Pantano & H. Timmermanns (Eds.), *Advanced technologies management for retailing: Frameworks and cases* (pp. 105–120). Hershey, PA: IGI global. doi:10.4018/978-1-60960-738-8.ch006

Tambo, T. (2014a). Collaboration on technological innovation in Danish fashion chains: A network perspective. *Journal of Retailing and Consumer Services, 21*(5), 827–835. doi:10.1016/j.jretconser.2014.02.016

Tambo, T. (2014b). Omni-channel retail information systems. In M. Khosrow-Pour (Ed.), *Encyclopedia of information science and technology* (3rd ed.). Hershey, PA: Idea Group Publishing.

Tang, C., & Guo, L. (2013). Digging for gold with a simple tool: Validating text mining in studying electronic word-of-mouth (eWOM) communication. *Marketing Letters*, 1–14. doi:10.1007/s11002-013-9268-8

Tardivo, G., Scilla, A., & Viassone, M. (2013). "Codice QR": Una risposta innovativa per la comunicazione e la soddisfazione del cliente. In *Proceedings ofReferred Electronic Conference Proceeding XXV Annual Sinergie Conference* (430-444). Verona: Sinergie.

Tardivo, G., & Viassone, M. (2011). Creating an innovative social assistential performance management system. beyond the economic financial perspective: Empirical research findings. *Journal of Financial Management and Analysis, 23*(2), 99–110.

Taylor, H., Dillon, S., & Van Wingen, M. (2010). Focus and diversity in information systems research: Meeting the dual demands of a healthy applied discipline. *Management Information Systems Quarterly, 34*(4), 647–667.

Taylor, S., Celuch, K., & Goodwin, S. (2004). The importance of brand equity to customer loyalty. *Journal of Product and Brand Management, 13*(4), 217–227. doi:10.1108/10610420410546934

Teece, D. J., Pisano, G., & Shuen, A. (1997). Dynamic capabilities and strategic management. *Strategic Management Journal, 18*(7), 509–533. doi:10.1002/(SICI)1097-0266(199708)18:7<509::AID-SMJ882>3.0.CO;2-Z

Terzis, V., & Economides, A. A. (2011). Computer based assessment: Gender differences in perceptions and acceptance. *Computers in Human Behavior, 27*(6), 2108–2122. doi:10.1016/j.chb.2011.06.005

Theodoridis, P. K., & Panigyrakis, G. G. (2011). Internal marketing, market orientation and organisational performance: The mythological triangle in a retail context. European Retail Research, 24, 33–67.

Thether, B. (2002). Who co-operates for innovation, and why, an empirical analysis. *Research Policy, 31*(6), 947–967. doi:10.1016/S0048-7333(01)00172-X

Thomas, S. (2013). Linking customer loyalty to customer satisfaction and store image: A structural model for retail stores. *DECISION, 40*(1-2), 15–25. doi:10.1007/s40622-013-0007-z

Thomson, M., MacInnis, D. J., & Park, C. W. (2005). The ties that bind: Measuring the strength of consumers' emotional attachments to brands. *Journal of Consumer Psychology, 15*(1), 77–91. doi:10.1207/s15327663jcp1501_10

Tidd, J., Bessant, J., & Pavitt, K. (2003). *Managing innovation*. Chichester, UK: John Wiley and Sons.

Timmor, Y., & Rymon, T. (2007). To do or not to do: The dilemma of technology-based service improvement. *Journal of Services Marketing, 21*(2), 99–111. doi:10.1108/08876040710737868

Tisseau, J. (2001). *Réalité virtuelle: autonomie in virtuo*. Habilitation à Diriger des Recherches, Informatique, Université de Rennes 1.

Tisseron, S. (2008). *Virtuel, mon amour: Penser, aimer, souffrir, à l'ère des nouvelles technologies*. Paris: Albin Michel.

Tornatzky, L. G., & Klein, K. J. (1982). Innovation characteristics and innovation adoption implementation: A meta analysis of findings. *IEEE Transactions on Engineering Management, 29*(1), 28–45. doi:10.1109/TEM.1982.6447463

Tornow, W. W., & Wiley, J. W. (1991). Service quality and management practices: A look at employee attitudes, customer satisfaction, and bottom line consequences. *Service Quality and Management Practices, 14*(2), 105–115.

To, W. M., Tam, J. F. Y., & Cheung, M. F. Y. (2013). Explore how Chinese consumers evaluate retail service quality and satisfaction. *Service Business, 7*(1), 121–142. doi:10.1007/s11628-012-0149-7

Towell, J., & Towell, E. (1997). Presence in text-based networked virtual environments or "MUDS". *Presence (Cambridge, Mass.), 6*(5), 590–595.

Treadgold, A. (1988). Retailing without frontiers. *Retail and Distribution Management, 16*(6), 8–12. doi:10.1108/eb018382

Treadgold, A. (1991). The emerging internationalisation of retailing: Present status and future challenges. *Irish Marketing Review, 5*(2), 11–27.

Tremblay, L., & Schultz, W. (1999). Relative reward preference in primate orbitofrontal cortex. *Nature, 398*(6729), 704–708. doi:10.1038/19525 PMID:10227292

Turley, L. W., & Milliman, R. E. (2000). Atmospheric effects on shopping behavior: A review of the experimental evidence. *Journal of Business Research, 49*(2), 193–211. doi:10.1016/S0148-2963(99)00010-7

Turner, M., Kitchenham, B., Brereton, P., Charters, S., & Budgen, D. (2010). Does the technology acceptance model predict actual use? A systematic literature review. *Information and Software Technology, 52*(5), 463–479. doi:10.1016/j.infsof.2009.11.005

Ulrich, D., Halbrook, R., Meder, D., Stuchlik, M., & Thorpe, S. (1991). Employee and customer attachment: Synergies for competitive advantage. *Human Resource Planning, 14*(2), 89–103.

Ünay, F. G., & Zehir, C. (2012). Innovation intelligence and entrepreneurship in the fashion industry. *Procedia: Social and Behavioral Sciences*, *41*, 315–321. doi:10.1016/j.sbspro.2012.04.036

Underhill, P. (2007). *La science du shopping: comment le merchandising influence l'achat*. Paris: Village mondial.

Underhill, P. (2008). *Why we buy: The science of shopping - Updated and revised for the internet, the global consumer, and beyond*. New York, NY: Simon and Schuster.

UNEP/Wuppertal Institute Collaborating Centre on Sustainable Consumption and Production. (2008). *A guidelines manual for retailers towards sustainable consumption & production*. Retrieved August 30, 2014, from http://www.unep.org/Documents.Multilingual/Default.asp?DocumentID=321&ArticleID=4019&l=en

Uner, M. M., Kocak, A., Cavusgil, E., & Cavusgil, S. T. (2013). Do barriers to export vary for born globals and across stages of internationalization? An empirical inquiry in the emerging market of Turkey. *International Business Review*, *22*(5), 800–813. doi:10.1016/j.ibusrev.2012.12.005

US Department of Labor. (2008). *Occupational outlook handbook, 2008-2009 edition*. Retrieved May 15, 2008, from http://www.bls.gov/oco/ocos121.htm

Utterback, J. M. (1974). Innovation in industry and the diffusion of technology. *Science*, *183*(4125), 620–626. doi:10.1126/science.183.4125.620 PMID:17778831

Utterback, J. M. (1996). *Mastering the dynamics of innovation: Mastering the dynamics of innovation*. Boston, MA: Harvard Business School Press.

Vaagen, H., & Wallace, S. W. (2008). Product variety arising from hedging in the fashion supply chains. *International Journal of Production Economics*, *114*(2), 431–455. doi:10.1016/j.ijpe.2007.11.013

Valerio Netto, A., & De Oliveira, M. C. F. (2002). Virtual reality for machine tool prototyping. *Proceedings of the ASME International Mechanical Engineering Congress and Exposition*, *13*, 15-22.

Välkkynen, P., Boyer, A., Urhemaa, T., & Nieminen, R. (2011). Mobile augmented reality for retail environments. In *Proceedings of Workshop on Mobile Interaction in Retail Environments in Conjunction with MobileHCI*. ACM.

Van der Heijden, H. (2004). User acceptance of hedonic information systems. *Management Information Systems Quarterly*, *28*(4), 695–704.

Van der Meijden, O. A. J., & Schijven, M. P. (2009). The value of haptic feedback in conventional robot-assisted minimal invasive surgery and virtual reality training: A current review. *Surgical Endoscopy and Other Interventional Techniques*, *23*(6), 1180–1190. doi:10.1007/s00464-008-0298-x PMID:19118414

Van Riel, A. C. R., De Mortanges, C. P., & Streukens, S. (2005). Marketing antecedents of industrial brand equity: An empirical investigation in specialty chemicals. *Industrial Marketing Management*, *34*(8), 841–847. doi:10.1016/j.indmarman.2005.01.006

Van Schaik, P., Turnbull, T., Van Wersch, A., & Drummond, S. (2004). Presence within a mixed reality environment. *Cyberpsychology & Behavior*, *7*(5), 540–552. doi:10.1089/1094931042403145 PMID:15667049

Van Slyke, C., Belanger, F., Johnson, R. D., & Hightower, R. (2010). Gender-based differences in factors influencing consumer e-commerce adoption. *Communications of the Association for Information Systems*, *26*(2), 17–34.

Van Slyke, C., Comunale, C., & Belanger, F. (2002). Gender differences in perceptions of web-based shopping. *Communications of the ACM*, *45*(7), 82–86. doi:10.1145/545151.545155

VanAuken, B. (2005). *The brand management checklist: Proven tools and techniques for creating winning brands*. London, UK: Kogan Page.

Varadarajan, R. (2010). Strategic marketing and marketing strategy: Domain, definition, fundamental issues and foundational premises. *Journal of the Academy of Marketing Science*, *38*(2), 119–140. doi:10.1007/s11747-009-0176-7

Varadarajan, R. (2011). Marketing strategy: Discerning the relative influence of product and firm characteristics. *AMS Review*, *1*(1), 32–43. doi:10.1007/s13162-011-0003-4

Vaughan-Nichols, S. J. (2009). Augmented reality: No longer a novelty? *Computer*, *42*(12), 19–22. doi:10.1109/MC.2009.380

Vecchiato, G., De Vico Fallani, F., Astolfi, L., Toppi, J., Cincotti, F., Mattia, D., & Babiloni, F. et al. (2010). The issue of multiple univariate comparisons in the context of neuroelectric brain mapping: An application in a neuro-marketing experiment. *Journal of Neuroscience Methods*, *191*(2), 283–289. doi:10.1016/j.jneumeth.2010.07.009 PMID:20637802

Velayudhan, S. K. (2014). Outshopping in rural periodic markets: A retailing opportunity. *International Journal of Retail & Distribution Management*, *42*(2), 151–167. doi:10.1108/IJRDM-07-2013-0136

Venkatesh, V. (2000). Determinants of perceived ease of use: Integrating control, intrinsic motivation, and emotion into the technology acceptance model. *Information Systems Research*, *11*(4), 342–365. doi:10.1287/isre.11.4.342.11872

Venkatesh, V. (2006). Where to go from here? Thoughts on future directions for research on individual-level technology adoption with a focus on decision making. *Decision Sciences*, *37*(4), 497–518. doi:10.1111/j.1540-5414.2006.00136.x

Venkatesh, V., & Davis, F. D. (1996). A model of the antecedents of perceived ease of use: Development and test. *Decision Sciences*, *27*(3), 451–481. doi:10.1111/j.1540-5915.1996.tb01822.x

Venkatesh, V., & Davis, F. D. (2000). A theoretical extension of the technology acceptance model: Four longitudinal field studies. *Management Science*, *45*(2), 186–204. doi:10.1287/mnsc.46.2.186.11926

Venkatesh, V., Morris, M. G., & Ackerman, P. L. (2000). A longitudinal field investigation of gender differences in individual technology adoption decision making processes. *Organizational Behavior and Human Decision Processes*, *83*(1), 33–60. doi:10.1006/obhd.2000.2896 PMID:10973782

Venkatesh, V., Morris, M., Davis, G., & Davis, F. (2003). User acceptance of information technology: Toward a unified view. *Management Information Systems Quarterly*, *27*(3), 425–478.

Verbees, F., Matthew, J. H. M., & Meulenberg, T. G. (2004). Market orientation, innovativeness, product innovation, and performance in small firms. *Journal of Small Business Management*, *42*(2), 134–154. doi:10.1111/j.1540-627X.2004.00102.x

Verhoef, P. C., Neslin, S. A., & Vroomen, B. (2007). Multichannel consumer management: Understanding the research-shopper phenomenon. *International Journal of Research in Marketing*, *24*(2), 129–148. doi:10.1016/j.ijresmar.2006.11.002

Verhoef, P., Lemon, K., Parasuraman, A., Roggeveen, A., Tsiros, M., & Schlesinger, L. (2009). Customer experience creation: Determinants, dynamics and management strategies. *Journal of Retailing*, *85*(1), 31–41. doi:10.1016/j.jretai.2008.11.001

Vieira, V. A. (2010). Visual aesthetic in store environment and its moderating role on consumer intention. *Journal of Consumer Behaviour*, *9*(5), 364–380. doi:10.1002/cb.324

Virvou, M., Katsionis, G., & Manos, K. (2005). Combining software games with education: Evaluation of its educational effectiveness. *Journal of Educational Technology & Society*, *8*(2), 54–65.

Visich, J., Li, S., Khumawala, B., & Reyes, P. (2009). Empirical evidence of RFID impacts on supply chain performance. *International Journal of Operations & Production Management*, *29*(12), 1290–1315. doi:10.1108/01443570911006009

Volpe, R. J. (2013). Promotional competition between supermarket chains. *Review of Industrial Organization*, *42*(1), 45–61. doi:10.1007/s11151-012-9352-x

Von Hippel, E. (2005). *Democratizing innovation*. Cambridge, MA: The MIT Press.

Vorhies, D. W., Orr, L. M., & Bush, V. D. (2011). Improving customer-focused marketing capabilities and firm financial performance via marketing exploration and exploitation. *Journal of the Academy of Marketing Science*, *39*(5), 736–756. doi:10.1007/s11747-010-0228-z

Vranca, S. (2009, September 21). WPP chief tempers hopes for ad upturn. *Wall Street Journal*, p. B1.

Vrontis, D., & Thrassou, A. (2013). *Innovative business practices: Prevailing a turbolent era*. Newcastle, UK: Cambridge Scholar Publishing.

Wachs, D. (2013). *Five reasons you should be using SMS based marketing.* Retrieved July 11, 2014, from http://venturebeat.com/2013/05/08/five-reasons-you-should-be-using-sms-based-marketing/

Wagner, G., Schramm-Klein, H., & Steinmann, S. (2013). Effects of cross-channel synergies and complementarity in a multichannel e-commerce system – An investigation of the interrelation of e-commerce, m-commerce and IETV-commerce. *International Review of Retail, Distribution and Consumer Research*, 1–11.

Wallace, D. W., Giese, J. L., & Johnson, J. L. (2004). Customer retailer loyalty in the context of multiple channel strategies. *Journal of Retailing, 80*(4), 249–263. doi:10.1016/j.jretai.2004.10.002

Wallbaum, H., & Meins, E. (2009). Nicht-nachhaltiges Planen, Bauen und Betrieben – Aus guten Gründen (noch) die Praxis in der Bauwirtschaft? *Bauingenieur, 84*(7/8), 291–304.

Wall, D. P., Kudtarkar, P., Fusaro, V. A., Pivovarov, R., Patil, P., & Tonellato, P. J. (2010). Cloud computing for comparative genomics. *BMC Bioinformatics, 11*(1), 259–271. doi:10.1186/1471-2105-11-259 PMID:20482786

Waller, M. A., Williams, B. D., Tangari, A. H., & Burton, S. (2010). Marketing at the retail shelf: An examination of moderating effects of logistics on SKU market share. *Journal of the Academy of Marketing Science, 38*(1), 105–117. doi:10.1007/s11747-009-0146-0

Wallis, J. D. (2007). Orbitofrontal cortex and its contribution to decision-making. *Annual Review of Neuroscience, 30*(1), 31–56. doi:10.1146/annurev.neuro.30.051606.094334 PMID:17417936

Walsham, G. (1989). Interpretive case studies in IS research: Nature and method. *European Journal of Information Systems, 4*(2), 74–81. doi:10.1057/ejis.1995.9

Walsh, G., Shiu, E., Hassan, L. M., Michaelidou, N., & Beatty, S. E. (2011). Emotions, store-environmental cues, store-choice criteria, and marketing outcomes. *Journal of Business Research, 64*(7), 737–744. doi:10.1016/j.jbusres.2010.07.008

Walter, F. E., Battiston, S., Yildirim, M., & Schweitzer, F. (2012). Moving recommender systems from on-line commerce to retail stores. *Information Systems and e-Business Management, 10*(3), 367-393.

Walters, D., & Laffy, D. (1996). *Managing retail productivity and profitability.* London, UK: Palgrave MacMillan.

Wamba, S. F., Lefebvre, L. A., Bendavid, Y., & Lefebvre, E. (2008). Exploring the impact of RFID technology and the EPC network on mobile B2B eCommerce: A case study in the retail industry. *International Journal of Production Economics, 112*(2).

Wang, H.-C., Pallister, J. P., & Foxall, G. R. (2006). Determinants of consumer loyalty in B2C e-commerce. *Technovation, 26*(12), 1366–1376. doi:10.1016/j.technovation.2005.11.003

Wang, H., & Wang, S. (2010). User acceptance of mobile internet based on the unified theory of acceptance and use of technology: Investigating the determinants and gender differences. *Social Behavior and Personality, 38*(3), 415–426. doi:10.2224/sbp.2010.38.3.415

Wang, J., Wang, L., Ye, F., Xu, X., & Yu, J. (2013). Order decision making based on different statement strategies under stochastic market demand. *Journal of Systems Science and Systems Engineering, 22*(2), 171–190. doi:10.1007/s11518-013-5217-6

Wang, K., Gou, Q., Sun, J., & Yue, X. (2012). Coordination of a fashion and textile supply chain with demand variations. *Journal of Systems Science and Systems Engineering, 21*(4), 461–479. doi:10.1007/s11518-012-5205-2

Wang, L. C., Baker, J., Wagner, J. A., & Wakefield, K. (2007). Can a retail web site be social? *Journal of Marketing, 71*(3), 143–157. doi:10.1509/jmkg.71.3.143

Wang, M. C. H. (2012). Determinants and consequences of consumer satisfaction with self-service technology in a retail setting. *Managing Service Quality, 22*(2), 128–144. doi:10.1108/09604521211218945

Wang, Y. J., Minor, M. S., & Wei, J. (2011). Aesthetics and the online shopping environment: Understanding consumer responses. *Journal of Retailing, 87*(1), 46–58. doi:10.1016/j.jretai.2010.09.002

Ward, J. L., & Saren, M. (2008). Second Life: Contours of a virtual marketing landscape. In *Proceedings of European Marketing Academy Conference*. University of Brighton.

Wargocki, P., Seppanen, O., Andersson, J., Boestra, A., Clements-Croome, D., Fitzner, K., & Hanssen, S. O. (2008). *Indoor climate and productivity in offices: How to integrate productivity in life cycle costs analysis of building services*. Brussels: REHVA.

Watson, B. C. (2011). Barcode empires: Politics, digital technology, and comparative retail firm strategies. *Journal of Industry, Competition and Trade, 11*(3), 309–324. doi:10.1007/s10842-011-0109-2

Watson, K., Klingenberg, B., Polito, P., & Geurts, T. G. (2004). Impact of environmental management system implementation on financial performance: A comparison of two corporate strategies. *Management of Environmental Quality: An International Journal, 15*(6), 622–628. doi:10.1108/14777830410560700

Webster, F. E., & Lusch, R. F. (2013). Elevating marketing: Marketing is dead! Long live marketing! *Journal of the Academy of Marketing Science, 41*(4), 389–399. doi:10.1007/s11747-013-0331-z

Weibel, D., Wissmath, B., Habegger, S., Steiner, Y., & Groner, R. (2008). Playing online games against computer- vs. human-controlled opponents: Effects on presence, flow, and enjoyment. *Computers in Human Behavior, 24*(5), 2274–2291. doi:10.1016/j.chb.2007.11.002

Weijters, B., Rangarajan, D., Falk, T., & Schillewaert, N. (2007). Determinants and outcomes of customers' use of self-service technology in a retail setting. *Journal of Service Research, 10*(1), 3–21. doi:10.1177/1094670507302990

Weitz, B. A. (2010). Electronic retailing. In M. Krafft & M. K. Mantrala (Eds.), *Retailing in the 21st century* (pp. 357–371). Berlin: Springer. doi:10.1007/978-3-540-72003-4_22

Weitz, B. A., & Whitfield, M. B. (2010). Trends in US retailing. In M. Krafft & M. K. Mantrala (Eds.), *Retailing in the 21st century* (pp. 83–99). Berlin: Springer. doi:10.1007/978-3-540-72003-4_6

Werkle-Bergner, M., Müller, V., Li, S. C., & Lindenberger, U. (2006). Cortical EEG correlates of successful memory encoding: Implications for lifespan comparisons. *Neuroscience and Biobehavioral Reviews, 30*(6), 839–854. doi:10.1016/j.neubiorev.2006.06.009 PMID:16904180

Westhead, P., Wright, M., & Ucbasaran, D. (2004). Internationalization of private firms: Environmental turbulence and organizational strategies and resources. *Entrepreneurship & Regional Development, 16*(6), 501–522. doi:10.1080/0898562042000231929

Wiedmann, K. P., Hennigs, N., Klarmann, C., & Behrens, S. (2013). Creating multi-sensory experiences in luxury marketing. *Marketing Review St. Gallen, 30*(6), 60–69. doi:10.1365/s11621-013-0300-4

Wiersema, M., & Bantel, K. (1992). Top management team demography and corporate change. *Academy of Management Journal, 35*(1), 91–121. doi:10.2307/256474

Wigley, S., & Moore, C. M. (2007). The operationalisation of international fashion retailer success. *Journal of Fashion Marketing and Management, 11*(2), 281–296. doi:10.1108/13612020710751437

Wigley, S., Moore, C. M., & Birtwistle, G. (2005). Product and brand: Critical success factors in the internationalization of a fashion retailer. *International Journal of Retail & Distribution Management, 33*(7), 531–544. doi:10.1108/09590550510605596

Williams, R., & Omar, M. (2009). Renaming services organizations for growth. In *Proceedings of Academy of Marketing Conference*. Leeds, UK: Leeds Metropolitan University.

Williams, D. (1992). Motives for retailer internationalization: Their impact, structure, and implications. *Journal of Marketing Management, 8*(3), 269–285. doi:10.1080/0267257X.1992.9964196

Wilson, C. (2010). Why should sustainable finance be given priority? Lesson from pollution and biodiversity degradation. *Accounting Research Journal, 23*(3), 267–280. doi:10.1108/10309611011092592

Wilson, M. A. (2002). Hippocampal memory formation, plasticity, and the role of sleep. *Neurobiology of Learning and Memory, 78*(3), 565–569. doi:10.1006/nlme.2002.4098 PMID:12559835

Winter, S. (2003). Understanding dynamic capabilities. *Strategic Management Journal*, *24*(10), 991–995. doi:10.1002/smj.318

Wise, R. A., & Rompre, P. P. (1989). Brain dopamine and reward. *Annual Review of Psychology*, *40*(1), 191–225. doi:10.1146/annurev.ps.40.020189.001203 PMID:2648975

Witmer, B. G., & Singer, M. J. (1994). *Measuring immersion in virtual environments.* ARI Technical Report 1014. Alexandria, VA: U.S. Army Research Institute for the Behavioral and Social Sciences.

Witmer, B. G., & Singer, M. J. (1998). Measuring presence in virtual environments: A presence questionnaire. *Presence (Cambridge, Mass.)*, *7*(3), 228–240. doi:10.1162/105474698565686

Wolf, M., & McQuitty, S. (2011). Understanding the do-it-yourself consumer: DIY motivations and outcomes. *AMS Review*, *1*(3-4), 154-170.

Wong, C. Y., Arlbjørn, J. S., Hvolby, H. H., & Johansen, J. (2006). Assessing responsiveness of a volatile and seasonal supply chain: A case study. *International Journal of Production Economics*, *104*(2), 709–721. doi:10.1016/j.ijpe.2004.12.021

Wong, W. K., & Guo, Z. X. (2010). A hybrid intelligent model for medium-term sales forecasting in fashion retail supply chains using extreme learning machine and harmony search algorithm. *International Journal of Production Economics*, *128*(2), 614–624. doi:10.1016/j.ijpe.2010.07.008

Wood, S. L. (2002). Future fantasies: A social change perspective of retailing in the 21st century. *Journal of Retailing*, *78*(1), 77–83. doi:10.1016/S0022-4359(01)00069-0

Wren, B. M. (1997). The market orientation construct: Measurement and scaling issues. *Journal of Marketing Theory and Practice*, *15*(3), 31–54.

Wright, P., Blythe, M., & McCarthy, J. (2006). User experience and the idea of design in HCI. *Lecture Notes in Computer Science*, *3941*, 1–14. doi:10.1007/11752707_1

Wu, J., Ju, H. W., Kim, J., Damminga, C., Kim, H. Y., & Johnson, K. K. (2013). Fashion product display: An experiment with Mockshop investigating colour, visual texture, and style coordination. *International Journal of Retail & Distribution Management*, *41*(10), 765–789. doi:10.1108/IJRDM-08-2012-0072

Wu, K., Zhao, X., Zhu, Q., Tan, X., & Zheng, H. (2011). A meta-analysis of the impact of trust on technology acceptance model: Investigation of moderating influence of subject and context type. *International Journal of Information Management*, *31*(6), 572–581. doi:10.1016/j.ijinfomgt.2011.03.004

Xia, M., Zhang, Y., Weng, L., & Ye, X. (2012). Fashion retailing forecasting based on extreme learning machine with adaptive metrics of inputs. *Knowledge-Based Systems*, *36*, 253–259. doi:10.1016/j.knosys.2012.07.002

Xiao, S. S., Jeong, I., Moon, J. J., Chung, C. C., & Chung, J. (2013). Internationalization and performance of firms in China: Moderating effects of governance structure and the degree of centralized control. *Journal of International Management*, *19*(2), 118–137. doi:10.1016/j.intman.2012.12.003

Xiao, Y., Palekar, U., & Liu, Y. (2011). Shades of gray—The impact of gray markets on authorized distribution channels. *Quantitative Marketing and Economics*, *9*(2), 155–178. doi:10.1007/s11129-011-9098-z

Xi, Y., & Peng, S. (2010). The effects of two kinds of corporate publicity on customer-brand relationship. *Frontiers of Business Research in China*, *4*(1), 73–100. doi:10.1007/s11782-010-0004-4

Yang, C., Hsu, Y., & Tan, S. (2010). Predicting the determinants of users' intentions for using YouTube to share video: Moderating gender effects. *Cyberpsychology, Behavior, and Social Networking*, *13*(2), 141–152. doi:10.1089/cyber.2009.0105 PMID:20528269

Yang, D., & Wang, X. (2010). The effects of 2-tier store brands' perceived quality, perceived value, brand knowledge, and attitude on store loyalty. *Frontiers of Business Research in China*, *4*(1), 1–28. doi:10.1007/s11782-010-0001-7

Yang, K. (2010). Determinants of US consumer mobile shopping services adoption: Implications for designing mobile shopping services. *Journal of Consumer Marketing, 27*(3), 262–270. doi:10.1108/07363761011038338

Yang, K., & Young, A. (2009). The effects of customised site features on Internet apparel shopping. *Journal of Fashion Marketing and Management, 13*(1), 28–139. doi:10.1108/13612020910939923

Yang, Z., Cai, C., Zhou, Z., & Zhou, N. (2005). Development and validation of an instrument to measure user perceived service quality of information presenting web portals. *Information & Management, 42*(4), 575–589. doi:10.1016/j.im.2004.03.001

Yan, R. (2010). Cooperative advertising, pricing strategy and firm performance in the e-marketing age. *Journal of the Academy of Marketing Science, 38*(4), 510–519. doi:10.1007/s11747-009-0171-z

Yarbrough, L., Morgan, N. A., & Vorhies, D. W. (2011). The impact of product market strategy-organizational culture fit on business performance. *Journal of the Academy of Marketing Science, 39*(4), 555–573. doi:10.1007/s11747-010-0238-x

Yasin, N., Nasser Noor, M., & Mohamad, O. (2007). Does image of country-of-origin matter to brand equity? *Journal of Product and Brand Management, 16*(1), 38–48. doi:10.1108/10610420710731142

Yee, N., Ellis, J., & Ducheneaut, N. (2009). The tyranny of embodiment. *Artifact, 2*, 1–6.

Ye, J., Marinova, D., & Singh, J. (2012). Bottom-up learning in marketing frontlines: Conceptualization, processes, and consequences. *Journal of the Academy of Marketing Science, 40*(6), 821–844. doi:10.1007/s11747-011-0289-7

Yen, D. C., Wu, C.-S., Cheng, F.-F., & Huang, Y.-W. (2010). Determinants of users' intention to adopt wireless technology: An empirical study by integrating TTF with TAM. *Computers in Human Behavior, 26*(5), 906–915. doi:10.1016/j.chb.2010.02.005

Yi, M. Y., Fiedler, K. D., & Park, J. S. (2006). Understanding the role of individual innovativeness in the acceptance of IT-based innovations: Comparative analyses of models and measures. *Decision Sciences, 37*(3), 393–426. doi:10.1111/j.1540-5414.2006.00132.x

Yi, M. Y., Jackson, J., Park, J. S., & Probst, J. C. (2006). Understanding information technology acceptance by individual professionals: Toward an integrative view. *Information & Management, 43*(3), 350–363. doi:10.1016/j.im.2005.08.006

Yi, Y., Gong, T., & Lee, H. (2013). The impact of other customers on customer citizenship behavior. *Psychology and Marketing, 30*(4), 341–356. doi:10.1002/mar.20610

Yong, C., Gruca, T. S., & Klemz, B. R. (2003). Internet pricing, price satisfaction and customer satisfaction. *International Journal of Electronic Commerce, 8*(2), 31–50.

Yoo, B., Donthu, N., & Lee, S. (2000). An examination of selected marketing mix elements and brand equity. *Journal of the Academy of Marketing Science, 28*(2), 195–211. doi:10.1177/0092070300282002

Yoo, C., Park, J., & MacInnis, D. J. (1998). Effects of store characteristics and in-store affective experiences on store attitude. *Journal of Business Research, 42*(3), 253–263. doi:10.1016/S0148-2963(97)00122-7

Yoo, Y., & Alavi, M. (2001). Media and group cohesion: Relative influences on social presence, task participation, and group consensus. *Management Information Systems Quarterly, 25*(3), 371–390. doi:10.2307/3250922

Yuen, S., Yaoyuneyong, G., & Johnson, E. (2011). Augmented reality: An overview and five directions for AR in education. *Journal of Educational Technology Development and Exchange, 4*(1), 119–140.

Zahorik, P., & Jenison, R. L. (1998). Presence as being-in-the-world. *Presence (Cambridge, Mass.), 7*(1), 78–89. doi:10.1162/105474698565541

Zahra, S., Ireland, R., & Hitt, M. (2000). International expansion by new venture firms: International diversity, mode of market entry, technological learning and performance. *Academy of Management Journal, 43*(5), 925–950. doi:10.2307/1556420

Zarantonello, L., & Schmitt, B. H. (2010). Using the brand experience scale to profile consumers and predict consumer behavior. *Journal of Brand Management, 17*(7), 532–540. doi:10.1057/bm.2010.4

Zar, J. H. (2000). *Biostatistical analysis*. New York: Prentice Hall.

Zeithaml, V. A., Berry, L. L., & Parasuraman, A. (1996). The behavioral consequences of service quality. *Journal of Marketing, 60*(2), 31–46. doi:10.2307/1251929

Zeithaml, V., Bitner, M., & Gremler, D. (2009). *Services marketing* (5th ed.). New York, NY: McGraw-Hill.

Zentes, J., Morschett, D., & Schramm-Klein, H. (2007). *Strategic retail management – Text and international cases.* Wiesbaden: Betriebswirtschaftlicher Verlag Dr. Th. Gabler.

Zhang, J., Farris, P., Irvin, J., Kushwaha, T., Steenburgh, T., & Weitz, B. (2010). Crafting integrated multichannel retail strategies. *Journal of Interactive Marketing, 24*(2), 168–180. doi:10.1016/j.intmar.2010.02.002

Zhang, S., & Schmitt, B. H. (2001). Creating local brands in multilingual international markets. *JMR, Journal of Marketing Research, 38*(3), 313–325. doi:10.1509/jmkr.38.3.313.18869

Zhenxiang, W., & Lijie, Z. (2011). Case study of online retailing fast fashion industry. *International Journal of e-Education, e-Business, e- Management Learning, 1*(3), 195–200.

Zhou, J.-Y., Song, A.-B., & Luo, J.-Z. (2013). Evolutionary game theoretical resource deployment model for P2P networks. *Journal of Software, 24*(3), 526–539. doi:10.3724/SP.J.1001.2013.04229

Zhou, K. Z., Yim, C. K., & Tse, D. K. (2005). The effects of strategic orientations on technology- and market-based breakthrough innovations. *Journal of Marketing, 69*(2), 42–60. doi:10.1509/jmkg.69.2.42.60756

Zhou, M., & Lin, J. (2014). Cooperative advertising and pricing models in a dynamic marketing channel. *Journal of Systems Science and Systems Engineering, 23*(1), 94–110. doi:10.1007/s11518-013-5221-x

Zickuhr, K. (2013). *Location-based services.* Retrieved June 8, 2014, from http://www.pewinternet.org/Reports/2013/Location.aspx

Zielke, S., Toporowski, W., & Kniza, B. (2011). Customer acceptance of a new interactive information terminal in grocery retailing. In E. Pantano & H. Timmermans (Eds.), *Advanced technologies management for retailing* (pp. 289–305). Hershey, PA: Business Science Reference. doi:10.4018/978-1-60960-738-8.ch015

Zijlmans, O. M. (2010). *De veranderende vraag naar winkelvastgoed onder invloed van online winkelen: een onderzoek naar toekomststrategieën van (r)etailers.* Eindhoven: University of Technology.

Zyda, M. (2005). From visual simulation to virtual reality to games. *Computer, 38*(9), 25–32. doi:10.1109/MC.2005.297

About the Contributors

Eleonora Pantano is Lecturer in Marketing at Middlesex University of London (UK). Prior to joining Middlesex in February 2015, she was post doc research fellow at University of Calabria (Italy) and researcher at Technical University of Eindhoven (The Netherlands). She has a Ph.D. in "Psychology of Programming and Artificial Intelligence" and a Master Degree in Business Engineering. Her research activities explore marketing management and mainly relate to consumers attitude and acceptance towards new technology-based retail settings, and how business and retail models are implemented in terms of innovation and technology management. Her findings appear in numerous international journals such as Journal of Marketing Management, International Journal of Information Management, and Journal of Retailing and Consumer Services (she was also guest editor of two special issues for this journal and got the Certificate of Excellence in Reviewing for 2013).

* * *

Fabio Babiloni is currently Professor of Physiology at the Department of Molecular Medicine at the University "Sapienza" of Rome. Prof. Babiloni is author of over 200 scientific publications in peer-reviewed journals with impact factor and he has more than 250 communications in international conferences, abstracts and book chapters. His total impact factor is 400 while his h-index is 50. He is Editor of several international journals.

Daniel Baier is Professor of Marketing and Innovation Management at Brandenburg University of Technology Cottbus-Senftenberg. His research interests are in market-oriented design of products and services, adoption and diffusion of new products and services, multivariate statistics, data and web mining. He studied computer science at the University of Karlsruhe where he also completed his dissertation and habilitation in business administration. He has published in journals like *Advances in Data Analysis and Classification, Annals of Operations Research, Creativity and Innovation Management, Journal of Econometrics, Journal of Retailing and Consumer Services*, and *R&D Management*.

Marta Blázquez Cano is Research Associate in University of Manchester. She hold a PhD in Marketing, MSc in Marketing and BA (Honors) in Advertising and PR. She is actually collaborating in different research projects with the University of Oxford and University of the Arts among others. Her primary research interests include Multichannel Retailing - especially e-commerce, m-commerce, and physical stores - International Retailing, Experiential Retailing, Consumer Experience, Consumer Behaviour, and Social Media.

Aloys Borgers is associate professor in urban planning at Eindhoven University of Technology, The Netherlands. He is interested in how people behave in urban environments. His main research theme is modelling individuals' preferences and behaviour in urban contexts in order to predict or simulate how people react to changes in the urban environment or how they respond to new societal and technological trends. His scope is mainly on residential preferences, shopping behaviour, and pedestrian behaviour.

J. Joško Brakus is a Professor in Marketing at Leeds University Business School. He earned his Ph.D. at Columbia University. He conducts experimental research in consumer behaviour. He studies experiential marketing and branding practices as well as managerial and consumer judgment and decision processes, with specific emphasis in the areas of selective information processing and biased processing. He also investigates how individual differences (e.g., self-regulation) affect adoption of new products and responses to marketing stimuli in general. His work has been published in leading academic marketing journals such as the *Journal of Marketing Research* and the *Journal of Marketing*.

Patrizia Cherubino is graduated in Economics and Business Administration at the University of Calabria in the 2009. After degree, she attended a master on "Marketing Intelligence and Techniques market for Public Administration" (2010) Since 2010 Dr. Cherubino is also working with BrainSigns srl, a spin-off of University of Rome "Sapienza", in the generation and validation of biometric tests using EEG, Heart Rate and ERMs related to the perception of commercial TV advertisings for several companies such as Eni S.p.A., Telecom Italia S.p.A., Vodafone S.p.A., Segugio.it S.r.l., Opel, GfK Eurisko. Dr. Cherubino is also co-author of several publications on neuromarketing on peer-reviewed scientific journals and since 2013 enrolled in PhD course "Economics Management and Communication for Creativitiy" at the IULM University of Milan.

Charles Dennis is Professor of Marketing and Retailing at Lincoln Business School, the University of Lincoln (UK); and Associate Editor (Retailing) of the European Journal of Marketing. His main teaching and research area is (e-)retail and consumer behaviour – the vital final link of the Marketing process. Charles is a Chartered Marketer, elected a Fellow of the Chartered Institute of Marketing for helping to modernise the teaching of the discipline. Charles was awarded the Vice Chancellor's Award for Teaching Excellence for improving the interactive student learning experience at Brunel University. Charles has published in journals such as *Journal of Business Research, Journal of Marketing Management,* and *European Journal of Marketing*. Books include *Marketing the e-Business* (1st & 2nd editions) (joint-authored with Dr Lisa Harris); the research monograph (combined textbook) *e-Retailing* (Routledge), and *China Logistics Publishing House*; and research monograph *Objects of Desire: Consumer Behaviour in Shopping Centre Choice* (Palgrave). His research into shopping styles has received extensive coverage in the popular media including TV appearances with Sir Trevor McDonald OBE and Adrian Edmondson.

Gianpiero Di Blasi received his degree (summa cum laude) in Math in 1999 at the University of Palermo and his PhD degree in Computer Science in 2006 at the University of Catania. From 2006 to 2011, he was a Post-doc in Computer Science at the University of Calabria and in Numerical Analysis at the University of Palermo; since 2012 he is a Post-doc in Computer Science at the University of To-rino. Due to the numerous scientific experiences, his research interests cover different areas including image analysis, processing and enhancement, computer graphics algorithms, non-photorealistic rendering techniques, SVG applications, Java/Java3D programming, chaos theory, applications of meshless methods to engineering problems, intelligent systems, and data mining. He has published more than 50 papers in international journals and conference proceedings. From 2003 to 2008, he has taught computer graphics, mobile programming, and computer-human interaction at the University of Catania. Finally, He has excellent programming skills thanks to some industrial experiences.

Marion Garnier is an Associate Professor in Marketing at SKEMA Business School - Université de Lille and graduated from Université Pierre Mendès-France Grenoble 2 and Université de Lille II (Habilitation à Diriger des Recherches - qualified researcher and PhD supervision French diploma). Her research focuses on consumption experiences, especially virtual ones, on consumers' avatars and embodied virtual agents, as well as more generally on online consumer behavior (loyalty to a website, e-consumer productivity, savvy consumer). She has published in *Recherche et Applications en Marketing, Information and Management, Journal of Marketing Management, Journal of Retailing and Consumer Services, Advances in Consumer Research, Journal of Internet Marketing and Advertising,* and *Journal of Virtual Worlds Research.*

Ilenia Graziani obtained her Degree in General and Experimental Psychology at the Faculty of Medicine and Psychology of "Sapienza – University of Rome" in July 2012. Since September 2012 she has been carrying out her post-lauream apprenticeship in Neuromarketing, Neuroaestethics and Neuropolitics at the Department of Physiology and Pharmacology of "Sapienza – University of Rome" in collaboration with BrainSigns s.r.l. and the Department of the Developmental and Social Psychology of "Sapienza – University of Rome".

Young Ha is an assistant professor of Fashion Merchandising and Design in the department of Family and Consumer Sciences at California State University, Long Beach. She has published articles in journals such as *Psychology & Marketing, Journal of Service Management, Journal of Fashion Marketing and Management, Journal of Retail and Distribution Management, Journal of Research in Interactive Marketing,* etc. Her current research interests focus on Internet and mobile marketing/retailing that covers consumer behavior, visual merchandising, online interactivity, social networking, and store image.

Eva Helberger is an expert in brand experience and in particular in retail branding and retail experiences. She is a lecturer at the London College of Fashion and an international brand consultant. As a consultant, she is specialised in re-branding exercises with leading brands over a broad array of industries, with a particular emphasis on consumer and retail experiences. She has published and presented work at the British Academy of Management and other branding and retail conferences, and is currently working on several retail studies exploring the merging of the physical and the digital retail experience.

Hyunjoo Im is an assistant professor of retail merchandising at the University of Minnesota. Her research interest includes online consumers' responses to website features and visual information presentation, online engagement, impact of retail technology on consumer behavior, mobile technology in retailing and consumers' and retailers' technology adoption. Her work appeared in academic journals such as Journal of *Research in Interactive Marketing, Journal of Service Management,* and *Journal of Retailing and Consumer Services.*

Katrin Kallweit holds a degree in Marketing and Channel Management from the University of Göttingen (M.Sc.). She is an external PhD student at the chair of retailing in Göttingen and works for a management consultancy in Munich. Her research focuses on mobile marketing in retail and multi-channel integration.

Kijpokin Kasemsap received his BEng degree in Mechanical Engineering from King Mongkut's University of Technology Thonburi, his MBA degree from Ramkhamhaeng University, and his DBA degree in Human Resource Management from Suan Sunandha Rajabhat University. He is a Special Lecturer at Faculty of Management Sciences, Suan Sunandha Rajabhat University based in Bangkok, Thailand. He is a Member of International Association of Engineers (IAENG), International Association of Engineers and Scientists (IAEST), International Economics Development and Research Center (IEDRC), International Association of Computer Science and Information Technology (IACSIT), International Foundation for Research and Development (IFRD), and International Innovative Scientific and Research Organization (IISRO). He also serves on the International Advisory Committee (IAC) for International Association of Academicians and Researchers (INAAR). He has numerous original research articles in top international journals, conference proceedings, and book chapters on business management, human resource management, and knowledge management published internationally.

Astrid Kemperman is an associate professor of urban planning and quality of life at the Eindhoven University of Technology. Her research focuses on the impacts of urban environments on human behavior to improve planning and design of built environments that support livable communities for its residents and visitors. She has specific interest in shopping behavior in both offline and online retail environments.

Anthony Kent is Professor of Fashion Marketing at Nottingham Trent University. After studying Modern History at the University of Oxford, he worked in both manufacturing and fashion retail. He was latterly Associate Dean for Research at the London College of Fashion. He has published widely on retail and design management, and his publications include *Flagship Marketing: Concepts and Spaces* (Routledge 2009). He is a Fellow of the Royal Society for the Arts.

Ivan Kovač, Ph.D., Department of trade, Faculty of Business and Economics, University of Zagreb, Croatia, is author of numerous articles about retail trade, marketing, sales and international trade. He teaches Procurement management, Logistics and Wholesale and retail trade. In his career, he has been Director General of Croatian Bureau of Statistics, Operating Executive of Badel 1862 (spirits and vines), CEO of Marin Getaldić-Gethaldus (optical industry), CEO of Essilor Croatia (optical industry).

Zui Chih Lee received his PhD at University of North Carolina, Greensboro. He is a Marketing Professor in the Department of Business Administration at Susquehanna University. His research interests include both business-to-business as well as business-to-consumer consumption behaviour. He has conducted researches on consumer behaviour in electronic contexts.

Tasha Lewis, PhD., is an Assistant Professor in the Department of Fiber Science & Apparel Design at Cornell University where she teaches in the area of fashion design management. Her research interests include the disruptive impact of technology in the apparel industry, the behavior of fashion brands, global and domestic apparel production ("glocalization") issues, and the significance of social responsibility and sustainability throughout the apparel supply chain. Dr. Lewis has also worked in the apparel industry in areas of production, sourcing, and retail operations and maintains ongoing contact with industry professionals to inform her research. She is a faculty fellow of both the Cornell Institute of Fashion & Fiber Innovation and the Atkinson Center for a Sustainable Future.

Michael Lewrick received his PhD from Napier University Edinburgh and holds a MBA from Bristol Business School. He studied - in New York, Munich and Nice - Business Administration with an emphasis on IT and organization. His research interests centres on the management issues related to the design, development and commercialisation of technological and business model innovation. Specific areas of focus include developing capabilities for innovativeness and business success. A number of publications have been produced in this area. Michael worked as a Managing Partner in a strategy consulting company as well as for major industry players like Siemens, Allianz, Fraunhofer-Gesellschaft and Swisscom in various positions. Over the years, he developed skills to address design, innovation and entrepreneurial challenges. Michael collaborates with Stanford University on design thinking and research. He offers university courses at master level as well as workshops for industry partners on design thinking.

Suzanne Loker is a Professor Emerita in the Department of Fiber Science and Apparel Design at Cornell University. She has published widely on topics about the apparel industry, international apparel production and marketing, and home-based work. Her research focuses on innovative business strategies in the apparel industry, specifically socially responsible approaches to business and the use of body scanners and mass customization technologies to improve apparel design and manufacturing. She recently co-authored the book, Social Responsibility in the Global Apparel Industry, with Drs. Marsha Dickson and Molly Eckman.

Anton Giulio Maglione achieved his Bachelor degree in Clinical Engineer and Master degree in Biomedical Engineer at University "La Sapienza" of Rome in 2008 and 2011. Since 2011, he is Ph.D. Student at the Dept of Anatomy, Histology, Forensic Medicine and Orthopedics at the University "La Sapienza". Anton Giulio is working with the EEG,HR and EDA recording and them analisys. He collaborated in some Neuromarketing research with BrainSigns company.

Virginie Maille is a professor of marketing. She received her Doctorate in Management Studies from Montpellier I University and her Habilitation à Diriger des Recherches (French Qualification for Ph.D. Supervisors) from Paris-Dauphine University. She has 20 years of experience in teaching and academic administration. Her primary research interest is information processing - how the consumer is affected by various marketing cues, more particularly sensory information and incongruent information. She has published articles in peer reviewed journals such as Journal of Business Research or Recherche et Applications en Marketing and has been presented at major marketing conferences such as ACR, EMAC and AMS.

Maktoba Omar, PhD, is a Reader in Marketing Strategy at Edinburgh Napier University, Edinburgh, Scotland, specialising in international marketing, emerging markets, and foreign direct investment. She has undertaken a range of knowledge transfer and commercial projects with business in the areas of international marketing and marketing strategy. This has included academic supervision of a Knowledge Transfer Partnership and a number of consultancy projects. Maktoba is a Director of Studies and supervises a number of Ph.D and DBA students nationally, and internationally. She has also published, edited and refereed a number of academic journals. She is a member of a range of professional organisations including the Academy of Marketing, the Academy of International Business and the Institute of Learning and Teaching in Higher Education.

Ingrid Poncin is professor of Marketing at UCL (Université Catholique de Louvain- Belgium) – LSM (Louvain School of Management). Her expertise areas are in marketing research and consumer behavior. She also holds qualified researcher diploma – (Habilitation à diriger des recherches from – Lille II University). Dr. Ingrid PONCIN's research is dedicated to the importance and measurement of affect in marketing and to consumer behavior in 3D commercial web site as well as in multichannel context. She published several articles in peer reviewed journals in the last 5 years: *Journal of Business Research, Journal of Advertising, Advances in Consumer Research, Recherche et Applications en Marketing, Management et Avenir, Journal of Retailing and Consumer Services.*

Sanda Renko is the Full Professor at the Department of Trade, Faculty of Economics and Business in Zagreb, Croatia. She is the course co-ordinator for Retailing Management, Benchmarking, Distribution Strategies, Category Management, Fashion retailing, Wholesale and retail business, Business Logistics, and Retail Services. She is the member of the editorial board of some distinguished journals, and was the guest editor in special issues of some journals, such as: *Food Product Marketing* and *British Food Journal.*

Alexandra Rese is Assistant Professor at the Chair of Marketing and Innovation Management, Brandenburg University of Technology Cottbus-Senftenberg, Germany. She received her PhD in sociology and entrepreneurship from the University of Karlsruhe while working at Fraunhofer Institute for Systems and Innovation Research ISI in Karlsruhe. Her works have appeared in journals like *R&D Management, Creativity and Innovation Management*, and *Journal of Retailing and Consumer Services*. Her current research focuses on the acceptance of innovative applications in retailing, e.g. augmented reality, as well as abilities and roles in innovation management.

Stefanie Schreiber completed her Master of Science degree in Business Administration at Brandenburg University of Technology Cottbus-Senftenberg, Germany, and now works as Research Assistant at the Chair of Marketing and Innovation Management. Her PhD thesis focuses on consumer's acceptance of augmented reality technologies. She has published in journals like *Marketing ZFP - Journal of Research and Management* and *Journal of Retailing and Consumer Services.*

Philipp Spreer is a PhD candidate at the Chair of Retailing at the University of Goettingen, Germany. In addition, he works as a lecturer at the University of Applied Sciences Munich and as a management consultant for a business consultancy. His research is funded by the Rid Foundation and focuses on consumer and salesperson behavior in the context of digital innovations in retail. He has published his work in peer-reviewed journals such as the Journal of Retailing and Consumer Services, Transactions on Marketing Research and Marketing Review St. Gallen and contributed to several books.

Torben Tambo is M.Sc., GDBA, and associate professor at AU Herning, Aarhus University, where he is programme coordinator for MSc in Technology-based Business Development. Previous to this he served 17 years in IT, management and consultant roles within manufacturing and trading/retail companies. Research interests include information systems, enterprise architecture, retailing and supply chain management. Within retailing, larger, specialty retailing organisations has the key focus. Torben has previously published with *International Public Policy Review, Journal of Economic Dynamics and Control, Journal of Enterprise Architecture*, and contributed to several books published by IGI Global.

Nathalia C. Tjandra is a marketing lecturer at Edinburgh Napier University Business School. Nathalia completed her PhD at Edinburgh Napier University in 2013. Her PhD investigated the management of a triadic relationship between long-term savings and investments provider(s), IFAs, and customers; IFAs' view of branding and brand equity; and the development of a co-creation model in a triadic relationship network. Her key research interests are branding, business-to-business marketing, co-creation, country-of-origin, marketing ethics, retail marketing, emerging market and international marketing. She has published a number of articles in peer-reviewed journals and conferences in these areas.

Arianna Trettel has a long job experience in committing marketing research to test efficacy and ROI of fund raising communication materials and strategies (in advertising and below the line communication, information campaigns, volunteers management). Since 2012 became co-founder and President of BrainSigns srl, a spin-off company of the University of Rome Sapienza devoted to the application of neuroscience in industrial and marketing contexts.

Lieke van Delft started the studies Building Sciences at the University of Technology in Eindhoven, where she gained her bachelor degree in 2011. For her master degree, Real Estate Management & Development, she studied the omni-channel shopping behavior of consumers in The Netherlands.

Giovanni Vecchiato achieved his Bachelor and Master degree in Telecommunication Engineering at University "Federico II" of Naples in the 2004 and 2007, respectively. Then he attended the Ph.D. course in Neurophysiology at University "Sapienza". Since 2010, he is Ph.D. fellow at the Dept of Physiology and Pharmacology of "Sapienza". In his research, Ing. Vecchiato is currently investigating cognitive and emotional correlates of the EEG related to the observation of advertisements, emotional pictures and faces. He is author of several scientific publications on international peer-reviewed journals and books. In the 2012, Ing. Vecchiato won the grant funded by "Officina dell'Innovazione" (Province of Rome) to develop a system for the biometric measurement and analysis of cognitive and emotional variables during the observation of TV commercials and fruition of exhibitions. He is team leader performing Neuro-marketing research with BrainSigns working for companies such as ENI, Telecom, Vodafone, Segugio.

Milena Viassone ESCP Europe Ph.D., Paris and Ph.D in Business Management-University of Cassino; Researcher in Business Management-University of Turin; Member of the Aidea (Italian Academy of Business Administration) Research Group (GSA) on the topic "Management for the sustainability of touristic development and the destinations competitiveness"; Member of the EuroMed International Group of Research on "Tourism"; Member of the International ESCP Europe Group of Research on "International Development". Member of the Editorial Board of important international journals. Main Research Areas: Management of tourist destinations, Territorial competitiveness, Measure of sectorial performances, Mergers and Acquisitions.

Robert L. Williams, Jr., PhD, is an Assistant Professor of Marketing at the AACSB International-accredited Sigmund Weis School of Business at Susquehanna University, Selinsgrove, PA, USA. He has published in peer-reviewed journals such as *Journal of Product & Brand Management* (Emerald Literati 2008 Award for Excellence international), *Marketing Intelligence and Planning, Journal of Brand Management*, and *International Journal of Leisure and Tourism Management*; published textbook chapters, as well as served as presenter and track reviewer at numerous global conferences and workshops. He currently serves on the Editorial Review Board of the *Transnational Marketing Journal*, and was most recently the Associate Editor for the Special Issue on *Branding for the Journal of Marketing for Higher Education*. After 20 years as a management practitioner in Fortune 50/500 companies, he is in his 11th year of university teaching. His current academic research interests focus on competitive advantage, branding, innovation, Higher Education, and market entry strategies.

Index

T

U

Lightning Source UK Ltd.
Milton Keynes UK
UKOW07n0831250515

252225UK00012B/144/P